Simone de Beauvoir and the Demystification of Motherhood

Simone de Beauvoir and the Demystification of Motherhood

by
Yolanda Astarita Patterson

U·M·I Research Press
Ann Arbor / London

Produced and distributed by
UMI Research Press
an imprint of
University Microfilms Inc.
Ann Arbor, Michigan 48106

Library of Congress Cataloging in Publication Data

Patterson, Yolanda, 1933-
  Simone de Beauvoir and the demystification of motherhood / by Yolanda Astarita Patterson.
    p. cm.—(Challenging the literary canon)
    Bibliography: p.
    Includes index.
    ISBN 0-8357-1978-2 (alk. paper)
    1. Beauvoir, Simone de, 1908- —Criticism and interpretation.
2. Motherhood in literature. 3. Mothers in literature. 4. Women in
literature. I. Title. II. Series.
PQ2603.E362Z864   1989
848'.91409—dc20   89-30480
                                                                    CIP

British Library CIP data is available.

The paper used in this publication meets the minimum requirements of
American National Standard for Information Sciences—Permanence of
Paper for Printed Library Materials, ANSI Z39.48-1984. ∞ ®

Dedicated to
the five Candela sisters,
Kathleen,
and Germaine,
all of whom were an integral part
of a very special "mother package" for me

Contents

Foreword

Simone de Beauvoir's stature as a proponent of women's emancipation in the mid-century years is by now clearly established. In 1949 *The Second Sex*, her historical survey of the situation meted out to women and its consequences, though it generated some violent controversies at the time, inspired to a large degree the explosion of vitality that fueled a new cosmopolitan and action-oriented phase in women's collective determination to put an end to the social inequities and the bland myths concerning "feminine nature" on which such discriminations rested. Since the mid-century years much has changed for the better in the status of women; much remains to be done. *The Second Sex* may soon take its place as history, an influential document whose theses define a past era.

But this leaves the scene wide open to an exploration of Simone de Beauvoir herself, to the complexities that shaped her itinerary from her childhood in a particularly tradition-oriented stratum of society to her intransigent rejection of the models of life it held in store for her. "While Simone de Beauvoir had an intense and elevated sense of her vocation as a writer, she had an ambivalent and conflicted view of herself as a writer of novels," writes a perspicacious critic, Marthe Noel Evans (*The Masks of Tradition*, 1987). The origin of her discomfort is pretty clear: fiction is a genre connected with feminine sensibility and imagination; the conceptual mode calls for the male "superior" qualities of rational order and ideological coherence. Beauvoir was ill at ease with her "feminine" being in-the-world. By concentrating on a specifically feminine function—motherhood—and by treating alike autobiography, fiction, drama, essays, and interviews spanning all Beauvoir's writing, Yolanda Patterson goes to the source of a deep emotional conflict in Beauvoir's life; the ambivalent feelings that linked her to her mother, Françoise. That conflict she describes persuasively as basic, because it is early woven into Beauvoir's awareness that it is an active threat to her own passionate dreams of becoming an independent woman and a writer. Patterson explores the topic chronologically as it appears in Beauvoir's collection of short stories, *When the Things of the Spirit Come First,* to *Adieux: A Farewell to Sartre,* her poignant account of Sartre's physical deterioration and death. She notes the unraveling of the tight knot of rejection in *A Very Easy Death,* Beauvoir's account of her vigil at her mother's death-bed.

"This book," Patterson explains, "is an attempt to explore Beauvoir's attitudes toward motherhood, to examine her relationship with her own mother, her lingering memories of the mother of her best friend Zaza during their adolescence, her portrayal of mothers in her fictional works, and her pronouncements on motherhood in her essays and interviews." There is a further unannounced dimension in Patterson's book: sustained references to the resonance of Beauvoir's writing whether in France or abroad, more specifically the U.S.A. A first introductory chapter, which may surprise readers, briefly but pertinently supplies a compendium of the predominant contemporary views on the topic of motherhood. After each chapter, Patterson introduces a section presenting the reactions to the book she has previously discussed. Besides their documentary interest, these sections serve a deeper purpose, which, ever wary of theorization and conceptualization, Patterson does not spell out: the existence of an underlying historical and social magma of trends which gave Beauvoir's specific itinerary its resonance and significance in a continuum of evolving events and thought. Patterson's topic, which crosses the boundaries of genre, is situated in the area of the history of ideas, or as the French call it "l'histoire des mentalités." It zeros in on one of the more explosive realms of socio-political concern, the family and the woman's role therein.

As Engels noted in his history of the family, there is no single preordained, universal model for family life; nevertheless each society holds its own established model as sacred. In nineteenth-century bourgeois society, "motherhood," the joys and fulfillment it promised, was the blissful lure set out to "trap" women, so Beauvoir felt, in the narrow prison of the housewife. Beauvoir felt that the trap had closed down on her mother and destroyed her friend Zaza. To question the pattern was to draw much righteous indignation on one's head. But French society was changing. Simone de Beauvoir was to live that central event of the twentieth century, the opening of educational institutions to women, and the possibility of economic emancipation bringing new freedoms. Why, in her case, this emancipation was accompanied by a fundamental resentment of the mother she had as a child passionately loved is the problem Patterson's study traces. She suggests that for Simone, the maternal code, religious and moral, collided with basic abstract ideals: existentialist freedom and responsibility; political commitment; a negative view of power; the sense of free bonding that makes for a real community. Beauvoir herself stressed the connection between her childhood and her subsequent participation in the politics of feminism and socialism.

Yolanda Patterson moves from book to book, examining Beauvoir's statements on facts and situations; she stresses the coincidence between these and the circumstances and destinies the writer creates for the characters she sets in motion. Her readings are quite literal with very few recourses to sub-texts or "decodings." Abundant quotations in the notes recall the particularity of the text and keep open a welcome line of communication between text and reader. In this respect the three levels of Patterson's presentation—analysis, critical reactions, notes— will make it a helpful reference book for young scholars.

Patterson is pleasingly detached from intransigent *partis-pris*. In her preface she recalls her early interest in Beauvoir's work and the bonds of friendship and confidence that ultimately linked her to Simone and to Simone's sister, Hélène, a gifted painter. She presents herself as a happy daughter, wife, and mother; and besides she is a successful teacher and scholar. She may on occasion draw our attention to Beauvoir's particularly extremist statements, but never with any acerbity. As she goes through many years and pages of writing, focusing on the single topic chosen, she moves toward her own contribution, the rectification of the major accusation thrown at Beauvoir, attributing her discomfort with regard to motherhood to hatred of all bodily functions. Beauvoir, Patterson notes, was fighting for her right *not* to be forced into motherhood, a fight which is not yet entirely won for women as a whole. She was *not* claiming the right to impose her choice on others.

The friendship and confidence Patterson inspired, her many contributions to the prestige of Beauvoir in the USA (the founding and editing of the *Simone de Beauvoir Studies* not the least among them), and her integrity endeared her to the Beauvoir sisters. She is thus able to bring to her study facts, documents, and interviews not available elsewhere. She gives an exceptionally humane picture of the highly intelligent Simone, often depicted as arrogant, who moved away from a restrictive milieu, not without cost to herself, and ironically became for many women the inspired "mother-figure" of their emancipation.

Germaine Brée

Preface

I first became acquainted with the works of Simone de Beauvoir not, like many of her readers, through *The Second Sex,* but rather through her 1954 novel *The Mandarins,* which I chose as a text for a second-year French class for which I was a teaching assistant in the mid-1950s. It was not a particularly wise choice for that level of French—my Stanford University students were lacking the vocabulary and cultural and political background necessary to appreciate it fully—but there was something about the forthright style and the presentation of ideas that drew me to its author and set me to reading everything she had written up to that point. When it came time to choose a Master's thesis topic, I decided to write about "The Problem of Communication in the Works of Simone de Beauvoir."

The years went by and I completed my degree and began teaching at California State University, Hayward. I spent my first sabbatical catching up on all of the books Simone de Beauvoir had written since I had finished my doctorate in 1964. A graduate course devoted entirely to her works drew the largest enrollment we had ever had at that level in the Hayward French Department. A colleague of my mother's in the French Department of New York City's Julia Richman High School suggested that since I returned to France on a regular basis each summer I should try to interview Simone de Beauvoir. My first reaction was, "Why would she grant an interview to *me*?" Then I recalled her comment in her autobiography that she was always pleased to talk to people doing serious research on her work and I decided it was worth a try. She answered my letter immediately and indicated how and when to get in touch with her when I was in Paris. I spent an hour at her apartment on the rue Schoelcher in June 1978, having approached the doorbell with much trepidation, but realizing as soon as we began to talk that beneath the rapid-fire responses was a great deal of warmth and caring. As I was leaving, she thanked me for being so interested in her work. There was no problem of communication there.

In December 1981, after a fiery and provocative special session at the Modern Language Association convention in New York City, Professor Jacques Zéphir suggested that we form a Simone de Beauvoir Society. Its membership has been constantly expanding ever since. I took over as its president in 1983. Simone de Beauvoir remained in close touch with the Society and expressed her appreciation for its role, through its newsletters and its journal, the *Simone de Beauvoir Studies,* in making her writing better known in the United States and indeed throughout the world.

In 1978 I had become acquainted with Hélène de Beauvoir, the "Poupette" of her sister's memoirs. She had never been to the San Francisco area, so I decided that we would see about arranging an exhibition of her paintings that would provide that opportunity for her and also give the Bay area a chance to observe the talents of the younger sibling of the Beauvoir family. By 1985 I was hard at work on the manuscript of this book. In September of that year I spent another hour at the rue Schoelcher apartment, talking with Simone de Beauvoir both about the art-exhibit project and about her ideas on motherhood. That interview appears in appendix A of this book. Beauvoir was very supportive of my plans for the exhibit, which I was able to coordinate with a three-day conference on "Autobiography and Biography: Gender, Text and Context" sponsored by the Center for Research on Women at Stanford University in April 1986.

April 1986. A fateful date for Beauvoir admirers and scholars. Hélène was our houseguest, a lively and successful *vernissage* had been held for the opening of her exhibit at the Office of the President at Stanford. Hélène Wenzel, editor of the special issue of *Yale French Studies* devoted to Simone de Beauvoir, Deirdre Bair, Beauvoir's official biographer, and I had participated in a panel discussing "Simone de Beauvoir and Biography" for the CROW conference on Saturday, April 12. Despite the beautiful weather and the excitement of the conference, a cloud hung over all of our activities: Simone de Beauvoir was in the intensive-care unit at the Hôpital Cochin. The phone call came early on the morning of April 14: Simone de Beauvoir had just died. My first priority was to facilitate Hélène's return to Paris. Once she had walked down the ramp to her plane, I realized what a tremendous sense of loss I felt for the woman whose ideas and writing had so influenced my own.

When Hélène de Beauvoir called to tell me about the funeral arrangements for Saturday, April 19, I knew I had to be there. Only in that setting could I feel a part of the kind of mourning I needed to do for the loss of someone with whom most Americans had only a passing acquaintance. I quickly arranged to fly to Paris, where I followed along in the cortège which blocked traffic on the Boulevard du Montparnasse on a drizzly spring afternoon as five thousand people paid tribute to the author of *The Second Sex*.

In reading through Simone de Beauvoir's works, I had always been disturbed by her very negative attitude toward the family. I was fortunate enough to have been raised in a very loving Italian-American family with parents who were my best cheering squad for anything I wanted to attempt. My mother taught French, Spanish, and Italian at Julia Richman High School, a public high school in New York City which enrolled only girls until the 1970s. Her students adored her and I loved being fussed over by them when I was a little girl and she would take me to school to sit in on one of her classes. When I went on to become a French teacher too, she would say quietly but with great pride, "Oh, I only teach at the high-school level, but my daughter is a university professor." Perhaps naively, I was never aware of the kind of wrenching rivalry that seems to exist between many mothers and daughters.

Since I belong to the much-maligned college generation of the 1950s, most of my contemporaries were producing three, four, and five children while I was busily working away on my Ph.D. at Stanford. I would have very much liked to follow suit after I married in my late twenties, but my biological clock was to allow us only one child, a son who has been a real joy for both of us. Motherhood certainly did take some juggling of schedules so that I could continue to teach full-time. We were fortunate to find a reliable baby-sitter who remained with us for seven years. There were some raised eyebrows when I told friends that I intended to return to the classroom when our son was a year old. Today the raised eyebrows appear when mothers say they plan on quitting their jobs and staying home to raise their children.

Simone de Beauvoir once remarked that people have children in the hope of producing replicas of themselves for posterity. If anything became patently clear to me as our son was growing up, it was that he had no intention of becoming a replica of either me or my husband. When he was about ten years old and struggling through a French class in private elementary school, he remarked cannily to me one afternoon as I was drilling him on irregular verbs, "You know, Mom, just because you like to spend your time talking French and playing tennis doesn't mean that I have to like those things too." Never the compulsive straight-A student that both of his parents were, he wondered when I came home one day enthralled with the challenge of taking a beginning German course, "How can anyone be that enthusiastic about something you have to study?" After some early years of trying to push him in the directions I had found most satisfying, I realized that I needed to back off and let him follow his own instincts. Our relationship, always a close one, was much more relaxed once I had learned that lesson. I put the bulk of my energy into teaching, and he managed to wend his way through college into a challenging career as a sports journalist. Motherhood, at least in my case, has never represented the enslavement and abandonment of autonomy associated with it by Simone de Beauvoir and other militant feminists.

For the past five years, I have been teaching a Women's Studies course at Hayward State which I call "Mothers, Daughters, and Sons." It is through the students in that class that I have become aware of both the joy and the pain that can exist in mother-child relationships. In the backgrounds of those students who come to my office to confide in me, I see some of the pitfalls of the misdirected motherhood Simone de Beauvoir describes so vividly in her works.

This book is an attempt to explore Beauvoir's attitudes toward motherhood, to examine her relationship with her own mother, her lingering memories of the domineering presence of the mother of her best friend Zaza during their adolescence, her portrayal of mothers in her fictional works, and her pronouncements on motherhood in her essays and interviews. In the Introduction, I have tried to survey key American and French attitudes toward the role of motherhood in twentieth-century society. Despite her personal choice not to marry and not to have biological children of her own, Simone de Beauvoir would be the first to admit that this is obviously not a path to be recommended unilaterally for all women. In my opinion, feminists and women in general need to deal with the question of motherhood and to look beyond the issues of contraception and abortion to determine how best to incorporate the birth and raising of children into the feminine experience.

Introduction: "Throw Momma from the Train": American and French Views of Motherhood in the Twentieth Century

"Throw Momma from the train ... a kiss, a kiss." These lyrics of a popular 1940s tune seemed reasonably appalling when they were first heard, suggesting for a moment the unthinkable, the possibility that the sacrosanct mother idolized for one Sunday every May and theoretically for the rest of the year as well could ever inspire rage and an urge toward violence and destruction. There was an audible sigh of relief when the second line of the lyrics, "a kiss, a kiss," was vocalized. In late 1987, however, a film adopted that very song title, but with the kiss deleted. It is no longer considered sacrilegious to admit that the mother-child relationship is fraught with feelings of ambivalence and even of violence.

Simone de Beauvoir was one of the first modern feminists to articulate the problems inherent in the rapport between mother and children and to warn of the dangers of this often all-too-symbiotic relationship both for the independence and sense of identity of the mother and for the healthy development of the child. In her moving account of the last weeks of her own mother's life, *A Very Easy Death,* the author referred to her relationship with Françoise de Beauvoir as a dependence she both cherished and detested. Beauvoir evolved from a little girl who adored her beautiful and affectionate mother to a rebellious adolescent isolated from that same mother by her loss of faith at age fifteen to an independent intellectual continuing to maintain polite but somewhat distant contact with her aging mother. These stages reflected an ongoing struggle in the author between a certain nostalgia for the lost paradise of childhood and the firmness of her feminist convictions. This struggle is clearly mirrored in almost all of her writing, be it autobiography, fiction, or the still resonating essays of *The Second Sex*. It is a struggle which has come to occupy center stage for younger feminists torn between a need to be liberated from everything their mothers represent and a longing to participate in the maternal experience both as daughter and as mother.

The Questioning of the Mom–and–Apple Pie Mentality in the United States

Margaret Sanger

The chapter of *The Second Sex* entitled "The Mother" brought cries of outrage in 1949 from readers offended by its frank emphasis on contraception and abortion, on avoiding motherhood rather than on basking in its touted joys. Yet Simone de Beauvoir was certainly neither the first nor the last respected author to question the validity of enshrining the institution of motherhood beyond the reach of all discussion or analysis. As early as 1928, Margaret Sanger published *Motherhood in Bondage*,[1] a collection of excerpts from the plaintive letters of women from all parts of the United States and Canada who had written to her in the hope that she could do something to free them from what she labels "the bondage of enforced maternity." (xi) The mothers are presented as "enslaved" (xi) by Sanger, who spearheaded a birth control movement long before modern medicine had invented the pill. She contrasts the intellectuality of the arguments presented against birth control with the very real suffering of the mothers appealing to her for help.

Sanger emphasizes the particular hardships to which farm mothers and those from poor families are subjected as well as the medical hazards of childbearing in the early twentieth century. She is adamant in pointing out the disastrous effects of excessive childbearing, which she calls "a type of slavery that is a disgrace to American ideals and that constitution which guarantees to every citizen the right to life, liberty and the pursuit of happiness." (xvix) In her conclusion, Sanger calls upon the families of the future to control procreation voluntarily and to concentrate on cultivating the art of parenthood so that each child born may be a wanted child. Large families, high infant and maternal mortality rates, long considered "normal," are no more so than an epidemic of typhoid, Sanger proclaims. In the final sentence of her book, Sanger calls for the immediate abolition of enslaved motherhood.

Philip Wylie, Hans Sebald, and "Momism"

Philip Wylie's 1942 *Generation of Vipers*[2] is one of a number of books depicting mother as monster. With outrageous cynicism, Wylie coins the term "momism" and calls up legendary images of the female devouring her young. He accuses the United States of being overrun by "megaloid momworship" (185) and berates the American male for never having had the courage to "[pronounce] the one indubitably most-needed American verity: 'Gentlemen, mom is a jerk'" (186). Focusing primarily on the mother-son relationship, Wylie espouses the Freudian concept of the castrating woman, blaming Mom for having taken away her son's sense of adventure and for having used psychological blackmail to discourage him from seeking new horizons far away from her apron strings. Philip Wylie greatly admired the audacity of the ideas Simone de Beauvoir presented in *The Second Sex,* and the unnamed heroine of the Beauvoir story "Age of Discretion" bears some resemblance to the possessive mother against whom Wylie is railing.

Wylie's description of the middle-aged matron of the 1940s absorbed in bridge games, cocktails, the sentimentality of the radio soap operas, and lunch with the girls, the perennial clubwoman keeping a tight grasp on the family checkbook, is laden with hyperbole. He fearlessly depicts women as self-serving, domineering, and hypocritical in their expression of concern for the fate of their offspring and accuses them of undermining their sons' sense of their own worth. Wylie compares mom to Hitler and labels her "the American pope," (195) albeit a female pope preparing her daughters for "a place in the gynecocracy" (195). Slipping into a bit of comic relief, he declares that all the material for his chapter entitled "Common Women" was gleaned from his observations as a department-store clerk. "Clerks see moms in the raw" (200), he proclaims. In the final paragraphs of this irreverent tirade, the author calls upon all self-respecting males to join together in a battle aimed at "the conquest of momism, which grew up from male default" (203).

More than three decades after *Generation of Vipers* hit the bookstores, Hans Sebald wrote a more scholarly and seemingly less emotional analysis of Wylie's theories in a study entitled *Momism: The Silent Disease of America.*[3] In this later book, mom and momism have evolved from Wylie's spelling with lowercase "m's" to the more formidable abstraction of the upper case. Treating the middle class as the "breeding ground for Momism," Sebald describes in detail what he labels the "Momistic child" (41). He defines Mom as an "incompletely emancipated woman" (43) who espouses an intellectualized approach to child rearing and seeks self-expression and career satisfaction within the family. That this phenomenon has in no way been confined to American women will be seen when we examine Simone de Beauvoir's analysis of the frustrations which led her mother to invest all of her energy and talent in the raising of her two daughters.

Sebald makes a distinction between the fully emancipated woman's conscious and free choice of a domestic career and the partially emancipated woman's grudging acceptance of it as her unavoidable destiny. He uses imagery similar to Beauvoir's in his portrayal of women trapped in the wife-and-mother role as victims of "psychological self-incarceration" (45). Suggesting that motherhood often proves to be quite different from the blissful state depicted by the media, Sebald comments wryly, "Unlike a disappointing marriage, disappointing motherhood cannot be resolved by divorce" (47). The children are there and must be dealt with, he notes, and the trapped woman on whose shoulders the entire responsibility for their upbringing may fall often creates a psychologically damaging home situation for all concerned out of sheer frustration and exhaustion.

Sebald differentiates between a mother, who does not need to manipulate her children through conditional love, and a Mom, who does, postulating a craving for love in Moms, who, in his opinion, have an inordinate and obsessive need for some kind of recognition. Like Simone de Beauvoir, he feels that a salaried job is an effective way of breaking out of the hothouse atmosphere of the nuclear family for both mother and children and he attributes the relatively lower incidence of neurosis in lower-class children to the fact that so many more lower-class women than middle-class women have traditionally worked outside the home.

The presence of siblings may well diffuse the impact of what Sebald labels "Momistic practices," in his opinion (62). This certainly seems to have been the case for the Beauvoir sisters, who banded together in a concerted effort to win some degree of privacy and independence for themselves during an adolescence clearly dominated by the authoritarian personality of the well-meaning but emotionally awkward Françoise de Beauvoir. In his discussion of Arnold W. Green's report on "The Middle-Class Male Child and Neurosis," Sebald begins to sound more like the caustic Philip Wylie as he praises Green for "pinpointing the crippling peril and unveiling the hidden savagery of Mom's repressive transactions" (65). Green considers the constant threat of the withdrawal of parental love as the basis of "the most characteristic modern neurosis" (69). This threat produces infantile adults who are continually searching for the acceptance and approval they felt was denied them during their childhood. Sebald refers to such individuals as "Momistically impaired persons" (70–71) who tend to avoid being alone, preferring what Jean-Paul Sartre would call the judgmental look of the Other to relying on themselves for approval and love.

Focusing on the general lack of rites of passage in contemporary American society, Sebald emphasizes their importance, particularly for young men who must repress their early symbiosis with their mother and clearly proclaim their masculinity. The absence of the kind of public manifestation of maturity which is commonplace in many primitive tribes "robs a child of his last chance of escaping from a mother-imposed, continual childhood" (82). Like Philip Wylie, Hans Sebald is articulate and persuasive in placing the blame for neuroses and myriad other ills of modern society squarely on maternal shoulders.

Betty Friedan

It is apparent that both Philip Wylie and Hans Sebald have cast mothers in the villainous role of monsters responsible for all of the problems afflicting their offspring, and particularly their male offspring. Women writers dealing with motherhood tend to see the issues from a dual perspective, identifying both with the problems inherent in the maternal role and with the effects of inept mothering on children in general and occasionally on the children they once were. Betty Friedan's *The Feminine Mystique*,[4] admittedly influenced by her reading of *The Second Sex*, was a landmark in the development of American feminism, highlighting as it did the lack of identity and fulfillment sensed by women who had followed the traditional path from college to marriage to motherhood. Published in 1963, the book questions the direction taken by the lives of women who graduated from college in the 1940s and 1950s, as Friedan recalls her own ambivalence about continuing graduate work rather than settling into the cocoon of the suburban housewife and the subsequent painfulness of the loss of her career orientation when she chose the latter alternative.

When Betty Friedan returned to her alma mater to interview Smith College seniors in 1959, she was aware of the dread with which these talented young women viewed life after the age of twenty-one, of the escapism involved in relying on imminent wedding plans as a solution to the problem. Noting that many young women were adamant about not wanting to follow in the footsteps of their mothers, the author found that this vacuum of female role models was being filled by the supercilious images of womanhood provided by the media. High-school girls she interviewed would opt to become female Peter Pans rather than grow up and become like their mothers. In a devastating appraisal, one seventeen-year-old told Friedan, "My mother doesn't serve any purpose except cleaning the house." A college junior who had seen her own mother's frustration at having given up a career as a reporter to raise her family admitted, "I don't want to be interested in a career I'll have to give up. . . . Maybe education is a liability" (74).

Betty Friedan herself remembers being haunted by the negative impression left by career women, who were often cruelly labeled old maids by middle class society:

> None of these women lived in the warm center of life as I had known it at home. . . .
> I dreaded being like them, even the ones who taught me truly to respect my own mind and use it, to feel that I had a part in the world. I never knew a woman, when I was growing up, who used her mind, played her own part in the world, and also loved, and had children (75).

Returning to the impression she gleaned from talking to the Smith seniors of the class of 1959, Friedan muses: "What if the terror a girl faces at twenty-one is the terror of freedom to decide her own life, with no one to order which path she will take, the freedom and the necessity to take paths women before were not able to take?" (76). This is perhaps the other side of the coin on which Alain-Fournier imprinted in indelible fashion Augustin Meaulnes's reluctance to settle into married life and abandon the adventures of the wanderer. Is it not a choice which the women of the 1980s, particularly those who are college-educated, are forced to make now that it is no longer socially acceptable to be labeled "just a housewife"?

Betty Friedan concludes that those in her Smith class who married right out of college simply postponed confronting the terror of finding their own identity, a terror which returned to haunt them after their children had left home and they found themselves in their forties, isolated between the walls of their meticulously appointed houses. Like Simone de Beauvoir in the concluding chapters of *The Second Sex,* Friedan came to look upon salaried jobs as a focal point for woman's liberation. According to Friedan, a woman "can find identity only in work that is of real value to society—work for which, usually, our society pays" (346). In the United States, and undoubtedly in many other cultures as well, a paycheck is tangible evidence of appreciation of work well done, an appreciation which both Philip Wylie and Hans Sebald found their "Moms" desperately and neurotically seeking from family members whose words would never be quite reassuring enough.

Focusing once again on the problems of motherhood in her 1981 book *The Second Stage,* Betty Friedan recognizes the importance of allowing

modern women to choose to have their own children or "to be genera-
tive in other ways."[5] She notes that the only child is rapidly becoming
the norm in American families, that "the choice to have a child becomes
for many women and men a profound statement of human values, an
assertion of human priorities in defiance of pressures to material and
career success" (259). Such a choice must include consideration of who
will take care of the child in a family where both father and mother are
very likely to be involved in full-time careers. In a chapter entitled
"Take Back the Day," Friedan proposes a variety of practical approaches
to the ever-present question of effective child care, a question which has
yet to be resolved satisfactorily for the vast majority of working mothers.
Issues of part-time work, maternity and paternity leaves, extended families, flextime schedules, and the phenomenon of the superwoman all
figure in Friedan's analysis of the second stage of the women's movement, many of them echoing suggestions sketched by Simone de
Beauvoir in *The Second Sex* more than thirty years earlier.

Shirley L. Radl

The bookstore shelves of the 1970s contained a number of books written
by American women tackling the increasingly complex question of the
balance between liberation and motherhood. Entitling her analysis
Mother's Day Is Over,[6] Shirley L. Radl examines the contrast between the
ageless, ever-patient mothers of television situation comedies such as
"The Brady Bunch" and "My Three Sons" and the reality of everyday
life. Radl describes as insidious the television-commercial implication
that if you buy the right products you too can find motherhood "easy,
fun and vastly fulfilling.... The cumulative message of the media is
that motherhood is beautiful and a woman without children is an unhappy woman indeed" (6). Radl's book articulates her resentment of the
trivializing and demeaning aspects of the television version of the feminine mystique and declares, "Neither love nor sudsier suds can make
you like the responsibility, drudgery, or boredom that all mothers know
deep down go with caring for their children" (7). Observing women
who, despite their experience with the reality of maternal responsibility,
continue to produce child after child, Radl suggests that this is perhaps
a vain attempt to make the motherhood myth come true.

A number of women interviewed by Shirley L. Radl were honest
enough to admit that, although they loved their children, they might
well opt to have none if they had it to do all over again, that they felt
guilty about their inability to be perfect mothers. "When our media-fed
cultural attitudes, telling us that parenthood is normal, natural, fun and

easy, collide with a child-centered society that makes parenthood a very hard job indeed, a kind of schizophrenia results. . . .," Radl comments (16). Her analysis includes a hard look at the myriad and conflicting "expert" opinions on child-rearing and suggests that we were perhaps better off when we simply followed our own instincts. In an admirably frank appraisal of the situation, Radl confesses, "Many women come to feel, as I do, that the scales of motherhood do not really balance out for them, that the rewards of motherhood . . . are not great enough to offset the difficulties and plain unpleasantness of so much of the job" (18–19). Proclaiming that there is nothing unnatural about the logical evaluation of the pros and cons of having children, the author labels motherhood "both a career and an affliction," a situation in which the mother gives and the children take (20).

Jessie Bernard

In 1974, Jessie Bernard examined *The Future of Motherhood,* [7] seeing both motherhood and the isolated home as relatively recent products of an affluent society. She contrasts the shared care of infants in tribes in Kenya, India, Okinawa, and Mexico with the total responsibility for child raising assumed by the twentieth-century American mother, commenting, "It is as though we had selected the worst features of all the ways motherhood is structured around the world and combined them to produce our current design" (9). Bernard's research into studies of mothering suggests that maternal warmth is present in inverse proportion to the burden of child care placed on the individual mother. Entitling her introductory chapter "Mother Is a Role, Women Are Human Beings," she quotes the assertion made by Ibsen's Nora in the 1879 play *A Doll's House* that, more than a wife and mother, she is primarily a human being, just as her husband is.

Like Shirley L. Radl, Jessie Bernard was very much aware that many women were "daring to say that although they love children, they hate motherhood" (14). These women were objecting to being saddled with the sole responsibility for child care and to the isolation from the outside world which this entails. Children who were the victims of the "smother-love" so sharply criticized by Philip Wylie and Hans Sebald had come to look upon their mothers as "devouring vultures" rather than flawless madonnas, according to Bernard (15). Seeing the Victorian model of the family as an anachronism in the twentieth century, Bernard concludes, "We can't go home again. Not, at least, to the Victorian home" (16).

Jessie Bernard is one of several authors who agrees with psychoanalyst Erik Erikson's call for a new balance between the sexes rather than a concentration of nurturance in women and of power in men. She urges mothers to take an active role in the political process, to organize in fighting for their children's right to live in a healthy, peaceful, and secure environment. In the concluding sentence of her study, she proclaims, "We cannot . . . afford to deprive either sex of the strengths of the other. Motherhood . . . is too important to leave to women. Inside or outside of the home" (365).

Adrienne Rich

One of the most poetic and most anguished studies of motherhood in the late twentieth century can be found in Adrienne Rich's 1976 study *Of Woman Born*, subtitled "Motherhood as Experience and Institution."[8] Her first chapter, "Anger and Tenderness," immediately plunges the reader into the ambivalence of the maternal experience with a passionate entry from the author's own journal written in November 1960: "My children cause me the most exquisite suffering of which I have any experience. It is the suffering of ambivalence: the murderous alternation between bitter resentment and raw-edged nerves, and blissful gratification and tenderness" (21). Like Shirley L. Radl and the women she interviewed, Rich once saw it as her ineluctable fate "to serve a function for which I was not fitted" (21). In one poignant passage after another, Rich articulates the depths of maternal emotion, commenting on protectiveness, anger, jealousy, hope, and fear, on the assumption that maternal love "is, and should be, quite literally selfless" (22), on her concern that she might be an abnormal monster because she could not slip easily into the myth of motherhood.

Reminiscing about her children's early years, Adrienne Rich recalls vividly the way in which each of her three sons attempted to monopolize her completely, her rage at having her needs "always balanced against those of a child, and always losing" (23). Jumping from her journal entries of the 1960s to a 1975 meeting of women poets who were discussing the case of a depressed mother of eight who had murdered and decapitated her two youngest children on her suburban lawn, Rich notes, "The words are being spoken now, are being written down; the taboos are being broken, the masks of motherhood are cracking through" (24–25). Like Beauvoir, Friedan, Radl, and Bernard, Rich was willing to do her part to help destroy the masks which had effectively falsified the image of motherhood for so many centuries.

Adrienne Rich shares a good deal of herself with her readers in the candid lines of *Of Woman Born*. She acknowledges that she became a mother without ever questioning what she herself wanted, sensing that "to have a child was to assume adult womanhood to the full, to prove myself, to be 'like other women'" (25). As a teenager, she had written poetry and dreamed of going to postwar Europe as a journalist. Yet she married, and, she confesses, "As soon as I was visibly and clearly pregnant, I felt, for the first time in my adolescent and adult life, not-guilty" (26). Peer pressure, the images promulgated by the media, and family expectations all combined to encourage a mindless acceptance of her so-called female destiny as a wife and mother.

Recalling her husband's laudable willingness to help at home, she nonetheless reflects, "It was clearly understood that this 'help' was an act of generosity; that *his* work, *his* professional life, was the real work in the family" (27). This is reminiscent both of Virginia Woolf's *A Room of One's Own* and of Betty Friedan's analysis of the validating quality of the regular paycheck in *The Feminine Mystique*, written more than a decade earlier than Rich's book. Expecting her third child yet determined to forge an identity of her own, Rich notes in her journal, "It is really death that I have been fearing—the crumbling to death of that scarcely-born physiognomy which my whole life has been a battle to give birth to—a recognizable, autonomous self" (29).

Throughout her recounting of her experiences as a mother, the reader senses in Adrienne Rich a constant tug-of-war between societal demands and the imperatives of her vocation as a poet. When people asked her why she didn't write poems about her children, she insisted that "poetry was where I lived as no-one's mother, where I existed as myself" (31). Recording with pleasure the gradual evolution of her sons from dependent and demanding beings to equals with whom she could share meaningful and difficult moments of her life, she admits, "For years I believed I should never have been anyone's mother, that because I felt my own needs acutely and often expressed them violently, I was ... the unwomanly woman in flight from womanhood" (32).

As she remembers her first pregnancy in her chapter focusing on mothers and sons, Adrienne Rich explains:

> I wanted to give birth, at twenty-five, to my unborn self, the self that our father-centered family had suppressed in me, someone independent, actively willing, original. . . . If I wanted to give birth to myself as a male, it was because males seemed to inherit those qualities by right of gender (193).

She points out the enormous influence of Sigmund Freud's theory of the Oedipus complex, which has made women afraid to show their sons physical affection and tenderness for fear of being overly seductive. Twentieth-century women have been encouraged to facilitate the loosening of the bond linking them to their sons and the strengthening of their sons' identification with their father. According to Rich's analysis,

> The fundamental assumption here is that the two-person mother-child relationship is by nature regressive, circular, unproductive, and that culture depends on the son-father relationship. . . . Through the resolution of the Oedipus complex, the boy makes his way into the male world, the world of patriarchal law and order. (197)

Sons have thus been conditioned to espouse power and aggression and to turn their backs on what have traditionally been considered the more "feminine" virtues. Summing up the feminist attitude toward mother-son relationships, Rich articulates a desire for sons "to discover new ways of being men even as we are discovering new ways of being women" (211).

Like Beauvoir, Friedan, and others before her, Adrienne Rich urges men to participate fully in the care and nurturing of their children, suggesting that "In learning to give care to children, men would have to cease being children" (216). She equates "patriarchal" with "anti-maternal" and discusses "the pressure on all women—not only mothers—to remain in a 'giving,' assenting, maternalistic relationship to men. . . . This is infantilizing to men, and it has meant a trapping of female energy" (213). She warns against the tendency to view the women's movement "as a potential healing of men's pain by women, a new form of maternalism, in which little by little, through gentle suasion, women with a new vision will ease men into a more humane and sensitive life" (214).

As she reread her old journals, Adrienne Rich experienced feelings of both grief and anger, "grief at the waste of myself in those years, anger at the mutilation and manipulation of the relationship between mother and child, which is the great original source and experience of love" (33). In the ninth chapter of *Of Woman Born*, she records the degree to which the relationship between a mother and a newborn child resembles an all-encompassing love affair, as well as the way in which giving birth automatically dredges up a woman's long-repressed and often ambivalent feelings about her own mother. Rich describes herself as a woman who had intermittently "tried to return to her mother, to repossess her and be repossessed by her, to find the mutual confirmation from and with another woman that daughters and mothers alike hunger for, pull away from, make possible or impossible for each other" (218).

Rich admits that she has found it painful to write about her own mother, who had trained seriously as a concert pianist and a composer before getting married after a ten-year engagement during which her future husband completed his medical training:

> My father, brilliant, ambitious, possessed by his own drive, assumed that she would give her life over to the enhancement of his. . . . She would "keep up" her music, though there was no question of letting her composing and practice conflict with her duties as a wife and mother. She was supposed to bear him two children, a boy and a girl (221).

Instead, like Françoise de Beauvoir, she produced two daughters, of whom Adrienne was the older. She taught both girls at home until the fourth grade, following a study plan carefully laid out by her husband, and undoubtedly being made to feel responsible for any failures or imperfections produced by that plan, according to her daughter. Adrienne Rich articulates the resentment this schedule engendered in her, her conviction that "my mother had chosen my father over me, had sacrificed me to his needs and theories" (222). In the hospital room in which she gave birth to her first child, the author sensed the presence of "the tangled thread running backward to where she had labored for three days to give birth to me, and I was not a son" (222). At age twenty-six, Rich had succeeded in producing a son. "Part of me longed to offer him for her blessing; part of me wanted to hold him up as a badge of victory in our tragic, unnecessary rivalry as women" (223).

The author is painfully aware that it is what she labels "the guilt of Everymother" that stands between her and the woman who "had been expected to help create, according to my father's plan, a perfect daughter" (223). Like Simone de Beauvoir reminiscing about the mother both cherished and detested, Adrienne Rich records being torn apart by "grief and anger *for* her, and . . . anger at her: the ancient, unpurged anger of the child" (224). It is of interest that Hélène de Beauvoir, in a 1986 interview contained in appendix B of this book, attributes her older sister's sometimes harsh pronouncements about their mother to the unresolved resentments of childhood and adolescence. Rich's admission of her ambivalent feelings toward her mother in *Of Woman Born* might be applied equally as appropriately to the poignant memories of *A Very Easy Death:*

> I no longer have fantasies . . . of some infinitely healing conversation with her, in which we could show all our wounds, transcend the pain we have shared as mother and daughter, say everything at last. But in writing these pages, I am admitting, at least, how important her existence is and has been for me (224).

That "infinitely healing conversation" calls to mind the focus of Ingmar Bergman's film portrayal of the mother-daughter relationship in *Autumn Sonata*. The healing aspect of it is indeed a fantasy, however, as actresses Ingrid Bergman and Liv Ullman portray the mother, a concert pianist who did not abandon her career priorities, and the affection-hungry daughter tearing each other apart emotionally throughout an anguished night of wine drinking and recriminations. According to Adrienne Rich, no matter what kind of mother any woman has had, "the child in us, the small female who grew up in a male-controlled world, still feels, at moments, wildly unmothered" (225).

Referring to the use of the term "matrophobia" by poet Lynn Sukenick, Rich defines it as "the fear not of one's mother or of motherhood but of *becoming one's mother*" (235), a fear eloquently recorded by Betty Friedan in her interviews with high-school and college-age women documented in *The Feminine Mystique*. According to Rich, "The loss of the daughter to the mother, the mother to the daughter, is the essential female tragedy" (237). She concludes that women who grow up feeling "unmothered" often spend their lives looking for someone, male or female, to mother them and footnotes this theory with a reference to Simone de Beauvoir's recollection of a dream in which her mother blends with Sartre, happily for a moment and then as a nightmare. This is part of the same passage in *A Very Easy Death* in which Beauvoir speaks of her both cherished and detested dependence on Françoise de Beauvoir.

Adrienne Rich suggests that a woman who has felt "motherless" often focuses her energies on "mothering" others, thereby depending on their neediness to reinforce her own sense of usefulness. What all women need, according to Rich, is "courageous mothering" (246), mothers who refuse to become victims, who help their offspring to focus on the myriad possibilities life holds for any human being, male or female. "The quality of the mother's life ... is her primary bequest to her daughter," Rich declares (237).

Noting that throughout history "childless" women have been regarded as somehow unwomanly, Rich refers to Albert Memmi's criticism of *The Second Sex*,[9] which suggests that Simone de Beauvoir "is suspect because she did not exercise what Memmi glibly describes as her 'woman's right' to bear children." (Rich, 251) Listing such "childless" women as Charlotte Brönte, George Eliot, Emily Brönte, Emily Dickinson, Christina Rossetti, Virginia Woolf, and Beauvoir, Rich declares that without them "we would all today be suffering from spiritual malnutrition as women" (252).

Rich's discussion of motherhood and daughterhood points out the societal pressure on adolescent girls to draw away from the women who have nurtured them and direct their attentions toward men. Only men, she proclaims, are considered " 'worthy' of our profoundest love and loyalty. Women are made taboo to women . . . in reuniting with our mothers, we are breaking this taboo" (255). Like so many other women writers, Adrienne Rich urges women to see themselves as something more than their husband's wife or their children's mother. "Motherhood," she points out, " . . . is *one part* of female process; it is not an identity for all time. . . . It is not enough to let our children go; we need selves of our own to return to" (37). Recalling her own experience, she confides, "I realize that I was effectively alienated from my real body and my real spirit by the institution—not the fact—of motherhood" (38–39). It is this institution, as it is delineated by patriarchal society, that she has joined Simone de Beauvoir in the battle to redefine.

Dorothy Dinnerstein

In her 1976 book entitled *The Mermaid and the Minotaur* . . . ,[10] Dorothy Dinnerstein sets out to analyze the roots of what are considered "normal" masculinity and femininity in a society in which child rearing is almost exclusively female-dominated, and to highlight "the depth of the necessity for shared early parenthood." (xiii) Emphasizing "the overwhelming power, attractiveness, and hatefulness of the person or persons who tend the body and support the emerging personality of the pre-verbal child," (xiii) she draws her title from half-human beasts like the mermaid and the minotaur, who reflect the inconsistency of the female and male roles children are raised to assume in contemporary society:

> The treacherous mermaid, seductive and impenetrable female representative of the dark and magic underwater world from which our life comes and in which we cannot live, lures voyagers to their doom. The fearsome minotaur, gigantic and eternally infantile offspring of a mother's unnatural lust, male representative of mindless, greedy power, insatiably devours live human flesh (5).

Dinnerstein notes the long span of time during which human offspring need physical care and the degree to which the female caretaker is limited in mobility and in her contact with the world extending beyond the hearth, a situation which has prevented most women from assuming an active role in the making of history. She points out the small percentage of the current female adult life span required for child bearing and lactation, the only parental tasks in which men cannot fully share.

"The human male's tendency to claim one-sided access to a female, and the human female's tendency to consent to this claim, are rooted first of all in infancy...," Dinnerstein proclaims (40). She notes the contrast between the all-encompassing influence of the mother and the relatively late impact of the father's presence on the developing child, a contrast which in her opinion encourages sons to assume "that love for a woman ... must not be allowed to interfere with the vital ties between men" (49) and young girls to have essentially positive feelings toward their father while reserving the negative ones for their mother.

Dinnerstein dwells extensively on the rage toward the mother felt by both male and female infants and on the ensuing need to punish, humiliate, and dethrone the mother. She sees the loss of the infant illusion of omnipotence as the source of human grief as well as the motivation for trying in vain to recapture the lost delight of infancy and perhaps recreate thereby the mother-infant relationship. Lovemaking appears to the author to be aimed at recapturing the harmony of this relationship, a motivation which Dinnerstein claims inhibits women from giving full rein to their sexual impulses and calls upon men to incorporate "*both* the worshipful and the derogatory, the grateful and the greedy, the affectionate and the hostile feeling toward the early mother" (69) into their attitude toward the women they love.

Acknowledging the body of literature currently devoted to the criticism of mothers and mothering, the author recognizes that nonetheless "most of us go on feeling that the mother-child tie is in some real sense sacred: ... it is clearly the most fundamental, universal, biologically sturdy tie we have" (76). She attributes the overwhelming power of mothers to the fact that their influence is strongest "in that emotionally crucial period when feelings are formed entirely without words, feelings which then survive without ever being touched by words, so that they never fall under the sway of more mature rational processes" (84). Adults are thus haunted by their recollection of what the author labels "the magically powerful goddess mother of infancy" (85).

Dinnerstein sees adult life as a masquerade carried on generation after generation by "childishly self-important men ... and childishly play-acting women" (87). Her central thesis is that men and women cannot achieve equality until women stop shouldering both the responsibility and the blame for the initial introduction of all infants to the human condition. She uses a maternal image of the "dirty goddess" associated with flesh and mortality and insists that the need to keep women subordinate would be mitigated by the participation of both male and female in the "dominion over the early flesh" (155). One of the author's deepest concerns is the tendency of women to step back and allow men to rule and run the world, to take refuge in "a sane world of food and flowers, houses and children, weddings and wakes, friendship and love" (158). Suggesting that both men and women fear female domination because they wish at all costs to avoid reverting to the helplessness of infancy which such power evokes, the author asserts that "to mother-raised humans, male authority is bound to look like a reasonable refuge from female authority" (175).

Dorothy Dinnerstein poses the interesting question of why human beings need bosses at all after the inevitably painful psychological struggle they have waged to depose the first despot in their lives, their mother. She highlights the degree to which most adults yearn to return to the childhood paradise in which someone else assumed full responsibility for their protection and their happiness and suggests that man makes use of woman "to hide from himself the depth of his capitulation to societal coercion, the depth of his failure to leave childhood behind and take his fate in his own hands" (188). In her opinion, the abiding resentment of the female domination of the early years of human life also deprives adult women of "the quasi-parental nurturant support" (194) that both sexes need in order to participate fully in the affairs of the world. Throughout this discussion, the author tends to emphasize the resentment of early nurturing, placing mother and child in the role of antagonists rather than that of beneficiaries of a mutually satisfying dependency.

In a perceptive analysis of Simone de Beauvoir's attitude toward the disenfranchisement of women in contemporary society, Dinnerstein states:

> In de Beauvoir's view, the central bribe to which woman succumbs is the privilege of enjoying man's achievements and triumphs vicariously, honored and treasured by him as arbiter, witness, nurturant servant-goddess, while enjoying immunity from the risks he must take (211).

A subsequent passage dealing with the female outsider pays tribute to Simone de Beauvoir as the author proclaims, "I rest —as anyone who is examining our gender arrangements must—on de Beauvoir's shoulders" (220). After several pages of quotations from Beauvoir's work, Dinnerstein concludes, however, that despite her insight, Beauvoir "still takes the male worldmaking enterprise at face value" (224).

Dorothy Dinnerstein sees in the fast-moving history of recent decades a renunciation of the magical roots of infancy in favor of a compulsive and frenetic focus on the present and the future. Her answer to

Sigmund Freud is that "what women want is to stop serving as scapegoats ... for human resentment of the human condition" (234). She points out that women have always known

> that large-scale politics are pompous and farcical; that science and logic are a limited and overrated part of our array of techniques for exploring reality; that face-to-face relations are in a basic sense the point of life; that flowers, gossip, the smell of food, the smiling of babies, embody and symbolize central human values. . . . (267)

This instinctive understanding of what is really important in life has remained unheeded, in Dinnerstein's opinion, because of the human tendency to disparage and denigrate female opinion and authority. She urges men to seek more from women than "maternal applause, menial services, and body contact" (269) and "to share overt formal responsibility for the human self-creative enterprise" (270). Emphasizing the importance of maintaining the bridge between generations that makes human beings aware of the continuum from past to present to future in face of new feminist rhetoric against the family and against childbearing, Dorothy Dinnerstein urges the human race to facilitate and support true collaboration between male and female in order to survive and maintain some historical sanity.

Nancy Friday

"I have always lied to my mother. And she to me."[11] The starkness of these two short sentences, which are the opening lines of Nancy Friday's 1977 best-seller *My Mother/My Self*, is reminiscent of the impact made by Camus's Meursault when he informs the reader in the very first words of *The Stranger*, "Mother died today. Or, maybe, yesterday; I can't be sure."[12] Whereas Camus's novel does not focus on the relationship between Meursault and his recently deceased mother, Friday's study concentrates on the frustrations felt by the author because of the way in which her widowed mother brought her up.

Nancy Friday regrets that her mother was unwilling to admit, as have Shirley L. Radl and Adrienne Rich, that she was "not really good at this mothering business" (19), and to suggest that Nancy look to other women to complete what she labels "the whole mother package" (20). She recognizes the value of daughters using as role models women whose "great virtue is the paradoxical one that they are not mother" (229). The fact that these surrogates do not have the symbiotic ties that their mother does with them allows them to encourage the younger person to try new things and to risk failure. Friday ties the sense of failure to an unarticulated societal imperative that a daughter should follow in her mother's footsteps: "So long as we have not repeated the model of our mother's life, most of us will live with a suspicion of failure, of being incomplete" (248).

As in Adrienne Rich's *Of Woman Born*, the reader of *My Mother/My Self* learns quite a bit about the author and her family. Widowed when she was twenty and left with the care of two small daughters, Nancy's mother invested all of her energies in their upbringing, just as Françoise de Beauvoir did when she found herself emotionally and physically abandoned by her husband. Unlike Françoise de Beauvoir, however, Nancy's mother had had an affectionate and almost reverent relationship with her own mother, who had summoned the courage to leave an unsatisfactory marriage with a written explanation to the four children she left behind about her reasons for doing so. In it she assured her oldest daughter, Nancy's mother, who was fourteen at the time, "To me motherhood has been the most beautiful thing in my life. . . . This is the hardest, bitterest moment of my life, leaving you, but I cannot do anything else" (51–52). Nancy interprets this letter in the following way:

> While she was a mother, she was a woman first. She would not go through all her short life celebrating only self-abnegation and the maternal emotions. She loved other ideas and people besides her children. She was their mother, but would not be their martyr—which is one reason they loved her so (52–53).

Instead of resenting this act of abandonment, Nancy's mother and her siblings admitted to nothing but admiration and adulation for their mother and her decision to live her own life.

Acknowledging the importance of symbiosis between mother and child during early infancy, Nancy Friday anticipates Nancy Chodorow's thesis in *The Reproduction of Mothering* when she states that "when one woman gives birth to another, to someone who is like her, they are linked together for life in a very special way" (39). Friday also points out the degree to which symbiosis can encroach on the emotional growth of both mother and child if it is allowed to continue too long. She warns against the maternal tendency to treat one's offspring as possessions rather than as individuals, to manipulate them by never quite giving them total approval. This keeps them trying unrealistically, throughout their entire adult lives, to gain that elusive assurance that they are doing things "right," i.e., in a way that can win Mother's unqualified praise and support.

Dr. Betty Thompson is quoted by Nancy Friday as equating Eden with the emotional relationship that once existed between the mother and the dependent infant, an Eden with which the individual is continually attempting to reconnect. According to psychoanalyst Dr. Richard Robertiello, women are ambivalent about taking the step toward maturity represented by an acceptance of their own sexuality. He indicates to Friday that "you can't be sexual and symbiotic with mother at the same time" (332). Friday sees the fundamental lie to which she refers in the opening sentences of her book as the inability of mothers and of daughters to admit to one another that they are both sexual beings.

Chapter 11 of *My Mother/My Self* is entitled "Marriage: The Return to Symbiosis." Nancy Friday theorizes that what most women are looking for when they marry is the same sense of security and affection, of Eden, that they had as babes in arms. Marriage is thus another attempt to reunite with Mother. Marriage is what Mother, society, and the happily-ever-after fairy tales have prepared young girls for all their lives, the "hidden agenda" (257) which encourages little girls to become anything they want, as long as they also become mothers: "Our marriage ... is proof that she has been a good mother.... In marriage we become the little girl who once took down the cookie sheet and imitated mommy. We also become mommy" (388–89). Like many of her predecessors, Nancy Friday focuses on the refrain played over and over for young girls suggesting that they will not be "real" women until they are mothers. She attacks the notion of maternal instinct as a tyrannical concept which "idealizes motherhood beyond human capacity" (35) and notes that many women in the 1970s are desperately trying to conform to all of society's mandates by combining careers and full-time motherhood, a task next to impossible for all but a very few exceptionally energetic individuals. Friday cautions that "you cannot base a rational society on all women being superpeople" (257).

It was not necessarily her mother, but rather society and convention, which pressured Nancy Friday into reconsidering her decision not to have children. Oft-quoted psychologist Helene Deutsch, interviewed by Friday when she was ninety-three years old, told Nancy categorically that she would always regret not having had children. Like both Simone and Hélène de Beauvoir, Friday insists that she has never regretted that decision.

Nancy Friday points out the counterproductive quality of blaming one's mother for everything that has gone wrong in one's life: "*Blaming mother keeps us passive, tied to her*. It helps us avoid taking responsibility for ourselves" (83). Focusing on anger, Friday asserts, "*It is not today's mother we are in a rage with*" (414). She notes how much time and energy are wasted being angry at one's mother and makes a distinction between anger and blaming. Indicating the evolution which has taken place within her since she began writing her book, she confesses:

> I am beginning to see that there is nothing I can ever do that will destroy my mother. I can be as sexual, as free, as different from her in my work and life as I choose, but can have a relationship with her too. It will be far more real than the mythic All-Loving Mommy I had been unconsciously holding out for (422).

Like many of the women writing on the subject before her, Nancy Friday urges women to make a conscious choice about becoming mothers: "Motherhood furnishes great feelings of worth and value, function and pleasure. The question some women are beginning to ask is, Is there something else I would rather do with my life that would be more satisfying still?" (446). For Simone de Beauvoir, the time to devote to her writing was clearly more satisfying, for Hélène de Beauvoir the time to devote to her painting.

When Simone de Beauvoir published *A Very Easy Death*, there was some criticism of her recounting the details of her mother's last weeks for the reading public. Nancy Friday quotes Dr. Richard Robertiello as stating that people who consider it cold and calculating to analyze their relationship with their mother "are still trying to hold on to her as children ... at some deep level they still fear she can be hurt by their thoughts. They are also demanding that she be immortal, postponing their separation" (454). In writing about her mother's death, Beauvoir was struggling with the symbiosis, the guilt, the need to separate as passionately as Nancy Friday does in *My Mother/My Self*.

Nancy Chodorow

Nancy Chodorow's 1978 study entitled *The Reproduction of Mothering*[13] focuses on the ramifications of the fact that mothering, and child rearing in general, have traditionally been the exclusive realm of women in Western society. This fact has meant, according to the author, that "women's mothering role ... has come increasingly to define women's lives" (4). Women thus tend to reproduce a desire to mother in their daughters and curtail the "nurturant capacities and needs" of their sons (8).

Chodorow's analysis reinforces Adrienne Rich's observations about the link between childbirth and a woman's emotional attachment to her mother: "Mothering is invested with a mother's often conflictual, ambivalent, yet powerful need for her own mother" (212). Both male and female children are often torn between the desire so eloquently expressed by Simone de Beauvoir in her recounting of her dream both to escape from and to return to their mother. Chodorow feels that everyone has a haunting desire to recreate the "exclusive symbiotic mother-child relationship" (201). The nature of this relationship underlies societal expectations that women will devote their entire energy to caring for other human beings and forgo separate interests of their own.

Highlighting the effect of the social structure on the way in which mothers relate to their children, Chodorow posits that women who "do meaningful productive work, have on-going adult companionship while they are parenting, and have satisfying emotional relationships with other adults ... are less likely to overinvest in children" (212). Along with Jessie Bernard and others who have studied the historically changing situation of the individual family, Chodorow emphasizes the importance of the female support network, which has gradually been disintegrating as families move more frequently and suburban living tends to isolate mothers of small children from daily contact with what she labels "female kin" (212). She suggests that "mother-daughter relationships in which the mother has no other adult support or meaningful work and remains ambivalently attached to her own mother produce ambivalent attachment and inability to separate in daughters" (213). This thesis will be echoed in the relationship between Françoise de Beauvoir and her daughters and particularly in Simone de Beauvoir's astonishment at the depth of her emotions when she realizes that her mother is indeed dying.

Like Beauvoir, Friedan, Rich, and many others, Nancy Chodorow considers it imperative that men begin to assume a more major role in the raising of children. She notes that men are beginning to regret the little time they have to spend with their children, feeling "that they are missing what remains one of the few deep personal experiences our society leaves us" (213). To bring about equality of the sexes, she states, it will be necessary to undertake "a fundamental reorganization of parenting, so that primary parenting is shared between men and women" (215). Chodorow clarifies her position in the final pages of her book:

> My view is that exclusive single parenting is bad for mother and child alike. . . . Mothers in such a setting are liable to overinvest in and overwhelm the relationship. Similarly, I think, children are better off in situations where love and relationship are not a scarce resource controlled and manipulated by one person only (217).

Her stance echoes opinions articulated by Philip Wylie, Beauvoir, and Hans Sebald. Such a sharing of child care would, in Chodorow's opinion, help women develop an autonomy which is often denied to them by what she labels "too much embeddedness in relationship" (218). Like Dorothy Dinnerstein, she feels that the present system "creates a psychology of male dominance and fear of women in men" (219). Chodorow urges men and women to join together in an effort to transform the current "social organization of gender" (219) with a view to bringing about equality of the sexes.

The 1980s

Moving into the 1980s, we find Kim Chernin's very personal 1983 book entitled *In My Mother's House*.[14] Chernin, a writer by profession, reluctantly acquiesced to the request that she write down the story of her mother's life. Rose Chernin wanted to assure that the events of the years that led her from her childhood in a Jewish *shtetl* in Russia to her septuagenarian existence in Los Angeles in 1974 would be recorded. As Kim Chernin interacted with both her mother and her daughter in her mother's home, she became aware of the fundamental difference between the generations they represented: "Hers, with its eye fixed steadily on survival. Mine freer, more frivolous, less scarred and, in my own eyes, far less noble" (6). Chernin explains her hesitation in the following words:

> I am torn by contradiction. I love this woman. She was my first great aching love. All my life I have wanted to do whatever she asked of me, in spite of our quarreling. . . . But . . . This enterprise will take years. . . . It will bring the two of us together to face all the secrets and silences we have kept. . . . I'm afraid. I fear, as any daughter would, losing myself back into the mother (12).

Her reluctance is an eloquent illustration of Dorothy Dinnerstein's theories. What Kim Chernin is attempting to produce is not the angry condemnation of a *Mommie Dearest* best-seller,[15] but rather an honest attempt to hear what her mother has to pass on to her about the way in which she has lived her life. Whereas Simone de Beauvoir's *A Very Easy Death* was clearly an effort to deal with the trauma of the loss of her mother's physical presence, Kim Chernin's book is a perceptive dialogue between mother and daughter, with the voices of grandmother and granddaughter adding to the spectrum of feelings presented. She assesses it as a tale of four generations:

> It is a tale of transformation and development—the female reversal of that patriarchal story in which the power of the family's founder is lost and dissipated as the inheriting generations decline and fall to ruin. A story of power. . . . I see generations

of women bearing a flame. . . . And now, . . . my mother imparts the care of it to me. I must keep it alive, I must manage not to be consumed by it, I must hand it on when the time comes to my daughter (16).

Like Nancy Friday and so many other independent women, Kim Chernin's mother Rose was determined to be different from *her* mother, to forge a life of her own once the family emigrated to America: "I loved my mother, I wanted to help her. . . . [But] I would not be my mother and no child of mine would be my mother" (39). She obviously still feels a certain amount of guilt about having left her mother to face a miserable and depressing life as the victim of an unloving husband's violence and caprice, yet justifies her decision by explaining, "I put aside everything to go after my own life" (54). In the course of the narrative, mother and daughter come to understand the ways in which each is unusual, liberated, and unwilling to sacrifice her own identity to her role as a mother. Kim Chernin followed up this moving and sensitive family biography with a 1985 study entitled *The Hungry Self,*[16] in which she traces eating disorders sych as anorexia and bulimia, which have become rampant among young women in the 1980s, to an unwillingness or inability to break the symbiotic relationship between mother and daughter.

A 1984 study by Carole Klein focuses on the mother-son relationship.[17] Noting that in primitive societies "giving birth to a son was a woman's only way of achieving status," (ll) Klein remarks that in the contemporary world it is the act of giving birth, rather than the wedding ceremony, which represents the crossing of the line between girlhood and womanhood. She suggests that for some women producing a son is a way of winning the attention and approval of a father who has seemed indifferent to them.

Commenting that we live in a society in which men are more valued than women, Carole Klein also points out that in the contemporary American world "the cultural belief persists that a good mother is an asexual person" (21), thereby echoing once again Nancy Friday's comments in *My Mother/My Self* about the basic lie separating mothers from daughters. Yet Klein is also aware of the erotic aspect of the mother-son relationship, stating that "whether the statement is made by Michelangelo, Renoir, or Picasso, . . . we immediately understand that even without father, mother and son together are remarkably complete" (25).

Another book focusing on the mother-son relationship is *The Hand That Rocks the Cradle,* published in 1985 by Mercedes Lynch Maloney and Anne Maloney.[18] The authors identify the source of the statement "The hand that rocks the cradle is the hand that rules the world" as a poem by William Ross Wallace. The book proposes to look at various historical figures in an attempt to determine the degree to which Wallace's statement can be considered accurate. In questioning how much actual influence mothers have on their children, the authors hope to arrive at some conclusions about the importance of motherhood itself.

The Maloneys point out the ambivalence of society's attitude toward mothers, combining as it does deference, reverence, neglect, and dismissal. As a counterbalance to a certain general skepticism about motherhood in modern society, Rose Kennedy is quoted as having declared, "I looked on child rearing not only as a work of love and duty but as a profession that was fully as interesting and challenging as any honorable profession in the world and one that demanded the best I could bring to it" (3). The authors note that motherhood currently is considered only one facet of a woman's life rather than its central focus. Questioning whether the cultural significance of motherhood will diminish now that it has become an option rather than an imperative, the Maloneys suggest that the crucial nature of the mother-child relationship makes it unlikely that maternal influence will be drastically reduced in the future despite the enormous changes in society that have taken place over the last century.

Commenting on how little information is available about the mothers of such American statesmen as Thomas Jefferson and Benjamin Franklin, the Maloneys remark that "motherhood is revered as a hallowed, even sacred calling, yet the women who do actually give their lives to the rearing of children are all but forgotten"(9). The authors note the uniqueness of the task placed before all mothers, who must display "both total dedication and the ability to let go. . . . the most selfless and the most difficult love of all: the love that fosters not dependency but freedom" (10). They feel that human history cannot be recounted truthfully unless it includes the stories of the mothers who formed the men who shaped it.

Books on motherhood continue to appear in American bookstores as the years of the twentieth century move to their conclusion. Among 1986 titles one finds *My Mother before Me,* subtitled "When Daughters Discover Mothers,"[19] *The Shock of Motherhood,*[20] and *Mothers on Trial,*[21] in which Phyllis Chesler focuses on the battle for custody of the children in a divorced family and discusses at length just how one can determine who is a "good enough" mother. A similar dilemma is examined in fictional form in Sue Miller's popular novel *The Good Mother.*[22] These books and others too numerous to cite in this study suggest the entanglement of emotions evoked by the whole question of motherhood and its place in late-twentieth-century American society. Before moving on to the presentation of mothers and motherhood in the works of Simone de Beauvoir, let us look briefly at the French counterparts to the titles which have appeared in the United States on the subject.

A Francophone Look at Motherhood

"Les Femmes s'entêtent"

The April–May 1974 issue of *Les Temps Modernes* entitled "Les Femmes s'entêtent" (Women Are Adamant) contains numerous articles dealing with the French feminist view of maternity. It is of interest to note that one French author after another refers to an almost official policy on motherhood promulgated by the Mouvement de Libération des Femmes, whereas American authors tend to rely almost exclusively on personal experiences and observations for the derivation of their theories. Introduced by Simone de Beauvoir, the special 1974 issue of *Les Temps Modernes* contains some very personal passages focusing on the problems of motherhood. Contributors are identified only by first names and discuss experiences with abortion, childbirth, child care, and reconciling feminism with motherhood.

As in *The Second Sex,* the sensitive issue of abortion in traditionally Catholic France becomes an immediate focus for the discussion of maternity. When Danièle speaks of aborting her second child, she declares emphatically, "No one will ever make me believe that an abortion is simply a medical intervention like having a tooth pulled,"[23] thereby challenging a certain prevalent feminist attitude which minimizes the emotional impact of having an abortion. She nonetheless contrasts the informative and supportive way in which her abortion was handled with the psychological horror of childbirth in a sterile and impersonal hospital. Another woman who gave birth to one child and then had five or six abortions suspects that she was trying to kill her mother in herself. A chilling story is told by an unidentified mother who, having given birth to a mongoloid child, planned successfully with supportive friends to smother the baby in order to spare it and her family a lifetime of pain.

Acknowledging that most people are delighted to welcome a new baby into the family, one article suggests that the experience would continue to be a positive one if the sole responsibility for bringing up that baby did not always fall squarely on the mother's shoulders. A discussion taken from a collective book entitled *Maternité esclave* (The Enslavement of Motherhood) concludes that the only logical choice for women who wish to be independent is to refuse to become mothers as long as procreation and exclusive responsibility for child rearing continue to be confused. A contrasting point of view is presented by a contributor who affirms that the great hope of the world lies in its children. Noting that the women's movement has tended to concentrate on the refusal to have children, this article suggests that women's desire for children be articulated rather than hidden as a guilty secret. Another contributor observes that emphasis on autonomy and independence for women is beginning to be replaced by an awareness of the importance of affection and emotion. "One is nothing all by oneself," she declares.[24]

The importance of the nurturing aspect of the mother-child relationship is highlighted by one contributor, who points out that partaking of food together is one of the main symbols for communication between two human beings in contemporary society, a symbol originating in the symbiotic rapport existing between the mother and the infant feeding at her breast. In the "Postface" to this special double issue of *Les Temps Modernes,* the "official" line of reasoning of the women's movement which labels enjoyment of motherhood as backward is questioned by a mother who feels that having a child makes one aware of the solidarity of all mothers. She asserts that by taking charge of her child, a mother is simply seeking an alternate path toward the realization of the revolution which will bring about a radical change in societal structure.

Les Cahiers du GRIF

Several issues of the Belgian-based *Cahiers du GRIF* (Groupe de Recherche et d'Information Féministes) comment on the problems associated with motherhood by the feminists of the 1970s. In her introduction to the pilot issue of this journal, Françoise Collin sees the modern family as the product of a capitalistic patriarchy whose children the mother is expected to take sole charge of reproducing and educating. [25] A 1975 article regrets the degree to which mothers are obliged by the social system to transmit traditional patriarchal values to the next generation. Emphasizing once again the burden of responsibility which falls upon the mother of the family, Collin remarks, "Married or not, we are all, . . . to some extent, single mothers. . . ."[26] Collin and her collaborators urge a change in society which will replace the nuclear family with collective parental responsibilities and encourage women to become happy human beings rather than what society has heretofore defined as good mothers.

In a double issue published in 1977, Collin refuses to "condemn" maternity, yet highlights the paralyzing nature of the responsibilities it entails.[27] Françoise d'Eaubonne, who wrote a book about Beauvoir after her death, disagrees with the latter's denial of the existence of maternal instinct. The essence of what we call maternal instinct, in d'Eaubonne's opinion, is the need inherent in all human beings, male or female, "to seek a continuation of themselves and to pass on the best of themselves to a young person whom they may help toward adulthood, toward becoming a useful and happy individual."[28] More recently, in 1985, psychoanalyst Julia Kristeva reiterated in an interview for the journal her conviction that maternal influence is the essential component of all passionate relationships.[29]

L'Histoire des mères

In 1980, history professors Yvonne Knibiehler and Catherine Fouquet put together the extremely well-documented and beautifully illustrated *L'Histoire des mères, du Moyen Age à nos jours* (The History of Mothers from the Middle Ages to the Present Day).[30] In their introduction, they point out that recent laws liberalizing contraception and abortion have allowed women the negative freedom of avoiding motherhood, but that little has been recorded about existing collectively and actively as mothers. Their book aims at helping mothers build a future based on a knowledge of their past.

From the Middle Ages onward, history shows that mothers have been expected to pass on values, traditions, and conventions, particularly to their daughters. In the seventeenth century, Madame de Maintenon cited a taste for hard work and obedience as the primary virtues a mother should instill in her daughter. Jean-Jacques Rousseau wanted his fictional Sophie to be raised to keep Emile happy and to dedicate herself to the care of their children. Knibiehler quotes the nineteenth-century historian Michelet, for whom every woman was a "school" teaching beliefs to succeeding generations.[31]

It is suggested that the triumph of Rousseau's permissive theories of child raising led to two centuries of emphasis on the welfare of the child rather than on that of the mother. Theories, however, were adopted primarily by those in the upper echelons of society. Knibiehler notes that all the working-class mother generally handed on to her daughter was the image of her suffering, her resignation, and occasionally her rebellion.

Much discussion centers on the degree to which the male establishment, medical, political, and educational, has taken upon itself the instruction and protection of society's mothers. Birth has become a medical rather than a private event in the twentieth century. Knibiehler accuses obstetricians, gynecologists, and pediatricians of favoring the child's interest to the exclusion of the mother's. Noting Freud's influence on child rearing, she observes a progressive infusion of psychiatric theories and guilt into the lives of mothers striving to fulfill their role conscientiously. Women are told that they are an irreplaceable part of their children's early years and that they are at the same time likely to be responsible for any problems, complexes, and traumas these children develop later in life. As responsibilities increase, the mother's self-assurance declines and her authority begins to be questioned by her children even while they are still quite young.

Like Simone de Beauvoir and Yvette Roudy, who headed the Ministry for the Rights of Women during the first years of François Mitterrand's presidency, Knibiehler is suspicious of laws granting allocations of funds for mothers who stay at home. She fears that such incentives will further insulate women from the real world and leave them without marketable skills or a sense of purpose once their children have grown up and moved away. The creation of professional mothers will also risk reversing the trend of having young fathers assume an active and pleasurable role in the raising of their children.

In the final pages of the book, Knibiehler quotes the findings of a study examining the changing role of the family in the late twentieth century. Whereas the family was once considered the vehicle for transmitting a name, property, and culture to the ensuing generation, it has become primarily a refuge from the workaday world, a source of recreation and affection focused on the pursuit of happiness. With the ready availability of contraception and abortion, having children becomes an individual choice made for the pure pleasure of enjoying an intimate relationship with a newborn child. Knibiehler acknowledges that the present-day image of the mother is confused and ill-defined, and suggests that it is contemporary women who must join together to create a satisfactory definition of motherhood in the modern world.

Elisabeth Badinter

Elisabeth Badinter's *L'Amour en plus* (And Love Besides)[32] is a study of the history of maternal love in France from the seventeenth to the twentieth century. In it, Badinter discusses at length the so-called "maternal instinct" and concludes that there is essentially no such thing. She demonstrates that mothers have traditionally followed the social patterns of their day, which, particularly in eighteenth-century France, involved sending newborn infants off to spend their first years with a wetnurse, at great peril to their lives in a period of rampant infant mortality and apparently at little emotional cost to their mothers. In her 1981 preface to the Livre de poche edition of her book, the author expresses surprise at the passionate reactions the study has inspired and realizes that maternity continues to have a sacred aura about it, an association with an all-loving Virgin Mary who remains firmly embedded in our collective unconscious.

Badinter questions the 1971 Larousse definition of maternal instinct as an innate tendency in all "normal" women to have children and to watch over the physical and moral well-being of such children. She suggests that a woman can be perfectly normal without being a mother, and that there are surely mothers who do not instinctively wish to care for their newborn infants. Badinter sees the attacks of her critics as an indication that the one unthinkable "sin" in the eyes of modern society is a lack of interest in one's own child, that people will go to any length to explain away any information indicating that such indifference is indeed possible. Like Simone de Beauvoir and other modern feminists, the author accepts the idea of a multiplicity of feminine experiences rather than the notion of a feminine nature. Badinter asserts her conviction that maternal love has existed from the beginning of time but that it is not an innate quality in all women, noting that other women, fathers, and other men are just as capable of "mothering" as biological mothers. Who does the mothering is essentially a factor of the moral, social, and religious values of the era, in her opinion. By allowing for the possibility of significant variations in the degree of maternal love felt by individuals, Badinter feels that society can arrive at a better understanding of motherhood which can benefit both the child and the mother.

After a detailed analysis of almost four centuries of maternal love in France, Elisabeth Badinter concludes that the idea of maternal instinct is a myth, that maternal love cannot be taken for granted but is rather an extra, hence the title *L'Amour en plus*. She suggests that statistics should take into account paternal as well as maternal love as the influence of modern feminism and the women's movement alters the traditional relationships within the nuclear family. "Apparently," she theorizes, "maternal love is no longer the exclusive domain of women."[33]

Luce Irigaray

In two slender volumes published in 1979 and 1981, psychoanalyst Luce Irigaray has recorded her passionate interpretation of the mother-daughter relationship. The ambivalence of that dependence both cherished and detested by Simone de Beauvoir is poetically evoked in the opening line of *Et l'une ne bouge pas sans l'autre:* "With your milk, my mother, I drank in ice. And here I am now, frozen within."[34] The entire text is addressed directly to the author's mother, repeatedly evoked by the familiar pronoun *tu.*

Irigaray feels herself a prisoner of her mother's desire to protect her, to keep her always literally under her eye. Like Kim Chernin, she speaks of the legacy of generations of mothers and daughters, but in more pessimistic terms, suggesting that at some point in the future only a photograph will mark her mother's passage from her own mother to her daughter. The implication is that once her nurturing role is fulfilled, a mother is somehow no longer quite alive. The ice that she found in her mother's milk has paralyzed the daughter and frozen all possibility of exchange between them. Irigaray describes herself as imprisoned in her mother's lack of identity, limited by society's insistence on confining her to a mothering role, a *maternage.* The final paragraph uses the title phrase "And one doesn't budge without the other," and expresses Irigiray's need to have her mother remain alive after she has given birth to this daughter who is analyzing their relationship in such sensitive and passionate terms.

A second text reproduces a lecture and two interviews given by Luce Irigaray at a colloquium on "Women and Madness" held in Montreal in May 1980. Irigaray feels that the historical moment has come when the whole meaning of maternity is being questioned because of such issues as contraception and abortion and posits that our society and culture have been based on a matricide. The primordial murder was not, as Freud suggested in *Totem and Taboo,* that of the father, according to Irigaray, but rather that of the woman-mother, a murder deemed necessary to establish a certain political order.

Drawing on her psychoanalytical training, Irigaray asserts that Sigmund Freud's theories neglect the situation of the mother, torn between son and father. She points out that in therapy the psychoanalyst always places himself behind his patient, "like the mother toward whom one must not turn back." [35] Comparing this phenomenon with the legend of Orpheus and Eurydice, Irigaray deplores the fact that Western culture insists upon making the mother taboo. She suggests that one is always both trying to return to the womb and fearful of being smothered, contaminated by such a regression. The infant, in her opinion, is seeking at its mother's breast the shelter, nourishment, and warmth that it has lost by leaving her womb, through the "irreversible, irreparable wound created by the cutting of the umbilical cord."[36]

The second section of this volume, entitled "Nietzsche, Freud et les Femmes," contains an interview conducted by Suzanne Lamy and André Roy on May 28, 1980 in which Luce Irigaray speaks both of sisterhood and of reciprocal mothering in relationships between women. She urges women to make their peace with the mother within them, the introjected mother, as well as with their real mother. Irigaray states that, as Simone de Beauvoir became deeply aware, the physical death of one's mother does not remove her influence on her children. In her opinion, many women feel they themselves are dead after their mothers die, worry that they may have killed their mother, that they needed to have her die in order to exist.

For Luce Irigaray, maternity is not limited to the production of babies. It includes the creation of one's identity, of a life-style, of love, desire, language, art, of social, political, and religious concepts. Like so many other feminists, she exhorts mothers and daughters to be women above all else, to avoid being reduced to a maternal function prescribed by society. She proclaims that all men look for and need a *femme-mère*, a corporeal object that remains at their beck and call.

Irigaray's definition of a mother is a devastating one: "Someone who always acts according to commands and stereotypes, who has no language of her own and no identity."[37] Blaming the family for imprisoning mothers in a role demanding that they satisfy the needs of others but never their own, she suggests that women form a woman-to-woman relationship with their mothers in which either one can play the role of mother or of daughter. Such a radical change in the pivotal mother-daughter relationship is, in her opinion, the only way to overturn the patriarchy.

"Merci, Sigmund!"

In her popular 1985 book *Moi, ta mère,* Christine Collange, mother of four sons, questions the contemporary permissiveness in child rearing and pleads for some reciprocal sensitivity between parents and children. Pointing out that a mother is a human being with moments of weariness and weakness, the author expresses a desire to be considered a partner in the lives of her grown children. She takes pity on the parents of today's young adults, who tend to be blamed for whatever problems their offspring encounter. No longer willing to wait until her own children are mature enough to continue a dialogue that has been interrupted for ten years, Collange articulates her intention to use her book to talk to them about herself, "moi, ta mère."

Noting that in earlier eras parents could be satisfied with a job well done once their children were grown up and on their own, Collange amusingly tosses off a "Merci, Sigmund!"[38] to underline the degree to which Freud and his theories have contributed to a never-ending sense of parental, and most particularly maternal, guilt in the twentieth century. She wants to be relieved of her responsibility for anything that might go wrong with the lives of her now adult children. Agreeing with Elisabeth Badinter that one does not necessarily love a child simply because one has given birth to it, Collange is nonetheless convinced that it is extremely rare for maternal love to be totally extinguished in a woman who has once experienced it. Addressing her children, she admits that they are irreplaceable for her, that they occupy an enormous place in her life and her conversation, a place that continues to expand as they grow older.

Collange acknowledges that the superhuman task of transforming little animals into socialized beings takes a great deal of patience, and asserts in bold type that she is her children's mother, not their maid. She amusingly describes the permissiveness of contemporary society as Jean-Jacques Rousseau's revenge on Queen Victoria. The author feels that modern mothers have been forced to become spectators in the life battles waged by their children, having the right only to watch and remain silent. Sometimes overwhelmed by her maternal responsibilities, she recalls a particularly trying day when she wanted to be someone's child instead of everyone's mother. In her opinion, a wall of silence often prevents mothers from sharing their human weakness with their children. In this statement one hears the echo of Nancy Friday's plea that mothers be honest with their children in admitting that they are incapable of conforming to the media stereotype of the all-loving, all-sacrificing mother.

Unlike the mothers who have done everything to prolong their children's dependency and keep them from growing up, Christine Collange asserts that her offspring no longer represent the sole justification for her existence, and perhaps never have, even when they were babies. She feels that when mothers are in their forties they have a second chance to live their own lives, one which they must not miss if they are to have no regrets later. Echoing the terminology used by Simone de Beauvoir when she speaks of motherhood as enslavement, Collange informs her children that she will now regain her freedom and they will lose a slave.

Collange comments on the phenomenon of the *Pauvre Maman* (Poor Mom), a mother admired by sons and pitied by daughters resolved never to fit into that category themselves. These women are described as "heroic women, pelican women who have sacrificed their personal destiny in order to fulfill their maternal mission."[39] Collange has here transformed Alfred de Musset's male pelican of "La Nuit de mai," the distraught father who has only his heart to offer as nourishment for his starving children, into a female sacrificial victim. These "pelican women" are the relative beings described in *The Second Sex*, individuals who find sole justification for their existence in their ability to fulfill the needs of others who seem dependent upon them. Today's women are less likely to accept this martyr's role so dramatically depicted by Musset, according to Christine Collange.

The author joins Luce Irigaray in attacking the accepted Freudian theory that adolescents must rebel against their parents to attain maturity. "The more I think about it, the less I am convinced that it is absolutely indispensable that my children 'kill' me in order to become adults," she states.[40] Collange realizes that by encouraging her children to grow up and leave home she may be running the risk of having them forget her. The book ends as she affectionately assures her children that she will always have a wonderful memory of their childhood and hopes that the same will hold true for them.

Maternité en Mouvement

Maternité en mouvement (Motherhood on the Move) is a collection of scholarly essays on feminism and maternity based on papers presented at a colloquium held in January 1984. The foreword points out that while contemporary feminists no longer assume that motherhood is necessarily either enslavement or destiny, they have seldom spoken of both the enjoyment and the power inherent in being pregnant, giving birth, and becoming a mother. This collection proposes "to analyze our ambivalent and complex relationship with our mother, with the Mother, with the maternal, on the one hand, and on the other hand to fill in the theoretical gap concerning maternity left by the French women's movement."[41]

Although the articles for *Maternité en mouvement* are written almost exclusively by French feminists, the inclusion of quotations from translations of works by Adrienne Rich, Phyllis Chesler, and Nancy Huston indicates the degree to which American and French feminists share similar concerns on the subject of motherhood. Anne-Marie de Vilaine and other contributors also refer frequently to Luce Irigaray's description of the mother-daughter relationship as the authentic "dark continent" to which Freud attempted to relegate childhood sexuality, and to Irigaray's analysis, in her 1985 book entitled *Parler n'est jamais neutre* (Speech Is Never Neuter), of the lack of a non-patriarchal language in which women can express themselves.

Françoise Laborie divides recent French feminist discussions about maternity into two categories: one which glorifies motherhood as an expression of woman's power and enjoyment and one which sees it as the primary basis for the oppression of women and therefore something to be avoided. She considers the second group to represent the majority point of view in the French women's movement, which has concentrated on making abortion generally available and legal, acting on the tacit assumption that maternity must be rejected if women are to be free of oppression. This is indeed the position adopted by Simone de Beauvoir in *The Second Sex*. Laborie has found that many militant feminists consider women with heterosexual relationships and with children *rétrogrades*.

Laborie and other contributors highlight the maternal role women tend to play in the daily lives of the men with whom they are closely associated, suggesting that women are constantly giving birth to men. This point of view will be of interest when the present study examines Beauvoir's relationship with Jean-Paul Sartre, which a recent biography of Sartre has posited as an essentially maternal one. A recurrent theme in the collection is the inclusion of the father as an equal partner in child rearing as a way of ensuring that he too becomes mature and no longer acts like just another needy child. This thought is echoed by Marie-Elisabeth Lanoë, who urges women to encourage their sons to be independent emotionally so that they will not spend their entire lives looking for another *maman*.

Lanoë emphasizes the notion that the only way mothers can ensure their children's happiness is if they themselves enjoy life to the fullest. When she herself became a mother, she felt that she was an institution rather than a living woman, a means of passing her children on to the conventions of patriarchal society. Lanoë sees the family unit as a prison over which society has appointed Mothers, with a capital M, as guards. She asks what would happen if mothers suddenly refused to turn their children over to the patriarchy. The society for which the Mother is expected to prepare her children appears to Lanoë to be an unlivable world of competition, violence, and destruction which has not changed substantially from the era of the 1950s, when someone, hearing that she had given birth to three sons, asked Adrienne Rich if she was working for the army.

Recalling Ibsen's Nora and her need to leave her "doll's house" to find her own identity, Jacqueline Feldman contrasts feminism and maternity. She labels feminism "the freedom to be, maternity the attachment to human beings, feminism the revolt against society, maternity the entire weight of social responsibility."[42] Elisabeth Badinter corroborates Feldman's view of maternity in her analysis of a child's insatiable appetite for love and unspoken desire that its mother prove her willingness to die so it may live, something she can do only by "graciously erasing the woman who resides underneath the mother."[43] The dream of being the perfect mother of the fantasy created by her children and by society conflicts with each woman's need to satisfy her own desires and ambitions, according to Badinter.

In the second section of this volume, the ambivalence and anxiety attached to the individual's feelings about his or her mother are associated by Anne-Marie de Vilaine and Marie Goudot with the fact that it is distasteful for most people to think about a time when they did not yet exist, or existed only as an inseparable part of another human being. Some radical feminists have rejected their connection not only to a father representing the law and society but also to a mother who reproduced and guarded the patriarchal values, according to the authors. They note that women who do not wish to become biological mothers often become symbolic and spiritual mothers as they create values, a culture, and a language which will help to liberate other women. This is certainly a category into which Simone de Beauvoir can easily fit.

In an interview on the subject of maternal love, psychoanalyst Julia Kristeva points out that maternity involves an intense confrontation with love in a way that is both regressive and sublimated. She sees "official" and visible feminism disassociating the active, professional, intellectual woman from the mother and housewife. Noting the enormous contribution to history and culture that has been made by women in the latter category, she urges feminists to find a way of expressing that particular experience. Kristeva acknowledges the impact that becoming a mother can have on the way in which a woman sees her own mother and her childhood, and here uses the term *continent noir* to refer to reminiscences of childhood which, in her opinion, can be luminous and warm as well as dark, hidden, and repressed. Kristeva expresses concern that the contemporary intellectual woman focuses excessively on aggressive behavior rather than on affection and love in her struggle to achieve equality. For Kristeva, maternity is the highest form of creation, one which women must find words to analyze. Author of a 1983 study entitled *Histoires d'amour,* Kristeva speaks of maternity as the essential nucleus of the complex experience which is the life of a woman.

Michèle Le Coadic stresses the importance of acknowledging and articulating conflict in parent-child relationships, seeing the alternative as "a risk of a death called self-sacrifice,"[44] something epidemic in her mother's generation. She recalls being unable to use vulgarity when she argued with her mother because she knew her mother would not understand that this did not signify a rejection of her and of the bond between them. Boys, on the other hand, are encouraged to rebel and to express their opposition aggressively. Le Coadic calls upon mothers to give voice to their feelings and their desires rather than smothering their needs in a vain attempt to maintain familial harmony at any cost, and advocates a "conflictual conviviality" as the basis for a new mother-child relationship which will teach children of both sexes not to be afraid that disagreement will be interpreted as a lack of love.

Françoise Gavarini resents the effort her own mother expended preparing her for the "universal man" she was to marry, "making of our relationship a preparation for his desires. You were totally mother and totally absent. Where was the woman in you? I never met her."[45] She feels that all her own children saw in her was the mother she did not wish to be. In an echo of André Gide's "Familles, je vous hais," she exclaims, "Maternity, I hate you.... You transformed my creative power into procreation, ... the lives that emerged from my life and from my coming together with an Other, into familial objects."[46] She calls upon women to become truly liberated by striking against maternity and refusing to participate in traditional family life.

Anne-Marie de Vilaine regrets a certain feminist rejection of one's mother, querying, "How can one seek the sisterhood of women and refuse all solidarity with one's mother? Why does a woman no longer have the right to be heard by us, to have our sympathy and our understanding simply because she is our mother?"[47] She remembers excluding her mother from her conversations with her father, assuming that if her mother didn't understand what she said or wrote this really proved how different they were. She admits, however, that she had a real need for the unconditional approval of this woman to whom she felt intellectually superior. This question of intellectual superiority will be seen to be a sensitive issue between Simone and Françoise de Beauvoir as well. Now that de Vilaine herself is a mother, she feels that the unattainable image of the perfect mother has plagued both her and her mother. She urges mothers to abandon the pursuit of perfection and concentrate rather on assuring each child that it is loved.

Eléna Gianini-Belotti joins Christine Collange in deploring the overwhelming psychological pressure brought to bear on mothers by the incredible proliferation of childbearing and child-rearing theories that have come to the fore in the twentieth century, each establishing rules imposed upon mothers from the outside. These theories have recently created new imperatives such as the importance of refusing anesthesia during childbirth, the necessity for the father to be in the room at the moment of his baby's birth, the need for the mother to be with her child constantly during the first years of its life, the obligation to breastfeed. As the ideal of what constitutes a "good mother" becomes increasingly elaborate, women succumb to feelings of inadequacy and guilt, the author affirms.

The entire third section of this volume is devoted to the question of the involvement of the father in child rearing. Radical feminists often advocate the abolition of the family unit and its replacement with a social unit consisting exclusively of a woman and her children. Annie Leclerc shares memories of childhood vacations during which her father was treated as an intruder and wonders if women are capable of allowing fathers to play as important a role in providing love and affection for their children as females have traditionally played for centuries. She now realizes that she and her siblings loved their mother too much, as their mother loved them, letting them understand that all of her devotion was concentrated on her children and not on her husband. Leclerc considers it essential that a child realize it can love its father without betraying its mother, noting that this is the only way it can be prepared to face a world in which its mother will not always be by its side. A child too well loved will never have the strength to separate from its mother and find its own way in the world, according to Leclerc.

Section 4 of *Maternité en mouvement* deals with the problems of juggling child care and work. Michèle Le Coadic states that feminists no longer think salaried jobs and collective child care will solve all of women's problems. She points out lucidly that it is when a child is born that a woman is forced to take stock of the value of the work or career she is engaged in. Housework continues to be devalued by society in comparison to salaried work outside the home. Various solutions to the problem have been proposed, including some innovative ideas by Renée Wormser about compensating both husband and wife for alternately working at home and in the workplace. The term *parentalité* is used frequently in this section to encourage a shift from the assumption of total responsibility for child rearing by the mother to its assumption by both parents.

Speaking from personal experience, Annie Leclerc does not think that a new mother whose emotional and physical energy is focused on her infant can possibly give equal concentration and devotion to any other creative endeavor. She herself found that she could teach but not write when her children were very small, explaining that she felt she belonged entirely to her child at that time. She discovered that when she was able to return to writing, it was with new understanding engendered by the experience of childbirth and caring for her infant. Acknowledging that some women substitute mothering for creation of works they have dreamed of, she feels that this is a dangerous practice: "When the child becomes the highest mode of expression possible for the mother, . . . what a loss of identity for the mother, what a burden for the child!"[48]

The fifth section of the collection focuses on maternity and the medical profession, highlighting the degree to which the essentially male medical establishment has for centuries controlled the way in which women approach pregnancy, childbirth, and childcare. Topics such as abortion, artificial insemination, home births, midwives, fashionable ways of giving birth, and surrogate motherhood are discussed, with the recurrent conclusion that it is society and often the notion of "baby as king" rather than the mother's needs and wishes that are being served. Some contributors express great concern about the manipulation of pregnancies and childbirth now possible because of new technological advances in medicine and question the validity of providing children on demand as if they were products to be ordered from a warehouse catalogue.

The collection of articles in *Maternité en mouvement* raises numerous issues which need to be addressed before women can fully enjoy the benefits of both motherhood and autonomy. The volume in no way claims to supply answers to all of the questions raised by the status of motherhood and the family in the 1980s. It is, however, persuasive in highlighting the many aspects of the problem and in cautioning against a simplistic suggestion that real feminists don't become mothers.

Autrement

The May 1987 issue of the magazine *Autrement* focuses on "La Mère," with articles written by both men and women about motherhood throughout the world. Of special interest for this study is an interview with Hélène de Beauvoir by Françoise Hurstel which complements the 1986 interview contained in appendix B of this book. Its title, "Sans regret," echoes Edith Piaf's passionate lyrical affirmation, "Non, je ne regrette rien," as the artist explains the reasons for her choice not to have children.

It is Hélène de Beauvoir's opinion that the creative strength one puts into raising one's children is then no longer available for one's work. Mothers never have the space or the time for an endeavor such as painting, she feels. Aware that children would have taken time away from her passion for painting, Hélène de Beauvoir states emphatically that she considers it irresponsible for women to bring children into the world and then neglect them. She also reveals that both she and her sister judged their mother rather severely and preferred to avoid having daughters of their own who might judge them accordingly.

Like Nancy Friday, Hélène de Beauvoir admits that she often lied to her mother, something she and Simone found necessary after both lost the religious faith Françoise de Beauvoir had worked so hard to instill in them. She did not consider her mother at all creative, and found the burden of being the justification for her existence an onerous one. Expressing relief that her father represented a different type of life from the one her mother was leading, thereby opening the door to wider horizons for both of his daughters, she suggests that the complete agreement between the parents of Simone's close friend Zaza "Mabille" Lacoin was the indirect cause of her premature death: "They simply smothered her. And madness and death were her only escape," she comments.[49]

Among a great variety of subjects discussed in this volume are the concept of a "mother tongue" and the importance of the mother as the original source of language for her child. Corinne Alexandre Garner analyzes *Portnoy's Complaint,* by American Philip Roth, as an example of the overwhelming possessiveness of the stereotypical Jewish mother. She notes that the novel's main character, Alex Portnoy, was convinced as a child that his mother was lurking behind the face of every one of his teachers: "If, as an adult, he knows that she cannot physically follow him everywhere, he discovers that she is still everywhere, always, not with him, but within him."[50] The number of literary works, both fictional and autobiographical, haunted by that image of the omnipresent mother suggests that Portnoy is not alone in having introjected a mother who will forever remain a part of him.

Vividly describing the child as "a vampire , a 'chronophage' who steals your time,"[51] Elisabeth Badinter underlines the current transformation taking place in accepted ideas of motherhood and predicts that its emphasis will become more cultural and less biological in the twenty-first century. Jean-Marc Terrasse concentrates on the negative image of mothers and particularly of stepmothers in traditional fairy tales and uses the tale of Snow White as an example of a mother who tries to kill her daughter because the latter has become a woman. He points out, however, that "it is the daughter who will kill the woman in the mother when she in turn becomes a woman. Her femininity excludes and annihilates her mother's."[52]

It is suggested by the contributors to this issue of *Autrement* that one of the ways to live with one's mother or the memory one has of her is to write or speak about her. The volume ends with the famous quotation from Jean-Jacques Rousseau's *Confessions* in which he states, "I cost my mother her life, and my birth was the first of my misfortunes."[53] This plaintively negative view of life is in sharp contrast to that of Simone de

Beauvoir, who, despite later conflicts and misunderstandings, always acknowledged the essential role her mother had played in providing her with an affectionate and secure childhood that allowed her to become a successful adult. As we examine her works of fiction, her autobiography, and some of her essays in chronological order, it will become apparent that her relationship with her mother was a key factor in her rebellion against middle-class conformity and that her attitude toward motherhood was strongly influenced by her observation of both Françoise de Beauvoir and Madame "Mabille" Lacoin in the traditional roles of wife and mother. Although some of her early fiction suggests that she might indeed have fantasized about "throwing Momma from the train" as the train carried her forward to a very different life from that lived by her conservative and devout mother, Simone de Beauvoir's later works show both an understanding of the impossible situation in which society has placed mothers for centuries and an impatience with women who are still willing to allow themselves to be limited by these traditional roles. A look at the roles played both by biological mothers and maternal figures in Beauvoir's fiction and autobiography will help clarify the outcome of the ongoing battle waged inside of the author between her need for autonomy and independence and the introjected specter of the first real love of her life, Françoise de Beauvoir.

1

Breaking Away:
When Things of the Spirit Come First

Simone de Beauvoir tells us in her memoirs that in her very first attempts at writing she had no intention of trying to reproduce the reality of her own experiences but was rather fascinated by the play of words on the page. She therefore created the story of the misfortunes of a courageous orphan girl in *Les Malheurs de Marguerite* and then a pastiche of the popular adventures of *La Famille Fenouillard* which she entitled *La Famille Cornichon*. In her family-centered universe, a life without parents was undoubtedly one of the greatest misfortunes she could imagine. Her tales of the Cornichon family were carefully copied by her Aunt Lili into a bound volume given her by her grandfather and she tasted her first success as an author, which was accompanied by the general approval of all the relatives.

This was perhaps the only time in Simone de Beauvoir's life when her family could look upon her writing with complete equanimity. As she passed through adolescence and began to rebel with increasing displeasure against the traditional role she as a female was expected to play, her daily diary and her creative work became an outlet for her raging need to break away from the destiny she saw represented by her unhappy mother and resigned women like her. Even more than Françoise de Beauvoir, however, Madame "Mabille" Lacoin became a symbol of maternal tyranny for the young Simone, who watched helplessly as her best friend Zaza struggled to free herself from the eventually fatal stranglehold of love and a sense of religious duty which characterized her ambivalent feelings toward her mother. Virtually all of Beauvoir's early adult attempts at writing fiction centered on transpositions of the story of Zaza's tragically premature death in 1929.

Between 1935 and 1937, as she was approaching thirty, Beauvoir wrote a collection of interwoven stories originally entitled *La Primauté du spirituel* (The Primacy of the Spiritual), an ironic reference to an essay by the Catholic philosopher Jacques Maritain. Turned down by both Gallimard and Grasset, the manuscript remained in a drawer until the late 1970s, when the author agreed, despite considerable hesitancy, to have it published for those interested in following the development of her thought. Because Maritain had since used the original title for a book of his own, Beauvoir changed hers to *Quand prime le spirituel,* which has appeared in English as *When Things of the Spirit Come First.*

Beauvoir's introduction to the 1979 publication clearly indicates her intentions in writing these stories:

> I had put a great deal of myself into this work. I was rebelling against the spiritual values which had long oppressed me and I wanted to express my distaste through the story of young women whom I knew who had been more or less willing victims of this morality.[1]

The mother to whom society entrusts the moral and religious upbringing of the children, who dominates one's early years and serves as a model to be emulated, seemed to Beauvoir the undeniable source of this morality from which she was struggling to free herself. Many more years were to pass before the author could put sufficient psychological distance between herself and her own mother to be capable of speaking directly about her mother in writing. Madame "Mabille" Lacoin, however, was a perfect target for her venom.

Occupying a central place in the sequence of stories, the section entitled "Anne" opens with a five-and-a-half page prayer addressed to the Good Lord by Madame Vignon, a merciless caricature of a matron who uses God as an excuse for manipulating the lives of her many children. Madame Vignon's strict religious upbringing has made her wary of men in general, of physical pleasure in particular. She considers it her God-given duty to protect her daughters from base male instincts, proclaiming to Anne, "I know what men are like; they speak of ideals, but they are full of ignoble desires."[2] Marriage and maternity appear to represent a distasteful fulfillment of social and moral obligations to this woman, who tells her oldest daughter, Lucette, "Rest assured that if I had thought only of my pleasure, you would never have been born."[3] The messages conveyed by this mother to her offspring portend a grim future for those who choose to follow in her footsteps.

Despite her own obvious disappointment with the state of matrimony, Madame Vignon expends a good portion of her very considerable energy pushing her daughters toward equally loveless matches. An unmarried daughter would represent a blot on the family escutcheon which she is unwilling to tolerate. The twenty-five-year-old Lucette is a prime target for her impatience:

> They seem to hold me responsible . . . I too want to get rid of her . . . I'm going to shake her up a bit. Your patriotic duty at this moment is to become a wife and mother. This refusal to fulfill your mission as a woman is immoral . . . she's going to become a pitiful parasite, a reject, like Cousin Marie. A fine state of affairs for the family! Jesus condemned the sterile fig tree. I'll find a way to make her accept her social role and fulfill the destiny You have assigned to her. All her girlfriends are married.[4]

This incredible diatribe, alternating among first-, second-, and third-person forms and mingling indiscriminately ideas of duty to family, society, nation, and God, is an angry cry of rebellion from an author still smarting from her overprotected and rigid upbringing. Her portrayal of a mother eager to rid herself of her firstborn daughter is decidedly heavy-handed in its hyperbole, yet undoubtedly reflects with great accuracy Simone de Beauvoir's view of the destructiveness and manipulativeness of family relationships when she was in her mid-twenties. Since her own father was an essentially absent and uninvolved parent after the years of her early childhood, it is the mother figure which bears the brunt of her resentment and criticism as she strives to separate herself from her bourgeois ties and from the aching memory of the death of a best friend for which she held those ties responsible.

Madame Vignon represents a maternal tendency to see one's offspring as a reincarnation of one's younger self, an opportunity to correct one's own mistakes by influencing the course of another human life. As she analyzes the temperament of her favorite daughter, Anne, she observes, "She is like I was at her age, too sensitive. It's up to me to be strong for her."[5] Madame Vignon is operating under the misguided assumption that she alone knows what is best for her spirited daughter. "I used to be like you. But one learns to stop listening to one's inner voice,"[6] she remarks in an outrageous attempt to reassure Anne that all will be well if she simply follows her mother's dictates. The appalling idea that a young woman should completely stifle her own instincts in order to conform to the mold which family and society have constructed for her is used ironically by Simone de Beauvoir in this passage in order to underline the need for each individual to establish a unique and separate identity. Were Madame Vignon to have her way, she would eradicate the very aspects of Anne's life which have made her a lively and passionate human being: her studies, her intellectual friends, the men to whom she has been attracted.

Madame Vignon is not above taking advantage of the very real devotion and affection Anne feels for her in order to impose her will, and readily admits that "it was atrocious to torture this child, but one had to think about her salvation, not about her happiness."[7] The full impact of the author's irony resonates in this statement, which recalls the adolescent Beauvoir's decision to opt for happiness here on earth rather than the postponed rewards of eternal salvation. Indeed the reader discovers through Anne's conversations with her close friend Chantal that she is tormented and exhausted by the constant arguments which occur between her mother and herself:

> For three years, I have never stopped fighting; for each of the books I have read, each outing, each thought, I have had to fight. I had sworn to myself that I would never hurt my mother and I have done nothing but torment her. Whenever I gave in to her, I lost my self respect; whenever I resisted, I hated myself.... I can't go on like this, Chantal.[8]

Raised in a tradition of Christian obedience, Anne neither can bring herself to defy her mother openly nor can she endure the thought of adopting the lusterless life-style which Madame Vignon is trying to force upon her. Her premature death seems to provide the only means of escape from this insoluble dilemma.

In this early story, Simone de Beauvoir presents the mother-daughter relationship as a trap which prevents a talented young girl from progressing beyond the limited confines of existence prescribed by the older generation to which her mother belongs. As she chats with her fiancé, Anne reminisces, "I was so happy when I was little.... One day I must tell you, Pascal, about the kind of world my mother was able to create for us during our childhood."[9] Happy memories, gratitude, nostalgia for a bygone era are all potent forces in determining the course of an adult life. The desire to keep things from changing, to perpetuate a symbiotic mother-child relationship which proved so satisfying during one's early years, is a strong counterbalance to the thrust toward independence and freedom, particularly when mother, God, and salvation are inextricably bound together in the mind of the young woman striving for maturity.

For Simone de Beauvoir as for Zaza "Mabille" Lacoin, advanced studies contributed to the distance separating the university student from her mother. Madame Vignon incarnates the busy housewife for whom the demands of domesticity leave no room for abstractions or intellectual diversion. She acknowledges that it has been years since she has even opened the cover of a book, that she is completely out of touch with current literature. It is not her own stagnation which she regrets, however, but rather her inability to exercise informed control over the books Anne is reading. Regret turns to indignation as Madame Vignon rails against the academic world and intellectuals in general as emissaries of the devil: "Never should I have allowed her to continue her studies. That was my first mistake. One becomes complex and haughty.... I hate those intellectuals.... I won't let those upstarts compromise her salvation. I must marry her off right away."[10] Marriage, to a family-approved mate, is thus the antidote to intellectual conviction in the eyes of Madame Vignon. In order to justify her own existence, such a woman must continue to persuade herself that her choice of life-style is also the most desirable one for her daughters to adopt. If they too choose to become wives of middle-class, conservative, appropriately educated Catholic gentlemen, and to have a large number of children of their own, she can, by her example and experience, maintain a certain control over their adult years.

It is precisely lack of control over her daughter's life which has provoked Madame Vignon's rage over the letters that Anne has received from Pascal Drouffe. "Before, her child's joys and tribulations had always depended upon her alone," she muses.[11] She is intent upon maintaining a firm grip on her daughter's emotions and deeply resents the intrusion of a young man upon the symbiotic relationship she and Anne have always shared. Even though this young man appears to have all of the appropriate credentials for a future son-in-law, Madame Vignon does everything she can to discourage the relationship. Simone de Beauvoir presents her as a possessive monster who interprets any indication of independent thinking on her daughter's part as an unacceptable lack of loyalty to the closeness she has cultivated between them.

In the final analysis, Beauvoir's story leaves the reader with a haunting image of a self-centered mother who has managed to persuade herself that she has been a mere instrument in the hands of a God who has selected her daughter for sainthood. Her final prayer is directed to Anne rather than to God: "Anne, my little saint, ... pray for me, a poor sinner. Help me to accept unquestioningly having been the instrument of your suffering and of your salvation."[12] Whereas Chantal sees both Madame Vignon and Pascal as murderers indirectly responsible for the death of her best friend, Anne's mother retreats into a self-imposed martyrdom which she justifies by her conviction that she has carried out God's will.

Beauvoir's portrayal of Madame Vignon allows her to vent her still-simmering rage over the loss of her best friend Zaza to what she perceived as martyrdom imposed by a manipulative mother whose uncompromising Momism, as Philip Wylie and Hans Sebald would label it, drove her daughter to illness and eventual death. She did not discover until many years later that the real reason the Lacoins objected to Zaza's plans to marry Maurice Merleau-Ponty, the Pascal of these tales, was their discovery that he was illegitimate. This revelation only added to her disdain of a narrow-minded morality that preferred to make lives miserable rather than to deviate from accepted social norms.

The depiction of Madame Vignon in this early collection is especially memorable because she is something more than the domineering Madame Lepic in Jules Renard's *Poil de carotte* or the malevolent "Folcoche" in Hervé Bazin's *Vipère au poing*. Whereas the male novelists appear to have no hesitation about painting an entirely black portrait of tyrannical mothers and stepmothers, Beauvoir offers her readers an insight into the rationalizations used by an outwardly well-meaning mother figure to paralyze her brood with feelings of guilt and ingratitude. In her late twenties and still smarting from the loss of Zaza, Beauvoir undoubtedly considered the Madame Vignons and their manipulative tugs on their daughters' heartstrings as far more insidious psychologically than the Madame Lepics and Folcoches, whose authority society encourages young boys at least to challenge and reject.

The only other mother featured in *When Things of the Spirit Come First*, Madame Drouffe, pales in comparison to the determined Madame Vignon. Her older daughter Marcelle has little respect for her intelligence. The narrator describes their relationship as follows: "Madame Drouffe was passionately devoted to Marcelle, but she was neither very intelligent nor very well educated; naturally, Marcelle adored her, but she felt very much alone when she was with her mother. Often she couldn't help answering her harshly."[13] In this early collection of stories, Beauvoir has made use of both of the Drouffe sisters to reflect her attitude toward her own mother. Marcelle's condescending appraisal of her mother's intelligence articulates what was an essentially unarticulated sentiment of the author's, one of which Françoise de Beauvoir proved herself to be only too aware when, perhaps under the influence of medication, she admitted that she had always been intimidated by her daughter's brilliant mind. The use of the expression "naturally" (*naturellement*) in the above quotation highlights the bind in which both Simone de Beauvoir and her best friend Zaza found themselves as adolescents. Their love for their mothers was considered "natural," a given; it would be unthinkable to consider the possibility of any emotion other than the one dictated by society, religion, and tradition for mother-daughter relationships. Older daughters in a family with younger siblings, both the author and Zaza were expected to conform to the dutiful-daughter image imposed upon them by their milieu. Neither the fictional Marcelle nor the tormented Zaza proves capable of mounting an outright rebellion against the mother who has watched over her since childhood.

It is Marguerite, youngest offspring of the Drouffe family, who acts out her rebellion against the mores imposed upon her by her mother in a far more direct manner than ever seemed possible to her creator. Whereas Madame Vignon is an exaggerated transposition of Zaza's domineering mother, Madame Drouffe is drawn from the author's recollections of Françoise de Beauvoir's retreat into soulful martyrdom when defied by her headstrong older daughter. Unlike the adolescent Simone, Marguerite makes no attempt to hide her nightly sorties from her mother, deliberately flaunting the fact that she far prefers bar-hopping with her bohemian brother-in-law to spending a quiet and dull evening at home. This leaves Madame Drouffe no alternative but to retreat behind a wall of tears, wearing her suffering as a halo sanctifying the torments of motherhood.

Marguerite's rebellion is based on her determination to become a part of the real and vibrant world she knows exists beyond the stifling confines of her family life, a world in which she visualizes her mother and older sister as parasitic "poor relations": "I felt like a visitor in life, one who doesn't dare touch anything; Mother and Marcelle seemed like poor relations: only Denis seemed at home and one would have to go to him to get the key which opens all the doors."[14] She will eventually realize her mistake in looking to someone else to provide her with that elusive key, yet she must make use of Denis just as Beauvoir used her cousin Jacques as a link to the outside world, the world that lies beyond family expectations and conventions. Marguerite's tale, along with the entire collection of stories, ends on a triumphant note of freedom and of independence from all inhibiting ties:"The world was as shiny as a bright new penny; I didn't know yet just what I wanted to do with it, but everything was possible because at the center of things, in the place that Denis had left empty, I suddenly found myself."[15]

Simone de Beauvoir has stated that Marguerite is the character with whom she identified most closely in these stories. Like her creator, Marguerite makes a successful transition from the constrained existence of a young girl forced to conform to the dictates of her mother and of middle-class society to the liberated life-style of an intelligent, independent young woman. For those critics who fault Beauvoir for not having created positive female protagonists in her fictional works, Marguerite Drouffe provides a convincing example that this was not always the case.

In addition to the images of Madame Vignon and Madame Drouffe, the reader finds maternal aspirations of a different sort in the stories of *When Things of the Spirit Come First:* those of a new bride toward her husband, those of a new lycée teacher toward her students. Marcelle Drouffe sees all men as children in need of maternal care and actually rejects the middle-class solidity of her symbolically named fiancé Desroches, who may or may not be as sturdy as a rock, for a husband for whom she is more eager to be a mother than a wife:

> These exceptional creatures were also men, big clumsy children just like all men. She would have liked to clean up their rooms, adjust the knot on their ties, and sew their buttons back on as she did for Pascal. Her admiration for them was tempered by a maternal affection.[16]

Everyone agrees that Marcelle looks like a madonna in her wedding dress, thereby reinforcing this image of wife-mother. She attempts to bring structure, inspiration, and frugality to Denis, the self-proclaimed poetic genius she has chosen to marry. How then to cope with the physical demands of this child-husband? Inadequately, it appears, as Marcelle finds herself "upset to see this child over whom she watched maternally during the day transformed into an imperious young male" at night.[17] This marriage seems doomed to failure from the beginning, its only hope lying in Denis's actual need for mothering and more specifically for the financial support both Marcelle and her younger sister Marguerite are ready to sell their souls to afford him. In this story of the Drouffe sisters, Simone de Beauvoir takes a wry look at a societal tradition which encourages women to live vicariously through the experiences and talents of the men with whom they become emotionally involved and to justify their need to incorporate these men into their lives by adopting an essentially maternal attitude toward them. In a predominantly puritanical milieu, such a mentality allows the young woman to sublimate her need for physical satisfaction in a morally acceptable way. If everyone agrees that men are mere children whose physical demands must be met as part of the marriage contract, sex can take its place on the list of late-evening household chores. Beauvoir treats with consummate irony this conjugal flight into a maternity which encompasses not only one's children but also one's husband.

Chantal Plattard, on the other hand, sees herself as a flaming torch lighting the way for the uninitiated adolescents in her lycée philosophy class. She fantasizes about their virginity, their youthful grace, appears almost physically attracted to the more seductive among them. She gives her adoring charges the impression that she is a liberated freethinker, a daring alternative role model to the one provided by their own mothers and their provincial families. "What an ideal image of a free, intelligent, and happy life she must represent for these children!" she muses, as the narrator allows us to hear her thinking to herself.[18] Beauvoir exposes the hazards involved in taking on such a responsibility in a manner which is more self-serving than sincere as she records Chantal's effect on fifteen-year-olds who supposedly see her as emerging from "an infinitely rich universe which is nonetheless within reach."[19] The girls take her at her word, look to her as mentor and savior, and are sorely disappointed when she retreats to the camp of parents and society after being approached for advice about an unwanted pregnancy.

The reader begins to wonder about how realistic Chantal's view of life can be when she rhapsodizes over her student Monique and her boyfriend, finding them like a fairy-tale couple right out of the pages of *Le Grand Meaulnes,* "both bursting with youth, both pure and beautiful."[20] As long as this young love remains problem-free, Chantal can continue to see herself in the maternal role of beneficent fairy godmother worshipping at the altar of true love: "On an invisible altar the mysteries of youth and love are being celebrated and I bow my head with religious fervor."[21] In Chantal one finds a forerunner of the thirty-year-old Françoise Miquel, who allows herself to become mesmerized by the unpredictable capriciousness of the adolescent Xavière in the novel *She Came to Stay.* Chantal is more of a romantic than Françoise, however, and takes very seriously the role of facilitator of young love which she sees cut out for her: "If some fairy godmother did not look after youth and love, these fragile flowers would be quickly destroyed by men's crude hands. I'm pleased that thanks to me a little more beauty, a little more happiness has lent its fragrance to the world for a short while."[22] The author's choice of a word I have translated as "lent its fragrance to," one which literally means "embalmed," is just one of the many ironical touches in this tale of misguided intentions. And young love is symbolically embalmed when it is forced to cope with an unplanned pregnancy. The invoked fragrance of petals of flowers is transformed abruptly into images of mud and murkiness as Chantal withdraws in disgust from any association with a relationship she has encouraged and fostered. Her experiment of playing at enlightened guide and mentor has resulted in a possible jeopardizing of her coveted social reputation, and she can think of nothing but the betrayal of her tenuous dreams as she exclaims, "They could have put me in a compromising situation. . . . What muck!"[23] Young Galahad has proved to be just another self-seeking adolescent eager to assure his future security by forcing his way into a wealthy family, while the erstwhile fairy godmother has laid aside her magic wand and exchanged it for a mantle of social conformity.

Chantal's final attempt at replacing her students' parents in their hearts takes place on awards day, when she is at first disheartened by the apparent regression into the bosom of the family which is happening before her eyes: "There they are, completely reabsorbed by their families.... For a moment she reflected sadly on the ingratitude of childhood."[24] Beauvoir's description of this young self-centered teacher is thick with irony throughout. It is only after the ceremonies are over, when some of her more naive students bid her adieu with tears in their eyes, that Chantal can once again take refuge in her fantasy of what she has represented for them: "At the dawn of these young lives, there would emerge forever her delicate silhouette,... somewhat enigmatic, somewhat paradoxical, whose appearance in an old provincial lycée had been so dazzling."[25] Shades of *Le Grand Meaulnes* and of André Gide's call to the freedom of the open road in *Les Nourritures terrestres,* both appeals to which Simone de Beauvoir herself responded but which she appears to view ironically in this portrait of an ambitious young secondary-school teacher with delusions of grandeur. Earnest in her existential pursuit of authenticity and good faith, Beauvoir seems to be particularly severe in analyzing her own motives and those of her colleagues in the early years of her teaching career, during which she was indeed a dazzling example of living with a flair for the students in her provincial classrooms in Marseille and Rouen.

What of the prospects of motherhood for the characters in this collection of stories? An unplanned pregnancy is presented as a disaster which will ruin Monique Fournier's life forever in this era before abortions became readily and safely available to the general public. No longer the virgin painted by Lippi either to Chantal or to herself, Monique is frightened and horrified at the prospect of being forced by her parents to marry a boy who has cleverly schemed to gain access to the family fortune for himself. For Monique's best friend Andrée Lacombe, the pregnancy is a catastrophe for the future and a source of disgust for the present. Simone de Beauvoir's images of childbearing and maternity are hardly the romanticized ones of television commercials. Fifteen-year-old Andrée describes one of the lycée teachers as having "a big bump in the middle of her belly,"[26] Monique's expected child as "a mysterious bit of rot in the process of developing."[27] Andrée imagines the life which Monique will lead as the wife of a man she resents, the mother of an unwanted child: "She would knit, listen to the radio in the evening, try to love her child, in order to console herself. Andrée would see her perhaps twice a year, and soon they would no longer have anything to say to each other."[28] A grim prospect, a direct result of a moment's mistake for which the woman alone will pay for the rest of her life. Maternity as presented in the story of Monique Fournier is a trap which prevents promising young women from developing their talents appropriately and confines them to quarters, forever immured in the socially acceptable role of middle-class wife and mother. In an era when pregnancy was a disaster for an unmarried girl from a "good" family, particularly a devoutly Catholic one, Beauvoir uses the story of Monique to reinforce her interpretation of motherhood as a form of imprisonment impeding individual progress.

When Things of the Spirit Come First reflects an underlying pessimism on the part of the author about the alternatives available to young women who try to escape the nets of marriage and maternity, as James Joyce's Stephen Dedalus attempted to fly free of the entanglements of family, religion, and country. For the studious Andrée Lacombe, following in the footsteps of the maiden aunt who has raised her and taking her place among the lycée teachers by whom she has been surrounded is a fate almost as terrifying as that of being married off to one of the "acceptable" young men chosen by her family for invitations to afternoon tea: "Wearing the same dress all year, having a six-franc lunch at school, never traveling, never going out, gave one permission to be married one day to an insignificant civil servant who wanted to better his station in life."[29] Chantal has proved disappointing as a role model because of her obvious lack of sincere interest in Andrée. Even with her keen intelligence, Andrée sees her future as a dead end, life as a cynical stage play with all the roles predetermined. As people congratulate her for her academic achievements after the awards ceremony, she realizes she would prefer to be dead. She feels alone and afraid, a prisoner of the life and the town in which she has been enveloped. Her only hope, a tragic one, is that the psychological pain will diminish as she grows older: "One day, in spite of everything, I will finally no longer be young."[30] Andrée conforms to the impression Beauvoir had of her classmates from the Cours Désir, who seemed to her faded and lacking in vitality as they strove to fit into the uninspiring mold laid out before them by the bourgeois expectations of their families.

Lisa Nardec is depicted in another of these stories as a bright young woman who resents the fact that a lack of family funds will force her to use her brain to make a living. The choice of marriage and maternity is a doubtful one for Lisa, as it was for the Beauvoir sisters, because of the lack of a dowry, a requirement which underlines the extent to which arranged marriages were based exclusively on economics. Lisa's rebellious spirit makes her persona non grata to the pious spinsters who run the school at which she is both instructor and boarder. She complains of her plight to Pascal, the vapid brother of her friend Marguerite: "I find it horrible that one can be reduced to using one's brain to earn a living. . . . My entire future, the bread I will eat, my coal, my shoes, all of that must be financed by my brain. A brain is fragile, so fragile."[31] This was the situation of the two Beauvoir sisters, whose father announced to them early on that he had no money for dowries. Unlike Lisa, however, they were both delighted to escape the artificial social events and arranged marriages which awaited their more affluent classmates, happy to have an authorized excuse to pursue the careers of writing and painting which they had envisaged for themselves since early childhood.

Lisa Nardec's imagined passion for Pascal Drouffe is, like Marcelle's for Denis, once again tinged with maternal sentiments: "Oh to be seated in a warm chair caressing the angelic head that he would finally put on my lap, without speaking; no kisses...."[32] She is realistic enough to realize that this image of their relationship exists only in her mind, and actually prefers her fantasies to Pascal's physical presence. She disdains the other boarders at her school for their lack of imagination, assuming that their only goals in life are to become farm wives and mothers. She and her friends joke about the principal's determination to marry off her daughter, yet demonstrate their total lack of self-confidence in the devastating comment, "She doesn't want her daughter to be like us; that's understandable."[33] "Like us" can here be interpreted as "without funds," therefore unmarriageable and forced to depend upon one's brains to survive.

In this early work which Simone de Beauvoir originally intended to leave unpublished, the reader is aware of the author's extensive use of irony and cynicism to help her make the transition from the protected, maternally dominated atmosphere of the family home to a world with infinitely expanding horizons. Mary Evans[34] sees these early stories as the most autobiographical and least distanced of Beauvoir's fiction, while for Judith Okely they represent "an important contribution to the literature of adolescent struggles lost or won."[35] Terry Keefe notes that "Mme Vignon is the first of a line of portraits that Beauvoir was to draw of the repressive mother who transfers her own psychological problems to her daughter."[36]

This collection can indeed be viewed as an anguished attempt on the part of the author to understand why she had been able to turn her adolescent struggle into a victory while her best friend had succumbed to permanent defeat. The separation from one's mother and the family values she represents, which is a necessary step toward maturity for the adolescent girl, entails varying degrees of suffering depending upon how close the relationship has been. For Zaza "Mabille" Lacoin, the suffering was so intense that it led to a premature death. The vindictive tone of *When Things of the Spirit Come First*, the sarcasm, the unsympathetic portrayals of practically all of the characters with the exception of Anne Vignon and Marguerite Drouffe, suggest a breaking away which was quite painful for the author. Through the ironic tone of these stories, Simone de Beauvoir struggled to put some distance between herself and her bourgeois upbringing, and most particularly between herself and her devoted but insecure, devout, overbearing mother. Although she considered these stories still another unsuccessful attempt to bring Zaza back to life, what she did succeed in rendering frighteningly alive was the age-old symbiotic struggle between mothers and daughters. By presenting Madame Vignon as a full-fledged Mom à la Philip Wylie, and her daughter Anne as a victim of what Wylie labeled "megaloid mom worship," Beauvoir vented her anger on the entire bourgeois social system, "threw Momma from the train," and prepared to move on to an autonomy in which she hoped to maintain a polite distance between herself and a mother who, as a representative of a spiritual approach to life which the adolescent Simone had long since rejected, might never again be capable of fully understanding the daughter who had once been such an integral part of her existence.

2

Independence vs. Surrogate Motherhood:
She Came to Stay

Just as the stories of *When Things of the Spirit Come First* served as a catharsis for Simone de Beauvoir's feelings of hostility toward her mother and the conservative society she and Madame Lacoin represented, *L'Invitée,* translated into English as *She Came to Stay,* reflects the tension between a young adult's need to establish a separate and independent identity and the lure of involvement in relationships which might provide a viable alternative to the nuclear family. In this fictional transposition of her experiment with a symbiotic trio, Beauvoir, although adamant about denying the mother-daughter subtext in her first novel in a 1985 interview with the author of this book,[1] does in effect trace the emotions of a mature young woman who invites a capricious and rebellious nineteen-year-old to become an integral part of her existence and who then experiences all of the pangs of nurturing, symbiosis, separation, and rivalry typically felt by biological mothers.

Raised in a milieu in which female maturity is measured by the ability to bear and raise children, the thirty-year-old protagonist of Beauvoir's first published work is unsure of her place in society, and is tempted by the possibility of assuming a nurturing role in her relationship with a younger woman. Françoise Miquel's supposedly successful writing career and her sexually fulfilling association with the playwright Pierre Labrousse, neither of which is convincingly depicted in the narrative, in no way protect her from a sense of isolation and unconnectedness which comes close to destroying her both physically and psychologically. She seems to be searching desperately for the kind of justification for her existence that more conventional women find at least temporarily in marriage and motherhood. Her dilemma highlights the emotional impact which the conscious rejection of the traditional paths of marriage and maternity may have on a woman brought up in a family-oriented middle-class environment.

The minimal role played by the only actual mother portrayed in *She Came to Stay* suggests the extent to which Simone de Beauvoir's own mother has temporarily receded into the background at this stage of her development. Madame Miquel is a reincarnation of the ineffectual Madame Drouffe, seldom uttering a word beyond a few carping comments about the way her daughter dresses or spends her money. There is virtually no communication between Madame Miquel and Françoise, who dispenses with her filial obligations by dropping in briefly to exchange polite platitudes with a mother who has taught her to smile convincingly at social gatherings, a mother who brings her gifts of gloves and bedjackets so that she may be at all times appropriately clad.

Like Françoise de Beauvoir, Madame Miquel is self-effacing and socially ill at ease. She is nervously effusive as she thanks the nurse who allows her to share her daughter's lunch at the hospital. Françoise Miquel is particularly sensitive to the dull stagnation of her mother's existence because she fears that it may mirror what the future holds for her: "Whenever Françoise found herself in [her parents'] apartment, it seemed to her that all these years had been leading nowhere for her; time spread out around her in a stagnant, acrid marsh. Living simply meant growing old."[2] Like her creator, Beauvoir's protagonist wants much more out of life than a routine of simply surviving through the twenty-four hours of each day.

In the collection of Beauvoir texts by Claude Francis and Fernande Gontier published in 1979,[3] one finds a manuscript originally intended as the opening chapter of *She Came to Stay* and eliminated before its publication on the advice of Gallimard editor Brice Parrain. It deals with Françoise Miquel's childhood and adolescence, reproducing in fictional form many of the incidents later recounted in the autobiographical *Memoirs of a Dutiful Daughter*. In it we see Françoise developing from a six-year-old paragon of virtue who tells her mother everything to a rebellious adolescent resenting her mother's awkward attempts to be her confidante and defying some of the incomprehensible rules to which Madame Miquel subjects her. As she attempts to imitate her vivacious classmate Elisabeth, a character clearly inspired by Zaza "Mabille" Lacoin, Françoise realizes that she can no longer conform to the understated feminine behavior her mother expects of her. She appears to lose both the affection and the respect she had for her mother during the early years of her childhood and concludes somewhat haughtily that there is nothing but a void inside her mother's head.

By choosing to use her mother's name for her main character, Beauvoir echoes her own struggle to separate herself from the expectations of family and middle-class society in this novel and suggests that there is much of the introjected mother that she is still carrying around within her. Both she and Françoise Miquel have found themselves in danger of suffocating in a psychological atmosphere that attempts to ensnare and immobilize them, one which looks forward to Luce Irigaray's poetic metaphor of a female child frozen by her mother's milk. The protagonist of *She Came to Stay* rushes from her mother's apartment to the relative freedom and fresh air of the Parisian streets after one brief dutiful visit home. Much later in the novel, we find her looking longingly out of her window after she has become inextricably caught up in the life of Xavière Pagès: "With astonishment, she looked out for a moment on that lucid, bustling street where everything seemed so reasonable. And then she turned back to the room mired in anguish where obsessive thoughts relentlessly pursued one another in a circle."[4] The unbreathable air of the apartment shared by Françoise and Xavière clearly replicates the atmosphere of the Miquel household as it is remembered by the thirty-year-old protagonist. The Paris streets represent an escape from overwhelming and exhausting emotional entanglements for Françoise Miquel just as they did for the adolescent Simone de Beauvoir and her younger sister, who would take advantage of the evenings their parents went out by wandering freely through the neighborhoods close to their apartment.

Simone de Beauvoir took her first step toward freedom by moving into a room in a boarding-house run by her grandmother while she was still a student. Her first job as a lycée teacher took her even further from the maternal sphere of influence by relocating her in Marseille. Yet her psychological escape from home undoubtedly occurred most completely when she began her liaison with Jean-Paul Sartre. As we recall psychotherapist Dr. Richard Robertiello's comment to Nancy Friday that a woman cannot be both symbiotic with her mother and sexual at the same time, we can see that the autobiographical aspects of *She Came to Stay* provide valuable insight into the further movement away from her mother that took place for Beauvoir after the period of anger and attack represented by her early stories.

Beauvoir's first novel shows Françoise Miquel at a moment in her life in which she appears totally free of whatever ties she may once have had to her mother but in need of reclaiming her identity as an individual in her supposedly ideal relationship with Pierre Labrousse. Early in the narrative, she finds herself savoring a few precious moments of solitude:

> She was not sorry that Pierre wasn't with her; there were joys she could not experience in his presence: all the joys of solitude; they had been lost to her for eight years,

and sometimes she missed them . . . it was strange to become a person in her own right once again, just a woman. . . .[5]

Françoise here reflects her creator's uneasiness about allowing herself to become so completely caught up in the life of the man she loves that she has no viable existence without him. In a traditional marriage, having a baby would be the next logical step in the pattern prescribed by society for giving the female half of the couple a sense of purpose and the assurance that she is a "real woman." A recent biography of Jean-Paul Sartre by Ronald Hayman[6] suggests that the role assigned to Beauvoir by Sartre was essentially a nurturing one, a role she willingly played for half a century. In *She Came to Stay*, her alter ego Françoise gradually becomes a mother figure both to her lover Pierre and to the puzzling young Xavière.

It is clear in the early pages of the novel that Françoise is responsive to certain maternal instincts within her aroused by some of the younger members of her entourage. She notices affectionately that twenty-year-old Gerbert's eyes are "as pink as those of a sleepy child."[7] She suggests that he take a nap before they continue working on the play they are rewriting, then takes off her shoes and slips under the covers beside him. Throughout *She Came to Stay*, Françoise's feelings toward Gerbert and Xavière alternate between a desire to mother them and a frustrated need to possess them both psychologically and physically. In the case of Gerbert, who was modeled after Sartre's student Jacques-Laurent Bost, she eventually succeeds in achieving both goals, thereby establishing what appears to be the most satisfying relationship in the novel, an honest and straightforward caring for one another which includes sensual pleasure and posits no anxiety-producing obligations for the future. Françoise is quite lucid about her feelings for Gerbert: "It was undeniable, she had maternal feelings toward Gerbert; maternal, with a slight tinge of incest."[8] Since the group which is the focus of the action in *She Came to Stay* is clearly based on the "family" of non-relatives formed by Beauvoir, Sartre, their friends, and their favored students, the definition of incest takes on a rather special meaning in this passage. It was only in late 1985, with the publication of the Francis and Gontier biography,[9] that Beauvoir's readers learned of her real-life liaison with "le petit Bost" during the years mirrored in this first novel.

Just before Pierre suggests that they support Xavière so that she can stay in Paris with them, Françoise has been clucking over him, worrying about the fact that he looks pale and may not be eating regularly. Pierre's suggestion may well be his way of redirecting this maternal attention. Like a woman who is considering having a child, Françoise is well aware of the commitment of time and energy the decision to take Xavière under their wing will entail. Pierre's generosity in wanting to share their good fortune with others is commendable, but Françoise knows that the burden of the responsibility for this magnanimous gesture will fall squarely upon her shoulders. She smarts under Pierre's accusation that she always recoils from anything which deviates from her well-ordered routine. Her willingness to go ahead with his plan is as much a taking up of the gauntlet as it is a fascination with the possibilities for their collective future offered by such involvement with Xavière.

During the early days of their relationship, Françoise seems convinced that Xavière is as much a part of her as if she had actually carried her in her womb for nine months and given birth to her. The verb "to belong to" (*appartenir*) is used repeatedly to express this sense of possession and domination: "Xavière belonged to her; nothing ever made Françoise so joyful as this type of possession. . . . Xavière's gestures, her face, her very life needed Françoise in order to exist."[10] Like a developing embryo, Xavière seems totally dependent upon Françoise, at least as she is depicted through the latter's eyes in the narration: "Xavière was riveted to her . . . everything that happened to Xavière happened through Françoise and, in spite of herself, Xavière belonged to her."[11] As is the case with expectant mother and fetus, the link is mutually binding. Françoise feels "riveted" to Xavière by a bond not of her own choosing, "inextricably bound" to her.[12] Once the decision has been made to "adopt" Xavière, it is cemented by the symbiotic attachment which quickly develops between Françoise and her young protégée.

Françoise's initial reaction to the inclusion of the nineteen-year-old Xavière in her life mirrors the wonderment of a new mother: "She finally understood what a miracle had erupted in her life . . . a thousand marvels would be created through the grace of this demanding young angel."[13] The terminology here is religious. Xavière's presence is a miracle. She is an angel sent from on high to bring divine grace to Françoise. Pierre reinforces this sense of expectation, associating witchcraft and Christmas in his image of Xavière: "That little sorceress . . . She looks at things from a brand new perspective; and suddenly things begin to exist for us just as she sees them. . . . Thanks to her, it will be a real Christmas for us this year."[14] Both Françoise and Pierre are depending on the magical power of youth to cast a new light on their lives just as parents tend to relive their own childhood through the experiences of their offspring. For Beauvoir and Satre as well, turning thirty was fraught with all of the anguish associated with that pivotal age by the rebellious students of the sixties, an anguish clearly reflected in the early novels of both authors.

Miracles and magic are, however, ephemeral experiences. Early in the relationship between the two women of different generations, the battle begins for self-assertion. Françoise naively assumes that she will be able to guide Xavière smoothly toward maturity and independence. She is completely taken aback the first time Xavière defies her: "It was scandalous: she was so sure of dominating Xavière, of being an integral part of her past and of the yet uncharted paths of her future! But there was that stubborn will against which her own will was being shattered."[15] Françoise realizes that she has overestimated the degree to which any human being can direct and influence the life of another. Like many a parent, she would like to assure the future happiness of her protégée: "From then on it would be Françoise who would carry [Xavière] through life. 'I will make her happy,' she decided with conviction."[16] The word "carry" (*emporter*) is significant here, suggesting that a young person is merely an object, a package to be toted about from one place to another and expedited in the direction of happiness. The distinction between *emporter* and *emmener* is psychologically revealing: one can carry off, *emporter*, an inanimate object with little difficulty, but one can only lead, *emmener*, a person in one direction or another. If that person chooses not to follow, the final destination may be quite different. Françoise would like to lead Xavière into the realms of music, theatre, literature, and art, but finds herself rebuffed by someone whose limited intellectual curiosity seldom lures her beyond the threshold of her hotel-room door.

As she interacts with Xavière Pagès, Françoise progresses through emotional stages which are often an integral part of the development of the mother-daughter relationship. Hesitant at first to assume responsibility for the existence and happiness of another human being, she soon becomes enchanted by the possibilities inherent in guiding and sharing her experiences with a younger person. She is initially delighted by Xavière's fresh outlook on life, accepting her moods and her capriciousness as part of a challenging new way of looking at the world.

However much she may be charmed by this youthful grace, however, Françoise would nonetheless like to be sure of her ability to control and dominate Xavière. As it becomes painfully evident that Xavière will never allow herself to be dominated or "possessed" in any way, Françoise's involvement with her begins to grow cumbersome, anguished, and infuriating. The initial fascination of finding a spirited young woman who reminds Françoise of herself and her own childhood rages gives way to a confrontation between a woman who has just passed the demarcation line from youth to maturity represented by age thirty and a rebellious adolescent reminiscent of that woman a decade earlier.

What began as an affectionate investment in a promising future is transformed into a desperate rivalry between two women competing for the attentions of the same men. Françoise can no longer delude herself into thinking of Xavière as an insignificant and naive little girl. In the final chapter of the novel, the rivalry escalates into a full-scale war, a battle to the death in which one of the protagonists must be eliminated in order that the other may survive. The invited guest of the French title is no longer welcome and must be dismissed through drastic measures by the hostess who can no longer tolerate her presence.

Xavière may well appear angelic, but she is a demanding angel. After the first glow of enchantment has worn off, Françoise begins to find herself resenting the burden which Xavière represents in her daily routine, comparing interaction with her young protégée to "walking through life with pounds of clay under your soles."[17] Françoise finds herself waiting interminably for Xavière to show up for appointments, trying desperately to adapt to the young woman's changing moods, taking whatever abuse Xavière may choose to dole out. Neither she nor Pierre can devote the necessary time to the work demanded by their careers as they cater to Xavière's eccentricities: "It was terrible to realize all the time she was eating up. They never had any leisure moments any more, any solitude, nor even any rest; they had reached a state of inhuman tension."[18] From a miraculous presence in their adult lives, Xavière has evolved into an intruder, a sea monster intent upon entangling Françoise and destroying her: "She would flee to the ends of the earth to escape those avid tentacles that wanted to eat her alive."[19] This poignant image recalls the metaphors used to describe the developing fetus in *When Things of the Spirit Come First*. The symbiosis which should be limited to the early stages of motherhood is shown here in a strikingly negative light. Rather than evolving into a mutually supportive relationship which allows both mother and offspring to grow, a maternal investment in another human being is described by Simone de Beauvoir as the prelude to a destructive and animalistic fight for survival between two mutually antagonistic entities.

Along with the frustrations occasioned by Françoise's assumption of responsibility for Xavière, the protagonist of *She Came to Stay* experiences the torments of physical rejection in her interaction with the young girl. Psychiatrists have compared the mother-child relationship to a passionate love affair, all the more sensual because of the fact that it begins with the complete union of two bodies during the nine months of gestation. Once the child is born and becomes a separate entity, there is a longing on the part of the mother to recapture a physical union which can never again be recreated. Françoise has "given birth" to Xavière only in a symbolic sense, yet is very much caught up in a similar need to return to a previous moment of symbiosis. She dwells upon the image of an early morning embrace in which she felt that Xavière truly belonged to her: "Their fingers remained entwined ... melting, yielding, [Xavière] gave herself over entirely to [Françoise]."[20] The nostalgia of this moment is underlined at a later point in the narrative when Xavière is beginning to lose her aura of wide-eyed innocence for Françoise: "She remembered another face, a childish one, a trusting one which was leaning on her shoulder early one gray morning; she hadn't been able to hang on to that face. It had erased itself. Perhaps it was lost forever."[21] Just as a mother cannot prevent her child from developing and growing apart from her after it is born, Françoise has found herself unable to freeze her relationship with Xavière and keep it as it was when the two women first made a mutual commitment to one another.

There is an evident ambivalence on the part of Françoise about the sensual aspect of her attachment to Xavière. The younger woman is occasionally coquettish with Françoise, inviting her to dance, commenting on her physical appearance. Speaking of a party which they both attended, Xavière exclaims: "I remember nothing about it but you ... how beautiful you were!"[22] Françoise is understandably flattered by such comments. She is both charmed by Xavière's adoration and aroused by any degree of physical contact which occurs between them. The verb "to melt together" (*confondre*) is used by Françoise to describe what it is she is seeking from Xavière: "a total union which would melt together their joys, their anxieties, their torments."[23] Such passages underline the symbiotic nature of the relationship Françoise is attempting to establish with Xavière.

Françoise is not sure just what label to assign to the feelings that overwhelm her when she is physically close to Xavière:

> She felt Xavière's lovely warm breasts against her chest, she breathed in her charming breath; was this desire? But what was it she desired? Her lips against Xavière's? That body yielding in her arms? She couldn't imagine anything concrete, felt only an undefined need to keep this loving face forever turned toward her and to be able to say passionately, "She belongs to me."[24]

Aware of the alluring quality of Xavière's sensuous, youthful body, Françoise is confused by this physical attraction with its nuances of incest. On one occasion, she sees herself as an overly timid suitor: "Did Xavière resent her discreet self-effacement? Had she hoped that

Françoise would make a violent claim to her love?"[25] As the intensity of feeling between these two women increases, so does the possibility of violence between them: violent passion or violent destruction.

As long as Françoise can continue to look upon Xavière as an insignificant child, she can succeed in keeping her own world intact. Xavière is at first described as a sad little individual, a brand-new little playmate whom Françoise takes by the hand to lead backstage during the dress rehearsal of Pierre's play. When she is in an affectionate mood, Xavière becomes "a loving and vulnerable little girl whose pearly cheeks one would like to cover with kisses."[26] The repetition of these diminutives highlights Françoise's attempt to keep Xavière cast in the role of a little girl whom she can mother. Pierre's assessment, "There is something childish about her which I find a bit distasteful; she still smells of mother's milk," [27] lulls Françoise into assuming that Xavière is nothing more than a mere child for both of them. Indeed she often acts like a child, a headstrong one sorely in need of discipline.

Françoise soon finds herself in the unenviable position of becoming an authority figure for both Xavière and Pierre. When she mentions to Pierre that Xavière must be disciplined, he requests peevishly that she stop scolding him. Like an irresponsible father who wishes to have a good time with his children without ever being cast in a position of authority, Pierre would like to leave all of the unpleasant tasks to Françoise. If the trio is to succeed, someone must keep things in line, even if it is at the expense of becoming an ogre in the eyes of the other two members of this surrogate family.

Just as Madame Miquel is sure that she has better taste in clothes than her daughter, Françoise is wary of anything done independently by Xavière. There is an amusing mother-daughter-type exchange between the two at a tea party carefully prepared by Xavière in her hotel room. As Françoise looks at the creative display of sandwiches before her, most of them composed primarily of tomatoes, which she loathes, the third-person narration describes her condescension: "She chose the least red of the sandwiches; it had a strange taste, but it wasn't too bad."[28] Françoise is sensitive enough to realize that she must not say anything critical but must rather encourage any effort the young girl makes to bridge the gap between herself and the adult world. Alone with Xavière in her room, Françoise is still trying to persuade herself that she is dealing with an innocent child: "Those charming features were part of the face of an honest child and not a worrisome magician's mask."[29] Right up to the end of the first part of the novel, Françoise is capable of looking up at Xavière from her sickbed and seeing an affectionate child who is precious to her. Indeed, this section ends with the words "Precious Xavière."

In the second half of *She Came to Stay*, Françoise is still trying to persuade herself that Xavière's presence represents something miraculous in her life. "Her look transfigured the most insignificant objects," she muses.[30] The verb "transfigure" is chosen from a lexicon of religious terminology, whereas the "joyous enchantment"[31] in which Françoise feels the trio is living is borrowed from a world of magic and wizardry. During the two-year span covered by the events in the novel, however, the relationship between the women progresses from one which simulates the interaction between a mother and a young child to the stormy period of adolescence when mother and daughter become rivals for the father's attention. The fact that Pierre Labrousse is not Xavière's father, but rather a man seeking conquests of ever younger women in order to reinforce his sense of virility, adds to the intensity of emotion experienced by the surrogate family represented by the trio.

Françoise is sincere in her desire to help Xavière lead a happy and satisfying life, offering her guidance as she remarks, "Life is so difficult for you. Let me help you." [32] In Sartre's play *Les Mains sales*, Hoederer says something very similar to his young secretary Hugo: "You're a kid who is having trouble becoming a man but you will be a very acceptable man if someone helps you make the transition. . . . I will keep you with me and I will help you."[33] However, just as Hoederer's decision to respond to the sensual advances of Hugo's wife destroys all possibility of his acting upon his paternal instincts, so does sensuality turn the affectionate good will of the trio into tormented rivalry. Once Pierre decides to try out his masculine charms on Xavière, Françoise becomes a useless appendage, a faceless chaperone with no identity of her own.

Like a mother approaching middle age and watching her adolescent daughter mature, Françoise is gradually forced to cope with the reality of Xavière's sexuality. The little girl has disappeared, replaced by "a woman face to face with a man" when she interacts with Pierre.[34] Françoise is uneasy when confronted with this budding sexuality: "That austere little bit of virtue—it seemed sacrilegious to think of her as a woman with feminine wants and needs."[35] Once again the terminology becomes religious as Françoise calls upon a higher authority to stem the tide of human sexuality by labeling it a sacrilege. She is clearly jealous of Pierre's ability to evoke a response in Xavière that she herself has been unable to arouse: "This black pearl, this austere angel—with his caressing male hands Pierre would make a submissive woman out of her. . . . She looked at him with a sort of horror."[36] An angel is supposedly asexual. As Xavière begins to respond to advances from both Pierre and Gerbert, Françoise finds it increasingly difficult to continue to look upon her as a disembodied spirit sent from above to enrich her own life.

Part of Françoise's discomfort centers around the difference in age between Xavière and herself. Whereas everything seems open and possible for Xavière, Françoise frets about options she has never explored: "Never would she be a woman in complete control of her body. . . . That's what being thirty meant: a woman who was already a finished product."[37] Beauvoir herself was just past thirty when she began writing *She Came to Stay* and, like Sartre, reluctant to see her youth slip away. For Françoise Miquel, it is not marriage but rather validation of the principles by which she has chosen to live that she is seeking at this stage of her life. Her opinions, her values no longer hold as much weight with Pierre as do Xavière's capricious judgments. Xavière's criticism of their life-style is making Pierre reevaluate all of his ideas, ideas on which he and Françoise were formerly in complete accord. A "flower child" *avant la lettre,* Xavière is challenging all of the values held by Françoise's generation: "How can anyone agree to live a programmed existence, with schedules and chores to do as if you were in boarding school!" she queries.[38] After having carefully observed Françoise's life-style, Xavière holds every aspect of it up to ridicule. She disdains art and culture, railing, "Concerts are still another one of your beautiful inventions! How extravagant to think that one might want to hear music at a predetermined hour!"[39] Françoise, like her creator, is an intellectual who values structure and logical thinking, while Xavière rebels against this Cartesian approach to life.

Françoise eventually becomes exhausted by these constant assaults on her value system. Having invested her energy in her studies, her writing career, her relationship with Pierre, and her commitment to Xavière, she does not have the stamina to reevaluate every premise upon which the first thirty years of her life have been based. Although she is loath to see Pierre sacrifice hours of his precious time prancing about after a whimsical nineteen-year-old, she is too tired to continue keeping a maternal eye on the two of them: "What good did that do? All she managed to do was spoil their pleasure and make herself hateful in her own eyes."[40]

Françoise Miquel discovers a reality known to many who have played maternal roles: one must be prepared to cope with a change of stature as one's offspring develops from a dependent to an independent entity. In the early stages of motherhood, the mother is essentially the sole occupant of the child's universe, a divinity upon whom it depends for all of its needs. Xavière admits to a similar sense of adoration when she tells Françoise, "You are spotless . . . . That fact dazzles me so much that

I can no longer believe you really exist."[41] This attitude puts Françoise in an impossible position. Xavière has placed her on an altar at which she worships when she has need of absolution. After she has slept with Gerbert, Xavière comes to Françoise as if to a confessional:

> [She] began to embrace her with ecstatic devotion: these were sacred kisses which purified Xavière of all stains and which gave her back her self-respect. Under those gentle lips, Françoise felt herself so noble, so ethereal, so divine, that it turned her stomach; what she wanted was a human friendship, and not this fanatical and demanding cult in which she had to play the role of docile idol.[42]

Relegated to the role of conscience, of arbiter of the proper thing to do, Françoise becomes mother confessor to both Xavière and Pierre, a listening ear forced to remain detached from involvement in their daily lives. Making a divinity out of someone is a convenient way of setting her aside, keeping her continually available to respond to the needs of the devout as they may occur. Françoise quickly resents being treated "as both an idol and a doormat."[43] She finds herself in exactly the same situation that many mothers of adolescent girls encounter as their daughters fight to separate from maternal authority and consider their fathers infinitely more interesting human beings than their mothers, a pattern perceptively analyzed by Dorothy Dinnerstein in *The Mermaid and the Minotaur.*

A doormat, a spoilsport, a useless appendage: all of these labels seem to apply to Françoise as Xavière and Pierre join forces against her. Pierre even has the cruelty to articulate the cumbersome nature of her role in the trio when he says of Xavière, "Even though she loves you with all her heart, for her little possessive soul you are still the greatest obstacle between her and me."[44] Beauvoir is here dealing with the classic Electra complex, one from which the incestuous aspect has been somewhat removed by the fact that Françoise and Pierre are not married to one another and Xavière is not their biological child. The unpredictable nature of Xavière's moods nonetheless keeps Françoise constantly off balance and gradually erodes her sense of identity. Although she can hardly be considered ancient at age thirty, she compares herself unfavorably to Xavière, feeling "so dried out" next to this epitome of youthful recklessness.[45]

Françoise seems unequipped to cope with the constant ego battering she is receiving from the other two members of the trio and gradually sinks into a state of depression. The unreal atmosphere exuded by Xavière is highlighted as Françoise prepares to enter the young girl's hotel room: "It was not only a sanctuary where Xavière worshipped her own religion: it was a hothouse where luxuriant and poisonous vegetation was blooming, a lunatic's cell whose clammy atmosphere stuck to your body."[46] These vivid images accentuate the impact which Xavière has had on Françoise's previously well-ordered existence. She is stifling under the nineteen-year-old's tyranny. She has tried on the garb of mother, mentor, divinity, friend, and potential lover, and none of them has proved to be the proper fit. This series of trials and failures leaves the dutiful Françoise psychologically annihilated: "Under the vain pretext of keeping herself pure, she had left nothing but a void inside herself."[47]

All three members of the trio seem to be caught in an unearthly existence, poignantly illuminated by the café scene in which Xavière holds the hands of the other two and Françoise has the feeling that they have all been turned into marble. She is faced with the choice of remaining immobilized, encased in this psychological marble, or finding a way to break out of it. Whereas Simone de Beauvoir needed to break away from the conventional milieu in which her parents lived, Françoise Miquel seeks to escape from the emotional entanglement of an experimental family structure of which she has become the unsuspecting and unwilling victim.

The trio in *She Came to Stay* becomes a metaphor for the prototypical family struggling through the adolescence of a difficult offspring. At one point in the novel, Françoise, in her symbolic motherhood, is willing to settle for Xavière's permission simply to continue to be a part of her life.[48] She is experiencing the pain of watching someone whom she originally looked upon as a child in need of her protection pull away from her in a bid for independence. In the course of the narrative, this bid for independence escalates into a full-scale rebellion and an eventual battle for identity between the two women. As one rereads the passages dealing with this relationship, one is struck by Beauvoir's repeated use of military terminology, which looks ahead to Luce Irigaray's assertion that Western society has always encouraged children to "kill" their mothers in order to attain maturity.

Françoise Miquel appears to sense that she is engaged in a mortal combat with the younger Xavière and to understand the necessity of girding for battle. Like a country greedy for territory, Françoise delights in having "annexed this sad little existence to her life."[49] She wants to "vanquish" Xavière's resistance to staying in Paris at her expense. As the threat of another world war hovers over France, Xavière is seen as "a living catastrophe which was stealthily invading [Françoise's] life."[50] The young girl is a "foreign intruder,"[51] an individual enemy whose assault prefigures that of the collective enemy which will soon disrupt the lives of millions of Frenchmen.

She Came to Stay vividly depicts the ostrichlike attitude which caused the pacifists of the 1930s to minimize the menace represented by Hitler's rise to power. This false sense of security is reflected in the microcosm of Françoise's universe as she continually tries to convince herself that Xavière is nothing more than "a loving, defenseless little girl,"[52] "a warm, defenseless little bit of humanity,"[53] with a face that is "childish and defenseless"[54] and a "disarming naiveté."[55] The repetition of the French word *désarmée*, defenseless because of a lack of weapons with which to fight, highlights the appeal of young children to the nurturing instinct of both men and women. As they mature, however, it becomes apparent that, like Xavière, they too have their weapons, disarming ones at that. Images of arms and weapons have found their way into the supposedly supportive relationship between Françoise and Xavière, underlining the adversarial positions which they have gradually come to occupy.

Françoise's initial reaction to the call to battle is to abandon arms and admit defeat. Xavière has made her feel antiquated and useless, a fossilized remnant of a prehistoric era. No amount of "heroism," she muses, can change that basic fact.[56] Françoise is painfully vulnerable, both physically and emotionally. She watches from the sidelines as Pierre and Xavière agree solemnly on a peace pact between them, sees Pierre as a warrior on the battlefield of love with a mania for conquests, a need to triumph over all female resistance. We know from the published *Lettres au Castor et à quelques autres*[57] that this was indeed the case for Jean-Paul Sartre, who, throughout his long association with Beauvoir, insisted upon enjoying an ever increasing number of "contingent loves," much like a roving husband who leaves his spouse at home to tend the fires. Although Simone de Beauvoir was never relegated to the role of an abandoned *Hausfrau*, Sartre's involvement with younger women, and most particularly with her student Olga Kosakievicz, certainly gave her a taste of the rivalry between generations of women which causes much of the psychological strain between mothers and adolescent daughters. The strain of battle is lucidly reflected in *She Came to Stay*, where Françoise feels vanquished, defenseless, incapable of fighting back.

Françoise's frustration is exacerbated by her ambivalent feelings toward Xavière. Her sensitivity to Xavière's physical charms makes her see Pierre as an obstacle to the communion she seeks with the younger woman because of his gender: "She had no hold on that stubborn little soul, nor even on the beautiful body of flesh and blood which defended it; a warm, supple body, accessible to male hands but which presented itself to Françoise like a rigid suit of armor."[58] Once again the terms are military: a body on the defensive, protected by impregnable armor. Françoise would like to break into Xavière's room, her solitude, her dreams. As the novel unfolds, her fantasies become more violent. Aware that Xavière is jealous of Pierre's continued devotion to her, Françoise is one day "overcome by a wild desire to beat Xavière up, to stomp on her."[59] The younger woman now represents an enemy presence working away at turning Pierre against her.

The reader senses that if only Xavière were willing to join forces with Françoise in a display of feminine solidarity, the latter would joyfully accept such a realignment of allegiances. Yet Xavière has moved from the essentially female associations of the latency period to a newly found sexuality which causes her to pursue relationships with men and to keep a safe distance between herself and older women. When Xavière refuses to confide in her, Françoise is once again driven to the brink of violence, at least mentally: "In a burst of ineffective rage, Françoise would have liked to crush that hard little head between her hands until it exploded."[60] Although the rage is ineffective at this particular point in the narrative, Françoise is gradually feeling more and more like a caged animal awaiting an opportunity to go on the rampage. Her maternal instinct is giving way to her need to reassert herself and assure her own psychological survival in the face of "this painful foreign presence which was continually blocking her path."[61]

The mutual animosity which develops between the two women makes each desirous of eliminating the other from the face of the earth. The narration informs us that "it was not only [Françoise's] presence, it was her very existence that Xavière would have liked to erase."[62] The verb "to erase" (*effacer*) is significant here, suggesting an effortless gesture which leaves no trace of the hand responsible. Eliminating the influence of another human being on one's life, and particularly of one who has played a maternal role, is seldom that easy, however.

Françoise feels that she and the older generation have won a preliminary skirmish when she establishes an affectionate and satisfying liaison with young Gerbert and Pierre simultaneously begins to tire of Xavière. The public and private wars merge in *She Came to Stay* when Pierre and Gerbert go off to the army and Françoise and Xavière decide to share an apartment in Paris. The threat of Nazi invasion outside its door and the petulant Xavière inside both represent an enemy presence for Françoise, who savors her letters from Pierre and Gerbert and seethes at Xavière's smug assumption that she is the one true love of both men. She wants to "annihilate" Xavière's pride,[63] to force her to proclaim her own defeat: "There was no victory possible without her admission of defeat."[64] This emerging taste for vengeance and domination is surprising in an intellectual who prides herself on her sense of morality and ethics. Xavière has battered the very core of her existence, however. It is Françoise's emotions rather than her intellect which take up arms against this menacing enemy.

It is not until Françoise despairs of ever achieving the kind of close relationship she has sought with Xavière that she first thinks of killing the younger woman: "Xavière never gave in; no matter how high you were in her esteem, even when she cherished you, you remained an object for her.... She smiled. Xavière would have to be killed."[65] Françoise smiles as this thought occurs to her, but the seed of the idea has been planted. Like the embattled mother of a rebellious and intransigent teenage daughter, Françoise is driven to contemplate murder as an alternative to the ongoing daily struggle for supremacy or even mutual understanding. The thought resurfaces after Xavière rifles through Françoise's desk and reads her letters from Pierre and Gerbert. Having prided herself throughout her life on her moral probity, Françoise cannot endure Xavière's assessment of her as treacherous and insincere. Two egos have clashed in open combat. One has retreated behind a closed door, refusing to engage in further skirmishes. Françoise can either accept defeat and live with Xavière's low opinion of her or reassert her own integrity by eliminating the source of that low opinion. The novel ends with Françoise's choice of herself over the younger intruder, the woman whom she invited to become a part of her life and from whom she can extricate herself emotionally only by turning on the gas and leaving her to die of asphyxiation.

In *She Came to Stay*, Simone de Beauvoir explores alternative lifestyles. The story suggests the existence of a nurturing instinct in most mature women which draws them toward the challenge of guiding and shaping the future of the younger generation. The lure of surrogate maternity contains a mixture of magical charm, religious aura, emotional turmoil, and provocation toward violence for Françoise Miquel, who is determined to avoid the complacent bourgeois existence of her own mother. The trio's attempt to become a surrogate family for all three of its members exaggerates the complications of the interaction of personalities found in the more traditional nuclear family.

Beauvoir presents the mother-daughter relationship, be it real or surrogate, as a battle to the finish, a clash of wills and of personalities which can only be resolved by the destruction of one of the combattants. The impression left by the novel is that the independent woman can successfully separate herself from her own mother by remaining detached and disinterested, dutiful but uninvolved, but that emotional indifference is

far more difficult to achieve toward a member of the younger generation whose very existence challenges the whole structure upon which
one has built one's life and one's sense of security. One can accept the
role of divinity or of doormat, sink into a state of depression, take refuge
in physical illness, or fight back, as Françoise decides to do only in the
final pages of the narrative.

Critical Reaction

In one of the earliest discussions of *She Came to Stay* to appear in English,
Hazel E. Barnes sees the trio as illustrative of "the Sartrean disintegration of a dual relation under the Look of a Third."[66] This description
suggests an analogy to the situation of the traditional nuclear family in
which a young couple's relationship is inalterably changed by the arrival
of the first child, *le Tiers* who will for at least seventeen or eighteen years
be a presence with which to contend. Barnes notes Françoise's attempt
to keep Xavière from progressing beyond the stage of the little girl from
the provinces in need of her guidance and points out the ambivalent
feelings experienced by Xavière after her first sexual experience with
Gerbert, which both establishes her autonomy as an independent entity
and plunges her into feelings of shame and disgust. As in the mother-
daughter relationship analyzed by Nancy Friday, both women find it
difficult to acknowledge that the outwardly angelic and virginal teenager is indeed a sexual being.

In *Sens et non-sens*,[67] Maurice Merleau-Ponty treats *She Came to Stay* as
a prime example of a metaphysical novel focusing on the problem of the
Other and the struggle to find one's identity. Analyzing the work from
a philosophical point of view, he does not mention the possibility that all
sense of alienation may stem from the unavoidable necessity for each
individual to separate from the symbiosis of the mother-child relationship and to acknowledge the otherness of all other human beings. Annie-Claire Jaccard's 1968 study notes the contradiction in the expectations the established couple, Françoise and Pierre, have of the new "addition" to their family: "On the one hand, they treat this other person
as an object to be annexed, and on the other hand they would like her
to be a source of creativity for the couple that they are."[68] This discussion, like Merleau-Ponty's, concentrates on the problem of the Other.

Jean-Raymond Audet recognizes the type of mother-daughter relationship implied in *She Came to Stay* from the moment that Xavière is
presented as a new possession for Françoise, and labels this relationship
a "rather dubious" one.[69] He notes that at the beginning of the novel
Françoise vacillates between the roles of protective mother and posses-

sive lover but that eventually the latter role will prevail and lead to "a sort of philosophical infanticide which is cruel and useless."[70]

Carol Ascher indicates her awareness of the mothering role played by Françoise Miquel in *She Came to Stay*.[71] She notes that Françoise "mothers" the affair between Pierre and Xavière and that she is essentially a mother figure for Pierre, giving him permission to seek pleasure with other women and remaining available to listen and provide moral support.[72] This indeed was a role taken on by Beauvoir herself, to whom Sartre wrote voluminous letters about his liaisons with a variety of "contingent loves."

In her 1987 book *Masks of Tradition,* Martha Noel Evans devotes one chapter to the murder of Xavière Pagès in *She Came to Stay*. Evans acknowledges the Oedipal-triangle aspect of the trio, but focuses on Xavière as an adoptive daughter representing the aspects of her femaleness with which Simone de Beauvoir feels uncomfortable and which she must therefore destroy: "The logic of this biological metaphor of motherhood inevitably introduces the possibility, the danger, of development and growth. Françoise is indeed troubled by any signs of independence in Xavière, any evidence that her daughter may be growing up."[73] According to Evans, it is Françoise's unwillingness to admit that she too is "a guilty, selfish, passionate, erotic woman" [74] that is at the root of her determination to eradicate the one person who judges her in those terms. Evans analyzes Simone de Beauvoir's reluctance to recognize that she is in some ways like Xavière, noting that alongside the patient, nurturing acceptance of anything Xavière/Olga and Pierre/Jean-Paul may decide to do there exists in her as in Françoise Miquel an unfulfilled desire to gratify her own emotional and sexual needs. She cites Beauvoir's inability to acknowledge and articulate these needs as the underlying explanation for what she perceives as "the debased and murdered heroines, . . . the failed sisterhood and the hostile mother-daughter relationships in her novels."[75]

Simone de Beauvoir admits to having put a great deal of herself into the protagonist of her first published novel. Her discussion of the writing of *She Came to Stay* in *The Prime of Life* suggests the extent to which the novel provided her with the opportunity to analyze her relationships with her contemporaries as well as with members of other generations. Françoise Miquel bears the same name as Françoise de Beauvoir, yet closely resembles Simone de Beauvoir, who began her novel when she herself was thirty years old. Xavière is clearly a fictional transposition of the author's former student, Olga Kosakievicz, to whom the novel is dedicated. She is also, however, partially drawn from Beauvoir's recollections of Zaza "Mabille" Lacoin. In *The Prime of Life,* the writer speaks of "that dizziness I had known in Zaza's presence"[76] and admits that Zaza, like Sartre, often made her feel inferior. Beauvoir's inability to communicate comfortably with her closest friend during their adolescence as well as the ultimate withdrawal and separation represented by Zaza's untimely death apparently left the author searching for the symbiotic relationship which she never achieved with her classmate.

Symbiosis, however, can endanger individual integrity. Responding to critics who did not consider Françoise's crime consistent with her character, the author revealed, "If I chose to make a murderess out of her, it is because I preferred any other alternative to that of being submissive." [77] Just as she would not allow her own mother to dominate her life once she reached an age at which she began to question the rules and values Françoise de Beauvoir imposed upon her daughters, she would not let a member of a younger generation, no matter how intelligent and alluring, compromise her sense of her own worth. Françoise Miquel, like a number of the protagonists in Sartre's fiction (Oreste in *Les Mouches*, Mathieu in *La Mort dans l'âme*, Hugo in *Les Mains sales*), resorts to an act of murder as a means of self-assertion, as the ultimate existential choice.

The writing of *She Came to Stay* gave Simone de Beauvoir the opportunity to analyze and reject the roles of surrogate mother and surrogate wife, which can be extremely tempting to a thirty-year-old woman. Referring to the novel's ending, she concludes:

> That ending . . . had a cathartic value for me. First of all, by killing Olga on paper, I liquidated the irritations, the grudges that I had felt toward her; I purified our friendship of all the bad memories which were mingled with the good ones. Above all, by freeing Françoise, through her crime, of the dependence in which her love for Pierre had imprisoned her, I won back my own autonomy.[78]

The elimination of Xavière thus erased unpleasant memories of dependency, inferiority, and frustration associated with Olga, Zaza, and Sartre. Through the successful publication of her first novel, Simone de Beauvoir established herself as an independent entity, a recognized writer, and a mature self-supporting adult. This represented another step on the path leading her away from her ties to her own mother. Her subsequent novels, however, continue to grapple with the problems generated by the emotional intensity of the mother-child relationship. Françoise de Beauvoir and her early training were never too far from the surface for the independent and self-confident young writer that her older daughter had become.

3

Passivity vs. Activism: *The Blood of Others*

Although more than half of Simone de Beauvoir's second published novel, *Le Sang des autres,* translated literally into English as *The Blood of Others,* is told from the point of view of a male character, the tension between the traditionally passive role of wife and mother and the new morality emerging as a result of World War II makes itself felt throughout the work. On the one hand, the reader is introduced to the masochistic Madame Blomart, the materialistic Madame Tellier, the demanding Madame Kotz, all mothers of an era in which parent-child relationships were very clearly defined by society. The children of these mothers are young people struggling to stay alive and to find an identity in a world in which war is all around them and traditional values are no longer taken for granted. For Hélène Bertrand, Denise Tellier, Yvonne Kotz, and Madeleine, becoming a wife and mother is no longer the only acceptable goal and dream. Their nurturing instincts find other outlets. This is a generation reaching maturity at a time when those who choose to bear children may suffer the fate of the nameless Jewish woman whose small daughter is torn away from her and sent off to a Nazi concentration camp as her anguished cries reverberate in Hélène Bertrand's ears.

Madame Blomart is another in the long line of submissive, passive women like Madame Drouffe and Madame Miquel who have allowed themselves to become what Beauvoir will later label "a relative being" in *The Second Sex.* Like Françoise Brasseur de Beauvoir, she is timid and self-effacing, filled with an overabundance of energy for which she has difficulty finding an appropriate outlet. Her adeptness at playing the martyr causes her son Jean to vacillate between guilt and resentment because of the unspoken accusations he senses behind his mother's resigned exterior facade.

Our entire impression of Madame Blomart is formed from what we learn of her through her son. Jean Blomart precedes ten-year-old Catherine in *Les Belles Images* by two decades in his concern for the poverty and misery which exist in the world. His sensitivity to the plight of others is quite clearly a result of his mother's early influence. As a child, he trotted along behind her as she visited "her" sick, "her" poor people. Her days are filled with the charitable activities expected of a well-off middle-class matron, yet Jean senses a frenetic quality in her charity, a busyness calculated to make her forget the basic injustice of class distinctions:

> From morning to night, she would run right and left, in an endless flight, spending hours pushing the wheelchair of the paralyzed old governess, talking with her hands and her lips with her deaf cousin. She didn't care for either the old governess or the cousin. It was not for them that she was putting herself out. It was because of that cheerless odor which permeated the house.[1]

Jean's sisters question the validity of the tedious tasks Madame Blomart sets for herself, the darning of socks, the making of layettes for the servants' babies, tasks she could easily pay to have done for her. He feels that he alone understands his mother's attempts to assuage her guilt and to deny the reality of her privileged existence by engaging in menial chores.

The sincerity of Madame Blomart's concern for others is brought into question when Louise's baby dies. Louise is a former family servant who, like the maid of the same name who took care of the Beauvoir girls, lives in near penury after she leaves her governess job to marry and have a child. Jean is taken by his mother to pay a duty call on Louise after her baby's death. He sees the overcrowded apartments, the lifeless form in the crib, and is struck by the difference between this abject misery and the well-dressed, well-washed, politely grateful poor people he usually visits with his mother. His father has little sympathy for his anguish that evening and forces him to eat his dinner. Although his mother appears to understand, Jean is later shocked to see her entertaining friends and laughing with them that same night. Even his apparently charitable mother cannot focus for very long on the plight of those less fortunate than she, he concludes.

Jean is clearly closely attached to his mother and follows the traditional Oedipal pattern in his conviction that she is married to an unfeeling, insensitive man whom she does not really love. A scene from a family trip to Seville remains in his mind as an indication of his mother's good intentions and of the ineffectiveness of well-meaning women whose efforts are not backed up by men. Reacting to a state of panic provoked by a coup d'état, his mother makes an admirable attempt to calm people down and restore order:

> She stopped and, to stem the mindless rush of people, she extended her little arms; I was convinced that if Papa had not grabbed her, if he too had put out his great big masculine arms, the tamed crowd would have begun to walk calmly again. But my father never dreamed of stopping the senseless way in which the world grinds along.[2]

The failure of this impulsive effort may well account for Madame Blomart's subsequent withdrawal from all political involvement, her horror at Jean's espousal of the Communist cause and of revolution. Jean paraphrases his mother's attitude toward political activism and action in general in the following words:

> It was crazy to want to change anything about the world or about life; things were already miserable enough if you were careful not to touch them. Everything that her heart and her reason condemned, she insisted upon defending: my father, marriage, capitalism. . . . The thing to do was to crouch in the corner, make oneself as inconspicuous as possible, and, rather than try something doomed to failure from the start, accept everything.[3]

Jean seems convinced that his mother instinctively agrees with his ideas and ideals, that she is a prisoner of her comfortable middle-class existence and of a loveless marriage: "With what a fierce sense of justice she took the part of that man she did not love!"[4] His childhood fantasy was to replace his puritanical father at her side and run through the streets holding his mother's hand and telling anyone who would listen how to remedy the ills of the world. As a child, Jean obviously considered his mother his ally and his soulmate, a friend whom he could sweep along with him toward the goals which seemed important to him.

Throughout the narrative, Jean makes several lighthearted references to his mother's high heels. In his fantasy, he is pulling her along as she struggles to keep up with him in those high-heeled shoes. When he visits his mother with Hélène Bertrand, he playfully grabs one of his mother's shoes and teases her about the heels, about her resentment of the fact that she is so tiny. In this playfulness there is an undertone of trying to minimize his mother's stature so that he can convince himself she no longer has too strong a hold on him. Jean is sometimes almost coquettish with his mother, who seems very young and vivacious to Hélène. Once Madame Blomart's only son has separated himself from her and from the family home, she appears less morose and resigned. Perhaps the prospect of Jean's engagement to Hélène has renewed her hope that he will return to a more traditional life-style and eventually have a family of his own.

Madame Blomart's initial reaction to Jean's leaving home is anything but cheerful, however. She is angry about his unwillingness to continue the family business, outraged at his lack of gratitude toward his father for his upbringing and his education, quick to point out the inconsistency of his taking advantage of the "capitalist" security of his home while he learns enough about the printing business to be able to walk out on his father. Jean has rationalized his decision to continue living at home during his apprenticeship by convincing himself that his mother needs him there. He feels betrayed by her arguments, yet senses that underneath them lies "another voice deep inside her which was begging, 'Don't let him talk [to his father], not yet; let me keep him here just a little longer.'"[5] They both know, however, that Madame Blomart will never articulate her own emotional needs, particularly not to her offspring.

Madame Blomart's attitude of silent suffering makes her son feel both guilty and resentful. Overtly, she is not a domineering mother: "We were free, free to sully our souls, to ruin our lives; her only freedom was to suffer from what we did."[6] Psychologically, she is a more stifling personality to her children than a mother who overreacts emotionally and makes continual demands on them. As he packs his things, Jean cannot get out of his mind the image of Madame Blomart isolated in the satin and velvet décor of their expensively appointed home: "I was all she had. . . . But how can anyone protect her against herself?"[7] Her laconic acknowledgement that he must do what he thinks best when he tells her he doesn't want to hurt her only adds to his burden of guilt. The reader wonders to what extent the Beauvoir sisters experienced similar feelings about moving out of the family apartment and leaving their mother to cope with the indifference and infidelities of their father without their supportive presence as they pursued their separate lives.

With a son who has become a Communist, one daughter whose marriage has turned out badly, another whose marriage seems empty and unfulfilling, Madame Blomart no longer appears to Jean to be as firm in her convictions as she was when he was a small child. He asks his mother's advice about telling Hélène, to make her happy, that he loves her, even though he is not sure of his feelings for her, and Madame Blomart demurs: "'Ah, I can't give you any advice. . . .' When we were small, she had been adamant about teaching us not to lie. But she too was no longer sure of anything: not of the value of caution, or of charity, or of truth."[8]

An adult responsible for the day-to-day survival of small children can be definite about opinions and values. Children grow up, however, to challenge all of the premises upon which their parents have built their self-assurance and their security. Like Françoise Miquel reacting to Xavière Pagès in *She Came to Stay*, Madame Blomart has been thrown off balance by Jean's coming of age. She simply cannot understand his decision to join the Communist Party, his determination to leave home and live like a member of the working class. She is no longer convinced of the validity of her principles or of a psychology of child rearing which allowed her offspring to make their own choices. "No matter what you do, you are always responsible,"[9] she tells her son, who seems so intent upon refraining from causing harm to anyone through his actions. There is a maternal resignation in Madame Blomart's tone which fore-shadows Laurence's sense of overwhelming responsibility for her children in *Les Belles Images* many years later.

Jean Blomart is afraid that he resembles his mother in her overly cautious, passive approach to life. Uncomfortable about his lack of in-volvement in the Spanish Civil War, he muses, "I felt just like my mother, clinging to the walls, running away from looks which might have made me reexamine what I was really like."[10] He goes into the army with a sense of exaltation. Here is a way of breaking all bourgeois ties, of becoming anonymous. Military regulations may even deliver him from his physical resemblance to his mother: "With what joy he had had those overly luxuriant, overly thick locks he inherited from his mother all shorn off!"[11] Anonymity is short-lived, however. Jean feels continu-ally drawn back into his mother's sphere of influence by the importance her opinions hold for him.

Jean's decision to become the leader of a terrorist Resistance group results in a strange realignment of allegiances for him. Suddenly it is his father whose chauvinism inspires him to help the Resistance cause and who participates vicariously but triumphantly in all of the group's activi-ties, his mother who becomes her son's adversary by questioning the validity of taking a single human life. Madame Blomart knows intui-tively what Jean is doing and blames him for the death of innocent Frenchmen shot in retaliation for Nazi casualties. Once again Jean is reduced to the status of a small child who must force himself to eat at the family dinner table: "I'm not hungry but I must eat. My mother isn't eating: she is looking at me. She mustn't know. *She knows. I know she knows. She will never forgive me.*"[12] When he was a child, his parents urged Jean to eat and literally to swallow his concerns for the injustice of the death of a baby, a death for which he apparently bore no responsibility. He is now a man who is indeed responsible, a murderer, an assassin in his mother's judgmental eyes. Despite the fact that he is past thirty, Jean still considers his mother the final arbiter of right and wrong. He desperately needs both her love and her approval: "Suddenly I'm five years old, I'm afraid and I'm cold. I would like to have my mother tuck me into my bed and give me a big long hug. I would like to stay here. I would stay in my old room, crouched in my past, and maybe I would sleep. 'I have to go.'"[13]

As Thomas Wolfe has so poignantly demonstrated, you can't go home again. The assumption of the responsibilities of adulthood places a return to childhood security forever out of reach. Jean must now live not only with his mother's silent suffering but also with her unarticulated condemnation. "She will die without having forgiven me," he muses.[14] This is a heavy burden of guilt to bear for a young man with a deep emotional attachment to his mother. It is a burden Jean must assume, however, if he is ever to separate himself psychologically from Madame Blomart. The novel's ending suggests that although Simone de Beauvoir has deep respect for Madame Blomart's insistence that human life must be preserved at all costs, she considers the particular circumstances of World War II and the Nazi occupation of France justification for the violence of terrorist activities.

The other mothers depicted in *The Blood of Others* are mere cameos, playing only very secondary roles in the narrative. Denise's mother Madame Tellier is a proud, wealthy woman who feels it her duty to set an example for the peasants by staying in her country villa when the arrival of the Nazi army is imminent. She becomes a caricature of bourgeois materialism when she tries to wear all of her jewelry at once in order to protect it from the invading soldiers. Harmless and hospitable, she is someone who is not taken seriously even by her own daughter.

Hélène Bertrand's mother is essentially a non-person in Beauvoir's novel. The reader never actually has a clear picture of her. We know Hélène will do almost anything to avoid eating at home. Spending time with Hélène's parents is a necessary chore Jean takes on when he becomes engaged to her, a chore he lets her know he finds distasteful. While Hélène is going out with a German officer who wishes to take her back to Berlin with him, she has nothing but disdain for her parents' vacillating attitude: "They were intrigued by the brilliant opportunity being offered to their daughter, but they blamed her for consorting with the enemy."[15] Madame Bertrand, unlike Madame Blomart, appears to have had virtually no influence on the development of her child's ideas and values. It is significant that she is never once mentioned during Hélène's long agony, which provides the framework for the novel.

Madame Kotz is an incarnation of the demanding mother who uses illness, imaginary or otherwise, to make a virtual slave of her daughter.

Yvonne cheerfully waits on this immobilized woman, who refuses to lift her arm out from under the covers of her bed to get anything for herself. Yvonne dismisses her friend Hélène's protests by assuming her invalid mother to be mentally deficient and by considering the outrageous demands made upon her the only pleasure Madame Kotz has in life. Because Yvonne has a traditional sense of duty which tells her she owes everything to her mother, Hélène knows she must lie in order to save her friend from the Nazi roundup of Jews. There is a dramatic contrast between Madame Kotz's reaction to the arrival of the police and Hélène's account of the scene to Yvonne. Madame Kotz emerges as an egotistical hypochondriac who wants her daughter to remain by her side and continue to satisfy her every whim despite the danger this may entail: "She'll be the death of me! ... Oh! I'm dying.... Give me my medicine, quickly.... Tell her to hurry back. They'll kill me!"[16] Hélène reassures her astonished friend that her mother is fine and wants her to save herself. Yvonne seems too naive to question Hélène's honesty and escapes to Spain, we assume, convinced that she is fleeing with her mother's blessing.

What of the daughters of this generation of mothers? They seem a confused lot, still dependent upon male approval to justify their existence, yet rejecting the wife-and-mother role expected of the women of earlier decades. The most fully developed character in this group is Hélène Bertrand, whose relationship with Jean Blomart is seen in flashbacks as he sits at her bedside watching her die of shrapnel from a terrorist bomb she has thrown. Beauvoir's novel recounts the story of the coming of age not only of Jean Blomart but also of Hélène Bertrand.

The reader watches Hélène develop from a self-centered, capricious child with no scruples to a socially concerned, politically committed activist who sacrifices her own life to save a former fiancé whose love she could never reciprocate. Unlike Xavière Pagès of *She Came to Stay*, Hélène has no female mentor, no surrogate mother like Françoise, to help her find her own identity. She feels caught in an oysterlike shell which keeps her from establishing contact with the real world. Although she has rejected the petit bourgeois mentality of her parents, she has found nothing substantial to replace it. Her fiancé Paul's visions of modest happiness, his promises of shelves that he will build for the books she reads, frames he will make for the pictures she paints, seem insipid and unexciting to her intense personality. Since marriage and motherhood are the paths which society expects girls of Hélène's age to follow, having a fiancé spares her from unwanted pressure applied by family and friends. As Paul begins to speak of getting married, however, she realizes that she has never really taken these plans seriously: "This marriage was just another myth; they spoke about it seriously, but no one really believed in it."[17] Hélène's rejection of Paul's physical advances, along with her reluctant admission that she does not really love him, ends the convenient framework which their engagement has provided for her life.

Marriage to Jean Blomart seems more promising. Like Marguerite Drouffe in *When Things of the Spirit Come First*, Hélène is sure that there is more to life than the protected and repetitive existence in which her family has encased her. She too looks to men with more than ordinary intelligence to guide her on her path. Her childlike trust is frightening to Jean Blomart: "She plied me with questions. You'd think she took me for God the Father."[18] Hélène is both childlike and domineering, however. It is her determination to mother Jean, to protect him from all harm, which ultimately destroys their original relationship. When he and his fellow workers are on strike, she arrives with an array of sweets from the family candy shop. She would undoubtedly like to reduce Jean to the level of a child who can be won over with candy and she demonstrates her impatience with his talk of workers, capitalists, and the efficacy of strikes. Although he finds Hélène charming and attractive, Jean is determined not to allow himself to become involved with her.

There is an interesting parallel between Hélène's attempts to manipulate Jean at will and Madame Blomart's long-suffering silences. Hélène tries to achieve with words and tears what Madame Blomart does indeed achieve through a self-imposed martyrdom. Both women want to make Jean feel guilty and responsible for them and to them. Both imply that if he really loves them he will do what they ask of him. The reader assumes that what Madame Blomart wants of Jean is that he remain at home and take over his father's printing business. Hélène at first merely wants more of Jean's time for herself, more of his attention and affection. His rejection of her after she breaks her engagement to Paul catapults her into an angry misuse of her sexuality. She considers becoming a prostitute just to teach Jean a lesson, then settles for a drunken evening in the apartment of an acquaintance for whom she has no feeling whatsoever, an evening which results in an unwanted pregnancy.

Hélène's pregnancy in *The Blood of Others* is treated as a biological accident, a disease to be summarily cured. "Hélène's keeping the child is out of the question, you understand?" Yvonne explains to Jean Blomart.[19] This was, of course, an era in which an illegitimate child was a lifelong stigma for any woman. Beyond the consideration of societal pressure, however, there is an obviously romantic implication that the bearing of children should be the result of a true communion between two people rather than of a chance coupling. Both Jean and Hélène are simultaneously fascinated and repulsed by this aborted reproductive process. The pregnancy seems to Jean an invasion of Hélène's innocence, an abrupt ending to her childhood for which he feels somehow responsible: "Under her childish skin, there was that thing which she was nourishing with her blood."[20] The "blood of others" of the novel's title surfaces unexpectedly here in the context of a woman's inability to escape the parasitical nature of reproduction. While Hélène dismisses the entire experience as "disgusting," "distasteful" (*dégoûtant*), Jean wallows in guilt as he watches her suffer: "I refused to play an active role in her destiny and I had used her as brutally as if I had raped her."[21]

It is primarily through Jean's eyes that we see the night of physical suffering which follows Hélène's abortion. For him as for Chantal in *When Things of the Spirit Come First,* the whole process is somehow obscene: "Her youth and her exuberance were flowing out of her womb with an obscene gurgling sound."[22] Simone de Beauvoir is here projecting upon Jean Blomart her interpretation of the male attitude toward pregnancy as well as her own squeamishness about the entire process. Jean is enough of an idealist to want to continue to look upon Hélène as an incarnation of capricious and innocent youth. The abortion night she spends in his room makes it impossible for him to maintain such a paternal attitude toward her. The degree to which Jean feels emotionally involved in this abortion presents a sharp contrast to Paul Périer's attitude. Pushed away by Hélène, Paul angrily demands, "You're not planning on remaining a virgin all your life, are you?"[23] to which Hélène retorts, "Do you think you're the only one in the world I can go to bed with?"[24] In this earlier scene, sexuality and self esteem are inextricably bound up in an adversarial situation which does not seem to take the possibility of pregnancy into account.

The issue of childbearing is raised once again after Hélène and Jean become engaged, but only in an extremely detached, philosophical way. The conversation between the two makes it evident that Hélène would like to bear Jean's children but is fearful of his reaction to the idea. "It would seem absurd to you to have children, wouldn't it?" she queries.[25] The ensuing discussion focuses on the questionable wisdom of bringing children into the world, both from the standpoint of the difficulties life may hold for them and from the standpoint of the positive or negative contributions they may make to the human experience. Hélène's optimism about the value of living, even if one lives unhappily, provides a sharp contrast to Jean's inertia: "Allowing a child to be born, preventing it from being born ... both are equally absurd. It really doesn't matter."[26] Does Jean really believe this, or is he playing the blasé intellectual in this scene? The question is never resolved because the war intervenes and with it the subsequent breakup of their relationship.

Because Jean has become Hélène's sole raison d'être, she fights fiercely to protect him from harm as war appears imminent. She has listened carefully to what he has told her about his mother, somewhat jealous perhaps of Madame Blomart's strong influence on her son, and uses many of the same ideas to try to persuade Jean to save his own skin. War is to her too a stupidity, one which no rational human being could possibly accept. Once it is declared, Hélène urges Jean to do as his mother did in Seville, to refuse to go along with the crowd. "You used to tell me that all you had to do was cross your arms and they couldn't do anything without your cooperation," she reminds him.[27] Jean is no longer convinced, however, that one should resist participating in the war. He welcomes the anonymity of soldierhood, of being a man among men, of simply responding to orders without having to reflect philosophically on whether they are right or wrong. This leaves Hélène and Madame Blomart on the home front preparing packages to send him and brooding about his safety. However, whereas Jean's mother is willing to accept the role of waiting patiently for others to determine her destiny and her happiness, Hélène is prepared to act to remove him from danger despite his protests. It is her decision to save him in spite of himself, to sacrifice their harmony as a couple to his physical security, that alienates Jean and causes him to end their relationship. He cannot prevent his mother from worrying about him and making him feel guilty, but he *can* eliminate Hélène from his life. He desperately needs to assert his independence from both of these women, to escape from under their maternal wings and establish his identity in a male-oriented society.

After Jean stops seeing Hélène, she tries to persuade herself that nothing matters, proclaims herself indifferent to the war, the occupying soldiers, the prospect of beginning a new life in Berlin. Her nurturing instincts continually draw her back toward caring about the plight of others, however. When she is fleeing from Paris, she attempts to help a poor peasant woman place a telephone call to her small provincial village. She empathizes with mothers concerned for their children's safety, gives up her place in a car returning to Paris to a bedraggled woman and her baby: "It suddenly seemed to her that she felt the weight of the child on her lap, and the appeal of those eyes full of reproach."[28] Reproach for what? one might ask. Perhaps for thinking only of herself, perhaps for being unfettered by children of her own in this time of crisis.

It is just as Hélène is trying to convince herself that her German friend is merely one man among many, like Jean Blomart, that people are essentially interchangeable, that she is jolted back to an awareness of her own identity by a chance connection with her anonymous mother, a box of chocolates from the family candy store being sold at an enormous markup to the German soldiers. She politely tells her German escort she cannot leave for Berlin the following Monday. Nor can she remain indifferent to the fate of her childhood friend Yvonne, who is in danger of being arrested because she is Jewish. Knowing Yvonne to be too trusting, too devoted to her demanding mother, Hélène takes over, providing security for both Madame Kotz and Yvonne, for whom she rescues a beloved teddy bear and finds an escape through Spain.

The imminent danger to her best friend reverberates in the larger-scale tragedy which Hélène observes as she is returning from Yvonne's home. Jewish children are being torn away from their parents, packed into buses, and sent off to concentration camps. An anonymous Jewish mother calls out after her little Ruth and pierces Hélène's shell. For perhaps the first time in her heretofore self-centered life, she realizes the value of group effort: "Suppose we were all to descend upon the policeman? Suppose we were to grab the child away from him? But no one budged."[29] The description of a desperate woman trying to stem the tide of events provides a clearcut parallel to the earlier passage depicting Madame Blomart in Seville. Slowed down by their high heels and their small stature, both women want to assure the security of their families and of the world they live in, and both fail.

Hélène decides that she must find some way to influence the course of events, to fight for a better future. She joins Jean Blomart's terrorist group and insists on taking all of the same risks the men do. The unspeakable tragedy of a Jewish mother separated from her daughter has catapulted Hélène into a willingness to act, a determination which eventually costs her her life. The exaltation she feels as she throws the bomb which saves the life of her former fiancé Paul is expressed in terms of breaking through the shell which has been her emotional prison. Having previously considered herself and Jean Blomart two oysters isolated in a shell,[30] she now senses that "the shell had broken: she existed for something, for someone."[31] Through action and commitment, Hélène enters into a communion with all those who look toward the future, toward a better tomorrow. Hélène Bertrand will never have the opportunity to marry, to have children, to grow old with Jean. Nonetheless, she dies with no regrets, acknowledging rather a sense of fulfillment derived from having participated wholeheartedly in a collective struggle in which she firmly believes. By rejecting the traditionally passive female tasks of preparing food and providing moral support for the men, and insisting on participating in the violent attacks against the Nazis, Hélène has translated Madame Blomart's good intentions into action and thereby found the perfect harmony she sought so desperately and so unsuccessfully in earlier years.

Most of Hélène's female contemporaries are far too much involved in the wartime struggle for survival to pay much attention to traditional family and maternal responsibilities. Each displays some form of nurturing instinct, however, an innate concern for what is happening to other people. Like Marcelle Drouffe in *When Things of the Spirit Come First*, Denise Tellier has attempted to mother her temperamental artist husband, with similarly disastrous results. A strong-minded eighteen-year-old at the beginning of the novel, Denise has ambition enough for herself and Marcel. "She planned on walking beside him unimpeded toward glory and happiness," we are told.[32] Marcel, based on both Giacometti and Duchamp according to *The Prime of Life*, will not allow himself to be pushed into becoming a popular society artist, however, and counters one day by dumping all of his paintings into the Seine. Denise must then find another outlet for her nervous energy. At the end of the novel, Denise is dedicated to Jean and to the Resistance, more protective of Jean's safety than of her own because she recognizes the group's need of his leadership ability. The war has shaken her faith in what Marcel has described as "that fraternal sheep-pen where Denise claimed to live, a well-raked human paradise, where abundant virtues flowed, where merit, truth, and beauty hung from trees like gilded fruit."[33] She continues to keep a maternal eye on her friends and associates, yet fears for her own safety and that of humanity in this new and violent world in which she must live.

Hélène's friend Yvonne Kotz appears to accept with good humor the traditional domestic role which society has delineated for a dutiful daughter. She spends her days waiting on her ill-tempered and demanding mother and sewing dresses for other people's weddings. Nonetheless, she has an inner strength, a peace of mind, which Hélène envies: "Yvonne did nothing else but sew, peel potatoes, and take care of an imaginary invalid; and yet her life did not seem absurd; it was even satisfying to think that Yvonne existed, just as she was, leaning over her work in her solitary room."[34] Although she is only a very minor character in *The Blood of Others*, Yvonne Kotz is nonetheless a liberated woman in her own way, precisely because she has taken the measure of the domestic chores which must be done and decided to do them willingly and cheerfully. She is intelligent enough to avoid arrest and ask for help in escaping the Nazis, empathetic enough to be concerned for her mother's health and Hélène's safety after she leaves. We are not informed about what happens to Yvonne after her escape to Spain, but can perhaps surmise that it is people like her, with equally strong instincts for nurturing and for survival, who will lead the way for future generations after the war is over.

Simone de Beauvoir's *The Blood of Others* takes the reader from the entanglement of interpersonal relationships in *She Came to Stay* to the collective experience of World War II in France. Whereas Madame Tellier and Madame Kotz react to wartime by trying to hold tight to their possessions and their idiosyncrasies, Madame Blomart represents a kind of collective conscience forcing the members of the younger generation to think hard about the taking of any human life, be it that of ally or of enemy. Throughout the narrative, Jean Blomart has railed against "that senseless caution"[35] which he inherited from his mother, a caution which has threatened to immobilize him because of his fear of hurting other people. His final confrontation with Madame Blomart seems to pit concern for human life against regrettably necessary violence, with the latter prevailing. The maternal instinct to preserve life represented by Madame Blomart's generation suddenly appears outmoded in an era in which action is valued over passivity.

In the concluding pages of the novel, Denise Tellier remains somehow suspect because she is afraid of death, while Hélène Bertrand wins the admiration of both Jean and her former fiancé Paul through her willingness to die for the cause. Hélène's death indeed provides the framework for the novel, which relates in a series of flashbacks both her story and Jean's as Jean sits by her bedside watching her life slowly ebb away. This long night of agony parallels the earlier night Hélène spent in Jean's room suffering through the physical and emotional pain of her abortion. During the first night, Hélène attained biological womanhood in Jean's eyes: "She was such a little girl. And already her body was acquainted with that acute suffering women must bear."[36] The final night brings her to emotional adulthood for Jean, who tells Paul that she has finally understood. This understanding, this willingness to sacrifice her own life, brings Hélène what appears to be universal approval, but most particularly male approval. The author's choice of words to describe Hélène's exaltation as she throws the bomb reinforces this sense of gaining entry into a masculine world: "The whole earth was a fraternal presence."[37]

By choosing a path of action which involves the taking and the risking of human lives, Hélène has automatically become a member of an exclusive fraternity into which women like Denise and Madeleine are not readily admitted. They provide the support system, the meals, the coffee, the deceptively domestic atmosphere needed to give an air of innocence to the Resistance activities. Hélène alone, however, goes beyond Madame Blomart's disdain of warfare as male foolishness and the older woman's anguished opposition to the taking of human lives to become a bonafide heroine in the novel. Whereas Françoise Miquel acts to eliminate an individual whose existence is challenging her own identity, Hélène participates in a collective effort to eradicate an enemy threatening the well-being and the survival of the human race. Prompted by her empathy for an anonymous woman who has suffered a brutal and definitive separation from her child, Hélène Bertrand transcends her adolescent dreams of finding the perfect mate with whom to settle down and have children of her own. She goes beyond the limits generally delineated for her sex to achieve a universal communion in which Simone de Beauvoir takes great pride. Reacting to Albert Camus's reference to *The Blood of Others* as a fraternal book, Beauvoir recalls, "I thought, 'Writing is worthwhile if one can create a feeling of fraternity with words.'"[38] This fraternity does imply a setting aside of traditional female concerns in order to cross the threshold into a more predominantly masculine realm of action which includes violence.

Hélène Bertrand is thus another positive heroine like Marguerite Drouffe, and also bears some resemblance to Françoise Miquel. All three of these protagonists grope their way through difficult moments while trying to find a balance between traditional expectations and the demands of a changing world. It is undoubtedly no coincidence that Simone de Beauvoir chose to name the heroine of *The Blood of Others* after her younger sister, with whom she had playacted military battles during the First World War and discussed ambitions for the future. Hélène Bertrand also traces the evolution of Simone de Beauvoir's own thinking from ostrichlike denial of the impending war to a wholehearted commitment to action, risk, and, if necessary, violence. Such exposure to choices and decision making during World War II changed forever the insulated life of the majority of women and prepared the way for the revolution in female perspectives which developed into the Women's Liberation Movement.

An interesting autobiographical echo in *The Blood of Others* is Jean Blomart's guilt and sense of responsibility for the death of his young friend Jacques, who joined the Communist Party and participated in the demonstration that killed him because of his admiration for Jean and his ideas. In the first volume of the memoirs, the reader perceives that Beauvoir felt somehow responsible for the death of her close friend Zaza "Mabille" Lacoin, essentially because she was too busy savoring her new relationship with Sartre to be available to help Zaza free herself from her mother's stranglehold. Beauvoir's subsequent use of her fictional works to warn others against the tyranny of maternal domination suggests that the author's feelings of guilt and rage over the loss of Zaza, who was perhaps the only woman of her own age other than her sister with whom she ever sustained a close friendship, remained with her for many decades after Zaza's death.

Critical Reaction

Most critical comments on the motherhood theme in *The Blood of Others* have centered on Madame Blomart. Hélène Nahas describes mothers like Madame Blomart in existential fiction as living "like a big, sensual, sleepy cat who has renounced all creative activity. She has produced a child and watched it move away from her."[39] Nahas nonetheless considers Madame Blomart a special case in Beauvoir's fiction because, like her son, she is sensitive to the suffering of others and seems to offer up her passive suffering as a kind of cosmic compensation for the capitalistic exploitations of her husband.

Georges Hourdin highlights the love and admiration Blomart has for his mother as well as his willingness to abandon her, his family, and the ready-made happiness his milieu has attempted to hand over to him, in order to fight for the happiness of others.[40] Hourdin suggests that Jean's leadership abilities are a direct result of the self-confidence he acquired during the happy childhood provided for him by his mother and compares Jean to Beauvoir herself, emphasizing the degree to which she too was profoundly marked by her early years.

Elaine Marks notes that Jean Blomart finds in his mother's face "the impotent guilt of the sensitive bourgeoise."[41] Robert D. Cottrell comments on Jean Blomart's assumption that his mother is secretly opposed to capitalism, marriage, and other bourgeois values, yet resists change because she is convinced that evil resides primarily within individuals rather than institutions:

> There is something decidedly Augustinian in this harsh vision of an evil force that is harbored within us and that we cannot eradicate. The teen-aged Jean seemingly rejects his mother's negativistic view and, wishing to see evil not within us but in our institutions, sets out to change the world. . . . His somber meditations by Hélène's bedside seem to echo his mother's unspoken desperation as it dawns on him that "there is perhaps no solution."[42]

Blomart is seen by Carol Ascher as an idealist striving to achieve a kind of sainthood through moral cleanliness; her analysis implies that this striving has its roots in the upbringing provided by Jean's mother.[43]

Each of the above critics assumes a symbiotic connection between Madame Blomart's view of the world and the social consciousness she has instilled in her only son.

Beauvoir's own comments about her novel in *The Prime of Life* indicate that she had put a great deal of herself into the depiction of Hélène Bertrand, whom she considers a more believable character than Jean Blomart. The author feels that Jean lacks depth and comes across more as a spokesman for a particular moral attitude than as a flesh-and-blood human being, and she therefore acquiesces in Blanchot's evaluation of her second book as a *roman à thèse*. Hélène, however, is struggling through some of the same questions of purpose and identity faced by her more intellectual creator in her late adolescence and early adulthood. After the aimless and essentially frivolous years Hélène spends concentrating her energy on ensnaring Jean Blomart, the young woman reaches a maturity characterized by both courage and independence, by a strong sense of having found a cause she can claim as her own. Like her creator, she has long since left her traditional family behind and opted to carve out a life-style more in keeping with her temperament. She represents one of the most positive female protagonists in Beauvoir's fictional universe.

The shadowy mothers who are secondary characters in *The Blood of Others* still echo Beauvoir's rage with her own mother and with Madame "Mabille" Lacoin. Madame Blomart suggests the resentment the author felt toward a mother who allowed herself to be victimized by her husband and his conservative values without ever thinking of articulating her own ideas, while Madame Kotz reproduces the tyrannical maternity of Madame Lacoin and the fictional Madame Vignon in *When Things of the Spirit Come First*. Throughout Beauvoir's early fiction, mothers tend to be rather neatly divided into two categories: relative beings who allow themselves to become martyrs, and monsters intent on manipulating the lives and emotions of their vulnerable offspring. In her second novel, the author is still looking at motherhood primarily from the point of view of a daughter who has escaped from the family circle and wants no part of the traditional roles it represents.

4

Women and War: *Who Shall Die?*

Simone de Beauvoir has dedicated her only play, *Les Bouches inutiles*, translated into English as *Who Shall Die?* to her mother. One wonders as one reads through the text whether Françoise Brasseur de Beauvoir interpreted this dedication as a tribute or as an object lesson. In the play we find anonymous mothers trying to protect themselves and their children from famine and death, an energetic maternal force in the character of Catherine d'Avesnes, and an expectant mother, Clarice d'Avesnes, whose feelings toward her unborn child change as her relationship with its father is altered by the political crisis facing their fourteenth-century town. The city of Vaucelles also takes on the role of both mother and mistress for the men of the community, encompassing their memories of past struggles and victories along with their hopes and dreams for the future.

Characters identified only as "a woman," "another woman," and "a mother" form a sort of Greek chorus for the action of *Who Shall Die?*, begging at first for food for themselves and their children, later for pity and for their lives. They try to appeal to the investment which they hope the hardened soldiers will have in future generations, asking for a little soup for children dying of hunger. These women represent a time-honored female characteristic: patience. They have waited through the nine-month period of gestation before producing their offspring. They must now wait in line endless hours, sustained only by the slim hope that something edible will eventually be distributed to them. They must oblige their children to wait with them rather allowing them to wander off to play, for fear that they will be deprived of whatever food and drink might appear if they are not in the right place at the right time. In the besieged and famine-ridden city of Vaucelles, all creative endeavor has come to a halt for the female characters, who are reduced to concentrating their attention on day-to-day survival for themselves and their children.

The anonymous women are condemned to passivity by their conviction that their only hope for survival lies in masculine hands. They appeal to Catherine d'Avesnes for material and psychological support, yet see her primarily as a means of influencing her politically powerful husband Louis, leader of the town council. "Master d'Avesnes has always listened to what you have to say. Beg him. Persuade him. He is good, he is just. He will give in to your pleas," they urge.[1] The just and good Louis appears more accessible than a just and good God to these women of fourteenth-century Flanders who are desperately seeking a solution to their misfortunes in some outside force. Like a Greek chorus, they are passive observers of events. Any hint of initiative, such as one woman's plan to hide from the soldiers who are to round up the "useless mouths" for destruction near the end of the play, is immediately squelched by fatalistic mass inertia. In many ways, the indistinguishable women of *Who Shall Die?* resemble the older, resigned Madame Blomart in *The Blood of Others*, who advised her son to remain quietly in a corner watching the world go by. It is quite possible that Simone de Beauvoir saw many of her own mother's traits in these women's passive acceptance of whatever cards fate had dealt to them.

Catherine d'Avesnes is the biological mother of Clarice and Georges and has raised Jeanne and Jean-Pierre Gauthier from childhood. She is also the spiritual mother of the community of Vaucelles. It is to Catherine that the destitute appeal for food, to her that the masons turn for encouragement and advice as they build the belfry planned to proclaim the glory of Vaucelles to the surrounding townships. She emerges as a kind of earth mother intent upon protecting all of her offspring from misery and disaster. Catherine is sensitive to the needs of others, overwhelmed to the point of exhaustion by the emotional strain of knowing that she simply has no more food to offer to the starving women and children whose cries she can hear outside her window.

When one looks at the children she has raised within her own family, Catherine emerges as a fairly typical mother, concerned with assuring the future happiness and security of her offspring. In the early scenes of the play, she appears willing to manipulate the girls in order to assure the future success of the boys. She speaks of "giving" her daughter Clarice to Jean-Pierre, who challenges such a possessive concept of marriage: "Give her to me? Do you think I would agree to shutting her up in my home and telling her, 'I'm all you have on earth'? I'm not made to be a jailer."[2] In this scene Beauvoir has clearly put her own ideas into the mouth of her male protagonist.

Catherine instinctively understands Clarice's feelings for Jean-Pierre and would like to spare her daughter the emotional trauma of what appears to be unrequited love: "Do you think I haven't heard you sighing every one of these nights? When he is gone, you cry. When he returns, you cry. Can this suffering flesh be my daughter?"[3] She has attempted to protect Clarice by forbidding her to see Jean-Pierre, but is now forced to deal with her daughter's announcement that she is expecting Jean-Pierre's baby. Catherine's immediate reaction is to defend Clarice against the insults of her jealous brother Georges and against the rage with which she anticipates that her husband Louis will greet this revelation. However, Louis's preoccupation with the council's decision to eliminate the "useless mouths" of the community, the women, children, and aged, superimposes a collective crisis on the family crisis which has just arisen, leaving Catherine no time to discuss their daughter's physical and emotional situation with him.

Until the end of act 1, Catherine's sense of identity and of accomplishment has been derived not only from her maternal role but also from the satisfying sense of communion she has maintained with her husband. Louis's willingness to agree to the council's callous remedy for starvation isolates her as a woman and as a wife. She feels reified, transformed into an old shoe, a vegetable peeling to be thrown out with the garbage. These vivid images used by Beauvoir depict dramatically the sense of betrayal felt by a woman who has hitherto been convinced that she and her husband are equal partners in family affairs and in hopes for the future and suddenly discovers that this is no longer the case.

Catherine d'Avesnes cares very much about what will happen to Clarice, who, reconciled with Jean-Pierre, proposes that her mother flee with them and share their future. Catherine does not want to live vicariously through her daughter, however. "It will be your child, Clarice; your future, your happiness," she asserts.[4] The older woman is convinced that she must allow Clarice to live her own life, to function independently as she prepares to start a family of her own. Like many a mother, she will feel that her maternal efforts have been justified and worthwhile if they lead to happiness for her adult children. "Be happy and my life will not have been completely useless," she tells Clarice.[5]

The course of events in the play effects an almost total reversal of attitudes in Catherine and Clarice. They are found side by side in the final scene, ladling out soup to the townspeople, but it is now Clarice who has acquired sufficient serenity to face whatever the future may bring. Catherine is anxious not only about her own future but also about that of the townspeople who have looked to her for guidance. She has achieved her goal, persuading her husband to reexamine the decision to eliminate the "useless mouths," but now worries that she is leading the entire population to certain extermination by the enemy waiting outside the town walls. Her greatest satisfaction is derived from the fact that she and her husband Louis will face whatever the future holds united once again in purpose and in love.

Catherine d'Avesnes's maternal influence is reflected in Jeanne Gauthier, who is relegated to the role of a grateful orphan who will do anything to please the only mother she has ever known. Catherine has chosen Jeanne as the future wife of her son Georges despite the fact that Jeanne has confided to her that she does not love Georges. When Jean-Pierre tries to save his sister from this disastrous marriage early in the play, Catherine assumes the role of omnipotent matriarch who knows what is best for her offspring. "She is only a child. She will realize later that I have acted for her own good," she assures Jean-Pierre.[6] Here, in a much more sympathetic character, we find once again the misguided omniscience of the Madame Vignon of the early stories.

Jean-Pierre, acting as a spokesman for his creator's horror of maternal tyranny, attempts to undermine Catherine's confidence in her own judgment by commenting sardonically, "I am impressed that you dare to cut, trim, and build with living flesh."[7] Devastating as this accusation may seem, it does indeed become apparent that Catherine is counting on the fact that Jeanne is too indebted to her to go against her wishes. Jeanne resigns herself to marrying someone she finds repugnant simply because of what she feels she owes Catherine both materially and emotionally. She joins Zaza and Anne Vignon in placing a strong commitment to filial obedience above her own needs and desires. All three young women provide unforgettable illustrations of the dangers of the kind of maternal authority which Simone de Beauvoir encountered during her own adolescence, and most particularly that exercised by Madame "Mabille" Lacoin over her favorite daughter Zaza.

Catherine d'Avesnes is considering only what may benefit a son she has found difficult to raise to maturity as she tries to convince Jeanne that she is indeed the wife Georges needs to have beside him. Jeanne becomes a mere pawn in Catherine's plans for the family future. Eventually Jeanne also becomes a sacrificial lamb whose outraged reaction to Georges's treacherous plotting against his father and his community costs her her life. As it did for Zaza and Anne Vignon, death proves to be Jeanne's only refuge from the manipulation of her future by a mother for whom she feels both love and indebtedness.

It takes Jeanne's dramatic death at Georges's hands to make Catherine realize that her son's faults cannot be blamed on his youth, that no one, not even Jeanne, could have done anything about the innate character disorder which has driven him to treachery and violence. Catherine bitterly regrets the unhappiness and the tragedy for which she feels responsible: "Who will give her back the love and the joy I deprived her of? Ah! what a criminal I am! I thought, 'Later, she will be happy.' But her life has stopped at this point, in suffering and hatred. She died with the weight of my stupid will crushing her heart."[8] Unlike Madame Vignon in *When Things of the Spirit Come First,* Catherine d'Avesnes is willing to admit her mistake, to be perfectly honest about her responsibility for Jeanne's demise. This death has made Catherine painfully aware of the limits of her own ability to shape the lives of those around her. Using a poignant image of domesticity, she muses, "How could I have dared to believe that the world was a docile lump of dough which it was up to me to fashion at will?"[9]

During a period of temporary discouragement, Catherine loses confidence in the value of everything she has accomplished over the years: the harmony of her marriage, the happiness of her children, the future of her community. This picture of despair hints at what is to come two decades later in "The Woman Destroyed," where Monique, a middle-aged matron convinced that she has been the perfect wife and mother, suddenly finds her world turned upside down by the revelation that her husband is having an affair with another woman. By contrast, Catherine finds a way to reestablish shared values and goals with her husband and to continue to influence the destiny of her township despite the irreparable sense of pain and guilt caused by the part she has played in Jeanne's death.

It is Catherine's political and psychological acumen which provides the key to the ultimate solution of Vaucelles's problems. In contrast to the passive Madame Blomart, Catherine uses her maternal influence to prod a reluctant Jean-Pierre into taking an active part in the political life of the township. Like Jean Blomart, like Sartre's Hugo in *Dirty Hands,* Jean-Pierre would prefer to remain uninvolved, to keep his hands clean. From her window, Catherine points out the stone of the belfry which she laid, the flag flying over the city hall which she sewed, and makes an eloquent case for existential *engagement.* "Won't you ever know the joy of looking around you and thinking, 'This is my work'?" she asks.[10] Jean-Pierre is considerably more articulate than Jean Blomart both about his debt to his adoptive mother and about his need to act independently of her judgment now that he has grown up: "I know how much I owe you. You have been more than a mother to my sister and me. But now you must allow me to live my own life without anyone's help."[11] The symbiotic link must be broken, separation achieved before he is willing to give his full attention to Catherine's proposals.

Despite the young man's apparently negative reaction to Catherine's suggestions, he eventually comes around to her point of view and realizes that he must act or assume responsibility for his passive acceptance of unacceptable events. Catherine's maternal advice thus becomes the indirect cause of Jean-Pierre's bold intrusion upon the council meeting during which he manages to persuade its members to reverse their original decision and to allow the entire community, men, women, and children, young and old, to face the future together.

Catherine d'Avesnes is a strong advocate for the value of marital and family ties. When Jean-Pierre proclaims that each individual is essentially alone in this world, she speaks ecstatically of the kind of union possible between a man and a woman who share similar goals: "If a man and a woman are forging ahead toward the same future, in the work they have accomplished together, in the children they have borne, in the entire world which has been shaped by their common will, they are united in an indissoluble way."[12] This idealistic statement undoubtedly reflects Simone de Beauvoir's own conception of her relationship with Jean-Paul Sartre at the time she was writing the play, with the significant difference that children never figured in their plans for the future.

In Catherine d'Avesnes, Beauvoir has created a woman who has shared everything with her husband, who has taken an active part in the political as well as the domestic life of her community. This is why Louis's willingness to cast aside women and children, to assume that they are a useless segment of the population, is such a devastating revelation to her. She is prepared to fight and to die, but always by his side. Her articulate presentation of her position and most particularly her awkward attempt to kill both her husband and herself so that they may at least be joined in death persuade Louis to try once again to change the council's decision.

Simone de Beauvoir has chosen a historically documented situation as the basis for her play and used it in a way that highlights, four years before the publication of *The Second Sex,* the extent to which women, in their traditional roles of wife and mother, have repeatedly been relegated to second-class status in Western society. Catherine d'Avesnes, like Marguerite Drouffe and Hélène Bertrand, does not hesitate to question these assumptions about the "useless" nature of her sex and to act to prove that they are built on very weak foundations.

One senses in the relationship between Catherine and her daughter Clarice some of the hostility which is often typical of the interaction between mother and adolescent daughter. Catherine apparently seems too traditional and conservative to the fiery Clarice of the first part of the play. Clarice disdains the conscientious role her mother has played at her father's side when she tells a devoted suitor, "I am not a suitable wife for a burgomaster. I'm not like my mother."[13] Jean-Pierre later reinforces this appraisal of the situation, assuring Catherine that "Clarice is a different breed from you."[14]

Unsure of Jean-Pierre's feelings toward her, Clarice at one point threatens to throw her expected child into the river after it is born. In this threat we find echoes of Xavière Pagès's violent nature in *She Came to Stay* and of Estelle in Sartre's *No Exit,* who has been assigned a place in hell partially because she threw an unwanted and illegitimate child from a balcony window into a lake far below. Until Jean-Pierre has declared his love, Clarice looks upon this developing embryo as a troublesome accident but at the same time as the only thing in the world which truly belongs to her. "Nothing is mine except this little life which is moving about in my womb and which will be wrenched away from me tomorrow," she declares.[15] Despite her apparent independence, the defiant young woman is overwhelmed by feelings of ambivalence toward a helpless creature for whom she may soon be called upon to assume full responsibility.

Once Clarice and Jean-Pierre have declared their mutual love, however, the child represents an investment in the future, a reason to keep on living and struggling for survival. She uses its existence to console her own mother and hold out the promise of future happiness through the emergence of a new generation of the family. "My child will be born. Won't you want to smile at it?" she asks.[16] She is aware of the strong attachment her mother has to her family and hopes to encourage her to go beyond her temporary passivity and fight for her own survival. Clarice's pregnancy comes to represent both union with the man she loves and the continuation of a family in which she has known a happy and affectionate childhood. The Clarice of the final scene of the play bears a strong resemblance to the Catherine of act 1.

The one situation in which Catherine d'Avesnes's maternal instincts appear to have backfired is in her relationship with her son Georges. Few words are ever spoken between the two in the course of the play, but one senses that Georges has been a spoiled child to whose every whim his mother has catered. Georges ignores Catherine when she twice tells him to put down the bow he is aiming at the crowd crying out for food in their courtyard, later continues to taunt his sister despite his mother's insistence that he leave her alone after she has revealed her pregnancy to them. Catherine orders, commands, and forbids, and Georges does exactly as he pleases. His total defiance of the kind of unity Catherine has worked so hard to create in her family is demonstrated both by his lustful feelings toward his sister and by his plot to kill his own father in order to appropriate Vaucelles for himself.

The pressure which Catherine has put upon Jeanne to accept Georges as her husband is one last desperate attempt to assure him a successful future. She is willing to sacrifice her adopted daughter's happiness to the hope of reforming her recalcitrant biological son. She would like to believe the words she speaks to the weeping Jeanne: "He is still young. He will change. You will change him."[17] One wonders, however, if Catherine has ever really thought that Georges could be changed. It is significant that when she is cataloguing the dreams she shared with Louis that have been transformed into nightmares by his betrayal of her, she mentions only Clarice: "You have turned the day I gave birth to Clarice into a lie...."[18] Georges represents Catherine's one big failure in life. When she learns that he has murdered Jeanne, she is ready to give up and die herself. Yet it is precisely her misery, her acceptance of personal responsibility for her son's misdeeds, which makes Louis realize that he cannot cast her off and allow her to face death alone.

In *Who Shall Die?* the city of Vaucelles is still another female protagonist to be reckoned with. She is alternately mother and mistress to the men of the town, whose decisions are strongly influenced by considerations of her well-being. Jean-Pierre is astonished when Clarice tells him that in his place she would not have returned home from the espionage mission—he is unable to comprehend that anyone could abandon his native city. For him the community is an extension of mother and family and he owes his allegiance to all of them. The masons are proud to be building the most beautiful belfry in all of Flanders for Vaucelles. One of Louis's arguments to justify the elimination of "useless mouths" is the fact that Vaucelles must live on even if its life depends upon the death of some of its citizens. Louis later regrets having tried to save Vaucelles at the expense of killing her soul and appeals to the council to hear him out for love of Vaucelles. For him and for the other men of integrity in the town, Vaucelles is a revered and respected matron whose well-being is always uppermost in their minds.

For the traitors of the community, Vaucelles is a virgin maid ripe for possession. Georges d'Avesnes has no patience with the idea of waiting a year before being invited to join the town council: "A year! My time will have passed! Vaucelles will either be lost or saved; now is the time she is there for the asking, in famine, in fear. Ah! to feel all of this strength in me and to do nothing with it."[19] Vaucelles here emerges as a trembling maiden ready to be conquered. The image is a clearly sexual one of a young man overflowing with energy for which he can find no acceptable outlet. Georges wishes to defile everything feminine with which he comes in contact, taunting both Jeanne and his sister with words like *garce, chienne, and putain* (tart, bitch, and whore). Unable to endure Jeanne's disapproval of him and repulsed in his advances by his sister Clarice, Georges turns his attention to his city, repeating to his collaborator François Rosbourg, "Vaucelles is there for the asking. We must take her."[20] It is François who combines the two images of Vaucelles as he attempts to explain his reasons for conspiring against his fellow councilmen: "It was for Vaucelles's good. Never will your weak hearts be capable of providing for her the destiny I dreamed of. In my hands, she would have become the queen of Flanders and of the world."[21] His attitude echoes Catherine's feelings in the opening scenes of the play as he articulates his conviction that his conception of what is best for the future is superior to that of anyone else. In both cases, the dough to be kneaded and shaped by the hands of a confident manipulator is female in nature.

Published in 1945 when Simone de Beauvoir was thirty-seven years old, *Who Shall Die?* reflects a period in the author's life during which she continued to be fascinated by younger women who, like her adolescent self, dared to defy convention. Clarice d'Avesnes follows in the tradition of Marguerite Drouffe and Hélène Bertrand, developing into a young woman who is independent, sure of herself, and actively seeking her own identity in the final scenes of the play. Her personality also contains echoes of Xavière Pagès's impulsiveness and violence. Beauvoir indeed designated Clarice's role in the staging of her play for her former student Olga Kosakievicz, who was the model for Xavière in *She Came to Stay*. At the end of the play, however, unlike her three predecessors, Clarice is pregnant, planning to carry the child to term, and anticipating a future shared with the man she loves. Although this pregnancy out of wedlock has been the source of some serious soul-searching for Clarice, she has come to accept it as a positive element in her plans for the future.

Critical Reaction

Very little critical analysis can be found of Beauvoir's only play, which she herself dismissed in *The Prime of Life* as an unsuccessful and overly didactic attempt to transpose her ideas to a theatrical setting. Most comments focus on the existential theme of "engagement" and the similarity between Jean-Pierre Gauthier and Jean Blomart. Hélène Nahas emphasizes the authoritarian aspects of Catherine d'Avesnes's maternity and focuses on her responsibility for the death of her adoptive daughter Jeanne.[22] Commenting on the female characters in *Who Shall Die?* Robert Cottrell asserts: "In Beauvoir's fictional world, if a woman is not a man's comrade in arms, if she does not join him in a common project (which seldom, if ever, involves raising a family), she tends to experience love as abdication of her identity, as servility."[23] Catherine d'Avesnes does, however, seem an exception to this generalization, since she does emphasize as part of her bond with her husband Louis the children they have produced together.

In an analysis of the play presented at a colloquium at Columbia University in April 1985, Marie-Claire Pasquier declines to consider the work feminist in spirit, finding in it "little of what has become an important theme for feminists, the relationship between mothers and daughters, or even between two generations of women."[24] Virginia M. Fichera, on the other hand, sees in the play a dramatization of feminist issues of the 1980s, pointing out the way in which the men of Vaucelles "appropriate women's reproductive labor" yet treat the individual women as replaceable.[25]

Catherine d'Avesnes presents a much more positive image of maternity than has previously been seen in Beauvoir's fiction. She is far from perfect, still attempting to manipulate and meddle in the lives of the younger members of her family, and she is certainly indirectly responsible for the death of Jeanne Gauthier. Yet she is a woman who is willing to admit her mistakes and accept their consequences, willing to rethink preconceived notions of how to interact with those close to her, willing to take risks in an attempt to assure the survival of those for whom she feels responsible, be they family members or the more unfortunate citizens of Vaucelles. She is a character acting in good faith whose positive nurturing instinct Beauvoir appears to respect. Throughout the scenes of the play, Catherine is presented in a sympathetic light as a woman beset with crises inside and outside the confines of her own home and struggling to cope with them as best she can.

It is apparent that, like Françoise de Beauvoir, Catherine d'Avesnes has been sincere in her attempt to provide a secure and happy childhood for her offspring. Is Simone de Beauvoir, in choosing to dedicate her only play to her mother, indicating that she understands better from the perspective of her own maturity the struggles, disappointments, and frustrations which led Françoise de Beauvoir into open conflict with her rebellious adolescent daughter? Or is she holding up Catherine as a model of how she wished her own mother had reacted when the Clarice of the Beauvoir family challenged every premise on which Françoise de Beauvoir had based her very traditional approach to life? The truth undoubtedly lies somewhere in between these two interpretations. Unfortunately, we have no documentation indicating just how Madame de Beauvoir reacted to those three words with which the text of *Who Shall Die?* opens, *à ma mère* (to my mother).

5

From Generation to Generation through the Centuries: *All Men Are Mortal*

Simone de Beauvoir's panoramic novel *Tous les hommes sont mortels,* translated into English as *All Men Are Mortal,* focuses on a male protagonist, a thirteenth-century Italian nobleman who becomes immortal by drinking an alchemist's potion. As Raymond Fosca wends his way through seven centuries of Western history, his tale reflects an innate desire on the part of both men and women to influence the future through their interaction with the generations which will replace them. The nurturing instinct, the drive to assure the security and happiness of one's progeny, is in no way limited to the biological mothers of *All Men Are Mortal.* Indeed Fosca, after an early failure to produce the type of son he desires, attempts to become both mother and father to a subsequent offspring, with equally disappointing results.

The framework of Beauvoir's novel is provided by the initial determination of a rather shallow twenty-eight-year-old actress to share in Raymond Fosca's immortality by causing him to fall in love with her. Régine has no husband or children and finds no solace from her fear of death and oblivion in the assurance that her reputation as an actress will live on after her. The mysterious, almost catatonic young man who sits in the garden for hours is a challenge to Régine's powers of attraction. She tells a friend that she wants to "cure" him, although she is not quite sure of what.

Like Françoise Miquel in *She Came to Stay,* Régine is not convinced that she wishes to maintain a possibly cumbersome level of involvement with her protégé once her efforts to reawaken Fosca's interest in life have succeeded. She has created an almost childlike dependence in Fosca, who refuses to allow her to ignore his resulting claims on her. "You prodded me into becoming interested in life again. Well, now it's up to you to make life bearable for me," he asserts.[1] Fosca here sounds like a spoiled child berating its mother for bringing it into the world.

Although Régine resents playing nursemaid to Fosca, the lure of achieving eternal glory through his association with her causes her to encourage him to relate the story of his long life. Régine thus plays a dual role in the novel, first as surrogate mother facilitating a type of rebirth for Fosca, then as Muse inspiring him to share his experiences with her and with the reader.

Raymond Fosca's early years are dominated by his father, who raises him from infancy after his mother dies shortly after his birth in 1279. The protagonist's childhood memories are therefore totally devoid of any mother image. He is raised in a male-oriented society which emphasizes physical strength and the martial arts. His first close contact with a woman is essentially dictated by his father, who urges his only son to marry so that he can "smile at his grandchildren" before he dies.[2] This choice of words is reminiscent of Clarice's urging Catherine d'Avesnes to fight to remain alive so that she can one day smile at *her* grandchildren in *Who Shall Die?* Simone de Beauvoir is patently aware that the decision to marry and have children is often prompted more by a generation of parents eager to see the family line continued than by the young people directly affected by that decision.

Raymond Fosca surveys the available candidates and chooses a lovely young noblewoman named Catherine d'Alonzo, who, he records, "gave me a son we called Tancrède."[3] The vocabulary used to describe the relationship among the generations is significant in this passage. Grandparents look forward to "smiling upon" their grandchildren, a gesture which implies a pleasant but detached relationship which involves no direct responsibility. A wife "gives" a son to her husband, thereby fulfilling the practical role for which she has been designated. She is permitted, however, to participate in the choosing of a name for the child she has dutifully produced.

As the story unfolds, Catherine d'Alonzo Fosca proves to be much more than a convenient brood mare. In the early history of Carmona, the Italian city of which Fosca eventually becomes the leader, Beauvoir repeats the theme of "useless mouths" which was the focus of her earlier play. This Catherine, like Catherine d'Avesnes, develops into a spokeswoman for the value of individual human lives, pleading with her husband as did her predecessor to have compassion on the women, the children, and the elderly whom he plans to allow to starve to death. Unlike Catherine d'Avesnes, however, she herself is not in danger, since Fosca will exempt the members of his own family from his edicts in his concern for maintaining his lineage. She also has no political leverage. She is politely ignored by a husband who tries to convince her that everything he is doing is in the best interests of the community and of the future generations of Carmona and that she simply does not have the breadth of vision to understand this. The young Catherine is a life force, a force for survival, whose pleas for clemency are cavalierly dismissed by the ruthlessly ambitious Fosca. Her entreaties and her logic are set aside as short-sighted by a husband for whom she thereafter appears to lose both respect and affection as she retreats to her sewing and to an essentially passive domesticity.

As she grows older, Catherine remains an ever-present voice of conscience for the brash Fosca. She tries to protect Tancrède's white mouse from becoming the first recipient of the experimental elixir of immortality, then pleads with Raymond not to drink the potion himself, instinctively aware of the dangers of insulating oneself from the time-honored passing of the torch from one generation to another. When Fosca expresses a desire to rid Carmona of its unsightly ghetto area, Catherine asks him what he plans to do with the people who have never known any other home, characteristically countering her husband's reliance on political expediency with her concern for the welfare of others. She tries to keep peace between Fosca and the impatient Tancrède, urging her husband to avoid provoking his son, who has now grown to manhood. Throughout the decades Fosca continues to ignore Catherine's well-intentioned advice, perhaps because he was raised to think that men alone are capable of guiding the course of events judiciously.

It is only after Catherine has succumbed to the plague that Raymond appears to recognize the value of her opinions. After her death he attempts to carry on a continuous conversation with her and is frustrated by the realization that he cannot ever again be sure of how she might answer his questions. As the novelty of immortality wears thin, Fosca comes to regret his original unwillingness to heed Catherine's maternal warning against drinking the elixir. Kept alive in his memory over the centuries, Catherine becomes very much the mother figure who was missing from Fosca's childhood, an understanding female companion who represents salvation and who is waiting patiently for him on the other side of eternity. He awakens in the eighteenth century to the agony of a recurring nightmare:

> On the top of the mountain, there was a woman beckoning to me: Catherine. She was waiting for me. As soon as I touched her hand I would be saved. But the ground sank down under my feet ... I barely had time to lift up my hand and shout "Catherine!" and I was swallowed up by the burning lava.[4]

Catherine, his first wife, his first contact with women, has become almost canonized in Fosca's mind as a representative of the wisdom and simplicity of an earlier era. She is a maternal figure willing to wait patiently throughout eternity for the impetuous young man on whose decisions she has long since despaired of having any palpable influence, condemned to watch helplessly as he is submerged in the violence he himself has created. In this memorable image, Fosca and Catherine act out the male and female roles which Dorothy Dinnerstein warns may lead to the eventual destruction of the human race.

What of Catherine's relationship with her son Tancrède? Although Beauvoir does not elaborate on this relationship, the reader senses that it is suffused with warmth and affection. Catherine is seen hugging her son at the festivities which mark the end of Carmona's famine. She seems more sensitive to his feelings for his pet dog and his pet mouse, to his youthful vulnerability, than his father, who urges him to stop crying and act like a man when the little boy finds his dog dead. The father-son relationship appears stormy from the outset.

Tancrède grows increasingly hostile toward a domineering parent whose authority he wishes to challenge. The young man is jealous of Fosca's stated preference for his grandson, Tancrède's son Sigismond, as his political successor, and undoubtedly of the open affection Fosca shows for Sigismond. Fosca has been an unbending taskmaster for his son's generation, insisting on imposing rigid military discipline on Tancrède and his friends. The boy's hostility explodes at an early age, when he complains to his father, "We will grow old without ever having been young. . . . Who will give us back the years you are stealing away from us?"[5]

Tancrède's respect for his mother is evidenced by the fact that he waits until after her death to challenge his father for political power despite the impatience which has been gnawing at him for years. Like Georges d'Avesnes in *Who Shall Die?* he is most articulate in expressing his feelings, throwing down the gauntlet to his equally irascible father with the words "As long as my mother was alive, I was willing to wait. But now I have had enough. . . . You have had your time to rule. Now it is my turn."[6] Rash like Fosca and unaware of the latter's immortality, Tancrède tries to assassinate his father in order to claim power for himself and is instead killed by his father's sword. There is certainly a symbolic significance to the outcome of this battle between two generations, an implication that while one can never effectively destroy the influence of one's parents and of one's upbringing, one can indeed be destroyed by them. Catherine emerges as a peacemaker whose physical presence has served to dilute the aggression building up between father and son and whose death has left a void filled all too soon by violence and lust for power.

Raymond Fosca's first experience with parenting has thus been an essentially negative one. There was never much affection existing between him and Tancrède even before their open confrontation and battle to the death, and the grandson he adored has died of the plague. For many years he remains aloof and alone, imposing hardship measures on his beloved city of Carmona in order to build up her strength and prestige, and keeping his distance from emotional entanglements. One day, however, he sees a little girl from a poor family looking with delight at the newly blossoming almond trees and decides that the essence of life is to be found in viewing it through the eyes of a child. Fosca's revelation here undoubtedly reflects Simone de Beauvoir's recollections of her pious days in catechism class, of Christ's assertion in the Gospel according to Saint Mark that "whosoever shall not receive the kingdom of God as a little child, he shall not enter therein." [7] Although Beauvoir and her protagonist are seeking the kingdom of man rather than the kingdom of God, it is nonetheless to youth that they both look for guidance. This was indeed the allure of Olga Kosakievicz for Beauvoir and Sartre, of Xavière Pagès for Françoise and Pierre in *She Came to Stay*. Although Olga and Xavière are not exactly children, they both represent a refreshing and unorthodox view of life seen from the perspective of a younger generation.

Raymond Fosca wants a child of his own, one he alone can raise and mold. The physically attractive Laure serves only as a receptacle for the seed which produces Antoine Fosca and she is quickly exiled after the baby's birth. "I did not intend to share my son with anyone," Fosca recounts.[8] One wonders if he felt that Catherine had been in some way responsible for the problems he had with Tancrède, and that a father could do a more effective job raising his son all by himself without having to cope with the female influence on a male offspring. Be that as it may, Fosca's immortality affords him an opportunity which few parents ever have, that of experimenting with diametrically opposed styles of raising children. Whereas both he and Tancrède were brought up in an atmosphere in which physical strength was considered the measure of a man's worth, Fosca now dreams of raising Antoine in idyllic surroundings of culture, peace, and harmony. He fills his court with artists, scientists, books, and paintings, employs the most knowledgeable men available as teachers, and surrounds Antoine with Carmona's brightest and most attractive children.

In contrast to the harsh discipline he imposed on Tancrède, Fosca tries to anticipate Antoine's every wish even before it is articulated. He fancies himself a kind of androgynous parent to this child who appears to possess an ideal complement of intellectual and physical talents, and muses as he hears his son laugh, "He owes me his life, he owes me the world."⁹ When Antoine almost drowns trying to prove to his daredevil playmate Béatrice that he can swim across the lake, Fosca develops an even stronger conviction that the boy owes his entire existence to him alone:

> I felt the warmth of my hands penetrating his flesh. I felt his young muscles, his tender skin, his fragile bones under the palm of my hand, and I had the feeling I was molding a brand new body for him. I thought passionately, "I will always be there to save you from all harm." Tenderly I carried off in my arms the son to whom I had twice given life."[10]

No one, however, can impede the relentless march of time and prevent a child from growing up. The idyllic parent-child relationship must inevitably develop into a testing ground for the establishment of the identity and autonomy of a new generation. *All Men Are Mortal* provides a poignant fictional illustration of one of the underlying themes of Beauvoir's 1944 essay, *Pyrrhus et Cinéas*,[11] in which she stresses again and again the fact that parents must not treat their children as objects to be molded in their own image but must rather be content with providing a point of departure from which their children can make their own choices and develop their own identity. Antoine Fosca will at first promise reluctantly to obey his father and not attempt to swim across the lake again, but Fosca cannot delude himself into believing that this obedience will continue indefinitely. Because of the Western heroic tradition, male children are far less likely to value obedience over adventure and independence than girls like Zaza "Mabille" Lacoin and her fictional counterpart Anne Vignon, who were brought up to follow patterns established by their religion, their social milieu, and their mothers.

Although Antoine appears to feel much more affection for Fosca than did Tancrède, he too reaches a stage in his life at which he no longer wishes to live in his father's shadow. Raised in an atmosphere almost totally devoid of violence, Antoine sees war and battle as vehicles for proving both his personal prowess and the superiority of Carmona over the communities which surround it. Fosca now experiences the agony of mothers and fathers alike who realize that they must loosen the reins as their children grow older but who fear the consequences of the younger generation's immature judgment: "All my love was useless to him.... He wanted to hold his life in his own hands, his new, clumsy hands; but could one enclose this life in a hothouse in order to cultivate it without danger? Stifled, bound, it would lose its spark and its flavor."[12] Antoine jeers at the harmonious existence Fosca has worked so hard to create for him, labelling it his father's peace (*votre paix*) and judging it boring and unchallenging.[13] Fosca gradually becomes resigned to the necessity of allowing Antoine to choose the paths he wishes to follow, admitting, "I didn't have the right to prevent him from accomplishing his destiny as a man, a destiny over which I could have no influence."[14]

This destiny takes the form of provoking a neighboring community into an unnecessary war and of offering up a young life for the glory of Carmona. It is not paradise on earth which will satisfy Antoine, but rather the opportunity to prove his courage on the battlefield. As Fosca stands looking down at the son whose happiness has been the focus of his life, he reflects:

> Just a hole in the belly; and twenty years of care, twenty years of hope and love were wiped out. . . . He was dying a glorious, fulfilling death; as if his victory had been a real victory . . . he was dying, having done what he wished to do; he would be a triumphant hero forever.[15]

There is a mixture of cynicism and futility in Fosca's questioning of the validity of the Western heroic tradition. His sensitivity to his son's feelings overrides all other reactions, however, and he provides the answer he knows Antoine wants to hear before he dies when he assures his son that both he and Carmona are proud of his sacrifice.

Frustrated by his failure to procure happiness for Antoine, Fosca is nonetheless undaunted in his determination to influence the destiny of others. He insists that Béatrice, the poor little peasant girl who enjoyed the blossoming almond trees and whom Fosca brought to his court as a companion for his son, become his wife. Béatrice obediently gives in to the wishes of the lord and master of the court, but insists that she will be his wife in name only. Together they discuss Fosca's need to control other people. Looking back on the tragedy of his son's death, Fosca comments, "I allowed Antoine to take control of his life, and he lost it; he died for nothing. I won't make the same mistake again."[16] Béatrice respectfully suggests that no one human being can wrap up happiness and give it to another: "Maybe that is why Antoine chose to die: you didn't leave him any other way to live."[17] In Béatrice's lexicon, living means taking risks. It was she who almost perversely encouraged Antoine to swim across the lake when she knew that he did not swim well enough to cover the distance, she who constantly urged him to test the limits of his ability, she who was in love with an Antoine who never looked upon her as anything more than an amiable playmate.

As Fosca's wife, Béatrice spends most of her time poring over books in the library. In Fosca's opinion, it is she who refuses to live. He gives her everything she might ever want, yet realizes after many years have passed that he has suffocated her just as he suffocated Antoine: "If I had not wanted so frantically to make her happy, she would have loved, suffered, and lived. I ruined her more completely than I ruined Antoine."[18] The little girl whose zest for life originally convinced Fosca that he wanted to be the sole parent of a child of his own has grown up, matured, and grown old, seemingly losing all enthusiasm for living after the death of Antoine, for whom her love will remain forever unrequited. Never a biological mother to anyone, Béatrice nonetheless adopts a maternal attitude toward Fosca as she comes to know him better and to pity the predicament which makes any gift of himself he might like to offer to others a disappointing misapplication of his good intentions. Fosca's experiment in raising two children, Antoine and Béatrice, in a protective cocoon which insulates them from the real world has proved a resounding failure.

When Fosca, convinced that both Carmona and Italy are too small for his ambitions, offers his services to Maximilian, he and the Emperor highlight an aspect of parenting which varies from male to female. For the man of the family, children, grandchildren, and future generations are a necessary continuation of the line of heredity. "What counts is my lineage," Maximilian remarks.[19] Having failed to produce satisfactory heirs to carry on his own lineage, Fosca decides to borrow Maximilian's, to make use of the Emperor's grandson Charles to further his own political goals. He hovers over the frail child, once again playing the role of androgynous parent, since Charles's mother Jeanne is in poor mental health and his father Philippe has died at a fairly young age.

The longer Fosca lives, the less respect he has for mortal man's ability to conduct his own affairs. Through Charles, whose election as Emperor he manipulates with well-placed bribes, Fosca still hopes to establish the paradise on earth of which he has always dreamed. "Nothing will be left to the caprices of men or to the chances of fate. Reason will govern the earth: my reason," he muses.[20] Charles is more malleable than Tancrède or Antoine and readily seeks the advice of his mentor, who he feels has been sent by God to guide him through his life. Fosca's pride is highly inflated as he promises that he and Charles will do great things together and that he, single-handed, will reestablish paradise on earth. Although Fosca is reasonably fond of Charles, he does not seem to have the emotional investment in him that he had in Antoine. Charles represents for him a convenient means to an end.

With each of the young men whom he attempts to nurture, Fosca begins with great confidence in the creativity of his role. He contemplates the strong young Charles in love with Isabelle and reflects, "His power is my doing, his happiness is my doing. I am building a world and I have given that man his life."[21] He has apparently paid no attention to what Béatrice tried to teach him about the impossibility of ensuring another person's happiness. Biologically, psychologically, or politically, Fosca appears to need to repeat the essentially maternal role of creating and molding the lives of members of the generations succeeding his own. There are without a doubt delusions of grandeur in his ambitions for these surrogate offspring for whom he represents a sort of divinity because of his immortality. His plans for their future, however, differ substantially from those which a mother might have for her children in that they subordinate all other considerations to a drive for power and control.

Fosca's projects turn sour when he visits the New World and realizes what devastation the Spanish forces he has sponsored have wreaked on the essentially ideal Inca civilization, which so resembled the paradise on earth he was hoping to establish. This reality, coupled with the loss of spark in a Charles mourning for his beloved Isabelle and regretting the missionary zeal which has caused so much destruction on the continent and in America, forces Fosca to reevaluate the role he has played in the development of this influential political figure: "How did I dare say to myself one day, 'I gave that man life and happiness'? Then I would have to say today, 'I am the one who gave him those listless eyes, that grieving mouth, and that chilled heart; his unhappiness is my doing.'"[22] If one is to take credit for the positive things that happen to one's protégés, one must also assume the blame for the negative aspects of their development. In his interaction with Charles, Fosca is grappling with a problem which besets parents of every era, that of determining the extent of one's responsibility and culpability toward the human beings to whom one has given life either physically or psychologically.

After another interlude during which Fosca becomes mentor and protector to the impassioned young explorer Pierre Carlier, our immortal protagonist reawakens as a cynical member of eighteenth-century Parisian salon society. As he once was with Béatrice's wide-eyed love of nature, Fosca is captivated by Marianne de Sinclair's passionate devotion to science, progress, and life in general. He looks to her to rekindle his own zest for living, commenting to Régine, "I needed her in order to live."[23] Marianne thus becomes not only Fosca's wife but also a surrogate mother to him. He is both puzzled and charmed by her capacity to make the most of every moment, loves her even more than he loved Catherine or Béatrice precisely because she is so very alive. It is she who insists upon having children, children with whom Fosca would have preferred not to share her attentions. His attitude toward pregnancy and childbirth is a mélange of awe, fear, and repugnance. "Why had I given in to her? She had wanted a child, and now strange and dangerous chemical interactions were taking place in her womb," he reflects.[24] His is a point of view which may have been fairly typical of expectant fathers in an era before the advent of natural-childbirth classes, literature, and lectures which openly discuss the biology and the psychology of childbearing from conception to postpartum blues. Until very recently, pregnancy and childbirth were mysteries known only to the initiated, the mothers of the community. The mixture of distaste and fear the reader senses in Simone de Beauvoir's treatment of the entire process reflects the secrecy in which female biology was cloaked during the formative years of her own development.

Fosca worries about Marianne's health but has little patience with her solicitous concern for the two children they eventually produce. His interest in his own offspring appears to have been exhausted after his experiences with Tancrède and Antoine. He confesses, "I was fond of these children because Marianne had carried them in her womb; but they were not my children. I once had a son, a son of my own: he died when he was twenty...."[25] This passage causes one to speculate on exactly what may constitute parenthood for a man. The biological realities of conception, pregnancy, and childbirth make at least the physical link between mother and child a fairly incontestable one. Does a father consider a baby his child simply because it is the product of his sperm? Fosca's attitude toward Marianne's children suggests a negative response to this query. It is clearly Marianne who has an emotional investment in their offspring, while Fosca remains so detached that he has practically no memory of little Jacques, who apparently died at an early age.

The life-giving forces which are important to Fosca reside entirely in his relationship with Marianne, who feels betrayed and cheated when she learns that he is immortal. Whereas it was originally Marianne who renewed Fosca's will to live and to participate actively in the world, it is he who hopes to keep her alive after her physical death by remembering her voice, her smile, her tenderness, her hopes. "Could I not make her live through me?" he wonders.[26] Living on in Fosca's memory is the type of immortality Régine is seeking so ardently at the beginning of the novel.

It is Armand, great-grandson of Fosca and Marianne, who takes over the role of surrogate offspring in the final section of the reminiscences. Armand knows that Fosca is immortal and is quite content to make use of him for his own political ends. Fosca has never forgotten Marianne's advice that he remain a man among men. He has devoted himself to the furthering of scientific knowledge and to humanitarian causes in an effort to live up to her expectations of him. In some ways Marianne has become, like his first wife Catherine, a maternal figure whom Fosca is determined to please, albeit posthumously.

Just as Fosca once predicted that he and the young emperor Charles would do great things together, it is Armand who sees all sorts of possibilities for the future in his alliance with his indestructible great-grandfather. Fosca remains unconvinced about the probability of ever changing things for the better in a world made up of imperfections, yet finds inspiration in the similarities he discovers between Armand and Marianne. Bringing Armand to his apartment to see Marianne's portrait one day, he reflects:

> I felt like talking about her; she had been dead for a long time; but for Armand today was the day she began to exist; she could be reborn in his heart as beautiful, young, and passionate as ever. — She had faith in science.... Like you, she believed in progress, in reason, in freedom. She was passionately dedicated to the happiness of humanity.... She was so alive; everything she touched was alive: flowers, ideas....[27]

Fosca's description of Marianne in this passage is a real hymn of love, the most stirring emotional pronouncement that he makes throughout the long story of his experiences.

Fosca vacillates between his desire to bring Marianne back to life through Armand and his practical realization that for the young man she is simply another dead ancestor. When Armand talks to him about what he would do with hundreds of years of existence, he recognizes the same passion for life which attracted him to Marianne. "He is our child," Fosca assures himself.[28] Here at last is the spiritual product of his marriage to Marianne, a young man with energy, ability, and commendable goals for the future. Fosca stays by Armand's side, saves him from death on several occasions, and participates actively in the projects organized by Armand to further his political ideals and ambitions. Armand is totally aware of Fosca's opinion of the transitory nature of all battles won, yet affectionately points out to him, "Tomorrow we will have to fight again.... But today we are victorious."[29] The two men learn a great deal from one another and profit mutually from the many decades of their association. Because he has survived to maturity thanks to Fosca's determination to keep him alive in spite of himself, Armand comes closest to being the son of whom Fosca once dreamed when he long ago took sole responsibility for the raising of Antoine. Fosca no longer tries to protect Armand in a hothouse atmosphere constructed exclusively for this purpose, but has rather come to recognize the wisdom of allowing the people for whom he cares to live their lives fully, according to their own plans and goals, and to encounter the risks and dangers which such a freedom must necessarily entail.

There is one final maternal figure in Beauvoir's novel, Laure, who takes care of everyone and everything while neglecting her own health and appearance. It is she who arranges in vases the same nameless flowers with which Marianne once decorated her home, she who worries about how much people are eating and how much sleep they are getting. Laure is instinctively maternal and tells Fosca, "I worry about everything and everyone. . . . That's the way I'm made." [30] She knows that Fosca is immortal and is still willing to offer him her friendship, her concern, and her love. He is tempted by the lure of affection and security which her straightforward offer of herself represents and wishes he could bring himself to tell her his feelings: "Of all the women I have known, she is the most generous and the most passionate, the noblest and the purest."[31] Yet he is tired and therefore incapable of uttering the words and executing the gestures which would initiate another few decades of commitment to a mortal, a woman destined to disappear from his life and from the earth in a time span which has now begun to seem insignificant to him, that of a normal human life. He rejects still another opportunity for sensual rebirth and prefers instead to coil up in womblike position and sleep for sixty years.

Raymond Fosca begins to lose interest in interacting with still another generation of humanity when he realizes that although the final result of the workers' revolution led by Armand is exactly what Marianne once dreamed of, the means to the end, violence and senseless loss of lives, is not at all what she had envisaged. It is at this point that he abandons his long-cherished hope of serving as a link from one century to the next. In *Force of Circumstance*, Simone de Beauvoir comments on his defection from the ranks: "His defection does not take away the meaning of History: it simply indicates that a break between generations is necessary for progress. . . . Fortunately, life is continually renewed from father to son."[32] The author focuses here on the necessary chain of action and reaction typifying the relationship between father and son. Her novel also highlights, however, the role of women as mothers and nurturers balancing the more typically masculine thrust for power and domination. Catherine, Béatrice, Marianne, and Laure are spokespersons for peace, harmony, affection, enlightenment through knowledge, and concern for the unfortunate. The most satisfying moments in Fosca's long life are perhaps those in which he adopts their perspective and cavorts happily with his grandson Sigismond on his shoulders, delights in Antoine's childish laughter or in Marianne's hectic redecorating of his home, responds to the touch of Pierre Carlier's or Armand's hand on his shoulder. Between Fosca's determination to force either rigid discipline or serene happiness on his offspring and his final indifference to the course of events around him lies somewhere a midway point which exemplifies the ideal relationship between generations.

Critical Reaction

All Men Are Mortal, like *Who Shall Die?* has received only scant critical comment among Beauvoir scholars. Very little has been said about the nurturing aspects of the relationships described in the novel. Hazel Barnes underlines Fosca's dilemma as he realizes that using his immortality to remove all risk from the lives of those he loves also deprives their lives of meaning.[33] Commenting on the disagreeable nature of many of Beauvoir's young heroines, including the actress Régine, Robert Cottrell postulates that the author's generally hostile attitude toward marriage and maternity may be "rooted in a reluctance to accept as genuine any form of happiness that is different from her own."[34] Yet it is precisely in *All Men Are Mortal* that the reader finds some of the most touching portrayals of both marriage and parent-child relationships: the respect existing between Fosca and Catherine, between Fosca and Béatrice, and most especially between Fosca and Marianne, the warmth of the feelings of Catherine for Tancrède, of Fosca for Antoine, of Marianne for her children, of Fosca for Armand. Terry Keefe makes special mention of the tenderness of Beauvoir's portrayal of Fosca's feelings for his son Antoine.[35]

As Beauvoir neared her fortieth birthday, her view of motherhood appears to have mellowed a bit. There is no overbearing maternal figure in *All Men Are Mortal* and the novel contains some of the rare glimpses of tender relationships between parents and offspring to be found in the author's works. The possibility of male involvement in the nurturing and raising of children represented by Fosca looks ahead to proposals for change in traditional family roles that will be presented in *The Second Sex* and in the numerous works by both French and American feminists which come after it.

6

Motherhood and *The Second Sex*

It is in *The Second Sex* that Simone de Beauvoir first goes beyond a fictional transposition of her observations of the female condition to an analysis of the many elements which contribute to explaining it. The author began to work on this book when she realized that before she could be ready to write her own autobiography she needed to understand what difference the fact that she was born a woman had made in her life. Published in 1949, this monumental text explores the biological, psychological, social, and economic factors which have traditionally limited woman's access to independence and equality. The childbearing function is a recurrent theme in Beauvoir's analysis of the problems inherent in being born a woman and her comments about maternity provoked outrage in many of the early readers of her study.

Speaking of woman's destiny, the author presents female biology as a battle between the individual and the species, with the latter inevitably prevailing. Puberty is described as the moment when "the species reaffirms its rights" over the previously carefree young girl.[1] In a comparison of the human and animal worlds, Beauvoir notes that, for females, only in the higher monkeys and in human beings is the reproductive process a recurrent monthly phenomenon rather than a seasonal one. The biological cycles are thus regarded as an unending series of crises for the individual woman, who progresses from the onset of menstruation through pregnancy, childbirth, and child care to the negation of her reproductive usefulness at the time of menopause.

In the two lengthy volumes of *The Second Sex*, Simone de Beauvoir follows the female child from birth through old age. She highlights the strong influence which the mother-child relationship has on the future development of the individual, pointing out that although the mother is the first love object for both boys and girls, boys quickly realize at an early age that they must break away from the maternal sphere of influence and are indeed encouraged by family and society to do so. Little girls, on the other hand, are expected to remain close to their mothers, to emulate them, eventually to help them with their daily chores. Traditionally, they play at being "Mommy," using their dolls as surrogate offspring. Children of both sexes are fascinated by their mother's ability to produce a new human being from her stomach, the author notes. "It's as beautiful as a sleight-of-hand trick. The mother appears endowed with the awesome power of fairies," she remarks somewhat ironically.[2] In early childhood, according to Beauvoir's research, a little girl generally considers herself privileged to belong to the sex capable of performing this magical feat.

In a later chapter on lesbianism, Simone de Beauvoir acknowledges the importance certain psychoanalysts of the period attached to the mother's treatment of her daughter in the development of the latter's sexuality. Overly possessive or overtly hostile, the mother is cast as the culprit in turning her child toward homosexuality:

> There are two cases in which the adolescent girl has difficulty escaping from [her mother's] grasp: if she has been passionately protected by an anxious mother; or if she has been mistreated by a "bad mother" who has left her with a deep feeling of guilt. In the first case, their relationship was often bordering on homosexuality.... The girl will seek this same happiness in a new embrace. In the second case, she will feel a burning desire for a "good mother" who can protect her from the first one, who can take away the curse hanging over her head.[3]

Words such as "grasp," "anxious," "mistreated," and "curse" suggest the negative feelings experienced by the author when she considers the extremes of mothering she has witnessed during her own childhood and adolescence.

Although Beauvoir does not completely concur with the above explanation of lesbianism, the paragraphs which she devotes to it underline her awareness of the overwhelming influence of the maternal attitude on the development of the captive child. Heterosexual or homosexual, the maturing girl's search for a love object will often be an attempt to recreate the comfortable paradise of her childhood, according to *The Second Sex:*

> A woman does not wish to reincarnate one individual in another, but rather to revive a situation: the one she knew as a little girl protected by adults. She has been a complete part of the life of her family, has enjoyed in her home the peace of quasi passivity. Love will give her back her mother as well as her father. It will give her back her childhood.[4]

Beauvoir is here drawing on her own experience as part of a loving and supportive family and as the daughter of an affectionate, committed mother. Her perceptive analysis challenges the Freudian theory that all women are seeking a father substitute in the men they love and marry. It suggests that beyond the obvious physical attraction which draws one human being to another lies the nostalgia of childhood, the desire to return to a phase of one's life clearly dominated by the figure of a mother who absorbs all cares and all responsibilities.

It is only in the very early years of childhood, however, that the female child accepts her mother unquestioningly. As she matures, she begins to wonder, as did the Beauvoir sisters, about her mother's limited role in society, to suspect that it is rather her father's activities which are validated by public opinion. The narrow confines of her home suddenly appear suffocating. The adjective *étouffant* is used repeatedly by Beauvoir to describe the family circle.[5] Like the young Simone, the little girl is portrayed as detaching herself from her mother's dominion in order to fill her life with more meaningful tasks than the daily repetition of never-ending household chores. As her father grows in her esteem, her opinion of her mother's worth diminishes. With the approach of puberty, pregnancy and childbirth become frightening rather than miraculous phenomena: "Often it no longer seems marvelous but rather horrible to her that a parasitical entity is to grow inside her own body; the idea of this monstrous growth terrifies her. . . . Visions of swelling, of tearing, of hemorrhaging come to haunt her."[6] This description of the reproductive process is a very personal one of Beauvoir's and can be found in numerous passages of her fictional works. The mother-child symbiosis which some women crave becomes in the author's eyes "parasitical," "monstrous," "horrible," and "terrifying." *The Second Sex* suggests that everything associated with her mother is devalued and distasteful in the young girl's mind as she becomes biologically capable of supplanting the woman who has most influenced her life.

With adolescence comes ambivalence about one's female identity. On the one hand there is the frightening prospect of pregnancy and childbirth described above, the haunting image of the parasitic embryo which we have already met in *When Things of the Spirit Come First* and *The Blood of Others*. On the other hand there is the familiarity of the role of wife and mother for which the girl has been psychologically prepared since the first years of her life. Convinced that she is "destined to keep the human race going and the home fires burning,"[7] she views marriage as a welcome escape from the decisions she must otherwise make about her future. Beauvoir here presents a point of view which will be reinforced by Betty Friedan in *The Feminine Mystique* more than a decade later. This comfortable choice of marriage and motherhood is seen by the author as an acceptance of passivity:

> The first twenty years of a woman's life are extraordinarily rich; the woman . . . discovers the world and her destiny. At age twenty, she is a housewife permanently attached to one man, with a child in her arms; her life is over forever. Real action and real work are done only by men.[8]

For Beauvoir, a willingness to take on the expected traditional female roles is thus interpreted as a rejection of vitality, as a reluctance to commit oneself to meaningful participation in the real world. There are undoubtedly many contemporary women who would disagree with her bias in evaluating women's options, particularly those currently labeled "superwomen" by the media who have somehow managed to juggle families and careers successfully.

When Simone de Beauvoir was writing *The Second Sex,* many women had indeed tasted the freedom and independence afforded by a career, or at least by being active participants in a wartime marketplace which needed their contribution. Like Betty Friedan, Beauvoir was one of the first to emphasize the psychological satisfaction derived from pursuing a career and being paid for one's efforts. The author cites the childbearing function as the culprit in keeping women from continuing to participate in the work of their choice: "In most cases, the birth of a child obliges them to retreat to their matron's role. It is extremely difficult at the present time to juggle work and maternity."[9] Persuaded by society that the path to true fulfillment requires the assumption of responsibilities as wife and mother, the working woman of the 1940s readily abandoned her career goals as extraneous to what she had been led to consider the more essential part of her existence. Although the atmosphere has changed considerably in the decades since the publication of *The Second Sex,* young women of the 1980s are still torn between their desire to forge ahead in their careers and the lure of participating in the creation of a new generation.

Many pages of *The Second Sex* are devoted to an analysis of the pressures brought to bear upon women by a society eager to keep them at home as wives and mothers. The unmarried woman has traditionally been treated as a useless appendage in many families, an attitude which leads young girls to assume that any husband is better than none. Until relatively recent advances in methods of contraception and abortion, a married woman was obliged to consume her youth and her energy in an endless series of pregnancies. According to Beauvoir: "The woman cannot actually be forced to bear children: all one can do is enclose her in situations where maternity is the only way out for her. The law and custom force her to marry, contraception and abortion are forbidden, as is divorce. . . ."[10] In the conservative atmosphere of the 1940s, motherhood thus became an imprisonment rather than a choice freely and joyfully made. Highlighting the physical weakening of women through menstruation, pregnancy, childbirth, and child care, Beauvoir ascribes the development of male dominance to women's inability to assume an equal share of the work of the community. Motherhood traps the woman at home, where countless chores repeated at exhaustingly frequent intervals gradually erode away her youth, her vitality, and her interest in the realm of life that extends beyond her doorstep. The author paints a rather grim picture here, a demystification of the media presentation of serenely happy mothers beaming at their rosy-cheeked, gurgling babies.

The perceptive wife and mother soon finds herself caught in "a most ingenious paradox," as Gilbert and Sullivan would put it: the society which has led her to believe that she will find fulfillment, respect, and admiration in her current situation values violence, danger, and risk of one's life far more highly than the creation and preservation of life. In Beauvoir's estimation "it is not by creating life, but rather by risking one's life that man proves himself superior to animals; that is why humanity grants superiority not to the sex which gives birth but to the sex which kills."[11] In Fosca's frustrated plans for his son Antoine in *All Men Are Mortal*, we have already observed the discrepancy between the lip service paid to creativity and peace and man's drive to prove his value through danger and violence. It is of interest to note that in a number of Jean-Paul Sartre's fictional works, the existential hero proves himself by killing someone else: Mathieu in *Troubled Sleep*, Oreste in *The Flies*, Hugo Barine in *Dirty Hands*, Goetz in *The Devil and the Good Lord*. Beauvoir's early female protagonists follow suit as Françoise Miquel turns on the gas and leaves Xavière to suffocate, as Hélène Bertrand chooses a much more masculine mode of action when she throws a grenade at the Nazi soldiers. In each case, the protagonists find fulfillment and a sense of identity in their acts of violence.

Having been raised by a devoutly Catholic mother, Beauvoir discusses the added pressure to bear many children felt by women raised in predominantly Catholic countries. Glorifying purity and abstinence, the church of the author's childhood has traditionally looked upon marriage as a concession to human weakness, justified primarily as a necessary evil for the perpetuation of the species. Women of Beauvoir's generation were therefore encouraged to marry young and to produce as many children as possible. The strong religious stand against planned parenthood reverberates in Saint Augustine's proclamation quoted in *The Second Sex:* "Any woman who takes any measures to prevent herself from giving birth to as many children as she can bear is guilty of that many homicides...."[12] The fact that such an authoritative statement comes from a man who has never had first-hand experience with the childbearing process does not escape Beauvoir's perceptive eye.

Having capitulated to religious and societal pressures, the young married woman depicted in *The Second Sex* finds herself faced with the physical discomforts of pregnancy. Beauvoir sees problems like morning sickness as an indication of "the revolt of the organism against the species which is taking possession of it."[13] The modern gynecologist might well take issue with this assumption and rather attribute such symptoms to chemical imbalances.

Beauvoir discusses in considerable detail male ambivalence toward the whole reproductive process. The husband who has himself been programmed to sire a new generation often has little emotional support to offer his pregnant wife, according to her research. From childhood he has been alternately fascinated, frightened, and repulsed by female fertility: "Man is repulsed by finding in the woman he possesses the qualities which he has feared in his own mother."[14] This analysis foreshadows the theme of Dorothy Dinnerstein's *The Mermaid and the Minotaur.* The mysteries attached to conception and childbearing have been surrounded by taboos and superstitions from primitive times on. In Simone de Beauvoir's opinion, "Underlying all the respect with which society endows it, the childbearing function inspires spontaneous repugnance."[15] If both husband and wife have ambivalent feelings about the pregnancy, there is little mutual comfort which they can offer one another as she experiences a series of physical changes over which she appears to have no control. "Repugnance" is a very strong word in this context, indicating once again Simone de Beauvoir's personal bias. Her analysis of the sense of helplessness which may overcome a young couple expecting their first child is, however, extremely perceptive.

The author suggests that throughout the centuries men have attempted to divest women of any autonomy in the childbearing process. She has uncovered a revealing quotation from the Greek playwright Aeschylus in support of her argument: "It is not the mother who gives life to what people call her child. She only nourishes the germ poured into her breast. The father is the one who creates life. Woman, like a foreign receptacle, receives the germ and, if the gods so will, she becomes its guardian."[16] Aeschylus would thus deprive women of any claim to an active contribution to society. Christianity, according to Beauvoir, is scarcely more generous. She sees in the cult of the Virgin

Mary "the supreme male victory ... the rehabilitation of woman through the accomplishment of her defeat."[17] Mary's eagerness to kneel down before her son thus represents for the author the ultimate capitulation of female to male. The cult of the virgin contributes to the myth of the ideal Mother, created, in the author's opinion, to allow man to avoid recognizing the woman who gave him life as an essentially carnal being. Deified, purified, sterilized, woman becomes less threatening. In this passage one is aware of echoes of Françoise Miquel's reluctance to play divinity for Xavière and Pierre in *She Came to Stay*. The glorified image of motherhood becomes a haunting standard for the all-too-human women often unwittingly cast in that role, women who quickly realize that they will never be able to conform to all of the expectations with which religion and bourgeois society have encumbered maternity.

Psychological studies point out that the attitude of the mother toward her newborn daughter is fraught with ambivalence: "The daughter is both a double and an Other for the mother. The mother feels both a fierce attachment and hostility toward her."[18] Treating the daughter as a double is effective as long as the child is willing to accept such a role. Gradually, however, each little girl begins to grow up and to pull away from her mother's sphere of influence. "The more the girl matures, the more cumbersome her mother's authority seems to her," Beauvoir notes.[19] The adolescent girl will often focus her admiration and affection on an older girl or woman outside of the family circle, thereby arousing jealousy and resentment in a mother whose maternal role has been the only justification for her existence.

Simone de Beauvoir is painfully aware of the frustrations inherent in the mother-child relationship. For some new mothers, the newborn baby represents a love object to whom they utter "words that are almost those of a lover."[20] For others, a child provides a long-awaited opportunity to dominate another human being and may be treated like a miniature slave or a performing circus animal. An extreme case of this type of relationship will be seen in "Monologue," the second story in the collection entitled *The Woman Destroyed*. Still another group revels in the role of martyr, dwelling on the sacrifices demanded by motherhood and creating a gnawing sense of guilt in its offspring: "the *mater dolorosa* creates from her suffering a weapon which she uses sadistically."[21] No matter what its nature, however, any obsessive attachment to one's children is destined to meet with disappointment and futility. "Whether a mother is passionately affectionate or hostile, her child's independence destroys her hopes," the author warns.[22]

It is the very lack of reciprocity in the mother-child relationship which accounts for both the problems and the "grandeur" of maternal love, according to Beauvoir. In a very revealing passage, she interprets the search for domestic bliss as an attempt to curb the passage of time, to insulate family members from the real world:

> The ideal of happiness has always taken concrete shape in the form of a house, be it a hut or a castle. The home is an incarnation of permanence and of separation. It is between its walls that the family establishes itself as an isolated cell and asserts its identity beyond the flow of generations. The past, preserved in the form of furniture and family portraits, prefigures a future without risk. . . .[23]

It is the mother alone, however, who operates only within the four walls of her home. Her husband leaves for work each morning, her children soon go off to school. She is left striving frantically to find fulfillment in an encapsulated existence which she shares only with other non-working mothers. In her solitude she bravely assumes the burden of creating "happiness" for the members of her family.

The Second Sex traces the gradual separation between mother and child which begins dramatically at the moment of childbirth: "The mother wants both to keep this treasure of flesh which is a precious part of herself in her womb and to free herself of something bothersome."[24] The recurrent emphasis on the bothersome aspect of childbearing in Beauvoir's work is echoed in this passage, which labels the developing embryo a *gêneur*. The author's attitude toward pregnancy and childbirth may be partially explained by the fact that a pregnant woman does not seem to have any control over what is taking place in her body. She cannot, for example, choose to keep the child inside of her womb. An irreversible biological process expels it and sets it on the path to independence. Never again can the mother completely recapture the intimacy of the nine months during which the developing entity has been an integral part of her physical being. She must gradually resign herself to seeing her son move beyond her limited sphere of influence into a broader world of masculine values, to watching her daughter develop into a young woman whose sexuality threatens to supplant the energy and vitality of her parents' generation. In Beauvoirian terms, the mother of an adolescent has no alternative but to "accept her defeat."[25]

The more her identity is tied up in her children, the more difficult it will be for the mother to allow them to have an individual existence of their own. It is the exceptional mother, according to Beauvoir, who has the "rare mixture of generosity and detachment which allows her to find enrichment in her children without becoming a tyrant for them or allowing them to tyrannize her."[26] During her own adolescence, Beauvoir watched her classmate Zaza be tyrannized and manipulated by the mother she adored and at the same time resented her own mother's awkward attempts to dominate the lives of her two creative and independent daughters. Although she had undoubtedly observed children who tyrannized their mothers, it is of interest that she did not choose to use any of them as models for her fictional characters. In her fiction, mothers are consistently manipulative or martyred, but the martyrdom is of their own choosing and never blamed by the author on ungrateful children.

Just as Nancy Friday analyzes the threat a daughter's budding sexuality represents for her mother,[27] Simone de Beauvoir observes many years earlier that for women who look to motherhood for the sole justification of their existence, the birth of a new generation can be extremely unsettling. The pregnancy of either her own daughter or a daughter-in-law can remind such a mother of her relative insignificance: "Life will go on without her; she is no longer THE Mother: just a link ... she is no longer anything but an outdated, finished individual."[28] Brought up to seek fulfillment in caring for and serving others, she suddenly finds herself with no one left who requires her attention. A continuance of the nurturing role with grandchildren or with protégés of a younger generation may help fill the void, although Beauvoir considers it "very unusual for the woman to find in her posterity—be it biological or handpicked—justification for her declining role in life.... She knows that she is useless."[29] It is in this feeling of futility and uselessness that the author finds the explanation for the depression which sometimes accompanies menopause.

Beauvoir's own pessimism is apparent in the change of tone that has occurred between her play *Who Shall Die?* and *The Second Sex*. The French title of the play highlights the assumption that there are indeed no "useless mouths," that everyone in Vaucelles, women, children, and the aged, has an important part to play and a compelling reason to go on living. The author is much more severe in her application of the term "useless" (*inutile*) to the family-oriented women without careers whom she describes in *The Second Sex*.

How then is the woman of the mid-twentieth century to deal with motherhood? It is significant that Simone de Beauvoir devotes the first fourteen pages of her chapter entitled "The Mother" to a discussion of contraception and abortion. The author reiterates throughout the two volumes of *The Second Sex* her firm conviction that motherhood should be assumed only willingly and joyfully. She casts a perceptive spotlight on the hypocrisy of a bourgeois society which on the one hand waxes lyrical about the glories of maternity and on the other hand is quick to pressure a pregnant female whose condition might undermine the financial and social ambitions of her partner into doing away with the product of their sexual union:

> Since her childhood, the woman has been told again and again that she is made to have children and has heard hymns to the splendor of motherhood . . . . Everything is justified by the marvelous privilege of bringing children into the world which is hers alone. And now a man, in order to keep his freedom, . . . asks a woman to give up her feminine triumph.[30]

This is very much the dilemma facing Sartre's Mathieu in *The Age of Reason* when his mistress Marcelle becomes pregnant and wants to have the child.[31] Mathieu spends the entire duration of the narrative rushing here and there trying to raise money for an abortion and is finally greatly relieved when his homosexual and masochistic friend Daniel offers to marry Marcelle so that she can keep the child.

Although Simone de Beauvoir is totally in favor of legalizing abortion so that it may be equally available to women of all social classes, she is also very much aware of the trauma it represents for those brought up with traditional middle-class values. She describes the emotional aftermath of abortion in graphically naturalistic terms: "The only thing [the woman] remembers for certain is that foraged and bleeding womb, those bits of red life, that absent child."[32] Between the exterior pressure to do away with the child and the inner sense of frustration at being unable to carry the pregnancy to full term and thereby complete the creative process it represents, the woman who has undergone an abortion is left with extremely ambivalent feelings about maternity.

Simone de Beauvoir chastizes Western mentality for denying women an active role in society while at the same time entrusting to them "the most delicate, the most serious undertaking one can imagine: the formation of a human being." [33] She sees fulfillment through motherhood as a possibility only for the altruistic woman capable of respecting her child as an individual: "Nothing is more rare than the woman who genuinely respects the human being in her child, who recognizes his freedom even in his failures, who assumes with him the risks implicit in any commitment."[34] Children bring joy rather than continual frustration only to "the woman capable of desiring the happiness of another person in a disinterested way," according to Beauvoir.[35] The author implies that since such individuals are truly exceptional, one should think seriously before having children simply because of social and family pressures.

Beauvoir sees great strides being made in modern woman's ability to control her reproductive functions. For those who willingly choose to have children, she advocates increased assumption of child care responsibilities by the society rather than by the individual family. "Because of a dearth of conveniently organized child care centers and nursery schools, all it takes is one child to paralyze a mother's activities completely," she proclaims.[36] Beauvoir's use of the verb "paralyze" in this context underlines the depth of her feeling about women who never realize their full potential because of the social and familial roles they are trapped into playing.

In her concluding chapter, entitled "The Independent Woman," Simone de Beauvoir emphasizes the need to disentangle modern motherhood from the emotional and often pathological bonds inherent in the closed circle of the nuclear family. A child raised in a more communal atmosphere, one that would allow men and women to participate more equally in the activities needed to assure the smooth functioning of the society in which they live, "would sense that she is surrounded by an androgynous rather than a masculine world," the author asserts.[37] This androgynous society is indeed the goal toward which Beauvoir directed all of the arguments presented in the two volumes of *The Second Sex*, the goal toward which she led innumerable groups of modern feminists after its publication in 1949. Her work, which inspired committed feminists of the next generation like Yvette Roudy, Elisabeth Badinter, Kate Millett, and Betty Friedan, was an eye-opener for women all over the world and did much to demystify the aura surrounding the idea of motherhood in the mid-twentieth century.

Critical Reaction

The Second Sex has received more critical comment than any other work published by Simone de Beauvoir. Immediate reactions at the time of its publication in 1949 ranged from appreciation of the author's courage in examining the details of female existence both frankly and exhaustively to vituperative attacks on both the ideas presented and the woman who originated them.

Writing in 1957, Hélène Nahas speaks of Beauvoir's exposure of the mythical nature of stereotypes of the virgin, the mother, the spouse, etc. and the degree to which these myths are deeply imbedded in Western consciousness.[38] Geneviève Gennari's 1959 study highlights Beauvoir's implication that the secondary position assumed by women throughout the centuries is one which they have been taught to accept by mothers limited to roles delineated in turn by their mothers in an endless chain of cause and effect.[39] Gennari supports Beauvoir's frank discussion of abortion in her chapter on "The Mother," observing that it is an issue which needs to be aired in an era during which overpopulation is threatening the survival of the human race. She concurs with Beauvoir's suggestion that the child, even before it is born, is at the heart of the problem facing the modern woman.

Noting the degree to which Beauvoir has been attacked for her seeming lack of understanding of the joys of motherhood, Gennari asserts that the author is indeed "a stranger to the very simple and very profound love story that plays itself out between mother and child."[40] Yet she feels that the basic pessimism of *The Second Sex* cannot be attributed solely to its refusal to accord to motherhood the place it occupies in the life of most women. Gennari explains Beauvoir's anti-maternal stance rather as a rebellion typical of atheistic existentialists against the absurdity of a life content with simply repeating itself. She concurs with Beauvoir's emphasis on the seriousness of the commitment implied by the decision to give birth to a child and with her insistence that maternity is only one of many ways in which a woman can accomplish her destiny. For Gennari, the essential question, and one which remains an issue of the 1980s, is how a woman with children to raise can still maintain a concrete, vital connection with the world outside her home without becoming totally exhausted.

Georges Hourdin finds in Simone de Beauvoir the makings of a saint as well as of a rebel, and blames her resolute turning away from religion on a poorly taught concept of Christianity and Catholicism. Analyzing the text with a strong religious bias, Hourdin questions Beauvoir's competence in talking about marriage and maternity without having experienced either. He states categorically, "Whether we like it or not, woman, until proven otherwise, is made in part to stabilize and civilize man, to carry, bring into the world, suckle, and raise children."[41] He feels that one must assign equal importance to conjugal and parental commitments and to political, social, and professional commitments and points out that only exceptional individuals like Simone de Beauvoir can follow the path she has chosen, one which, in his opinion, she presents as "the only path to salvation."[42] Hourdin holds up as examples many women he knows who have "accomplished their destiny and found freedom and fulfillment in the work associated with the family and motherhood, which it is ridiculous to reduce to pure animal instinct."[43]

In his 1966 study, Serge Julienne-Caffié traces Beauvoir's historical arguments in *The Second Sex*, noting her emphasis on the critical nature of the overturning of the maternal right of inheritance and her praise of Sparta for its egalitarian treatment of women in a community not based on the family unit.[44] He warns against the interpretation of the text as a rejection of everything male and prefers to see in it an appeal to both men and women to join forces in an effort to transform society so that there can be true equality between the sexes.

In her highly critical 1970 book entitled *Le Malentendu du "Deuxième Sexe,"* literally "The Misunderstanding of *The Second Sex*," Suzanne Lilar questions many of Beauvoir's theories, which she attributes to the palpable presence of Jean-Paul Sartre in the text, and accuses the author of drowning her reader in a sea of confusing details. Lilar objects to the generalizations implying that motherhood prevents women from playing an integral part in the history of the human race, that giving birth reduces women to an animal-like status which removes them from the center of the human drama. She takes issue with the idea that the hunter risks his life while the woman who gives birth does not and criticizes Beauvoir for a deplorable devaluation and lack of understanding of motherhood.

Noting that "Beauvoir is no less vicious about maternity than about marriage" in *The Second Sex,* Lilar underlines the fact that maternity is consistently presented by her in the context of something to be avoided.[45] The critic disagrees strongly with Beauvoir's insistence that there is no such thing as maternal instinct, blaming this idea on the pervasive influence of Sartrian existentialism in the 1949 document. Opting for her own theory of bisexuality as the goal feminists need to espouse in the 1970s, Lilar concludes, "There is nothing virile which cannot be found in woman, nothing feminine—including the maternal vocation—which cannot be found in man."[46]

Henri Peyre, in his foreword to Jean Leighton's 1975 book on the women in Beauvoir's works, highlights Leighton's analysis of the images of carrion and quivering gelatin associated with pregnancy as reflections of the "Jansenist disgust with the flesh" typical of Sartrian thought.[47] Leighton herself accuses Beauvoir of attempting "to destroy motherhood altogether . . . with a truly fearsome catalogue of sadistic and capricious mothers"[48] paraded before the reader in *The Second Sex* and of presenting marriage and motherhood as "cowardly evasions" rather than authentic choices.[49] She questions the validity of omitting motherhood from the conception of femininity presented in *The Second Sex* and staunchly opposes the suggestion that non-working mothers are guilty of "moral parasitism."[50]

Robert Cottrell sees *The Second Sex* more as the study of a particular woman, Simone de Beauvoir, than of women in general. Like a number of other critics, Cottrell points out that Beauvoir does not recognize a woman as an individual "through her functions as a wife, mother, housekeeper."[51] He concludes:

> Beauvoir no doubt fails to come to grips with maternity and family life. She no doubt
> advocates a kind of "virile independence" that is better suited to a woman who is
> unmarried, childless, exceptionally intelligent, violently ambitious, and relatively
> well-off (in short, like Beauvoir) than the majority of women.[52]

While praising the originality of some of Beauvoir's analyses in the chapter on "The Mother," Konrad Bieber nonetheless considers certain of her statements, and most specifically her denial of the existence of maternal instinct, as "clearly excessive."[53]

In her discussion of *The Second Sex,* Carol Ascher refers to some of the "expert" opinions published in a 1953 issue of the *Saturday Review.*[54] She paraphrases psychiatrist Karl Menninger's antifeminist argument as suggesting that "the goals of individual women must be sacrificed to the greater end of the Family and the grand flow of Civilization, which needs women to bear and raise children; and ... women therefore ought to focus on what is happy about their lot: the joy of creating and sustaining life."[55] Margaret Mead is quoted as having criticized Beauvoir in the following terms: "By denigrating maternity, she constructs a picture in which the only way a woman can be a full human being is to be as much like a man as possible."[56] Ascher notes that even in 1980 the chapter on motherhood receives mixed reactions from feminists, "many of whom are directing themselves toward a reconciliation with their bodies."[57] She comments on Beauvoir's "near rejection of any hope for mothers and their children"[58] in *The Second Sex* and on the fact that the author softened her position on the subject in subsequent interviews over the years.

Anne Whitmarsh sees in Beauvoir's existential discussion of motherhood "a rationalisation of a deeply felt disgust (the equivalent of Sartre's nausée) at the thought of pregnancy, the foetus, childbirth."[59] She seeks the origins of this disgust in the puritanical nature of the upbringing of both authors and considers Beauvoir's seeming inability to imagine the possibility of real love between mother and child a whole missing dimension in the author's sensibilities.

In his 1982 study of Simone de Beauvoir's "neofeminism," Jacques Zéphir devotes an entire section to "La Femme et la maternité."[60] In his opinion, it is maternity which Beauvoir sees as the permanent cause of inequality between the sexes and a major obstacle to true liberation for women. He notes the avalanche of mail Beauvoir received protesting her negative comments about maternity in *The Second Sex,* from men and women shocked by the vehemence of her condemnation of the institution of motherhood. Emphasizing that on several occasions Beauvoir acknowledged the positive aspects of mothering, Zéphir posits that she considered motherhood a commitment, perhaps the most serious commitment a woman can make, but still only one of many possible commitments through which she can find total fulfillment if she chooses it freely and sincerely.

According to Zéphir, it is not maternity per se to which Beauvoir objects, but rather society's insistence that motherhood is the only role through which a woman can justify her existence. Interweaving ideas from *The Second Sex* with comments made by the author in numerous interviews, Zéphir cites her strong statement in a 1972 issue of *Le Nouvel Observateur* indicating that she is well aware of the joys associated with having a wanted child but that she considers herself fortunate not to have had children of her own, who would have competed with her writing for her time. "I would never wish to impose my life-style on all women, since on the contrary I am fighting for their freedom: freedom of maternity, contraception, abortion; the fanatics are certain mothers who do not allow people to follow other paths than the one they have chosen," she states emphatically.[61] Her objections are not to maternity but to the family, which she sees as a bastion of capitalism and patriarchy, in Zéphir's opinion.

Jacques Zéphir goes on to point out the vast difference between the situation of women of earlier eras, when contraception was virtually unknown and women spent a significant portion of their lives giving birth to and raising one child after another, and the possibility of family planning which exists in the late twentieth century. Western families are having fewer children, many more of whom tend to be wanted children, and women's increased life expectancy has meant that a much smaller percentage of their lives is spent on pregnancies and child rearing. This explains Simone de Beauvoir's focus on contraception and abortion in the chapter of *The Second Sex* entitled "La Mère," which Zéphir interprets as a desire to encourage happy families rather than to limit large ones.

For Terry Keefe, Beauvoir's treatment of motherhood in *The Second Sex* lacks breadth and depth. He finds no clear-cut justification for her denial of maternal instinct and considers her statement that maternal devotion is only rarely authentic "singularly arbitrary."[62] Keefe also faults her for not presenting any specific guidelines for implementing her suggestion that children would be better off cared for by the collectivity than by their biological parents. On the other hand, he praises her ability to convey the degree to which motherhood was a near-impossibility for professional women in 1949.

Philosophy professor Donald Hatcher has devoted an entire book to facilitating the understanding of the ideas in *The Second Sex*. He discusses the modern use of motherhood as a means of achieving social recognition and self-fulfillment, as granting "a kind of hallowed status."[63] Like many other scholars, he underlines Beauvoir's insistence that women are essentially passive in pregnancy and motherhood and thereby reduced to an animal state. Hatcher quotes Nietzsche's questioning of man's desire for offspring and his distinction between producing children out of animal need or loneliness and out of a desire to "bring living monuments to your victory and your liberation."[64] He interprets Beauvoir's argument as seeking to prove that motherhood may not be in the best interests of either the mother or the child and concludes, "I believe that de Beauvoir is quite right when she says that in order to attain ... equality women must be raised like men, and the possibility of a woman choosing to be only a housewife/mother must be negated."[65]

Focusing on what she conceives as the male orientation of Simone de Beauvoir's thinking, Mary Evans finds in *The Second Sex* the assumption that "traditionally male activities ... are in some sense superior, and are instances almost of a higher form of civilization than those concerns—such as child care and the maintenance of daily life—that have traditionally been the preserve of women."[66] Recalling that it was Sartre who suggested that Beauvoir write a study of women, Evans asserts, "If de Beauvoir is the mother of contemporary feminism, then Sartre played the typically male role, analogous to the physical father of a child developed and nurtured by the attention of a woman."[67] Along with other contemporary feminists, Evans questions Beauvoir's insistence on the passive nature of pregnancy and childbirth. She objects to the conclusions the author draws from analogies to animal reproduction and to the distaste with which female biology is depicted in *The Second Sex*, a distaste based on an assumption of inferiority, in Evans's opinion. She finds Beauvoir's suspicious attitude toward marriage and maternity exaggerated, yet grants that "her discussion of maternity rightly raises crucial questions about the reasons for women's desire for children and the complex of male/female relations in which a desire for a child becomes paramount."[68] While agreeing with Beauvoir's skepticism about the existence of a maternal instinct, Evans at the same time faults *The Second Sex* for not taking the desire of women to bear children and of men to father them sufficiently into account.

In 1986, anthropologist Judith Okely's book on Beauvoir focused on her reading of *The Second Sex* when she was in her late teens and again several decades later. Okely paraphrases the author's description of maternity as "not the sugary experience it was made out to be, but painful, constricting and sometimes a disaster."[69] She joins other feminists of the 1980s in pointing out that *The Second Sex* "reflected the experience of the cloistered, middle-class and white woman, namely that of the author," an author writing from the margins of a bourgeois existence in which children seem to be invisible.[70]

Many young women of the 1950s were attracted to Beauvoir as the incarnation of the possibility of childlessness without sexual abstinence. Okely acknowledges the influence of *The Second Sex* in causing her to delay maternity in the absence of sufficiently available child care.[71] She notes that "in contrast to her extensive observations on other aspects of maternity [Beauvoir] is reticent on the details of childbirth."[72] As other critics have observed, it was particularly for her negative view of maternity that Beauvoir was attacked after the publication of *The Second Sex*. Okely quotes the same images of quivering jelly, viscosity, carrion, slime, and putrefaction used by other critics examining Beauvoir's treatment of the reproductive process and suggests that they "echo Sartre's extensive discussion of viscous substance ... and some of his own personal disgust with aspects of the sexual body."[73]

After years of study and work as a feminist anthropologist, Okely reveals, "Today I can criticise de Beauvoir for her suspect generalisation about humanity's spontaneous psychological reactions to the physicality of childbirth, but some twenty years ago I underlined it."[74] Speaking for those who read *The Second Sex* in the 1950s and 1960s, she acknowledges:

> Some of us gladly embraced these images of a growing monster in the belly, threatening our identity rather than extending it. We wanted the language to reject maternity and motherhood which then seemed to demand that women retreat to the marital home and nuclear family.[75]

Twenty years later, Okely finds most of Beauvoir's treatment of maternity consistently negative, and points out, as an example, that Beauvoir never discusses the sensual pleasure associated with breastfeeding. "The focus is on the woman as victim," Okely proclaims.[76] She states that "there is no *necessary* reason why a female should see maternity as a threat to her individuality,"[77] and asserts that "today maternity is explicitly reintegrated with feminism. . . ."[78]

Not surprisingly, critical reaction to *The Second Sex* is closely linked to the point of view of the critic in question. The more conservative thinkers portray Simone de Beauvoir as a monster out to destroy the world as we know it and to discourage the continuation of the species, while the more liberal and feminist writers hail her insight into the problems confronting the modern woman in her search for fulfillment. Opinions are divided on her denial of the existence of maternal instinct as well as on her suggestion that children be raised by the collectivity rather than by their biological parents. While certain writers focus on the ideas presented in *The Second Sex,* others look behind them to their author, who is sometimes accused of not being in a position to comment on maternity and child rearing because she has never experienced either situation, sometimes considered limited in her viewpoint because of her exceptional intelligence and drive and because the "existential others" with whom she continually interacted were almost exclusively members of the Parisian intelligentsia. Whatever the point of view adopted by critics, it is apparent that the publication of *The Second Sex,* with its challenging suggestions for freeing women from the chains of marriage and maternity, created echoes as resounding as those of Jean-Jacques Rousseau's call for a revolution in child-rearing theories when he wrote *Emile* some one hundred and fifty years earlier.

Mothers and Daughters in Postwar France:
The Mandarins

Simone de Beauvoir's novel *The Mandarins,* winner of the Goncourt prize, occupies a special place in the canon of her work, appearing five years after her extensive study of women in *The Second Sex* and four years prior to the first volume of her autobiography. Published in 1954, when the author was forty-six years old, the novel focuses on Anne Dubreuilh, wife, mother, and psychiatrist, who is approaching her fortieth birthday. *The Mandarins* is the first of Beauvoir's fictional works in which the relationship between a particular mother and daughter is a recurrent and significant theme from beginning to end. The intricacies of the interaction between Anne and teenaged Nadine pave the way for the portrait of the writer's stormy relationship with her own mother in *Memoirs of a Dutiful Daughter.*

Like many of Beauvoir's fictional heroines, Anne Dubreuilh has arrived at a point in her life at which her patterned existence appears meaningless. She questions the validity of helping her patients lead "normal" lives, wonders to what extent she is in any way essential to the well-being and happiness of either her husband, a well-known writer twenty years her senior, or her unpredictable daughter. Her self-image is hardly bolstered by the constant needling of eighteen-year-old Nadine, who plays a role quite similar to the disruptive one assigned to Xavière Pagès in *She Came to Stay.* As she approaches forty, Anne feels psychologically and physically drained, a mere shell of the vital university student she was when she met and fell in love with Robert Dubreuilh, who was her professor at the Sorbonne.

Trained as a psychiatrist, Anne is constantly analyzing her feelings toward her only child. She blames her maternal ambivalence partly on the hostility she felt toward her own mother, who does not appear at all as a character in the novel but is merely treated as Item One in a psychological case study: "A clearcut sense of aggression toward my mother.... The ambivalence of the feelings I have for my daughter is the result of my hostility toward my mother, of my indifference toward myself...."[1] The void represented by the generation of Anne's parents in *The Mandarins* seems to correspond to the minimal involvement Beauvoir herself had in her own mother's life during this exceptionally productive decade of her career.

Hostility toward her own mother, indifference toward herself: these are the symptoms upon which Anne Dubreuilh bases her explanation of her alleged ineptitude at mothering. Like Françoise Miquel in *She Came to Stay*, Anne looks into a mirror and finds "no one" reflected there. Having sought her identity in Robert's protective and mature arms, she had anticipated that marriage would be a one-to-one relationship which would make her feel both secure and needed. She therefore interpreted Robert's immediate desire to have a child as an indication of her inability to fulfill his needs: "If he wanted a child so quickly, it is undoubtedly because I was not enough to justify his existence; maybe he was also looking for revenge against that future on which he no longer had any hold."[2] After the lengthy discussion of childbearing in *The Second Sex*, it is of interest to see which reasons for having a child Beauvoir indirectly assigns to the intellectual Robert. Anne's interpretation of his motives may of course not coincide at all with the "reality" of his feelings, feelings which will never be revealed to the reader in the course of the narrative. Anne herself is aggressively articulate about Nadine: "I didn't want her; it was Robert who wanted a child right away. I resented Nadine for intruding upon our intimacy."[3] The birth of this child appears to have interrupted Anne's search for her own identity by putting unwanted demands on both her time and her energy. Cast into a maternal role against her will, Anne resents her child and at the same time feels guilty about this resentment.

Nadine's temperament does little to relieve her mother's sense of guilt. She is an impulsive, rebellious young woman who seems to derive great pleasure from keeping everyone off balance. Anne interprets Nadine's rejection of femininity as her way of disassociating herself from anything resembling her mother. She vividly recalls the full-fledged temper tantrum staged by Nadine when Anne attempted to explain menstruation to her: "Never has she resigned herself to belonging to the same species as I do...."[4] Nadine reacted to this unwelcome bit of news by breaking her favorite vase. Her first menstrual period provoked such anger in her that she did not have another one for eighteen months, her mother tells us. Nadine's rejection of femininity has been encouraged by her father, however. Robert chides Anne for being shocked at her daughter's sexual promiscuity, assuring her that he was exactly like Nadine when he was her age. This is scant consolation for Anne, who senses that Robert has never completely accepted the fact that the offspring they produced was a girl rather than a boy.

Nadine's ambivalence toward her own sexuality is underlined by the paradox of her attitude toward her physical appearance. Proclaiming herself ugly and awkward, she generally disdains any advice about making herself more presentable, yet willingly borrows dresses, jewelry, and even shoes from her mother before going out to a party. In her resentment of the limitations society puts upon her because she was born a girl, she becomes obsessed with driving her boyfriend's motorcycle, "the symbol of all the virile pleasures she could not generate and in which she could not share," according to Anne's analysis.[5] In Nadine we find a strong personality who wants to be in control of her own destiny and to manipulate others according to her whim, a complete contrast to the passive *êtres relatifs,* the "dependent beings" described in great detail in *The Second Sex.*

Nadine is discouraged by the options she sees open to women, taunting her mother with the fact that, despite her apparent success as a psychiatrist, she will never be Freud. The implication is that only a man ever achieves recognizable success. "All women can do is vegetate," Nadine declares.[6] The two characters are agonizing over sex roles in the late 1940s, when options for women were indeed still severely limited. In a subsequent discussion with her mother, Nadine resigns herself to accepting the pattern laid out for the vast majority of the women of her generation: "I suppose that I'm meant to have a husband and children like all women. I'll scour my pots and produce a brat a year."[7] This is hardly the glamorous picture of motherhood perpetrated by the glossy pages of the women's magazines of the era.

Despite her psychological sophistication, Anne Dubreuilh appears to have accepted the myth of the perfect mother-daughter relationship highlighted by the media. She is all too ready to interpret Nadine's recalcitrance as an indication of her own failure at motherhood. Anne is tormented by the fact that she has never known how to make her daughter obey her, and more particularly by the certitude that she has been incapable of loving Nadine enough. In a very poignant dialogue with herself, Anne muses: "Perhaps it would have comforted her if I had taken her in my arms and told her, 'My poor little girl, forgive me for not loving you more.'"[8] This passage provides an interesting parallel to the suggestion we have seen in Nancy Friday's *My Mother/My Self* that mothers simply admit to their children that they cannot supply what she labels "the whole mother package" for them, that they are themselves only limited human beings incapable of meeting all of the grandiose expectations associated with motherhood.

One can only retrace the development of the mother-daughter relationship in *The Mandarins* through Anne's recollections, since the reader is never privy to Nadine's thoughts. During the first years of Nadine's life, the two women seem to have lacked the sense of closeness and warmth which characterized Simone de Beauvoir's relationship with her own mother. According to Anne, Nadine's adolescence followed the classic pattern of teenaged girl setting herself up as her mother's rival for her father's attention and affection. Since much of Anne's uneasiness in her dealings with Nadine has stemmed from her sense of inadequacy, the one period during which mother and daughter got along extremely well was when Nadine was passionately in love with the young Jewish poet Diégo. "That particular year, we were friends, my daughter and I," she reveals.[9] Anne was relieved to discover that Nadine was actually capable of finding love and happiness. She lightheartedly reverted to an earlier phase of motherhood, obligingly tucking both Nadine and Diégo into their bed at night. This is an autobiographical detail echoing the role played by Beauvoir when her ex-student Nathalie Sorokine, whom she calls Lise in her memoirs, fell in love with the appealing young Bourla. Certainly no one can accuse Anne of being an old-fashioned mother as she actively condones her daughter's first affair. This idyllic situation was tragically short-lived, however. When Diégo was taken away and eventually put to death by the Nazis, all that Anne could offer Nadine was her physical presence. She cradled her distraught daughter in her arms until Nadine was finally able to sleep once again by herself.

Anne realizes that none of the traditional expectations of earlier eras can be applied to a generation whose adolescence corresponded to the years of World War II. She feels constantly on the defensive in all of her dealings with Nadine. Ever since the day on which she expressed her disapproval of Nadine's promiscuity and Nadine stayed away all night, Anne has felt it incumbent upon her to back off from giving any advice, to accept anything Nadine may do with feigned equanimity. Not even this approach guarantees peace between the two women, however. Extremely sensitive to Anne's moods and thoughts, Nadine knows when her mother disapproves of something she is doing and resents the unarticulated judgment this implies. Mother and daughter are thus caught in a vicious circle of defiance and resentment, a syndrome for which Anne is once again very quick to assume the blame: "If I had loved her more, our relationship would have been different. Maybe I could have prevented her from leading a life of which I cannot approve." [10] Anne's only moment of relief comes when she compares Nadine to someone she labels a "faded virgin" serving coffee at her mother's social get-together. Nadine is at least acting out all of her obsessions, sexual and otherwise, while this over-protected young woman seems to Anne, and certainly to Beauvoir, to be caught in a web of repression and middle-class convention.

The fact that Anne does not try to protect and shield her daughter from the world but rather opts for allowing her total freedom may be partially explained by the concern she shares with Beauvoir about having grown up with an innately puritanical approach to life. It was Simone de Beauvoir's close friend Zaza who originally wrote in a letter of the comment a German friend had made to her about her tendency to live life securely clad in kid gloves. This remark is echoed by Nadine in *The Mandarins:*

> Do you call that living! Frankly, my poor little mother, do you honestly think you have lived? Chatting with Dad half the day and taking care of a bunch of nuts the other half, what kind of an existence is that? . . . I'd rather end up in a brothel than meander through life with kid gloves on: you never take off those gloves of yours.[11]

Those symbolic gloves haunt Anne as she contemplates the choices available to her. She accepts Scriassine's invitation to sleep with him not because of any particular sexual attraction but specifically because of Nadine's challenge to her timidity. "What would happen if I took off my gloves? If I don't take them off tonight, will I ever take them off?" she wonders.[12] Anne is clearly intimidated by the thought of what might happen if she let down her defenses, and is disappointed when nothing significant does happen in this, her first foray into the world of daring. She resents the fact that her daughter's words have had such an impact on her and have led her to make a decision she regrets. Temporarily at least, she is determined to retreat to the comfort of the detached attitude she has always maintained toward everyone around her, resolving: "Never again will I try to take off my kid gloves. It's too late. . . . Now my gloves are grafted to my skin. To make me take them off, they would have to skin me alive."[13] Anne thus barricades herself behind her own conception of acting her age, which, at thirty-nine, she equates with resigning herself to expecting no further sexual or physical pleasure from life.

The kid-glove syndrome is one which had a very personal relevance for Simone de Beauvoir, who was accused by the young Nathalie Sorokine of acting like "a clock in a refrigerator."[14] Beauvoir, who loved life and the adventures it had to offer, always smarted at insinuations that she was more cerebral than sensual, and seems to have been trying to deal with these insinuations in her portrayals of Françoise Miquel in *She Came to Stay* and Anne Dubreuilh in *The Mandarins*. Nadine Dubreuilh is clearly modeled after Nathalie Sorokine, who was jealous of Beauvoir's total commitment to her writing. Like Nadine, she tried to denigrate her mentor's career, commenting in a condescending tone, "How sad it is to be a second-rate writer!"[15] Like Xavière and Nadine, Olga and Nathalie challenged every premise upon which Beauvoir had built her values and her serenity. Her fictional works attempt to deal on paper with this aggressive onslaught of a younger generation.

There is a period of uneasy stability in Anne Dubreuilh's life between the night she spends with Scriassine and her first encounter with the Chicago writer Lewis Brogan, a thinly veiled fictional counterpart of Beauvoir's first major "contingent love," Nelson Algren, to whom *The Mandarins* is dedicated. Anne enjoys the peace and quiet of her intimacy with Robert while Nadine is traveling in Portugal with Henri Perron. For the first time in many years, she does not have to cope with slammed doors, clothes tossed everywhere, constant interruptions, and verbal sparring. Upon her return, Nadine blows through her mother's life like a hurricane, criticizing Anne's unfashionable outfits, insisting that they hire a maid, taking offense when Anne appears to have no confidence in Nadine's ability to do small chores around the house.

When Nadine participates in the activities of a band of terrorists bent on punishing former collaborationists, Anne uses her very genuine concern for her daughter's safety as an excuse for postponing a decision about accepting an invitation to a professional conference in the United States. As she calls out Nadine's name in a wooded area in the middle of the night and receives no answer, Anne is terrified that she may have lost her daughter forever, that she too has disappeared just as her young lover Diégo had. Like the mother of a small child who has wandered off on her own, Anne is at first panic-stricken, then livid as Nadine strolls casually toward her. Her initial fear of losing Nadine is symbolic of a more generalized maternal reluctance to let a child go, to acknowledge fully the independence and maturity of one's offspring. When the actions of said offspring appear to prove that she does indeed still need maternal guidance, only a very unusual mother would refrain from reverting to earlier methods of dealing with misbehavior. Anne realizes as she forbids Nadine to have anything more to do with activist Vincent that she has not adopted this peremptory tone with her daughter for years. She senses, however, that it is somehow quite appropriate to the circumstances.

Nadine's escapade provides a temporary excuse for Anne's inertia in answering the invitation to the United States. Her daughter is clearly in danger, susceptible to all kinds of temptations. What will she think up next? Yet Anne is too honest not to realize that her physical presence can in no way protect Nadine from life: "Even if I stayed with her, I would not be able to protect her.... I couldn't give her either love or happiness. How useless I was to her! ... I understand her perfectly, but I can't do anything for her."[16] Once again the theme of the usefulness of one human being to another surfaces in Beauvoir's writing. A determination to make every moment count, which was almost an obsession during her adolescent years, echoes in her fiction as her characters try to justify the validity of the roles they play in the lives of those around them.

In *The Mandarins,* we see Anne Dubreuilh arriving at the moment of truth which eventually comes for parents of grown children. With all the good intentions in the world, there is no way that one can continue to protect one's offspring as one did when they were infants. At some point even the most devoted parent must be willing to let go. Anne's passing thought that she could at least pray for Nadine if she had any religious convictions herself is a scarcely veiled allusion to Françoise de Beauvoir's reaction to the discovery that Simone had lost her faith. The author will later comment in her autobiography that it is extremely difficult to communicate with someone who spends all her time ardently praying for your soul. Religion, however, is not a barrier between Anne and Nadine Dubreuilh, who both appear to be either agnostics or atheists.

When Anne finally departs for America, she leaves Nadine behind physically but certainly not psychologically. Sexually attracted to Lewis Brogan, she remains in limbo for an entire day because she cannot bring herself to suggest that she stay at his apartment with him, something she knows Nadine would not hesitate to do if she were there. When, after a series of trysts which closely parallel the various stages of Beauvoir's liaison with Algren, Brogan asks her to marry him and remain in the United States, Anne realizes the extent of her commitment to Robert, Nadine, and her entire past. The bonds of country, language, family, and friends are deep-rooted and inescapable for Anne Dubreuilh. Not the least of these is the link to the future represented by the child Nadine is carrying.

Anne is wary of Nadine's motives in becoming pregnant, rightly surmising that she has done so in order to trap Henri Perron into marrying her. Even when Henri assures Anne that he is quite pleased at the prospect of becoming a father, she comments, only half jokingly, "I hope that I will find equal equanimity in my role as a grandmother."[17]

She then begins noticing how old women her age look and quickly loses her last semblance of self-confidence when Brogan tells her he no longer loves her. It is at this point that she first thinks of suicide. The combination of being replaced by a new generation of mothers and daughters over whom she will have scant influence and of no longer appealing to the man who had restored her sense of her own desirability drags Anne down into a depression which has almost fatal consequences in the final chapter of the novel.

As Anne lies on her bed contemplating the vial of poison she once confiscated from her friend Paule's purse, she is convinced of the total inanity of her life. She has been fleeing from death since she was fifteen and is now too tired to continue the struggle. She no longer considers herself essential to the well-being of either Robert or Nadine. In her newborn granddaughter she sees the inevitability of her own decline and demise: "One day, she will be as old as I am now and I won't be around any more. . . . She is the reality of the future and of oblivion."[18] Just as in an earlier section of the novel Anne remained immobilized while waiting for Nadine to summon her to tea with her friends, she is now called back to life by the sound of her daughter's irritated voice coming from the garden below. She has left her granddaughter unattended and Nadine is angry. Could something have happened to Maria? Anne is jarred out of her indifference by the concern she still feels for the members of her family. Her inbred sense of responsibility and of guilt suddenly makes her realize the full implication of committing suicide:

> I imagined Nadine's voice, loud and indignant: "You shouldn't have done that! You had no right!" . . . I cannot inflict my cadaver and everything associated with it on their hearts: Robert bending over this bed, Lewis at Parker House with words dancing before his eyes, Nadine's infuriated sobs.[19]

Anne would have to agree with Nadine's predictable reaction to the situation: no one has the right to inflict such a psychological burden on her family.

In the last analysis, it is essentially Nadine's opinions and feelings which count more than anything else for Anne: "She would have come in, she would have seen me on the bed, my body convulsed. How horrible!"[20] All of her life Anne has tried in her awkward but well-intentioned way to bring happiness and security to her daughter. In the final lines of the novel she reverts to the self-sacrificing maternal role which has both ensnared and justified her existence. In *Force of Circumstance,* Simone de Beauvoir labels Anne's descent toward reinvolvement in the daily concerns of those who are close to her as a defeat rather than a triumph.[21] Analyzing a decade later the ending she chose for her novel, the author calls into question the self-effacement traditionally imposed upon women by a society which denies them even the right to control or dispose of their own lives as they wish. However, it is hardly likely that Beauvoir would ever advocate suicide as a solution to one's problems. When Anne Dubreuilh comes down from her upstairs bedroom, she is returning to the commitments to husband, daughter, and granddaughter whose validity she had previously questioned. Anne's decision to allow herself to become reabsorbed in a traditional family situation is to Beauvoir a defeat rather than a triumph.

It is Henri Perron who is most articulate about the strong bond which exists between Anne and Nadine Dubreuilh: "Those two women would have sacrificed their lives for one another and yet there was something between them that did not click. Nadine became much more aggressive and much more stubborn when her mother was there."[22] When Henri ventures a comment about the strange interaction between them, Nadine snaps at him: "I'm fond of her, but she often annoys me; I suppose it's the same for her. There's nothing unusual about that. That's the way all families are."[23] This mixture of affection and hostility is certainly part of Simone de Beauvoir's image of family relations. In the Dubreuilh family, both mother and daughter are constantly on the defensive, Anne sneaking back home after her evening with Scriassine so that Nadine will not know she has stayed out all night, Nadine being excessively frank about her sexual activities as she deliberately tries to shock her mother. Like Xavière in *She Came to Stay*, Nadine taunts both Anne and Henri for being intellectuals, questioning the validity of everything on which they have based their lives. Yet she herself feels useless living a non-intellectual existence. Is her lack of self-confidence a reflection of her mother's inability to find a satisfying niche for herself?

Nadine spends hours talking things over with Anne each evening, yet maintains a façade of hostility toward her mother's advice and guidance. After she announces that she is pregnant, she taunts Anne with the words "Go ahead, give me some advice. I can see you're just dying to."[24] Earlier in the narrative, when she was quarreling with her boyfriend Lambert, she assured her mother that she knew in advance everything that she might have to say and that it was of no interest to her. This testiness is undoubtedly typical of a young woman struggling toward maturity. Acknowledging her need of her mother's guidance would represent a step backwards, a regression toward childhood dependency.

There are moments when Nadine is full of bravado, attempting to give the impression that she is an experienced woman of the world. Her analysis of the effect which producing a child has on a man is a case in point. She assures Anne, "Of course if you ask a man if he wants a child, he gets frightened. But once the child is there, he's delighted."[25] This indeed proves to be true for Henri Perron. What of Nadine herself, however? Henri watches her poring over books on child care, knitting baby clothes in bright, non-traditional colors, conscientiously giving Maria her bottle:

> She was having a hard time getting used to being nothing more than a mother. She gave [the baby] its bottle with authority, with patience. She made a point of being a competent mother. She had acquired solid ideas about bringing up children and a lot of sterilized objects. But Henri never glimpsed any real tenderness in her eyes when she was taking care of Maria. . . . Even with this baby, she kept her distance, remaining forever walled up inside of herself.[26]

The second-class nature of motherhood as a career is clearly evident in Henri's above analysis of Nadine as he speaks of being "nothing more than a mother." Is it perhaps this sense of performing tasks that can be done by just about anyone which makes Nadine competent but unenthusiastic? Anne has always berated herself for her inability to devote herself wholeheartedly to Nadine. It would appear that Nadine is suffering from the same lack of emotional commitment to Maria, despite the fact that, unlike Anne's, her pregnancy was entirely her own choice.

Although she is married and has a baby of her own, Nadine still feels like a child in a household of adults. When her parents and Henri do not approve of something impulsive she has done, she shouts, "Don't you look wonderful staring at me like a tribunal of judges! . . . You are adults and I am only a child. What amuses me doesn't amuse you, that's quite normal."[27] These words are very similar to Xavière's accusation in *She Came to Stay* that Françoise and Pierre are treating her like a child. Until Nadine is convinced of her own maturity, she will undoubtedly continue to throw temper tantrums and to act like a child in the presence of her parents and of her much older husband. When the opportunity to realize her fondest dream and move to Italy with Henri and Maria presents itself, however, she backs off and chooses to continue to live with her parents. Unsure of her own identity and worth, she has no solidity to offer Maria, and can perhaps only perpetuate the mistakes which Anne has made in bringing her up.

In contrast to Nadine's determination to follow a life-style diametrically opposed to her mother's until she gets married, *The Mandarins* presents the mother-daughter team of Lucie and Josette Belhomme.

There is certainly a touch of irony in Beauvoir's choice of family name here, since the entire thrust of Lucie's mothering seems to center on pushing her very beautiful twenty-six-year-old daughter into the arms of any gentleman, "bel" or otherwise, who may prove useful to either or both of them. Henri Perron is the "bel homme" who brings Josette to our attention when he is prevailed upon to allow her to star in his new play. Lucie Belhomme is an outrageous caricature of the pushy stage mother, lifting her daughter's skirt up at a social gathering so that Henri can appraise her lovely legs. Although Josette, who eventually becomes Henri's mistress, tells him that her greatest desire is "not to need Mom any more and to be sure I will never be poor again,"[28] she appears to lack whatever initiative it might take to break away from the stranglehold her mother has on her. She is disappointed when her success in Henri's play does nothing to change the way her mother talks to her.

Lucie Belhomme's calculating approach to life anticipates Dominique Langlois's in *Les Belles Images*. When Henri accuses her of using her daughter for her own selfish purposes, she retorts, "Josette has never been the least bit useful to me. . . . She compromised herself in an utterly useless way."[29] She is here referring to Josette's infatuation and affair with a young German soldier, a useless contact for Lucie during the Occupation and a threat to her postwar prosperity now that certain letters and photographs Josette left lying around are being used to blackmail her. What a contrast to Anne Dubreuilh's indulgent encouragement of Nadine's love for Diégo!

Lucie has taught her daughter to make use of her youth and beauty to manipulate the male ego to her advantage. Josette tugs at Henri's heartstrings, telling him that she would rather commit suicide than go to jail. Partially out of emotional fatigue, partially from misguided pity, Henri agrees to compromise his own integrity and perjure himself in order to save this damsel in distress. "What weapons was she given? What principles? What hopes? There were her mother's slaps, manipulative males, and that humiliating beauty," he rationalizes.[30] Henri thus attempts to redress the wrongs of a social system which forces a young girl to depend upon a ruthless, unethical mother. In doing so, however, he must turn his back on the principles of honesty, sincerity, and integrity on which he has previously based his entire life. His reputation as a Resistance hero makes him a believable witness and his false testimony effectively clears the unsavory Merceau, who is blackmailing the Belhomme women, of charges of collaboration during the war. Henri thereby saves Josette but then will have nothing further to do with either mother or daughter.

Although she is not a biological mother, Paule Mareuil is worthy of mention as an example of misguided maternal instinct in *The Mandarins*. Like Marcelle Drouffe in *When Things of the Spirit Come First,* she has taken on a self-assigned protective role in her relationship with Henri Perron, ready to sacrifice her happiness and her own identity to the literary genius of the man she loves. In contrast to Marcelle, Paule was originally a source of sexual pleasure for Henri. His ardor has cooled, however, as she has become increasingly dependent upon him emotionally. Paule decides to accept martyrdom, to take on the role of the long-suffering female who faces every affront uncomplainingly, just as Madame Blomart did in *The Blood of Others*. Although Jean Blomart and Henri Perron feel guilty about the emotional trauma they are causing for these women who insist upon devoting their lives to them, both react to such suffocating female concern by moving away, by putting physical distance between themselves and the women who dote on them.

Paule tells her close friend Anne Dubreuilh, "I'm the one who made Henri. I created him just as he created the characters in his books. . . ."[31] Her statement raises the question of the degree to which one has the right to expect to influence and control the life of a person one has "created," be it biologically or psychologically. In Paule's case, her determination to "mother" Henri in spite of himself leads her to a nervous breakdown and a period of complete madness before she is returned to dull normalcy through psychotherapy.

In *The Mandarins* the reader thus finds a distinctive array of maternal roles. Having begun to write the novel when she herself had recently turned forty, Simone de Beauvoir had been observing other women her age cope with the problems created by the adolescence and maturing of their children. In her memoirs, she says of Anne Dubreuilh, "The focal point of her life was the lives of others: her husband, her daughter; this dependence, which made her resemble the majority of women, was of interest to me. . . ."[32] As she continued to anticipate writing her autobiography, Beauvoir had also undoubtedly been giving much thought to her relationship with her own mother and the effect it had had on her subsequent development.

Critical Reaction

Critical comment on *The Mandarins* has generally centered on its significance as a *roman à clef* depicting the political and intellectual scene in postwar Paris. Some analysis, however, has been devoted to Beauvoir's depiction of family relationships in the novel. For Hazel Barnes, Anne and Robert "are simply Pierre and Françoise [of *She Came to Stay*] after ten years of peace with Xavière."[33] Serge Julienne-Caffié comments on the degree to which the permissiveness of Anne Dubreuilh's treatment of Nadine is in direct contrast to the authoritarian manner in which Françoise de Beauvoir raised her two daughters.[34]

Despite his recognition of the literary value of Beauvoir's Goncourt Prize winner, Georges Hourdin feels compelled to point out that the period described in *The Mandarins* was experienced very differently by French families with more traditional relationships than those existing between Anne and Robert Dubreuilh. Hourdin expresses his disagreement with Beauvoir's thesis that social life is more important than family life[35] and sees in the marriage of Nadine and Henri Perron and the birth of their daughter Maria one of the themes contributing to a happy ending unusual in Beauvoir's fictional works. Robert Cottrell interprets the presence of Nadine's new baby at the end of the novel as an indication of a return to normalcy after the war, with the mandarins assembled in the garden choosing a name for a new journal to which they too are about to give birth.

Jean Leighton considers Anne Dubreuilh a "strong and reassuring mother-figure"[36] and a particularly admirable mother to Nadine:

> Her acceptance of Nadine's behavior while gently attempting to dissuade her from her more self-destructive impulses demonstrates mellow wisdom. . . . Anne as mother, calm, somewhat detached, yet affectionate and Anne as an emotion-tossed woman in love are . . . in reality the same affectionate nature which tries to imagine what the other feels. . . .[37]

Questioning the negative aspects of the women in Beauvoir's fiction, Leighton points out that as a psychiatrist Anne should be the very embodiment of the autonomous woman held up as an ideal in *The Second Sex*. Yet the ending of the novel, and Beauvoir's later analysis of Anne's rejection of suicide as a capitulation to dependency, immerse this woman who has successfully combined the roles of psychiatrist, wife, and mother in shades of "insufficiency, purposelessness and despair," in Leighton's opinion.[38] She goes on to comment on Paule Mareuil's "appalling delusion that somehow *she* is the fount from which all [Henri's] creative energies flow."[39]

Leighton notes Nadine's unsuppressed hostility toward her mother, which she, like Anne, attributes to the latter's inability to provide her daughter with "the requisite generous and spontaneous maternal affection."[40] For Leighton, however, Anne "is affection and patience incarnate in comparison with the vengeful and frustrated mothers of *The Second Sex* who maliciously rejoice to see their daughters forced to share their bitter fate."[41] Leighton considers Anne patient to a fault with

Nadine, and might well agree with Terry Keefe's opinion that Anne Dubreuilh's life is "bound up with her family to an unhealthy degree."[42] Noting the energy which Nadine expends in unprovoked vituperative attacks against her mother, Leighton points out the extent to which the young woman's comment about her mother's kid-glove approach to life influences Anne Dubreuilh's feelings and actions. She attributes Nadine's repeated insensitivity in dealing with her mother and others to her "forlorn rejected-child mentality." [43]

An interesting popular reaction to Beauvoir's prize-winning novel is reflected in Henri Clouzot's 1960 film *La Vérité* (The Truth), in which Brigitte Bardot plays a distraught young woman of dubious morals on trial for having killed her lover. In order to prove the wantonness of Dominique Marceau's background, the prosecution interrogates her about having read *The Mandarins* at a fairly impressionable age and then proceeds to quote from a rather graphic passage in which Anne Dubreuilh is in bed with Lewis Brogan. One wonders to what extent the fact that Anne is a wife and mother in bed with a man other than her husband added to the shock value of these paragraphs in an era in which tradition far outweighed liberation for the vast majority of women.

The interaction between Anne and Nadine Dubreuilh in *The Mandarins* is a straightforward portrayal of the difficulties created by the juxtaposition of women representing different generations when they attempt to live in close proximity. Although Simone de Beauvoir never had any children of her own, she maintained close ties with women several decades younger than she throughout her life. Speaking of the genesis of her 1954 novel in *Force of Circumstance,* she admits:

> At first Nadine was an attempt to take revenge on Lise and several other women younger than myself for certain traits which had grated upon me, among others a brutal approach to sex which revealed their frigidity in an unpleasant way, an aggressiveness which could not compensate for their sense of inferiority. . . . Little by little, I began to see excuses for the way they acted. Nadine seemed to me more a victim than a guilty party.[44]

The Mandarins thus represents for Simone de Beauvoir another step toward a fuller understanding of the relationship between generations. In her next published work, *Memoirs of a Dutiful Daughter,* she will turn from fiction to autobiography in order to explore directly in her writing for the first time her own experience as the daughter of a loving mother led by circumstances often beyond her control to overinvest herself in the raising of her two children.

8

In Search of a Lost Paradise:
Memoirs of a Dutiful Daughter

After depicting in her fictional works a vivid array of mothers who assume secondary but significant roles, Simone de Beauvoir, in the first volume of her autobiography, *Mémoires d'une jeune fille rangée*, offers her readers their first direct glimpse of her own mother and of other mothers who influenced her childhood and adolescence. The title selected for the English translation, *Memoirs of a Dutiful Daughter,* is not a literal rendition of the French *jeune fille rangée,* which refers to a well-organized and conscientious young lady rather than to a dutiful daughter. In this volume, Françoise Brasseur de Beauvoir is seen both as the tender, vivacious, loving personality who dominated Simone's early years and as the frustrated, unfulfilled parent of a precocious, intellectually gifted individualist upon whom she strove in vain to impose her own will. Madame de Beauvoir shares the spotlight with Madame "Mabille" Lacoin, mother of Simone's best friend Zaza and an increasingly determined adversary in the author's battle to assure future happiness for Zaza as well as for herself. Lurking in the background of the memoirs are an undemonstrative grandmother, whose older daughter spends her life craving the affection she never found in her childhood, and several doting mothers whose symbiotic relationships with their sons tend to render the latter reluctant to take an independent step toward adulthood.

Simone de Beauvoir's earliest recollections of her mother belong to the idealized fantasy world to which we all have a tendency to relegate our memories of childhood. Attractive and affectionate, twenty-one years old when she gave birth to her older daughter, Françoise de Beauvoir baked delectable sweets, played the piano, and basked in the attention of a gallant husband who lovingly showered her with flowers and affection. Almost obsessively conscientious about her moral and spiritual responsibilities as a mother, this devout convent-reared Catholic from the provinces took Simone to early-morning mass with her practically as soon as she could walk and led her to assume that she was watched over not only by her family here on earth but by a host of heavenly guardians as well.

When Simone started school at the Cours Désir, Madame de Beauvoir, like many other mothers of that era, listened to her lessons and even studied Latin and English herself so that she could keep up with her. Keeping abreast of what one's child is learning in school is possible, of course, only up to a certain point in her development, beyond which both her knowledge and her desire to share it with her mother may well outstrip the capacities of even the most well-intentioned parent. It is significant that in the last weeks of her life, poignantly recounted in *A Very Easy Death*, Françoise de Beauvoir articulated her fear of her older daughter's formidable intellect. The reader senses that early on Simone's academic successes made her mother feel both proud and inadequate, and that she became increasingly uncomfortable about trying to reason on an appropriately intellectual level with the brilliant daughter she had produced. Indeed, Hélène de Beauvoir affirms in a 1986 interview that her mother was afraid of Simone's intellectual superiority and of her older daughter's opinion of her.[1]

Called upon by the school to evaluate her daughter's conduct at home, Françoise de Beauvoir proudly assigned Simone a grade of ten out of ten each week. "A nine would have dishonored both of us," Beauvoir proclaims.[2] Madame de Beauvoir and the older daughter who so resembled her formed a well-coordinated team. Presenting her mother as her earliest female role model, the author comments:

> Thus she and I lived in a sort of symbiosis, and without making a real effort to imitate her, I was molded by her. She inculcated in me a sense of duty and the need for self-effacement and austerity. . . . I learned from *maman* to stay in the background, to control my language, to restrain my desires, and to say and do exactly what it was proper to say and do. I never rebelled and I seldom dared take any initiative.[3]

Ill at ease in Parisian circles, the attractive young matron from the provinces chose silence and conformity as the path to social acceptance. Looking to her mother to set the example for interaction with others, the young Simone understandably assumed that a certain serene timidity was commendable female behavior.

Françoise de Beauvoir was hardly the even-tempered, unruffled mother of television situation comedies, however. Both of her daughters were afraid of her sharp tongue and quick hand. This may help to explain the young Simone's ambivalence about physical contact. While she recalls being attracted to the sensuality of her mother's arms, she also remembers her own solitary rages, during which Madame de Beauvoir once remarked, "When someone touches Simone, she turns purple."[4] This tendency to recoil from physical closeness to others is a trait of which Simone de Beauvoir is painfully aware and of which she often speaks either indirectly in her fiction or directly in her autobiography. Did she perhaps learn as a child to keep her distance from the potential slaps doled out by a mother much beloved but recognizably temperamental?

As we have seen, the comment made to Zaza "Mabille" Lacoin by a young German friend about going through life wearing kid gloves struck a responsive enough chord in Beauvoir to resurface many years later in a dialogue between Nadine and Anne Dubreuilh in *The Mandarins*. Both Zaza and Simone were brought up in families in which acceptable patterns of behavior were considered far preferable to spontaneous reactions to the situation at hand. Although both girls made repeated attempts to dispense with the kid gloves, those gloves remained hauntingly in the background, an integral part of an upbringing which was not easily cast aside.

It is apparent throughout *Memoirs of a Dutiful Daughter* that Simone de Beauvoir is very willing to acknowledge the debt she owes to her mother. In a touching tribute, she admits, "The warmth of her affection made up for her fits of temper. Had she been more perfect and more distant, she would not have had such a profound influence on me."[5] The author is also very much aware that the family's financial situation had a great deal to do with her mother's ill humor. The family resources dwindled as a result of the First World War and a promised dowry was never paid because of the basic ineptitude of Françoise de Beauvoir's father as a businessman. This left Madame de Beauvoir forever beholden to her husband Georges and therefore unwilling to complain about or even discuss the problems which eventually arose between them.

After the war, the Beauvoirs moved from their spacious apartment on the Boulevard du Montparnasse to the more cramped quarters of the rue de Rennes in order to save money. Once the beloved Louise was married and no longer available as governess and maid and several unsatisfactory replacements had been tried, Madame de Beauvoir decided to manage without domestic help. Having grown up in an era during which housework was traditionally relegated to hired servants, she was unaccustomed to taking care of the menial chores of everyday living and soon came to detest them.

The option of working outside the home was not a socially acceptable one for married women with children in the bourgeois milieu of the early decades of the twentieth century. Françoise de Beauvoir thus had no choice but to resign herself to the daily drudgery of housework in her determination to keep her family solvent. She appears in her daughter's memory as an earlier version of Belgian film director Chantal Ackerman's Jeanne Dielman, compulsively making use of every moment as she knits and reads at the same time, mends socks while talking to friends, and enters in a huge black ledger every cent that the family spends. In these activities, she is surely the prototype for Madame Blomart in *The Blood of Others*. Since, as the years passed, Georges de Beauvoir spent more and more time away from home, it is little wonder that his wife, feeling frustrated and abandoned, had scant patience with her daughters as they began to claim separate identities for themselves. Simone de Beauvoir understands all of this intellectually, analyzes it sympathetically, yet recalls in painful detail the emotional agony which her increasingly frequent confrontations with her mother caused her during her adolescence and early adulthood. While asserting that the portrait of their mother in *Memoirs of a Dutiful Daughter* was a very accurate one, Hélène de Beauvoir remarks nonetheless that she feels her sister's judgments were occasionally quite harsh because she was dealing with "childhood resentments that one doesn't forget, things that gnaw at you, wounds that never heal."[6]

When she was about seven or eight, Simone began to realize that it was sometimes best not to be totally honest with her mother about what she was thinking. As she matured, she kept her thoughts to herself both because she feared her mother's disapproval and because she preferred not to upset this woman whose nerves had already become so frayed. Françoise de Beauvoir quickly sensed her reticence and resented it. On one occasion she used uncharacteristically risqué imagery to berate her older daughter for her secretive nature. "Simone would rather prance around in the nude than say what is on her mind," she complained.[7] Given the fact that Simone had been raised to be equally as inhibited as her mother, the hypothesis is a marvelously outrageous one.

As Simone studied in the only heated room of the apartment, her mother wandered in and out, asking her what she was reading, why she had such a peculiar expression on her face, what she was thinking, and finally exclaiming in exasperation, "Naturally, you won't ever tell your *mother* anything. . . ."[8] The author recalls being so exhausted by this constant badgering that when her mother at last went to bed Simone had no energy left to take advantage of the quiet of the sleeping household. This description evokes echoes of the precocious Josyane in Christiane Rochefort's *Les Petits Enfants du siècle*, another bright young girl who finds the tranquillity necessary for doing her homework and for meditating on life in general only after her *famille nombreuse* is safely tucked away in bed each night.[9]

Madame de Beauvoir was extremely reluctant to let her daughters escape her control. She refused to allow her husband to buy bicycles for them or to facilitate their learning how to swim. She tried to restrict their reading to books of which she approved, opened their mail before they were allowed to see it, and even attempted to keep them from spending very much time together out of the range of her watchful eye. In a 1985 interview, Beauvoir recounts with a certain bemusement: "She was afraid that I would have a bad influence on my sister, so she forbad us to see one another when we were in the country. So we would each go out through a garden gate and meet. It was really absurd."[10] Françoise de Beauvoir did, however, have some mellow moments when she insisted that Simone continue to play tennis rather than spend all of her waking hours studying, when she went out to the movies with her daughters, when she replied graciously to Simone's summer letter, assuring her that one day she would be famous. As painful as it may have been for Françoise de Beauvoir to loosen the reins, she seems to have been sensible enough to realize that unless she did so she might drive Simone into open rebellion. As the author states:

> If she had often opposed me, I think she would have driven me to rebel. But in the important things—my studies, the choice of my friends —she seldom intervened; she respected my work and even what I did with my spare time, asking me only to do some minimal chores: grind the coffee, take down the garbage. I was used to being docile and I believed that this was essentially what God expected of me; the conflict between my mother and me did not come to a head.[11]

Although Simone refused to ask her mother's pardon for all her faults, as she had been advised at school to do before her first communion, although she resented being asked to sit in the living room when her mother was entertaining friends and relatives, she seldom openly defied maternal authority as long as her pious young mind continued to associate obedience to her mother with obedience to God.

It was Simone's realization that she no longer believed in God that set up an almost insurmountable barrier between the author and her mother. Beauvoir was fifteen years old when she came to this conclusion, one she was aware that she simply could not share with her excessively devout mother. For years she suffered in silence, having nightmares about the nothingness she believed awaited her when she died. One summer evening while vacationing with her father's relatives in the

Limousin area, she was so terrified at the thought of this eternal void that she almost pretended to be sick in order to seek the comfort of her mother's protective arms.

Françoise de Beauvoir had always avoided initiating conversations which might be emotionally charged. She had therefore to summon all of her courage to broach the subject of Simone's religious faith shortly before her daughter was about to embark on her university studies. The scene was an extremely dramatic one, one through which Simone had lived many times before in her imagination:

> She asked me with some embarrassment where I stood as far as my religious faith was concerned. My heart began to pound: "Well," I said, "I haven't been a believer for quite some time now." Her composure left her: "My poor little girl!" she said. She closed the door so that my sister wouldn't hear what we said next: in an imploring tone she sketched out a demonstration of God's existence, then gave a gesture of futility and stopped, tears in her eyes. I was sorry to have hurt her, but I felt immensely relieved: finally I would be able to live without hypocrisy.[12]

Simone could indeed now live without hypocrisy, but also without the former closeness which had once existed between mother and daughter.

Françoise de Beauvoir, already concerned about her daughter's adolescent attempts to establish her independence, became frantic once she realized that Simone no longer believed in God. She ran about asking advice from any friends or family members with some to offer, spent much of her time praying for her daughter's lost soul. "With her eyes toward heaven, my mother prayed for my soul; here on earth she moaned about my shortcomings: all communication between us was cut off."[13] However well Beauvoir understood her mother's predicament intellectually, the breach between them left her feeling abandoned and resentful:

> My mother had often told me that she had suffered from Grandmother's lack of warmth and that she wanted to be a friend to her own daughters. But how could she talk with me as one human being to another when she considered me a soul in danger, a soul to be saved, an object? The solidity of her convictions forbad her the slightest concession.[14]

Thus the religion which had represented one of Simone's earliest bonds with her mother became the obstacle that precluded real communication between them for many years.

Apparently Madame de Beauvoir could not bring herself to follow up on her first instinctive reaction to Simone's loss of faith, expressed so touchingly in her exclamation "My poor little girl!" Had she been able to approach the problem from the point of view of a friend regretting that something she considered one of life's greatest comforts was no longer available for someone she cared about, perhaps the two women might have maintained their earlier closeness in spite of this crisis. Her retreat into prayer apparently made this impossible, at least in the eyes of her older daughter. It is of interest that her younger daughter Hélène, referred to as Poupette throughout the autobiography, chose never to confront her mother on the religious issue. In her book entitled *Souvenirs* she speaks of spending Sunday mornings in the Louvre when her mother thought she was at mass, of giving her mother to understand that she was married in a Catholic rather than a civil ceremony in Portugal.[15] Whereas Simone felt called upon to tackle each issue head-on, Hélène chose a smoother path and avoided open conflict, thereby maintaining a closer bond with her mother throughout her adult years.

Françoise de Beauvoir's convent training had taught her to treat sexuality more as a necessary evil than as an integral part of life. Like so many women of her generation, she was extremely ill at ease with any allusion to the physical or the sensual. As a result, she did not prepare her older daughter for the "surprises" puberty held for her. When the probing questions asked by her younger daughter Hélène forced Madame de Beauvoir to say something about where babies came from, Simone recalls her explanation with both humor and irony:

> Mother gave us to understand that newborns came out through the anus and without causing pain. She spoke in a detached tone; but there was no follow-up to this conversation. Never again did I broach these questions with her and she never breathed another word about them.[16]

Realizing that a dress she intended to have Simone wear to a cousin's wedding was far too tight and consequently too revealing, Madame de Beauvoir wrapped her daughter's breasts in bandages to conceal her developing figure: "I was so bandaged up that I felt all day as if I were hiding a cumbersome infirmity inside my blouse."[17] Many such incidents during her childhood and adolescence alerted the author to the association which existed in her mother's mind betwen sexuality and danger: the pinning together of certain pages of novels, the reluctance to take her daughters to the movies where she had no control over what was projected on the screen, the horror in her eyes the day she discovered Simone reading a book "not meant for her." Such recollections underline both Madame de Beauvoir's inhibitions and her reluctance to accept the eventual development of her two daughters into women like herself, sexual and sensual human beings.

The first pages of the memoirs recount the strange story of Charlotte, a little girl who at first refuses to eat anything but a huge egg made of pink sugar and gradually shrinks to minuscule proportions. Almost thrown away with the garbage one day, Charlotte then decides to stuff herself with food and becomes as huge as an inflated balloon. She finally agrees to follow a diet prescribed by the family doctor and returns to normal size. Simone was fascinated by this story read to her by the maid Louise and comments in retrospect, "I would emerge safe and sound from the adventure that had in turn reduced me to a foetus and changed me into a matron."[18] This interpretation of the story in terms of the changing forms of the female body looks ahead to Kim Chernin's study of *The Hungry Self*, which theorizes that the eating disorders of the women of the 1980s are directly related to their reluctance to grow up and risk surpassing their mothers in terms of achievement and fulfill-ment.[19] Chernin sees the obsession with slenderness typical of anorexics and bulimics as an indication of a desire to emulate the male physique and thereby to be authorized to compete in the world beyond the mater-nal realm of influence, just as sons have always been encouraged to do.

The young Simone's fascination with Charlotte's story suggests a sense of danger associated in her mind with her original symbiotic attachment to her mother as a foetus as well as with her potential for becoming the pregnant mother-to-be of a member of the next generation. The sugary egg will be transformed in her later novel, *Les Belles Images*, into two rotten eggs that the protagonist Laurence, who subsequently becomes anorexic, finds totally indigestible. Charlotte's return to normalcy in-volves a careful and sane approach to eating and to living, one which detaches itself from obsessive concern with the vagaries of the female reproductive cycle. The author's recurrent comments about her distaste for things maternal suggest that Charlotte's tale struck a sensitive chord and lingered on, only partially repressed, during the twenty-one years of Beauvoir's existence as a "jeune fille rangée" when she was deter-mined to remain "safe and sound," comfortably protected from the looming menaces of pregnancy and childbirth.

It is highly likely that the distaste displayed by Françoise de Beauvoir for the physical aspects of female biology had a profound influence on her daughter's attitude toward maternity. Simone remembers that she was made uncomfortable by the presence of babies when she was a little girl, that she would only play mother to her dolls if she could dispense with the nurturing aspects of the role. At a fairly early age the author seems to have become aware of the cumbersome nature of the daily existence of women whose lives centered entirely on their reponsibilities as wives and mothers. She and Poupette always pretended that their husbands were away when they played with their dolls:

> I knew this was not so in real life: a wife and mother is always flanked by her spouse. A thousand tedious chores weigh her down. When I thought about my future, this servitude seemed so cumbersome that I gave up the idea of having children of my own. What I cared about was forming minds and souls: I will become a teacher, I decided.[20]

Beauvoir knew even at a very young age that she would have no patience with the daily routine of the homemaker.

The ultraconservative religious view of sexuality espoused by her mother actually made the young Simone decide at one point that marriage was "promiscuous," causing her to proclaim that she would become a Carmelite nun when she grew up. She thus rejected, at least temporarily, the mysterious physical coupling which she knew was somehow essential to producing children of her own. Beauvoir repeats in several passages of her autobiography that she was basically indifferent to babies, sex, and childbearing as a young girl: "I don't remember having pondered over the phenomena of pregnancy and childbirth or having considered them a part of my future. I was put off by marriage and maternity and I probably didn't think they concerned me."[21] She apparently sensed that the implications of Charlotte's story were best left unexamined at this stage of her life.

The adolescent Simone was embarrassed by her mother's discussions with the doctor about the changes taking place in her body, repulsed by the "ballooning" of a torso over which she seemed to have absolutely no control. Unprepared for her first menstrual period, she was at first afraid she had done something wrong, then rather proud of the fuss her mother was making with friends and relatives about her sudden maturity. She was horrified, however, when her mother shared this essentially female information with her father: "I had imagined that the confraternity of women kept its secret blemish carefully hidden from men."[22] The use of the French word *confrérie* in this passage is extremely significant, suggesting as it does that only groups of men manage to band together successfully. That menstruation should be labeled a *tare* in French, a blemish or defect, emphasizes the negative light in which women and their reproductive processes were viewed not only by the masculine world but also by the adolescent Beauvoir. Ill at ease with her newly acquired sexuality, Beauvoir was relieved when her father informed her and her sister mournfully that because he had no money to

provide dowries for them they would have to earn a living for themselves and would probably never marry.

Beauvoir relates that, during her adolescence, she set herself up as a
rival of her mother's for her father's attentions in a pattern she recognizes as typically Freudian. She was convinced that her mother deliberately dressed her in unattractive clothes in order to keep her asexual as
long as possible. She quickly realized that her father, impatient with her
adolescent awkwardness, was not about to ally himself with her against
her mother. Confused by his ambivalence about her outstanding academic achievements, she later analyzed her father's impatience as an
indication of his sense of failure in not being able to provide her with
the dowry which would make her marriageable and thereby traditional
and acceptable according to bourgeois standards.

As she matured, Beauvoir refused to play out the role of docile
daughter that would allow her mother to continue to find fulfillment in
the family responsibilities to which she had chosen to dedicate her life:
"Her upbringing and her social circles had convinced her that for a
woman maternity is the most glorious of roles. She could not play this
role unless I played mine, and I refused as tenaciously as I had when I
was five years old to take part in adult playacting."[23] Aware of how easily
her mother was upset by sexuality and emotion, however, she did everything in her power to spare them both embarrassment. When she found
that the story of *Adam Bede,* a book bought for her by her mother,
contained an unwed mother in it, she was terrified at the thought that
Madame de Beauvoir might want to pick it up and read it:

> Then she would know that I know. I couldn't stand that idea. I wasn't afraid of being
> reprimanded. I hadn't done anything wrong. But I was panicked at the thought of
> what would go through her mind. Maybe she would feel obliged to sit down and talk
> to me. This possibility terrified me because, from the silence she had always main-
> tained about such things, I was well aware of how repugnant it was for her to
> consider them. . . . The fact that I knew they existed would become, in my mother's
> mind, a scandal that would besmirch both of us.[24]

The use of the French verb *souiller* (besmirch) in this passage reflects the
attitudes toward sex and sensuality that were prevalent in the milieu in
which Beauvoir was raised. While trying to pull gradually away from
her mother's authority, the author nonetheless attempted to protect the
skittish Madame de Beauvoir from being upset by a side of life of which
she would prefer to remain ignorant. Throughout her entire campaign
to win her own freedom, Simone de Beauvoir remained a caring daughter whose memory of the happy childhood for which her mother was

essentially responsible made her intent on avoiding causing the older woman's life to become any more difficult than she made it for herself.

The question of what constitutes creativity became an important one to Beauvoir as she matured and looked forward to becoming a writer. She recalls being scandalized by Zaza's assertion that "bringing nine children into the world as my mother did is just as worthwhile as writing books."[25] Simone did not agree at all, feeling that artists and writers create a new world, whereas childbearing merely amounts to "playing the same old song over and over again."[26] Unlike many adolescent girls, Beauvoir found nothing particularly attractive about newborn babies. Once again she contrasts her sentiments with Zaza's: "I thought of marriage without repugnance. The idea of maternity was foreign to me and I was astonished that Zaza could go into ecstasy over wrinkled newborn babies."[27] During her adolescence, Simone became more open to the possibility of interacting with the opposite sex, but the often inevitable result of such interaction in this era many decades before the invention of the pill remained an idea totally outside of her realm of comprehension.

As a student at the Sorbonne, Beauvoir was struck by the fact that her philosophy teacher Mademoiselle Zanta had managed to reconcile her intellectual and her emotional needs by adopting a young niece who lived with her. At the same time the author's nostalgic feelings about the happy childhood her mother created for her made her consider the possibility of marrying her cousin Jacques, whom she admired for his knowledge of modern literature and art, and thereby incorporating her early memories into her adult life. Yet as soon as family members seemed to be smiling benevolently on this union, she became alarmed. "I no longer saw it as my salvation but rather as my perdition," she recollects.[28] On the other hand, an exclusively intellectual existence seemed extremely limited to her. She remarks about one of her teachers, "Mademoiselle Lambert was not really 'living.' She was teaching courses and working on her thesis: I found that a very dry kind of existence."[29] As she attempted to sort out her plans for her future, the young Simone was torn between the intermittent attraction of her cousin Jacques and the apparently bohemian world he represented and the lure of the life of the intellect.

A moment of profound discouragement is recorded as the author, approaching her nineteenth birthday, looks around her and finds no obvious outlet for her boundless energy:

> What would be the point of getting married? Raising children or correcting home-work amounted to the same useless routine. . . . Like my mother, Mademoiselle

Lambert was marking off one lifeless day after another, content simply to keep occupied.... Actually, what was bothering me was having been chased out of my childhood paradise without having found a place for myself among men.[30]

The French word *hommes* is used in the generic sense here, yet this statement may also be interpreted as an indication of Simone de Beauvoir's desire to fit into a male-oriented rather than a female-oriented style of life. Marriage and teaching both involve repetition and routine, and for Beauvoir routine is "useless." It is creativity which she values most highly, and this she clearly associates with the male world.

The author is far too perceptive not to have become aware of the inadequacies of a childhood paradise which prepares a woman for a lifetime commitment as a wife and mother. Both she and her best friend were struggling to free themselves from the domination of devoted and affectionate mothers who would have liked to perpetuate the family-centered existence of their respective broods indefinitely. In a letter she wrote to Simone, Zaza admitted, "I have lived too much in the past, unable to wrest myself away from the marvels of my childhood memories."[31] Both young women resisted falling into the far too comfortable roles society would have liked to assign to them. At the same time, they were both deeply disturbed by the necessity of hurting mothers they really cared about in the process of seeking their own separate identities.

Liberated from the yoke of belief in Christian obedience, the adolescent Simone chafed under the tyranny of a mother who insisted on continuing to dominate her life. She smarted at the slap she received when she put on some of her cousin Madeleine's rouge, was infuriated by her mother's overreaction to the evening she spent with Jacques, the embarrassment of her mother's shouting up from the street outside of her aunt's window about her daughter's lost honor. Although she seldom directly refused to do as her mother said, she took delight in finding furtive ways of getting out of the house at night in order to enlarge her horizons. Attending a performance of the Ballets Russes was a revelation, her first experience interacting directly with culture. "When I went out with my parents or the Mabilles, an insurmountable barrier separated me from the world," she realized.[32] She became fascinated with bars and dance halls, specifically because she knew her mother would disapprove of them: "Never would my mother have agreed to set foot inside them.... There was great satisfaction for me in knowing that I was doing something absolutely unacceptable."[33] She had found her own way of separating from her mother, of breaking away from the symbiosis of her early years.

Whether it was because Françoise de Beauvoir had come to realize the need to let go or simply because she was growing tired of battling with her headstrong daughter, Simone gradually obtained her mother's permission to live a life of her own. She was delighted to be free of the necessity of coming home for lunch each day, to be allowed to go out occasionally in the evening with friends. Her thoughts at age twenty about marriage and motherhood are tellingly ambiguous: "All I wanted was to find love, to write good books, to have a few children, 'and friends to whom I could dedicate my books and who would teach my children to think and to appreciate poetry.' I assigned a very minimal role to my husband."[34] This is one of the few places in all of Beauvoir's work in which she actually envisages having children of her own. The section in single quotation marks appears to come directly from her diary. It is significant that she planned to pass the responsibility of making creative human beings out of her children on to a few special friends. Only a few pages later, she recalls seeing her Sorbonne classmate Paul Nizan and his wife pushing a baby carriage in the Luxembourg Gardens one day. "I hoped against hope that such a picture would not be a part of my future," she records.[35] It is of course impossible to determine to what extent such remarks are the result of more than three decades of hindsight. Be that as it may, Simone de Beauvoir clearly recognized the fact that while married men like Nizan and René Maheu, referred to as André Herbaud in the memoirs, were free to pursue their studies at the Sorbonne and to go off in whatever direction their careers might take them, their wives remained at home with the dishes and the baby carriages.

Whereas Simone de Beauvoir struggled valiantly and successfully to escape from the maternal stranglehold, her best friend eventually succumbed tragically to her mother's tyranny. It is only toward the end of the first section of the memoirs that we meet Madame "Mabille" Lacoin, a militantly devout Catholic, mother of nine children. The author describes her as "an attractive brunette in her forties with sparkling eyes and a studied smile. . . . She ruled over her brood with carefully measured affection."[36] Beauvoir was amazed at the ease with which this mother of nine handled bruised knees, spilled food, broken dishes. She was appalled by the daring with which Zaza stuck out her tongue at her mother in public after flawlessly executing a piano piece Madame Mabille had considered too difficult for her to play. Even more incomprehensible was Madame Mabille's acceptance of this shocking gesture with a bemused hug. This incident caused the young Simone to assess the difference between Mabille spontaneity and Beauvoir timidity: "If I had done something inappropriate, my mother would have been mortified. My conformity was a reflection of her timidity."[37] It was precisely Zaza's vivaciousness, her casual directness in dealing with the teachers at the Cours Désir, which first attracted Beauvoir to her.

As the girls visited at each other's homes and spent time together in the country during the long summer vacations, Simone gradually came to recognize the fundamental difference between the two families in which they were being raised. Whereas Françoise de Beauvoir had, at least in the early years of her marriage, been sexually attracted to and satisfied by her dashing young husband, Madame Mabille did not conceal from Zaza the physical repulsion she felt for her mate:

> Zaza confided to me that Madame Mabille—whom she considered full of charm, sensitivity, and imagination—had suffered from being misunderstood by a husband as dull as an algebra book. . . . I realize today that she felt a physical repulsion for her father. Her mother told her at an early age, and with ill-intentioned crudeness, what sex was all about. Zaza realized precociously that her mother had hated carrying out her conjugal duties from the very first night.[38]

Clearly we have here the prototype for the Madame Vignon who, in *When Things of the Spirit Come First,* tells her older daughter that if her sexual activity had depended upon the pleasure she found with her husband, none of her children would have been born. While Françoise de Beauvoir and everyone else in her family accepted unquestioningly the superiority of Georges de Beauvoir, Madame "Mabille" reigned supreme in her household and in the mind of her third child, Zaza.

Secure in her authority, Guite Larivière "Mabille" manipulated her children at will. Looking back on her early impressions of the mother of her best friend, Beauvoir decides that "her patience, her smiles, masked, I believe, an enormous lack of warmth."[39] This is a woman who, in the author's opinion, wanted above all to control other human beings. When Simone put a great deal of effort and love into making a special purse for Zaza's name day, Madame Mabille directed her thanks to Françoise de Beauvoir. "She was trying to fit what I did into the framework of adult etiquette. At that moment I realized that I no longer liked her at all."[40] Her original fascination with the Mabille flair turned to disenchantment and finally to hatred as she watched Zaza writhing in the grip of a mother she loved and respected too much.

After approximately three decades had gone by, Beauvoir analyzed Madame Mabille's manipulative psychology with deadly accuracy: "When [her children] were very small, she treated them with playful indulgence. Later, she remained liberal about little things. When something important came up, her credit was intact."[41] She had always demonstrated a certain favoritism toward Zaza and, like Françoise de

Beauvoir, had taken great pride in the resemblance people saw between her and her daughter. Although Beauvoir continued to feel an emotional attachment to her mother, she was puzzled by the symbiotic relationship which persisted between Madame Mabille and her daughter even after Zaza turned eighteen, nineteen, and twenty. She tries to explain Zaza's passionate love for her mother as a possessive bid for the attention any member of a family of nine children must grow up craving. She also calls into question the genuineness of Madame Mabille's feelings for her daughter, suggesting that Zaza had been "taken in by her smiles. Love as well as respect paralyzed her whenever she thought of rebelling."[42] The idea of a daughter being "taken in" by her mother's wiles underlines the author's view of maternity as a type of power play on the part of bourgeois women seeking control over some aspect of their lives, a power play which can prove dangerous and even fatal to the offspring they are intent upon manipulating.

The essential difference between the author and her best friend lay in the fact that Zaza continued to be a believing and practicing Catholic until her premature death. She had been brought up to live by the Ten Commandments, one of the most straightforward being the admonition to all Christians, regardless of age, to honor their fathers and their mothers. Since Zaza's feelings toward her father were of a dubious nature, all of her respect and love was focused upon her mother. She was convinced that, however trivial they might seem to her, whatever chores she was asked to do were simply a part of her Christian duty. The young Simone was exasperated to see her wasting her time trying to find the least expensive material for dresses for her younger siblings, preparing meal after meal, canning. She comments wryly on the daily routine at the Mabille summer home: "Nourishing oneself became a harrowing, long-winded procedure."[43]

Because the Beauvoir family did not have the financial resources to provide a dowry for Simone and Hélène, their parents had been forced, however grudgingly, to orient both daughters toward a career. The social activities of the Mabille clan, on the other hand, centered on finding appropriate mates for each of the offspring, in chronological order. To Madame Mabille everything, including intellectual development and emotional happiness, took second place to the arranging of an economically and socially acceptable marriage. Zaza was painfully aware of her mother's plans for her as she watched her older sister being dragged from interview to interview, as if she were applying for a job, in search of the perfect partner. Zaza remarked indignantly to Simone that she saw no difference between a woman who accepts a marriage of convenience and a prostitute. Despite these strong feelings, she was aware of being trapped by the social customs of her milieu and most particularly by the ironclad law that a proper young girl does not choose her own mate. When she protested that she simply did not love the men her mother had chosen as candidates for her hand, Zaza was told firmly, "My little one, it's not the woman, it's the man who loves."[44]

Both Madame Mabille and Françoise de Beauvoir resented the closeness that existed between the two young women, the former because she considered the atheistic Simone a bad influence on her daughter, the latter more a victim of jealousy over an intimacy Simone had found with someone other than herself. For Madame Mabille Simone represented the dreaded intellectual who was jeopardizing Zaza's sense of filial duty. Zaza was reproached for spending too much time on her studies, her reading, and her music, and for thereby neglecting her so-called social duties. Madame Mabille did everything she could to keep the two girls apart. She was condescending to Simone because she had lost her faith, and infuriated by the books Simone chose to lend to her daughter. She was not above enlisting Simone's help, however, to dissuade Zaza from contemplating marriage to her cousin André. Simone recalls some agonizing summer visits to the Mabilles during which she often felt painfully isolated from Zaza, with "that mother and that entire family between us."[45] She vacillated between a determination to save Zaza from these nefarious influences and a resignation to the inevitability of eventually losing her best friend to Madame Mabille's tyranny.

What fundamentally separated the course taken by the lives of these two close friends was Zaza's willingness to compromise. Her fear of hurting her mother caused her to exhaust herself in an attempt to comply with as many of Madame Mabille's demands as she could. Beauvoir, on the other hand, felt incapable of playing a role of which she did not approve:

> My friends, and Zaza herself, played their social roles with ease. They made an appearance at their mothers' open houses, served tea, smiled, said pleasant little nothings. I had a hard time smiling. I didn't know how to be charming, or witty, or even how to make concessions![46]

Simone de Beauvoir was always a pragmatist unwilling to expend energy uselessly. Social obligations were undoubtedly right at the top of her list of useless activities.

Despite the different directions their lives took as they completed their teenage years, Beauvoir remained an important sounding board for Zaza, who occasionally poured out her heart to her in her letters. She seems to have been the only person to whom Zaza could reveal in total honesty the full weight of the emotional battle she was waging. The outcome of that battle would determine whether it was Zaza or Madame Mabille who prevailed. "I love her so, you see," she wrote in a summer letter, "that the most difficult thing in the world for me is to cause her all this pain and to go against her will."[47] For Beauvoir, establishing one's own identity apart from any role imposed by parents or society was the essence of individual freedom. Watching Zaza give in time and again because of the obedience to her mother which she considered a religious obligation, Beauvoir worried that "in the long run, Zaza will allow herself to be convinced that it is her Christian duty to settle down and start a family."[48] As we have seen from previous comments in the memoirs, such a situation was long considered by the maturing Simone as the proverbial "fate worse than death" for a bright young woman.

Accustomed to being in control of her children's lives, Madame Mabille ranted and raved against intellectuals, expressed regrets that she had ever let Zaza set foot inside the Sorbonne, and decided to send her daughter off to Berlin for three months to remove her from the negative influence of Beauvoir and others who did not think as she did. Away from her mother's constant demands on her time and on her emotions, Zaza blossomed in Berlin. She missed her family, wept for joy when she saw her mother at the train window coming to visit her, yet was frightened at the prospect of coming back to live at home again. The household was about to be turned upside down by preparations for her older sister's wedding, and she wrote to Beauvoir:

> I must admit that I am frightened at the thought of going back to the life I was living three months ago. That extremely respectable formality which characterizes the lives of most of the people in "our social circle" has become unbearable to me.[49]

From her vantage point back in Paris, Beauvoir was painfully aware of the psychological blackmail Madame Mabille was quite ready to use to keep Zaza in line. Complaining to Madame de Beauvoir one evening about Simone's influence on her daughter, Madame Mabille concluded with the words, "Fortunately, Zaza loves me very much."[50] It is apparent that to Madame Mabille a mother's love involved insisting on what she alone knew to be best for her offspring, while a daughter's love was equated with obedience and capitulation. A maternal concern for the happiness of one's child seems to be glaringly absent from this equation.

Beauvoir hoped that the love which had developed between Zaza and Jean Pradelle, a fictional transposition of philosopher Maurice Merleau-Ponty, would secure happiness for them both. She was naive enough to tell her best friend that she was no longer a child, that her mother surely wanted her happiness above all and would therefore accept her choice of a mate. Such logic seemed ludicrous to Zaza, who pointed out that marriages were simply not set up in that way in her social circle. With a great deal of good will, Beauvoir continued to make practical suggestions about ways to resolve the differences between Zaza and her mother. She also became increasingly exasperated with her friend for her willingness to sacrifice her own interests to those of everyone else.

When Zaza finally succumbs, the reader wonders if it is to some medical fatality or rather to the gradual grinding down of her willpower by her domineering mother. Her final words to Madame Mabille are heart-rending. "Don't be sad, my beloved mother. Every family has someone who is expendable. I am that someone," she whispers in a resigned voice.[51] Zaza thus goes to her death cherishing her mother to such an extent that she virtually eliminates herself from the face of the earth so that her mother's will might prevail.

There are a number of maternal figures in *Memoirs of a Dutiful Daughter* who are not directly on stage but whose attitudes have had a profound influence on the future development of their offspring. The lack of affection displayed by Beauvoir's maternal grandmother made her older daughter Françoise insecure and emotionally vulnerable. It was because of her inability to evince real tenderness and care from her own mother that Françoise de Beauvoir was so intent on doing a perfect job of mothering Simone and Hélène. Such determination had both advantages and disadvantages. The author gives full credit to her mother for the happy childhood she created for her. She also recognizes, however, that the fact that motherhood had become the sole justification for Françoise de Beauvoir's existence was a heavy burden for her daughters to bear. The ambivalent feelings inspired in Beauvoir by her mother's total dedication to her and her sister are highlighted by her yearning for a return to her childhood paradise. Despite her instinctive sense that marriage to her cousin Jacques would be a disaster for all concerned, she admits at one point that the prospect of making everyone happy again was very tempting:

> His mother and his sister would surround me with their tenderness, my parents would soften. I would become once again that person whom everyone loved and would take my place once again in that society outside of which I could see nothing but exile.[52]

A happy childhood, particularly when it includes a symbiotic relationship between mother and daughter, thus emerges as a trap perhaps every bit as dangerous as that set by a miserable childhood.

Simone de Beauvoir's father was a favorite son of a doting mother whom he did everything to please. She died when he was thirteen, however. After that, he curtailed his academic efforts, giving full attention only to those subjects which really interested him. His greatest passion throughout his life, according to his daughter, was the theatre. Georges de Beauvoir appeared to have found in the applause of his audiences the unequivocal approbation and admiration which he once commanded first from his mother, then from his young provincial wife eight years his junior, and, at least temporarily, from his growing daughters.

Because his father had died when he was still an infant, Beauvoir's cousin Jacques was convinced by the attention he received from a doting mother and sister that it was his duty to take over as the man of the house at a very early age. He took this role seriously and was thus devastated by his mother's decision to remarry five years later and by the subsequent birth of another son. Despite his bravado and a certain intellectual precociousness, Jacques never seemed to recover his self-confidence. After marrying a friend's sister because of her generous dowry and having a number of children, he literally drank himself to death. There are some similarities between the family situations of cousin Jacques and Jean-Paul Sartre, whose father died shortly after he was born and who had an extremely symbiotic relationship with a mother whom he treated more as an older sister than as a parent until her remarriage during his early adolescence. Unlike Jacques, however, Sartre did not allow his resentment of his stepfather to impede his progress toward a brilliant career in philosophy and literature.

In contrast to Jacques, the Jean Pradelle portrayed in the memoirs had an older brother of whom he seldom spoke with his friends. It was therefore not incumbent upon him to become the man of the house after his father's death. The lack of a male parent in the household, however, may well explain the close attachment he felt to his mother. At one point he confided to Beauvoir that he "had little hope of ever falling in love with any woman because he was too exclusively bound to his mother."[53] Although he was seemingly quite interested in Zaza, his immediate family always came first in his thoughts. He declined to see Zaza for an entire week because he felt obliged to console his mother after the departure of his married brother for Togo.

While Zaza approved intellectually of Pradelle's fulfilling his Christian duty to his mother, it is clear that she subconsciously saw Madame Pradelle as a rival. She arrived one day at the Pradelles' in a feverish state and asked Jean's mother if she hated her. When Madame Pradelle assured her that this was not the case, Zaza then wanted to know why she was opposed to their getting married. Although Madame Pradelle can hardly be cast in the role of wicked witch, the dependent relationship which she had allowed to develop between herself and her grown son appears to have kept Jean from moving out of his closeknit family circle and making adult commitments of his own. Zaza's intuition was supplying an explanation for Jean Pradelle's lukewarm treatment of their mutual feelings for one another.

The entire situation existing between Zaza and Jean Pradelle is presented in *Memoirs of a Dutiful Daughter* as Beauvoir saw it when she was twenty-one years old. In her opinion, Zaza "Mabille" Lacoin was assassinated by bourgeois society and its demands on young girls. What the author did not learn until after the publication of this volume of the autobiography was the real reason the Lacoins did not approve of the promising young student Maurice Merleau-Ponty as a suitable husband for their daughter. During the Lacoins' investigation into his family background, it was discovered, according to biographers Claude Francis and Fernande Gontier, that Merleau-Ponty was an illegitimate child. Both Maurice and his sister were the products of a very open liaison between his mother and a university professor in La Rochelle who was also married and who often sat between his wife and his mistress at public functions. Not only did the Lacoins react with horror to this threat to the family honor, they also hastened to enlighten Maurice Merleau-Ponty about the circumstances of his birth, information which his mother, now a widow living in Paris, had never seen fit to share with him. The young man agreed to give up Zaza in exchange for a promise of secrecy from Monsieur Lacoin so that his sister's approaching marriage would not be compromised by this scandalous revelation. After seeing the anguish and depression caused by their insistence that Zaza give up any thought of marrying Merleau-Ponty, the Lacoins finally told her the truth. Intellectually she understood that a Lacoin could not contemplate marrying an illegitimate child. Emotionally she was unable to handle the strain. When her parents finally decided to relent and give their permission for this marriage, it was already too late. Zaza died several hours later. It was not until thirty years after the fact that one of Zaza's sisters explained to Simone de Beauvoir the full circumstances of her death.

Had Beauvoir known the details of the Merleau-Ponty situation, would her conclusions have been any different? A family which bases all decisions on the necessity of keeping up appearances is still capable of "assassinating" a bright and sensitive daughter torn between devotion to her parents and love for one of her contemporaries. Merleau-Ponty's mother and her fictional counterpart Madame Pradelle would undoubtedly have been considered less suspect, since it appears that at no time did she oppose the union between her son and Zaza. The strong attachments existing between Zaza and her mother, and between Merleau-Ponty and his mother, might still end up, however, as the primary culprits in the tragedy which resulted in the premature death of Simone de Beauvoir's best friend.

In this first volume of Beauvoir's autobiography, numerous vignettes of mother-child relationships thus illuminate the author's experiences with maternal roles as she was growing up. *Memoirs of a Dutiful Daughter* can be read almost as a case study of the varying degrees of success with which members of Beauvoir's generation separated themselves from their parents. The story of Zaza "Mabille" Lacoin explains the bitterness with which the writer portrays such characters as Madame Vignon in *When Things of the Spirit Come First* and Murielle in "Monologue," the second story of *The Woman Destroyed*. The fictional portraits of mothers are not exclusively negative, however. Underlying Beauvoir's recollections is a warm nostalgia for a childhood made special by a woman whose affection and concern for her two daughters was clearly genuine.

Critical Reaction

The first volume of Simone de Beauvoir's memoirs has elicited a great number of critical comments over the years. Georges Hourdin considers Françoise de Beauvoir "as solid as her husband was frivolous"[54] and a strong influence on her young daughters, to whom she transmitted the traditionalist, jansenist, and "falsely puritanical" religion in which she herself had been brought up.[55] Hourdin, a devout Catholic who knew Zaza's father and was a close friend of her uncle's, deems the atmosphere in which Zaza was raised a much more authentic one than the "spiritual mediocrity" in which the Beauvoir sisters were brought up.[56]

Despite, or perhaps because of, his connection with the "Mabille" Lacoin family, Hourdin has very little to say about the death of Zaza, which he attributes in one short sentence to the exhaustion brought on by her long-term struggle against her mother's opposition to her marriage plans. His final chapter is entitled "God's Orphans" ("Les Orphelins de Dieu"). In it he attacks Beauvoir's rejection of the creativity involved in having children, stating, with the pronoun *nous* representing "we believers," that:

> We wish to be part of God's plan by participating in his act of creation by giving birth, through the uniting of two freedoms, to new freedoms.... Jean-Paul Sartre and Simone de Beauvoir are God's orphans. It is perhaps because they refuse the simple

creative love of men. Having rejected their family past, having no child's face at their side, having no future other than in their books, they are truly alone. . . .[57]

The critic thus suggests both that the interpretation of the Catholic faith handed down by Françoise de Beauvoir to her daughters was incomplete and somewhat false and that the anguish expressed in some passages of Simone de Beauvoir's autobiography is directly attributable to her decision not to have children of her own.

Francis Jeanson stresses the carnal nature of the love the small Simone felt for her mother, something he considers directly related to "the remarkable sensitivity to feminine charm with which almost all of [Beauvoir's] work seems to me to be impregnated."[58] Jeanson sees Françoise de Beauvoir as coming to represent for Simone an image of the kind of woman she spent her life reproaching for the wasteful squandering of a vitality that could have been utilized in so many more effective ways. According to Jeanson, Beauvoir eventually achieved an effective separation from her mother, who seemed to her "stuck in her feminine condition, physically irresponsible (her uncontrolled vitality, her temperamental nature) and morally bamboozled (by a triple submissiveness, to God, to her husband, to the conventions of their social circle)."[59] He senses in Simone de Beauvoir a resentment of the symbiotic attachment she once felt to her mother and a determination never to become a "woman," i.e. like her mother.

Annemarie Lasocki focuses on Beauvoir's oft-quoted refusal to allow Zaza to equate bringing nine children into the world with the creativity inherent in writing books.[60] Pointing out the common usage of such words as "prolific," "conception," "brought to term," and "gestation" to apply both to childbirth and to the writer's craft, Lasocki sees the author's obsession with writing as an attempt to assure herself a different type of immortality from the one promised her when she was a devout young Catholic. Beauvoir thus turns her back on the immanence she assumes to be an inescapable characteristic of the maternal role and searches rather for the transcendence she associates with male creativity, according to Lasocki.

Elaine Marks observes that the goal of Beauvoir's creativity from 1932 on was to describe Zaza's death, which "became with time the symbol of all of Simone de Beauvoir's formative years. Her revolt against church and family, her passionate hatred of the bourgeoisie, and her exacerbated sense of responsibility seem to have crystallized around this death."[61] Robert Cottrell notes the way in which Beauvoir presents her mother's religious convictions as "superficial and conventional."[62] He attributes Zaza's insistence on continuing to be a dutiful daughter to "a deep-rooted sense of insecurity as well as unwavering devotion to her mother (who is portrayed as totally unworthy of her daughter's affection)...."[63] The words "totally unworthy" seem a bit strong when one considers Beauvoir's initial depiction of Madame "Mabille" Lacoin as essentially sympathetic and lively and her later sincere attempts to understand and explain Zaza's obsessive and inescapable attachment to her mother.

Jean Leighton suggests that "the general lugubrious feminine atmosphere of her own family and class did not help to instill a desire for motherhood" in Simone de Beauvoir.[64] Highlighting the descriptions in *Memoirs of a Dutiful Daughter* of Aunt Hélène spending day after day inspecting her closets, Leighton elaborates upon her contention that Beauvoir harbors a basic distaste for traditionally feminine virtues:

> Motherhood can never lead to "la gloire" and all of Simone de Beauvoir's philosophical arguments and emotional bias against motherhood reflect a fundamental distaste for the classic feminine virtues which do not include power, success, and changing the face of the world in the sublime masculine manner.[65]

Leighton sees Beauvoir's portrayal of her mother as "sympathetic but detached,"[66] remarking that Françoise de Beauvoir "lacked the kind of prestige and imposing presence to make her daughter wish to emulate her."[67]

In Beauvoir's fiction, Leighton remarks, no one really embodies the maternal qualities of generosity, compassion, and warmth which Zaza "Mabille" seems to her to epitomize. She sees Madame Mabille as "a classic dominating mother" and comments, *"The Second Sex* is peopled with female gorgons of this type."[68] Sardonic but respectful toward her mother, Zaza wages what Leighton labels "a long war of attrition."[69] Had Zaza lived, Leighton feels that "she should have been a mother, since she had in such abundance those qualities motherhood demands."[70]

Carol Ascher stresses the role of religion in Françoise de Beauvoir's raising of her daughters, describing her as "an ardent Catholic who sought guidance from the Union of Christian Mothers."[71] She comments on the degree to which Zaza's mother "had increasingly pulled her away from the university world, demanding of her the restraint of a young Catholic woman of good breeding, with dowry, about to be married off."[72] The implication in many of these analyses is that religion was used by the generation of Beauvoir's and Zaza's parents as a tool for keeping daughters firmly under the maternal thumb.

Anne Whitmarsh emphasizes Beauvoir's "rejection of the family as a valid institution and her equation of parenthood with tyranny." She notes her depiction of "the powerful hold on these children of the bourgeoisie of the moral and spiritual absolutes inculcated from the cradle onwards."[73] Whitmarsh considers the author's espousal of leftist causes part of her rebellion against family and class ties, but posits that "while rejecting the outward forms of religion, she was deeply influenced by her mother's rigid moral attitudes."[74]

For Terry Keefe, Beauvoir's early "decisions" about becoming a teacher rather than a mother "sprang from a rather objectionable sense of her own superiority ... but her arrogance was only a thin surface, through which a deep need for self-justification and the approval of those she loved was always ready to break."[75] Keefe notes the author's impatience with Zaza's inability to break loose from her family but adds that she "was scarcely aware that some of her own deeper problems were relics of her upbringing."[76] The writing of *Memoirs of a Dutiful Daughter* was, in his opinion, a way of working some of these problems out of her system. He dismisses speculation about how fair a portrait of Françoise and Georges de Beauvoir can be found in this volume, insisting that "the real significance of the book is that it presents her own view of her childhood in a coherent and powerful form."[77]

Mary Evans underlines the atmosphere "of warmth and physical delight, of the softness of her mother's body" conveyed in the early pages of Beauvoir's memoirs.[78] She describes Françoise de Beauvoir as "the traditional martyred wife who maintains her own values and her own integrity by the passive rejection of the standards of the male world and by the elevation of spiritual values,"[79] the epitome of the suppressed, long-suffering woman so actively rejected by contemporary feminists. It is in the relative autonomy possessed by Georges de Beauvoir and denied to his wife that Evans seeks an explanation for the attraction the male world held for the adolescent Simone.

Evans suggests that Zaza's untimely death made Simone de Beauvoir realize that "values can be life-and-death matters, particularly when the values in question are associated with emotionally powerful figures."[80] The "emotionally powerful figure" in question is clearly the imposing and manipulative Madame "Mabille" Lacoin. Examining Beauvoir's relief that she, at least, had quite literally "escaped with her life" from the constraints of family and religious ties, Evans posits that, had Zaza lived, the two young women might nonetheless have lost contact rather quickly: "In the world which [Beauvoir] was entering there was less and less place for those bound by the moral and religious systems that she had come to despise."[81]

In Judith Okely's 1986 study, it is suggested that Simone de Beauvoir, "as a brotherless daughter, ... was treated more like a son and escaped a rigid gender demarcation."[82] Okely credits Georges de Beauvoir's early interest in his older daughter's intellectual development with having provided her with the necessary ammunition to adopt a life-style very different from the one epitomized by the more passive and resigned Françoise de Beauvoir. Analyzing the relationship between the young Simone and her mother, Okely speaks of "the delegation to women of the task of policing women for subordination."[83] She senses a great deal of anger in Beauvoir's depiction of her mother in these early memoirs and states, "In the desire to disassociate herself from the 'bad' or victim mother, she risked simultaneously rejecting the positive aspects of womanhood."[84]

In an article appearing in the special issue of *Yale French Studies* devoted to Simone de Beauvoir, Catherine Portuges treats the first volume of the memoirs as the author's attempt to analyze the pre-Oedipal stage of her development, with its strong attachment to the maternal figure represented by Françoise de Beauvoir. Portuges underlines the maternal role adopted by the young Simone in her interaction with her younger sister "Poupette" and suggests that "it can be argued that a central motivation for writing the Memoirs is an act of reparation to the mother and sister cast aside in favor of the freedom promised in the person of Zaza. . . ."[85]

Renée Winegarten treats *Memoirs of a Dutiful Daughter* as a theatrical presentation of Simone de Beauvoir's struggle toward freedom, one which requires "an obstacle, an opponent, a villain to be challenged, for its drama: the role fulfilled by the bourgeoisie in the person of her parents and others encountered in the course of her early education."[86] Winegarten considers that the major villainess in the spiritual drama reproduced in this first volume of Beauvoir's autobiography was not Françoise de Beauvoir but rather the formidable Madame "Mabille" Lacoin.

A great deal of analysis has thus been focused on the maternal presence in *Memoirs of a Dutiful Daughter*. The degree to which Simone de Beauvoir's relationship with her mother and Zaza "Mabille" Lacoin's anguished battle with hers have caught the attention of almost three decades of critics highlights the effectiveness of this first volume of memoirs in dramatizing a young girl's traumatic struggle to free herself from a symbiotic attachment to the woman who raised her in order to achieve an autonomous identity of her own. Both Simone and Hélène de Beauvoir refer to their mother as *maladroite* (clumsy) in her methods of dealing with them during their adolescence. When asked in an interview why her mother could not simply be proud of the intelligence and accomplishments of her two daughters, Simone de Beauvoir shook her head sadly and remarked, "Oh, no. She just wasn't like that."[87] Hélène de Beauvoir, while reinforcing her sister's description of the difficulties of dealing with a nervous and unhappy mother during their adolescence, nonetheless credited Françoise de Beauvoir with instilling in both of them a sense of discipline which helped her throughout her artistic career.[88] The writing of this first volume of her autobiography was clearly cathartic for Simone de Beauvoir, who was able to set aside the memories and resentments associated with her mother for several years after it was published and to devote her energies to recounting the details of an adult life lived quite independently of the influence of Françoise de Beauvoir.

Independence and a New "Family":
The Prime of Life

The second volume of Simone de Beauvoir's autobiography, which covers her life from 1929 to 1944, shows a significant absence of interaction between the author and her parents. During this period she was indeed the dutiful daughter of the English title of her memoirs, dropping by for lunch or an occasional visit but carefully avoiding serious discussions which might emphasize the conflicts in ideology and value systems that separated her from the bourgeois milieu represented by Françoise and Georges de Beauvoir. Busily establishing her identity as a teacher, a writer, and a human being, she was also making far-reaching decisions about maternal instincts, both biological and psychological, and about the true meaning of the word "family" in her lexicon.

After a scene straight out of a comic operetta in which Beauvoir's parents marched through the Limousin fields in a vain attempt to persuade Jean-Paul Sartre to leave the area and stop compromising the family reputation, the two generations appear to have arrived at an uneasy truce. At age twenty-one, Simone de Beauvoir felt that she had "liquidated" her past and was ready to devote herself unequivocally to her relationship with Sartre.[1] While she remained cordial in dealing with her parents, she was delighted to be free of their domination and control. "I remained on good terms with my parents, but they had lost any hold they once had on me," she remarks.[2] They were horrified when she sold her childhood jewelry in order to finance purchases which seemed more important to her, and distressed by her categorical refusal to participate in family get-togethers. She recalls: "I had dropped almost all of the obligations which bored me: aunts, cousins, childhood friends. I had lunch with my parents rather often: since we avoided quarrels, we had few things to talk about. They knew practically nothing about my life."[3] Although this willingness to discard family members and childhood friends may appear somewhat heartless, it is not unusual for a bright twenty-one-year-old university graduate to withdraw, at least temporarily, from active participation in the social events and reunions of the family from which she is trying to break away. The dual circumstances of living away from home and earning her own paycheck finally bestowed upon Simone de Beauvoir the autonomy she had craved since her adolescence.

As one reads through the 622 pages of *La Force de l'âge,* translated into English as *The Prime of Life,* one finds only passing references to the senior Beauvoirs. They visited her in Marseille while she was teaching there, and her father, still the master of the *beau geste,* took them to the best restaurant in town for bouillabaisse. Her mother accompanied her on sightseeing trips during their stay in Marseille and knitted elegant sweaters for her daughter to wear to class. She visited her every morning at the clinic where she later recuperated from pulmonary congestion, a recurring problem and one to which her death on April 14, 1986 has been partially attributed.

Simone de Beauvoir had a sandwich and a beer with her father the day France declared war on Germany, later stopped by to see her mother, who warned her to get back to her hotel before curfew time. Throughout the war she and her parents commiserated about the Occupation, about the problem of getting enough food to eat. Although it was specifically the Nazis, and not the "Boches" in general, whom Simone detested, she did not argue with her parents' chauvinistic hatred of Germany. "Thanks to this misunderstanding," she relates, "I did not find myself in conflict with my parents."[4] She was no longer above leaving enough things unsaid so that she could maintain polite contact with right-wing parents whose ideas and ideals seemed diametrically opposed to her own.

It was early in the war, while her sister Hélène was caught in Portugal for the duration, that Beauvoir was called upon to cope with her father's death. The two had been at opposite ends of the political and social spectrum since Simone's adolescence. Georges de Beauvoir had never adapted to the changes brought about by World War I and was therefore able to accept his own death with indifference. The author admired the calm way in which he confronted the nothingness which awaited him, a confirmed agnostic, and became his accomplice in assuring that no priest was called to his bedside. Noticeably absent from the author's recollections of Georges de Beauvoir's agony and death is any detailed account of her mother's reaction to the loss. The devout Françoise de Beauvoir surprisingly offered no objection to her husband's request to avoid the traditional visit of the clergy and administration of the last rites of the Catholic church during the final hours of his life. This is, however, the only mention of her involvement with his death, which occurred on July 8, 1941. The author's role in consoling her mother and Françoise de Beauvoir's method of coping with life as a widow are not touched upon in this second volume of the autobiography.

In *Memoirs of a Dutiful Daughter,* Simone de Beauvoir emphasized the happiness of her childhood and her tendency to want to cling to its security as she found herself growing older. Both she and Zaza admitted to a nostalgic longing for this period, which was remembered as one of almost unmitigated bliss. The author's recollections of her early years have turned somewhat sour, however, in *The Prime of Life.* As part of her reason for not wanting to have children, she explains: "I felt so little affinity to my parents that a priori the sons and daughters I might have seemed like strangers to me. I expected either indifference or hostility from them because I had such an aversion to family life."[5] Despite the closeness she once felt to a caring and affectionate mother determined to bring her happiness, the adult Beauvoir has a selective memory which causes her portrayal of family life in the second volume of her autobiography to be both pessimistic and somewhat cynical. She contrasts her casual approach to traveling as an adult, backpack filled and little else to worry about, with her recollections of the monumental task of getting the family from Paris to Uzerche in the summertime: "My mother would grow furious with the station employees, my father would insult the travelers who shared our compartment, and both of them would argue with each other. . . . I had promised myself that my life would be different!"[6] The pleasant memories of the first section of *Memoirs of a Dutiful Daughter* have faded almost into oblivion and what appears to remain is a mixture of embarrassment and resentment.

As a young lycée teacher who genuinely cared for her students, Simone de Beauvoir dreaded thinking about the type of home environment they had. "At the end of the school year," she recalls, "it pained me to think that these girls would return to a household as limited and drab as the one in which I had been suffocating when I was their age."[7] Teaching adolescent girls brought back into focus her own years of rebellion against familial constraints. Like Chantal Plattard in *When Things of the Spirit Come First,* Beauvoir was reluctant to loosen her grip on the students who had been her captive audience during the academic year. Serving *in loco parentis* during the school day, she had experienced the satisfaction of having a hand in molding and shaping the minds and attitudes of a younger generation of scholars, a satisfaction felt by many new teachers.

The messages encouraging family life, virtue, and religion broadcast by Maréchal Pétain from Vichy during the Occupation filled Beauvoir with disgust. "I recognized that warmed-over stupidity that had darkened my childhood. It was now descending officially on the entire country," she recollects.[8] Such a statement provides resounding evidence of the hostility which had been building up inside the author since her adolescence and which is now brutally articulated as she completes the first half-century of her life. She rails against her parents' stupidity, sees even her childhood years as dark and bleak. Almost every vestige of the warm feelings Beauvoir once had toward her early years seems to have been cast aside and discarded during this period of her life. Even the beloved summer homes at Meyrignac and La Grillère had lost their charm, overrun as they now were by her cousin Jeanne's many children and by statues of the Virgin amidst the trees. "I didn't find much of the past there," she confesses.[9] A moment had arrived for Simone de Beauvoir as for most adults when childhood had become little more than a faintly glowing memory and it was clearly time to move on. For writers, capturing the past on paper is often a liberating gesture which paves the way for turning one's attention more fully toward the challenges of the present and the future. This was certainly the case for Beauvoir as she "liquidated" her past, year by year, by sharing it with her readers.

Is an unmarried woman ever considered a bonafide adult by society? This is a question which Simone de Beauvoir had to ask herself at this critical period of her life. Frantic at the thought of being separated from Jean-Paul Sartre while he would be teaching in Le Havre and she in Marseille, she had to decide how to respond to his suggestion that they marry in order to be able to request a double assignment in the same geographical area. She assures the reader that she never seriously considered Sartre's proposal, knowing that maintaining independence from family obligations was essential to the happiness of both of them. The only possible justification for marriage, in her eyes, would be a desire to have children, a desire she insists that neither she nor Sartre ever felt.

Knowing that she has often been criticized for her categorical rejection of motherhood, Beauvoir explains her position in detail in *The Prime of Life*. She begins by assuring her reader that she has never had anything against maternity but has simply not seen it as a personal option for her. She analyzes the desire to produce in one's offspring a replica of oneself and protests that neither she nor Sartre ever felt any such need: "He was sufficient unto himself. He was all I needed. And I was sufficient unto myself," she proclaims.[10] In this passage, the omission of any claim that she was all Sartre needed is a significant one.

The author goes on to explain that she did not consider motherhood compatible with her career as a writer, noting that one must have both time and freedom in order to write. "In order to risk compromising [my time and my freedom]," she admits, "a child would have had to represent in my eyes an accomplishment as essential as a creative work. Such was not the case."[11] Here she repeats the strong stand she took many years earlier in her argument with Zaza "Mabille" Lacoin about the relative merits of producing children and of producing works of art. Although she launched this diatribe with the assertion that she was not categorically opposed to motherhood, her statement that "having children is a way of adding uselessly to the number of human beings on earth, without justification" seems to contradict that disclaimer.[12] Once again we find the idea of what is useful a dominant one in Beauvoir's reasoning. Whereas adding to the number of books on library and bookstore shelves seems eminently justifiable to her, adding to the number of human beings on earth does not. She will repeat this line of reasoning when talking with American feminist Betty Friedan in an interview to be discussed in chapter 15.

Beauvoir concludes this presentation of her reasons for choosing not to have children by suggesting that some women have a natural inclination to become mothers while others do not. "I didn't feel I was refusing maternity. It wasn't my lot. By remaining childless, I was fulfilling my natural condition."[13] In this carefully thought-out explanation, the author also assures the reader that the decision to remain childless is one which she has never regretted.

Having liquidated her own past and teamed up with Sartre, whose father died when he was an infant and whose life was never really controlled by either his mother or the Schweitzer grandparents in whose home he grew up, Beauvoir felt that both of them were "without a family" and therefore open to all the possibilities life had to offer.[14] Not only did they become "family" to each other, without any of the binding legal ties which were a part of the lives of most of their contemporaries, but they also began to expand their social circle to include some of their students and "disciples." In interpreting this phenomenon, Beauvoir issues a note of caution:

> People will probably say that Sartre was a surrogate father for me, Olga a surrogate child. Those who adhere to this theory never recognize the existence of adult relationships. They are not acquainted with the dialectic which transforms emotional relationships . . . from childhood days right up to the moment of maturity.[15]

It is certainly true that not every relationship between unmarried people can be accurately assigned a slot in a surrogate family. Differences in age and the assumption of a nurturing role do however suggest a pattern which replaces the more traditional responsibilities taken on by a majority of young adults in their twenties and thirties.

Beauvoir and Sartre enjoyed associating with younger people both because this made their lives more exciting and because they were rebelling against the inevitable maturity and loss of youthful status society wanted to impose upon them as they turned thirty. Because they were neither married nor parents of small children, they were eminently available to follow through on any emotional attachments which seemed attractive to them. These human attachments are generally waiting in the wings for almost everyone and it is indeed the availability of time and energy which determines whether or not they will develop into some sort of permanent association. A pervasive curiosity about ideas, places, and people made Sartre and Beauvoir exceptionally open to exploring associations which would take them beyond the confines of the exclusive unit they had at first formed as a couple.

Those who have done any significant amount of teaching will undoubtedly agree that there is often a sense of surrogate parenthood involved in a dedicated teacher's relationship to his or her students. A teacher sees these young people on a daily basis, can sometimes discuss certain issues with them more openly than their own parents can, and feels responsible for guiding their development toward maturity. Each of these nuances of feeling was experienced by Simone de Beauvoir during her career as a lycée teacher, first in Marseille, then in Rouen, and finally in Paris. She was particularly delighted to be teaching a subject, philosophy, which her students had never encountered before: "It was up to me to teach them everything. This idea intrigued me.... I rejoiced almost as much at their progress as if I had made it myself."[16] She much preferred the company of her more intelligent students to that of some of her older colleagues, most of whom she found far too rigid in their ways.

Both Beauvoir and Sartre tried to escape from what they considered the "pallor" of adulthood by plunging into a kind of youth cult. The author realized, however, the somewhat ambivalent position they were in as lycée teachers: "What were we exactly? No husband, no children, no home, no social veneer, and twenty-six years old. At that age, one wants to be able to influence the world."[17] In this passage the author acknowledges that society does indeed tend to refuse credibility to the marginal people who do not fit into the molds it has set out for them. Being without visible family connections definitely labeled one as marginal during the 1930s.

One of Beauvoir's ways of trying to influence the world was through her total frankness with her students about her ideas on family life and middle-class society. Understandably, it did not endear her to the parents or the school authorities when she proclaimed that women should not be conditioned to seek justification for their existence solely through producing children. Her opposition to Maréchal Pétain's family-oriented politics brought her to the attention of a conservative group with the intriguing name of "Departmental Commission on Childbearing and the Protection of Childhood."[18] She was nonetheless intrepid in her determination to present to her students a point of view very different from the one they were hearing at home.

It was in her philosophy class in Rouen that Beauvoir first encountered the precocious Olga Kosakievicz. Both she and Sartre were attracted to Olga's total lack of inhibition, just as the young Simone was drawn to Zaza's non-conformity. Free to form any associations which appealed to them, they decided to experiment with a trio. Beauvoir was nine years older than Olga and ready to step into her life at a moment when the adolescent had reached an impasse in her relationship with her parents, parents who, having formerly encouraged Olga to think for herself and avoid conformity, had suddenly decided that they wanted their daughter to lead a more normal existence:

> The classic conflict between an adolescent and her parents was particularly painful for Olga because hers suddenly incarnated everything they had taught her to condemn: the moral order, chauvinism, established customs, and that serious side of adulthood which Olga was horrified to see bearing down on her. She was unhappy with herself for having disappointed them, because their esteem had always been of enormous importance to her. But she deeply resented their about-face, their defection. . . .[19]

Olga was therefore emotionally available, as was Beauvoir, who was touched by the extent to which Olga seemed to need her.

The trio at first appeared to be united in complete harmony, in a total sharing of values. "Together we hated Sunday crowds, proper ladies and gentlemen, the provinces, families, children, and all humanisms," the author informs us.[20] In this passage there are many echoes of Jean-Paul Sartre's sardonic depiction of Bouville in *Nausea:* the mechanical tipping of the hat in the columns of provincials out for their obligatory Sunday walk, the pompous town fathers pictured in the official portraits adorning Bouville's museum, the sentimental humanism of the homosexual Autodidacte. One also hears echoes of André Gide's cry of rebellion, "Families, I hate you."[21] On these points the members of the trio undoubtedly did think as one.

In retrospect, however, Simone de Beauvoir realizes the extent to which she and Sartre were in fact acting out parental roles with Olga:

"Her role was nonetheless that of a child dealing with a couple of adults united by an unshakable complicity.... We had not established real equality with her, but had rather annexed her."[22] *The Prime of Life* indicates that Beauvoir was fond enough of Olga to be willing to sacrifice some of her hard-earned freedom, a freedom she was unwilling to give up to childbearing and rearing, in order to take the young girl under her wing and thereby persuade her parents to allow her to live away from home. She knows, again with the benefit of hindsight, that both she and Sartre were depending on Olga to restore their lost youth. "With her impetuous manner, her extremism, Olga was a stunning incarnation of youthfulness," she asserts.[23] Olga was also a living question mark, constantly challenging the dedication to hard work, structure, and culture which had been the essence of Beauvoir's life.

The trio was a noble experiment that failed. It died a natural death when Olga made it a four-way relationship by including Sartre's former student, Jacques-Laurent Bost, in the "family" circle. Beauvoir explains that she set aside the myth she and Sartre had created of Olga when she penned the dramatic ending for her novel *She Came to Stay:* "By killing Olga on paper, I liquidated the irritations, the resentment, that I might have felt toward her. I purified our friendship of all the bad memories that were mingled with the good ones."[24] Olga Kosakievicz Bost is said to have had ambivalent feelings about this fictional assassination she underwent in her former lycée teacher's first published novel. She nonetheless remained a member of the Beauvoir- Sartre clan until her death in 1985.

Olga is just one of a number of young people who became a part of Beauvoir and Sartre's inner circle of friends. The author admits to her willingness to put up with certain unpleasant traits as long as the person involved had something to contribute to her life. This was the case with her student Nathalie Sorokine, referred to as Lise in the autobiography. Lise lay in wait as Beauvoir came out of her hotel or out of class each day and insisted on taking up more time than Beauvoir would have liked to give to her. Nonetheless, the author admits, "In my eyes, her vitality, her talents far outweighed the things she did to annoy me."[25] When Lise began to live with the young Spanish poet Bourla, Beauvoir obligingly tucked them both into bed each night, thereby playing the maternal role she assigned to Anne Dubreuilh in *The Mandarins*.

As the war dragged on, food became increasingly scarce. Beauvoir decided to find a hotel room with a kitchen. She had always objected to the enormous amount of time most women spent preparing food, yet was now ready to attack the problem of feeding "the family" as diligently as she worked at her writing, doing everything she could to keep them all as well nourished as possible. It was now essentially Olga and her sister Wanda, Jacques-Laurent Bost, Lise, and Bourla whom she and Sartre considered "family." Madame "Lemaire" Morel, with her financial resources and her country home, became a sort of surrogate mother to this Parisian family, sending whatever food she could, some of it scarcely edible by the time it reached Beauvoir. In introducing the reader to Madame Lemaire, Beauvoir recounts her very liberal, male-oriented upbringing, her amazement at the strange rules of polite society which she found in Paris, and her conscious choice to devote herself to others after her husband decided to live like an invalid. "Madame Lemaire devoted herself to her husband, her children, elderly relatives, various down-and-outers. She had given up living her own life," Beauvoir recounts.[26] This is perhaps one of the first "relative beings" the author encountered as an adult, one for whom she appears to have felt great affection and respect.

As we have seen, the adolescent Simone was horrified when Zaza suggested that bringing children into the world was just as valid an endeavor as producing a work of art. It was now incumbent upon Beauvoir to produce the books which she felt would justify her existence. Her father, impatient with her rejection of solid bourgeois values, had evidently heard her make the above comparison. Somewhat crudely, he told relatives and friends, "If she has something in her belly, let her bring it forth!"[27]

One of the gnawing embryos which had been developing for almost a decade within Beauvoir was the tragic story of Zaza "Mabille" Lacoin. Several early attempts at transforming that tale into fiction failed because the author substituted an unsympathetic husband for a domineering mother. "A mother cherished and revered from the time one is a baby can maintain a terrible hold on a child, even if that child deplores the narrowness of her ideas and her abuses of authority," Beauvoir notes in this second volume of her autobiography.[28] This conviction led her to create the devastating Madame Vignon of *When Things of the Spirit Come First*. Husbands can sometimes be taken to task as obstacles preventing their wives from realizing their full potential, but their influence begins only after most women have reached adulthood. The stranglehold mothers have on their offspring is, in the author's opinion, much more dangerous because it begins the moment the child sees the light of day and is the dominant influence throughout the most formative years of its life. "Give me a child until (s)he is seven, and (s)he is mine forever," admonishes an old adage. It is not until one reads some of

Beauvoir's later works that one realizes the extent to which this statement applies to her relationship with her own mother every bit as much as it does to Zaza and Madame "Mabille" Lacoin.

Although several of the author's early attempts at fiction remained in drawers and the collection of stories originally entitled *La Primauté du spirituel* was rejected for publication, only to be reconsidered many decades later, the appearance of *She Came to Stay* and the positive recognition that it received did indeed justify Simone de Beauvoir's claim to being a writer, just as the birth of a child confers not only motherhood but maturity upon a woman in the eyes of society. The publication of this first novel, which occurred after the death of the father who appears to have scoffed at her writing ambitions, gave her a clear sense of identity, a confidence in her ability to stake out a place for herself in the literary world. Her creativity was no longer in question and even her mother was proud to have a daughter who could earn money by writing books.

Until the beginning of World War II, Simone de Beauvoir felt that hers was a privileged existence. She realized the value of being capable of earning her own living. "The curse which weighs heavily on most women, dependence, was spared me. Earning one's living is not a goal in itself; but it is the only way to attain a solid sense of one's autonomy," she proclaims.[29] Beauvoir was enjoying her teaching, had the time she needed to continue writing, and was completely comfortable interacting on a daily basis with those she had chosen as her new "family." Speaking of herself and Sartre, she remarks, "Not only were we protected from need, like all bourgeois, and from insecurity, like all civil servants, but we had no children, no family, no responsibilities: we were elves."[30] This passage provides an amusingly accurate image of the detached life-style of those in their mid-twenties and early thirties who have avoided becoming tied down to family commitments. They are the Peter Pans who never really want to grow up.

Even the war and the concomitant loss of young lives did not shake the author's conviction that she had chosen the right path for herself, one along which she could find both self-fulfillment and a way of serving others. She was already looking toward the future as she answered criticisms of the points of view she presented in her classes by accusing these parents of "supporting Hitler's doctrines when they demand that women be confined to the home."[31] She read with interest of an Institute of Sexology founded by a Dr. Hirshfeld in Berlin which insisted that "procreation in particular should not be passively accepted but rather the result of lucid consent."[32] Simone de Beauvoir's breaking away from the influence of her middle-class upbringing seemed to be complete as she rejoiced with her friends on Liberation Day and looked ahead to the role that she as an intellectual and a writer could play in creating a better future for everyone. Her concerns would soon expand to encompass not only Sartre and their young friends but an entire world of fellow human beings.

Critical Reaction

Critical comment on the second volume of Beauvoir's autobiography has generally highlighted the details of the development of the relationship between the author and Sartre and the accurate picture of life in occupied France which it provides. Annie-Claire Jaccard, however, focuses one of her chapters on the invention of the trio fictionalized in *She Came to Stay* and later elaborated upon in *The Prime of Life*. She analyzes the need for a couple closed in on itself and threatened with psychological suffocation to seek a breath of fresh air in the presence of a third individual. "Thanks to the trio," she states, "the human being thinks he can approach the exterior world and enter into contact with it while remaining all the while within his protective shell."[33] The inclusion of a third person in the closed circle originally established by the couple is, in Jaccard's opinion, still another manifestation of the human need to reach out toward other people. Much of what Jaccard discusses here in ontological terms can be applied equally as well to the traditional family and its thrust toward extending its influence beyond the couple into the future represented by the next generation.

For Anne-Marie Lasocki, Simone de Beauvoir's autobiographical works contain a recurrent warning against the individual tendency to want to possess and dominate another human being. Pointing out the catastrophic nature of both domination and self-sacrifice in interaction among individuals, Lasocki refers to "political or familial enslavement in social relationships"[34] as an extreme form of domination and sees in martyred devotion to another human being a veiled means of manipulation. Both of these extremes can be found reflected in the maternal monsters and maternal martyrs who people Beauvoir's fictional works and can help explain why, during the period reflected in *The Prime of Life,* the author did everything she could to distance herself from traditional family relationships.

Terry Keefe reinforces the impression conveyed earlier in this chapter of the almost total absence of Beauvoir's biological family from the pages of *The Prime of Life*. "Having broken away from her family, she barely mentions her mother now, and only one paragraph is devoted to her father's death," he notes.[35] The motherhood theme is thus hardly considered a prominent one in this second volume of the autobiography. During the years between her twenty-first and her thirty-sixth birthdays, Simone de Beauvoir was giving birth not to children but to the first of her published works, maintaining a precarious balance in her relationship with her parents and particularly with her mother, and forging new "family" ties for herself, many of which were to last for a lifetime.

10

Expanding Horizons: *Force of Circumstance*

The third volume of Simone de Beauvoir's autobiography covers the period from 1944 to 1963. Between her mid-thirties and her mid-fifties, the author expanded her concerns beyond her "family" of close friends to encompass the poor, the underprivileged, the tortured people of the world. In the 900 pages of these memoirs, one finds scant mention of Beauvoir's own mother, occasional references to Sartre's, and scattered information about individuals in whose lives the author has become involved. *La Force des choses,* translated into English as *Force of Circumstance,* focuses rather upon the writer's espousal of political and humanitarian causes, on her travels through such countries as Cuba and Brazil, and on the degree to which she feels drawn to the younger generation of intellectuals who reciprocally look to her for moral leadership.

Throughout the many chapters of *Force of Circumstance,* there are only two passages in which Françoise de Beauvoir is mentioned. The first is a journal entry for May 1, 1946, indicating that Beauvoir had lunch on that day with her mother, who was reading Arthur Koestler's *Darkness at Noon.* The second reference appears in the much discussed Epilogue at the end of this third volume of memoirs and is part of an impassioned reaction to critics who suggest that Simone de Beauvoir would have been just as influenced by any man she happened to meet when she was twenty as she was by Jean-Paul Sartre and his ideas: "I find once again, fifty years later, my father's old idea: A woman is what her husband makes of her. He was sorely mistaken. He did not alter a single hair on the head of that pious young woman molded by the nuns of her convent school."[1] This is an understated and touching tribute to the solidity of Madame de Beauvoir's convictions. Although her deep-rooted Catholicism created an almost insurmountable gap in communication between her and her daughter, Françoise de Beauvoir is here accepted by the mature Simone as an individual who commands respect for the strength with which she resisted becoming a pale reflection of her husband's ideas.

After the death of her second husband, Jean-Paul Sartre's mother, Madame Mancy, played a substantial role in the daily lives of both Beauvoir and Sartre, primarily because the latter chose to share an apartment with her at 42, rue Bonaparte, in 1946. The reader glimpses her in the background, making donuts for a *Temps Modernes* staff meeting, listening to music, reacting to a false report that her son has died in an automobile accident, fleeing from terrorists threatening to blow up Sartre's apartment because of his political stand during the Algerian crisis. The passing references to Madame Mancy suggest a sense of closeness and affection which existed between her and Simone de Beauvoir as they came to know one another better. Their relationship will be discussed in considerably more detail in the fourth volume of Beauvoir's autobiography, *All Said and Done*.

The fact that Sartre agreed to comply with his mother's wishes and share an apartment with her indicates that she in no way represented the threat to his autonomy that Françoise de Beauvoir might have if she had ever shared living quarters with her older daughter after the latter became an adult. In *A Very Easy Death*, Simone de Beauvoir recalls a recurrent dream to which we have referred previously in which her mother and Sartre somehow blend into one androgynous individual:

> She often played the essential role in [my dreams]. She blended with Sartre. We were happy together, she and I. And then the dream turned into a nightmare. Why was I living with her again? How had I fallen into her clutches once again? Our former relationship therefore lived on in me in its double image: a dependence both cherished and detested.[2]

Beauvoir apparently never outgrew the psychological ambivalence she felt toward her mother. The relative lack of tension between Sartre and Madame Mancy may be partially explained by the fact that her relationship to him seemed more like that of an older sister as the young "Poulou" was growing up in his Schweitzer grandparents' home after the death of his father.

It is of interest that Simone's younger sister Hélène and her husband, Lionel de Roulet, actually lived with Françoise de Beauvoir in her Paris apartment for a year when they returned from a diplomatic assignment in Milan.[3] Hélène de Beauvoir does not mention any particular problems associated with this arrangement in her book of reminiscences. She simply indicates that her mother was appalled when she and her husband arrived at her doorstep at five in the morning with a Siamese cat in tow. Françoise de Beauvoir eventually became comfortable sharing her studio apartment with Hélène and her husband and with the first pet she had ever harbored in her own home.

As a younger sibling, Hélène apparently felt she had less to prove than did her formidable and more uncompromising older sister and was therefore able to relate to her mother with considerably less strain in her adult years. When asked in a 1986 interview about the difference in the rapport she and her sister were able to establish with their mother in their mature years, Hélène explained:

> Simone intimidated her. I didn't intimidate her. . . . Simone was very careful but she had a hard time communicating with *maman*. I managed to talk to her. I found it easier to make small talk, to talk woman-to-woman, if you will. I talked to her about her friends, about the things she did each day. She sensed that Simone wasn't interested in those things. She was a little afraid of Simone's intellectual superiority. She was afraid Simone might judge her harshly.[4]

Simone found it expedient to limit her conversation to neutral topics and to maintain a certain emotional distance from her mother, whom she did indeed judge to be less intelligent than she. She admitted this very candidly in a 1985 interview:

> One never likes to feel that someone thinks herself more intelligent than you are. And this is indeed what I thought about my mother. She did *not* seem intelligent to me. Not only was she very Catholic, but she did not seem intelligent because of her ways of doing things . . . she must have sensed that I felt this way, and she was not happy about it. That is the main reason she didn't want my sister to be an intellectual. . . . My sister wanted to study for an *agrégation* . . . and my mother would not allow it.[5]

Throughout the years covered by *Force of Circumstance*, the author thus continued to play the role of a dutiful daughter properly attentive but deliberately detached from the intricacies of her mother's day-to-day routine.

During their years of lycée teaching, both Beauvoir and Sartre developed close ties to certain of their students. Olga and Jacques-Laurent Bost continued to belong to their circle of intimate friends and Beauvoir kept a maternal eye on Olga's battle against tuberculosis during the many months when Olga was confined to a sanitarium. The catharsis involved in writing *She Came to Stay* indeed seemed to have purified their relationship of all former resentment. This was not the case, however, for Nathalie Sorokine, the "Lise" who served as a model for Nadine Dubreuilh in *The Mandarins*. This former student, rebelling against a domineering mother, was always frustrated by Beauvoir's unwillingness to devote more of herself and her time to her. It is she who compared Beauvoir to a clock in a refrigerator, complaining about her single-minded devotion to her writing career. The young woman rightfully assumed that the author's books were rivals for her attention: "She still resented the fact that I had sacrificed her to my work and took out this resentment on what I was writing."[6] Those books were indeed Simone de Beauvoir's surrogate children and vied fiercely with anyone who attempted to usurp their role in her life. Thus Lise's childish bid for attention took the form of denigrating the offspring of Beauvoir's mind, who competed all too successfully for her time and energy.

Simone de Beauvoir saw in "Lise" a tendency of which she had become aware in many women, the effort to compensate for an unhappy childhood by attempting to provide perfect mothering for a new generation. For a young woman who had always had difficulty interacting with others, the prospects for success in such an undertaking were rather discouraging. "She had hoped to make up for the sadness of her early years by becoming a mother," Beauvoir informs us, "but this sadness had prepared her inadequately for nurturing a little girl with whom she identified too much and too little."[7] The relationship between the author and her former student became more distant, both literally and figuratively, once Lise settled in America, and was eventually limited to an exchange of Christmas cards. Neither did Beauvoir prove to be the surrogate mother whose affection and approval Lise had been seeking nor did motherhood provide this young woman with the panacea of emotional fulfillment she had hoped it might bring.

"You remind me of my mother," a woman in her thirties told Simone de Beauvoir one day.[8] And indeed, the author of *The Second Sex,* the recipient of the Goncourt Prize for *The Mandarins,* had become a figure of international stature, the undisputed "mother" of the women's movement. She listened carefully to the women who came to talk to her about their problems, read all of her mail, and responded conscientiously. She dismissed male critics who claimed she had no right to speak about motherhood because she herself had never had a child, pointing out succinctly that they too had never given birth. She openly denied having undermined the value of maternal instincts: "I have supposedly refused to grant any validity to maternal instincts and to love: that is not the case. I have asked women to face these feelings truthfully and freely, rather than use them as excuses...."[9] Beauvoir is here raising an issue which is critical for women brought up in a society which hints that one is not really a woman unless one has had a child. Until recent years, many women succumbed to this pressure, resigning themselves to their roles as wives and mothers and using these roles as a convenient excuse for avoiding putting forth the effort necessary to make full use of their creative talents.

Simone de Beauvoir was a firm believer in treating motherhood as one of several options available to young women. She therefore did not hesitate to join in the battle to make contraceptives and abortion available to women of all social classes. She participated in a press conference promoting "happy maternity,"[10] willingly wrote a short preface for Madame Weil-Hallé's book on family planning. Thirty-five years after Beauvoir's frank discussion of these issues in *The Second Sex,* United States Democratic Vice-Presidential candidate Geraldine Ferraro was being asked how she could reconcile her Catholic faith with her pro-abortion stand. In a country with a predominantly Roman Catholic heritage, it is little wonder that Beauvoir was involved in an uphill battle all the way on the issues of contraceptives and abortion.

Without having biological children of their own, Sartre and Beauvoir remained in close contact with the young intellectuals of the postwar era: "To be twenty or twenty-five in September 1944 seemed an incredible bit of luck. All sorts of possibilities were opening up. . . . The gaiety of the young people fortified my own. When I was with them, I was their age. . . ."[11] She was happy to set aside time to speak with students who knew her work and Sartre's well, eager "to learn what young people are thinking, what they know, what they want, how they live."[12] As aging and eventual death began to haunt her, however, Beauvoir developed a certain ambivalence toward these young people in whose company she had always taken such pleasure:

> The future is in their hands and if I recognize my values in theirs, it seems to me that my life will be prolonged beyond my grave. I enjoy their company. However, the comfort they bring me is suspect. By perpetuating this world, they are stealing it away from me. . . . What a superiority it is to be alive![13]

This passage echoes Anne Dubreuilh's ambivalent feelings toward her baby granddaughter in *The Mandarins.* One of the psychological problems of motherhood is the gradual recognition that as a woman's children grow older and more independent, she comes progressively closer to extinction. Ever since her loss of faith at age fifteen, Simone de Beauvoir was haunted by the nothingness she was sure awaited her at the moment of her death. Valuing every moment of life as she did, it is no wonder that she harbored a certain resentment toward those members of a younger generation who would live on after she was gone.

Simone de Beauvoir was deeply touched by the welcome accorded her by leftist students to whom she lectured about the novel, caught up in the youthful enthusiasm of the demonstrations for Algerian independence. "I ached to be young," she confesses.[14] In the camaraderie of these massive demonstrations, the author found the same exhilaration she experienced during the days of the Liberation, the warmth and solidarity of becoming once again a member of the human family after the feelings of horror and guilt aroused by case histories of torture and mutilation in Algeria had temporarily caused her to withdraw into morose isolation.

Beauvoir claims that with the publication of *Memoirs of a Dutiful Daughter* she detached herself from her early years. In *Force of Circumstance* she contrasts her point of view with that of philosopher and former classmate Maurice Merleau-Ponty, revealing: "Our devout bourgeois upbringing created a bond between us; but we reacted to it in different ways. He was still nostalgic about this lost paradise. I wasn't. He was comfortable with older people, on the defensive with the young, whom I far preferred to the old."[15] Here is the Jean Pradelle of *Memoirs of a Dutiful Daughter* whom Beauvoir held partially responsible for Zaza's death precisely because his sense of obligation to his mother and perhaps to his Catholic religion had appeared to outweigh his commitment to Zaza's happiness. Intent upon liquidating her own past, the author continued to look to a younger generation to lead the way into the future and was highly critical of anyone who did not do likewise. She felt great empathy for the Irish wife of Italian author Ignazio Silone because she had had a childhood "still more suffocating than my own."[16] The French adjective *étouffant* (suffocating) reappears again and again as the writer looks back on her years of living under the parental roof, a period during which she apparently found the atmosphere at home literally and figuratively unbreathable.

Simone de Beauvoir was soon to realize, however, as she coped with her mother's terminal illness and death, that her nostalgia for the lost paradise of childhood security had not completely disappeared. Even in *Force of Circumstance* the smell of haystacks, a gurgling fountain, other sensual pleasures afforded by nature suddenly evoke happy memories of earlier years. Eighteen months of her adulthood were devoted to bringing the little girl who once delighted in such phenomena back to life in *Memoirs of a Dutiful Daughter*. As cathartic as the writing of the first volume of her autobiography may have been for the author, she was still keenly aware of the impact childhood has on each individual. "One's early years carry a lot of weight, a lot of resistance," she asserts.[17]

When Beauvoir was taken by Simone Berriau to visit Colette in the late 1940s, she described the famous writer as "a formidable Mother-

Goddess."[18] This is a role Beauvoir herself soon assumed for a whole new generation of women. A young American student brought her an offering of eighteen volumes of her personal journal and sought both her presence and her advice. With the cooperation of Albert Camus, Beauvoir facilitated the publication of Violette Leduc's first book. She met with politically committed women who were willing to get up several hours earlier than usual to help put up posters and expressed her admiration for their ability to juggle housework, child care, and jobs. She exchanged ideas with writer-gynecologist-mother Han Suyin. Of lawyer Gisèle Halimi, she says, "She has children and a career that must be hard on the nerves and the heart: still another of these superactive young women to whom I take off my hat."[19] Convinced of the appropriateness of her own total dedication to her writing career, Beauvoir nonetheless watched with great interest as the options for women began to open up and was quick to appreciate the validity of the choices made by other women on their way to personal fulfillment.

Much critical ink has been expended analyzing the final lines of the Epilogue to *Force of Circumstance*. The concluding paragraph begins with a frank admission of Beauvoir's horror of death, of the nothingness it represents for her. Considering the ensemble of her work, she penned the words read by Claude Lanzmann at her funeral: "At best, if my work is read, the reader will think, 'She's really seen a lot!'"[20] In her opinion, however, her books would be no more effective than any children she might have produced in bringing her experiences back to life. In a moment of extreme pessimism, she was unwilling to grant that any individual could have a particular impact on the world he or she leaves behind after death. What then must one create, to what must one give birth, in order to continue to influence future generations? "If she had at least enriched the earth; if she had created ... what? a hill? a rocket? But she hadn't. Nothing will have taken place," she muses.[21] She remembers a time when, like Marguerite Drouffe in *When Things of the Spirit Come First*, she contemplated the future which lay before her, "that gold mine at my feet, a whole life to live." [22] The promises that future held had been kept, she admits, yet she nonetheless felt cheated and discouraged. "Looking incredulously at that credulous adolescent, I am stupefied to realize to what extent I have been duped," she reveals in the concluding sentence of this section of the autobiography.[23]

Despite her success as a writer, the pleasure she took in her ongoing association with Jean-Paul Sartre, the knowledge and understanding she acquired through a wide variety of friends and extensive travels, Simone de Beauvoir reached her fifty-fifth year with a sense of emptiness and depression. Did she blame this perhaps on the bourgeois ethic she was taught at her mother's knee which suggested that if one works hard and maintains one's integrity all will be well with the world? Neither producing nine children, as did Zaza's mother, nor producing nine books, as the author had done by the time she wrote the concluding words of *Force of Circumstance,* led to the sense of self-justification, satisfaction, and fulfillment which she had been seeking since her adolescent days.

Critical Reaction

For Francis Jeanson, the first three volumes of Beauvoir's autobiography represent a coming of age, a transcendance of "an adolescent attitude (rather typical of the petty bourgeoisie) characterized by extreme reserve toward her closest friends and absolute secrecy concerning her own dialogue with herself."[24] This reserve is, of course, something she learned in the cradle from her convent-reared and socially timid young mother. The difficulty that she had overcoming it is apparent in her sensitivity to the aforementioned images of the white kid gloves and the clock in the refrigerator. However much she prided herself on having left her bourgeois upbringing behind her, the caution with which Françoise de Beauvoir approached any display of emotions or feelings remained an integral part of her older daughter's personality throughout her life. Only on paper, in Jeanson's opinion, did she "choose to bare herself before our eyes, much more than any strip-teaser will ever do."[25]

Madeleine Descubes contrasts the relative ease with which Beauvoir appears to have left her individual past behind her with the haunting torment of the collective past she describes in *Force of Circumstance.*[26] Anne-Marie Lasocki notes, on the other hand, that once Beauvoir had worked her way on paper through the bitterness of her adolescent memories, she returned again and again in her autobiography to her recognition of the extent to which her early childhood years had contributed to her penchant for happiness and optimism. In an extremely perceptive use of quotations from *Force of Circumstance,* she underlines the degree to which the author's affair with Claude Lanzmann represented a rebirth, a return to the youthful exuberance, joy, and sense of adventure that characterized her early years at her mother's side.[27]

In spite of the pessimistic tone of the Epilogue, Simone de Beauvoir appears to have been a woman in full command of her faculties, sure of her abilities, and confident that she could make use of them to help not only individuals with whom she came into contact but also humanity in general as she completed this book of memoirs covering her life through March 1963. Although she was convinced that she had long since left her childhood far behind, dealing with her mother's terminal illness was suddenly to catapult her back into those early years and into a reassessment of her relationship with Françoise de Beauvoir.

11

Mother and Daughters United: *A Very Easy Death*

In one of her most poignant works, Simone de Beauvoir shares with her readers the experience of watching her seventy-eight-year-old mother succumb to illness and die. The drama of *Une Mort très douce,* translated into English as *A Very Easy Death,* is enacted by three protagonists: the author, her younger sister Hélène, to whom the book is dedicated, and Françoise de Beauvoir. Their reactions are seen through the eyes of Simone de Beauvoir, who finds herself much more embroiled in the emotions of this crisis than she would ever have anticipated. Although she had long felt comfortably detached from the symbiotic relationship she once had with her mother in the early years of her life, Beauvoir could in no way insulate herself from the depths of feeling evoked by this elderly woman's valiant struggle against cancer and mortality. When the battle was over, and lost, she attempted to deal with its impact as she had always dealt with each crisis in her life, committing it to paper and articulating for her readers an experience in which almost all of them would one day participate. The result was a gripping account which Jean-Paul Sartre and several critics have suggested may be her finest work.

The center of attention in this heartfelt tribute is Françoise de Beauvoir, whose fall in her rue Blomet apartment on October 24, 1963, brought the author back from Rome to the gloomy atmosphere of a hospital room. The fall and the subsequent diagnosis of cancer forced Beauvoir to acknowledge her mother's mortality. Until this moment Madame de Beauvoir had been a fixture in her life, taken somewhat for granted and assumed to be there forever. "For me my mother had always existed and I had never seriously considered that I would see her disappear one day, soon. Her end was situated, like her birth, in a mythical time slot."[1] Illness and the stark reality of a hospital room, however, oblige one to reevaluate this comfortable avoidance of thoughts about mortality.

When Jacques Bost telephoned her in Rome to inform her of her mother's accident, the author had a double-edged reaction. She reassured herself that her mother was in excellent shape and would certainly recuperate easily. At the same time, she told herself that her mother was "of an age to die."[2] This reflection may at first glance appear somewhat callous. Is it not, however, primarily a defense mechanism devised to ward off the full impact of the realization that one's parents are indeed not immortal and that once parents die it is their children who achieve the dubious distinction of becoming the older generation? Being "of an age to die" suggests that death is part of the natural order of things. Despite all the philosophical efforts of a Marcus Aurelius or a Montaigne, there are few individuals who can accept mortality with sanguine disinterest, and Simone de Beauvoir was surely not one of them.

Once the writer saw her mother suffering and looking very much her age, she began to admit to herself the effect that this incident had had on her emotions: "I realized that my mother's accident was affecting me a great deal more than I had anticipated. I wasn't quite sure why. It had wrested her out of the framework, the role, the set images in which I had been imprisoning her."[3]

Beauvoir often speaks of the way in which one person can "imprison" another in stereotypical roles, in expectations that have produced an action and reaction syndrome that has continued unquestioned for years. *A Very Easy Death* is the author's attempt to reconstruct the framework which had allowed her to set her mother apart from the main current of her own life and to pull together everything she remembered about Françoise de Beauvoir in as coherent a way as possible.

As the reader examines the portrait of Françoise de Beauvoir presented by her daughter, the words uttered by the former at the time of the publication of *Memoirs of a Dutiful Daughter* echo hauntingly through the text: "Parents don't understand their children, but the reverse is also true. . . ."[4] Since Françoise de Beauvoir revealed so little of herself during her lifetime, we will never know how accurate a picture her daughter was able to paint of her in this short work. As we have seen, Hélène de Beauvoir considers her sister's descriptions of their mother quite authentic but infused with childhood resentments that had never been erased. *A Very Easy Death* is the only detailed account we have of the life of the woman whose influence permeates the writings and the ideas of one of the foremost authors of the twentieth century.

Simone de Beauvoir attributes the insecurity and vulnerability which plagued her mother throughout her life to a childhood virtually devoid of affection. Born and brought up in provincial Verdun, Françoise Brasseur had a passionate and loving nature to which she found her parents essentially unresponsive. Her daughter recalls:

> More than once she complained to me about her mother's lack of warmth. Grandmother, when she was fifty, was a distant and even haughty woman who seldom laughed, gossiped a great deal, and showed *maman* only the most conventional type of affection. Fanatically devoted to her husband, she accorded her children only a minor place in her life.[5]

Indeed, Hélène de Beauvoir has commented that in their family the women were consistently better spouses than mothers. [6] The festering wounds caused by this maternal lack of affection never healed for Françoise de Beauvoir. When, at age fifty-five, she was called upon to cope with her mother's death, she was so overcome by emotion that she was unable to attend the funeral. This death ended forever any hope she may have had of inspiring the sought-after affection in a woman apparently incapable of providing the psychological nurturing which is considered such an integral part of motherhood. As Simone de Beauvoir has recorded earlier in her memoirs, Françoise de Beauvoir was determined to provide her daughters with the emotional support she never received from her own mother, a goal which had both advantages and disadvantages for the Beauvoir sisters as they were growing up.

Whereas she found her mother emotionally detached from all three of her children, the young Françoise was also hurt by her father's obvious preference for her younger sister Lili. Simone de Beauvoir has remarked on several occasions that her sister Hélène had a more difficult childhood than she did. In this book she explains this partially by the physical resemblance between Hélène and their Aunt Lili:

> Until my adolescence, *maman* attributed the highest intellectual and moral qualities to me. She identified with me. She humiliated and underestimated my sister. She was the younger sister, pink-cheeked and blond, and, without realizing it, *maman* took her revenge out on her.[7]

Although Hélène herself does not see a significant physical resemblance between her and her aunt, the position of younger daughter in a family which had hoped to produce a son to carry on the family name created an awkward situation for her which undoubtedly influenced her mother's way of treating her. It is said that those who have not had a positive parental role model have difficulty interacting with their own offspring. With all the good intentions in the world, Françoise de Beauvoir appears to have made her younger daughter's early years less than pleasant, identifying almost exclusively with her brunette older daughter and refusing to recognize Hélène's equally strong intellectual and creative talents.

With her love for both of her parents thus virtually unreciprocated, Françoise de Beauvoir had only bleak memories of her early years. When Simone commented on the pretty costume she was wearing in a photograph taken when she was eight years old, all her mother could remember was how the green dye in the stockings ran and took three days to wash off. "She was ruminating on a past full of bitterness," the author remarks.[8] Beauvoir feels that her failure to communicate effectively with her mother after her adolescent years can be traced directly back to Françoise de Beauvoir's unhappy childhood. In a moving scene that takes place after her mother's death, she looks at family photographs taken when her mother was close to forty and she was eighteen and expresses pity both for the young girl who did not then understand the problems confronting her mother and for the middle-aged matron whose future was closed off and who, in her opinion, never understood anything: "The sadness of our failure, to which I thought I had resigned myself, disheartened me once again. . . . It wasn't in my power to erase the childhood unhappiness which condemned *maman* to make me unhappy and to suffer from doing so."[9] In this passage, Françoise de Beauvoir becomes a tragic figure, a victim of years of patriarchy and of bourgeois tradition which her crusading daughter would eventually challenge and help to transform. The depth of the author's emotion as she thinks back on her relationship with her mother is clearly indicated by her choice of such strong words as "failure," "condemned," and "suffer," while her frustration is evidenced by her sense of lack of "power" to change the unalterable. Thus convinced that the early years of a child's life provide an unshakeable foundation for its future development, Beauvoir had long since formulated firm opinions about the role played by the person who almost inevitably exerts the most important influence during this period, opinions which surfaced in a vast majority of her works.

Simone de Beauvoir relates the story of her mother's life as she has pieced it together from discussions, chance remarks, and anecdotes. It was during her years as a day student in a convent school that the young Françoise Brasseur first developed a modicum of confidence and self-esteem. The Mother Superior of the school became a surrogate mother to this adolescent girl so in need of attention and affection. Encouraged and nurtured for the first time in her young life, Françoise wholeheartedly embraced the Catholic religion in which she had been raised and which seemed incarnated in the sympathetic nuns at her school.

Beauvoir is here careful to establish a psychological rather than a spiritual foundation for her mother's religious faith.

The author relives once again the days following her admission of her loss of faith to her mother: "Our brief discussion about my lack of faith demanded a considerable effort from both of us. It hurt me to see her tears. But I quickly realized that she was crying about her failure without worrying about what was happening to me."[10] This passage reveals a great deal not only about Françoise de Beauvoir but also about her older daughter. Both women found it extremely difficult to confront emotions, to discuss important personal matters in any kind of depth. In this Simone was indeed her mother's daughter. As we have seen in earlier chapters, her realization of her lack of ability to articulate feelings made her particularly sensitive to Nathalie Sorokine's labeling her "a clock in a refrigerator." Simone's early attachment to her mother persisted in her reluctance to make her unhappy, her inability to view her mother's tears without being pained by them. This is indeed an exceptionally painful experience for most people, who remember Mother as the one who comforted *them* and dried *their* tears, hardly as someone even capable of weeping herself.

Is Simone de Beauvoir fair in assuming that her mother was concerned only with her own failure to raise a devout Catholic daughter? We have seen that in her recollection of the same scene recounted in *Memoirs of a Dutiful Daughter* she noted that her mother's immediate response to her confessed loss of faith was "My poor little girl!" This certainly does not indicate a lack of empathy on her part. Françoise de Beauvoir's religious faith was, however, clearly something she did not wish to question. According to her daughter, she simply accepted her husband's agnosticism without ever discussing it with him. She complied with his wishes by not insisting upon his seeing a priest before his death. She evidently felt no direct responsibility for *his* salvation. Simone, on the other hand, was the proud product of her upbringing, the star of the youngest class at the Cours Désir who was honored by being allowed to play the role of the Baby Jesus in the Christmas pageant. If this carefully nurtured daughter had lost her faith, it was one more resounding blow to the self-esteem of a woman who had prided herself on fulfilling her maternal responsibilities impeccably. It is no wonder that she became frantic when her worst suspicions were confirmed, and grasped at prayers, friends, and relatives to provide psychological and moral support. It is this recourse to prayers rather than to direct communication upon which the adult Simone looks back with considerable bitterness:

> We could have come to an understanding if, instead of asking everyone to say prayers for my soul, she had given me a little confidence and sympathy. I know now what kept her from doing that: she had too many things to avenge, too many wounds to dress to be able to put herself in someone else's place.[11]

The author is once again looking to her mother's unhappy childhood for an explanation of an attitude she still remembers with resentment. Like Meursault in Albert Camus's *The Stranger,* the young Simone was outraged at the idea of anyone, even her devout mother, presuming to pray for her soul.

Throughout Françoise de Beauvoir's terminal illness, the two sisters were put on the defensive by friends and relatives who suggested that they were keeping their mother from seeing a priest. Neither did Madame de Beauvoir ask that her confessor be sent for after she found herself too tired to see him the first time he was scheduled to come nor did she make use of the rosary beads and prayer books brought to her by her grandniece. Simone understood and respected her attitude, explaining it in terms of the depth of her religious conviction:

> Religion was the focal point and the very substance of her life . . . . Her abstention convinces me . . . that for her praying was a practice which demanded attention, reflexion, a certain state of grace. She knew what she should have said to God: "Cure me. But may Your will be done. I accept death." She didn't accept it. At this moment of truth, she did not want to say anything insincere. She would not allow herself the right to rebel, however. She said nothing. . . .[12]

This passage represents one of the most moving tributes to her mother that Simone de Beauvoir ever wrote, bearing witness not only to the power of Françoise de Beauvoir's faith and sincerity but also to the enormous effort her daughter made to understand something in which she no longer believed.

Madame de Beauvoir's life centered around her religious faith and her daughters. There is touching evidence that she never abandoned her hope that Simone would one day return to the fold, in letters found after her death from people who attempted to reassure her that her daughters would eventually attain salvation. Both Simone and Hélène recall hearing her comment that, though she of course hoped to go to heaven after she died, she did not want to be there without her daughters. Hélène sums up her dilemma in the following passage:

> Papa, Simone, and I had in her eyes led lives that were not at all acceptable. She refused to think about that, to think about death, about the other world, because, good Lord! would she find Papa there, Papa who was far from being a saint? Would we join her, we who were far from being saints? We who were her whole life.[13]

As they reflected on such considerations, both sisters were trying to understand why their devoutly Catholic mother regularly refused to see a priest or to consider asking for confession and last rites during her terminal illness. Unable to reconcile the demands of her faith with her passionate attachment to life and to her daughters, did Françoise de Beauvoir simply decide in those final weeks of hospitalization that she needed all of her energy to cope with the insults ravaging her body and had none left to devote to the concerns of the spirit?

In this book written after Françoise de Beauvoir's death, her daughter's feelings, both positive and negative, seem much closer to the surface than those expressed in *Memoirs of a Dutiful Daughter*. She relates that at the time of the publication of the first volume of her memoirs she sent her mother a bouquet of flowers and an apology. Thus, even in that earlier book, she sensed that her presentation of Françoise de Beauvoir and of their relationship would upset her mother, and quite probably not only because it represented an invasion of privacy. The fact that her mother could never read and be hurt by the words in *A Very Easy Death* allowed Simone de Beauvoir to use her writing cathartically, just as she had done in exorcising the painful experience of the trio in *She Came to Stay*.

Unlike her own mother, Françoise Brasseur de Beauvoir was a passionate child and a passionate young woman. The author recalls being struck by the sensuality of her mother's appearance as she emerged from her bedroom in the morning. Her older and more experienced husband both aroused her senses and satisfied them for almost a decade. Rather than blaming her father, Beauvoir imputes her mother's frustrations to the unnatural aspect of bourgeois morality and family life: "We are well enough aware that habit kills desire in men. *Maman* had lost the first bloom of youth and he had lost his ardor. To reawaken it, he resorted to professionals...."[14] This analysis raises the question of the double sexual standard applied to men and women. It is somewhat surprising to hear a leading feminist excuse a man's growing indifference to his wife simply because he is a man. Beauvoir goes on to use her mother's case history as an argument against bourgeois marriage:

> Her case would be enough to convince me that bourgeois marriage is an unnatural institution. The wedding ring slipped on her finger had authorized her to know pleasure. Her senses had become demanding. At thirty-five, in the prime of life, she was no longer allowed to satisfy them.[15]

On the one hand, Beauvoir is sympathetic to her mother's plight, understanding the acute sexual frustration involved in sleeping night after night beside a man whom she loves and who seldom touches her. On the other hand, the ill humor which this situation produced was vented on Simone and her sister and colors all of her memories of her adolescence. It is perhaps as difficult for the writer to put herself in her mother's position as it was for her mother to empathize with her older daughter's loss of faith. The issue becomes hopelessly complicated by the fact that the Catholic wedding ceremony leads a devout, innocent young girl to expect eternal devotion and fidelity from her spouse, while European mores tend to question the virility of a man whose sexual experience has been limited to one woman.

Be that as it may, the fact remains that in her mid-thirties Françoise de Beauvoir was essentially left to fend for herself with her daughters, her household chores, and precious little money. Grateful that her husband had never made an issue of the dowry which remained unpaid because of her father's bankruptcy, she said nothing of his nightly outings, of his physical and psychological absence from the family circle. She was hardly reticent and resigned with her daughters, however:

> She rushed headlong into the only outlet available to her: nourishing herself on the young lives in her charge. "I at least have never been selfish, I have lived for others," she told me later. Yes. But also through them. Possessive, domineering, she would have liked to hold us both entirely in the palm of her hand. But it was just at the time when this compensation was something she needed that we began wanting some freedom, some solitude.[16]

This description of Françoise de Beauvoir feeding on the lives of her daughters is a striking metaphor for the vampirelike relationship the author had observed between certain mothers and their children, one which she will later explore in some depth in *The Woman Destroyed*. Once again there is an ambivalence evident in Simone de Beauvoir's recollections of her relationship with her mother. She understands her mother's need to find some acceptable outlet for her pent-up energy while at the same time resenting the inevitable result of this frustration, Françoise's determination to control the lives of her growing daughters. Madame de Beauvoir becomes a perfect example of the type of "relative being" the author has so eloquently cautioned women against becoming in *The Second Sex*, a frustrated human being living through others rather than living a life of her own.

Despite Beauvoir's straightforward declaration that she did not blame her father for the gloominess of their family life during her adolescence, there is indeed a very strong undercurrent of resentment toward Georges de Beauvoir in *A Very Easy Death*. The reader learns that as early as his honeymoon he insisted on going to Nice for the races instead of taking his young bride to the Italian lakes she would have liked to see. He refused to entertain her friends because their husbands bored him. He kept a picture of his most recent mistress on the desk in his den. All of these details help the reader understand what might otherwise seem a callous statement on the author's part, "When my father died, I didn't shed a tear. I had said to my sister, 'It will be the same for *maman* .'"[17] Both because she realized that her father was indifferent to his own death and because she had had virtually nothing in common with him since her early years, Beauvoir was indeed able to sail unscathed through his agony and death. The very existence of this book indicates that her anticipation of being able to do the same for her mother proved to be unfounded. No matter how convinced one is that one has shaken loose from the tentacles of one's family and one's upbringing, the bonds remain, ready to resurface in times of crisis.

The picture of Françoise de Beauvoir painted by her older daughter is essentially one of a woman struggling against herself. Simone describes her as entering adulthood "corseted in the most rigid principles: the social mores of the provinces and the morality of the convent."[18] This tight-fitting corset was one she seldom removed, particularly after being psychologically abandoned by her husband. She justified her loss of interest in clothes and even in cleanliness by a pious disdain of the body. Resignation was not her forte, however. If she could not live a satisfying life of her own, she would try to live through her daughters. Her insistence on being present when they entertained friends, her refusal to allow them to learn to swim or to own bicycles, were all transparent maneuvers aimed at forcing the two girls to include her in everything they did. She was jealous of the friendship which existed between Simone and "Poupette," a jealousy of which they were so painfully aware that even as adults they refrained from telling her about the things they did together. Hélène de Beauvoir provides a perceptive analysis of Françoise de Beauvoir's attitude toward motherhood in her book of reminiscences:

> Nothing had prepared my mother for raising two little girls who could never lead the same kind of existence she did, and in the city of Paris at that. *Maman* had a totally tyrannical concept of maternity: girls must be closely, unconditionally linked to their mother. Her favorite saying, which she had found in a book by Marcel Prévost, was, "A girl has two friends, her mother and her needle." That was the type of principle she taught us.[19]

It is obvious to anyone acquainted with the creative talents of both Hélène and Simone de Beauvoir that those two little girls were not going to remain symbiotically attached to mother and needle for very many years of their lives.

We have seen in *The Blood of Others* the way in which a mother can manipulate adult children by making them feel guilty of neglecting her. Françoise de Beauvoir's first words to Simone when she arrived at the hospital from Rome berated her for not having written for two months. Many years earlier she had accused her older daughter of neglecting her family after she moved out of her parents' home, although she had only moved a short distance away to a building in which her grandmother rented out rooms. Throughout her adult years, Simone had attempted to be a conscientious daughter, dropping by the family apartment for meals or a friendly chat, even inviting her mother to pose with her for the press when she was awarded the Goncourt Prize for *The Mandarins* in 1954. These efforts were commendable, but the sensitive Françoise de Beauvoir was undoubtedly always aware that they represented more of a duty than a pleasure for her older daughter.

Simone de Beauvoir's description of her mother in *A Very Easy Death* contains a mixture of pity and resentment:

> My mother . . . lived in opposition to herself. Rich in appetites, she used all of her energy to repress them and this renunciation made her angry. During her childhood, her body, her heart, her spirit were compressed under a harness of principles and sanctions. She was taught to rein herself in tightly. There was still a woman of blood and fire inside her, but one who was deformed, mutilated, and a stranger to herself.[20]

This image of an animal harnassed and trained to rein itself in is a vivid one, reminiscent of André Gide's *The Immoralist,* whose main character expresses his complete freedom by turning away from the careful dressage of an earlier period in his development and allowing horses, crops, and people to develop with no control whatsoever. The choice of such words as "repress," "compress," "harness," and "rein" indicates the frustration experienced by Simone de Beauvoir as she watched her mother waste precious years conforming to the dictates of a life-style which was not appropriate for her passionate nature. Because Françoise de Beauvoir tried to raise her two daughters to be equally constrained in their behavior, Simone, who considered herself more influenced by her mother than Hélène, expended a good deal of energy fighting against this early conditioning, pulling off those kid gloves and removing that clock from the refrigerator.

A close reading of *A Very Easy Death* suggests that there were indeed some moments of self-fulfillment in the life of Françoise de Beauvoir. After her husband's death, followed closely by the death of her mother, she seems to have broken out of her shell, to have decided to follow the dictates of her own feelings and desires. She moved from the rue de Rennes apartment,"which my father, as he grew old and became a hypochondriac, used to fill with his bursts of bad temper," the author informs us.[21] Her new apartment, gloomy as it may have seemed to her daughter, was her very own, filled with the things she had chosen to take with her from her former home, the walls proudly adorned with Hélène's paintings. She took courses in order to earn a certificate and work as an assistant librarian, learned to ride a bicycle again, renewed old acquaintances, read, attended lectures and concerts. At fifty-four, she appeared to have found a new life for herself. Her daughter admired her ability to "turn the page," as she put it, to set aside the very real grief she experienced at the death of her husband and to move on. Simone de Beauvoir became painfully aware of just how difficult this must have been when Jean-Paul Sartre died many years later, in April 1980.

The positive traits resurfacing in this elderly woman fighting for her life endeared her to her sometimes judgmental daughter. Allowed by her illness to concentrate for the first time in her life on her own needs rather than on those of others, she took delight in simple sensations: the feel of cold metal against her skin, the color of the roses brought to her from Meyrignac, the song of the birds in the trees outside her hospital window. She savored every minute, was unhappy when her medication caused her to sleep through a lost day. She was considerably more honest with herself and with others than she had been in her earlier years, confessing, as she became exhausted by her disease, that she felt indifferent to everything and everyone, that she was perhaps no longer capable of loving anyone. She was finally willing to admit that she had grown old. This dropping of all pretense was profoundly moving for her daughter, who realized that the strong attachment she once felt to her mother was still very much a part of her:

> I had become attached to this dying woman. As we talked in the shadows, I rectified something that had been bothering me for a long time. I took up once again the dialogue which had been broken off during my adolescence and which our differences and our similarities had never allowed us to renew. And the former tenderness that I had believed completely extinguished was reborn, now that it was possible for it to be couched in simple words and simple gestures.[22]

Forty years had passed since the fifteen-year-old Simone had decided she no longer believed in God, forty years during which she had maintained a polite but detached relationship with a mother for whom she had once felt great love and affection as a young child.

It is of interest to note that the author recognizes not only the differences but also the similarities between her mother and herself as the cause of the breaking off of the dialogue between them. Like her mother, Simone de Beauvoir loved life and rebelled against the inevitability of death. As she accompanied Françoise de Beauvoir through this final battle against suffering and mortality, she found once again the close bond of her early years which paradoxically had given her the self-confidence and the individuality to separate herself from the very person who had launched her so effectively into life. Just like a child's view of the world, the specter of death simplifies all relationships, straining out all that is not essential.

A Very Easy Death is on the one hand a portrait of Françoise de Beauvoir, on the other a sharing of emotions by the author, the emotions of the story of a mother and a daughter trying to find equilibrium in their relationship. There are moments when the writer cannot suppress her impatience with her mother's prejudiced view of the world. She is stung by comments about the moaning of working-class women in the hospital, about nurses working only for money: "They were stock phrases, as mechanical as breathing, but nonetheless an indication of her mentality. It was impossible for me to hear them without being disturbed. I was saddened by the contrast between her suffering body and the rubbish with which her head was stuffed."[23] There is no doubt that Simone de Beauvoir was a severe judge as far as her mother was concerned, impatient with what she considered her limited and bigoted bourgeois perception of the world around her.

Because of Madame de Beauvoir's middle-class morality, it had behooved her daughter to say as little as possible about her unorthodox life-style. Only when *She Came to Stay* was published did her mother begin to make certain assumptions about how she was living. Accustomed to using an ostrich-like approach to realities she would prefer not to face, Françoise de Beauvoir carefully avoided asking too many questions. This unfortunately created uncomfortable silences between mother and daughter when they did spend time together. The author shares with her reader her vivid recollections of her visits to the rue Blomet apartment:

> I would knock. I would hear a little sigh, the shuffling of her slippers on the floor, another sigh, and I would promise myself that this time I would find something to talk about, some common ground for conversation. After five minutes, all was lost. We had so few interests in common! I would thumb through her books: we didn't

read the same ones. I would get her talking, I would listen to her, I would make comments. But, because she was my mother, the unpleasant things she said displeased me more than if they had come from someone else's mouth.[24]

Her remarks were considered unpleasant undoubtedly because they did not coincide with Beauvoir's socialistic, leftist ideas. Having become politically aware and committed during World War II, the author was unable to compromise her ideals, to set aside her convictions, bite her tongue, and chat innocuously with her ultra-conservative mother. The conversations described above were particularly difficult for her because the symbiosis which existed between mother and daughter when Simone was a young girl had not been totally dissolved and the author could not detach herself completely from the prejudices expressed by this person who was not just some bourgeois matron of limited intelligence but rather her own mother. The time she had dutifully spent with Françoise de Beauvoir had therefore been awkward and uncomfortable, reinforcing her expressed distaste for the responsibilities imposed upon individuals by family ties.

A key factor in Madame de Beauvoir's attitude toward her older daughter was her awe-filled evaluation of Simone's intelligence. Just as the two sisters did everything in their power to avoid being judged ridiculous by their mother in their early years, Françoise de Beauvoir was now afraid of appearing unintelligent to *them*. "I know you don't consider me intelligent,"[25] she told Simone one day, a statement which bothered her daughter a great deal even though a number of passages in her autobiographical works as well as my 1985 interview with her (appendix A) indicate that this was indeed the case. Left alone and financially dependent on her two daughters, she frequently consulted with them and with Hélène's husband Lionel de Roulet before making decisions. "She was afraid of 'looking like an idiot' to us," the author notes. "She therefore continued her fuzzy thinking, saying yes to everything without ever questioning anything."[26] This is indeed an attitude for which Simone de Beauvoir continually reproached her mother, one she originally attributed to the reluctance of a young provincial to express her opinions in a Parisian setting.

The fact that Françoise de Beauvoir was indeed intimidated by the superior intelligence of the offspring she had produced is corroborated by her younger daughter's recollection of her opposition to her studying for her baccalaureate degree: "If my daughters continue their studies, they will be more intelligent than I am. Simone is already more intelligent than I. I don't want to have two daughters more intelligent than I. Therefore, Hélène will not study for her baccalaureate degree."[27]

Hélène, however, was convinced that she needed this degree in order to win her independence and escape from her mother's oppressive domination. With Simone's support, she managed to persuade her parents to allow her to pursue her degree, although, as we have seen earlier, Françoise de Beauvoir drew the line at advanced studies for her younger daughter.

When Simone de Beauvoir proposed staying at the hospital one night so that her sister could get some rest, her mother first asked if she was sure she knew how to care for a sick person. Then, her defenses down because of the drugs she was taking, she admitted, "You frighten me."[28] A sensitive and vulnerable woman, she was painfully aware of her daughter's impatience with her ideas, an impatience which is evident in Beauvoir's choice of images such as the "rubbish" (*billevesées* and the "mists" (*brumes*) which she envisaged inside of her mother's head. The author blamed her mother's upbringing for teaching her never to use her own judgment about anything, commenting, "She had been conditioned neither to understand herself nor to make her own decisions. She always felt she had to resort to some authority outside of herself."[29] She also noted that her mother did not seem to retain the ideas found in the many books she read despite her innately good memory. All of these remarks corroborate Françoise de Beauvoir's fears that her older daughter did indeed judge her to be of limited intelligence.

Raised in a very traditional social environment, Madame de Beauvoir had also grown up deferring to masculine opinions. It is significant that after her husband died it was her daughters, both with successful careers, who essentially took his place in her life: "I was the family breadwinner, her son to some degree. In addition, I was a well-known writer. . . . Often shocked by the content of my books, she was flattered by their success. But the authority that success conferred upon me aggravated her sense of uneasiness."[30] Just as Honoré de Balzac had illustrated a century earlier, money was still the focal point of middle-class relationships. As long as her daughters were living under her roof, Françoise de Beauvoir felt justified in controlling their lives in whatever way they would allow her to. Once they were supporting her financially, her attitude toward them was the same as it had been toward her parents and subsequently toward her husband, one of humble gratitude.

Françoise de Beauvoir was terribly afraid of being a bother, of costing her daughters too much money. Olga Kosakievicz Bost, who helped with the arrangements to get her to the clinic after her fall, told Beauvoir, "She seemed so embarrassed about disturbing us, so frantically grateful for what we were doing for her, it was heartbreaking."[31] Her upbringing had made her feel that she had no right to receive favors from anyone.

During her first days in the hospital, she urged her daughter to send flowers to the doctor in her building who came to her rescue as well as to the policemen who arranged for her ambulance. She worried about taking up too much of Simone's precious time, about causing too much trouble for the nurses. Throughout her life, she had essentially sacrificed herself and her identity, ignoring her own needs and desires. Like Madame Blomart in *The Blood of Others,* she had decided that it was best to stay quietly in a corner and hope no one noticed you. For the first time, her illness authorized her to be the center of attention, to be waited on, and to concentrate her efforts on herself, on her body, on recuperating. No longer the helpmate to a male head of household or the handmaiden of the Lord, she was a person in her own right, with demands that needed to be met.

Like any hospital patient, Françoise de Beauvoir was first and foremost a suffering body. It was the sight of her mother's nakedness which precipitated one of her daughter's most violent reactions to the accident. Lying there uncovered, Madame de Beauvoir admitted to Simone that she no longer had any sense of shame. The author articulated her approval to her mother, yet confessed to her readers:

> No body existed less—existed more—for me. As a child, I had cherished it. As an adolescent, I felt an uneasy repulsion toward it. That's a classic reaction, and I considered it normal that it had retained this double character, repugnant and sacred, for me: a taboo. Just the same, I was astonished by the violence of my displeasure. My mother's carefree consent made it worse. . . .[32]

It is the pubic area of her mother's body which lies uncovered, the area through which Simone de Beauvoir was conceived and born. Elsewhere, the author recalls spending the night before her grandmother's funeral sleeping at her mother's side, "forgetting my disgust for that nuptial bed where I was born, where my father had died . . . ."[33] Here as in certain passages of her fictional works, Beauvoir attests to the physical repulsion which conception and childbirth seem to have inspired in her. It was only after she succeeded in detaching herself psychologically from the fact that this was indeed her own mother's body that she could deal with the nakedness. "Her nudity no longer bothered me," she remarks. "It was no longer my mother, but rather a poor suffering body."[34] These passages corroborate Nancy Friday's suggestion that the great lie which separates mothers from their daughters is the implication that mothers are totally asexual, aphysical even, disembodied spirits whose attempts to emphasize the spiritual rather than the carnal were so perceptively satirized in Beauvoir's early short stories originally entitled *La Primauté du spirituel*.

As is so often the case with adult children and elderly parents, there is a final reversal of roles in the Beauvoir family as Simone and Hélène "mother" Françoise through her illness and death. It is they who make decisions about how best to have her treated, they who are in possession of privileged information about her condition. The author promises that she will take charge of finding a good rest home for her mother, that she will not have to return to the apartment which will forever be associated in her mind with the trauma of her fall and her two-hour crawl toward the telephone for help. The sisters hold their mother's hand, mop her forehead, do all of the things which she undoubtedly did for them during their childhood illnesses. Simone de Beauvoir is both surprised by what she labels the childish anxiety with which her mother anticipates the battery of tests to which the doctors plan to subject her, and infuriated by the self-importance of some of these doctors and their haughty condescension toward the helpless old woman her mother has become.

For six weeks Simone's energies were totally focused on Room 114: "The world had reduced itself to the dimensions of her room.... My real life was being lived next to her and had only one goal: to protect her."[35] The great question for the two sisters, as for any conscientious mother, was how they could best protect this person they loved. One of the older nurses advised Simone in hushed tones not to let them operate on her mother. Faced with the recommendation of the specialists and her sister's desperate hope that it might after all be peritonitis rather than cancer, she agreed to the operation anyway. Once the cancer diagnosis was confirmed, she fought to keep her mother as comfortable as possible, agonizing over any moment when she was in pain.

Throughout this long and unsuccessful fight against death, Simone de Beauvoir once again entered into the symbiotic relationship with her mother which she had had when she was a little girl. Obsessed by the tic which distorted her mother's mouth, she was told by Sartre that her own mouth was mimicking those distortions:

> I spoke to Sartre about my mother's mouth, as I had seen it in the morning, and about everything I saw in it: an appetite she had repressed, an almost servile humility, hope, distress, solitude—the solitude of her death, the solitude of her life—which she didn't want to acknowledge. And my own mouth, he told me, no longer obeyed me. I had put *maman*'s on my face and in spite of myself I was imitating its tics. Her entire person, her entire existence materialized there and compassion was tearing me apart.[36]

This focus on the mouth and female appetites for living foreshadows Kim Chernin's association of eating disorders with problems of separation in the mother-daughter relationship.

Simone de Beauvoir suffered physically and mentally with her mother during the latter's terminal illness. Fifteen minutes of waiting for a morphine injection to take effect seemed like hours of agony. She identified with Françoise de Beauvoir's love of life, with her horror of death. Beyond the barrier of a faith they did not share, the two women found once again that there were indeed more similarities than differences between them. Both had always agreed that Simone had inherited her vitality from her mother. Both were passionately fond of living. When her mother related over and over again, like a litany, the story of her fall and of her anguished crawl toward the telephone, Simone understood perfectly: "I could imagine her distress. She believed in heaven, but despite her age, her infirmities, her discomforts, she was fiercely attached to the earth and had an animalistic horror of death."[37] This horror of death is one clearly shared by her older daughter. Simone de Beauvoir expresses great admiration for this elderly woman, who, when her arthritis became so severe that it took her an hour to walk around the block, continued to do just that and to remain as involved in life as possible despite her physical ills.

The mouth through which so many alienating statements had passed throughout the years became a fixation for the author, who comments, "I was fascinated by that sucking motion, both avid and restrained, by that lip shaded by a slight fuzz, which swelled up as it did in my childhood when *maman* was unhappy or disturbed."[38] This was a lip which had expressed not only anger and frustration but also sensuality and radiance. Among Beauvoir's earliest memories is the following image of her mother emerging from her bedroom:

> *Maman*'s face, with the slight fuzz which shaded her upper lip, betrayed a warm sensuality. . . . I was struck by the radiance of her smile, associated for me in a mysterious way with that room from which she was emerging. I hardly recognized in that fresh apparition the respectable adult that was my mother.[39]

Watching their mother delight in simple sensations during the days when she was feeling reasonably comfortable, the sisters were able to recapture the memory of that long-forgotten smile. "We found once again the smile which had dazzled our early childhood, the radiant smile of a young woman. Where had it been lost in the meantime?" Beauvoir queries.[40] In the fuzzy upper lip of this seventy-eight-year-old woman, her daughter can retrace the story of her life: the joys of sexual fulfillment in young adulthood, the disillusionment and frustration of middle age, the final struggle for survival. The prejudices, the anger, the resentment, the silences in which these lips had played their part suddenly receded into the background as the relationship between mother and daughters was concentrated on issues of life and death.

As sick as she was, Françoise de Beauvoir still took pride in the good looks she once had, in the vitality which astonished her doctors, in the optimistic personality which her friends appreciated. Her daughter was touched by the courage of her fight against death, particularly because it provided a common battleground on which they could struggle side by side. "*Maman* loved life as I love it and when faced with death she experienced the same sense of rebellion as I do," she realized.[41] Her mother had waited a long time to rebel, but did so at last during the final weeks of her life. Beauvoir was struck by the way in which she gradually divested herself of all of the defense mechanisms which had made communication between them so difficult: "Her illness had broken through the protective shell of her prejudices and her pretentions. . . ."[42] As an individual who had been an integral part of her life confronted death, the author suddenly found social and political ideologies far less important than this primal battle against mortality.

Admitting that for many years her attitude toward her mother had been essentially one of indifference, Simone de Beauvoir discovered that her renewed attachment to this frail and vulnerable woman stirred up violent emotions within her. She fantasized about finding a revolver so that she could put her mother out of her misery instead of continuing to watch her writhe in pain. Torn between this desire to keep her mother from suffering and her unwillingness to accept her death, the author found some solace in the recapturing, however short-lived, of the happy images of earlier days: "Surfacing once again, her beauty, her smile expressed a peaceful harmony within her and, on this deathbed, a kind of happiness."[43] This harmony existed not only within her mother but also as part of a childhood paradise recaptured by the two Beauvoir sisters during the final weeks of Françoise de Beauvoir's life.

A Very Easy Death is dedicated simply "To my sister." The closeness of the bond which existed between Simone and Hélène is strong evidence that their mother's jealousy never succeeded in weakening the intimacy of the relationship between the two sisters. In the course of the narrative, Beauvoir notes several essential differences between "Poupette" and herself. "More intimate with [*maman*] than I, she was also more attached to her," she reveals.[44] In an attempt to explain the fact that their mother was more comfortable having her younger daughter remain at the clinic with her at night, the author notes: "She thought that

I was judging her. Poupette, 'the little one,' less respected than I was—
and who, less influenced by *maman,* had not inherited her rigidity—
interacted more easily with her."[45]

In her book of recollections, Hélène de Beauvoir remembers her
efforts to convince her mother that she was just as good a student as
Simone, to point out to her that she too was always first in her class.
Somehow Françoise de Beauvoir could never be as impressed by anything Hélène did, simply because Simone had done it first. Although
Hélène resented this lack of recognition of her talents, there was less
tension in her relationship with her mother than in Simone's precisely
because Françoise de Beauvoir was less intimidated by Hélène, who
therefore passed through adolescence less traumatically than her older
sister. In recalling her mother's authoritative role during her childhood
and adolescence, Hélène appreciates the fact that being forced to work
conscientiously at her studies, to sleep in an unheated bedroom, to dress
without elegance or vanity, prepared her effectively for the vicissitudes
of adult life.

Throughout the narrative, the reader is aware of Simone de
Beauvoir's protective instincts toward her younger sister. Seeing her
own feelings reflected in Hélène's despair, she found some outlet for
her frustrated energies in calming her sister down, in taking her out for
a cup of coffee, requesting a tranquilizer for her, relieving her on the
night shift. Caught in Portugal for the duration of World War II,
Hélène had not been present at their father's deathbed. In assuming the
burden of the responsibility for her mother's care at the clinic, she had
found a way of expiating her sense of guilt for her earlier absence. She
told Simone, "You saw Father and Grandmother die. I was far away . . .
I'll be the one to take charge of *maman.* Besides, I feel like staying with
her."[46] Through her own choice, it was thus Hélène who held her
mother's hand throughout the long operation which confirmed the diagnosis of cancer, Hélène who saw her mother die.

What then is the effect of a mother's death on her surviving children?
Simone de Beauvoir generalizes perceptively about the effect of any
death on those left behind:

> When someone dear to us disappears, we expiate our guilt as survivors with a thou-
> sand piercing regrets. Her death reveals to us her uniqueness . . . it seems to us that
> she ought to have had a larger place in our lives: in the extreme, to have occupied
> our lives completely. We shake ourselves loose from this obsession: she was only an
> individual among others. But since one never does everything one can for anyone—
> even within the questionable limits that one has set for oneself—one can always find
> many reasons to reproach oneself.[47]

Beauvoir's reference to the questionable limits one sets for oneself in relating to another human being is an indication of her reexamination of the amount of time and attention she chose to give to her mother during her adult years. From this lucid analysis of the guilt feelings precipitated by any death, the author goes on to consider the particular case of Françoise de Beauvoir and her daughters:

> As far as *maman* was concerned, we were certainly guilty, during recent years, of negligence, forgetfulness, abstention. We felt as if we had made up for all of this through the days we devoted to her, through the peace of mind our presence brought her, through the victories won over fear and pain. Without our stubborn vigilance, she would have suffered a good deal more.[48]

These thoughts compensated for Beauvoir's sense of having betrayed her mother by allowing her to be operated on, by not being honest with her about the true nature of her illness. She also reminded herself that while the constant presence of her daughters did indeed, as the nurse at the clinic suggested, make Françoise de Beauvoir's end "a very easy death," every individual is essentially alone when facing that final moment. She chose not to dwell on her mother's remark that when, for the first time in decades, she had both of her daughters with her, she was too ill to enjoy their company as fully as she would have liked.[49]

As one closes the book on the final sentence of this thin volume, one is left with a sense of the great complexity of the relationship between Françoise de Beauvoir and her older daughter. Its tangled emotions are perhaps best represented in the dream the author describes, one to which we have referred in several earlier chapters but which bears repeating in the context of this chapter:

> Ordinarily, I thought about her with indifference. However, in my sleep . . . she often played a major role. She blended in with Sartre, and we were happy together. And then the dream turned into a nightmare. Why was I living with her again? How had I fallen back into her clutches? Our former relationship thus survived in me with all of its ambivalence: a dependence both cherished and detested. It rose again in all its strength when *maman* 's accident, her illness, her death had broken the routine which had been governing our contact with one another. . . . The "chère petite maman" I knew when I was ten was no longer distinguishable from the hostile woman who was so oppressive during my adolescence. I wept for both of them as I wept for my elderly mother.[50]

Simone de Beauvoir often attributed her confidence in her own ability, her success, to the happy childhood lovingly created for her by her mother. It is the beloved mother of those early years whom she found once again in this suffering woman so avidly hanging on to life.

Both Simone and Hélène were struck by the complete change in their mother's attitude as she approached death. When her grandnieces were at her bedside, she advised them to live life to the fullest, even to kick up their heels, expressing regret that she hadn't done so herself when she was their age.[51] When asked if she would ever have given her daughters that same advice, she quickly abandoned her bantering tone to reply categorically, "To my daughters? Oh, no!"[52] As a mother, she had a mission she took very seriously, an obligation to raise her daughters with the same standards of ethics and morality with which she herself had been imbued in her convent school. Nonetheless, Hélène sensed that they were seeing for the first time what their mother might have been like had she been less inhibited, less "corseted" by the demands of her upbringing and her conditioning.

"Nothing ever abolishes our childhood," Beauvoir remarks as she explains her mother's lack of confidence and retreat into conformity.[53] This statement holds true just as strongly for her and her sister. The resentments, the differences in outlook, the guilt all faded into the background as mother and daughters joined together in the common struggle against mortality. The united front the three women presented against the inevitable perhaps justified Simone's conclusion that Françoise de Beauvoir's was, after all, "a very easy death."

Critical Reaction

Serge Julienne-Caffié sees *A Very Easy Death* as an opportunity for Simone de Beauvoir to clarify the misunderstandings which had characterized her relationship with her mother since her adolescent days. Laurent Gagnebin records the complaints by some readers of a lack of delicacy on Beauvoir's part in her detailed descriptions of her mother's agony and death. He, however, praises the authenticity of the work and considers it a masterpiece in its appeal to its readers to dispense with the mascarades and hypocrisy which often surround death and dying. He finds in the work the expression of a tenderness long smothered by silences and misunderstandings during Beauvoir's adult life.

Agreeing with Gagnebin that this small volume is perhaps Simone de Beauvoir's best work, Elaine Marks devotes an entire chapter of her study of encounters with death to the 1964 text. Marks finds Beauvoir's portrayal of her mother that of "a rather attractive but silly woman" and claims that the author "is quite explicit about her own preference for her non-conformist father."[54] Although this was certainly true for the adolescent Simone, it is, in my opinion, a debatable assumption. Discussing Beauvoir's tendency to equate her mother with bourgeois Catholicism and an elitist milieu, Marks notes that Francoise de Beauvoir's illness and impending death suddenly placed her on the side of the victims, and therefore among those with whom her older daughter could more readily sympathize. It was then Madame de Beauvoir's animalistic dread of death which reunited the two women, proving "stronger than the barriers erected between them by her mother's religious beliefs and the difference of generation," according to Marks.[55] In an ironic analysis of Simone de Beauvoir's propensity for judging everything in black-and-white terms, Marks calls Françoise de Beauvoir's illness her "salvation" in the eyes of her older daughter.

In this critical study, Elaine Marks is quite harsh on Simone de Beauvoir for what she perceives as the writer's inability to put herself in another's place. She considers this autobiographical work "a courageous desire to break through some of the simplistic left-wing ideology that often replaces intelligent analysis in her other books." Beauvoir appears to her to have been a "faithful but inattentive daughter," unaware of signs that made friends and relatives show concern about Françoise de Beauvoir's physical condition even before her fall in her apartment.[56] She labels the author's expressed empathy with her mother's distress as she crawled painstakingly to the phone after her fall a rare instance of her "imagining what it is like to be someone else, to see and feel differently."[57]

Marks highlights Beauvoir's instinctive understanding of the need for her to return to Paris from a trip to Prague with Sartre so that her mother would not die without seeing her again. "Never," she points out, "as companion to Sartre, or mistress or passionate friend, did Simone de Beauvoir allow herself to be caught in a situation in which someone else was so dependent on her."[58] The depth of the author's emotion is illustrated, according to Marks, by the continual emphasis on protecting her mother and the repetition of the word "maman" throughout the text. "There is no sentimentality here, only an extreme human compassion which moves the reader more profoundly than her ponderous maxims." [59] Yet Marks faults the writer for her tendency to use language as a means of evading confrontation with deep emotion, focusing on her Jansenistic division of the protagonists of this drama into those of "bad faith" like Françoise de Beauvoir, and those of "good faith," like herself. Marks's interpretation here is jarringly acerbic, leaving the reader with the disturbing impression that she finds the tone of *A Very Easy Death* more vindictive than sincerely anguished.

Robert Cottrell labels Simone de Beauvoir's style in *A Very Easy Death* "almost clinical, at times harrowingly dispassionate . . . all the more striking because it is understated."[60] Like Elaine Marks, he finds a dichotomy between the author's "compassion for the suffering body and ironic contempt for the old woman herself, for the life she led, and for the values she professed."[61] He is extremely caustic in assessing the severity of Beauvoir's judgment of her mother, commenting that her "inability to see her mother except through ideological lenses is chilling. . . . The cavalier way in which she passes judgment on her mother borders on arrogance."[62] Cottrell feels that the course of Simone de Beauvoir's life was dictated by her determination to choose paths diametrically opposed to those of which her mother would approve. He recognizes the anguish caused by the fact that the author found in her mother's demise an intimation of her own to come and concludes rather harshly that, rather than an expression of grief, "the book is an elegy in which Beauvoir laments the dissolution of her own being."[63]

For Konrad Bieber, this thin volume is a "beautiful memorial" to Françoise de Beauvoir.[64] He notes that most of what Simone de Beauvoir wrote after *A Very Easy Death* centered on fundamental human problems. Emphasizing Beauvoir's skill as a chronicler, Bieber comments: "The daughter continues her dutiful life in recording for mankind this intimate experience . . . to create a monument for her mother . . . but also as an example for others to live and die by."[65]

Carol Ascher suggests that Beauvoir found a certain relief in her mother's inability during her final weeks to follow the dictates of the religion she had embraced so devoutly throughout her life. Religion had created the barrier between them and they could now unite, as they once did when Simone was a very small girl, in a common cause, only this time it is the struggle against death rather than attendance at morning mass.

A Very Easy Death is considered by Terry Keefe a very strong indictment of Françoise de Beauvoir's overly conservative view of the world and of its adverse effect on the young Simone. Keefe mentions Beauvoir's apparent forgiveness of her mother's strictness and autocracy in the pages of her book but surprisingly faults her for failing to record "any serious sense of loss."[66] He expresses the vital nature of the author's relationship to her mother in the following passage:

> The intense relationship, begun when Beauvoir was brought into the world, did not come to an abrupt end with her mother's death. That she felt the need to write a book about it already provides evidence of this, but many of her other writings, fictional as well as autobiographical, suggest that this primary relationship is both a vital permanent thread in the texture of Beauvoir's mental life and too complex or fundamental to be tidily encapsulated in rigid formulas.[67]

Critics have sometimes judged the author rather severely for a certain condescension they sense in her portrayal of Françoise de Beauvoir as the epitome of the "relative being" described so vividly in *The Second Sex*. Few have been unresponsive, however, to the depth of feeling which took Beauvoir beyond the resentment and studied detachment that had characterized her relationship with her mother since her late adolescence into the empathy and anguish which cry out to the reader from behind the pages of *A Very Easy Death*. Through her daughter's literary talent, "this retiring woman whose name was so seldom heard pronounced" had at last become someone worthy of attention.[68] In Hélène de Beauvoir's opinion, this small book revealed the degree to which her sister had arrived at a real understanding of their mother and of what their mother's life had been all about.[69]

Just as 1939 and the outbreak of World War II marked a turning point in the life of Simone de Beauvoir, so did 1963, the year when she suddenly found herself a member of the older generation, a daughter whose interaction with her mother could henceforth take place only in her memories and in her psyche. The mother-daughter relationship was hardly over, however. It lived on in the fictional works to which she turned her talents immediately after the publication of *A Very Easy Death*.

Georges de Beauvoir as a Young Man

Françoise de Beauvoir as a Young Woman

Françoise de Beauvoir

Françoise de Beauvoir

Georges de Beauvoir

Françoise de Beauvoir and Baby Simone, 1908

Hélène de Beauvoir as a Little Girl

Hélène and Simone de Beauvoir Visiting Cousins in Lyons, 1913

Hélène and Simone de Beauvoir Visiting Cousins in Lyons, 1913

Georges de Beauvoir

The Beauvoir Family on Their Paris Balcony

Three Generations of Women in *Les Belles Images*

In the fourth volume of her autobiography, Simone de Beauvoir informs her readers that, after the deeply personal pages of *A Very Easy Death*, "I promised myself that I would not talk about myself again for a long time."[1] She therefore plunged into a fictional format in her 1966 novel *Les Belles Images*, her first work of fiction in more than a decade. Although the upwardly mobile family she depicts moves in social circles very different from those in which she herself was brought up, there is a haunting similarity between the three generations of women the author has created for her novel and the women of the Beauvoir family with whom we have become better acquainted through the revelations of *A Very Easy Death*. The main character, Laurence, is faced with a much more trivial crisis than the terminal illness of Françoise de Beauvoir, but is nonetheless called upon to provide moral support for a mother toward whom she has felt detached and even hostile, a woman who perhaps resembles Beauvoir's maternal grandmother in her lack of affection and sensitivity. Laurence is the mother of two young daughters clearly patterned after the Beauvoir sisters and, like Françoise de Beauvoir, feels an enormous sense of responsibility for them and their future. As the narrative progresses, the reader watches the gradual disintegration of Laurence's self-protective mechanisms as this outwardly capable, intelligent, attractive career woman yields to the anxieties created by the pressures of the many roles she is trying to fill. It is tempting to see in Laurence a reflection of the devastated emotions of the author who, only three years earlier, felt "cheated" by the promises life had held out to her, and who was still recovering from the sense of loss occasioned by her mother's death.

When we first meet Laurence, she is attending a very trendy garden party given by her mother, whom she always addresses as Dominique. We discover that Dominique left Laurence's father as soon as her younger daughter was married and that she is a ruthless career woman:

"She went into radio work by the side door in 1945, and she has grappled her way up, working like a horse, trampling anyone in her path."[2] This vision of a woman who will stop at nothing to get her own way appears on the surface to provide as stark a contrast to the Madame Drouffes and Madame Blomarts of Beauvoir's earlier fictional works as it does to Françoise de Beauvoir. Yet the effect of a materially deprived childhood parallels that of Françoise de Beauvoir's emotionally deprived childhood in fueling Dominique's determination to raise her daughters in a way totally different from the way in which she herself was raised. The novel's title refers in part to Dominique's methods of child rearing, for she stopped at nothing to create two picture-perfect little girls.

When she is alone with her older daughter in an upstairs room, Dominique launches into her usual diatribe about the mediocrity of her estranged husband. Here again she provides a striking contrast to Françoise de Beauvoir, who refused to admit that her life with Georges de Beauvoir was anything but idyllic. Whereas Madame de Beauvoir carried Christian humility to the point of dressing shabbily and downgrading the importance of physical appearance for herself and her daughters, Dominique sports all of the latest fashions and worries about beginning to show her age. Laurence seems repulsed by her mother's viciousness, snobbishness, and shallowness, and reproaches herself for her instinctive malevolence: "This is her mother, she feels affection for her. But she is also a stranger. Behind the images that are dancing about in the mirrors, who is hiding? Maybe no one at all."[3] Laurence responds mechanically to her mother's query about the children, musing sardonically, "Dominique asks these questions as a matter of principle, but she would find Laurence indiscreet if she gave her disturbing answers or even detailed ones."[4] The distance between mother and daughter is underlined by a narration in which Laurence refers in a detached journalistic style to both herself and Dominique in the third person.

At age fifty-one, Dominique has a well-paying job, a fifty-six-year-old lover who is one of the wealthiest men in France, an expensive country home, a Ferrari, and an impressive set of friends. Her life at the beginning of the novel corresponds to the elegant, seductive images created by Laurence in her advertising work. Her existence has not always been picture-perfect, however. As she was raising Laurence and her sister Marthe, Dominique would frequently recite her reasons for insisting that they be impeccably dressed:

> You don't know what it's like to have threadbare soles on your shoes and to feel through your sock that you have stepped on spittle. You don't know what it's like to be looked up and down by classmates with sparkling clean hair who are nudging

each other with their elbows. No, you will not go out with that spot on your skirt. Go change.[5]

Whereas emotional deprivation during her childhood made Françoise de Beauvoir determined to lavish affection and attention on her two girls, financial deprivation made Dominique obsessive about having her daughters always look, as the novel's title suggests, "as pretty as a picture." As Laurence thinks back on her childhood days while working at her drawing board, she recalls the story of the king who turned everything he touched, including his little daughter, into gold. This variation on the King Midas story is perhaps unfamiliar to American children but hauntingly appropriate for Dominique's child rearing goals. Laurence often feels like "a magnificent metal doll," one who may no longer be capable of either enthusiasm or emotion.[6]

In the course of the narrative, however, Laurence's emotions will be profoundly stirred both by her mother and by her daughter. Enlisted by the egotistical Gilbert to help break the news that he is planning to leave Dominique in order to marry the nineteen-year-old daughter of his former mistress, Laurence reacts to this soap-opera scenario with painful empathy for her mother: "*Maman!* My poor *maman!*"[7] Her words echo Françoise de Beauvoir's spontaneous reaction years earlier to Simone's revelation that she had lost her faith: "My poor little girl!" It is significant that the endearing term *maman* is what instinctively comes to mind for Laurence rather than her habitual detached use of "Dominique" to refer to her mother.

The self-possessed Dominique is viewed differently by her daughter after this conversation with Gilbert has transformed her from a heartless social climber into a pitiful victim. Like Simone de Beauvoir, Laurence has tended to look disdainfully at her mother's life-style and values. Yet her heart is pounding and she feels nauseated as she leaves Gilbert's apartment. Just as it fell to Simone and Hélène de Beauvoir to protect their mother during her illness, Laurence feels it incumbent upon her to see Dominique through this emotional crisis. She is amazed to find Dominique's eyes swollen the following day, having been previously convinced that this woman who always seemed in control of everything, including her feelings, was physically incapable of shedding tears. Here again there is an outward contrast to Françoise de Beauvoir, whom her daughters often found dissolved in tears during their adolescence, but who faced physical suffering courageously and with dry eyes during the weeks of her final illness.

Searching for some helpful advice to offer, Laurence draws upon the maxims which were drummed into her by her mother as she was growing up: "She chooses her words from those which used to be on her mother's lips: dignity, serenity, courage, self-respect, keeping up appearances, behaving with class, taking things on the chin. Dominique doesn't answer."[8] The reversal of roles which was effective when the Beauvoir sisters cared for their mother during her terminal illness cannot take place unless both parties are willing to accept such an exchange of responsibilities. The fifty-one-year-old Dominique is clearly unreceptive to her daughter's suggestions, which she undoubtedly recognizes as the platitudes by which she had tried to guide her children. She fixates rather on finding out the identity of her rival for Gilbert's affections. Laurence is devastated by the animalistic vengeance she senses in her mother: "Has Dominique ever loved anyone? Is she capable of love? . . . Even her suffering doesn't make her more human. It's like hearing a lobster creaking, an unarticulated noise, evoking nothing but raw pain. Much more intolerable than if it were something one could share."[9] Dominique's tenacity as she meticulously plots to recapture Gilbert reinforces Laurence's image of her mother as someone who has "hacked her way through life, crushing, pushing aside everything in her path and is now suddenly ineffective and battling furiously."[10] Laurence is cast into the role of a spectator with privileged information since Gilbert does not at first reveal his marriage plans to Dominique. Like Beauvoir dealing with her mother's cancer, she feels guilty knowing more about the older woman's circumstances than Dominique herself does.

Despite a very apparent lack of warmth in her feelings toward her mother, Laurence, like Beauvoir, cannot bear to see another human being suffer. When Gilbert warns her that he plans to tell Dominique about his nineteen-year-old fiancée the following day, Laurence muses, "The only remedy would be to kill him: Dominique would suffer a good deal less."[11] Death does indeed seem to be a solution to psychological problems favored by a number of Beauvoir's protagonists: Françoise Miquel in *She Came to Stay* actually manages to eliminate Xavière by turning on the gas and leaving her to be asphyxiated, Anne Dubreuilh in *The Mandarins* seriously considers suicide in the final chapter of the novel. Simone de Beauvoir herself recalls in *A Very Easy Death* her temptation to find a gun and shoot her mother to spare her the inevitable suffering of those final weeks of struggling with cancer. Laurence is however only fantasizing. Having become aware over the past month that Dominique has many acquaintances but essentially no friends, she realizes that the burden of helping her mother through this crisis will fall squarely on her shoulders and that there is clearly no easy way to cope with it.

When Dominique becomes vengeful and threatens to reveal Gilbert's earlier liaison with his fiancée's mother, Laurence is both fearful and repulsed: "That heart is so black, full of writhing snakes."[12] The metaphor calls to mind the title of Hervé Bazin's powerful novel about a tyrannical and black-hearted mother, *Vipère au poing*, with its literal image of a viper writhing in one's hand, as well as François Mauriac's depiction of the provincial family in *Le Noeud de vipères* as a vipers' tangle. Just as Simone de Beauvoir was strongly repelled by the sight of her mother's nudity in the hospital, Laurence is equally taken aback by the vulgarity of Dominique's language. It is as if both women, though far from being innocent and pure themselves, wish to preserve the myth of the virginal-mother-above-reproach promulgated by society and the media.

Laurence's ambivalence toward this woman with such primitive instincts who just happens to be her mother is constantly highlighted by Beauvoir's narrative:

> How easy it would be if Laurence could take her in her arms and stroke her hair as she does Catherine's. What is tearing her apart is this repulsion mingled with pity: as she would pity a wounded toad, without being able to bring herself to touch it. Gilbert horrifies her, but so does her mother.[13]

A trampling horse, a creaking lobster, snakes, a wounded toad. For Laurence, her mother seems more animalistic than human. Raised to be picture-perfect herself, the younger woman has difficulty understanding someone who has taught her one set of values while herself living more by the law of the jungle. Certain critics had reacted to a judgmental tone in the portrayal of Françoise de Beauvoir in *A Very Easy Death*, and Laurence's negative feelings about her mother are clearly evident throughout the pages of *Les Belles Images*.

Laurence, who has always considered her father a member of a superior race and her mother mediocre, is devastated physically and psychologically when the two decide to reconcile. She attempts to cope with the visceral shock of losing her father to Dominique for a second time by analyzing her own Oedipal complex. Freudian terminology may be helpful in pinpointing what is going on, but it does not prevent Laurence from succumbing to an anorexia that is both psychological and physical.

Laurence's greatest disappointment comes from her realization that the father she has adored all these years is not really the superior being she had always imagined. Here we find echoes of the mature Simone's disenchantment with a father who once seemed to her to embody all that was exciting, intellectual, and cultural in the world. Laurence's father rationalizes his former criticisms of Dominique by telling his daughter that "he realized that he had misjudged her, that her worldliness, her ambition, were a form of vitality. And someone vivacious at his side was precisely what he needed."[14] It is of interest that the question of vitality surfaces again here, as it did in *A Very Easy Death*, where it represented a cherished legacy passed on from Françoise to Simone de Beauvoir. In *Les Belles Images*, on the other hand, Dominique Langois seems to regain her former strength and ability to cope with life at the expense of her daughter's vitality, as Laurence is tempted simply to remain in bed for the rest of her life and refuse all offers of nourishment. Her anorexic response to psychological trauma might well be analyzed by Kim Chernin as symptomatic of a daughter's guilt over the repressed rage she has felt toward her mother since early childhood.[15]

Laurence cannot allow herself to give in to anorexia and depression, however, because she continues to feel a deep sense of commitment to her two young daughters. Ten-year-old Catherine is as sensitive to the existence of famine and poverty in the world as the young Laurence was to the plight of Jewish children during World War II and to the dropping of the bomb on Hiroshima. Raised in a non-religious atmosphere, Laurence had been encouraged by Dominique to discuss her concerns with a Catholic priest: "[She] had tried to believe in God, in another life in which all the suffering would be rewarded. Dominique had been perfect: she had allowed her to speak to a priest. She had even chosen an intelligent one for her."[16] Religion is treated in *Les Belles Images* with a certain amount of cynicism and irony, both in Dominique's magnanimous gesture of supplying an intelligent priest for her daughter to consult and in the more fanatical saintly demeanor of Laurence's younger sister Marthe, who is the target of much family scoffing.

As Laurence compares her childhood to that of her own daughters, one senses her resentment of Dominique's authoritarianism. Dictating what her daughters would wear, where they would go for vacation, what friends, if any, they might have, the fictional Dominique clearly shared with Françoise de Beauvoir a need to dominate her children's lives. Laurence deeply regrets never having been allowed to have a close friend when she was growing up. This has become an obsession over the years, one which surfaces again as she watches Catherine play with her new friend Brigitte, whose influence on her will gradually be brought into question:

> I would have liked to sit in the dark with a little girl my own age and laugh and whisper. But Dominique would always say, "Your friend is certainly very nice, but,

my poor child, she is so ordinary." Marthe had a friend, the daughter of one of Papa's friends, a silly girl of limited intelligence. I didn't. Ever.[17]

Dominique has always assumed that Laurence, more intellectual and outwardly capable than Marthe, fared quite well without childhood friends, an assumption Laurence contradicts at the family dinner table shortly before nausea and anorexia make her take to her bed. "Friendship is something precious," she declares. "If I had a friend, I would talk to her rather than lying here exhausted."[18] There is an underlying implication in the novel that Laurence's problems are partially due to just this lack of childhood friendship, a gap in her experience which has made it extremely difficult for her to communicate with others as an adult. Lucien, her rejected lover, is horrified when she calmly assures him that losing her is not terribly tragic because people are totally interchangeable.

The reader learns that five years earlier Laurence had experienced rather severe mental depression, which she explains as the result of marrying and having children at an early age. Her analysis of the problem typifies Beauvoir's treatment of marriage and motherhood as a drain on female creativity: "I felt as if I no longer had any future. Jean-Charles and the children did; I didn't. So what was the use of learning anything? A vicious circle: I neglected myself, I was bored, and I felt more and more dispossessed of my own identity."[19] It was Dominique who found the solution for Laurence's first crisis by suggesting that she take a job in advertising, a field which interested her and for which she had considerable innate talent. That job was an effective cure for the first depression.

Two years later Laurence fell apart emotionally once again after reading a newspaper article about a woman who had been tortured to death. In this anguished identification with human suffering, she closely resembles Simone de Beauvoir and the emotional crisis which the Algerian war stirred up within her. The remedy for Laurence, however, was to avoid reading magazines and newspapers, to rely upon her husband Jean-Charles to keep her informed about what was going on in the world. Since then Laurence had attempted to keep the outside world from intruding upon her life and her thoughts, to avoid asking herself any unsettling questions.

What can she do, however, when ten-year-old Catherine is the one who asks the questions? The little girl's first question is an essentially metaphysical one about why people exist. After throwing out some superficial and hopefully comforting answers, Laurence begins to brood about the whole issue: "Why do we exist? That's not my problem. We do exist. The thing to do is to take no note of it, to keep moving along straight toward death."[20] This is an extremely pessimistic evaluation of the value of existence, predicated on a life lived out with blinders effectively blocking any investigation into the world around us. For Laurence, the specter of earlier depressions is enough to make her intent on hanging on to her security at all costs and avoiding any thoughts which might again bring about an unravelling of the comfortable cocoon in which she has ensconced herself.

In Laurence's family, Beauvoir has reproduced her own childhood experience, portraying a mother who identifies symbiotically with the older daughter, who reminds her of her younger self. Like Françoise de Beauvoir, Laurence is extremely conscientious about her obligations to her daughters. She is even willing to force herself to learn more about current events if it will help Catherine to achieve a better understanding of the world around her. She decides to end her relationship with her co-worker Lucien in order to spend more time with her family, noting her chilling impression "that people are merely juxtaposed, that they are not a part of her, with the exception of her daughters, but that must be organic."[21] Jean-Charles is a perfectly acceptable husband, Lucien a perfectly acceptable lover, yet Laurence feels a close connection only to the two young girls who were once a physical part of her body.

Despite her good intentions, Laurence finds that it is not particularly easy to sit down and talk things over with Catherine, that they do not really speak the same language. Her efforts to communicate with her older daughter echo Françoise de Beauvoir's misguided attempts to force the adolescent Simone to share her thoughts with her. Laurence is here experiencing the other side of the problem felt by Simone de Beauvoir as she knocked dutifully on the door of her mother's apartment and wondered what they would find to talk about. Communication between two human beings is never easy and can be especially complicated between mothers and daughters because of all the emotional baggage that each carries around with her.

Laurence admires Catherine's warmth and sensitivity in dealing with the younger Louise's jealousy of Catherine's friend Brigitte, an autobiographical detail which parallels the relationship between the young Simone and her sister Hélène at the time she and Zaza "Mabille" Lacoin became such close friends. When Laurence's father assures her that Catherine is very much like her, Laurence is both pleased and troubled. Her self-confidence is shaky enough that she is not quite sure she wants Catherine to grow up to be like her. As she lies exhausted on the couch, she clings to the solicitous Catherine, wondering, "Will she have to become a woman like me, with stones in her chest and sulphur fumes in her head?"[22] Having suffered from Dominique's authoritarianism and from the unspoken rule that emotions are always to be kept well hidden, Laurence is determined to raise Catherine differently.

Motherhood is certainly not a source of security for Laurence. She is both drawn to her daughters and resentful of the responsibility their existence has imposed upon her. When Jean-Charles declares in anger that Catherine has inherited her exaggerated sensitivity from Laurence, the latter is taken aback:

> It's frightening to think that one marks one's children merely by what one is. . . . Daily moods, a chance word, a silence, all of these contingencies which should be erased behind me become inscribed upon this child, who ruminates and who will remember, as I remember the inflexions of Dominique's voice. It seems unfair. One cannot be responsible for everything one does or doesn't do.[23]

From an existentialist point of view, this statement would be a quintessential example of bad faith. One must indeed take responsibility for what one does or doesn't do. But what of the responsibility which society cavalierly foists upon mothers, ever ready to blame them for anything that goes wrong with their children? Laurence is sensitive enough to be fully aware of this tradition which she considers an injustice and to feel weighted down by the heavy burden of the task she assumed simply by giving birth to Catherine and Louise.

When Laurence travels to Greece with her father, she hopes to find in him the answers to all of her own questions and then pass them on to her daughters. What she finds instead is some disturbingly negative images of motherhood. In Delphi she watches a little girl totally absorbed in her dancing:

> Placid and fat, her mother was gossiping with another enormous woman, rocking a carriage with a baby inside it back and forth. Insensitive to the music, the night, she occasionally cast a bovine glance toward the inspired child. . . . A charming little girl who would one day become that matron.[24]

Popular tradition has it that anyone wanting to look into the future to see what a young girl will be like after she matures need only observe the girl's mother closely. In this scene, Laurence is charmed by the spontaneity and passion of the little Greek girl, appalled at the insensitivity of her mother, at the limited scope of the life which awaits her. Like Simone de Beauvoir recalling Zaza's death, Laurence cries out against the tragedy of a life whose potential will never be realized:

No. I didn't want that to happen. . . . I refused to allow her to resemble her mother one day, no longer remembering that she was once this adorable reveler. A little girl condemned to death, a frightful death without a corpse. Life was going to assassinate her. I thought of how they were assassinating Catherine.[25]

In this passage the reader finds a poignant contrast between childhood and adulthood, between the ability to be moved which is innate in most children and the blasé indifference of the adult world. The scene also echoes a theme from *The Mandarins,* where psychology and psychiatry become killers destroying individual spirit in favor of social conformity. Before Laurence left on the trip with her father, she reluctantly gave in to Jean-Charles's insistence that they send Catherine to see a psychologist. As she watches the little Greek girl and her uninspired mother, Laurence is convinced that the psychologist will mutilate her daughter's sensitivity and is tempted to take the next plane home in order to protect her. A few days later, seeking some nourishment in Andritsena, all she can find is two rotten eggs. Whether the symbolism is intentional or not, there is a strong implication that these eggs may parallel those produced both by Dominique and by Laurence unless the latter acts quickly to reorient the course of her daughters' lives.

It is while fighting for Catherine's independence against the psychologist and everyone else in the family that Laurence finds herself literally unable to stomach what is going on around her or within her after her return from Greece. Her father, who seemed earlier to agree with her opinion of psychologists, is now just one of a chorus of voices urging her to entrust Catherine to a specialist. She has the impression that everyone is in league against her, that everyone else is content with a false picture of family bliss in which she sees so many imperfections:

Once again she is overwhelmed by the image she represses as vehemently as she can, the one which emerges as soon as she lets down her guard: Jean-Charles, Papa, Dominique, grinning as if they were part of an American poster advertising some brand of oatmeal. Reconciled, participating together in the joys of family living.[26]

The metaphor of the American oatmeal poster is delightfully sardonic, recalling Beauvoir's observations of the perennial smile which followed her in her travels across the United States in 1947. She undoubtedly considered the American smile as shallow as Laurence finds the family unity suddenly surrounding her. Unable to participate in this Pollyannaish existence, Laurence retreats to her sickbed, refusing to see a doctor and preferring not to eat: "They will force her to eat, they will make her swallow everything . . . everything that she is regurgitating: her life, the lives of others with their false loves, their money concerns, their lies.

They will cure her of her rebellions, of her despair. No."[27] For Laurence as for Simone de Beauvoir there is value in rebellion, authenticity in refusing to accept the pablum of the media's "beautiful images." If anorexia is the only effective way in which she can rebel against the hypocrisy she senses all around her, Laurence will remain anorexic to the end.

As long as Laurence continued to act like the exemplary young woman Dominique had raised her to be, Jean-Charles knew how to deal with her, how to impose his will on the entire family. She began to lose patience with his paternalistic attitude, however, the day he ranted and raved about Catherine's mediocre report card: "He is so sure of his rights. Furious if we disturb the image he has formed of us in his mind, exemplary little girl, exemplary young woman. He doesn't give a damn who we really are."[28] Here as in several other passages, Laurence feels inextricably bound to her daughters and to all women who have been forced to assume passive roles in their families. The symbiotic feelings she has for her older daughter are very much in evidence when Jean-Charles's cavalier dinner-table discussion of Catherine's problems in front of all the adult members of the family makes her cringe.

By identifying too closely with Catherine, however, Laurence cannot effectively mother this child who is looking to her for guidance. She must first take close stock of herself. This involves reacting to Lucien's angry statement that she has a frigid heart—echoes once again of the kid gloves and the clock in the refrigerator—to Jean-Charles's complaints about her overly sensitive nature, to his suggestion that she too would benefit from therapy. She is uncomfortable with her own inability to respond to her emotions, aware that she is hopelessly indecisive. Until the last few pages of the novel, the reader fears that Laurence may simply continue to allow things to happen to her, that this passivity, this unwillingness to ingest anything, may literally kill her.

Just as the thought of Nadine kept Anne Dubreuilh from committing suicide at the end of *The Mandarins,* however, it is Laurence's very real concern for Catherine's future that shakes her from her torpor and inspires her to do battle with Jean-Charles: "And Catherine? Nail her eyelids shut? No! . . . I will not allow them to make of her what they have made of me. . . . This woman who loves no one, who is insensitive to the beauties of the world, incapable even of crying, this woman I am regurgitating."[29] As she thinks of her older daughter, Laurence regains some sense of her ability to influence the course of events. She is determined, with missionary zeal, to lead Catherine out of darkness, ignorance, and indifference, to encourage her to follow the dictates of her own emotions. The novel ends on an ambivalent rather than triumphant note, however, as Laurence sits up in her bed brushing her hair and muses, "For me the die is cast.... But the children will have their chance. Chance for what? She doesn't even know."[30]

The final lines of the novel raise a question that all parents eventually ask themselves: what are their hopes for their children, for future generations? "Happiness" would perhaps be the first word that comes to mind as an answer to this question, but it merely leads to more queries about the definition of happiness. Laurence is too perceptive to accept the images of contentment promulgated by the media and by middle-class values. She is honest enough to admit that although she wants something different for her children, she cannot identify exactly what it should be.

In *Les Belles Images,* Simone de Beauvoir traces the painful process through which Laurence comes to accept her own maturity, a maturity that forces her to rely upon her own resources. As she watches her younger daughter Louise drawing contentedly in her room with her crayons, Laurence remembers similar happy moments in her own childhood: "Precious moments lost forever. For them too, one day, they will be lost forever. What a shame! Let's keep them from growing up. Or else ... what?"[31] Despite her ambivalent feelings toward Dominique, she too would have preferred never to grow up. Growing up can mean losing that glow, that sensuous appreciation of life that Laurence was aware of in the little Greek dancer, as one assumes the responsibilities and burdens of everyday existence. Seeing one's children grow up is a bittersweet experience. The maturing of the younger generation can weaken the parent-child relationship irreparably as young adults move away from home both physically and emotionally, leaving their parents, but particularly their mother, to face the slow but unyielding approach of old age and death. In the cozy image of Louise and her crayons one finds a taste of the nostalgia Simone de Beauvoir felt for the lost and comfortable paradise of her childhood.

It is no coincidence that *Les Belles Images* is the first of Beauvoir's works to follow *A Very Easy Death.* Despite some critical commentary to the contrary, it is my opinion that the two works deal with many of the same themes, with the novel sometimes parodying subjects still too painful for Simone de Beauvoir to treat directly. Dominique's newly found financial and social security represented by her reunion with her husband is portrayed as a kind of living death not unlike the one Beauvoir felt had imprisoned her mother in a cage of passive conformity. The two women's life-styles may be diametrically opposed, but the lack of authenticity in their respective existences joins them together in the author's mind. Both women evoke both condescension and pity in their older daughters.

Laurence is headed for another type of demise if she cannot change the course her life is taking. Not only is she physically threatened by her refusal to ingest the hypocrisy of the technological world in which she lives, but she is also psychologically in danger of emotional paralysis. She shares Beauvoir's disillusionment with a father once adored, her difficulty understanding a younger generation more articulate about emotions than hers was raised to be. She is in many ways a woman in limbo, caught between the traditional responsibilities of wife and mother and a professional, trendy world. Her intelligence, her sensitivity, and her success in her advertising career would suggest that she should represent the independent modern woman described in *The Second Sex*. It is perhaps Beauvoir's adamant feelings about the dangers of family life that caused her to turn Laurence into a confused, suffering matron unsure of the road she must take in order to find a satisfactory identity of her own.

Critical Reaction

Looking back on her intentions in writing *Les Belles Images,* Simone de Beauvoir proclaims that she set out to depict the technological society in which she lived but from which she made every effort to distance herself.[32] Several of her early critics suggest that she reproduced so well the platitudes and shallowness of this society that her novel suffered accordingly. Robert Cottrell, ever caustic in his analysis of Beauvoir's works, finds Laurence's nausea "a rather worn image, coming nearly thirty years after Sartre's *La Nausée.*"[33] He does not consider the degree to which her eating disorder may be a specifically female malaise, one which will later be clinically associated with the trauma of the mother-daughter relationship by Kim Chernin in her 1985 book *The Hungry Self.* Discussing Laurence's empathy with her mother's plight, he notes that "grief, anguish, rage are not 'lovely images.' They are the raw stuff of authentic experience as contrasted to the artificiality of carefully contrived images."[34] In Cottrell's opinion, the novel is too didactic to portray rejection of bourgeois values in a dramatically effective context.

It is of interest that Jean Leighton, in a book focused on the analysis of Beauvoir's heroines, does not touch upon either *Les Belles Images* or *The Woman Destroyed* or even list the titles in her Selected Bibliography. There appears to have been a tendency among the critics of the 1970s to pass over both works as lightweight and unworthy of serious attention. Like Robert Cottrell, Konrad Bieber finds *Les Belles Images* rather shallow, the characters presented closer to caricatures than to believable human beings. He sees a parallel between Laurence's adored father and Jean-Paul Sartre, yet considers Dominique and Laurence "miles away from Simone de Beauvoir in their tastes, opinions (except Laurence's on torture), and mannerisms."[35] In reviewing other critical comment on the novel, Bieber notes:

> Critics have taken Beauvoir to task, in *Les Belles Images* as well as in *The Mandarins*, for failing to convincingly depict the relationship between mothers and daughters. Because the author often stated her determination not to give birth, the critics, conveniently ignoring the reasons why the author never wanted children, have concluded that she must be ignorant about child psychology and motherly feelings altogether. That this is untrue is easily verifiable for any reader of *The Second Sex*, *A Very Easy Death*, and *The Coming of Age*.[36]

For Bieber, Laurence is "a somewhat less than fully satisfying heroine,"[37] one he suggests may have been used by Beauvoir to indicate "the futility and frivolousness of women's professionalism without strong ideological commitment."[38]

Carol Ascher refers to *Les Belles Images* as a modern *Doll's House* depicting a mother who must pass her own uneasy conscience on to her daughters.[39] Terry Keefe is one of the few critics presenting a detailed and serious analysis of *Les Belles Images*. He finds the novel's beginning brilliantly ironical. Pointing out the degree to which Laurence's admiration for her father's articulated values is responsible for her hostility to those of her mother, he notes that it is surprising to see her deciding when she is apparently only in her early thirties that she can do nothing to change her life or the "social web" in which she is "ensnared."[40] This attitude will be seen as a reflection of Beauvoir's when we examine some of the interviews she granted and her comments about the trap in which married women with children found themselves. Keefe emphasizes the fact that Laurence's upbringing was totally dominated by her mother and that her anxiety over Catherine's future is the result of a long-simmering rebellion against the way in which she herself was raised. He assumes, unconvincingly in my opinion, that Catherine was the result of an unplanned premarital pregnancy. Keefe pays tribute to Beauvoir's literary talent, stating that "the depth and resonance of the final sections of *Les Belles Images* are unmatched anywhere in Beauvoir's fiction and the ending itself confirms that one of the principal themes of the book is that of the complex ramifications of upbringing."[41] Finding it surprising that some critics treated the novel "as some kind of inferior imitation of the fiction of Françoise Sagan," Keefe suggests that they have missed the point, and credits the author with having successfully carried out the goal she claimed for the novel in *All Said and Done,* that of making silence speak out.[42]

Simone de Beauvoir expressed in a number of interviews her dismay with the lack of serious critical comment on her fictional works. A close analysis of *Les Belles Images* and the collection of three stories published a year later indicates that her autobiographical works and her fiction formed a dialectic in which such crucial issues as the mother-child relationship were examined by the penetrating gaze of an increasingly militant feminist who found herself torn between her debt to a happy and secure childhood and her conviction that motherhood and family life prevented women from capitalizing on their full potential.

Motherhood and Disillusionment:
The Woman Destroyed

One of the major themes in each of the three stories which make up the 1967 collection *La Femme rompue,* translated into English as *The Woman Destroyed,* is that of unfulfilled motherhood. The sixty-year-old protagonist of "Age of Discretion" finds her career and her maternal responsibilities coming to an end at the same time. In "Monologue," forty-three-year-old Murielle has been a blatant failure at motherhood in the eyes of society. She spends New Year's Eve trying to justify the way she has chosen to raise her children and to live her life. In the title story, Monique is obliged to revise all of her convictions about her success in creating a happy and secure home for her husband and her two daughters when she learns that her husband is interested in another woman.

The protagonist of "Age of Discretion" remains unnamed. We first meet her as she waits impatiently for the arrival of her thirty-year-old son Philippe, wondering if her watch has stopped because time seems to be moving so slowly. She wanders nostalgically about his old room, where "books, papers, an old gray pullover, a pair of purple pajamas are still lying around, this room I cannot bring myself to change because I don't have the time, or the money, because I don't want to believe that Philippe no longer belongs to me."[1] The use of the verb "belong" (*appartenir*) is something we have seen previously when Françoise Miquel spoke of Xavière Pagès in *She Came to Stay.* In Beauvoir's opinion, mothers and those who take on maternal roles sometimes assume, wrongly, that the human beings they are nurturing "belong" to them and tend to treat them like material possessions.

The above passage accurately records the reluctance of most mothers to admit that their children, and perhaps particularly their sons, are grown up and independent and can never realistically be expected to live at home again. The opening scene of this story echoes the section in *The Blood of Others* in which Jean Blomart hesitatingly leaves his mother to the quiet and the luxury of his childhood home, torn between his need to prove his maturity and his sense of guilt at abandoning her both physically and emotionally. The passage also recalls Laurence's plaintive wish in *Les Belles Images* that she could find some way of preventing her two little girls from growing up, of keeping them forever as happy and secure as they are at that particular moment coloring with their crayons in their room. A psychiatric social worker talking about the death of a five-year-old leukemia victim once remarked cannily that all mothers mourn the disappearance of the five-year-olds their children once were.

The protagonist of Beauvoir's first story is not a woman who has confined her energies to her home. She is a recently retired professor, author of several books. She has attempted to inspire in her son the same kind of enthusiasm she herself feels for literature and writing: "Why did I insist on making an intellectual out of Philippe when André would have allowed him to become involved in other pursuits? As a child, as an adolescent, I was saved from despair by books. That persuaded me that culture is the highest of values."[2] This query gives us one of our few insights into the protagonist's past, suggesting that she, like the author who created her, found solace and escape in literature as she was growing up. She understandably wishes to share this appreciation of culture with her only child.

As the story progresses, it becomes obvious that orienting Philippe toward a university teaching career has been no easy task. His mother recalls battles over unfinished homework, an Easter vacation when he was left behind to complete his schoolwork while his parents traveled in Holland. The young boy often defied his mother and her ambitions for him, swearing that he would not write a single word of his assignment, begging her in vain to provide him with parental excuses for not having completed his work while he was in elementary school. Echoing through these reminiscences are the painful experiences of many academically oriented parents who have attempted to propel their offspring toward an equally enthusiastic approach to their studies, with only minimal success. As Beauvoir's story opens, Philippe has only to finish his thesis and he will become a colleague of his mother's. She is looking forward to hearing his comments on the proofs of her latest book, which she left for him to read a few weeks earlier.

While the protagonist is awaiting her son's arrival, it becomes apparent that she would also like to relate to him in a way that is much more seductive than intellectual. When he commented several years earlier that she was growing plump, she quickly bought a scale, went on a diet, and was annoyed by the fact that he never really noticed her subsequent loss of weight. On this particular evening, she has prepared Philippe's favorite dishes and donned her prettiest dress. She hastens to embrace him as he crosses the threshold, thinking as she does so, "Suddenly he appeared . . . he gave me a big hug as his words expressed his joy and I abandoned myself to the tenderness of his flannel jacket against my cheek."[3] If the reader had not already been informed that Philippe was her son, this passage would undoubtedly make one jump to the conclusion that she was talking about a long-lost lover. Studies have shown that often the most passionately romantic feelings women have are for their children rather than for their husbands or lovers, and most particularly for their male children. This theme will be taken up again by Beauvoir in the second story of the collection, "Monologue."

Another surprise for the reader, who is dependent upon the protagonist for all of the information about this family, is the realization that Philippe is married. His mother would apparently much prefer to forget this fact. She thinks to herself peevishly, "I always forget her and she is always there. . . . I quickly erased her from my mind. I was alone with Philippe as I used to be when I awakened him every morning with a kiss on the forehead."[4] From Marcel Proust on, childhood memories of being tucked into bed at night and awakened in the morning by a loving mother have been depicted as poignant reminders of a lost past, of a time when mother and child related to each other in a very special and intimate way. In this story it is the mother who wishes to hang on to that past, in contrast to the scene in *The Blood of Others* in which Jean Blomart would like to forget his Resistance responsibilities and have his mother tuck him into his comfortable old bed. Anne Dubreuilh's willingness to tuck Nadine and her young lover into bed in *The Mandarins* provides still another example of maternal nostalgia for the less complicated relationships of early childhood. We know from the autobiography that that particular detail is based on Beauvoir's adopting a similarly maternal attitude toward her former student Nathalie Sorokine and the latter's young lover Bourla. That maternal gesture of tucking in at night and awakening gently in the morning is poignantly symbolic of the degree to which mothers and mother figures attempt to encompass the lives of those they nurture and protect them from outside harm.

It becomes considerably more difficult to imagine oneself alone with one's child when that child is thirty years old and has his new bride standing right beside him, however. Beauvoir's protagonist would like to "erase" Irène from her mind, indeed from the world if only she could, as she makes vivid use of a teacher's favorite method of making things disappear from the classroom blackboard with the verb *effacer*. Daughters-in-law cannot be so easily erased, however. Philippe's mother has never approved of his taste in women, we learn, undoubtedly because each of them has represented to her a rival for his affections. She remembers how her heart pounded when he announced that he planned to marry Irène, assuring her that she would like Irène because she too was a career woman. It is evident that Philippe had made up his own mind and was simply conveying his decision to his mother, not asking her for advice.

A member of an older generation who has in her own way managed to juggle home and career responsibilities, the protagonist is nonetheless severely critical of the modern "superwoman":

> I know these fashionable young women. They have some vague career, they claim to be cultured, to participate in sports, to dress well, to keep a spotless home, to raise their children perfectly, to have an active social life, in short to be successful at everything. And they don't really care about anything. They make my blood run cold.[5]

The utter disdain in her attitude is underlined by the use of the pronoun *on* rather than *elles* to refer to these young women in the original French. Philippe's mother is quick to judge this younger generation and most particularly Irène, ready to dislike her because she comes from the wealthy upper-middle-class milieu which is anathema to leftist intellectuals like her husband and herself.

The anticipation of Philippe's visit turns into frustration, first when he sheepishly admits that he has not even glanced at the proofs of his mother's book, then when he announces that he has decided to abandon his plans for a university career in order to be available for a lucrative position his new father-in-law has hopes of procuring for him. As Irène helps Philippe explain his decision, his appalled mother interprets everything that is said as a direct attack on her values:

> In well-measured phrases, she let us know what she thought of us. . . . We are cut off from the world, our lives confined to laboratories and libraries. . . . Irène is not as stupid as I had thought. She exists, she counts, she has nullified the victory I won with Philippe, against him, for him.[6]

Her relationship with her son has indeed been one long battle, a battle which she thought she had won until Irène appeared on the scene. Now that she realizes the important role Irène plays in Philippe's life, she senses that her whole value system is under attack by the younger generation. She is put in the same position as Françoise Miquel was in *She*

Came to Stay when Xavière taunted her about her well-programmed life, as Anne Dubreuilh was in *The Mandarins* when her daughter Nadine questioned the validity of her psychiatric work and of the sheltered intellectual life led by both of her parents. She reacts, however, more like the Françoise of the final pages of *She Came to Stay* than like Anne, with utter rage rather than suicidal depression.

All of this mother's anger is concentrated on the daughter-in-law who, she feels, is taking her son away from her irrevocably. Although she is intellectually aware that it is quite normal for a sexually attractive young woman to replace an aging mother in a young man's affections, this in no way softens the impact of the blow: "I am the one who fashioned his life. Now I will remain outside of it, a distant spectator. This is the fate common to all mothers; but who has ever found consolation in the fact that one's fate is shared by others?"[7] She realizes that she has been trying to delude herself into believing that Philippe was coming home to stay. From now on he will never again be anything but a visitor, a visitor who owes his allegiance to his bride rather than to his doting mother, a visitor twice removed who has turned his back on the cultural and intellectual values of his parents in order to join the technocracy.

Philippe's scientist father André is small consolation. He is convinced that his creative days are over and is brooding over his own aging. While Philippe was still at home, it was he who would accompany his mother to the races, to art exhibits, to a bar for a late-night drink. Now she is frantic at the thought of the silence that will permeate the household without her son's cherished presence. André is not terribly sympathetic to his wife's plight, reminding her that Philippe had never been very enthusiastic about pursuing a university career, that he only did so to please her. She counters by accusing him of negativism, complaining that his limited expectations of Philippe are responsible for his recently proven mediocrity. Like many a mother, she feels that she alone understands her son, that together mother and son have created a human being of whom she has until this moment been duly proud. This carefully concocted creation is now evaporating:

> What did I think would happen? Because he was demanding I thought I was indispensable. Because he allows himself to be easily influenced I thought I had created him in my image.... I was the only one who knew the real Philippe. And he is choosing to put distance between us, to destroy our complicity, to refuse the life which I had built for him with such effort. He will become a stranger.[8]

In the words chosen here by Simone de Beauvoir, we see her view of the overpossessive mother who takes on godlike proportions in her own mind, feeling that she has created her children in her own image, and who attempts to mold and manipulate psychologically these lives for which she is physically responsible. There is obviously a much more charged emotional bond between Philippe and his mother than between Philippe and André, a discrepancy which casts André in the unenviable position of mediator for the other members of his family.

In many ways the protagonist acts like a rejected lover. She admits her awareness of Philippe's faults, her willingness to accept them as an integral part of this young man she loves. She cannot understand why he does not call immediately after their first confrontation to smooth things over with his usual sweet talk. When she learns through André that their son has actually accepted a position with the Ministry of Culture, she explodes, rushes to the telephone, and angrily accuses him of opportunism. Having evidently inherited his mother's volatile temperament, Philippe counters with the devastating assertion, "A person is not a bastard just because he refuses to share in your senile obsessions."[9] For a woman who is concerned about aging, who fears that her recent retirement will keep her out of the mainstream of life, such an accusation from the person in whom she has invested a major part of herself is intolerable. She slams down the phone, swearing that she will never see Philippe again, and announces dramatically to her husband, "It's all over between Philippe and me."[10] These words sound as if they come straight out of the melodramatic exaggerations of nineteenth-century theatre and opera.

During the ensuing days, the protagonist returns her son's letters unopened, hangs up immediately when she recognizes his voice on the telephone. Here again she is acting like a rejected mistress. In one poignant scene, she returns to Philippe's old room which she contemplated so lovingly in the opening paragraphs of the story, tears up his papers, throws away a number of his things, and packs what is left in suitcases. The author gives us privileged access to her thoughts: "Faced with the bare shelves, I felt tears welling up in my eyes. So many moving, upsetting, delightful memories rose within me. I would twist their necks. He had left me, betrayed me, ridiculed me, insulted me. I would never forgive him."[11] The violence of this mother's reaction to the inevitable separation that must take place between her and her adult son is underlined by her desire to "twist the neck" of the happy images that arise in her memory. Her pride is wounded both by Philippe's angry words implying that she is outdated and useless and by the reality of his allegiance to Irène. "Married. Gone over to the other side," she reflects angrily.[12] Apparently, in her view humanity is divided between idealistic intellectuals on one side and, on the other, the technocrats and materialists whose lack of scruples will one day destroy the world. In her opinion her son has just joined the enemy.

Hour after hour the protagonist ruminates about her loss of control over her son. She has heretofore thrived on the symbiosis of their relationship, speculating, "Had he been less capricious, less casual, he would have needed me less. He would not have been so delightfully tender if he hadn't had to ask my forgiveness continually."[13] Simone de Beauvoir's negative feelings about motherhood are reflected in her treatment of this fictional character. This mother has evidently fed on her son's weaknesses, using them to manipulate and control his life. Like Anne Dubreuilh in *The Mandarins,* she needs to feel needed. Philippe has grown up, however, and is ready to stand on his own two feet. He is nonetheless willing to act out his old role of beloved offender to a degree. Having written, phoned, and sent his wife, all to no avail, he himself appears at the doorstep and insists that his mother let him in. Putting his arms around her, he coos seductively, "My little one, my beloved, I beg of you, don't hate me. I can't live cut off from you. I beg of you. I love you so!"[14] Her first instinct is to return her "little boy's" embrace. He is no longer a little boy, however.

Philippe continues to use a psychology which has undoubtedly worked in the past, acting essentially like a rejected lover. "I can't sleep thinking about this," he laments. "I don't want to lose you. Take pity on me. You are making me so unhappy!"[15] There is undoubtedly a great deal of irony in Beauvoir's choice of dialogue for this story as she highlights the emotional entanglements that can occur between a manipulative mother and her seductive son. In this scene, the protagonist steels herself, forcing herself not to succumb to this assault on her well-worn emotions by continually reminding herself that this young man is essentially Irène's husband and no longer really her son. This rationalization raises the issue of mother-child relationships, suggesting that a son is no longer a son once he refuses to follow the dictates of his mother's plans for him.

Philippe clearly senses the implications of his mother's tyrannical ways. Failing to convince her of the validity of his choice of career, he allows all of the resentments that have accumulated over the years to roll off his tongue:

> In your mind, love must be deserved. I certainly tried hard enough not to be judged unworthy of it. All my wishes—to be an aviator, or a race car driver, or a reporter, to find action, adventure—you treated as whims; I gave them up to make you happy. The first time I don't give in to you, you cut off all communication with me. . . . After all, I wasn't going to obey you all my life. You are too tyrannical. Basically you have no heart, just a will to power. . . . Very well! Farewell! Look down on me all you like. I'll manage without you.[16]

These are powerful words, spoken in anger, an anger which seems quite justified. It is apparent that Philippe's temperament has encouraged him to seek adventure, to want to pull away from the more intellectual life led by his parents. His very real emotional attachment to his mother has kept him from rebelling earlier. Her domineering ways have made him passive, willing to travel the roads she has mapped out for him rather than risk incurring her displeasure. Now that his self-confidence is bolstered by his wife, he is for the first time willing to criticize his mother's determination to control him, and to declare his independence, even if it means losing her approval.

Even after Philippe has slammed the door and left, his mother expects him to return so that they can cry together and be reconciled. These emotionally charged scenes have obviously been an integral part of the interaction between mother and son over the years. This time, however, Philippe does not come back. As André later tries to explain to his wife, the young man has desperately needed to take a stand against the pressure applied by his mother, against the expectations of two very successful parents who have assumed that he shares their goals and ideals.

Only with time can the protagonist begin to think of her son without anger and pain. Without pleasure either. She and her husband agree that things will never again be the same between them and Philippe. For this particular mother, psychological maturity brings her to accept her son as a separate entity in whom her vested interest has turned out to be a disappointment, and to realize that her emotional commitment during the years that remain in her life must be rather to her aging husband than to her grown child. Perhaps her contacts with former students and younger colleagues can indeed lighten the burden of aging, carrying her along into their future, "beyond [her] own grave."[17] Perhaps she will find a cause that will absorb the energy she once put into her relationship with Philippe and into her teaching, just as André's eighty-four-year-old mother seems perfectly satisfied with her life as an actively militant member of the Communist Party who still looks forward to the future with a sense of adventure.

Whatever the future may hold, the reader has the impression that the protagonist's spirit has been sadly broken. Time alone will help to mend her bruised sense of identity, an identity inextricably bound to her ill-placed satisfaction with having a son who was to be a successful academic created in her own image. Even though she eventually agrees to see and speak to Philippe again at the end of the story, the hopes and dreams for the future which he once represented for her have evaporated, leaving her uninspired and resigned to spending her last decades crawling with her husband relentlessly toward death, according to Simone de Beauvoir's vivid metaphor.

For the mother of this first story, the age of discretion is reached when she accepts the fact that she has lost control over her son, that she can no longer count on him to keep her from feeling old. If ever a Beauvoirian character had absolutely no discretion, it is Murielle, the owner of the voice we hear in the second story, "Monologue." One might well label Murielle a maternal megalomaniac. The reader keeps her company throughout New Year's Eve and the dawn of another year as she rails against the injustices of her life.

Forty-three-year-old Murielle has had two husbands and two children, none of whom is living with her at the moment. She nervously anticipates making a bid to get her eleven-year-old son Francis back, repeating again and again that it is not normal to deprive a child of his mother. The degree of Murielle's neurosis becomes apparent as she thinks of ways to force her second husband Tristan to move back in with her: "I'll throw a fit in front of the child open my veins on their doorstep . . . . All those other old bags have a man to protect them kids to wait on them and I have nothing. Things can't go on like this."[18] Murielle's diatribe is essentially unpunctuated, giving the impression of an uninterrupted attack on humanity in general. In her determination to manipulate others, she is obsessed by the possibility of traumatizing her family members with a messy suicide: "If I were to kill myself in front of [Francis] wouldn't that be a nice memory for him? . . . I'll shoot myself in [Tristan's] living room I'll open my veins when they come home there will be blood everywhere and I'll be dead."[19] Unlike Anne Dubreuilh, who abandoned her suicidal thoughts precisely because of the effect such an act might have on the people she most loved, Murielle uses suicide threats as a weapon to force others to pay attention to her. She takes a sadistic delight in imagining the gory blood-bathed scene and the trauma it might produce for the son she is supposedly eager to take to the circus, the zoo, the ice capades.

Murielle's obsession with suicide becomes more understandable when we learn that her seventeen-year-old daughter Sylvie killed herself five years earlier. Murielle has been particularly affected by this suicide because her own mother publicly accused her of murder at her daughter's funeral. Almost everything which is said throughout this monologue is an attempt by Murielle to persuade an invisible listener, and herself, that she is not guilty as charged. The reader would be more sympathetic to Murielle's plight if every word she uttered did not seem to be impregnated with the proverbial existential bad faith. As she proceeds to prove that she always had Sylvie's best interests at heart, she reveals that she read through her daughter's private diary, that she tore up the note Sylvie left for her father asking for his forgiveness and explaining that she could no longer go on. The implication of this note is that Sylvie decided death was preferable to living under her mother's roof, to coping on a daily basis with Murielle's manipulative and neurotic ways. Murielle attributes this attitude to the interference of family members who made Sylvie feel like a martyr. She would like to believe that the death was an accident, a miscalculated melodramatic bid for attention. She would also like to convince herself that it was an unwanted pregnancy or blackmail rather than her relationship with her mother which prompted Sylvie to take her own life. All of this rationalization points clearly to the fact that Murielle is experiencing a good deal of guilt about the fatal results of her relationship with her daughter but is unwilling to face the reality of her own shortcomings as a mother.

As she continues her monologue, Murielle directs much of her anger at Sylvie and her "ingratitude": "I kept her under surveillance yes. I was firm but I was tender always ready to chat with her I wanted to be her friend.... But what an ungrateful temperament! She's dead. What of it? The dead aren't saints. She didn't cooperate she never confided in me."[20] The extremes of Murielle's reactions suggest a manic-depressive personality, exalting one moment in the wonderfully symbiotic relationship she would like to think she had with Sylvie, furious the next at her daughter's audacity in killing herself and leaving her mother with this burden of guilt. Anne Dubreuilh in *The Mandarins* visualized the outrage her daughter Nadine would express were she to leave her to cope with her suicide. Beauvoir does an excellent job of portraying such outrage as she depicts Murielle reminding us that people are not saints just because they have died. This passage echoes sardonically the author's more sober analysis, in the final pages of *A Very Easy Death,* of the guilt we all feel after the death of a loved one.

Whereas Beauvoir confessed to her readers that she and her sister had not always taken enough time out of their busy lives to spend with their aging mother, however, Murielle is incapable of admitting that she has ever done anything wrong. She extols her own maternal virtues and bemoans her daughter's lack of appreciation, proclaiming, "I had a lot to give to Sylvie I would have made a fine girl of her. And I didn't ask anything of her. I devoted myself entirely to her. Such ingratitude!"[21] This rationalization is reminiscent of the characters in Sartre's *No Exit,* two of whom protest with wide-eyed innocence that they have no idea why they have been relegated to hell. The popular aphorism that the road to hell is paved with good intentions blends well with the existentialist notion of acting in bad faith, which is illustrated so dramatically both in Beauvoir's short story and in Sartre's play.

The litany of Murielle's sacrifices includes her marriage to Tristan, for whom she abandoned another promising lover. "Sylvie the little ingrate," she exclaims, "I wanted her to have a real home and an irreproachable mother a married woman the wife of a banker."[22] This wonderfully naive assumption that being married, and to a respectable middle-class banker at that, makes a woman a perfect mother is treated with consummate irony here by Beauvoir. Murielle, playing the martyr to the hilt, would like others to conclude that her conscientious concern for her daughter not only influenced her choice of a second husband but ruined her life, a life she would have lived much more happily with the more attentive Florent.

Like the protagonist of "Age of Discretion," Murielle feels that her child's decision, in this case a fatal one, has undermined years of careful maternal planning: "So much effort so many struggles scenes sacrifices: in vain. The work of my life up in smoke. I left nothing to chance; and the most cruel of chances fell across my path."[23] The mothers in both of these stories appear to consider their children their life work. To the protagonist of "Age of Discretion" Philippe is more emotionally significant as a gauge of success than the books she has had published, the classes she has taught. In contrast to Philippe, Sylvie never seems to have cooperated with her mother's plans for her. Murielle is deceiving herself when she labels Sylvie's suicide "the most cruel of chances." Sylvie chose suicide as the only viable means of escaping from her mother's domination. Murielle appears to be a hopeless neurotic who has attempted to use her children to justify her own existence. We learn that when Sylvie ran away and expressed her desire to live with her father and his new family, Murielle refused to allow her this freedom, protesting that her decision was for her daughter's own good, that Sylvie would become a mere maid in a household of younger children. Murielle spends a good deal of time searching for justifications for her past acts. The reader senses that she has been put on the defensive by the judgments of family, friends, and society, and that this monologue represents a violent catharsis as she spews out all of the bitterness and anger that has been accumulating inside her since her life ceased to conform to traditional bourgeois standards.

Rage mingles with self-justification as Murielle relives the day on which the maid could not awaken Sylvie:

> Yes, if I were one of those mothers who gets up at seven o'clock in the morning we would have saved her but my life has a different rhythm there's nothing criminal

about that how could I have guessed? I was always there when she came home from school many mothers can't say the same ready to chat with her to question her she was the one who would shut herself up in her room on the pretext of doing her school work. I never failed her.[24]

In this passage she is trying to prove two contradictory things. First she prides herself on being a bit eccentric in her life-style, sleeping late in the morning, "marching to a different drummer," and loudly proclaims that there is nothing wrong in that. Second she tries to convince her invisible listener that she was more traditional than the most traditional of mothers in raising Sylvie, insistent upon being home when her daughter returned from school so that she could be available to her. Once again she attempts to place all of the blame squarely on Sylvie's shoulders, Sylvie who did not appreciate her friendly overtures and who shut herself off from Murielle's well-meant efforts at nurturing. Just as Laurence in *Les Belles Images* asserts that if her ten-year-old daughter is crying out at night it must be her fault, Murielle is all too aware that society holds a mother accountable for the suicide of her adolescent daughter. Whereas Laurence was more than willing to assume responsibility for Catherine's unhappiness, however, Murielle performs all sorts of psychological acrobatics in her determination to prove herself innocent.

The unkindest blow of all and an admittedly cruel one was the public accusation made at Sylvie's funeral by Murielle's mother, who shouted out, "You killed her!"[25] The reader learns early in the monologue that there has been little love lost between Murielle and her mother, whose closeness to her young son Nanard has always been a thorn in Murielle's side:

> Nanard was king. She would take him into her bed in the morning I could hear them tickling each other ... she would prance around her bedroom bordello half naked in her white silk nightgown with cigarette burns and holes in it he would hang on to her thighs mothers with their little males are enough to make you sick.[26]

Simone de Beauvoir is here depicting a sibling rivalry she never experienced, the jealousy aroused in a daughter by her mother's distinctive sensual preference for her brother. Murielle's way of dealing with anger is to use vulgarity, and she here accuses her mother of acting like a whore in a bordello with her younger brother. Both Nanard and their mother deny that there was ever anything more than a normal mother-son relationship between them, but Murielle thinks otherwise. Although Murielle's sex life has undoubtedly not been beyond reproach, she exults in vilifying her mother, whose supposedly loose morals she uses to explain her rigidity in what she would allow Sylvie to wear: "I didn't want my daughter to become a whore like my mother. At seventy skirts up to her knee paint all over her face!"[27] The simile used here by Murielle, and indeed much of the language in her monologue, shows an uncharacteristic audacity on Beauvoir's part, a willingness to allow her protagonist at least to "throw Momma from the train."

Intent upon forcing her mother to retract what she said at the funeral, Murielle telephones her during the early hours of the morning on New Year's Day. The reader must of course take into account the unbalanced state of Murielle's mind. Her vulnerability when she finds herself rebuffed once again is nonetheless a poignant indication of the impact of a mother's judgment on her daughter:

> My mother; a mother is a mother after all I didn't do anything to her she's the one who botched up my childhood she insulted me she dared say to me . . . I want her to take back what she said I will not continue to live with that cry in my ears a daughter can't stand being cursed by her mother even if that mother is the worst of whores.[28]

Murielle is here again trying to diminish the value of her mother's pronouncement in her own mind by labelling her a whore while at the same time indicating how very painful it is for her to have no support from her own mother in dealing with her daughter's suicide. The degree of pain is clearly evidenced by the fact that she cannot even bring herself to repeat her mother's words in this passage.

Murielle becomes almost a caricature of Françoise de Beauvoir as she explains that the methods she used in bringing up Sylvie were an attempt to give to her daughter the affection she never had from her own mother. Insisting that she really tried to become Sylvie's friend, she reflects bitterly, "I would have kissed my mother's hands if she had behaved that way with me."[29] Her recollection of her relationship with her mother suggests, however, that emotional deprivation, real or imagined, was only one facet of it. We learn that as a child Murielle felt close to her father, who died when she was quite young. Her mother takes on the role of wicked witch in her portrayal of her, beating her at the least provocation after her father's death. She finds herself drawn to the concierge's little girl Jeanne because the latter reminds her of herself as a child, "shabbily dressed neglected slapped around snubbed by her landlady mother always on the verge of tears." [30] Yet her description of the martyred Jeanne turns out to be just another attempt at justifying one of her tyrannical episodes with Sylvie, whom she forced to play with this child despite Sylvie's reluctance to do so, proclaiming that she was merely trying to teach her some Christian charity.

Just as Dominique in *Les Belles Images* feels she must have a man in her life in order to maintain her social respectability, Murielle is aware that a woman alone is generally considered an outcast. She fantasizes about forcing Tristan and Francis to move back in with her so that she can have the last laugh and lord it over the neighbors once again. She wants to take Francis on special outings not necessarily to please him but so that she can make others swallow their words about the type of mother she has been. "I'll spoil him," she promises. "That will make them take back their slanders and their lies."[31] In almost the same breath she criticizes the freedom allowed other children by their mothers, stating her firm belief that one must raise a child as if one were training a performing horse. Her major problem is that no one here on earth will allow her back into the circus ring. In an ironic reflection of Madame Vignon's prayer in *When Things of the Spirit Come First*, Murielle appeals to the ultimate authority:

> My Lord! Let it be that you exist! Let there be a heaven and a hell I will stroll along the paths of paradise with my little boy and my beloved daughter and the rest of them will all be writhing with envy in the flames I'll look at them roasting and moaning I'll laugh and laugh and the children will laugh with me. You owe me this revenge my Lord. I demand that you give it to me.[32]

It is on this marvelously ironic image of an eternally triumphant Murielle, coercing the Good Lord into reuniting her in paradise with her two children so that she can laugh at her detractors as they burn in a Dantesque inferno, that Beauvoir's story ends.

Murielle's vulgarity, her self-deception, the torment she must have caused her daughter, all make her an unsavory character with whom the reader has difficulty identifying. Along with Madame Vignon, she is the most exaggerated caricature of the monster mother in all of Simone de Beauvoir's fiction. Her final "prayer" is a rather sardonic variation on Françoise de Beauvoir's sincere statement in a letter to a young nun that although she would like to go to heaven, she would not want to be there without her daughters. Whereas in *A Very Easy Death* Simone de Beauvoir seemed touched by this evidence of her mother's continuing concern for her salvation, "Monologue" suggests that the young Simone's resentment of the barrier her mother's devoutness and prayers for her soul set up between them is still a source of unresolved anger for her. Through Murielle as through Madame Vignon, she launches a brutal attack on the misuse of religious faith and on the inherent psychological abuse with which self-serving, self-deluding mothers can eventually wear down and destroy their offspring.

The choice of the name Sylvie for Murielle's psychologically battered daughter has an important autobiographical resonance. Simone de Beauvoir, as her readers will learn in *All Said and Done,* first met the young philosophy student Sylvie Le Bon in November 1960. As the two grew closer, Sylvie gradually opened up and spoke to Beauvoir about her difficulties with a mother who had attempted to live vicariously through her and her successes during her early childhood and who became manipulative and vindictive when Sylvie began to insist on living a life of her own. Madame Le Bon went so far as to force her daughter to repeat a whole year in school in order to separate her from a favorite friend, belittled her repeatedly during her adolescence, and engineered a temporary rift between Sylvie and Beauvoir in her determination to come between her daughter and any friends who threatened to take on too important a role in her life. Sylvie's intelligence and strength of character eventually triumphed and she was legally adopted by Simone de Beauvoir a few years before the latter's death. As we have seen, the Sylvie of "Monologue" was not so fortunate. In that story, Beauvoir appears to have been speculating about the fate of daughters psychologically abused by the kinds of mothers represented by Madame Le Bon and the manipulative matrons described so vividly in *The Second Sex.*

In the title story of this collection the reader watches Monique deteriorate from a fairly self-assured matron to a person with no sense of her own identity. She is perhaps the most haunting incarnation of Simone de Beauvoir's warnings against the pitfalls of marriage and motherhood. When we first meet Monique, she is alone for what may well be the first time in her life, traveling by car from Nice to Paris, surprised that she feels reasonably comfortable unaccompanied by either her husband Maurice or her two daughters. She has just rejected Maurice's suggestion that she think about getting a job, telling him that she is looking forward to living for herself, for just the two of them, now that both daughters are out of the house and on their own. The seriousness of her intentions is immediately brought into question, however, when she cuts her trip short and hurries back to Paris because she discovers that her older daughter Colette has the flu.

The relationship between Monique and Colette is a very close one. Monique becomes gravely concerned about her daughter's health, annoyed by her doctor husband's casual assumption that there is nothing seriously wrong with her. This situation reinforces her decision not to look for a job:

That's one of the reasons—the main one—why I have no desire to be tied down to a job. I wouldn't be able to endure not being totally available for people who need me. I'm spending almost every day at Colette's bedside. Her fever isn't dropping. . . . Terrifying thoughts are going through my mind.[33]

Monique is a typically anxious mother whose dedication to her children is so consummate that anything threatening their well-being causes her to become frantic. She needs to be needed. Her family has teased her about being too much of a mother hen. It is a role, however, which she has relished and in which she has found her niche.

Sensing a certain amount of tension between herself and Maurice, Monique wonders if she has perhaps been too much caught up in her sense of obligation to their children. Once she learns that Maurice is seeing another woman, she immediately blames herself for not having been attentive enough to her husband's needs the previous spring when she insisted that Colette accompany her on a trip to the mountains. Colette is her most effective support system, a loving young woman who adores her mother and has opted to follow in her footsteps, abandoning plans for a scientific career in order to marry at an early age. This is something which makes Monique feel vaguely guilty, particularly since Maurice appears to blame her for the fact that Colette chose to marry someone he considers mediocre and uninteresting. Monique reflects, "She is no less intelligent than her sister. Chemistry interested her, her studies were going well. It's a shame she gave them up. What is she going to do with her days? I ought to approve of her decision; she has chosen the same path I did. But I had Maurice."[34] Here once again we meet up with Beauvoir's equation of marriage and domesticity with meaningless activity, boredom, and mental stagnation for the woman. While the protagonist of "Age of Discretion" is infuriated by her son's decision to turn his back on a career in which she herself has found success and satisfaction, Monique is equally uncomfortable with Colette's desire to pattern herself too exclusively on the model her mother has provided for her. Simone de Beauvoir's portrayal of mothers in her fictional works thus suggests that a strongly committed and involved parent will be uneasy about finding either the antithesis of herself or a carbon copy of herself in her mature offspring.

Colette's existence is the reason Monique is married to Maurice, the reader discovers as the plot unfolds. Monique became pregnant when she and Maurice were both medical students. Their decision to get married, a joint one, she insists, forced Maurice to give up his internship and take a rather uninteresting position with Simca. The pregnancy also obliged Monique to abandon any thought of becoming a successful doctor like her father. It is suggested, however, that marriage and mother-hood offered Monique a convenient excuse for giving up a career for which she felt ill-suited emotionally: "I thought there was no more glorious career than medicine as Papa practiced it in his Bagnolet office. But during my first year I was upset, disgusted, overwhelmed by the daily horror of it all. I lost my nerve several times."[35] A girl's admiration for her father may propel her into following in his footsteps when she chooses a specialty, yet Monique's recollection of her reaction to her first year of medical studies implies that a traditionally male career like medicine may be too horrible, too gory, too unesthetic for a delicate feminine mind. It is significant that Beauvoir is careful to highlight the success of the young women in her fiction in male-oriented fields of study. Both Colette and Nadine Dubreuilh in *The Mandarins* do extremely well in chemistry. Maurice had hoped that his younger daughter Lucienne would become a doctor and eventually his partner in a Paris office. Yet both Colette and Nadine turn their back on scientific careers in order to marry and have children, while the information provided by the narrator about exactly what Lucienne is studying in New York is rather vague. For Monique, her fellow student Maurice brought passion, love, pregnancy, and the opportunity to avoid a commitment to a medical career.

Maurice's decision to leave his Simca job for a more research-oriented position ten years before the story begins and his obvious preference for his younger daughter Lucienne both point to a simmering resentment of having been trapped into family life before he was quite ready to give up his freedom. As arguments proliferate between husband and wife, Maurice leaves no doubt in Monique's mind about the bitterness of his feelings:

> I was the egotist, I was the one who hadn't hesitated to make him give up his internship, who would have liked to confine him to mediocrity all of his life in order to keep him at home, the one who is jealous of his work: a castrating female . . . he didn't want to get married right away, I knew that, and something could have been done about the child.[36]

These are angry words, meant to hurt Monique, who has earlier noted that under Pétain in 1944 there was no question of having an abortion. The words are quoted by Monique as she heard them and interpreted them, the all-encompassing accusation of being a manipulative, controlling, castrating female ringing loudly in her ears. Maurice is in effect implying that she used an unplanned pregnancy to trap him into marriage before he was ready, thereby bringing into question the entire image of happiness and security which she has prided herself on having provided for her husband and children. Here as in Beauvoir's earlier novel, the *belles images* begin to disintegrate early in the narrative.

Aware that the raising of her daughters has been her greatest source of pride, Maurice takes aim at his wife's sense of achievement by telling her she has been "possessive, demanding, and invasive" with him as well as with the girls.[37] It is of interest that she records his accusation as pertaining to "my daughters" (*mes filles*) rather than "our daughters," a choice of words which suggests that she does indeed consider herself to have a proprietary claim on them. Maurice goes on to blame her for everything the girls have done of which he does not approve. "You pushed Colette into an idiotic marriage and Lucienne left home to get away from you," he taunts.[38] Although Colette does everything she can to reassure her mother, Monique discounts much of what her older daughter says because of the symbiotic bond which still exists between them. She is tormented by the possibility that she has indeed had a destructive influence on this daughter she loves so much. "He held me responsible for her sentimentality, her need for security, her timidity, her passivity," she ruminates.[39] This is reminiscent of Laurence's concern in *Les Belles Images* that, as Jean-Charles has suggested, she is the source of Catherine's painfully sensitive reactions to the problems of the world.

Like Laurence, Monique has stopped reading the latest books, listening to current records. She urges her daughter to take time to keep up with the world so that she will not become dull like her mother. She is both flattered and disturbed by Colette's reaction: "She laughed. If I am stupid, she wants to be stupid too. She loves me so, that at least is something no one can take away from me. But have I crushed her? . . . Did she languish in my shadow?"[40] Until this point, Monique has been able to convince herself that Colette has chosen the right path, that she is a competent and happy housewife. When she and Maurice are invited to Colette's for dinner, however, her former convictions begin to crumble:

> The poor thing, she had gone to so much trouble and nothing had worked out. I looked at her from Maurice's point of view. Her apartment certainly has no charm. . . . They don't go out, they have few friends. Again I asked myself in terror: is it my fault that the brilliant fifteen-year-old high-school girl has become this uninspired young woman?[41]

There is a certain amount of humor, reminiscent of Françoise Miquel's comments about Xavière's tomato sandwiches, in this matronly woman's appraisal of her recently married daughter's domestic skills. Yet in Monique's world a poorly decorated apartment and a tasteless meal take on tragic proportions. Her evaluation of domestic happiness by such yardsticks as the "charm" of one's apartment, the frequency of one's outings, and the number of one's friends is a none-too-subtle attack on middle-class social standards. The author is quite evidently using Monique as a mouthpiece as she returns to a theme we have already seen in *Memoirs of a Dutiful Daughter,* that of the brilliant high-school student whose life begins to go downhill when she starts concentrating on finding and ensnaring a suitable mate rather than on more intellectual pursuits.

All of these unsettling thoughts plague Monique because Maurice has skillfully managed to undermine her self-confidence. Nothing that Colette can say or do can counteract the erosion of her mother's personality which Maurice has initiated. Knowing that it will be excruciatingly painful for Monique to watch her husband move out of their apartment, Colette insists that her mother fly to New York for a two-week visit with her younger daughter Lucienne. Even at this point Monique is still seeking an explanation of what she has done wrong, hoping that if she can correct her mistakes she can somehow make everything right again between herself and Maurice. The person to whom she looks for objective criticism is Lucienne.

Each time Lucienne is mentioned, it is apparent that she has been a difficult child to raise. Monique recalls her demands during family trips, her bids for independence. When Maurice expresses his regret that his favorite daughter did not stay on to study medicine in Paris and eventually become his partner, Monique points out that such an arrangement would have prevented her from being on her own. Her husband's assertion that Lucienne could have worked with him and maintained her freedom at the same time causes Monique to reflect upon the differences in parental attitudes:

> Fathers never quite have the daughters they wish for because they have a certain image to which they want them to conform. Mothers accept them as they are. Colette needed security more than anything else, Lucienne freedom. I understand them both. I consider both of them totally successful in their own way, Colette so sensitive, so human, Lucienne so energetic, so brilliant.[42]

This passage echoes Simone de Beauvoir's evaluation of her own parents during her childhood. In *Memoirs of a Dutiful Daughter* she remarks, "My father treated me like a finished product; my mother took care of the child I was."[43] A variation on the same theme, treated with more resentment, can be found in Laurence's impatience with Jean-Charles's expectations that she and Catherine will always be *belles images,* with his cavalier and inflexible attitude toward any problems which may arise when they prove to be more human than picture-perfect. The implication is that mothers are generally more sensitive and understanding about their children's imperfections whereas fathers want their illusions about the serenity, happiness, and achievements of family members to remain unchallenged.

Since Monique's thoughts about the different views of child rearing she and her husband have are registered more than a month after she has found out about Maurice's affair with Noëllie Guérard, they may indicate hopeful rationalization rather than real conviction. She would like to continue to believe that she has encouraged both daughters to develop according to their bent and that they are both happy as a result. Colette has repeatedly assured her mother that she is content with her lot. What of Lucienne? Why did she leave home and move to America? "Would Lucienne have adapted better to family life with a different mother, one who was less anxious, less hovering?" her mother wonders.[44] Plagued by uncertainty about the kind of job she has done as a parent, Monique flies from Orly to New York, intent on getting her younger daughter to tell her the truth about herself. "She doesn't love me; she'll tell me," she assures herself.[45] The extent of Monique's insecurity is underlined by this almost casual affirmation that her younger daughter does not love her and will therefore not hesitate to utter words which may be painful for her. Suddenly this difficult child is transformed in Monique's mind into a psychological magician who can put her tattered existence back together again. "Then I will erase everything bad, everything which is harming me. I'll put things back in place between Maurice and me," she speculates.[46]

When Monique first sees Lucienne at the New York airport, she is proud of the elegant, self-sufficient young woman her daughter appears to be. The point of view Lucienne has to offer is a cynical one, however. Like Simone de Beauvoir reflecting on the relationship between her own parents, Lucienne considers it normal for men to look elsewhere for sexual satisfaction after fifteen years of marriage, and certainly after twenty-two. Speaking as a woman of the world, she pontificates, "When marital love has been the focus of your existence, you run the risk of being left empty-handed at age forty."[47] Although she is sorry that her mother is experiencing such emotional agony, she frankly admits that she sees no reason why her father should sacrifice his desires to Monique's. Being female in no way prevents Lucienne from applying a double standard which allows men to seek their pleasure while their wives are expected to stay at home and busy themselves with housework, children, and grandchildren.

Lucienne is carefully building a wall around herself to protect herself from being similarly hurt. She tells her mother in a matter-of-fact tone that as soon as she finds herself really caring for some man, she leaves him for another. Horrified, Monique exclaims that she will therefore never love anyone. Lucienne's blasé reply is "No, of course not. You've seen where that gets you."[48] As far as Monique is concerned, life is not worth living if you can't love someone. Mother and daughter are obviously endowed with conflicting temperaments, the one a sentimental romantic, the other a cynical pragmatist. Words like "happiness" and "love" are meaningless abstractions for Lucienne, whereas they have always been the essence of Monique's goals and dreams.

Lucienne tries to be as reassuring as Colette was about the way in which Monique has brought her up, insisting that she left Paris not to get away from her mother but rather simply to prove that she could live successfully on her own. "You have always had a very exaggerated sense of your own responsibilities," she chides when Monique blames herself for Colette's attraction to the first boy she met.[49] Lucienne's theory that much of what happens between people, and particularly between parents and children, is on a subconscious level that cannot be controlled: "According to her, what counts in childhood is the psychoanalytical situation which exists without parents being aware of it, almost in spite of parents. The conscious, deliberate part of child raising is supposedly very secondary. My responsibilities are non-existent."[50] This very modern logic is small consolation for Monique, whose entire sense of identity is inextricably tied up in her maternal role. If all of a mother's efforts to raise her children well have had essentially no influence, then her whole adult life has been a waste of time and energy.

After spending two weeks in close association with Lucienne, Monique is much less convinced of her younger daughter's ability to cope with life than she was on the day she first arrived in New York: "I find her existence a very dry one.... Her rejection of love must surely also be my fault. My sentimentality disgusted her, so she worked hard at not being like me.... She is not the strong, radiant, well-balanced young woman I imagined when I was in Paris."[51] Monique has clearly not been listening to Lucienne's attempts to free her of her guilt and much prefers to assume all the blame for the imperfections she finds in her grown daughters. Uneasy about the type of existence each of her daughters has chosen for herself, Monique must now reevaluate the sense of all of her efforts over the past two decades to prepare Colette and Lucienne for a life of happiness, security, and achievement.

Unlike the protagonist of "Age of Discretion," Monique has been ready and willing to make plans to transform the girls' room into a den now that Lucienne has left home. Early in the narrative she seems to accept the fact that neither of her daughters will live at home again, and to be planning for the future. This, however, is before she learns of her husband's affair. Until that moment she is confident that she has raised the girls well, that they are both mature, happy individuals, and that she can look forward to many good years alone with Maurice. Once that bubble bursts, her self-confidence is gradually eroded. She spends hour after hour rehashing past events in an attempt to put them in a different perspective. She remembers how hurt she was the first time her daughters lied to her, confessing, "I had trouble accepting the truism that all children lie to their mothers. Not to me! I am not the type of mother one lies to; not the type of woman one lies to. Idiotic pride!"[52] Just like the protagonist of "Age of Discretion," Monique would prefer to think that she is different, so special that the normal psychological traits listed in the textbooks do not apply to either her or her family. Monique's vain hope has been that if she did everything "right," family life would be perfect, an idyllic, peaceful harmony that would continue forever. She has somehow been able to gloss over Lucienne's pointed attacks on the myth of ideal happiness, but it is impossible for her to ignore Maurice's attachment to another woman.

It is perhaps symbolic that Noëllie met Maurice when she brought her fourteen-year-old daughter to him for treatment of anemia. There appears to be nothing anemic about Noëllie's life-style. She is a divorced lawyer, elegantly dressed, very articulate, active in many social circles. By comparison, Monique seems an uninteresting homebody. Monique would like to consider Noëllie a selfish, egotistical individualist who neglects her adolescent daughter, something which no one can accuse Monique of having done with her children. Maurice, however, argues that his paramour "is not neglecting her daughter at all. She is teaching her to get along on her own, to depend on her own resources, and she is certainly right."[53] He also makes the devastating comment that "women who do nothing can't stand women who work."[54] He thus equates running a household and raising children with doing nothing and suggests that, at least from his male point of view, Betty Friedan was indeed right when she stated in *The Feminine Mystique* that nothing is considered a real achievement unless it is rewarded with a salary check.

With the modern emphasis on independence and fending for oneself, the traditional mother-hen approach to raising a family begins to seem outdated. Gradually Monique starts to question the validity of her devotion to others: "Do I really know who I am? Maybe some sort of blood-sucker nourishing itself on the lives of others: Maurice's, our daughters', all those strays I claimed to be helping. An egotist who refuses to let go."[55] The bloodsucker image is a vivid metaphor for the kinds of mothers Beauvoir has warned against in *The Second Sex*. Here again the reader is aware of her distaste for the symbiosis of the mother-child relationship, which she describes as essentially parasitic. The embryo drains off energy from the pregnant mother, the young child from the frantic young housewife. As time goes on, Beauvoir suggests that the roles are reversed and that the mother feeds on the lives of her children as the only justification for her existence.

A fifteen-year-old girl whom Monique takes into her home for several nights is a "stray" whom she has befriended during the course of the narrative. Marguerite eventually runs away from the juvenile hall where she has been kept, impatient when Monique's frustrated attempts to have her placed in more interesting surroundings produce no results. Here too, as with her daughters, she can only conclude that her efforts have failed:

> [My sole ambition] was to create happiness around me. I haven't made Maurice happy. And my daughters aren't happy either. What next? I don't know any more. I don't know who I am or how one should be. . . . How can I go on living without believing in anything, including myself?[56]

Monique goes through an anorexic episode like Laurence's in *Les Belles Images,* and thinks about suicide as a solution to her problems just as Anne Dubreuilh did in the final chapter of *The Mandarins*. She does indeed appear to be a broken woman, as the title suggests, a woman with nowhere to go and no faith in herself.

Like Laurence, like Anne Dubreuilh, like Murielle, however, Monique will indeed go on living. Although she will no longer have two small children at home as Laurence does, she will have the support of her affectionate older daughter Colette and a certain degree of detached understanding on the part of Lucienne. She will live in an apartment where there will never be anything but a dark window awaiting her at night, an apartment filled with memories behind each door. Here she must now stop ruminating about the past and face the future. Along with the other women in this collection of stories, Monique will at last be obliged to abandon her secondary role as wife and mother and to live primarily for herself.

The "broken women" of these three stories have been destroyed partially by the myth of motherhood promulgated by Western society. Each protagonist has internalized an image of the close-knit, happy, harmonious family which exists only on television and in glossy magazine advertisements. It is the mother of that hypothetical family who is expected to keep all the wheels turning smoothly. The inevitable moment of disillusionment depicted in these tales causes depression and resignation in the retired professor of "Age of Discretion," illness and dejection in Monique, and madness in Murielle. The collection reinforces the impact of *Les Belles Images* in presenting an eloquent warning against the pitfalls of life in a traditional nuclear family.

Critical Reaction

In looking back at her original intentions when she wrote "Age of Discretion," Simone de Beauvoir indicated in *All Said and Done* that she was more interested in the relationship between the aging intellectuals than in the interaction between parent and son.[57] The lack of meaningful communication within the family circle experienced by Laurence in *Les Belles Images* and Murielle in "Monologue" was attributed by the author to the fact that both protagonists were lying to themselves and were therefore incapable of being sincere with others. Beauvoir acknowledged that the inspiration for the title story came from letters she had received from hundreds of women who had been abandoned by their husbands and did not understand what had happened to them. Disappointed by the critical comments of some feminists, she stated that nothing precluded drawing feminist conclusions from Monique's misfortunes, caused in her opinion by her choice of dependency rather than autonomy.

The author's artist sister Hélène illustrated the title story for a special edition of the work. When asked in a television interview why she had chosen one of her sister's least effective efforts to illustrate, she was adamantly articulate in her defense of the story, stating that it had been appreciated both by those who read it on a literal level and were touched by the drama of Monique's predicament, and by real intellectuals who could read between the lines to capture her sister's true intentions. She went on to accuse those who reacted negatively to "The Woman Destroyed" of being *demi-intellectuels* with minds not subtle enough to understand its nuances and attitudes too pretentious to allow them to appreciate the literary value of the story line.[58]

Robert Cottrell views each of these three stories as a warning against female dependence on husband and children. He compares Murielle's monologue to Molly Bloom's at the end of James Joyce's *Ulysses*. Judging the collection inferior to Beauvoir's earlier fictional works, he criticizes "the hysterical voices of women who are too monstrously selfish, too lacking in perception to be entirely credible."[59]

In Annie Ophir's detailed analysis of *The Woman Destroyed*, the need felt by the protagonist of "Age of Discretion" to reify her son and thereby continue to possess him is tied to her insistence that the present and the future perpetuate the past. Ophir identifies Philippe as the "detonator" of the crisis that forces his parents to confront the aging process.[60] She points out the irony of Philippe's decision to take a job at the Ministry of Culture after his mother has clearly articulated her conviction that culture is the highest of values. "The irony of fate or a warning against intellectual mothers?" Ophir queries.[61] Discussing the way in which society strips the elderly of their human dignity, Ophir points out that Philippe transgressed all limits when he accused his mother of clinging illogically to her senile obsessions, that he "broke the social conventions which allow us to maintain before all the idea of human dignity."[62]

In Ophir's opinion, the specter of the castrating, possessive, abusive mother hangs over all three of the stories in Beauvoir's collection. She finds in "Monologue" thirty-one pages throughout which the need of other people pierces through the articulated rejection of the Other. Attributing Murielle's need for vengeance and feelings of frustration to the birth of her younger brother many years earlier, she notes that the only person the protagonist considers pure like herself is her deceased father. Yet even he has betrayed her on two occasions: by having a son with her rival, her mother, and by dying. Ophir focuses on the protagonist's recurrent obsession with her father's refusal to put her on his shoulders so she could see the fireworks when she was a little girl, a refusal explained by the fact that that privileged position belonged rather to her younger brother. The critic deduces from this scene that symbolically neither of Murielle's parents ever succeeded in raising her toward the light.

Noting that Murielle accuses her mother of every conceivable moral sin, Ophir suggests that this mother has monopolized, and therefore stolen, both father and brother from the jealous Murielle.[63] Worse yet, she has stolen from her daughter, whom she has accused in public of being responsible for her own daughter Sylvie's suicide, the picture-perfect image Murielle tried to paint of herself as a conscientious and understanding mother. It is Murielle's mother rather than Murielle, in Ophir's opinion, who is the vampire figure in this tale, feeding on the lives of others and particularly on that of her daughter.[64] Ophir's analysis of "Monologue" gives evidence of a sympathetic interpretation of Murielle, whom Beauvoir in a 1978 interview cautioned against casting in the role of victim.[65]

Ophir notes in the title story Monique's obsession with proving that everything she has done since she decided to abandon her medical studies has been a failure. No longer able to hide behind the double role of beloved spouse and indispensable mother,[66] she realizes that admitting that her husband and daughters have evolved beyond their need of her would be tantamount to admitting that she no longer has any identity of her own.[67] Ophir identifies as Monique's enemy not her husband's mistress Noëllie Guérard but rather the passage of time. While her younger daughter Lucienne has done everything possible to develop into the exact opposite of her mother, the older daughter Colette, described by Ophir as her "drab double,"[68] is equally incapable of helping her mother face up to the march of time and the confrontation with her own identity.

Konrad Bieber finds the mother-son relationship in "Age of Discretion" "hardly credible. Even a Spartan mother had more feeling for her own flesh and blood than this intellectual shrew, who condemns Philippe in the name of a principle." He sees in the unnamed protagonist "a rigidity totally uncharacteristic of the author."[69] Her husband André is in his opinion patterned after Jean-Paul Sartre. In Murielle's monologue Bieber finds "the vulgar, spiteful jargon of a woman obsessed by her many failures."[70] Considering the title story of the collection an important literary document, Bieber notes Monique's "monstrous egotism" in being so obsessed by her problems with Maurice that she talks of nothing else during her brief stay in New York with her younger daughter Lucienne.[71]

The relationship between mother and son in "The Age of Discretion" is considered fairly well delineated by Terry Keefe, who regrets that this aspect of the story was not developed further. He considers "Monologue" an attempt by Beauvoir to look at the whole question of raising children from a different angle and, like Konrad Bieber, deems it a tour de force. Keefe points out the emphasis in the three stories of this collection, as in *Les Belles Images,* on the potentially disastrous influence of the traditional family on the children it produces.

In a 1987 article comparing *The Woman Destroyed* to Marie Cardinal's *Une Vie pour deux,* Carolyn A. Durham finds that all three of the stories in Beauvoir's collection are essentially about a conflict between two women. She notes that "Beauvoir's abandoned wives and mothers attribute their rivals' power to their sexual availability. . . . The dependent, other-oriented wife and mother opposes the independent, self-affirming career woman."[72] Using Monique's attempt to "become" Noëllie Guérard as her example, Durham sees in this confrontation with the otherness of women a vehicle for female self-definition. She finds in Beauvoir's replacement of the alternating first- and third-person narration of her earlier fiction with three variations on the subjective voice in these tales a possible indication of "her rejection of women's alienating 'otherness' and her belief that their most important task presently lies in the creation of selfhood."[73]

Simone de Beauvoir's last fictional work thus takes its place in the chain of books that reflect the author's personal experiences with maternal behavior as well as the observations she gleaned from her contact with female friends and relatives and from the letters she received from desparate women seeking encouragement, consolation, and a sense of their own identity. In a protagonist like Monique, the reader cannot help finding many of the traits which Beauvoir regretted in her own mother's choice of a nurturing but passive role within the confines of the family. Rather than validating the kind of care and affection through which Françoise de Beauvoir created a solid base for her daughters' future security and self-confidence, the author tends to dwell on the negative and occasionally fatal consequences of a continuing and overly possessive symbiosis between mother and child. The broken women of the French title have allowed motherhood to overshadow all other activities in their lives, with disastrous results both for themselves and for their offspring.

14

Aging Researched and Experienced:
The Coming of Age and *All Said and Done*

When she was in her thirties, Simone de Beauvoir coped with disruptions in her life by transposing them into fiction and attacking them obliquely through the characters she had created. As she grew older, her work tended to tackle problems head on, sometimes after exhaustive research, sometimes in words painfully wrenched from deep within her. In her frank and disturbing study of old age, *La Vieillesse,* euphemistically translated into English as *The Coming of Age,* the author confronts the loneliness and frustrations of the elderly and examines the degree to which close family ties can in any way alleviate these misfortunes. The fourth volume of her autobiography, *All Said and Done,* contains comments about her own mother and Sartre's and about mother-child relationships she has observed over the years. When she was writing these two works, Beauvoir had already celebrated her sixtieth birthday. The members of her parents' generation were rapidly dying off and she was beginning to look closely at the young people in whose company she had always delighted and who, she hoped, would carry her ideas and values into the future with them.

The Coming of Age

Simone de Beauvoir proceeds painstakingly in her study of old age, addressing the biological, ethnological, economic, and historical aspects of aging. She notes that in women "the reproductive function is brutally interrupted at a relatively young age"[1] and comments on the degree to which Western culture tends to glorify vigor and fertility and to fear the sterility of old age.[2] In this study as in *The Second Sex,* Beauvoir uses the word "reproduce" in a pejorative sense, stating that as soon as the individual trapped in a job senses he is limited to "reproducing" his life, his universe begins to shrink.[3] This is reminiscent of her comments in *Mem-*

oirs of a Dutiful Daughter about the repetitive nature of household chores and of child rearing. Reproduction and repetition are closely linked in the author's mind and contrasted with the more desirable goal of transcending oneself by a choice of activities which lead to new, challenging, expanding horizons.

In her extensive research into a variety of family patterns, Beauvoir finds primitive tribes in which the elderly are honored and respected and states that one of the most effective forms of protection against old age can be found in the love and nurturing provided by well-adjusted and happy members of the younger generations of a family.[4] This is a concession to the positive aspects of family life rarely found in the canon of Beauvoir's works. Addressing the problems of aging in contemporary Western culture, the author warns, however, of the dangers of moving away from a familiar area and pattern of life to be close to one's children: "The children don't pay attention to [their parents], who have given up their familiar habits in vain," she asserts.[5]

It is Beauvoir's thesis that women have an easier time with old age than men because they are generally accustomed to being passive observers rather than active participants in the world. She posits that women are therefore less bothered than men by their eventual dependence on their children or on other younger relatives or friends. She uses the case of her own maternal grandmother as an example of someone who adapted fairly well to living with her adult daughter and grandchildren, attributing this to the fact that her grandmother herself made a considered decision to move in with her older daughter's family. Yet even she, we learn in another passage, stashed away bits of food in her room, apparently insecure about her status in a household that was not her own. Statistically, Beauvoir has found, many elderly people die within a year of moving in with their children, often feeling disoriented and desperately isolated from the contacts and projects which had previously made their lives meaningful.

Like Yvonne Knibiehler and other feminist historians, Beauvoir notes that the extended period of dependency of the twentieth-century child is a relatively recent phenomenon and that childhood was essentially non-existent during the Middle Ages. "As soon as they ventured forth from their mothers' apron strings, children were immediately treated as little adults," she records.[6] As a result, the whole question of the joys and responsibilities of motherhood did not become an issue until women were programmed by Western society to remain at home and to invest all of their energies in the raising of their children. Old age was not an issue either, however, since in earlier centuries few women survived beyond their childbearing years.

The Coming of Age contains extensive documentation of the generally negative treatment of older women in society and in literature throughout Western history, highlighting the proliferation of witches and wicked stepmothers in fairy tales and legends. Beauvoir at the same time expands on her hypothesis that the contemporary matron has a decided psychological advantage over her aging male counterpart. The aging woman has experienced a period of crisis when her children grew up and left home, but has since found something to do with her time either at home or through an outside job. Despite the negative comments made by the author in *The Second Sex* about the burdens of taking care of one's grandchildren, she suggests in this study that becoming a grandmother opens up new horizons for the mature woman.[7] A grandmother's continued involvement with her family allows her to maintain some sense of identity, an identity that for her male contemporary has been inextricably bound to a salaried job.

Beauvoir speaks at length about the effect on aging persons of dealing with the death of people who have played important roles in their lives. Her comments about the death of a parent apply poignantly to the feelings she experienced when her mother died. Buried with parents or close relatives, in her opinion, are the memories of childhood and adolescence they alone shared with the adult children who mourn them.[8] This was certainly true in the case of Françoise de Beauvoir's "disappearance," a common euphemism in French for dying. With her disappeared the images of the devout and obedient little girl who accompanied her mother to mass every morning and who shared with her mother all of the events and adventures of her young life.

The author is convinced that the complexes of childhood one represses during adulthood come back to haunt one in old age. She speaks directly of her own mother in this context, recounting, "All her life my mother was marked by her childhood, but at the end she recalled even more often with bitterness the favoritism her father had shown her younger sister."[9] One is thus possessed by one's childhood, according to Beauvoir, and tends to ruminate over certain incidents, both positive and negative, as one grows older. Reflecting on childhood memories, Beauvoir suggests, "If the emotional memories that reawaken our childhood are so precious, it is because, for a brief moment, they put us back in possession of a future without limits."[10] For her, the reality of the limited amount of time she has left to accomplish what she would like to achieve here on earth is one of the most disturbing aspects of growing old.

Beauvoir makes some very perceptive observations about the vertiginous rate of change in the modern world, change which leaves the elderly insecure and off balance. In her opinion, the family unit has fallen apart almost everywhere. [11] Although parents can sometimes find satisfaction in seeing a continuation of themselves and their values in their children, the author feels that the inevitable generation gap in modern society makes this more and more unlikely. Citing the words put in the mouth of the venerable old man who is the focus of a work by Rétif entitled *La Vie de mon père,* she refers to the exile represented by a long life in which one becomes an alien in one's country and one's family and has no particular feeling for one's great-grandchildren. She highlights Rétif's pessimistic view that the great-grandchildren are at the same time scarcely aware of the existence of the family patriarch. [12]

Speaking of her own experience with aging, the author records her surprise when she determined that she must now consult members of a generation twice removed from her own in order to understand the point of view of young people. Becoming a member of the older generation is in her mind associated with the threat of solitude and the sadness it can bring.[13] She feels that the most effective way to deal with aging is therefore to maintain warm relationships and communication with other people and states categorically that "the emotional equilibrium of the elderly depends especially on their relationship with their children."[14]

Focusing on the lack of ambivalence in a mother's love for her son, the author notes that if he remains a bachelor, he is a source of happiness for her in her old age. If he gets married, his mother may feel abandoned and resentful of her daughter-in-law. This was indeed the case for the unnamed protagonist of "Age of Discretion." As far as daughters are concerned, Beauvoir feels that mothers tend to identify closely with them. They, however, may still be influenced by the adolescent hostility they felt toward their mother and may therefore insist upon maintaining their distance from her as adults. The mother too may still have a residue of hostility left over from the period during which the daughter's youth threatened her own vitality and sexuality. Their adult relationship will depend a great deal on the way in which these former crises have been resolved, according to Beauvoir's analysis.[15]

The author suggests that quite frequently there is a close relationship between a mother and her daughter-in-law, particularly when the latter did not get along well with her own mother. Although she and Sartre were never legally married, it would appear from certain passages in *All Said and Done* that her relationship with his mother during the final years of the latter's life was considerably more comfortable and open than her relationship with her own mother.

Beauvoir states unequivocally that "the warmest and happiest feelings of the elderly are those they have for their grandchildren."[16] Once a woman gets over the ambivalence of the first impact of becoming a grandmother, she can enjoy a perfectly gratuitous relationship with her grandchildren, for whom she generally has no direct responsibility and therefore no sense of the guilt and frustration typical of parenthood. Ever sensitive to conflict between mother and daughter, Beauvoir posits that a woman may at first resent her grandchildren because their very existence proclaims that her daughter has finally escaped from under her wing and become an adult in her own right. An additional concern is that their birth automatically makes her a member of an older, displaced generation. "Because women ordinarily justify their existence through motherhood, competition with their daughters or their daughters-in-law on this ground can be very bitter," she adds.[17]

The author notes nonetheless a great deal of tenderness existing between grandparents and grandchildren and feels that this relationship helps the older generation to continue feeling young. This is also true of friendship between the elderly and members of a younger generation, in Beauvoir's opinion: "It revives their own youth, and carries them along into the infinite future: it is the best defense against the morosity which threatens old age."[18] She takes away some of the glow of this picture, however, by pointing out that close relationships between different generations are rare because old and young generally belong to two distinct worlds between which there is very little communication.

Beauvoir does assume that under favorable circumstances old age can represent a kind of deliverance for women: "All of their lives submissive to their husbands, devoted to their children, they can finally think about themselves."[19] In speaking of the carefree attitude that for women occasionally accompanies old age, she refers to the delightful film *La Vieille Dame indigne*, called *The Shameless Old Lady* in English. It is based on Bertolt Brecht's short tale of a grandmother who abandoned the traditional patterns of her daily existence after her elderly husband had died and thereby shocked and dismayed her adult children.

In her conclusion, Beauvoir underlines once again the importance of maintaining close relationships with others: "Life remains valuable as long as one sees value in the lives of others, through love, friendship, indignation, compassion. Then one still has a reason for acting or speaking."[20] Despite the unaccustomed tenderness with which she describes certain family relationships in this study, she urges her readers to work to overhaul the entire societal structure so that members of every social class can find a place in the collectivity which will allow them to maintain their dignity even in old age. Since she has consistently attacked the family unit as a source of unhappiness and neurosis, it is incumbent upon her to suggest alternative structures that will provide for the elderly the kind of nurturing and connection with other generations which has traditionally been supplied by family members.

In her analysis of *The Coming of Age,* Anne-Marie Lasocki notes that the death of Françoise de Beauvoir caused her daughter to reassess her opinion of parent-child relationships, which she had effectively "swept aside" in the majority of her works, "having thought that she had resolved her relationship with her own parents."[21] Lasocki goes on to quote sections of *The Coming of Age* analyzed above, emphasizing Beauvoir's reexamination of the parent-child relationship in this study published seven years after her mother's death, and her theory that adult children tend to treat their elderly parents in much the same way that they themselves were treated during their childhood.

In her discerning study of the theme of death in Simone de Beauvoir's works, Elaine Marks cites a passage from *The Coming of Age* in which the author notes that "anxious parents, like anxious couples, are not those who love the most, but those who find that something is lacking in their feelings."[22] Marks goes on to compare this tension to the individual sense of anguish about one's own death. Beauvoir's generalized observation about parental anxiety undoubtedly has its roots in her memories of the frantic possessiveness of a mother whose emotions found their only outlet in confrontational interaction with her two daughters during the "stifling" years of the author's own adolescence.

Konrad Bieber devotes a substantial chapter of his study of Simone de Beauvoir to *The Coming of Age.* He notes that here as in previous works the author looks to early childhood for the explanation of the totality of one's life. In an article entitled "Simone de Beauvoir: Aging and Its Discontents," Kathleen Woodward attributes the author's dark portrait of old age "in part to her personal revulsion for changes in the human body and to her particular temper of mind which does not value certain forms of memory."[23] Woodward is persuasive in tracing the author's celebration of the strong, unchanging body of the pre-adolescent girl and her repulsion for the soft, unformed masses of the fertile female body. She notes that Beauvoir's life, "never punctuated by the birth and growth of children, ... was ... distinguished by immense continuity."[24] The article suggests that the anguish underlying *The Coming of Age* is associated not with Beauvoir's own death but rather with her dread of losing Sartre to death, and attributes her emphasis on the meaningful nature of "a relationship with an equal partner, not with a parent or a child," to her continuing despair over the irreplaceable loss of her best friend Zaza.[25]

Most critics sense in *The Coming of Age* an attempt on the author's part to distance herself through documentation and abstract theory from the inevitable onslaught of the aging process she is observing in herself and in her contemporaries. Two years after her study of old age appeared, the fourth volume of her memoirs afforded her readers an up-to-date glimpse of her life and thoughts as she turned sixty-four.

All Said and Done

Having reached her early sixties, Simone de Beauvoir looked back upon the turbulent 1960s in the fourth section of her autobiography, *Tout compte fait*, translated into English as *All Said and Done*. In the chapters of this volume published in 1972, she provides further insight into her relationship with her own mother, observes mother-child relationships among her friends and acquaintances, and takes a strong stand on feminist issues such as abortion, the raising of children, and the role of the family in modern society.

Agreeing with Bruno Bettelheim and Freud that early childhood leaves an indelible mark on every human being, Beauvoir recalls once again the affection with which her mother surrounded her during the first years of her life. "Young, cheerful, and proud of her success in producing her first child, she had a tender, warm relationship with me," she reveals.[26] The author still enjoys traveling through Verdun because of all of the memories Françoise de Beauvoir shared with her of her own childhood there. In a touching tribute to her parents and the family life they provided for her, Beauvoir acknowledges, "My example proves to me in a striking way the degree to which an individual is the product of his or her childhood. Mine allowed me to get a good start in life."[27]

Simone de Beauvoir's expressions of appreciation are counterbalanced, however, by her recollection of the frustrations and emotional pressures of her adolescent years. She felt suffocated by the attitudes and behavior expected of her by the traditional middle-class society in which she was brought up, impatient with what she judged to be limited intellectual capacity in her mother. Returning to a theme we have already encountered in *A Very Easy Death*, the author reveals, "If my mother had been less indiscreet and less tyrannical, her limited intelligence would have bothered me less. Resentment would not have obliterated the affection I felt for her."[28]

Here for the first time in print Beauvoir frankly admits to a feeling of intellectual superiority which her mother sensed and occasionally articulated during her lifetime. In this section of her autobiography, as she speculates on what might have happened if certain aspects of her life had been different, she clearly suggests that her mother's limited intelligence would have been less offensive to her had Françoise de Beauvoir not been so insistent upon imposing her will on her. More humble and less confrontational, Françoise de Beauvoir might have had a more harmonious rapport with her older daughter once the latter reached adolescence and adulthood. Yet had she been more passive, she might at the same time have lost the respect Beauvoir so often expressed for her vitality and passionate nature.

The sting of the years during which Beauvoir's parents disapproved of practically everything she did still smarts more than forty years later:

> If both [of my parents] had been more pleasant, I would still have been opposed to their way of living and thinking. I would have felt more or less stifled at home and I would have felt alone. But not rejected, exiled, betrayed. . . . This is the only period of my life about which I have regrets. . . . Between the ages of seventeen and twenty, I was deeply hurt by the attitude of my parents.[29]

It is of interest to contrast Beauvoir's recollections with the lot of American girls seventeen to twenty, who, if they are college material, often live in university dormitories or in their own apartments while attending classes and are perhaps working their way through school. This arrangement provides a socially acceptable transition from maternal domination to independence and maturity which serves to ease the kind of tension the adolescent Simone found unbearable at home.

Despite her intellectual comprehension of the reasons for her mother's frantic tyranny after the First World War, the author still blames Françoise de Beauvoir for her rigidity: "My mother was so easily intimidated and so despotic that she was incapable of thinking of ways to make life more pleasant for us and reluctant to allow us to have a good time without her."[30] Beauvoir seems to understand that her mother's authoritarian manner compensated for the uneasiness she had always felt in Parisian society and that her daughters were clearly the only human beings who could give her a much-needed sense of power. The picture she paints of her mother is that of an unsatisfied, petulant woman unable to meet the problems of daily living with anything but grim resignation. Watching the drab monotony of the family's domestic routine, the young Simone often wondered, "Would I one day be obliged to lead the same dull gray existence my mother did?"[31] The kind of life her mother led, and the negative attitude her mother had toward the daily chores she was obliged to take on when the family could no longer afford maids, helped convince Beauvoir never to have anything to do with either marriage or motherhood. Hélène de Beauvoir corroborates the effect that their mother's unhappy domestic situation had on the two sisters:

> *Maman* was a very good, very devoted wife. She adored Papa, but he did not make her happy. And she was often very clumsy in her dealings with us. So Simone and I had no desire whatsoever to have children of our own.[32]

The life-style of the Beauvoirs was complicated by the loss of the family fortune during World War I. The author speculates on how different her life might have been had her father had sufficient funds to set up a dowry for her. Had that been the case, she realizes, she might well have married her cousin Jacques and settled into the role of wife and mother. "I would have known the wrenching experience of so many young women bound by love and maternity who have not forgotten their earlier dreams."[33] The French word *ligotées* (tied and bound) is a strong metaphor for the fate toward which Beauvoir so regretted seeing her intelligent young girlfriends headed. Throughout her mature years, she continued to equate the traditional pattern of falling in love, getting married, and having children with intellectual suicide on the part of bright young women. While the availability of a dowry might have made her a more desirable candidate for the role of Madame Champigneulles, Beauvoir also suggests that more family funds might have made her home life more pleasant, her mother less authoritarian, and cousin Jacques less appealing in the role of knight in shining armor come to rescue a damsel in distress.

The dreams in which Françoise de Beauvoir continued to appear to her daughter underlined the amount of unfinished business still separating them. One of these dreams is strikingly symbolic of the inability of the two women to reach out to one another:

> I saw my mother—her silhouette young and beautiful, but faceless—standing on the edge of an expanse of illuminated water which I had to cross to get to her . . . but there was no boat available. One had to venture into the water and risk drowning. Yet I had to warn my mother somehow that she was in great danger.[34]

This frustrating barrier to communication echoes Fosca's dream of his first wife patiently awaiting him on the other side of mortality in *All Men Are Mortal*. When Beauvoir thinks of her mother, she often seems to return to the early years of their relationship before the situation soured, hoping undoubtedly to find a different resolution for the problems to come, at least in her dreams. In this particular dream she remembers her mother's youthful beauty, with the lure of her tender affection reflected on the illuminated water. The author has told us in her autobiography that Françoise de Beauvoir's smile illuminated her childhood. Her mother is faceless here, however, without identity, like Françoise Miquel, Anne Dubreuilh, Laurence, Monique, and many other female characters who, in certain passages of Beauvoir's fictional works, stand before their mirrors and see no one looking back at them.

This dream reflects the adult Simone's ambivalence toward her mother. On the one hand she would like to cross over that expanse which separates them, both to reestablish their former intimacy and to warn her mother of impending danger. On the other hand, she feels totally helpless, unable to traverse the liquid barrier which is keeping them apart because there is no vehicle to transport her. We remember that her mother long ago objected to her learning how to swim, and the fear of drowning in this dream may well echo Simone's adolescent rage at being prevented from learning a life-saving skill. The water image evokes the amniotic fluid that once protected an embryonic Simone in her mother's womb, a fluid through which she can never again pass to recapture that initial biological symbiosis. Venturing into the water may well carry along with it the risk of drowning in the kind of somber and repetitive existence her mother led during Simone's adolescent and adult years. The metaphor of the boat suggests language as a necessary tool for communication between two human beings. The adult Simone feels responsible for her mother even beyond the grave, thinking that perhaps more effort on her part in finding the right words to express her ideas might have made Françoise de Beauvoir's existence more palatable, might have allowed her to find joy and fulfillment in each day of her life before old age and death consumed her completely.

Simone de Beauvoir records that she often dreamed of the family apartment on the rue de Rennes, where she would see her mother waiting to serve her dinner or to repair a hem that had come apart. Sometimes she would try in vain to get to the apartment. On other occasions, her mother was no longer there when she arrived. Once again, her good intentions of resuming the dialogue broken off many years earlier were constantly thwarted and nothing but the guilt remained. Her regrets about the unfulfilling life her mother had led were highlighted by a dream in which she saw a young woman dressed in white, possibly in a bridal gown, falling from a height and hitting the pavement. She would lethargically announce to Sartre and other friends, "My mother has just killed herself."[35] The juxtaposition of wedding gown and suicide provides a dramatic illustration of Beauvoir's conviction that marriage literally takes the life out of the young woman who has pinned all of her hopes for the future on the promises it appears to hold for her. The author, however, does not venture to interpret these images.

As she relates these frustrating dreams, Simone de Beauvoir speaks again of the anguish that gripped her at the time of her mother's death. She is obviously disturbed by those who have suggested that she sat by her mother's bedside and took notes for her book *A Very Easy Death*. She carefully explains the cathartic value of writing that account, the need to share her experience with others as she evoked those days "forever engraved within me."[36] She also admits that for a time all literary endeavors seemed pointless to her once she had completed the wrenching task of recounting her mother's death. It is hardly surprising that this short book, considered by many critics to be her most poignant, should have taken such an emotional toll on her as she committed her thoughts and her feelings to paper and as she reflected on the regrettably limited existence led by the beautiful and affectionate young woman who had brought her into the world so many decades earlier.

The tragedy of Zaza "Mabille" Lacoin's death still echoes through *All Said and Done*. Beauvoir once again compares her own struggle for freedom and independence with Zaza's:

> Why did she falter into death when she would have preferred to live, to love, perhaps to write? What went wrong for her? I think that above all her early years were to blame: less appreciated by her father than her older sister, passionately attached to an affectionate but seldom available mother, under an apparent calm she was very vulnerable and lacked self-confidence. This was confirmed by the last words she uttered: "I am a reject."[37]

Beauvoir was somehow better able to separate herself from her parents as she grew older, more capable of seeing them as flawed human beings who could not maintain their hold on her throughout her life. Attributing Zaza's apparent inability to question the tenets of her Catholic faith to the fact that both of her parents were practicing Catholics, she notes that she and her sister had the example of their agnostic father as a counterbalance to the devout model of unquestioning belief represented by their mother.

In the concluding pages of these memoirs, the author speculates that her friend's insistence upon clinging to the religion of her childhood was an indication of her unwillingness to separate herself emotionally from her mother: "Zaza had a critical mind and many aspects of her religion perplexed her. If she did not lose her faith, it was because of the unconditional and painful love she had accorded her mother. She did not want to become emotionally separated from her."[38] The assumption in this passage is that any intelligent person will give up her religious faith unless she is tied to it by emotional bonds beyond her control. Although her own loss of faith precipitated a painful separation between her and her mother, it also cleared the way for Simone de Beauvoir to become an independent adult. Religion and motherhood continue to be inextricably bound together in her mind and replete with negative associations. The haunting image of Guite Larivière "Mabille" remains with Beauvoir more than four decades after the demise of her best friend, a demise for which she still holds Zaza's mother accountable.

Whereas for many years Beauvoir's association with Sartre's mother, Madame Mancy, was polite but distant, the relationship between the two women became considerably closer during the final years of the latter's life. Beauvoir at first appraised Madame Mancy much as she did her own mother, seeing both as traditional women deriving their entire sense of identity from the men in their lives. "Like many 'relative' women, she lived in a constant state of anxiety," she writes of Madame Mancy,[39] noting her tendency to use diminutives to weaken the impact of any opinion she articulated.

We learn that, like Françoise de Beauvoir, Sartre's mother suffered much of her life from the influence of an authoritarian and self-centered mother who was unable to provide the warmth and encouragement she needed as a child. Examining Western society in *The Coming of Age*, Beauvoir posited that women, whatever their chronological age, are treated as eternal minors in patriarchal societies. A poignant example of this phenomenon can be found in Madame Mancy, who, after the death of her first husband, returned to her parents' home and seemed to her son more like an older sister than like a mother responsible for his upbringing. In the autobiographical *Les Mots,* translated literally into English as *Words,* Sartre describes how the young Anne-Marie reverted to her status as a child in the Schweitzer home and remained under the domination of her very opinionated parents until she eventually remarried. He perceptively records the subtle triumph his grandmother, Louise Schweitzer, felt when her daughter came home, a baby in her arms, leaving behind a deceased husband who had proved "useless." Describing his grandmother as someone who was sure she was indispensable, Sartre highlights his mother's plight: "Poor Anne-Marie: if she did nothing, they would have accused her of being a burden; if she helped around the house, they suspected that she was trying to take control of it. . . . It didn't take the young widow long to become a minor once again: a tainted virgin."[40] The reader senses a mixture of affection and condescension in many of the passages of both *Words* and Sartre's 1974 conversations with Beauvoir dealing with Anne-Marie Schweitzer Sartre Mancy.

Madame Mancy's reaction to her son's autobiography was similar to Madame de Beauvoir's evaluation of *Memoirs of a Dutiful Daughter.* "He didn't understand a thing about his childhood," she remarked.[41] She was touched by Sartre's description of the closeness of their relationship in *Words,* shocked by his portrait of her father, disturbed by the realization that her remarriage to "Uncle Jo" had destroyed something very precious which had previously existed between mother and son. On several occasions she took Simone de Beauvoir aside to explain that she had remarried in order to provide some independence for herself and a father for Jean-Paul, indirectly seeking forgiveness for a decision which had apparently disrupted the young Sartre's life more than she had originally suspected.

Beauvoir's initial superficial appraisal of Madame Mancy focused on her poor taste in art and literature as well as on her musical talent and excellent singing voice. She noted the degree to which Madame Mancy needed to feel that she had an essential role to play in her son's life after the death of her second husband, and records her cheerful assertion, as she made plans to move in with Sartre, that this would be her third marriage. Subconsciously Madame Mancy was here expressing the same maternal ambivalence we have seen in the protagonist of "Age of Discretion," who would have been all too happy to be assured of the primary place in her grown son's affections.

Shocked at first by Sartre's political ideas, Madame Mancy gradually came to agree with them. During her final years, she acquired, in Beauvoir's opinion, an insight into herself which she had never before possessed. On one occasion, she confided to Sartre and Beauvoir, "Although I have been twice married and am a mother, I am still a virgin."[42] This delightful appraisal of intellectual and sensual innocence by a woman in her eighties is a strong indication of the effect sharing an apartment with her brilliant son had had on her ideas. Beauvoir comments approvingly on the evolution which had taken place in her:

> By rebelling against the prejudices which had plagued her in her early years and against the ideas her husband had imposed upon her, she took vengeance on all those who had tyrannized her. Toward 1962, she felt totally liberated. 'It's only now, at the age of 84, that I have really been able to break away from my mother's influence,' she told us.[43]

Here again we find the mother cast in the role of villain, a tenacious villain who maintains her grasp on her daughter from beyond the grave.

Simone de Beauvoir's psychological explanations of the problems many women have in becoming liberated and independent repeatedly center on harmful mother-daughter relationships.

The publication of *Words* inspired Madame Mancy to write her own memoirs. In the course of gathering her thoughts together, she was struck, Beauvoir tells us, by the superficiality of family ties she had always considered very close. "I can see us in the evening, gathered under the lamp, my parents, my brothers and I. But I realize that in fact we did not really talk to one another. Each of us was entirely alone," she reminisced.[44] This analysis probably reflects the substance of many conversations with both Sartre and Beauvoir about solitude and authentic communication with other people. Since both authors tended to consider family life anathema, they appear here to have won a convert to their anti-bourgeois cause.

Formerly a chronic complainer, Madame Mancy faced the physical ills of old age with a positive spirit and the determination to remain independent and self-sufficient as long as possible. Even when taken to the hospital after a serious heart attack, she displayed a lively curiosity about her surroundings. In January 1969 Simone de Beauvoir shared with Sartre the emotions of the final weeks of Madame Mancy's life. She reports that Sartre, looking at his mother's lifeless body after her death, was "struck by the fierce determination in her face. He had the impression that life had crushed and worn down a woman whose temperament was passionate, tenacious, and even violent, but had never managed to break her."[45] Both Sartre and Beauvoir appear to have taken pride in discovering in their elderly mothers traits which they could admire and applaud, traits which made the biological connection an easier one to accept. When Madame Mancy was hooked up to a full array of medical machinery designed to maintain her existence artificially, Beauvoir was painfully reminded of the "heroic measures" which had resulted in a few more days of life but also in unbearable suffering for her own mother. Although the death of Madame Mancy was not as wrenching for her as that of Françoise de Beauvoir, she was sincerely affected by the loss of a woman who had managed, like Bertolt Brecht's shameless old lady, to come to terms with her own identity in the final years of her life.

All Said and Done is dedicated, simply, "To Sylvie." In the course of the narrative, the reader becomes acquainted with Sylvie Le Bon, a young philosophy student whom Beauvoir met for the first time in 1960. Her childhood experiences, reluctantly related to Simone de Beauvoir, substantiated the author's strong conviction about the dangers of maternal possessiveness: "[Sylvie's] mother had as a young girl nourished ambitions which she herself had never managed to fulfill. She wanted to avenge herself through her daughter. When [Sylvie] was very young, she had her take piano lessons, singing lessons, and dancing lessons."[46] Here was another mother assuming the bloodsucker role so vividly described by Monique in "The Woman Destroyed," a mother who looked to her offspring to make up for all of her thwarted ambitions and dreams. When Sylvie was old enough to make her own decisions, she gave up the lessons and the theatrical performances which had brought her mother such vicarious pleasure. No longer able to exert sufficient control over her daughter's life, Madame Le Bon became jealous and possessive. In her determination to force Sylvie to devote full attention to her, she went so far as to tear up her favorite books and, as indicated earlier, to hold her back a year at school in order to separate her from a special friend.

Beauvoir listened sympathetically to this tale of woe, which corroborated her worst suspicions about the misuse of maternal power. She could easily identify with Sylvie's struggle to separate herself from her parents:

> In public, her parents expressed their pride in her. At home, they were exasperated by her restive attitude. They wanted to be an integral part of her life and she would not let them. They wanted to break her spirit but she couldn't be tamed. . . . This story had a familiar ring for me. But I was older, I depended less on my parents when I suffered from their ill will, and they did not react with as much brutality.[47]

Ill will and brutality can indeed make the already difficult life of an adolescent close to unbearable. At age fifty-two, Beauvoir had found a soul mate in Sylvie Le Bon, who instinctively understood the real sense of the oft-quoted epilogue to *Force of Circumstance* and who provided much-needed comfort during the trying days of Françoise de Beauvoir's terminal illness. Thirty-three years her junior, Sylvie came to represent a stake in the future for Simone de Beauvoir and was adopted by her a few years before Beauvoir's death in April 1986.

As the reader is reintroduced to the author's former student Nathalie Sorokine, "Lise" in the memoirs, it becomes apparent that herein lay part of the inspiration for the delineation of Murielle in "Monologue." Since leaving France to live in the United States with her GI husband, Lise had been divorced and remarried, had given birth to two children and adopted another. Her mothering appears to have left a great deal to be desired, however, as we learn that one child after another has had serious emotional problems. When Beauvoir asked Lise if she had read any interesting books, the latter replied indignantly, "Read! How could

I possibly do that? I don't even read a newspaper! You don't know how absorbing it is to train a child!"[48] Here we see reflections of Laurence, of Monique, of Monique's daughter Colette. The fictional Laurence and Monique, however, had a sincere interest in raising their children as tenderly as possible. For Lise, child rearing was more akin to training a circus animal. Beauvoir was aghast at Lise's sudden determination to whip everything and everyone into shape, a mania which even extended to teaching the dog to use the toilet.

Like Murielle in "Monologue," Lise had as many problems with her mother as with her children. It was Lise's mother who had accused Beauvoir of corrupting a minor and was therefore responsible for her temporary suspension from her teaching job in 1943 during the Occupation. Although her mother spoke no English, Lise insisted that she move to the United States to be near her. A subsequent quarrel made Lise refuse to see her mother ever again, even when the latter lay dying of cancer. Lise's own untimely death put an end to an apparently turbulent and emotionally confused existence, which once again sustained Beauvoir's conviction that the early years of a child's life mark it forever.

Throughout the years covered by *All Said and Done*, Simone de Beauvoir had remained an interested observer of the social scene. Asserting that she had never regretted the joint decision she made with Sartre not to marry, she assessed the life-style of more traditional couples in the following words: "The only novelty in their lives is that provided by the birth and development of their children. Even this becomes lost in the monotony of their everyday existence."[49] Beauvoir was clearly never able to envisage the possibility that a traditional family with children might be just as intellectually and culturally alive as unmarried members of the intelligentsia. With the numerous examples of unhappy childhood experiences she had heard about from friends and acquaintances, she continued to emphasize the importance of early affection and support from parents: "When one has not had enough love as a child and one has adopted the point of view held by one's parents, one has formed a self-image which can never be shed."[50] Unable to understand why Charles Dullin's mistress "Camille" drank herself to death, Beauvoir speculated that the answer could only lie in a childhood "Camille" never chose to reveal to her friends. Just as in *A Very Easy Death* the author blamed the lack of affection in her mother's childhood for the latter's emotional and psychological handicaps, so did she consistently look to the same critical years for explanations of the personalities that surrounded her.

Particularly after 1970, Simone de Beauvoir was an active participant in demonstrations for feminist causes. She was especially adamant in her support of legalized abortion and added her signature to a list of women, many of them well known in France, who claimed to have had abortions. She also used her influence to help unwed mothers win the right to bring up their babies themselves. Although articulate about allowing women to choose whether or not to have children, she continued in this fourth volume of her autobiography to display a consistently negative attitude toward maternity and family life. She depicted the housewife as an unhappy human being determined to foist her misery on future generations, as a sadist "unhappy with her lot, [who] doesn't want her daughters to have it any easier. The more she suffers, the more fiercely she demands that the status quo be maintained."[51] This is a rather sweeping generalization based once again on Beauvoir's assumption that family life is the closest thing to hell on earth.

This conviction is clearly spelled out in the following passage condemning the family as an institution:

> I deplore the enslavement imposed upon women by their children and the abuses of authority to which children are exposed. Parents make their children enter into their sado-masochistic games, projecting their fantasies, their obsessions, their neuroses on them. This creates an extremely unhealthy situation. . . . Like many feminists, I favor the abolition of the family, but without quite knowing what to suggest as a substitute.[52]

Therein lies the problem, of course. Granted, the traditional nuclear family has had its quota of emotional and psychological traumas. Nonetheless, it has also assured a stable, generally secure environment in which children can grow up nurtured by adults who usually care about what happens to them. Kibbutzim and child-care centers do not seem to provide the same sense of identity, of being special, that a nuclear family like the one formed by Françoise and Georges de Beauvoir supplied for their two very successful daughters.

In *All Said and Done*, Simone de Beauvoir reaffirmed her interest in young people. Konrad Bieber notes the disappointment she expressed with the refusal of young people to read not only her books but any books at all. He shows his admiration of her determination to comprehend the new generation, commenting: "The young now appear to her . . . like another nation to acquaint herself with, to explore, and to conquer. Dynamic and patient, full of the desire to understand, more than to persuade, she is bound to succeed in reaching today's youth."[53] Bieber sees in *All Said and Done* a "sense . . . of usefulness in bringing hope to many readers, of elation in seeing young people acclaim her efforts and encourage her to continue her work."[54]

Carol Ascher focuses on the sections dealing with Sylvie Le Bon in *All Said and Done* and on the author's assertion that she sometimes saw in Sylvie a reincarnation of her younger self. Addressing the author's denial of any maternal relationship between them, Ascher notes: "In fact, it seems that there is a much closer 'we' here than in most mother-daughter relationships, where the need to separate creates rigid and at times cruel barriers. Yet Sylvie obviously does play the role of projecting into the future, a daughter's role."[55] Like Konrad Bieber's, Ascher's attention is caught by Beauvoir's focus on the future. She highlights the author's acknowledgement of the fact that her own generation will only be fully understood by those who, precisely because they have not been intimately connected with it, can assess it with far more perspective than she.

Citing Beauvoir's expressed desire for the abolition of the family in *All Said and Done,* Jacques Zéphir situates her ideas on the subject in the context of her humanitarian and "neo-feminist" commitments. He strongly disagrees with those who claim that her opposition to the family and to marriage is based on some kind of perverse desire to keep other women from finding happiness in domesticity.[56] For Terry Keefe, in this fourth volume of her memoirs. Simone de Beauvoir's "underlying assumptions about the crucial influence of childhood need further elucidation."[57] Keefe finds the account of the author's friendship with Sylvie "touching,"[58] but regrets that most of the information she supplies about her relationship with her friends is more anecdotal than analytical. He too notes that after the gloomy tone of *Force of Circumstance* this segment of the autobiography attests to the author's renewed interest and hope in the future.

Simone de Beauvoir's choice of title for the fourth volume of her memoirs suggests that she visualized this 1972 text as her last major publication. The emotional shock of Jean-Paul Sartre's death on April 15, 1980, however, sent her back to her desk, just as Françoise de Beauvoir's demise in 1963 had precipitated a cathartic sharing with her readers of the anguish of the loss of a loved one.

15

Illness, Memories, and Posterity:
Adieux: A Farewell to Sartre

It is not within the purview of this book to examine in depth the long-lasting relationship between Simone de Beauvoir and Jean-Paul Sartre. Since my analysis has centered on both fiction and autobiography, however, I would be remiss if I did not include some comments about the last of Beauvoir's published works. A look at *La Cérémonie des adieux*, translated into English as *Adieux: A Farewell to Sartre,* reveals that the author assumed a nurturing and often maternal role toward the man with whom she shared her life and her dreams for over fifty years. The 1974 interviews which make up the second section of *Adieux* provide further insight into Sartre's upbringing, his relationship with his mother, and his long-festering resentment of her remarriage during his early adolescence. The theme of seeing a continuation of oneself in a member of a younger generation is a prominent one in the passages dealing with Sartre's relationship with the militant Maoist Benni Lévi, who is generally referred to in the text by his pseudonym, Pierre Victor. The conversations recorded in this volume address the general question of posterity in both philosophical and personal terms.

Earlier volumes of Beauvoir's autobiography contain sections indicating the degree to which she worried about Sartre's self-destructive habits, begging him to curb his drinking, his use of stimulants, his tendency to work for long hours without sleep when he became absorbed in his writing. When faced with the unmistakable physical decline of the philosopher's final decade of life, Beauvoir fought as tenaciously to protect him and spare him from suffering, both physical and mental, as she had for her mother during the final weeks of the latter's illness. She was touched by Sartre's determination not to be a burden to her, frantic when she sensed that he was facing death with indifference and resignation rather than defiance. From 1970 to 1980, she had to be both watchdog and source of moral support, encouraging Sartre to follow essential medical advice while at the same time helping him to maintain a sense of dignity and of involvement in the world around him.

Throughout the text, Beauvoir seems intent upon proving to the world that Jean-Paul Sartre maintained a high level of meaningful activity during the final decade of his life. She defends his vitality, asserting that "if old age is, as certain people say, the loss of curiosity, then he wasn't at all old."[1] She recounts his continued involvement in political issues with a kind of maternal pride. Occasionally, however, she acknowledges the inappropriateness of some of his ventures, such as his enthusiastic support of the February 1971 occupation of the Sacré-Coeur by a group of Maoists, a project she deems, "a rather silly undertaking."[2] One sometimes has the impression that she was skeptical about a good number of the causes into which Sartre threw himself headlong, but that she nonetheless admired the energy and conviction with which he did so.

The aging Beauvoir looks indulgently on the pleasure Sartre takes in the company of a variety of young women, something she has had to do throughout their long association. The reader of *Lettres au Castor et à quelques autres*,[3] a collection of his letters edited and published by Beauvoir after his death, senses that Sartre, while taking full advantage of their mutual agreement to expand horizons through what he had labeled "contingent loves," always felt the need to check back with Simone de Beauvoir for her reaction and approval. She is delighted when he reports that his Greek friend Mélina makes him feel thirty-five again, teases him gently when he complains that he doesn't have enough time to work by suggesting that he is spending too many hours with his young friends. When he protests that such company is "useful" to him, she muses, "I think that indeed they were the ones to whom he owed his taste for living. He declared to me with a naive complacency, 'I have never pleased women more.'"[4] There is something touchingly childlike in Sartre's admission to Bost that the only time he worries about death is on Saturday afternoon, because he doesn't want to miss out on his evening with Castor and Sylvie. In several of the scenes recollected in Beauvoir's text, Sartre gives the impression of being a spoiled but charming little boy indulged by a maternal companion who loves him too much to interfere with his wishes.

Despite repeated warnings from an array of doctors that he must give up smoking and alcohol or suffer dire medical consequences, Sartre childishly resists doing what he knows is best for him, thus leaving it to Beauvoir to worry and impose rules, to limit his supplies and police his daily activities. As he and Beauvoir leave the doctor's office after hearing an unequivocal statement that he must give up cigarettes altogether, he stubbornly announces that he intends to continue to smoke.[6] Although he sometimes repents of his stubbornness and promises to make an effort to change his habits, his good intentions are generally short-lived. The occasional scoldings Beauvoir and Sylvie administer bother him but not sufficiently to make him alter his ways. Simone de Beauvoir, having always been scrupulously honest in her relationship with Sartre, does not relish playing the kind of games necessary to force him to comply with doctor's orders, subterfuges like having Sylvie water down the whisky, but this seems to be the only way to save him from himself.

Just as Francoise de Beauvoir's rapidly diminishing stamina forced her two daughters to reverse roles and take care of her during the last weeks of her life, Simone de Beauvoir must again become a reluctant maternal caretaker as Jean-Paul Sartre's condition deteriorates. When a combination of false teeth and failing eyesight makes it difficult for him to eat properly, she finds that he resists having her cut his meat for him. She is hesitant to tell him to wipe his mouth in a restaurant for fear he will become annoyed. She packs his things for him and sees him off on his annual trips with Arlette El Kaïm, whom Sartre had adopted in 1965. She is constantly walking a fine line between helping with tasks Sartre is apparently incapable of managing for himself and encouraging him to maintain a sense of independence and identity. Knowing that he doesn't take criticism easily, she finds it particularly difficult to refrain from contradicting him when he is clearly wrong about past events. Those events are part of a life they have shared and which she sees rapidly drawing to an end.

The section of *Adieux* devoted to Beauvoir's 1974 conversations with Sartre contains some illuminating passages about the philosopher's relationship with his mother and his stepfather. One has the impression that Sartre was extremely close to his mother until she remarried. His childhood memories contain idyllic scenes of listening to the musically talented Anne-Marie play the piano and of playing duets with her. The "wicked stepfather" syndrome enters into his reminiscences as he recalls that his mother played the piano a great deal less after her remarriage, allegedly because her second husband did not like music. Sartre attributes his own continuing appreciation of music to his mother's influence.[7] Just like Beauvoir, he considers himself privileged to have been born into a family which valued intellectual pursuits.

We discover that the young Jean-Paul once made a habit of taking money from his mother's purse in order to buy popularity by treating his schoolmates to babas at the local pastry shop in La Rochelle. The money was never missed by Madame Mancy until one day when she inadvertently shook some rather large sums out of his jacket pocket.

Beauvoir registers amazement that she did not realize money was missing, recalling her own mother's habit of counting every sou that passed through their household. The theft undermined the young Jean-Paul's integrity in his mother's eyes and in the eyes of his adoring grandfather Schweitzer, and resulted in fairly stringent discipline methods imposed by his stepfather. Despite this incident, however, Sartre claims to have been essentially indifferent to money throughout his life. He explains his total disdain for accumulating money by recalling that his mother always carefully pointed out to him as he was growing up that the money they were spending did not belong to either of them. Whatever they had at their disposal was made available first by Sartre's grandfather, Charles Schweitzer, and then by his stepfather, "Uncle Jo" Mancy. Insisting on emphasizing the distance between himself and his stepfather, he proclaims, "My stepfather's money was even less mine than my grandfather's."[9]

Speaking of his conviction, at the tender age of eleven, that God did not exist, Beauvoir asks a question which reveals a great deal about the struggles of her own adolescence: "Didn't it bother you to find yourself in opposition with your family, which you respected and cared for, on so important a point?" Sartre unhesitatingly assures her, "Heavens, no."[10] It is apparent that, unlike Françoise de Beauvoir, Jean-Paul's mother had not felt compelled to instill strong religious beliefs in her son. The emotional shock of his young life was his mother's remarriage, not his loss of faith and any ensuing awkwardness it might have created between him and his mother. This very basic difference in the coming of age of these two intellectuals, who shared so many of their ideas and values throughout their adult lives, reinforces the theory that mothers have traditionally been intent upon passing on their own spiritual values to their daughters but have not necessarily felt the same obligation toward their sons.

Asked by Beauvoir if the excessive attention and affection he received from his mother and his grandfather during his early years have perhaps caused him to resist displays of emotion as an adult, Sartre replies with a laconic, "It's possible."[11] He admits that he found it disagreeable to see his mother acting uninhibited, something she rarely did. There is a condescending note to this memory, as he refers to the young Anne-Marie as la pauvre (poor thing).[12] Sartre reveals with a certain irony that he was treated like "a little prince" in his grandparents' home and was the center of attention both for his grandfather and for his doting mother. This status made her decision to remarry all the more difficult for him to accept. He expresses his resentment of this decision very articulately in the interviews:

I had had a privileged role in my mother's life the years preceding [her remarriage] and it was taken away from me because now there was that man who was living with her and who became the most important person in her life. Before, I was a prince to my mother, and now I was only a second-rate dignitary.[13]

These feelings reveal a good deal about Sartre and help explain his reluctance to grow up, to be labeled an adult, and to maintain lasting relationships with members of his own generation, particularly when they were male. The reader wonders if Sartre's many breaks with previously close intellectual friends, documented in these interviews, can perhaps be attributed to Sartre's desire to remain, unencumbered by competition from other males, the "little prince" of the childhood paradise that disappeared abruptly with his mother's remarriage. His resentment of that marriage continued to fester throughout the years and was still a bitter memory even during his old age: he was adamant about not wishing to be buried between his mother and his stepfather at the Père-Lachaise cemetery, not even willing to share her in death with the man who had successfully intruded on their intimacy.[14]

The aging philosopher recalls finding his mother and women her age very attractive when he was small, and being proud that his classmates also commented on her beauty. Sharing with Beauvoir the memory of watching his mother undress in his hospital room when she stayed overnight with him during a childhood illness, he asserts, "I certainly had rather sexual feelings for my mother."[15] He suspects that his need to dominate the women with whom he becomes involved has its roots in his childhood. "My grandfather dominated my grandmother. My stepfather dominated my mother," he recalls.[16]

Like Simone de Beauvoir, Sartre often sounds rather smug in his evaluation of his mother's intelligence. He remarks, for example, that she did not do much reading, and that when she did, her choice always ran toward popular literature.[17] When Beauvoir gets him to talk about his upbringing, he admits that the entire family dwelled constantly on his supposedly prodigious intelligence. It is quite likely that his mother, like Françoise de Beauvoir, was rather intimidated by the intellect of the child she had produced. Sartre remarks that his mother knew nothing about politics and that neither she nor his somewhat overwhelming grandfather had ever even heard of the class struggle.[19] In Sartre's estimation, his family was living fifty years behind the times, particularly as far as culture was concerned.[20] He speaks condescendingly though affectionately of his mother's naïveté in signing papers that would have resulted in his being awarded the Legion of Honor, a bourgeois-capitalist anathema in his eyes: "The poor woman didn't know anything about all that. She had had a father who had been awarded the Legion of Honor, and a husband who had the Legion of Honor. It seemed to her that her son should have it too."[21]

In spite of any suspicions he might have had during his childhood about his mother's limited intellectual capacity, Sartre reveals that he showed her everything he wrote until he was about fourteen years old, and that she was always duly appreciative. She didn't share his literary endeavors with her second husband, however, who, Sartre assumes, would not have been at all interested in them. Everything he has written, he declares, has been "against " his stepfather.[22] There is a persistent rebelliousness against members of the older generation throughout Sartre's life, even after he himself has long since become a member of that generation. He asserts that when he was a boarder in a Paris lycée he read authors like Stendhal "*with* people my age and *against* those older than I, even the teachers" (italics mine).[23] The word "adult" was consistently used derogatorily in his lexicon.

Despite his passion for literature, Sartre claims to have never owned a book of his own until, at age forty, he moved into his mother's apartment on the rue Bonaparte after his stepfather had died. He had clung until then to his decision never to own anything.[24] This total denial of possessions, a major theme in his novel *Nausea*, appears to have been associated with his determination to avoid accepting anything material from the intruder who had destroyed his intimacy with his mother. Once the stepfather was no longer in the picture, Sartre somehow was ready to allow himself to enjoy owning or at least taking advantage of some material items, items such as books and a piano which are generally associated with the enhancement of culture.

There is an evident abruptness in Simone de Beauvoir's handling of certain subjects in these 1974 interviews, particularly when references are made to Madame Mancy. When Sartre mentions that his mother wanted him to live with her after her husband's death, Beauvoir interrupts with a quick "Yes, I know. Well, then, getting back to your reading . . . [25] Despite the apparently good relationship that developed between Beauvoir and Madame Mancy during the latter's final years, the reader wonders if a certain amount of jealousy underlined the author's unwillingness to dwell too long on the closeness that existed between Sartre and his mother.

Simone de Beauvoir questions Sartre at length about his repeatedly stated admiration for the young, an admiration which she herself shared. Speaking of the young Maoists who seemed so attentive during his final years, he asserts:

> I still prefer the young to the old . . . when I speak with the Maoist leader who is not yet thirty, I am more at ease than with someone fifty or sixty. . . . Most of the Maoists do not feel friendship for me, nor I for them, we are simply working together . . . there is [only] one for whom I feel real friendship, and that is Victor.[26]

He offers two concrete explanations for his preference for young people: they are not set in their ways and he feels he can help them. One thinks in reading these words of Hoederer's offer, in *Les Mains sales,* to help the idealistic young Hugo become an acceptable adult.

In one of these interviews, Sartre firmly denies that the company of young men makes him feel young, assuring Beauvoir that he does not feel old and never has. She, on the other hand, reveals that she is feeling the weight of her age and finds that speaking with younger women makes her feel younger.[27] It seems to be important to Sartre to deny any significant age difference between himself and the young Maoist leader who is spending so much time with him. He analyzes the relationship in the following words: "I am happy to see Victor, but after a moment our conversation is from one individual to another, rather than between a young man and the old man he has come to see."[28]

It is in the first section of *Adieux* that Simone de Beauvoir traces the development of the relationship between Sartre and Victor, from the early moments when she shared Sartre's idealism and joy in the young man's energy and political commitment, to the bitterness of the final months of Sartre's life, when she was convinced that Victor was taking unfair advantage of the aging philosopher's failing capacities. Knowing that their associations with people young enough to be their grandchildren would be seized upon and subjected to close scrutiny, Beauvoir seems on the defensive in asserting for Sartre as she had for herself the total lack of any regret about their decision to remain childless. She quotes his statement in an interview he granted to Michel Contat when he was approaching seventy: "I never wished to have a son, never, and I am not seeking a substitute for fatherhood in my relationships with men younger than I."[29]

Beauvoir keeps a benevolent eye on Sartre's fascination with young Maoists like Pierre Victor and Philippe Gavi, and records his comment that his friendship with them keeps him young,[30] which is a direct contradiction of his above statement that he feels young with or without the company of those many years his junior. In this passage, he registers his regret that he is too old to take full advantage of the vitality and creative approach to life his young friends have to offer. In a very telling conversation with Pierre Victor reminiscent of Fosca's discussion with his great-grandson Armand in *All Men Are Mortal,* Sartre indicates his awareness that he is merely a useful tool for this ambitious young man. Nonetheless, much of the energy of his last years is concentrated on the joint intellectual effort that is meant to culminate in the book they plan to write together, a book to be entitled *Pouvoir et liberté* (Power and Freedom). Sartre's goal is to assure that there will still be a place for philosophers, and for the "new man," who will combine manual and intellectual talents, in the future society he will have had a hand in creating.[31] It is this goal which appears to keep him going despite the onslaught of physical ills that would completely hobble a lesser man.

When Sartre takes on Pierre Victor as a second secretary, Beauvoir accepts this with good humor. She approves of anything that gives him pleasure. The new arrangement will also allow her more free time for her own work. It is as they are preparing a television series on Sartre's personal view of the history of the twentieth century that Beauvoir begins to grow wary of Victor and his tendency to claim that he is speaking for Sartre. There is a definitive break between Victor and Beauvoir after Victor gives *Le Nouvel Observateur* an article based on a trip he and Sartre took with Arlette to Jerusalem. The article is "signed" with both his name and Sartre's and clearly reflects only Victor's point of view. When Beauvoir prevails upon Sartre to retract the article, Victor is furious that he was not informed. All communication between him and Beauvoir is eventually cut off. Critical of Victor's self-importance and arrogance, Beauvoir nonetheless remains convinced of the close bond existing between him and Sartre and regrets being shut out of a significant part of Sartre's life.[32]

Learning from Sartre of the constant arguments he and Victor are having about their book, Beauvoir worries that Sartre will make too many concessions to the young man's ideas. With reference to an interview they plan to publish, she recalls fearing that "rather than helping him enrich his own ideas, Victor was pressuring Sartre to repudiate them." [33] Sartre registers surprise at her assessment of the situation, which only makes him that much more determined to have the interview published as quickly as possible.[34] In this headstrong gesture, it seems as if Sartre is deliberately playing the person who has most influenced his life and his ideas against a member of a younger generation that to him represents hope for the future.

At least in retrospect, Beauvoir makes a heroic effort to understand Victor's enormous influence on Sartre. She posits that Sartre saw the young man as an incarnation of the new intellectual he hoped his work had created. He therefore could not bring himself to doubt Victor's ability or motives, because this would be tantamount to "giving up this living continuation of himself" which was so important to him.[35] Her assessment in this section of *Adieux* emphasizes Sartre's need to find continuity in a younger generation, whereas her earlier emphasis on his denial of any desire to establish a fatherly relationship with the young men in his entourage suggests that such a "continuation of himself" was a matter of complete indifference to him.

On several occasions throughout the interviews, Beauvoir probes Sartre's thoughts about the immortality of artistic endeavor. Although he eventually rejected the idea of salvation through artistic creation presented in the final pages of *Nausea*, he nonetheless continued to care a great deal about the way in which posterity would view his works. Toward the end of the interviews, he analyzes his relationship to future generations of readers in the following words: "If the work that one does is to succeed, it must go beyond the present, living, existing public and address a future public as well."[36] The important place given in these interviews to reaching future generations through the art one has created contains echoes of the conversation Simone de Beauvoir held many years earlier with her best friend Zaza. Tragically, Zaza did not live long enough to produce the children who would have represented her investment in posterity. Beauvoir's children, like Sartre's, are the books she published, as well as the readers who have absorbed and appreciated her ideas and will transmit them to the generations of readers who come after her.

It is apparent that the relationship between Simone de Beauvoir and Jean-Paul Sartre was one which defies easy categorization. Surely in the early years of their association it was filled with passion and a mutual attraction that was both sensual and intellectual. As time went on, Beauvoir often assumed the role of spouse, mediating, discussing, providing a stable environment in which Sartre could make maximum use of his talents. Although she uses his statement as an example of his tendency to confuse words in his final years, it is no coincidence that Sartre gratefully comments to her one morning as she is giving him his medication, "You are a good spouse."[37] She apparently shudders at such bourgeois terminology, and yet in many ways she did indeed play the role of devoted wife during the mature period of their relationship. In their final embrace the day before Sartre's death, both the passion and the maternal nurturing are evident, as Beauvoir responds to his gesture of lifting up his mouth toward her by bestowing a kiss first on his lips and then on his cheek.[38] The same mixture of the sensual and the maternal can be seen in her insistence on lying down on the hospital bed next to Sartre the morning after his death. She thus becomes both lover reluctant to part with her life companion and mother intent upon protecting her child from the harm that awaits him in being eternally separated from her and from life.

Critical Reaction

In a 1981 article in *Le Canard enchaîné*, Jean Clémentin suggests that *La Cérémonie des adieux* was written by Simone de Beauvoir in order to protect Sartre posthumously from those who claimed to be close to him toward the end of his life. According to Clémentin, Arlette El Kaïm and Pierre Victor went to Sartre's apartment the day after his death and removed everything of any value to them. Clémentin's description of Pierre Victor is less than charitable: "Lacking the ability to become someone on his own, he maneuvered to make himself the spiritual heir, the intellectual executor of Jean-Paul Sartre."[39] Clémentin is more forthright in his suspicions of the good intentions of Victor and of Sartre's adopted daughter than Simone de Beauvoir chose to be in her recounting of the last decade of her famous companion's life.

In his analysis of *Adieux,* Terry Keefe is rather hard on Simone de Beauvoir, finding, in her hostility toward Pierre Victor and her furor at Michèle Vian's willingness to encourage Sartre to drink so that he might have a cheerful death, a possessiveness, a "rigid determination to hang on to her own particular image of Sartre." He interprets some of the quotations of Sartre's words in the text as being included "largely in order to establish that she has a unique claim upon him, or conceivably to reassure herself that this is so."[40] Judith Okely finds in the details of Beauvoir's nurturing provided by *Adieux* strong parallels to the supportive roles generally played by more traditional women within the context of the family.[41]

Among the reactions of the American press to the Patrick O'Brian translation of *La Cérémonie des adieux* that was published in the United States in 1984, an article by Richard Sennett notes that Sartre's political involvement in 1970 was essentially with people thirty to forty years younger than he, "people who could have been his children or grandchildren." He points out the degree to which Beauvoir's tale focuses on "how some young radicals began to exploit Sartre as he grew weaker, and how he lost the power to resist them, emotionally as well as physically," and notes that "she does not conceal her own bitterness...."[42] Turning to Sartre's entourage of younger women during this same decade, Sennett remarks cannily:

> The intrusion of these young women bringing him danger, like the more purposeful intrusion of the young men making use of him, raises the most arresting question

in this diary: How is a woman living in freedom with a man, outside of marriage, to protect him when he can no longer take care of himself?[43]

This is indeed a dilemma with which Simone de Beauvoir struggled throughout her association with Sartre and most particularly during the final years of his life. Richard Sennett sees in Beauvoir's 1974 interviews with Sartre a more cogent presentation than appeared in print anywhere else of "the peculiar trauma that came to him in his last years: his troubled relations with the generations that followed him."[44] Recalling Sartre's tendency to associate youth and openness, the critic analyzes the sometimes unfounded idealism of the philosopher's attitude toward the members of a younger generation: "Not being a rigid person led him to identify with the young and unformed, as though in their innocence they could do no harm and would never become intellectual landowners themselves."[45] Despite Beauvoir's earlier euphoria about their associations with young people and her pointed criticism of contemporaries who appeared suspicious of them and their rebellious ways, the problems she encountered when Pierre Victor usurped too prominent a place in Sartre's life appear to have disillusioned her somewhat about the hope to be found for the future in these younger generations.

Berkeley writer Ruth Rosen, commenting on the 1974 interviews, records, "At times one feels irritated by the maternal tone de Beauvoir adopts in her separate effort to force Sartre to see the worth of his work."[46] Anatole Broyard interprets Beauvoir's role as "Sartre's nurse at the end—in both a physical and spiritual sense—and this is not the best position for a biographer."[47] Writing in *The New York Times Book Review*, Douglas Johnson suggests that Beauvoir needed to reveal all because she found "rivals who offend her sense of accuracy and challenge her possessiveness.... Arlette,... Victor,... Olivier Todd...."[48] Like Rosen, he objects to Beauvoir's maternal prompting of Sartre in the interviews.

In her perceptive article entitled "Beauvoir and Sartre: The Forms of Farewell," Hazel E. Barnes speaks of Sartre's "desire to feel himself actively at work with young people molding the future."[49] Documenting the break between Beauvoir and Pierre Victor, she notes the ironic parallel between reality and the story of Beauvoir's earlier novella, "The Age of Discretion." Its protagonist, we remember, angrily cuts off communication with her son Philippe and reproaches her husband André for remaining in touch with him. According to Barnes:

It is an ironic coincidence that Beauvoir felt not only excluded but indignant at Sartre's overindulgence of the young Benny Lévy. It could not have been predicted, but perhaps it was inevitable that Sartre's wish to go beyond himself would at last put him beyond Beauvoir's willingness to follow him.[50]

Like many other critics interpreting *Adieux*, Barnes considers the generation gap and the consequences it had for both Beauvoir and Sartre during their later years as one of the significant themes of the text.

Hazel Barnes is eloquent in taking issue with the suggestion by certain critics that the details of Sartre's physical deterioration contained in *Adieux* represent Simone de Beauvoir's revenge on him for all of the years of "contingent" relationships. Considering such an accusation slanderous, Barnes finds in the text of *Adieux* an indication of "the profound respect which Sartre and Beauvoir had for each other, something deeper than the obvious affection, companionship, and commonality of values, more bedrock than love. . . . Sartre's conduct toward her consistently displayed that basic equality that he declared has always existed between them."[51]

In the emphasis placed by critics on the relationship between Victor and Sartre, we are brought back to the question of the individual desire to influence the future by inspiring a continuity of one's ideas and values in a member of a younger generation. Whereas the traditional means of achieving this is through one's biological children, the decision by Beauvoir and Sartre not to have children of their own in no way eliminated the hope that the future represented for them. The fact that they never had daily exposure to young people whom they themselves had raised from infancy may account for the idealized view they both held about the leadership, lucidity, and spontaneity of youth. Observant parents are generally well aware that during adolescence and early adulthood most young people are too self-centered, too intent upon grasping at independence and autonomy, often too ambitious, to be particularly philosophical about the path their lives are taking. Yet Jean-Paul Sartre, to Beauvoir's dismay, appears to have looked to Victor and his Maoist cohorts for some kind of absolute truth about the contemporary world. It is little wonder that she tried to remain protective of him both physically and intellectually and that she felt hurt and displaced by some of the young people to whom she and Sartre had traditionally looked for inspiration. The enlarged circle of their intellectual "family" managed in the end to leave Simone de Beauvoir on the outside looking in. An examination of her statements about the family and motherhood in interviews spanning several decades will provide further insight into her views and the extent to which they evolved over the years.

16

Feminism and Motherhood: Communicating with the Media

Beginning in the early 1960s, Simone de Beauvoir granted a substantial number of interviews, wrote prefaces for numerous books, and expressed her opinions in newspaper and magazine articles published internationally. Through the media she spoke directly about the world and woman's place in it, much as she did in *The Second Sex*. The degree of militancy with which she presented her ideas varied, sometimes according to the identity of her interviewers, who generally probed beyond theory and abstractions to discover more about the author's private life. Questions about childhood, motherhood, and the family recurred with impressive frequency. Beauvoir's answers underlined just how central the general problem of reconciling feminism and motherhood is among the dilemmas facing the women of the second half of the twentieth century.

Whenever she talked about her own life, Simone de Beauvoir emphasized the fact that the positive experience of her childhood years laid the foundation for her future achievements and success. In 1965 she described these years to Francis Jeanson as extremely stable and happy.[1] Speaking with John Gerassi in 1976, she explained that she and Sartre were able to combine their lives so effectively because they had both had very solid, very secure childhoods. She considered this a gift from their families, and particularly from their mothers, asserting that as a result of their upbringing neither she nor Sartre had anything to prove to themselves or to each other.[2] Asked by Claude Lanzmann how it felt to be living to a relatively advanced age, she admitted nostalgically, in a 1978 film directed by Josée Dayan, that the slowing down of the pace of her daily routine had allowed her to enjoy a kind of agreeable laziness she hadn't encountered since her childhood.[3] Furious with Claude Francis and Françoise Gontier for the misconceptions of her childhood and of her life in general that she found in their 1985 biography of her, she told *Le Matin* in December 1985, "I was born in total happiness. . . . I was born in serenity."[4] All of these statements corroborate what the author said in her memoirs about her appreciation of the loving atmosphere provided by her family during the formative years of her life.

An occasional comment in her interviews sheds further light on Beauvoir's relationship with her parents. Talking to Francis Jeanson, she analyzed her interaction with them in typically Freudian terms, just as she had in the first volume of the memoirs: first a fixation on her mother, then an Oedipal attachment to her father and jealousy of her mother, accompanied by a romantic conviction that her mother was not worthy of her father. Yet she admitted that her father was always very detached in his dealings with her and her sister:

> No interaction on a moral, or on a physical level, or on a . . . human level, for all intents and purposes! All of that came exclusively from my mother. . . . She was the one who counted first. And when he began to count for me, she still counted for me too, but, of course, my attitude toward her had grown more hostile.[5]

Jeanson suggests cannily that since Beauvoir could not simply get rid of her parents as she had of God, she managed to neutralize their influence on her life by playing their opposing views against each other in her mind. She recalled in the interview that her father's lack of religious faith helped her when she lost hers and found herself cut off from real communication with her mother, who had until then dominated her spiritual life.

Georges de Beauvoir's influence on his older daughter appears to have been primarily intellectual. When he ridiculed as childish the books her mother had chosen for her to read, she rationalized that whatever Françoise de Beauvoir suggested had some useful purpose for her life. Analyzing the contradictory influences her parents had on her, she admitted, "Yes, in fact, I felt authorized by my father to be intelligent and by my mother to remain a child."[6] Beauvoir had already elaborated in her memoirs on the balance between her mother's spiritual influence and her father's intellectual one, a balance that allowed her to develop her strong sense of individual identity and specifically to escape, with little guilt, from the grasp of the Roman Catholic faith in which she had been raised. In these words the reader continues to hear echoes of the tragedy of Zaza "Mabille" Lacoin.

Françoise de Beauvoir, her daughter noted as she chatted with her sister Hélène in the Josée Dayan film, always tried to avoid any unpleasantness, to keep human relations within the realm of the conventionally acceptable. She once said that Simone had shown no signs of jealousy when Hélène was born. The author realized that any such statement could not be taken at face value because her mother would have considered it "bad" for her older daughter to be jealous of her newly born sibling and would therefore never have admitted to such a possibility. Madame de Beauvoir's attempt to ignore potential sources of conflict, at a time when the family was suffering financial and emotional difficulties, led to an oppressively tense atmosphere which made the young Simone eager to escape from the family circle and strike out on her own, as she confessed to Catherine David in a 1979 interview.[7] As late as September 1985, Beauvoir still vividly recalled the antagonism that existed between her and her parents during her adolescent years. Asked about the effort adult children eventually make to understand their parents' shortcomings, she admitted that though she fully comprehended the reasons for her mother's nervousness and retreat into piety and for her father's rightist political views, "that did not bring me one inch closer to them."[8] She certainly never regained any feeling of emotional closeness to her father, and here seems to deny that her sensitivity to her mother's plight in any way facilitated renewed empathy between them.

As we have noted earlier, the disagreement over religion was central to the author's problems with her mother. She commented in a 1960 interview with Madeleine Chapsal that most American readers of the first volume of her autobiography did not realize how essential the crisis of her loss of faith should be in any analysis of the ideas presented in these memoirs.[9] Assuming that religious faith does not have the emotional hold in America that it has in traditionally Catholic France, Beauvoir pointed out that her mother, her teachers, and her friends all considered it scandalous that she had ceased to be a believer. It does indeed seem clear from the reading of the autobiography that once Simone de Beauvoir admitted her loss of faith to her mother she remained a "dutiful daughter," but the spark of vitality and almost sensuous affection that had existed between mother and daughter during Simone's early childhood grew gradually more faint until the final weeks of Françoise de Beauvoir's life.

Interviewers repeatedly suggest that Simone de Beauvoir must have had some regrets about never having had children of her own. Her answer over the decades never changed. She told Jeanson in 1965, "I have not had any children, but I never really wanted any, and I do not in any way regret not having any."[10] She remarked to him, however, that she would probably be more interested in observing the behavior of a small child from morning to night at age fifty-five than she was when she was twenty. A 1972 article in *Le Nouvel Observateur* from which we have quoted earlier bears repeating as an unequivocal indication both of her understanding of the joys other women might find in having children and of her dismay at the limited vision of those who insist that this is the only viable choice for a woman to make:

> For me who did not want children and who wished above all to pursue a writing career, it was fortunate not to have any. I am not one who wishes to impose my life-style on all women, since on the contrary I am fighting for their freedom: freedom to become mothers, to use contraception, to have abortions. The fanatical ones are certain wives and mothers who do not allow women to follow a path other than the one they have taken.[11]

This is one of the author's most strongly worded expressions of frustration at the constant carping of critics about her decision to remain childless.

In a 1973 interview with Alice Schwarzer, Beauvoir denied that she found the idea of having and raising children repugnant, an accusation made by a number of her detractors. During the period in her youth when she contemplated marrying her cousin Jacques, she assumed that her future would include having children of her own. With Sartre, she explained, the relationship was complete without children: "My relationship with Sartre was such ... that I never felt the desire to have a child. I had no particular desire to have a carbon copy of Sartre—he fulfilled me completely—nor of myself. I felt totally fulfilled."[12] Asked by Schwarzer if she had ever had second thoughts about her decision, her response was again categorical: "Absolutely not! I have never regretted not having any children."[13] When the question was brought up again in a 1976 interview with Schwarzer, she elaborated that rather than regretting her decision, she rejoiced in it. She even went on to express pity for grandmothers obliged to take care of their grandchildren when they could be pursuing their own interests in their leisure time. For Simone de Beauvoir, the possibility of deriving pleasure from being with small children appears to have seemed quite unthinkable, although this statement about grandmothers contradicts her treatment of the joys of grandparenting in a section of *The Coming of Age* discussed in an earlier chapter.

In contrast to some younger women authors like Marie Cardinal, Beauvoir was convinced early on that a writing career and motherhood were mutually exclusive. In the 1978 Dayan film, she stated a strong preference for intimate relationships freely chosen by adults over biological family ties, reiterating, "I have never regretted not having children. I much prefer friendships, relationships I have chosen, to those which would have been imposed upon me by maternity."[14] She pointed out with annoyance that no one had ever suggested that Jean-Paul Sartre was not a "real man" because he was not a father. Why should a woman writer be treated any differently, she wondered? Some readers would answer that while Sartre never expressed theoretical opinions about fatherhood, Beauvoir did indeed have a great deal to say about motherhood, much of which represented an emotional challenge forcing those who had decided to become wives and mothers to justify their choices and indeed their existence.

An aspect of motherhood which was not extensively explored by Beauvoir in her writings was suggested by her reaction to a comment by a young woman who told her she reminded her of her mother. She was shaken by the realization that she was indeed of an age to be somebody's mother, and even somebody's grandmother: "My former self-image, one of a certain youthfulness which would go on more or less indefinitely, had been destroyed, and I couldn't quite manage to recognize myself in that woman who could indeed be a mother, almost a grandmother."[15] Thus motherhood was associated in her mind with a recognition that one is growing older, is indeed old enough both to create a new generation and eventually to yield one's place to it. We remember how fiercely both Beauvoir and Sartre fought against the implications of turning thirty, how they sought out younger, more capricious friends like Olga in order to maintain the illusion that they were not yet staid adults. Would the transition have been more or less difficult for them had they married and had children of their own as they approached thirty?

Simone de Beauvoir was cognizant of the fact that, in addition to the responsibilities which ensue after the birth of a child, the awareness that one can no longer lead the carefree, spontaneous life associated with youthfulness is a painfully sobering one for a new mother. This sense of giving up the freedom one has enjoyed all of one's life is undoubtedly an important factor in post-natal depression and in the general sense of frustration and disillusionment with which Beauvoir depicted the existence of young mothers. The fleeting distaste with which the author greeted the possibility that she could indeed be someone's mother reflected her instinctive understanding of the psychological problems inherent in the choice made by the vast majority of women to become mothers and thereby to spawn the generation that will eventually replace them.

Did Beauvoir herself ever resort to an abortion to avoid pregnancy? In the fall of 1970, she signed the Manifesto of the 343, subsequently published in an April 1971 issue of *Le Nouvel Observateur*, indicating that she had had an abortion. Nowhere in her autobiography, however, did she discuss this experience or its impact on her. When asked by lawyer Gisèle Halimi during the Bobigny trial if she had ever had an abortion, she answered quickly, "Yes, a long time ago."[16] After this hasty response, she immediately changed the focus of the inquiry from her personal life to the efforts she had made to help other women have safe abortions. This left her public wondering whether the signature on the 1970 manifesto was an indication of an event in her own life or rather an effective act of political support for an issue which she had openly espoused since the writing of *The Second Sex*. The question was not answered definitively until April 1984, when, in an article in *Le Journal du dimanche* by Michèle Stouvenot entitled "Les aveux de Simone de Beauvoir" (Simone de Beauvoir's Confessions), Beauvoir spoke of signing the Manifesto of the 343 and then revealed, smiling, "I added my name to the others, without hesitation. And yet it was a lie: that act, abortion, was something of which I had no personal experience."[17] Her pronouncement was again printed two days later as a news story in *Le Monde,* under the title "Mme Simone de Beauvoir et l'avortement." This information is interesting in light of the comparison Beauvoir made between having a tooth pulled and having an abortion. Someone who had actually experienced the emotional pain of deciding to end a life developing inside her might have found such an equation much more difficult to suggest.

What of Simone de Beauvoir's maternal instincts towards those who were close to her? She and her younger sister Hélène obviously had a very special relationship. Hélène paid a touching tribute to her sister in the Dayan film, revealing to her, "You were the one who gave me a sense of my own worth."[18] In her book of reminiscences, Hélène makes it apparent that Simone was a second mother to her, more appreciative of her talents than Françoise de Beauvoir, who had hoped that her second-born would be a boy. As a young girl, Simone delighted in teaching "Poupette" everything she knew and in seeing the rapid progress made by her bright pupil. It was indeed this teaching experience which made her decide that she would prefer to put her nurturing instincts to use as a teacher rather than as a mother. She admitted, however, that her attitude toward her lycée students was quite elitist. She had little patience with the less gifted members of her philosophy classes. She felt that true communication between teacher and student was very difficult because "knowledge is a type of oppression; in a sense I oppressed them with my knowledge."[19] She did, however, develop lifelong friendships with certain of her students, but only after they were no longer in her courses and therefore were supposedly beyond the authoritative structure of the classroom.

Even before Beauvoir chose to adopt Sylvie Le Bon, it was widely suggested that the latter had become her surrogate daughter. The author was most emphatic about denying the validity of this assumption. In 1976 she exclaimed to Alice Schwarzer, "Absolutely not! . . . Relationships between mothers and daughters are generally catastrophic."[20] She had always been so categorically opposed to traditional family ties that any suggestion that she herself might be engaged in a relationship even remotely resembling them appears to have horrified her. Again, during the shooting of the 1978 Dayan film, she emphasized the fact that her association with Sylvie was far more satisfying than most mother-daughter relationships.[21]

Forever intrigued by the psychological intricacies of the writer's private life, critics have also posited a maternal aspect to Beauvoir's liaison with Claude Lanzmann, seventeen years her junior. Curtis Cate of *The New York Times* stated authoritatively in a 1971 article that such a relationship between an older woman and a much younger man is always incestuous.[22] Beauvoir, however, never considered her associations with either Lanzmann or Sylvie as anything more than chosen ties which helped her remain young in spirit.

For many younger feminists, Simone de Beauvoir has become a spiritual mother. As Alice Schwarzer asserted, "She has no children—and yet many members of the younger generation look to her as a model."[23] As early as 1960 the author mentioned to Madeleine Chapsal a letter from a young woman who objected to her devoting her energies to writing her memoirs when she should be telling other women how to balance their commitments to their husbands, their careers, their children, and themselves. The letter writer quite obviously wished to see Beauvoir assume direct responsibility for the women who had been inspired by her works. In the 1978 Dayan film, she seemed somewhat exasperated by the expectations of her public. "It's not up to me to provide solutions for people and people should not expect solutions from me," she stated.[24] She had been careful not to assume the responsibilities of biological parenthood and clearly wished to avoid being trapped into psychological parenthood by several generations of women seeking the kind of liberation to which her books and her life had introduced them.

At an April 1985 colloquium held at Columbia University in New York City, there was much discussion of Beauvoir's role as surrogate mother, of a tendency among feminist scholars who greatly admire and respect her to be reluctant to criticize her in any way. One panelist described this hesitancy as motivated by a desire to "remain good little girls for Mommy." In an amusing countersuggestion, Kate Millett retorted, "Not mother. Try aunt. Aunts are really safer."[25] Still, many women through-out the world are so beholden to Simone de Beauvoir for the impact that the reading of *The Second Sex* had on their lives that they have indeed looked upon her with the same kind of affectionate awe that characterized their early relationships with their own mothers. Asked about this attitude in a 1985 interview, she replied:

> To be a mother, you have to take care of someone over a long period of time. And then in general children do not accept their mothers' ideas. So when women say they have been influenced by me, that means that I am not their mother, because most of them would not be influenced by their mothers.[26]

Although mothers would often agree wholeheartedly with the author about the tendency of their offspring to avoid following any advice they might offer, the thrust of this book is to suggest that Françoise de Beauvoir, like the mothers of many other successful women, was never as far from the surface of her brilliant daughter's psyche as the adult Simone may have believed.

An article appearing in *Le Monde* on April 16, 1986, two days after the author's death, was entitled "Une mère symbolique" (A Symbolic Mother). In it Josyane Savigneau stated persuasively:

> In her private life as in her public battles, Simone de Beauvoir, our "symbolic mother," forced the hand of history. Starting out as an innovator, she became our companion. She was everywhere .... Whether or not they know of Simone de Beauvoir, the women who are today in creative and influential positions, those the world will need to reckon with, owe her something. Those women are the progeny of that woman without children, of that elderly woman with the outdated turban, with the tense look, who, obstinately, for more than sixty years, despite slander, insults, and even worse, derision, kept affirming that being born a woman was not a fault.[27]

Beauvoir might quibble over the semantics of the word "mother," stat-ing that "in order to be a mother, you must first have given birth, and then diapered the child for months and months, and then taught it to walk and to talk. That is what a mother is."[28] Nonetheless, I think that, despite her reluctance to take on the role of maternal mentor, Simone de Beauvoir would have been pleased with Savigneau's moving tribute quoted above.

Because of her deep concern for the situation in which contemporary women find themselves, Beauvoir reflected a great deal on the impact of motherhood on individual lives. Her seemingly negative pronounce-ments about maternity have attracted volleys of protest from the more conservative of her readers. Until this point, we have concentrated on the way in which the author presented mothers in her fictional works and on what she said about the maternal role in *The Second Sex* and in her autobiography. The interviews, articles, and prefaces which appeared during the last twenty-five years of her life provide us with considerable additional insight into her view of the contemporary scene and of the dilemmas facing the modern woman.

Did Simone de Beauvoir ever actually suggest that women should not have children? Not in so many words. She told Jeanson in 1965 that it would be wrong to think that in order to be considered a true feminist a woman should not have children. "Far from it!" she emphasized.[29] She articulated her appreciation of the value of becoming a mother in the following terms: "Maternity can *always* have a positive value, even if it is only to help women to get to know themselves better ... if one does not have more pressing things to do, it must be quite exciting to discover what a child is like."[30] Her statement here hardly implies an overwhelming appreciation of maternity as a viable focus of energy for women. Instead it is apparent that Beauvoir would prefer to leave the childbearing and rearing to those who are not talented enough to have better things to do with their time. This point of view was elaborated upon and reinforced in later interviews.

In a dialogue with Beauvoir, Betty Friedan asked her directly if she believed that women should not become mothers. She again replied in the negative, "No, I'm not saying that, but since you're talking about choice, a girl should not be conditioned from her childhood to want to be a mother."[31] Returning to the question of the validity of the maternal role, she was considerably less positive in 1976 than she was in 1965. "Yes, there are values, but doubtful, dubious values ... ," she mused.[32] Given Beauvoir's gloomy pronouncements about motherhood, Betty Friedan finally asked her how she suggested that the human race be perpetuated. Yielding to an abrupt attack of impatience, she retorted, "There are already enough people on earth!"[33] As she explained in her introduction to this dialogue, Betty Friedan was alienated by this answer and questioned whether or not Simone de Beauvoir was interested in the real world in which most ordinary people must live out their lives. She did explain, however, that Beauvoir was eager to get to the hospital to be with an ailing Sartre on the day of their dialogue and that this may well have influenced the curtness of her remarks. The fact that the interview had to be conducted through interpreters undoubtedly compromised the spontaneity of the question-and-answer format, which, as it reads in Friedan's English transcription, can hardly qualify as a dialogue.

Speaking with Alice Schwarzer in 1976, Beauvoir expanded considerably on her ideas about maternity. Asked if she rejected the whole concept of motherhood, she replied:

> Oh no! I do not reject it! I just think that in today's world it is an incredible trap for a woman. That is why I would advise a woman not to become a mother. But I am not making a value judgment. What needs to be condemned is not mothers, but the ideology which incites all women to become mothers, and the conditions in which they must play out this role.[34]

Her answer indicates that she clearly wished to avoid pronouncing herself categorically against motherhood, at least in a published interview, yet would still strongly caution young women about what she considered a dangerous trap. She continued to fight against the societal pressures which imply that no one can be a "real woman" without experiencing the joys of motherhood and to encourage young women to seek out an identity for themselves that goes beyond being John's wife or Sally's mother. Her response to a similar question posed in the 1978 Dayan film was somewhat more mellow:

> If one could remove the bad conscience women inherit from their own mothers and grandmothers, then why not maternity? It's a rather lovely thing indeed to watch a human being be born, grow, and develop. But considering the present-day situation, it represents a trap in which women cannot avoid losing their freedom and their happiness.[35]

In all of these interviews, Beauvoir's pronouncements on motherhood maintain a precarious balance between recognition of the very real values of the experience and awareness of the sometimes overwhelming problems entailed in the raising of a child. This same balancing of divergent, emotionally charged points of view is found in her 1979 discussion with Margaret A. Simons and Jessica Benjamin:

> Women want to have children, and I have nothing against that. However, I believe that in today's world . . . maternity is a trap for women because it ties them to a man, to their home. . . . If it were possible to change the conditions which are an integral part of motherhood, then it could be a viable option. There are certain ties between a woman and her child that can be very strong. . . . If the world were made in a different way, if the woman did not become a slave as soon as she became a mother . . . then, what would be the need for eliminating motherhood?[36]

The words "trap" and "slave" occur again and again in the author's lexicon whenever she is questioned about motherhood. Being a mother was clearly associated in her mind with the images of domestic drudgery, unhappiness, and tyranny in which her memories of her own mother were embedded. This is perhaps the "bad conscience" inherited from mothers and grandmothers of which she speaks in her film, where her conviction that motherhood is the antithesis of freedom and happiness certainly tilts the scales in favor of avoiding it at all cost.

What place did Simone de Beauvoir assign to motherhood in the social structure of the modern world? As early as 1960 she commented to Maria Craipeau that while men know they must find some kind of paying job for themselves, women are forever torn between the choice of pursuing a career or of marrying and staying home to take care of household and children.[37] This, of course, is no longer so much the case in the late 1980s, when many women refuse to make an either/or choice and attempt to juggle careers and home responsibilities. It is the undue influence of what she labeled the myth of maternity which Beauvoir saw as a bourgeois plot designed to trick women into doing unsatisfying but necessary work for nothing. She painted a sorry picture of bright young women who have allowed themselves to be lulled into apathy by the myth:

> If [the woman] has children, it's the end of her career. In general, it's over. There is a huge distance between everything to which an adolescent who loves life, who loves to read, to study, looks forward and what happens when she finds herself limited to doing the housework, taking care of the children, etc. Many things die within her.[38]

This point of view, expressed in June 1978, echoes the author's disapproving attitude toward her classmates from the Cours Désir whom she watched many years earlier pouring tea for their mothers and waiting for their families to choose acceptable mates for them.

Beauvoir was angered by her perception that women have essentially been tricked into accepting the role of wife and mother without complaint by a system dedicated to the continuation of the patriarchy. In her deposition at the Bobigny trial, she analyzed how this is accomplished:

> Instead of telling a little girl, when she is two, three, or four years old, "Your destiny is to wash dishes," she is told, "Your destiny is to be a mother." She is given dolls, she hears maternity exalted, so that, when she becomes mature, she thinks of only one thing, getting married and having children. She has been convinced that she would not be a complete woman if she didn't have any children.[39]

Here, very articulately stated, is the myth Beauvoir set out, almost single-handedly, to demystify. The lure of motherhood, as she saw it, is a hoax perpetrated by society to encourage women to do menial tasks and to stay out of the workforce. It is not motherhood itself, but rather the aura with which society and the media have surrounded it which is the villain in keeping women in a secondary, oppressed, and ineffectual position. She saw this as a situation which men would never want to change because it allowed them to remain in control. "As long as having children is considered woman's main role in life, she will not be concerned with politics, with technology—and she will not challenge male supremacy," Beauvoir proclaimed.[40] Motherhood thus emerges as an economic ploy designed to keep women firmly in their place; it is treated in some interviews by Simone de Beauvoir in much the same tone as jaded U.S. liberals use to utter the words "Mom and apple pie."

Again and again the author referred to motherhood as a servitude, a form of slavery which she was delighted to have escaped. Although she tempered her 1982 statement to Alice Schwarzer by asserting that not every woman who becomes a mother is automatically transformed into a slave, she went on to proclaim that slavery is indeed the status of the vast majority of mothers. In an extremely penetrating observation made in a 1966 lecture in Japan, Beauvoir characterized the Western woman as having no control over her life:

> She belongs to her husband, to her children. At any moment the husband or the children can come to ask her for an explanation, for help, for a favor, and she is obliged to satisfy them. She belongs to the family, to the group. She does not belong to herself.[41]

Women thus become possessions, objects, and gradually lose any sense of their own identity. They exist merely to serve others, never to satisfy their own goals and desires. Any woman who has ever attempted to accomplish serious work, work which demands concentration, in the midst of the daily family routine can undoubtedly relate easily to the above scenario, which restates in updated terms the theme of Virginia Woolf's *A Room of One's Own*.

Considering the pitfalls involved, why, Beauvoir was asked, would any intelligent woman choose to have children? It was the author's perception that contemporary society is permeated with feelings of loneliness and solitude. Women therefore give birth in order to have someone to keep them company, she suggested. This plan is doomed to failure in the long run, since the child will grow up and move away from the family circle in order to live a life of its own, she remarked to Alice Schwarzer in 1976. Women who try to be both mother and pal to their children find this an impossible goal. The expectation that the gratitude of husband and children will justify a lifetime of devotion and self-effacement generally results in a growing sense of frustration and bitterness, she warned in a 1961 article published in *La Nef*.[42]

The predominantly negative pictures of motherhood painted by Simone de Beauvoir in her interviews and lectures make it apparent why she was always such a militant supporter of liberalized contraception and abortion. As early as 1961 she wrote a preface for Dr. Lagroua Weill-Hallé's *La Grand'Peur d'aimer*, a book whose provocative title can be translated literally as "the great fear of loving." In it Beauvoir deplored the martyrdom of women, subjected to one exhausting pregnancy after another, who were afraid of seeking sexual satisfaction for fear that still another child would be conceived, women who were depressed, nervous, cut off from the "real" world which lay outside the confines of their home.[43] Beauvoir considered it monstrous that the arrival of a new baby should represent a catastrophe for so many families. She saw pregnancy and motherhood as a kind of ordeal which wore women out both physically and psychologically as they struggled to fulfill the impossible demands imposed upon them by a society which saddled them with almost sole responsibility for the raising of their children. "The man can get away from this domestic hell, while [the woman] is totally consumed by it," she noted.[44] Whereas Jean-Paul Sartre's character Garcin in *No Exit* arrived at the conclusion that hell is other people, this passage, with its images of the destructive flames of a Dantesque inferno, suggests that for Simone de Beauvoir hell could be found in the day-to-day existence of the housewife and mother.

Liberalized abortion laws appeared to the author to be the first step in relieving women of such overwhelming pressure. In her preface to the book on the Bobigny case she declared, "An abortion properly executed is an operation as benign as the extraction of a tooth: less dangerous than childbirth."[45] In her deposition at the Bobigny trial, the author went on to say that legalizing abortion would eliminate the trauma associated with it. Abortion, in her opinion, is traumatic only because women have been conditioned by their upbringing to consider motherhood a sort of divine mission. Although one can certainly agree with the importance of making it possible for women to plan their pregnancies so that each child born is a wanted child, the analogy between an abortion and a tooth extraction is one that is a bit difficult to accept. The tooth is not the result of two people engaged in the most intimate of relationships, nor does it have the potential to grow into a sentient human being. Psychiatrists and psychologists who have worked with women traumatized by abortions can attest to the fact that the decision to cut off a potential life through medical intervention is never one which can be taken lightly.

It is certainly true, however, that the legalization of abortion has minimized the physical risks involved. Simone de Beauvoir was justly proud of the fact that the battle she waged with other French feminists resulted in the availability of legal, free abortions in France. Although she still saw much more left to do, there was a tone of satisfaction in her appraisal of the accomplishments of recent years in a March 1984 interview in *La Vie en rose:*

> We now have free abortion, which is an enormous victory, and contraception is very widespread. And there are really laws which insist on the equality of rights, of salaries, of hiring, and on antisexism in the schools. And that all seems very important to me.[46]

Thus things appear to be falling into place, as schools pay more attention to how they are conditioning both girls and boys, as women have a greater possibility of arranging their lives to include both childbearing and careers.

Work outside the home was emphasized by Simone de Beauvoir as an absolute necessity for maintaining a sense of self-respect and dignity. She stated categorically in her 1966 lecture in Japan: "As far as what I will call her personal dignity is concerned, as far as her happiness and her equilibrium are concerned, a woman cannot find self-fulfillment if she limits herself to being a wife and mother."[47] While in agreement with Betty Friedan's highlighting of the importance of a paycheck for women in *The Feminine Mystique,* Beauvoir was categorically opposed to Friedan's idea of paying women for the work they do at home while raising their children. She felt that this would only encourage women to remain on the fringe of life, playing a secondary role forever. "No woman should be authorized to stay at home to raise her children," she pontificated in her dialogue with Friedan.[48] One wonders what verb is here being translated as "authorized," which seems very heavy-handed in its assumption that someone, the patriarchy or perhaps Beauvoir herself, must dictate to women what they will or will not be allowed to do with their lives. The issue was raised once again at the April 1985 colloquium at Columbia University, where in a heated exchange with Betty Friedan, Yvette Roudy, then Minister of the Rights of Women, restated the French feminist position opposing salaries for housewives. Working outside the home obliges you to remain in contact with the world, Beauvoir commented to me in June 1978. It also relieves the pressure of some of the power politics which she saw as an integral part of the nuclear family: "If [women] work outside the home, they are not on their children's backs so much, and they have a somewhat broader horizon. But those who stay at home all the time have nothing else. They therefore exert power over their children."[49] Working, Beauvoir noted cannily, also gives the woman the ability to support herself and her children should her husband die or decide to leave her. It is therefore basic to the acquisition of the independence and freedom which Beauvoir advocated for all women.

Despite her own happy childhood, Simone de Beauvoir had a very low opinion of the nuclear family. When I asked her in 1978 what role she felt the family played in modern society, she quickly retorted, "As far as I'm concerned, the family doesn't exist." [50] For decades she had been predicting the demise of the traditional family and she appeared to consider it close to extinction in 1978. In a 1972 article in *Le Nouvel Observateur,* previously cited, she portrayed the family in all its neurotic splendor, depicting it as a playground for sadomasochistic games and admonishing, "We must admit that the number of neurotic children our society produces is frightening."[51] It remains for other researchers to determine the degree to which the freely chosen members of one's entourage, often referred to by Beauvoir and Sartre as their "family," escape the neurotic entanglements of the more traditional biological family. The details of the final years of Sartre's life provided by *Adieux: A Farewell to Sartre* suggest that such arrangements can also be emotionally charged and draining.

Although Simone de Beauvoir occasionally acknowledged some of the positive aspects which have drawn women to motherhood throughout the centuries, she repeatedly urged women not to submerge their entire identity in their maternal role. This explains why she became exasperated with such movements as Mothers for Peace, convinced that any such campaign, like the efforts to secure wages for housework, tends to insulate women even more from the world at large:

> It is certainly not in the name of maternity that women should be pacifists. People try too often to enclose them in a sort of ghetto by saying, "It's because you are mothers." On that point, I don't agree at all. It is because they are human beings that they ought to fight for peace."[52]

Beauvoir never approved of the ghettoization of any group, be they feminists, mothers, Communists, or right-wing conservatives. The message conveyed throughout her life was that individuals must unite as caring beings with an equal stake in the fate of humanity in order to make the world a better place to live in.

In her 1979 interview with Simons and Benjamin, Simone de Beauvoir posited an underlying hostility between men and women which she attributed to the fact that each of us is, indeed, "of woman born." The moment of our birth sets us on a path which unavoidably leads to our death, thus making the woman responsible for our life also ultimately accountable for our mortality. Asked what effect feminism might have on the relationship between men and women, Beauvoir responded pessimistically, "I do not believe that feminism will prevent men from hating women because women are their mothers, consequently their death."[53] The use of the verb "hate" is particularly disturbing and somewhat surprising, coming from an author who has urged men and women to work together toward equality and who has disagreed with the radical-feminist tendency toward separatism and toward the development of a special style of women's writing. Borrowing from Freudian theory, Beauvoir here managed to identify motherhood as the source of the perennial battle between the sexes.

A statement made by Beauvoir to John Gerassi in 1976 suggests that she held the current maternal tradition responsible for much that is wrong with society. Speaking of both France and America, she declared:

> To change the whole value system of either society, to destroy the concept of motherhood, that is revolutionary. In a society where the male can be the mother, where . . . to be gentle or soft is better than to be hard and tough, . . . you have automatically set up equality.[54]

Her point here is well taken, as she seems to equate mothering with nurturing and to suggest that the latter can be done effectively by members of either sex. She elaborates on this point with Simons and Benjamin in 1979:

> I think that by changing the concept of motherhood, by changing the idea of maternal instinct, of the feminine vocation, society will change completely. Because it is through this idea of feminine vocation that women are enslaved. . . . If this concept were to be destroyed, I do not mean motherhood itself, but all the myths which are related to motherhood, without any doubt society would be completely transformed.[55]

Here as in earlier pronouncements, Beauvoir was careful to specify that she was not advocating the elimination of motherhood, but rather of the aura surrounding it in Western society. She was well aware that no one advising all women to give up having children would ever be taken seriously by the vast majority of the public she was trying to reach. Her goal was rather, as the title of this book suggests, the demystification of motherhood.

A comprehensive statement of Simone de Beauvoir's advice to women is contained in a 1976 interview which reflects her wary and predominantly negative attitude toward the family, marriage, and maternity at that time:

> I believe that a woman must not allow herself to be caught in the trap represented by children and marriage. Even if a woman wants to have children, she ought to think a great deal about the conditions in which she will have to raise them, because maternity, at the present time, is real slavery. Fathers and society leave to women, and to them alone, the responsibility for the children. It is the women who stop working to raise the children. It is the women who stay at home when the children are sick. They are the ones held responsible when the child fails. And if a woman wants a child anyway, it would be better for her to have it without getting married, because marriage is the biggest trap of all.[56]

This is a powerful assertion, which comes about as close as the author ever did to recommending categorically against motherhood. In it one sees reflections of Monique in "The Woman Destroyed" abandoning her medical studies when she became pregnant, cutting short her vacation to nurse her adult daughter back to health, of Laurence feeling guilty about her daughter Catherine's mediocre report card in *Les Belles Images*.

Beauvoir considered marriage an even more dangerous trap than maternity. Asked by Liliane Lazar in 1983 how she would suggest making marriage compatible with contemporary society, she responded without hesitation, "I think marriage should be abolished completely.... A commitment between two people who each have sixty years of life ahead of them ... is something absurd...."[57] Her dim view of family living, which surely had its roots in her adolescent experience under the authoritative but neurotic eye of Françoise de Beauvoir, appears to have been an issue on which she never wavered throughout her life.

Beauvoir clearly recognized, however, that most women, unlike herself, wish to become mothers. In a 1985 interview, she warmly endorsed women's fulfilling their innermost desires as far as maternity is concerned:

> If they wish to have children, why should they deprive themselves of that experience? One must follow one's profound desires. Then let them manage afterward to reconcile motherhood with a certain independence.... Let them try to avoid becoming slaves. But if they want children, let them have them, of course.[58]

She went on to advise that limiting a family to one child is perhaps the most effective way to combine motherhood and a career, noting that, among Sylvie's colleagues, those who had only one child managed to continue teaching at the lycée without great difficulty. When a second child arrives, she commented, "That begins to enslave a mother who has to juggle a teaching career and take care of changing diapers and correcting papers at the same time. With two, one becomes enslaved. One child is fine."[59] Her attitude toward motherhood seemed to have softened considerably in this 1985 interview, although the word *esclavage* (slavery) still appears prominently in her analysis of its pitfalls.

Simone de Beauvoir considered the lure of the ideal mother-child relationship the fatal link which keeps women at home and in the kitchen, sidelined from the activities of the real world. She urged women to rebel against the mindless conditioning which makes them consider motherhood as their only commitment, seeing this as the first necessary step in the struggle for equality. "The woman who rebels against forced maternity is on her way to a more general rebellion," she proclaimed in 1973.[60] Underlying this statement was Beauvoir's nostalgic longing for a socialist utopia, one in which the upheaval of capitalist society would automatically bring about equality of the sexes. Her sense that present society must be radically overhauled before maternity can become a viable option for independent women was articulated with increasing emphasis as she clarified her own feminist position and tried to reconcile it with her earlier commitment to socialism. In her later years she became much more skeptical about the alliance between socialism and feminism and concentrated her energies on feminist causes.

Beauvoir never abandoned her pragmatic view of maternity as an enslavement of mind, body, and spirit, yet some of the comments she made in interviews granted during the final years of her life suggest that she may have mellowed in her previously uncompromising view of the path to women's liberation. Her statements and her works serve as a warning to all those who might otherwise have followed the traditional call of marriage and maternity without considering alternative choices and indeed represent an articulate demystification of motherhood. It remains for each individual woman to decide whether or not she wishes to marry, whether or not she wishes to have children, and how she will best make use of her own talents and career goals if she does choose to do both. Simone de Beauvoir's works, ideas, and commitment to achieving autonomy for all women as she did for herself have made it possible for maternity to become a truly existential choice for the modern woman and thereby undoubtedly a more pleasurable experience for both mother and child.

Simone de Beauvoir and Motherhood: Private Struggle, Public Impact

What, then, can one conclude from this study of Simone de Beauvoir and her presentation of motherhood? The analysis of her fictional and autobiographical works suggests again and again that the author's inter-action with her own mother as well as her observation of the mothers of the bourgeois environment in which she was brought up made her attitude toward maternity an almost obsessive part of the legacy she was determined to pass on to her readers. Because of her repeated warnings about the enslavement represented by society's expectations of individual mothers, Beauvoir has had an enormous influence on the liberated approach to maternity characteristic of the 1980s. Many of the battles she fought have been won, as women in most Western countries find themselves able to avail themselves of contraceptive methods and of legalized abortions. A thorough reading of her work still leaves the question of the possibility of combining motherhood and a successful career among the most compelling issues confronting contemporary feminists.

As one proceeds chronologically through Beauvoir's works, it becomes apparent that the author was more comfortable tackling sensitive issues in fiction before discussing them directly in her autobiography. Her earliest works seethe with the resentment she felt toward her own mother and toward Madame "Mabille" Lacoin. The latter, in the persona provided for her by Madame Vignon in *When Things of the Spirit Come First,* has all of the villainous qualities of Jules Renard's Madame Lepic in *Poil de carotte*[1] and Hervé Bazin's "Folcoche" in *Vipère au poing.*[2] These two maternal monsters, depicted with precious little subtlety as having essentially no redeeming qualities, were both created by male writers. It is more difficult to find women authors who have peopled their fictional works with mothers as egotistical and harmful as Madame Vignon. Marie Cardinal's rendition of her mother in *Les Mots pour le dire,* for example, is as much an anguished recounting of the author's psychological insecurity as it is an indictment of the mother responsible for it.[3] This may well be due to the degree to which most women identify with their mothers—a symbiosis underlined by Nancy Friday's apt title *My Mother/My Self*—and are therefore reluctant to portray even fictional mothers in too negative a light.

For many years, Simone de Beauvoir appeared convinced that she had nothing in common with passive, conventional women resembling the mother from whom she had carefully distanced herself after her adolescence. The mothers she described in her fiction became more martyr than monster, pitiful victims of societal expectations that no one could ever fulfill. There are some sympathetic glimpses of Madame Blomart the pacifist, who objects to her son's responsibility for the taking of innocent lives in *The Blood of Others.* She is still depicted, however, as a "relative being" dependent upon her husband for both her support and her ideas. The kind of anguish and depression to which such a lack of identity can lead is found again in characters like Catherine Fosca in *All Men Are Mortal,* Laurence in *Les Belles Images,* and Monique in "The Woman Destroyed."

Not all the mothers portrayed in Beauvoir's fiction are ineffectual stay-at-homes, however. Catherine d'Avesnes in *Who Shall Die?* is a positive heroine capable of combining her maternal role with active participation in the political concerns of her community. Her daughter Clarisse, expecting her first child at the end of the play, is another activist with well-articulated opinions about the course of action she wishes her compatriots to take. Catherine Fosca, first wife of the immortal protagonist of *All Men Are Mortal,* is adamant in her demands that her husband reverse his decision about eliminating the "useless mouths" of Carmona. It is only after he refuses to acquiesce that she sinks into resignation and virtual silence. Fosca's eighteenth-century wife Marianne de Sinclair works hard to realize her idealistic vision of the betterment of humanity through scientific progress so that her children and grandchildren can live in a more harmonious world, thereby winning her husband's eternal admiration and love. Although not committed to a particular political cause, Anne Dubreuilh in *The Mandarins* represents a voice of conciliation and common sense that needs to be heard. Despite her bouts of depression and anorexia at the end of *Les Belles Images,* Laurence is determined to take an active role in raising her daughters to become much more than pretty faces.

None of these mothers represents the sheer determination and strength of character of such memorable protagonists as the mother in Marguerite Duras's *Un Barrage contre le Pacifique*[4] or Silla Boyce in Paule

Marshall's *Brown Girl, Brownstones*.[5] Both Duras's character, referred to only as "la mère" in the narrative, and Silla Boyce waste little time on introspection. Neither appears to have any ambivalence about her maternal responsibilities. Neither belongs to the middle-class society Beauvoir consistently depicts. Each is ready to fight tooth and nail to procure survival and eventual success for her children. Each does not hesitate to attack her daughter physically, in dramatic confrontations between a powerful maternal figure and a daughter trying to escape and find her own independence. Both Suzanne and Selena Boyce articulate love and respect for the formidable women who bore them. In all of Beauvoir's fiction, on the other hand, only Clarisse d'Avesnes seems capable of joining forces effectively with her mother in their pursuit of a common goal.

What of the younger generation of women found in Simone de Beauvoir's fiction? Those who reject marriage and maternity appear to lead more liberated lives than those following more traditional paths. Françoise Miquel in *She Came to Stay* triumphs psychologically over a surrogate daughter who has managed to turn her life inside out. Hélène Bertrand (*The Blood of Others*) chooses to abort a child conceived with someone to whom she is completely indifferent and goes on to play a tragically heroic role in the Resistance. In *All Men Are Mortal*, the sensitive Laure devotes herself day and night to the needs of suffering humanity, yet could indeed have been enticed into a relationship with Raymond Fosca had he been willing to comply. The caustic Nadine Dubreuilh (*The Mandarins*) deliberately becomes pregnant in order to force Henri Perron to marry her, yet clearly maintains her individuality and independence even as she conscientiously follows all the steps outlined in the child-care books in raising her newborn daughter Maria. These women each have a clear identity at the end of the respective works in which they appear.

A great many of the mothers in Beauvoir's fiction are abandoned in the final pages of the narrative in a confused and unsatisfied state, however. Madame Drouffe will never comprehend the vitality and drive of her younger daughter Marguerite (*When Things of the Spirit Come First*). Madame Blomart is disappointed and outraged to see the son she has raised in an atmosphere of Christian charity choose violence and terrorism as a means to an end in the Resistance (*The Blood of Others*). Catherine Fosca retreats to her needlework after her husband refuses to heed her voice of compassion and concern for the lives of others (*All Men Are Mortal*). Beauvoir tells us that Anne Dubreuilh's descent from the bedroom in which she contemplated suicide to the garden below, where her husband, daughter, and granddaughter await, is essentially a defeat (*The Mandarins*). Laurence does not know how she will go about making sure that her daughters do not follow in her footsteps (*Les Belles Images*). For the protagonist of "Age of Discretion," life will never again have the spark that it did when she looked forward to seeing her son share her enthusiasm for literature and the teaching profession. Murielle may well end up in a mental institution after the last word of her monologue pronounced, while Monique must learn to live with solitude and silence. Each of these characters seems designed by her creator to reinforce the thesis that family life is essentially isolating and counterproductive.

The fictional works must be examined, however, against the backdrop of Simone de Beauvoir's autobiography. *Memoirs of a Dutiful Daughter* is essentially the drama of two very bright girls from caring families who are struggling to establish their own identity in a society which makes demands upon them with which they do not choose to comply. Both the young Simone and Zaza "Mabille" Lacoin were raised with a great deal of tenderness and attention by families who recognized their intelligence and their vitality. We have noted how frequently Beauvoir attributed her success as an adult to the happiness of her early years, a happiness created almost single-handedly by her attractive and affectionate mother. What the perceptive classmates realized as they grew from childhood to adolescence was the degree to which family relationships and activities were based more on predetermined conventions than on freely chosen interaction with other human beings. It was at this point that Beauvoir began to see marriage and maternity as traps condemning the unsuspecting young woman to a routine of repetitious and uninspiring chores and isolating her from the vibrant activity of the world beyond the confines of her doorstep. The example of a mother abandoned psychologically by a husband with complete freedom to come and go as he pleased reinforced her determination to avoid fitting into such a mold.

The fact that Georges de Beauvoir did not have the financial means to provide a dowry for either of his daughters encouraged Simone and Hélène to pursue careers in which they could find satisfaction and fulfillment. As soon as Beauvoir began her advanced studies and moved away from the family apartment, she felt free to develop her talents and choose a life-style very different from her mother's. Having lost her religious faith during her adolescence, she felt no compunction about establishing her own identity and essentially turning her back on the uninspired existence her mother was forced to live. Her conviction about the validity of her choice was confirmed by her observation of the emotional trauma imposed upon her best friend Zaza by a manipulative mother, a rigid family structure, and a Catholic faith which demanded obedience to parents and to convention. Zaza's death was assuredly one of the most compelling reasons behind the crusading nature of Simone de Beauvoir's attack on family and motherhood throughout the canon of her work.

The depiction of Françoise de Beauvoir grows rather hazy during the years following the publication of *Memoirs of a Dutiful Daughter*. She seems to have been politely set to one side by her older daughter, who visited her dutifully but found little to talk about in her presence. Rather than the passionate admiration of a Colette for the Sido who declined an invitation to visit her in Paris at age seventy-six because she did not want to miss the spectacle of a cactus in her garden which only bloomed every four years,[6] Beauvoir's feelings for her mother during most of her adult life appear to have been uninspired and often tinged with impatience and condescension. Françoise de Beauvoir's relative lack of importance in her daughter's life lies in sharp contrast to the situation reflected in the works of Marie Cardinal, whose anguished recollections of a mother eternally mourning for a deceased older sister resulted in years of therapy and hundreds of pages of cathartic writing. Unlike Sylvia Plath's often impassioned letters to her mother Aurelia,[7] Beauvoir's missives addressed to her *Chère petite maman* were restricted to factual accounts of her trips and her daily routine.

In *A Very Easy Death*, the reader finds a gripping reflection of the emotional attachment between Françoise and Simone de Beauvoir. In this small volume, the adult Simone shares with her readers the agonizing experience of watching her mother's life ebb away and of realizing in the process that the bond between them was much stronger than she had dared to admit to herself during her mature years. The text is all the more poignant because of its straightforward, direct style. In its understatement it suggests comparisons to Yasushi Inoue's account of his mother's aging and eventual demise in *Chronicle of My Mother*[8] and to Annie Ernaux's tribute to the ambition and determination of her working-class mother in *Une Femme*.[9]

Given the impact of Zaza's death and Beauvoir's distaste for the traditional life her mother was leading, it is little wonder that her focus in *The Second Sex* and in numerous interviews was on the importance of free choice and careful deliberation on the part of women contemplating having children. She appears to have felt personally responsible for warning women about the dangers of becoming mothers simply because society and their families expected it of them. Her willingness to participate in demonstrations and her articulate support were clearly instrumental in helping to make contraception and abortion legally available in France. The often unpalatable metaphors she used to describe gestation and childbirth provided an image diametrically opposed to the myth of happy mother and chubby baby promulgated by the media.

Beauvoir repeatedly advocated the abolition of the family, admitting at the same time that she did not know what to suggest as its replacement. As we have noted earlier, she often referred to the circle formed by herself, Sartre, Olga, Bost, Lanzmann, Sylvie, and other close associates as her family, thereby replacing with specially chosen friends the biological ties usually implied in the use of the word. She mentioned in her autobiography that she maintained close contact with her sister Hélène because theirs was a freely chosen friendship rather than because they had been born into the same family. If one equates mothering and nurturing, arguments can be found for seeing in Simone de Beauvoir a surrogate mother for Olga, Sylvie, and even Bost, Lanzmann, and Sartre. The fact that both she and Sartre legally adopted daughters suggests that both wished to leave behind a member of a younger generation who cared about their work and their ideas and who could be entrusted to perpetuate them and make them available for future generations. The need for "family" was keenly felt by both authors, each of whom thrived on interaction and communication with other people and particularly with young people.

Simone de Beauvoir had a strong sense of responsibility toward those who looked to her for direction and who, despite her stated reluctance to accept such an idea, tended to elevate her to the role of surrogate mother in their lives. Deirdre Bair reveals that while Beauvoir once limited herself to answering the telephone in her rue Schoelcher apartment only during certain hours of the day, in her later years she felt that she had to answer it whenever it rang. "There are too many people who need something and time is too short," she explained somewhat apologetically.[10] The fact that even those who had never met her sensed her warm concern for the welfare of women and of humanity in general is reflected in the symbiotic tone of Carolyn Grassi's poetic tribute to Beauvoir in the memorial issue of the *Simone de Beauvoir Studies:* "We called her mother sister muse. . . ."[11]

Was Simone de Beauvoir's attitude a unilateral condemnation of motherhood then? I do not think so. "Obviously she never wanted to abolish marriage completely any more than she would try to prohibit the birth of children," Hazel Barnes concluded in an assessment of Beauvoir's blunt statements and radical positions on these issues.[12] Although the author might not agree with Barnes's interpretation of her views on matrimony, she did on several occasions articulate her recognition of the joys many women derive from having and raising children.

No one who has read *A Very Easy Death* can doubt that, despite her overt rejection of her mother's life-style, Beauvoir cared deeply for the painfully sincere and conscientious woman who raised her and appreciated the nurturing and affection she received from Françoise de Beauvoir during the critical early years of her life.

Simone de Beauvoir reiterated on numerous occasions that her quarrel was not with motherhood itself but rather with the institution of motherhood as it has developed in bourgeois society. We have seen that she considered this institution a trap paralyzing young women and preventing them from developing their talents and their autonomy. Through the vivid portrayals in her fictional works, through the documentation in *The Second Sex,* and through her impassioned pronouncements in her autobiography, Simone de Beauvoir made the women of the twentieth century take a long and hard look at the implications of having children. Perhaps the most compelling effect of the body of her work is indeed her success in demystifying the institution of motherhood.

Appendix A

Interview with Simone de Beauvoir, September 14, 1985

Yolanda Astarita Patterson: I would like to ask you some questions about the mother images in your fictional works. I will begin with *When Things of the Spirit Come First* and the mother of Marguerite and Marcelle in those stories. Does she resemble your own mother somewhat?

Simone de Beauvoir: Who is that? Whose mother?

YAP: Marcelle and Marguerite's. She doesn't have a big role, but there is a moment when Marguerite decides to go out with Denis, her sister's husband. Her mother tells her she can't, absolutely not, and she goes out anyway. She is rebelling against her mother's authority at that moment.

SdeB: Yes, of course. There were moments in my life that were in fact like that. When I was almost an adult, my mother on one or two occasions forbade me to go out in the evening, because we didn't go out in the evening. I was almost twenty, and I went out anyway.

YAP: I remember that you talked of this incident in your autobiography. And Madame Vignon in that collection of stories?

SdeB: She was very much like my friend Zaza's mother.

YAP: Did you exaggerate your depiction of her a great deal because of your feelings about what happened to Zaza? She seems almost a caricature. Was Zaza's mother really like that? Did she think she was carrying out God's will?

SdeB: Yes, certainly. Oh, certainly she thought she was carrying out God's will.

YAP: Do you think that if Zaza had lived, she would have been able to rebel against her mother after a while?

SdeB: Oh, I don't know about that. She loved her a great deal, so she might not have rebelled, but she perhaps might have separated a bit through marriage, for example. I don't know. I can't know what would have happened.

YAP: You have spoken a great deal about psychological manipulation by Zaza's mother. When the children were very little, they could do whatever they wanted . . .

SdeB: Yes, that's very true. That corresponds exactly to the reality of the situation. Whatever they wanted is a bit of an exaggeration, but she was in fact very liberal. She left them alone, she didn't bother about little things. If they overturned a chair, it wasn't a big thing, whereas in my family, a much bigger fuss was made. She didn't bother her children about a lot of little things and was therefore more assured of their obedience in the matters that really counted.

YAP: Do you think that mothers today continue to manipulate their children in the same way?

SdeB: Oh, I don't know exactly how they manipulate them now, but I think that in fact mothers do try to manipulate their children.

YAP: And there is the role of religion and the idea that one must always obey one's parents, isn't there?

SdeB: Yes, that's true. I no longer know anything about religious circles, but I think that when they raise their children they probably still have that idea of honoring your father and your mother. Yes, in religious circles, which I know very little about, that approach continues. I suppose that it still exists.

YAP: In *When Things of the Spirit Come First,* a student of Chantal Plattard's finds herself pregnant, and you described her pregnancy almost as something disgusting. There are other sections in your fictional works where you describe a sort of parasite developing inside the woman's body.

SdeB: I think that when the girl is very young and her pregnancy was an accident that is the impression she has. When the pregnancy is wanted and a matter of choice, and the woman is mature and knows about the responsibility it entails, it is not at all the same thing. In that story the girl is too young, I think she is fifteen, or fourteen, when that happens to her, when she finds out [that she is pregnant]. In that case, generally it is a frightful situation.

YAP: In *She Came to Stay,* can one compare the relationship between Françoise and Xavière to the one existing between a mother and her daughter?

SdeB: Oh no, not at all. I actually discussed that at length in ... *The Prime of Life* ... yes, that's where it was ... the fact that it is not at all a mother-daughter relationship, absolutely not. Oh no, not at all.

YAP: Without speaking of maternal instinct, because it has been said that what is called maternal instinct is the responsibility one feels toward another individual ... Françoise, at least at the beginning of the novel, feels somewhat responsible for Xavière.

SdeB: But you know, people also feel responsible for a sister, a brother, a friend. That isn't exclusively maternal. Of course, in maternal feeling, since in fact I reject the idea of instinct, there must be a very important sense of responsibility, which pleases certain women, moreover, because it makes them feel important to feel responsible for someone. But a feeling of responsibility is not necessarily maternal.

YAP: It is evident that in *She Came to Stay* you are talking about your own relationship with Olga. I understand that Olga just died this year. Did you always maintain a very close relationship with her?

SdeB: Yes, oh yes. Yes, yes, yes.

YAP: I read in the Francis and Gontier book the original first section of *She Came to Stay,* and I wondered why you decided to eliminate that section in which you speak of Françoise's early childhood.

SdeB: I'm not the one who decided. It was Gallimard who told me it wasn't good, and he was right.

YAP: From the point of view of the mother-daughter relationship I found it interesting, because Françoise's mother is almost never seen in the finished version of the novel.

SdeB: Yes, but it was really useless, not at all necessary.

YAP: But you have so often said that early childhood is so important ...

SdeB: Yes, of course. But I wanted to tell a very definite story, the story of the trio. I didn't want to recount all of Pierre's childhood, all of Françoise's childhood, all of Xavière's childhood. I took them at a moment of crisis when they were all developed personalities. You could assume certain things about their childhood. Quite a lot about Xavière's, at any rate, because a great deal is said about it. As for Pierre and

Françoise, one has the impression that they emerged from childhood as rather stable individuals, that they knew what they were doing. Therefore it wasn't worthwhile to elaborate on that aspect of their lives.

YAP: Between Françoise and Madame Miquel, it seems as if the relationship is one of polite distance.

SdeB: That's right, the normal, superficial relationship that many mothers and daughters seem to have.

YAP: And especially when the daughter is an adult . . .

SdeB: When the daughter is an adult, definitely.

YAP: In *The Blood of Others,* one has the pregnancy and abortion of Hélène Bertrand. That is the first time you spoke about an abortion in a fictional work. At that time were you beginning to think about the importance of making abortion legal for women?

SdeB: No, I had already been thinking about it for a long time. I even remember one of my first reactions as a young teenager when I was told that abortion was very bad. I thought that one should have the right to control one's body. No, I believed in the right to abortion well before writing *The Blood of Others.* And later, when the feminists took up this theme and wanted to use it as an issue to fight for, I was completely in agreement and I fought with them.

YAP: The scene in the novel is very compelling.

SdeB: Yes, it is realistic.

YAP: Back to the mother-daughter relationship: I would like to discuss the scene in which the Jewish mother calls after her little daughter when they are about to be separated, and the effect of this scene on Hélène Bertrand. Would it have been very different if it had been a woman who was going to be separated from her husband, for example? Do you think that the relationship between the mother and the daughter is much more emotional from a dramatic point of view?

SdeB: I don't know about that, but being separated from her husband would have been entirely different because the husbands had already gone underground. A little girl is helpless, totally helpless, and that is why I chose that situation. And then there were indeed really wrenching scenes. They put the children in buses to take them away and the mothers were there crying out, running after the bus, just as I described it.

YAP: Did you actually see this happen?

SdeB: I didn't see it but I heard about it. I knew about it. I wasn't in Paris at that time. It was July. I was not around when it happened.

YAP: I'd like to discuss Madame Blomart in *The Blood of Others*. She interests me because she seems to be a maternal martyr to some degree, the mother who knows that she has lost all control over her adult children. But she also has good intentions, for example her idea of extending her arms in Seville to stop the wild rush of the crowds. And when her son is responsible for the death of Germans, she says that it will cause the death of innocent Frenchmen. Is she perhaps the model for a mother who is not going to try to play too large a role in the life of her adult children but who . . .

SdeB: Her children? She only has one child, doesn't she?

YAP: She has two daughters we never see. But I think that you talked about their marriages. There again their mother said nothing but she suffers because she does not approve of the choice of husbands they have made.

SdeB: Ah yes. In fact, I had in mind a friend whom I call Madame Lemaire but whose real name was Madame Morel. She was a women with such a mentality. She was the one who acted like that. She was an absolutely charming woman but her relationship with her son was not at all like the one in the novel because her son was not a very interesting person. But that character was based on her. A pleasant woman, very pleasant indeed, and very beautiful, one who hated violence. One has to show the other side of the question.

YAP: And you have Jean Blomart, who would like to have his mother's approval, but if he continues to direct terrorist activities, and he believes he must continue, he can never have it. He would even like to become a little child again so that he can remain with his mother, yet he knows he cannot do this. He leaves her without winning her approval.

SdeB: Yes, that's right.

YAP: In the play *Who Shall Die?* there is Catherine, who is the mother of a detestable son and of an independent daughter. She is also somewhat the mother of her township, isn't she?

SdeB: Yes, because she is the wife of an official, of a political leader.

YAP: The poor people appeal to her. And with her daughter, who is pregnant, there is the whole idea of that baby's future, of the hope of another generation.

SdeB: Yes, indeed.

YAP: In *All Men Are Mortal,* you depict the difference between a father raising a child, and a mother. Antoine, who was raised in an atmosphere of peace and harmony, must rebel against Fosca in order to prove himself. Do you think that this rebellion is necessary between a mother and daughter as well as between a father and son?

SdeB: Oh, it's stronger between father and son.

YAP: What do modern sons do in order to gain power? There are no more military battles for proving one's prowess, by killing someone, for example.

SdeB: No. That's partly the reason they group together, take drugs, wander off, because they don't have many ways of proving themselves.

YAP: It is in *The Second Sex* that you spoke of the choices possible for women. Do you still think that motherhood keeps a woman from finding her own identity?

SdeB: I think that such as she is today, yes. Because the woman is too enslaved.

YAP: You still think that she . . .

SdeB: Ah, yes, I do.

YAP: Even with modern conveniences?

SdeB: Oh, modern conveniences, you know! It's nonetheless always the woman who takes care of the children, it's not the husband, even if he plays a small role. And it is often a very very heavy burden for the woman. At least in France, day-care centers and nursery schools are very very very inadequate.

YAP: Really? And I think that it is better here than in the United States, where we have very few day-care centers.

SdeB: The same is true for us. One has to sign up I don't know how many months in advance. It is very difficult.

YAP: In *The Mandarins,* there is the relationship between Anne and Nadine.

SdeB: I think that down deep Anne always reproaches herself for not loving her daughter but that she loves her a great deal. Several things suggest that. She says she doesn't love her enough because she demands a lot of herself but in fact she loves her a lot. On the other hand, she cannot live her daughter's life for her. She prefers to let her live her own life. And she does so.

YAP: And the guilt feeling she speaks about all the time. Do you think that is in general a part of motherhood?

SdeB: I think that for *many* women it is a part of motherhood. Because one feels so responsible, as you were saying. One is so responsible that the least thing, the slightest hitch, makes you feel guilty, because the entire burden is on you, the mother.

YAP: It is never the father who is blamed.

SdeB: No, it is never the father. No, no, no, no. That doesn't change. I think that now fathers try to be a little closer to their children, try to be more fatherly, at least . . . in certain sectors of society, especially among young people, young people and intellectuals. But on the whole it is always the mother who is responsible, and if she is responsible, since there are more or less grave misfortunes in every life, if she is responsible for the lives of her children, she will evidently often feel guilty about their misfortunes.

YAP: And it is always the mother who remains with the child when the child is sick and both parents work.

SdeB: It is almost never the father, always the mother.

YAP: There is Nadine, in *The Mandarins,* who reads all the books on child rearing but who doesn't seem to feel true affection for her daughter Maria.

SdeB: Yes, I think that Nadine is very egotistical, very self-centered. She really doesn't possess the kind of generosity one needs to take care of a child. She lacks warmth.

YAP: Will she perhaps develop that warmth?

SdeB: I really don't know. I think that she lacks warmth and that that is something one cannot learn.

YAP: And that is not simply a result of the tragic death of Diego?

SdeB: Oh no. It's her whole character that comes . . . I don't know exactly from what, I didn't go into that in depth. But she is frigid first, evidently, definitely frigid. And then cold; she is cold and hostile toward everyone.

YAP: When Anne Dubreuilh thinks about committing suicide, she changes her mind the moment she thinks about Nadine, about Nadine's reaction . . .

SdeB: Not only about Nadine, but about her husband, too.

YAP: About her husband, too, but especially about Nadine's indignation, about Nadine's saying "She didn't have the right to do that." Another example of a mother who feels a responsibility for her child and the next generation.

SdeB: Yes, certainly. Then that also shows that Nadine is cold on the one hand, but that she is less cold than her behavior would lead one to believe. Because, if she were to find that her mother had committed suicide, she would become enraged. That is her way of suffering, and that means that she cares a great deal about her mother.

YAP: The character of Nadine was modeled after "Lise," wasn't she?

SdeB: Yes, somewhat after "Lise." That's right.

YAP: In *Les Belles Images,* you have three generations of women, with Laurence caught between the other two. Is Laurence a "dutiful daughter"?

SdeB: Yes, I think she is rather dutiful, a rather dutiful young woman.

YAP: She feels responsible for her mother, whom she does not really love, and especially for her daughter.

SdeB: Her daughter, yes. That feeling is very strong.

YAP: Toward the end of the novel, there is a moment of despair when Laurence wants to do something to change her daughters' lives but doesn't know what to do. What can one do to make the life of the next generation more worthwhile?

SdeB: She actually says what she will do about that. She doesn't want Catherine's eyes to be closed, she doesn't want them to make her live as she herself has, divorced from reality. She wants her daughter to be not only free but as conscious as possible of the world around her. And that is why she does not want them to break up her friendship with her schoolmate. She doesn't want them to get a psychoanalyst who will numb her daughter completely. She does not want them to make *her* a pretty picture too.

YAP: Do you still feel that psychoanalysis tends to try to force women to conform to certain societal norms?

SdeB: That depends on the psychoanalyst. But there are evidently many who try to rehabilitate women and make them good wives and mothers satisfied with their lives, picking up on the Freud and Lacan tradition. Evidently there are psychoanalysts who don't follow those guidelines.

YAP: Your description of Paule, in *The Mandarins,* after months of psychoanalysis, suggested that she no longer had a personality of her own. Madness is terrible, but perhaps preferable to becoming too normal.

SdeB: Sometimes that is really the case, definitely.

YAP: In "Age of Discretion," I sensed an almost incestuous relationship between the mother and son.

SdeB: Yes, one can say that it was a somewhat amorous relationship. Many mothers adore their sons, love them very much, and if things don't go well, they feel as if they have been betrayed, and they suffer a great deal.

YAP: In "Monologue," I have labeled Murielle a monster mother.

SdeB: Yes, that's right. Definitely. Basically she is the one who made her daughter commit suicide.

YAP: And Monique, in "The Woman Destroyed," is really essentially a relative being.

SdeB: Absolutely. Absolutely. She has sacrificed everything. She preferred marriage to everything else. She had the opportunity to have a career, a job, something. And then she left everything to devote herself to her husband and daughters. And the daughters did not appreciate it at all. Yes, there is one, the younger, the less intelligent, but the older one, the one who has left for America, doesn't appreciate what she has done at all. [In fact it is Lucienne, the younger daughter, who leaves for America, and the older daughter, Colette, who gets married and remains in Paris—YAP] And then the other daughter, the one who really cares for her and who sees her more often, has married too. She no longer seems very close to her mother.

YAP: And that relationship does not justify the mother's life.

SdeB: No, certainly not. That's right. It is not a justification at all.

YAP: In the autobiography, it seems to me that one of the themes is the story of the two mothers, yours and Madame "Mabille," and the contrast between them.

SdeB: Yes, at least in the very first volume, because after that, the rest . . .

YAP: In *Memoirs of a Dutiful Daughter.* And your mother also wanted to keep control and authority until . . .

SdeB: Yes. Only that was very hard for her once I was at the Sorbonne and I admitted to her that I had lost my faith. Then she didn't have any idea of how to deal with me. She was very inept. For example, she was afraid that I would have a bad influence on my sister, so she forbad us to see one another when we were in the country. So we would each go out through a garden gate and meet. It was really absurd.

YAP: And her idea of not allowing you to have bicycles . . .

SdeB: That was a sort of mean streak that made her forbid us to have bicycles. And then it was especially because we would have gone too far from where she could keep an eye on us.

YAP: In *A Very Easy Death,* toward the end, you look at two photos, of you and your mother, and you decide that you could never have done anything to change your relationship, especially because of your mother's early childhood.

SdeB: That's right. First there was her religious upbringing, which was very strong, which prevented this. And then . . . I definitely got along very well with her until I was ten, maybe twelve years old. It was after that, when I changed my way of looking at things, my ideas. My father was also unhappy with me. Even though he was not a believer. But at any rate, when I became an intellectual, they were not at all pleased, because that word always had a negative connotation for them.

YAP: And you have suggested that your mother was a little afraid of your intelligence.

SdeB: She finally told me so. In effect, she told me, "You frighten me." Yes, she was definitely a little afraid of that, because one never likes to feel that someone thinks herself more intelligent than you are. And this is indeed what I thought about my mother. She did *not* seem intelligent to me. Not only was she very Catholic, but she did not seem intelligent because of her ways of doing things . . . Well, she must have sensed that I felt this way and she was not happy about it. That is the main reason that she didn't want my sister to be an intellectual. Of course, it was fortunate for my sister, who derived a great deal of pleasure from her painting, et cetera, but she wanted to complete an *agrégation* in English or something like that, and my mother would not allow it.

YAP: But after all, she had produced two very intelligent daughters of whom she could simply have been very very proud.

SdeB: Oh, no, not at all. She just wasn't like that... Moreover, I talk about that in ...

YAP: ... in *A Very Easy Death?*

SdeB: Yes, but especially in *Memoirs of a Dutiful Daughter.* My father too was proud that I was collecting degrees, but he was not happy to see me become an intellectual, because he didn't like that. That wasn't the way he looked at things.

YAP: A double message. He seemed to be proud, but you sensed that something wasn't quite right.

SdeB: Yes, I sensed that. It was easy to tell because he actually said so.

YAP: I wonder if fathers prefer not to have their daughters become too intelligent and if it is different for mothers. Does that depend on the mother's or father's own intelligence?

SdeB: Ah yes, it depends on their life goals, it depends on many many things.

YAP: You reversed the situation in "Age of Discretion," where you depicted two very intellectual parents and a son who decided to leave the academic world to become a businessman.

SdeB: Yes, that's right, that's right.

YAP: Did you feel that you had found the mother of your early childhood again during those last weeks you spent with her?

SdeB: Oh no, not at all. I was the one who was protecting *her,* she wasn't the one protecting me as she did when I was very small.

YAP: You spoke of seeing her vitality resurface ...

SdeB: Ah, yes, her vitality, but I sensed that throughout her life. Especially when I didn't agree with her, with her ideas, because my parents were totally, totally conservative. And that made things difficult. My mother was conservative and religious, my father conservative and an atheist, but it all came down to the same thing. And then the break that took place when I began to think differently was very dramatic, of course.

YAP: And even at the end, there was no reconciliation with your mother?

SdeB: Oh, there had never been a real break. We always visited one another, we always talked politely. But evidently I avoided talking about ideas with my mother, or about the books I loved, or things like that. That would not have been . . . no, I had to . . .

YAP: I remember that you said that when *Memoirs a Dutiful Daughter* came out, you sent Hélène to your mother with a bouquet of flowers and an apology.

SdeB: No, no, I brought the bouquet to her myself and I told her myself . . . maybe Hélène spoke to her a little about it too. It's possible.

YAP: You were afraid she would be upset by what you had written.

SdeB: Of course. And she *was* unhappy, but for funny reasons. For example, because I had said that the bed wasn't really an antique. Things like that.

YAP: And your mother said that children don't understand their parents.

SdeB: That is true. But that is not their role. It is the parents who have them, who raise them, and who must try to understand *them*. In general, children understand later. When one becomes an adult, one says to oneself, "Ah yes, my poor mother," etc., etc., but that doesn't bring you closer together because if antagonism has existed, one simply admits to feeling sorry for the poor woman. She was so pious and my father was politically conservative. I understood why they were like that, but that did not bring me one inch closer to them.

YAP: And the reversal of roles at the end of your mother's life, when you have to mother your own mother . . .

SdeB: In a sense, yes, that is what happens. You have to take care of her, etc.

YAP: You have no biological children, but there are hundreds of women like me who consider you a surrogate mother. You read in the Simone de Beauvoir Society newsletter the discussion in which people spoke of you as a maternal figure and Kate Millett said, "No, not our mother. I prefer to say that she is our aunt rather than our mother. Relationships with aunts are less complicated." [Laughter] Do you feel that link?

SdeB: No, not at all. No. I am happy when there are women who are fond of me, when I think that I have may have helped them live their lives, that I have helped them to think more clearly, to liberate themselves. I am very happy. But that doesn't in any way link us like a mother and daughter.

YAP: There are so many women who say after having read *The Second Sex* that you are the one who showed them the right path.

SdeB: Yes, but that is not what a mother does. In order to be a mother, you must first have given birth, and then diapered the child for months and months and then taught it to walk and to talk. That is what a mother is.

YAP: The relationship developed in early childhood . . .

SdeB: Yes, that counts a great deal, of course. And then afterward, one can choose to be more or less involved with the child. But to be a mother, you have to take care of someone over a long period of time. And then in general children do not accept their mother's ideas. So when women say that they have been influenced by me, that means that I am not their mother, because most of them would not be influenced by their mothers. Perhaps they would be in a few cases. There are daughters who love their mother a great deal and are influenced by her. But in many cases, even if they love their mothers a great deal, they are not at all influenced by them.

YAP: And Sylvie's role in your life? You are very close to her . . .

SdeB: Yes, I am very close to her, but precisely because I am not her mother. We are of different ages. Let's say that we are very very good friends, that's all. Moreover, I have always placed friendship above family ties, above imposed relationships.

YAP: In the interview you had a long time ago with Betty Friedan, she spoke to you about women who wanted to have children and you said that there were already enough of them in the world. [Laughter] She really reacted against that idea. You certainly didn't mean that no woman should have a child.

SdeB: Naturally, naturally. I said that it's fine if a woman wants children but it is not a necessity, because the planet is already overpopulated.

YAP: In conclusion, what advice would you give to young women who are pregnant at the moment or who would like to have children and at the same time maintain their own identity and independence?

SdeB: Well, if they wish to have children, why should they deprive themselves of that experience? One must follow one's profound desires. Then let them manage afterward to reconcile motherhood with a certain independence. Let them try to reconcile the two, to avoid becoming slaves. But if they want children, let them have them, of course.

YAP: You have sometimes been criticized and reproached for not being practical when you advise women not to have children and I have always maintained that that is not what you said.

SdeB: That is not at all what I said. No, no. I said that one must really follow one's deepest desires. Otherwise one feels unfulfilled. Absolutely. A woman who wants a child feels unfulfilled if she doesn't have children, just like a woman who has children and has abandoned a career that was important to her. One must not sacrifice what one really feels and wants. Otherwise one feels unfulfilled.

YAP: So one should not be conditioned to be a mother if one doesn't wish to be, and on the other hand . . .

SdeB: That's right. If one wishes to be, one should be. But one should be very careful not to become enslaved. That is possible. I think that if one has one child, it is very easy. It becomes more difficult with two children. With three or more, I think that then . . . unless you are very rich and the case of very rich women is not particularly interesting . . . that makes it too easy.

YAP: I have only the one son, so I have not had the experience of having a great many children. It works well with one child.

SdeB: Yes. I see Sylvie, who is a lycée teacher. Her colleagues who are thirty and forty years old, perhaps a little younger, say they want a child. And that's fine. With two, that begins to enslave a mother who has to juggle a teaching career and take care of changing diapers and correcting papers at the same time. With two, one becomes enslaved. One child is fine.

YAP: And now one can control the number of children one has.

SdeB: Yes indeed. That makes a big difference. There is no longer any reason why women should be enslaved by motherhood.

Interview with Simone de Beauvoir: Original Transcript

YAP: Je voudrais vous poser quelques questions sur l'image de la mère dans vos oeuvres de fiction. Je vais commencer par *Quand prime le spirituel* et la mère de Marguerite et de Marcelle dans ces nouvelles. Est-ce qu'elle ressemble un peu à votre mère à vous?

SdeB: Qui ça? La mère de qui?

YAP: De Marcelle et de Marguerite. Elle n'a pas un grand rôle à jouer, mais il y a un moment où Marguerite décide de sortir avec Denis, le mari de sa soeur. Sa mère dit non, absolument non, et elle sort quand même. Elle se révolte contre l'autorité de sa mère à ce moment-là.

SdeB: Oui, bien sûr. Il y a eu des choses en effet dans ma vie qui ont été comme ça. Quand j'étais presque adulte, enfin, ma mère une ou deux fois m'a défendu de sortir le soir, parce qu'on ne sortait pas le soir, quand j'avais déjà presque vingt ans, et je suis sortie quand même.

YAP: Je me rappelle que vous avez parlé de cet incident dans votre autobiographie. Et Madame Vignon dans ce même recueil?

SdeB: Ça, c'est beaucoup la mère de mon amie Zaza.

YAP: Est-ce que vous l'avez beaucoup exagérée à cause de vos sentiments envers ce qui est arrivé à Zaza? Elle semble presque une caricature. Est-ce que la mère de Zaza a vraiment été comme ça? Pensait-elle qu'elle faisait toujours la volonté de Dieu?

SdeB: Oui, certainement. Oh, certainement elle pensait qu'elle faisait la volonté de Dieu.

YAP: Pensez-vous que si Zaza avait survécu, elle aurait pu se révolter contre sa mère à un certain moment?

SdeB: Oh, ça, je ne sais pas. Elle l'aimait beaucoup, alors elle ne se serait pas révoltée, mais elle se serait peut-être, je ne sais pas, un peu émancipée, par son mariage, par exemple. Je ne peux pas savoir ce qui se serait passé.

YAP: Vous avez beaucoup parlé de manipulation psychologique de la part de la mère de Zaza. Quand les enfants étaient tout petits ils pouvaient faire n'importe quoi . . .

SdeB: Oui, oui. Ça, c'est tout à fait vrai. Ça correspond absolument à la réalité. N'importe quoi, c'est un peu exagéré, mais enfin elle était très libérale, elle les laissait tranquilles, elle ne les ennuyait pas pour les petites choses. S'ils renversaient une chaise, ce n'était pas une histoire, tandis que chez moi, ça faisait beaucoup plus une histoire. Donc elle les laissait tranquilles sur beaucoup de points et du coup elle était plus sûre de leur obéissance dans les cas plus importants.

YAP: Est-ce que vous pensez que de nos jours les mères continuent à manipuler leurs enfants de la sorte?

SdeB: Oh, je ne sais pas quelle est leur manière de les manipuler, mais je pense qu'en effet les mères essaient beaucoup de manipuler leurs enfants.

YAP: Et il y a le rôle de la religion, n'est-ce pas, l'idée qu'il faut toujours obéir à ses parents?

SdeB: Oui, c'est ça. Moi je ne connais plus du tout les milieux religieux, mais je pense qu'en élevant les enfants on doit garder cette idée d'honorer le père et la mère. Oui, dans les milieux religieux, que je connais mal, ça dure quand même, ces histoires-là. Je suppose que ça existe encore.

YAP: Il y a une étudiante de Chantal Plattard dans *Quand prime le spirituel* qui se trouve enceinte et vous avez décrit sa grossesse presque comme quelque chose de dégoûtant. On retrouve dans d'autres passages de fiction l'idée qu'il s'agit d'une sorte de parasite qui se développe dans le corps de la femme.

SdeB: Je pense que quand c'est une très jeune fille et que c'est un peu un accident si elle est enceinte, c'est l'impression que ça lui fait. Quand c'est une grossesse voulue et choisie, une femme un peu adulte et qui prend la responsabilité de sa grossesse, ce n'est plus du tout la même chose. Parce que dans cette histoire c'est quelqu'un de trop jeune, je crois qu'elle a quinze ans, ou quatorze ans, la petite, quand ça lui arrive, quand elle en a la nouvelle. Alors là c'est un peu affreux en général.

YAP: Dans *L'Invitée*, peut-on comparer le rapport entre Françoise et Xavière à celui qui existe entre une mère et sa fille?

SdeB: Ah non, pas du tout. Ça justement je l'ai dit longuement dans ... *La Force de l'âge* ... oui, c'est ça ... , que ce n'est pas du tout un rapport de mère à fille, absolument pas. Ah non, pas du tout.

YAP: Sans parler d'un instinct maternel, parce qu'on a dit que ce qu'on appelle l'instinct maternel, c'est la responsabilité qu'on sent envers un autre individu ... Là, Françoise, au moins au début du roman, se sent un peu responsable de Xavière.

SdeB: Mais on a l'impression, vous savez, qu'on est responsable aussi bien d'une soeur, d'un frère, d'une amie, de n'importe quoi. Ce n'est pas uniquement maternel. Oui, bien sûr, il doit y avoir dans le sentiment maternel, puisqu'en effet moi je refuse l'idée d'un instinct, il doit y avoir dans le sentiment maternel une très grande idée de la responsabilité, qui plaît à certaines femmes d'ailleurs, parce que ça leur donne de l'importance, de se sentir responsables. Mais il ne suffit pas qu'on se sente responsable pour que ça soit maternel.

YAP: Alors, évidemment dans *L'Invitée* il s'agit de vos propres rapports avec Olga. J'ai entendu dire qu'Olga vient de mourir cette année. Vous avez toujours gardé des rapports très étroits avec elle?

SdeB: Oui, ah oui, oui, oui, oui.

YAP: J'ai lu dans le livre de Francis et Gontier la première partie de *L'Invitée* et je me suis demandé pourquoi vous avez décidé de supprimer cette partie où vous parlez de l'enfance, de la petite enfance de Françoise?

SdeB: Ce n'est pas que j'ai décidé, c'est Gallimard qui m'a dit que ce n'était pas bon et il avait raison.

YAP: Du point de vue des rapports entre mère et fille, je l'ai trouvé intéressant, parce que la mère de Françoise, on ne la voit presque jamais dans le roman comme il existe.

SdeB: Oui, mais c'était inutile vraiment, ce n'était pas du tout nécessaire.

YAP: Mais vous avez tant dit que la petite enfance est tellement importante ...

SdeB: Oui, bien sûr. Mais je voulais raconter une histoire très précise, cette histoire du trio. Je ne voulais pas raconter toute l'enfance de Pierre, toute l'enfance de Françoise, toute l'enfance de Xavière, non. Je les prenais à un moment de crise où ils étaient déjà des individus formés. On devinait un peu leur enfance. Celle de Xavière, en tout cas, on la devine beaucoup, parce qu'on en parle beaucoup. Et Pierre et Françoise, bon, on a l'impression qu'ils sont sortis de l'enfance assez équilibrés, ils savaient ce qu'ils faisaient, donc ce n'était pas la peine de raconter ça en détail.

YAP: Ce sont simplement des rapports de politesse entre Françoise et Madame Miquel, semble-t-il.

SdeB: C'est ça, ce sont des rapports normaux et superficiels comme pour quantité de mères et filles.

YAP: Et surtout quand la fille est adulte . . .

SdeB: Quand la fille est adulte, bien sûr.

YAP: Dans *Le Sang des autres,* il y a la grossesse et l'avortement d'Hélène Bertrand. Ça c'est la première fois que vous avez parlé, dans une oeuvre de fiction, d'un avortement. Est-ce que c'est à ce moment que vous avez commencé à penser à l'importance de rendre l'avortement légal pour les femmes?

SdeB: Non, j'y avais déjà pensé depuis longtemps. Je sais même qu'une de mes premières réactions de toute jeune adolescente ç'a été quand on m'a dit que l'avortement c'était très mal. J'estimais qu'on a le droit de contrôler son corps. Non, j'avais l'idée qu'on a le droit d'avorter bien avant d'écrire *Le Sang des autres.* Et par la suite quand les féministes ont pris ce thème et ont voulu se battre sur ce thème alors là j'ai été tout à fait d'accord et j'ai lutté avec elles.

YAP: La scène du roman est très frappante.

SdeB: Oui, c'est réaliste.

YAP: Mère-fille encore une fois. Je voudrais parler de la scène où la mère juive appelle sa petite fille quand on va la séparer d'elle et de l'effet de cette scène sur Hélène Bertrand. Est-ce que ça aurait été très différent si c'était une femme qui allait être séparée de son mari, par exemple? Est-ce que vous pensez que ce rapport entre la mère et la fille est beaucoup plus émouvant du point de vue dramatique?

SdeB: Ça, je ne sais pas, mais une séparation d'avec son mari ç'aurait été entièrement différent parce que les maris étaient déjà dans le maquis. C'est désarmé, une petite fille, c'est tout à fait désarmé, c'est pour ça surtout que j'ai pris ça, et puis en effet il y a eu des scènes vraiment déchirantes. On a embarqué les enfants dans des autobus pour les emmener et les mères étaient là à crier, à courir après l'autobus, comme ce que j'ai raconté.

YAP: Et vous l'avez vu vous-même?

SdeB: Je ne l'ai pas vu, mais je l'ai entendu raconter. Je l'ai su. Je n'étais pas à Paris, ces jours-là. C'était le mois de juillet. Je n'ai pas assisté moi-même à ces scènes-là.

YAP: Prenons maintenant Madame Blomart dans *Le Sang des autres*. Elle m'intéresse parce qu'elle semble la mère martyre jusqu'à un certain point, la mère qui sait qu'elle a perdu tout contrôle sur ses enfants adultes. Mais elle a aussi de bons sentiments, par exemple cette idée d'étendre les bras à Séville pour empêcher les foules de courir. Et quand son fils est responsable de la mort des Allemands, elle dit que ça va causer la mort de Français innocents. Est-elle peut-être le modèle d'une mère qui ne va pas essayer de jouer un trop grand rôle dans la vie de ses enfants adultes mais qui a . . .

SdeB: Ses enfants? Elle n'a qu'un enfant, n'est-ce pas?

YAP: Il y a deux filles qu'on ne voit jamais. Mais je crois que vous avez parlé de leurs mariages. Là encore une fois leur mère n'a rien dit mais elle souffre parce qu'elle n'approuve pas le choix des maris qu'elles ont fait.

SdeB: Ah oui. En fait, j'ai beaucoup pensé à une amie que j'appelle Madame Lemaire mais qui s'appelait en vérité Madame Morel. C'était une femme d'une telle morale. C'est elle qui avait agi comme ça à Séville. C'était une femme tout à fait charmante mais ses rapports avec son fils n'étaient pas du tout ça parce que son fils n'était guère intéressant. Enfin j'ai été inspirée par elle pour ce personnage. Une femme sympathique, très sympathique même, et très belle, qui a horreur de la violence, et il faut montrer l'autre côté en effet.

YAP: Et vous avez Jean Blomart, qui voudrait avoir l'approbation de sa mère, mais s'il continue à diriger des activités terroristes, et il croit qu'il doit continuer, il ne peut jamais l'avoir. Il voudrait même redevenir petit enfant pour rester avec sa mère et il ne peut pas. Il la quitte sans avoir son approbation.

SdeB: Oui, c'est ça.

YAP: Dans la pièce *Les Bouches inutiles,* il y a Catherine, qui est la mère d'un fils haïssable et d'une fille indépendante. Elle est aussi un peu la mère de toute la ville, n'est-ce pas?

SdeB: Oui, parce qu'elle est la femme d'un notable, d'un gouverneur.

YAP: Les pauvres s'adressent à elle. Et avec sa fille, qui est enceinte, il y a toute l'idée de l'avenir de ce bébé, de l'espoir d'une autre génération.

SdeB: Oui, en effet.

YAP: Dans *Tous les hommes sont mortels,* vous dépeignez la différence entre le père qui élève l'enfant et la mère. Il faut qu'Antoine, qui a été élevé dans une ambiance de paix et d'harmonie, se révolte contre Fosca pour s'affirmer. Est-ce que vous croyez que cette révolte est nécessaire entre mère et fille comme entre père et fils?

SdeB: Oh, c'est plus fort entre père et fils.

YAP: Que font les fils modernes pour se procurer le pouvoir? Il n'y a plus de batailles militaires pour s'affirmer, en tuant quelqu'un par exemple.

SdeB: Non. Eh bien c'est en partie pour ça qu'ils se mettent en groupe, qu'ils se droguent, qu'ils vagabondent, parce qu'ils n'ont plus beaucoup de moyens de s'affirmer.

YAP: C'est dans *Le Deuxième Sexe* que vous avez beaucoup parlé des choix possibles pour la femme. Est-ce que vous croyez toujours que la maternité empêche la femme de trouver sa propre identité?

SdeB: Je pense que telle qu'elle est aujourd'hui, oui. Parce que la femme est trop esclave.

YAP: Vous pensez toujours qu'elle . . .

SdeB: Ah, oui, je le pense.

YAP: Même avec les commodités modernes?

SdeB: Oh, les commodités modernes, vous savez! C'est quand même toujours la femme qui s'occupe des enfants, ce n'est pas le mari, même s'il participe un petit peu. Et pour la femme souvent c'est un très très grand fardeau. En tout cas en France, les crèches, les écoles maternelles, tout ça, c'est très très très insuffisant.

YAP: Ah vraiment? Et je crois qu'ici c'est mieux qu'aux Etats-Unis où on a très peu de crèches.

SdeB: Et nous aussi. Il faut s'inscrire je ne sais combien de mois d'avance. C'est très difficile.

YAP: Dans *Les Mandarins,* il y a les rapports entre Anne et Nadine.

SdeB: Je pense qu'au fond Anne se reproche toujours de ne pas aimer sa fille mais qu'elle l'aime beaucoup. Ça se devine à plusieurs choses. Elle dit qu'elle ne l'aime pas assez parce qu'elle est très exigeante pour elle-même mais en fait elle l'aime beaucoup. D'autre part elle ne peut pas vivre la vie de sa fille à sa place, elle préfère la laisser vivre telle qu'elle est. Et elle le fait.

YAP: Et ce sentiment de culpabilité dont elle parle tout le temps. Pensez-vous que ça fait partie de la maternité généralement?

SdeB: Je pense que pour *beaucoup* de femmes ça en fait partie. Parce qu'on se sent justement tellement responsable, comme vous disiez, on est tellement responsable qu'à la moindre chose, la moindre anicroche, on se sent coupable, puisque c'est sur vous, la mère, que tout repose.

YAP: Ce n'est jamais le père qu'on blâme.

SdeB: Non, ce n'est jamais le père, non, non, non, non. Ça ne change pas. Je crois que les pères maintenant essaient un peu de se rapprocher de leurs enfants, essaient d'être un peu plus paternels, enfin ... dans certains secteurs de la société, parmi les jeunes surtout, les jeunes et les intellectuels. Mais dans l'ensemble c'est toujours la mère qui est responsable, et si elle est responsable, comme il y a des malheurs plus ou moins grands dans toute vie, si elle est responsable de la vie de ses enfants, elle se sentira souvent évidemment coupable de leurs malheurs.

YAP: Et qui reste avec l'enfant quand l'enfant est malade et que les deux parents travaillent?

SdeB: Ce n'est presque jamais le père, c'est toujours la mère.

YAP: Il y a Nadine, dans *Les Mandarins,* qui lit tous les livres sur la puériculture mais qui ne semble pas sentir une vraie affection pour sa fille Maria.

SdeB: Oui, je pense que le personnage de Nadine est quand même très égoïste, très renfermé sur soi et qu'elle n'a pas vraiment le genre justement de ... enfin de générosité qu'il faut pour s'occuper d'un enfant. Elle manque de chaleur.

YAP: Est-ce qu'elle va peut-être développer cette chaleur?

SdeB: Ça, je n'en sais rien. Je pense qu'elle manque de chaleur et que ça, ça ne s'apprend pas.

YAP: Et ça ne vient pas simplement de la tragédie de la mort de Diégo?

SdeB: Ah, non. C'est tout un caractère qui vient ... je ne sais pas exactement de quoi, ça je n'ai pas approfondi. Mais enfin, elle est frigide d'abord, évidemment, certainement. Oui, et puis froide, elle est froide et elle raille tout le monde.

YAP: Quand Anne Dubreuilh pense à se suicider, elle change d'avis au moment où elle pense à Nadine, à la réaction de Nadine ...

SdeB: Pas seulement à Nadine, mais à son mari aussi.

YAP: A son mari aussi, mais surtout à l'indignation de Nadine, qui dirait: "Elle n'avait pas le droit. " Encore un exemple d'une mère qui sent une responsabilité envers son enfant et la prochaine génération ...

SdeB: Oui, sûrement. Puis ça montre aussi que Nadine d'une part est froide mais qu'elle est moins froide qu'elle ne donne à penser par ses conduites, parce que, si elle voit sa mère se suicider, elle aura une crise de colère, c'est sa manière à elle de souffrir, et puis ça veut dire qu'elle tient beaucoup à sa mère.

YAP: Elle est inspirée par Lise, n'est-ce pas?

SdeB: Oui, un peu par Lise, oui, c'est ça.

YAP: Dans *Les Belles Images,* là vous avez les trois générations de femmes, avec Laurence coincée entre les deux autres. Est-ce que c'est une jeune fille rangée, Laurence?

SdeB: Oui, je pense qu'elle est assez rangée, une jeune femme assez rangée.

YAP: Elle a un sentiment de responsabilité envers sa mère, qu'elle n'aime pas tellement, et surtout envers sa fille.

SdeB: Sa fille, oui, c'est très fort.

YAP: Vers la fin du roman, il y a un moment de désespoir où Laurence veut faire quelque chose pour changer la vie de ses filles mais ne sait quoi faire. Qu'est-ce qu'on peut faire pour rendre la vie de la prochaine génération plus valable?

SdeB: Là quand même, elle le dit. Elle ne veut pas qu'on lui ferme les yeux, à Catherine, elle ne veut pas qu'on la fasse vivre comme ça loin de la réalité. Elle veut la laisser non seulement libre mais la rendre la plus consciente possible du monde. Et c'est pour ça qu'elle ne veut pas qu'on brise son amitié avec son amie qui elle est beaucoup plus éveillée, beaucoup plus mûre, elle ne veut pas qu'on brise cette amitié. Elle ne veut pas qu'on cherche une psychanalyste qui endormirait complètement sa fille. Elle ne veut pas qu'on en fasse enfin une espèce de belle image, elle aussi.

YAP: Est-ce que vous avez toujours l'impression que la psychanalyse tend à essayer de forcer les femmes à se conformer à certaines normes de la société?

SdeB: Ça dépend des psychanalystes. Mais il y en a évidemment beaucoup qui sont là pour récupérer les femmes et pour faire qu'elles se veulent épouses et mères et qu'elles soient satisfaites comme ça, en reprenant la tradition de Freud et de Lacan. Mais il y en a évidemment, des psychanalystes, qui s'échappent de ces chemins-là.

YAP: Votre description de Paule, dans *Les Mandarins,* après des mois de psychanalyse, suggérait qu'elle n'avait plus de personnalité. La folie, c'était terrible, mais peut-être mieux que cette femme trop normale.

SdeB: Certaines fois, c'est vraiment le cas, bien sûr.

YAP: Dans "L'Age de discrétion," moi j'ai senti entre la mère et son fils presque un rapport incestueux.

SdeB: Oui, on peut dire un rapport un peu amoureux. Beaucoup de mères adorent leurs fils, elles les aiment beaucoup et si ça ne marche pas, elles ont l'impression d'être trahies, et elles souffrent beaucoup.

YAP: Dans "Monologue," j'ai désigné Murielle comme la mère monstre.

SdeB: Oui, c'est ça, bien sûr. Au fond, c'est elle qui fait se suicider sa fille.

YAP: Et Monique, dans "La Femme rompue," est vraiment par essence l'être relatif.

SdeB: Absolument. Elle a tout sacrifié. Elle a préféré le mariage à tout. Elle avait encore des possibilités d'avoir une carrière, un métier, quelque chose. Et puis elle a tout lâché, pour se dévouer. Mari et filles. Et les filles ne lui en savaient aucun gré. Si, il y en a une, la plus jeune, la moins intelligente, mais l'aînée, celle qui est partie pour l'Amérique, ne lui sait aucun gré. [En fait c'est Lucienne, la plus jeune, qui part pour l'Amérique et l'aînée, Colette, qui se marie et reste à Paris—YAP] Et puis tout de même l'autre, celle qui l'aime bien, et qui la voit plus souvent, est quand même mariée à son tour. Elle n'a plus l'air très intime avec sa mère.

YAP: Et ça ne lui donne pas de justification pour sa vie.

SdeB: Non, certainement pas. C'est ça. Ce n'est pas une justification du tout.

YAP: Dans l'autobiographie, il me semble qu'un des thèmes, c'est l'histoire des deux mères, la vôtre et Madame "Mabille," et le contraste entre les deux.

SdeB: Oui, enfin dans le tout premier volume, n'est-ce pas, parce qu'après ça le reste . . .

YAP: Dans *Mémoires d'une jeune fille rangée.* Et votre mère aussi, elle a voulu garder le contrôle et l'autorité jusqu'à . . .

SdeB: Oui. Seulement ça lui était bien difficile une fois que j'étais à la Sorbonne et que je lui avouais que je n'étais plus croyante. Alors elle ne savait plus du tout par quel bout me prendre. Elle était très maladroite. Par exemple, elle avait peur que j'aie une mauvaise influence sur ma soeur, alors elle nous défendait de nous voir à la campagne. Eh bien, nous partions chacune par une porte du jardin et nous nous rencontrions. Alors, c'était vraiment absurde.

YAP: Et l'idée de refuser que vous ayez des bicyclettes . . .

SdeB: Ça c'était une espèce de méchanceté de nous interdire la bicyclette. Et puis c'était surtout parce que nous aurions été trop loin de son regard.

YAP: Dans *Une Mort très douce,* vers la fin vous regardez deux photos, de vous et de votre mère, et vous décidez que vous n'auriez rien pu faire pour changer vos rapports, et surtout à cause de la petite enfance de votre mère.

SdeB: Oui, c'est ça. D'abord c'était sa formation religieuse, très forte, qui l'empêchait. Et puis . . . Je me suis très bien entendue avec elle jusqu'à l'âge de dix, douze ans, c'est sûr. C'est après, c'est quand j'ai changé d'orientation, d'idées. Mon père aussi était mécontent de moi. Quoique lui ne fût pas croyant. Mais enfin, de toute façon, quand je suis devenue intellectuelle, au sens qu'ils donnaient à ce mot, qui était péjoratif, ça ne leur plaisait pas du tout.

YAP: Et vous avez suggéré que votre mère avait un peu peur de votre intelligence.

SdeB: Elle me l'a dit à la fin. Justement elle m'a dit: "Toi, tu me fais peur." Mais, oui, elle avait un peu peur de ça, bien sûr, parce qu'on n'aime jamais sentir que quelqu'un se croit plus intelligent que vous. Et c'était bien ce que je croyais par rapport à ma mère. Elle ne me semblait *pas* intelligente; non seulement elle était catholique à fond, mais elle n'était pas intelligente, parce que ses manières d'être . . . Bon, eh bien alors, ça elle a dû le sentir, elle n'était pas contente. C'est beaucoup pour ça d'ailleurs qu'elle n'a pas voulu que ma soeur soit une intellectuelle. Bien sûr, ça lui a porté bonheur, puisque ma soeur a très bien réussi, elle a été très heureuse de peindre, et cetera, mais enfin, elle aurait voulu au début faire une agrégation d'anglais, quelque chose comme ça, et ma mère n'a pas du tout voulu.

YAP: Mais après tout, elle avait produit deux filles tellement intelligentes qu'elle aurait pu tout simplement en être très très fière.

SdeB: Non, pas du tout, ce n'est pas comme ça qu'elle était. D'ailleurs, ça je le raconte dans . . .

YAP: . . . dans *Une Mort très douce?*

SdeB: Oui, mais surtout dans les *Mémoires d'une jeune fille rangée*. Mon père aussi était fier quand j'accumulais les diplômes, mais il n'était pas content que je doive être une intellectuelle, parce qu'il n'aimait pas ça. Ce n'était pas dans ses idées.

YAP: Un double message. Il semblait être fier, mais vous sentiez qu'il y avait quelque chose qui clochait.

SdeB: Ah bien, oui, je le sentais, c'était facile, parce qu'il le disait d'ailleurs.

YAP: Je me demande si les pères préfèrent que leurs filles ne soient pas trop intelligentes et si c'est différent pour les mères? Est-ce que ça dépend de l'intelligence de la mère, et du père?

SdeB: Ah oui, ça dépend de leurs projets de vie, ça dépend de beaucoup, beaucoup de choses.

YAP: Vous avez renversé la situation dans "L'Age de discrétion," où vous avez deux parents très intellectuels, et le fils qui a décidé d'abandonner le monde académique pour devenir un homme d'affaires.

SdeB: Oui, c'est ça. C'est ça.

YAP: Est-ce que vous avez eu le sentiment de retrouver un peu la mère de votre toute petite enfance pendant ces dernières semaines que vous avez passées avec elle?

SdeB: Ah non, pas du tout. C'était plutôt moi qui la protégeais, ce n'était pas elle qui me protégeait comme dans ma petite enfance.

YAP: Vous avez parlé de retrouver sa vitalité . . .

SdeB: Ah, sa vitalité, je l'ai sentie toute sa vie. Surtout quand j'étais en désaccord avec elle, avec ses idées, enfin, parce que c'était des gens tout à fait, tout à fait conservateurs, mes parents. Et ça ne marchait pas alors. Ma mère de droite pieuse et mon père de droite athée, mais ça revenait au même. Et alors la cassure qu'il y a eue quand moi j'ai commencé à penser autrement, ç'a été très fort, évidemment.

YAP: Et même à la fin, il n'y a pas eu de réconciliation avec votre mère?

SdeB: Oh, il n'y avait jamais eu vraiment de brouille. Nous nous sommes toujours vues, nous avons toujours parlé aimablement et tout ça. Mais enfin évidemment j'évitais de parler d'idées avec ma mère, ou des livres que j'ai aimés, ou des choses comme ça. Ça n'aurait pas été . . . non, il fallait . . .

YAP: Je me rappelle que vous avez dit que quand les *Mémoires d'une jeune fille rangée* sont sorties, vous avez envoyé un bouquet de fleurs et vos excuses par Hélène.

SdeB: Non, non, je le lui ai apporté moi-même et je le lui ai dit moi-même . . . peut-être bien qu'Hélène en avait parlé un peu aussi. C'est possible.

YAP: Vous aviez peur qu'elle ne soit froissée par ce que vous aviez écrit.

SdeB: Bien sûr. Oui. D'ailleurs elle a été mécontente, mais pour de drôles de raisons; par exemple, parce que j'avais dit que le lit n'était pas vraiment ancien, enfin, des choses comme ça.

YAP: Et elle a dit que les enfants ne comprennent pas leurs parents.

SdeB: Ça c'est vrai. Mais ce n'est pas leur rôle. C'est les parents qui les ont, qui les élèvent, et qui doivent essayer de les comprendre. Les enfants en général comprennent plus tard. Quand on devient adulte, on se dit: "Ah oui, ma pauvre mère, " et cetera, et cetera, mais ça ne rapproche pas beaucoup parce que si on a quand même été antagonistes, on avoue avoir pitié de cette pauvre femme. Elle était si pieuse et mon père était de droite. Bien, j'ai compris pourquoi ils l'ont été, mais ça ne m'a pas rapprochée d'eux d'un pouce.

YAP: Et le renversement des rôles à la fin de la vie de votre mère, quand on devient la mère de sa propre mère . . .

SdeB: En un sens, oui, c'est ça. Il faut la soigner, et cetera.

YAP: Vous n'avez pas eu d'enfants biologiques, mais il y a des centaines de femmes comme moi qui vous considèrent comme un succédané de mère. Vous avez lu dans le bulletin de la Société Simone de Beauvoir la discussion où on vous a traitée de mère et Kate Millett a dit: "Non, pas notre mère. Je préfère dire qu'elle est notre tante plutôt que notre mère. Les tantes, c'est moins compliqué." [Rires] Est-ce que vous sentez ce lien?

SdeB: Non. Pas du tout. Non. Je suis contente quand il y a des femmes qui m'aiment bien, quand je pense que je leur ai peut-être rendu service dans leur vie, que je les ai aidées à mieux penser, à se libérer. Je suis très contente. Mais ça ne me donne pas du tout un lien de mère à fille.

YAP: Il y a tant de femmes qui disent après avoir lu *Le Deuxième Sexe,* que c'est vous qui les avez guidées sur le bon chemin.

SdeB: Oh, une mère ce n'est pas ça. Pour être la mère, il faut d'abord avoir accouché, et puis ensuite avoir torché l'enfant pendant des mois et des mois et puis il faut lui avoir appris à marcher, à parler. C'est ça une mère.

YAP: Les rapports de la toute petite enfance . . .

SdeB: Oui, ça compte beaucoup, bien sûr. Et puis alors après, d'accord, on peut s'occuper plus ou moins de l'enfant. Mais enfin pour être mère, il faut s'en occuper longuement. Et puis généralement, précisément, les enfants ne prennent pas les idées de leurs mères. Alors quand les femmes disent qu'elles ont été influencées par moi, ça veut dire que je ne suis pas leur mère. Parce qu'elles ne seraient pas influencées par leurs mères, la plupart d'entre elles. Dans quelques cas, c'est peut-être comme ça, il y a des filles qui aiment énormément leur mère et qui sont influencées par elle. Mais dans des tas de cas, même si elles les aiment beaucoup, leurs mères, elles ne sont pas du tout influencées par elles.

YAP: Et le rôle de Sylvie dans votre vie? Vous êtes très liée avec elle . . .

SdeB: Oui, je suis très liée avec elle, mais justement parce que je ne suis pas sa mère. Alors, bon, nous sommes d'âge différent. Disons que nous sommes de très très grandes amies, c'est tout. Et d'ailleurs, j'ai toujours mis l'amitié au-dessus des rapports de famille, au dessus des rapports imposés.

YAP: Dans l'entretien que vous avez eu il y a longtemps avec Betty Friedan, elle vous a parlé des femmes qui veulent avoir des enfants et vous avez dit qu'il y en avait déjà trop dans le monde. [Rires] Elle a vraiment réagi contre cette idée. Evidemment vous ne vouliez pas dire qu'aucune femme ne devrait avoir d'enfant.

SdeB: Naturellement. Naturellement. Mais j'ai dit qu'enfin bon, c'est bien si elle les désire mais que ce n'est pas une nécessité, parce que la planète est déjà très encombrée.

YAP: Bon, alors, en conclusion, quels conseils donneriez-vous aux jeunes femmes maintenant enceintes ou qui voudraient avoir des enfants et garder à la fois leur identité et leur indépendance?

SdeB: Eh bien, si elles souhaitent avoir des enfants, pourquoi s'en priveraient-elles? Il faut suivre ses désirs profonds et puis qu'elles se débrouillent après pour concilier ça avec une certaine indépendance. Qu'elles essaient de les concilier, qu'elles essaient de ne pas se rendre esclaves. Mais bon, si elles veulent des enfants, qu'elles aient des enfants, bien entendu.

YAP: Oui, parce qu'on vous a quelquefois critiquée, on vous a reprochée de ne pas être pratique en conseillant aux femmes de ne pas avoir d'enfants et j'ai toujours dit que ce n'est pas ça ce que vous avez dit.

SdeB: Ce n'est pas du tout ce que j'ai dit. Non, non. J'ai dit qu'il faut suivre vraiment en effet ses désirs profonds. Sans ça, on se sent injustifié. Absolument. Une femme qui désire un enfant se sent injustifiée si elle n'a pas d'enfants, autant qu'une femme qui a des enfants et qui comme j'ai dit a refusé le travail. On ne doit pas refuser ce qui est profondément senti, voulu par vous. Sans ça on se sent injustifié.

YAP: Alors on ne devrait pas être conditionnée pour être mère si on ne veut pas l'être et dans l'autre cas . . .

SdeB: C'est ça. Voilà. Si on a envie de l'être, qu'on le soit. Seulement qu'on prenne bien des précautions pour ne pas être esclave. Ça c'est possible. Je crois que si on a un enfant, c'est très facile. Deux enfants, c'est déjà difficile. A partir de trois, je crois que là, à moins d'être très riche, bon, mais ça ce n'est pas très intéressant, le cas des femmes très riches . . . enfin c'est trop facile alors.

YAP: Moi, je n'ai qu'un fils, alors je n'ai pas eu l'expérience d'avoir beaucoup d'enfants. Avec un, ça marche bien.

SdeB: Oui, c'est ça. Je vois justement Sylvie, qui est professeur dans un lycée, dont les collègues ont dans les trente, quarante ans, justement, enfin un petit peu moins, et ils disent qu'ils veulent un enfant. Et c'est bien. Deux, ça commence à être un esclavage quand on a en même temps à faire le métier de professeur et qu'il faut s'occuper à la fois des couches de l'enfant et des copies des élèves. Déjà avec deux, on est vraiment esclavagé. Un enfant, ça va.

YAP: Et maintenant on peut contrôler le nombre des enfants qu'on a.

SdeB: Oui, en effet. Ça fait une grande différence. Il n'y a plus de raison pour que la femme soit l'esclave de la maternité.

Appendix B

Interview with Hélène de Beauvoir, June 22, 1986

Yolanda Astarita Patterson: I would like to begin by talking a little about your childhood memories. What do you remember about your mother when you were small?

Hélène de Beauvoir: Oh, *maman*. I adored *maman*. Only I had a rather difficult relationship with her as a little girl and particularly as an adolescent. But when I was little, I adored *maman* . She was beautiful. Children have a certain sensuality. I remember when *maman* went to a ball in the evening, I saw her, I breathed in her fragrance. She had a pretty dress, her hair was neatly arranged. When she leaned over my little bed, it was really a sensual pleasure. That is one of my memories. And then, she was an affectionate mother. Rather strict, but affectionate.

YAP: Did your feelings gradually change as you grew older?

HdeB: There was the prewar period, which didn't last very long for me since the war broke out in 1914. But until 1915, *papa* was at least at home. For me nothing had changed. I also loved *papa* a lot when I was very little. Afterward, our relationship deteriorated. But after 1915, when *papa* was gone, *maman* depended a great deal on us for companionship. *Papa* was first stationed on the outskirts of Paris before he left for the front. And sometimes *maman* and Simone went to see him. I stayed at home because I was too little. And then I remember *papa*'s leaves during the war. Naturally *maman* was often anxious and sad. She grew closer to us. She was more affectionate because *papa* was gone.

YAP: She was worried about what might happen to your father.

HdeB: Ah yes. *Papa* was in the Zouave regiment, which was one of the most dangerous ones. He became ill. His heart condition got worse. He was put in the hospital, which saved him, because his whole regiment was sent to Verdun and no one came back. The battle of Verdun was a slaughter, a complete slaughter.

YAP: And after the war?

HdeB: After 1919, things deteriorated a lot. *Maman* became very nervous ... I have told you about my grandfather's bankruptcy, so there was no more money. Before the war *papa* was a lawyer. After the war, he was not a very brave man. I have already told you that in my family it was really the women who worked. The men were not very hard workers. *Papa* didn't have the courage to go back to his law office, he couldn't bring himself to go to work. He never again did much of anything. And the war really destroyed something within him. He was used to the easy life, he had dreamed of a modern, easy life. He liked to act in the theatre, he liked to play bridge, he liked to watch the world go by. He was a worldly type. And then, all of a sudden he found himself very poor and without a job, and without the courage to rebuild his professional life.

YAP: Where did you live during that time?

HdeB: We had a lovely apartment which was on the Boulevard du Montparnasse, but the windows looked out on the Boulevard Raspail. It was very very pleasant, really a very pleasant and comfortable apartment. Then we moved to the rue de Rennes, to an apartment which seemed sad to Simone when she recalled it in the negative light of a difficult adolescence.

YAP: Your memory of it didn't coincide with Simone's then?

HdeB: It's true that the apartment wasn't comfortable. We were on the fifth floor without an elevator, and there were no toilets. But in 1919 in Paris, you know, comfortable apartments were considered a luxury. It was a luxury to have running water ... On the Boulevard Raspail we had a bathroom, but that was really a luxury.

YAP: What was your mother's reaction to the need to move?

HdeB: Maman was a product of a convent school in Verdun. Verdun was very provincial. She had this bourgeois idea that you have to maintain your social status. For example, she could have had different furniture. Today people don't have a living room, a dining room, and a den. Then you had to have living room, dining room, and den. You had to give elaborate dinners. She would wear herself out, but we did have a maid. We were not living in misery. We were very badly dressed because *maman* didn't pay any attention to how she looked. And then we must mention that she was very frugal and *papa* was not generous with her. When he had any money, he spent it on himself. He never gave me money without making a scene about it. Every day we had to ask him for money. *Maman* therefore became very nervous.

YAP: That's understandable.

HdeB: That's understandable . . . Besides, I have since understood that my father had certainly become completely unfaithful. He had started to go out all the time and I very often saw *maman* in tears.

YAP: Did she ever explain why to you?

HdeB: Maman gritted her teeth. You know that there was a family secret that I only learned after my mother's death. We knew that my grandfather had gone bankrupt, but what we didn't know was that he had been in prison. *Maman* never told us that, never, never, never. I learned it from an old friend of *maman*'s whom I visited after her death. I had gone to bring her a remembrance of *maman* and she told me that my grandfather had been in prison. "And your poor grandmother!" My grandmother was rather proud and I can imagine how difficult it was for her. First of all, she adored her husband. In my family, I think that the women were better wives than mothers. My grandmother was a rather cold mother but a very devoted spouse. *Maman* was a very good, very devoted wife. She adored *papa*, but he did not make her happy. And she was often very clumsy in her dealings with us. So Simone and I had no desire whatsoever to have children of our own.

YAP: Because of the misfortunes that befell your grandmother and mother?

HdeB: Perhaps. One day, when I was already fifty, I said to my mother, "Listen, *maman*, what was that family secret?" She said, "It was that your grandmother had to pawn her silver." She never told me, "Your grandfather spent time in prison." That was a terrible blow for her.

YAP: Her father's bankruptcy?

HdeB: Her friend also told me, "I am sure that your father made her very unhappy." But she never said anything to me, she never complained. However, she became very harsh because that hurt her and sometimes she took it out on us. She was unfair with us, she was bitter, angry without any good reason. She was a woman who was suffering. She pretended not to suffer from poverty. For example, at that time there were three classes in the trains and we traveled in third class. That really humiliated us, but we didn't say so. We would say, "Oh, I really like to travel in third class." I think it is better, if one is suffering from something, to say "I'm really suffering from that." It is healthier. It is rather unhealthy to hide the truth from oneself. I remember that she was unhappy. Children aren't aware. I said to myself, "Why is she crying? Why does she cry so much?"

YAP: She never tried to explain the reasons for her unhappiness to you?

HdeB: Ah no, and you don't ask your mother questions like that. And then *papa* was very egotistical. One day *papa* said to *maman,* "Françoise, there is a fakir at the circus. I'll take you to see the fakir for your birthday." *Maman* said, "Oh, listen, I don't like fakirs. I hate fakirs. I really have no desire to go see one." On her birthday, he said, "I have bought four seats for the circus so we can go see the fakir." He was always like that. He was very very egotistical.

YAP: That must have made life very difficult for your mother.

HdeB: Of course, *maman* suffered a lot more because she had a very unfaithful husband. I know that once—oh, I was already eighteen years old—he came home at eight in the morning. Maman had gone to mass. She had left for early mass in tears, and *papa* said to me, "You know, Hélène, I was playing bridge . . . " And I said, "Listen, *papa,* if you want to you can tell that to *maman,* not to me."

YAP: Did your mother accept everything he said without questioning?

HdeB: Even *maman* would not have believed him that time. *Papa* was ten years older than *maman.* He had led a full life, with pretty mistresses. He had decided it was time to get married and he went into the provinces to find a girl who was beautiful, rich, and virtuous. *Maman* was beautiful and virtuous, but she was no longer rich. She had a dowry but it was never paid. And I know that that always bothered her. And our maid, who was very fond of *papa,* told me, "Ah, your *papa* is a good man. He has never held the fact that the dowry was not paid against your *maman.*" Of course one should not hold it against one's wife if she doesn't bring in money. It would have been ignoble to hold it against her.

YAP: But that was the tradition, wasn't it?

HdeB: Yes. He had been cheated because he had married a rich girl and then in the end that girl was no longer rich. But that is what bourgeois France was like. You have read Balzac . . . Moreover, throughout my childhood, you know, I had no desire to get married and I said to myself, "I have the right to work because I don't have a dowry, and a girl without a dowry doesn't get married." My parents had friends in Limousin, a lady we went to visit every year. We would play tennis with her sons, who were good-looking boys, but whom we would never have wanted to marry. And every year the lady would say tactfully to *maman*, "You know, my sons will never marry a girl who doesn't have a dowry of at least a hundred thousand francs." At the time, a hundred thousand francs was a lot of money. What that woman was really saying to her was, "Your daughters are not for our sons." *Maman* would tell me that and it didn't matter at all to me. I had no desire whatever to marry them.

YAP: Society has really changed since then.

HdeB: Yes, although ... I told you that I recently had an interview for *Marie-Claire* with a thirty-five-year-old woman. I told her that our mother read our letters when we were eighteen and sixteen, or seventeen and nineteen. She told me, "My mother read our letters too, when I was fifteen ... I am sure that there are still women who read their daughters' letters." Not only that, but *maman* threw out the ones she didn't like.

YAP: So during your adolescence you began to rebel a little against the family tradition. And what exactly did you do?

HdeB: Well, our first act of independence was to go walking in the streets when our parents went out. They frequently went out to dinner. When they were invited to dinner, we knew that they would not come home before midnight. Then, oh, maybe from nine to eleven, we would wander about the streets, very properly, but it was an adventure to go walking alone in the evening. We would never have been allowed to go out alone in the evening.

YAP: Did you always have to have your parents with you?

HdeB: Oh yes, in the evening. In the daytime we could go about all alone, but in the evening we didn't go out alone. Once we even went so far as to have a *café crème* at the Rotonde. That was our great rebellion against family and country.

YAP: You apparently needed to escape a little from your parents' influence during your adolescence.

HdeB: Maman treated me very inappropriately. They did everything to make me hate Simone. Fortunately they did not succeed. They held her up as an example, and everything Simone did was right. I was the younger one who was not really accepted, you understand. They wanted a son. And that is why when pregnant women I meet say, "Oh, I want a son," I tell them, "Listen, you must not set your heart on a son or a daughter. You must accept the child you have, because it is frightful not to be accepted." You mustn't think that I was an abused child. *Maman* was very affectionate with me, but she made me feel that I didn't amount to much. She always tried to humiliate me.

YAP: In what way did she humiliate you?

HdeB: There is a story I always tell because it had a great effect on me. One day when *maman* was talking to the family about Simone's success in school, she said, "You know, Simone was first in her class again." And I said, "I was first too, *maman*." "Oh, for you it's easier." It wasn't easier. I was two-and-a-half years younger, I was two years behind her in school. It wasn't easier.

YAP: And Simone understood that.

HdeB: I have always said that if Simone had not been so kind and so intelligent, she could have destroyed me. I really could easily have become depressed. It is very bad for a child to be crushed. But Simone was supportive of me. And I admired her more than I admired my parents. And since I admired her more than anyone else, as long as she appreciated me, as long as I had Simone's esteem, it meant that I was worthwhile. That was very important. And you know, if I had not had enough self-confidence, I would never have been able to paint, because in order to create one must have a great deal of self-confidence. But Simone gave me that confidence. That is perhaps the most important thing I owe her.

YAP: She said in her autobiography that during your adolescence you were more beautiful than she was.

HdeB: She meant that I did not pass through an awkward stage. She had a very difficult awkward stage. I think that she had had a very happy life and then she had problems when she was fourteen. Her relationship with our parents was not going well, nor was her relationship with God, because she was beginning to wonder if God existed. You know, one asks questions when one has a very Catholic mother and a father who doesn't believe. A mother who says, "Oh, the Holy Virgin has been responsible for another miracle in Lourdes" and a father who tells her, "But if the Holy Virgin is capable of bringing about miracles, why doesn't she create a new leg for one-legged people?" And my mother would say that that would be too easy to believe. Because of all that, one begins to ask questions. At fourteen, Simone was a very very brilliant student, but she certainly had problems in her private life. Nothing was going right. She had been a very pretty little girl, and she became a very pretty adolescent, but there was a year between her fourteenth and fifteenth birthdays when I really was prettier. I just didn't go through an awkward stage.

YAP: Did you know Zaza's mother well when you were an adolescent?

HdeB: Oh, of course. Madame Lacoin was a real personality.

YAP: What was she like?

HdeB: A rather pretty woman. I only remember her with a hat on. I'm sure that she didn't wear a hat at home. She would leave our classes with a hat on her head, a big hat. She was very pleasant. She interacted with people much more easily than *maman.* Simone would say to me, "The Lacoin children really do whatever they please." One piano-recital day, Zaza was going to play a piece she was having a lot of trouble with and her mother swore, "You'll never get it, you'll never get it." She played it right and then turned around and stuck her tongue out at her mother. For Simone and me, it was an unthinkable thing to do. Sticking your tongue out at your mother was ... Zaza scandalized the Cours Désir students, but her mother just laughed. Her mother was very easygoing with the children. But, but, later on, when they were eighteen, then ... Zaza adored her mother. Since she had been very kind, very easygoing, very affectionate, you don't rebel against a mother like that. While *maman,* who didn't know how to deal with us, who was in conflict with us and sometimes very brutal, was someone you could rebel against.

YAP: And one needs to be able to rebel.

HdeB: It is much healthier. The rebellion is no doubt very painful for the parents, but I think it is very healthy. Zaza didn't rebel and it killed her. Simone told that story that you know very well. Madame Lacoin was a beautiful woman from the south of France, very affable, but at the same time very worldly. She thought that going to a dance was just as much a duty as going to mass. A social duty. Zaza never rebelled. Because one didn't rebel against Madame Lacoin.

YAP: Did *you* try very hard to please *your* mother?

HdeB: Usually, but not always. Simone had a friend whom I liked very much. Since she was getting married, she invited us to her wedding, and I said I would be delighted to go. I don't know why but *maman* said, "No, you don't have to go, you will not go to that wedding." "Why?" "You won't go, you won't go, you won't go." I said, "Yes, I will," and I went. Then she was very hurt and very angry. But *maman* was like that, when she got an idea into her head. Then she went to Madame Lacoin, and Madame Lacoin summoned me and told me, "I know that your mother hasn't always been too adept in the way she has raised you, but nonetheless you owe her respect," etc.

YAP: Madame Lacoin thought then that one should always obey one's mother.

HdeB: When I was small, of course I obeyed her, but in that instance I didn't. I went to the wedding. That is why she went to talk to Madame Lacoin. Ah no, I began to disobey, because I found some things idiotic. And so did Simone. *Maman* was beginning to feel that Simone was having a bad influence on me and she wanted to keep me from seeing Simone. How can you keep two sisters who are living together from seeing one another?

YAP: One would think that she would have preferred to have you do things together.

HdeB: No, because she realized that Simone had lost her faith. She still hoped to make a good little girl out of me. She had understood that Simone would never again be a good little girl.

YAP: Maybe she was jealous of the closeness between you.

HdeB: Maybe she was jealous too. I remember once when I had written to Simone without *maman*'s knowledge, when Simone was at Zaza's in Les Landes, and I was on my way to mail the letter. And *maman* caught me. I was already seventeen years old. She opened the letter and read it. I was enraged and I really resented it. It was so inappropriate. *Maman* acted very inappropriately. And at the same time, she didn't mean to hurt us, the poor woman, but . . .

YAP: She did her best but didn't know how . . .

HdeB: Ah, you know, she had prepared herself too well for her role as wife and mother. She had gone to lectures and then, as I told you, the mother-daughter relationship was set up on such a false basis. People would say for instance, "A girl has no better friend than her mother. A girl should tell everything to her mother." Now I don't think that any girl tells her mother everything. Did you always tell your mother everything?

YAP: No. When I was very small, perhaps, but after that . . .

HdeB: I am sure that even if one hasn't done anything out of the ordinary, one does not feel like talking about everything. And *maman* didn't allow us to have a life of our own. That is why we rebelled. When I was little and going to the Cours Désir, the mothers had the right to come to class. Until we were ten years old. And *maman* didn't miss a single one of my classes. With her sewing, she did petit point, chair covers . . .

YAP: She came to school every day?

HdeB: We had formal classes twice a week. Twice a week she was there, behind the table. And then if I said something stupid—children do say stupid things sometimes—what I said was broadcast so the whole family knew that I had said something stupid. There is a story that I find very very characteristic of the false relationship that was set up between mothers and daughters. We were good little Catholics. And before first-communion day, there was a retreat every year. We spent three or four days, all day long, at the Cours Désir, but we didn't go to class. We went to the Cours Désir chapel. We listened to the chaplain, who delivered long sermons, and the day was very calm and peaceful. And then we were supposed to write down our most secret thoughts in a notebook. But *maman* read my notebook and sometimes she made fun of me. That was ill-advised, because it meant that we didn't have the right to a life of our own. And children need to have a life of their own. That is why when I see parents today who want to be pals with their children and want to go to school with them, I think it's sad.

YAP: Children need to separate from their parents.

HdeB: We had a wide margin of freedom because *maman* went visiting all day long, did a lot of visiting, and Simone and I threw ourselves into our games. It was all very secretive, and if an adult came in while we were playing, we immediately stopped playing.

YAP: So you finally had a life of your own.

HdeB: But they stole that life away from us. And that still didn't satisfy *maman*. When *maman* heard us talking and playing, she tried to listen. And I am going to tell you a story I think will amuse you. It is about the retreat. The day before our first communion, the chaplain said—*maman* was there, naturally, she was always there, in the choir loft, listening to everything.—"My children, this evening you must sit down in your dear mother's lap and tell her, '*Maman*, I ask your forgiveness for all the ways in which I may have wronged you.'" And I said to myself, "*Maman* is expecting me to do that." And even though I was very small, I sensed that this was playacting. And I didn't do it. She said to me, "You didn't come to ask my pardon." And I didn't explain why but she must have understood. I really felt it was playacting, hypocrisy, stupidity. There were sometimes scenes between us. Sometimes *maman* would cry. She often cried because she was unhappy. She would cry and then I would hug her and we would make up.

YAP: There was a lot of affection in your relationship.

HdeB: In our family there was a lot of affection, a lot of shouting, a lot of anger. All four of us were strong personalities. *Papa* had a very violent temperament. And indeed *maman* was violent too. And I think that Simone and I each had a violent streak. I was the least violent. But nonetheless we would all get angry. We were capable of becoming very angry.

YAP: Sometimes it is very necessary to be able to express one's anger.

HdeB: Yes. Our family life was rocky, it wasn't peaceful. Not at all, not at all. And the older we got, the less peaceful it was. Simone always defended me. She was always on my side. She was able to help me more than I could help her because she was after all older than I was.

YAP: And the role of religion? You were raised to be a good little Catholic.

HdeB: I was very religious. I believed, all the while saying to myself, "How lovely life would be if God didn't exist." I think that if I had not been so religious, my rebellion would have been much more direct. I was really very religious.

YAP: Until what age? Did you ever talk to your mother about the change in your religious attitude?

HdeB: I had to hide that from her, because I knew that she had been very upset when Simone spoke to her. So on Sunday morning, every Sunday morning, I pretended to go to mass, and I went to the Louvre. I knew the Louvre like the palm of my hand. It has changed a good deal now. I knew every little room.

YAP: Maybe that was the beginning of your artistic inspiration.

HdeB: I certainly saw a lot of paintings, both good and bad.

YAP: And you never told your mother where you went?

HdeB: Oh no. And I never told her that Lionel and I only had a civil marriage. I always let her think that we were married in a church. And since I was married in Portugal during the war, it was easy to make her think that. She asked me how we could have a religious ceremony because usually you need to show a baptismal certificate. And I told her,

"But listen, it was wartime." I was baptized in Limousin, because my godmother was my Aunt Hélène, *papa*'s sister who lived at La Grillère. "But listen, in Portugal I couldn't ask for my baptismal certificate," I told *maman*. "And then Lionel is Protestant, but we were married in the sacristy. And it was wartime ..." You must know, since your family was Catholic, that it is worse to be married in a civil ceremony than to live together. *Maman* was not very sure that I still believed in God.

YAP: She didn't ask any questions. She preferred not to know.

HdeB: I think she preferred not to ask me personal questions. She said to one of my cousins, "Oh, what's the use of going to heaven if I can't be there with all my family." She wondered if *papa*, Simone, and I would go to heaven. And that worried her.

YAP: That must have been very difficult for her. Then there is that whole story about the reason Madame Lacoin didn't want Zaza to marry Merleau-Ponty, and it was because he was an illegitimate child, wasn't it? But Simone didn't know that.

HdeB: No. What she said in her memoirs was all she knew. She related everything she knew. But it was so horrible to go tell Maurice Merleau-Ponty, who knew nothing about it, "You are not your father's son. You are an illegitimate child. You and your sister are illegitimate." That is why Merleau-Ponty, who thought he was not good enough for Zaza, backed off from the marriage.

YAP: Zaza's family was very conservative.

HdeB: Oh, my. Oh, my. They all thought so much the same way that Zaza could not escape. While in my family, all the women went to mass and not a single man went. On Sunday morning, all the men—my grandfather, my uncles, *papa*—stayed in bed and the women went to mass. Then you begin to think that religion is fine for women and children. And they said that the men were the most intelligent and extraordinary members of the family. So why don't they believe in God then? One begins to ask that question. God seemed to be only for women and children.

YAP: And family members like Cousin Jeanne, for instance ...

HdeB: Oh, her father didn't go to mass either. He was *papa*'s brother. He didn't go to mass either. Her mother, like *maman*, was a young girl from the provinces. She was from Périgueux, *maman* from Verdun. We went to mass every Sunday and there was scarcely anyone but women and children there. Very few men were practicing Catholics, and people made fun of the ones who were. My father made fun of them. We had one or two men in the family who were practicing Catholics, and it pained me because the family rejected them. None of the men went to mass.

YAP: Was there a time in your life when you considered your mother a role model?

HdeB: Oh, no, never. Never. No, because I never felt that she was really happy. First because there was the war, and after that because *papa* made her unhappy. No, when I was very little, up to the age of five . . . there was no problem. But I don't think a five-year-old child says to herself, "My mother is a role model." She is unique, all is well, parents are perfect, everything is perfect. And then a day came when we started asking questions. We realized that *maman* was not happy. Basically, I was always a rebel. I think I became a feminist very young without realizing it, because I was rather repulsed by the life women led. For example, I remember when *maman* came back from an afternoon tea with her lady friends and said to me, "Madame So-and-So"—a woman who had lost a son in the war—"said, 'I have had twenty years of perfect happiness.'" Maybe to console herself for the loss of her son. And I said to myself, "That's the kind of happiness I don't want." I really rebelled even against the happiness those ladies professed: "I want a different kind of life." I don't know why, but I know that I began at a very very very very early age. I rejected the life of the women around me. I didn't know exactly what I *did* want, but that was already a step in the right direction.

YAP: Is it true, as Simone said in *A Very Easy Death,* that your mother felt more at ease with you than with Simone?

HdeB: Yes. Simone intimidated her. I didn't intimidate her.

YAP: Why do you think that was? What made the difference? Was Simone more outspoken with her?

HdeB: Simone was very careful but she had a hard time communicating with *maman.* I managed to talk to her. I found it easier to make small talk, to talk woman-to-woman, if you will. I talked to her about her friends, about the things she did each day. She sensed that Simone wasn't interested in those things. She was a little afraid of Simone's intellectual superiority. She was afraid Simone might judge her harshly. I don't know, I was more . . . she felt closer to me. She was a little afraid of Simone.

YAP: Do you think that the portrait of your mother Simone presented in her works was fairly accurate?

HdeB: Oh yes, very accurate. But I think her judgments are sometimes a little harsh. Sometimes she is a little harsh in her memoirs, because there were childhood resentments that one doesn't forget, things that gnaw at you, wounds that never heal. She related certain episodes in her childhood that hurt her. But I think that, in *A Very Easy Death*, she really understood *maman*, and what *maman* 's life was all about ... her suffering, her sadness, what made her the way she was as a young woman ... You know, you rebel against an authoritarian mother. But when you realize that her harshness was the result of a deep-seated unhappiness, then you understand. She was very nervous and it's true that it is not much fun for children to be raised by a mother whose nerves are always on edge, but she had good reasons for being the way she was. She was very unhappy and she seemed to think that if she said she was very unhappy that would mean, "Georges, you are making me too unhappy." Never, never, never would she say such a thing. She would say, "I am happy, I have a very happy marriage." Her close friend, the one who told me a lot about her, said to me, "But, you know, never, never did she admit that she was unhappy." I knew she was unhappy.

YAP: It would have helped her to admit it.

HdeB: It would have helped her to admit it to that friend. She was a well-meaning woman who was very fond of *maman* and whom *maman* liked very much. But she never confided in anyone.

YAP: That is probably because of her temperament. And that was not the way she was brought up.

HdeB: It's very true that that was not the way she was brought up. It was that way when she was young. And then she admitted that her mother had never been very close to her. Her mother had always been very cold.

YAP: Was she ever cold toward you and Simone?

HdeB: No, no, not cold. She hugged us a lot, she liked to hug us a lot. The whole family was affectionate. That's why I enjoy Italy so much. People hug a lot there. I think that in America there is very little hugging among family members. Is that right?

YAP: That depends. In families of European and particularly Mediterranean background, people hug all the time. Even the men. And that probably seems a little strange for Americans of a more Anglo-Saxon background.

HdeB: Once I saw a little boy who was leaving for school. His mother was going to kiss him and he said, "No, you don't kiss boys." I think it's important that in Europe a child isn't afraid to let his mother kiss him.

YAP: Did you ever consider the possibility of having children yourself?

HdeB: No. I have a friend who did research for the journal *Autrement* on the question of maternity and she came to interview me precisely about my non-desire for children. The editor-in-chief told her to ask me if creativity replaces children. I told her that was an idiotic question. I didn't replace a desire for children because I never had one and I don't think I was sterile. I have no reason to think that I was sterile. But I didn't want a child because my ambition to be a painter was so strong that I knew it would have been very very difficult to continue my career if I had children, even one child. A child absorbs you. You don't have the right to sacrifice a child. You can sacrifice a husband on certain occasions. If he is sick, you take care of him, but on the whole an adult has his own life. But a child lives through you. I didn't want to run that risk.

YAP: It's a question of having enough time.

HdeB: Partially. Many painters, especially artists like me, need time. I have always needed a great deal of time. I have always worked as if I were to live a hundred years. I don't know if I will live a hundred years. I am not young, but I will have had the time to work a great deal.

YAP: What do you think of the contemporary way of raising children?

HdeB: I think that in my village they are being raised very badly. I know young couples who raise their children very well. There are still people who raise them well. But I have the impression that people who raise their children well have understood that a child is not a pal. People were saying, "Let children do whatever they want." A long time ago, I had a friend who would say, "I must not give my son any complexes." And I knew a family that was rather well off, a good middle-class family. They had four sons. And their idea was that you should never frustrate a child. Even if the child is walking on the edge of a precipice, one should say nothing, because children must do what they want. As a result, those four children who really had no problems, who were wanted children, whose parents loved them, who had everything necessary for happiness, all became drug addicts. One began at age fourteen, one has recovered, and at twenty-five the oldest is a complete zombie. That is not a very good advertisement for a permissive upbringing.

YAP: A very different upbringing from your own.

HdeB: Ah yes. I don't think you should beat children either, but I think you have to exercise a little authority. *Maman* often treated us strictly, but that is something I would never reproach her for. She gave us a certain sense of discipline and that has helped me all me life. If one does something very freely, as I paint, if one is not disciplined one never gets anywhere. Sometimes people say to me, "Do you work when you are inspired?" And I say, "I work when it's time to work."

YAP: Your sister also had that need to work.

HdeB: I think that is not a bad thing. And I think that my parents must have provided me with that sense of discipline. In my village these days, the children and the parents are not assuming their responsibilities. I think that the peasants are always behind the bourgeoisie as far as social trends are concerned. The bourgeoisie's abdication of responsibility for child rearing is manifesting itself in my village now. As a result, the children are badly brought up and are little vandals. I know what I am talking about, because they have broken a great many things at my house. And that doesn't make those children any happier.

YAP: What advice would you give to a twenty-year-old woman about marriage, motherhood, and life in general?

HdeB: It is difficult to give advice. I would mainly tell her to do what she wants to do. I am sure that the only piece of advice one can give to young people is to do what they really want to do. The woman shouldn't do what she thinks is the right thing just because she has heard elsewhere that it is the right thing to do, or because she thinks that other people will think it is right. You have to do what you really want to do. I think that is the only advice I could ever give to young people.

Interview with Hélène de Beauvoir:
Original Transcript

YAP: Je voudrais commencer par parler un peu de vos souvenirs d'enfance. Quels sont vos souvenirs de votre mère quand vous étiez petite?

HdeB: Ah, maman. J'ai adoré maman. Seulement j'ai eu des rapports assez difficiles avec elle comme petite fille et surtout comme adolescente. Mais petite fille, j'adorais maman. Elle était belle. Les enfants ont une sensualité. Moi, je me rappelle quand maman allait au bal le soir, je la voyais, je la respirais, je respirais son parfum. Elle avait une jolie robe, elle était bien coiffée. Quand elle se penchait sur mon petit lit, c'était vraiment un plaisir sensuel. Ça c'est un souvenir. Et puis, c'était une mère affectueuse. Assez sévère, mais affectueuse.

YAP: Est-ce que vos sentiments ont changé peu à peu au fur et à mesure que vous grandissiez?

HdeB: Il y a eu l'avant-guerre, qui n'a pas duré très longtemps pour moi, puisque la guerre a éclaté en 14. Mais surtout, jusqu'en 1915, papa a été quand même à la maison. Pour moi rien n'a été changé. J'aimais aussi beaucoup papa quand j'étais toute petite. Après, nos rapports se sont détériorés. Mais après 1915, quand papa était parti, maman s'est beaucoup appuyée sur nous. Papa était d'abord cantonné aux environs de Paris avant de partir pour le front. Et quelquefois maman et Simone allaient le voir. Moi je restais parce que j'étais petite. Et puis je me rappelle les permissions de papa pendant la guerre. Maman était bien sûr souvent inquiète et triste. Elle s'est rapprochée de nous. Elle était plus affectueuse parce que papa était parti.

YAP: Elle s'inquiétait du sort de votre père.

HdeB: Ah, oui. Papa a été dans les zouaves, ce qui a été un des régiments les plus durs. Il est tombé malade, sa maladie du coeur s'est aggravée. Il a été à l'hôpital, ce qui l'a sauvé, car tout son régiment est allé à Verdun et personne n'en est revenu. La bataille de Verdun, c'était l'hécatombe, c'était l'hécatombe.

YAP: Et l'après-guerre?

HdeB: Après 19, les choses se sont beaucoup beaucoup détériorées. Maman est devenue neurasthénique ... La faillite de mon grand-père, je vous l'ai racontée, donc il n'y avait plus d'argent. Avant la guerre papa était avocat. Après la guerre, ce n'était pas un homme très courageux. Je vous ai déjà dit que dans ma famille, c'était plutôt les femmes qui travaillaient. Les hommes n'étaient pas de gros travailleurs. Papa n'a pas eu le courage de revenir à son cabinet d'avocat, il n'a pas pu se permettre un travail. Il n'a plus fait grand chose. Et la guerre vraiment a cassé quelque chose chez lui. Il était habitué à la vie facile, il avait rêvé d'une vie moderne, facile, il aimait jouer la comédie, il aimait jouer au bridge, il aimait voir le cours du monde, il était mondain. Et puis, tout à coup il s'est retrouvé très pauvre et sans situation, et sans le courage de se refaire une situation.

YAP: Où avez-vous habité pendant cette époque?

HdeB: Nous avions un bel appartement, Boulevard du Montparnasse, mais les fenêtres donnaient sur le Boulevard Raspail. C'était très très agréable, vraiment un appartement très agréable et confortable, et nous avons déménagé rue de Rennes, dans un appartement qui semblait triste dans le mauvais souvenir de Simone.

YAP: Votre souvenir ne correspond donc pas tout à fait avec celui de Simone?

HdeB: L'appartement n'était pas confortable, c'est vrai. Nous étions au cinquième étage sans ascenseur, il n'y avait pas de cabinet de toilettes. Mais en 1919 à Paris, vous savez, les appartements confortables c'était déjà un luxe, c'était un luxe d'avoir l'eau courante ... Alors Boulevard Raspail nous avions une salle de bains, mais c'était déjà un luxe.

YAP: Et la réaction de votre mère à la nécessité de déménager?

HdeB: Maman a été élevée au Couvent des Oiseaux à Verdun. Verdun c'était la petite province. Elle avait cette idée bourgeoise qu'il faut tenir son rang. Par exemple, elle aurait pu changer ses meubles. A l'heure actuelle, on n'a pas un salon, une salle à manger, et un bureau. Là, il fallait avoir salon, salle à manger, bureau. Il fallait donner de grands dîners. Elle s'éreintait, mais nous avions quand même une bonne. Ce n'était pas la misère. Nous étions très mal habillées parce que maman n'était pas coquette. Et puis tout de même il faut dire qu'elle économisait beaucoup et papa n'était pas généreux avec elle. Quand il avait de l'argent, il le dépensait pour lui. Il ne m'a jamais donné d'argent sans me faire une scène. Tous les jours on devait le lui demander. Maman est donc devenue vraiment neurasthénique.

YAP: Ça se comprend.

HdeB: Ça se comprend ... En plus, j'ai compris depuis que mon père est certainement devenu très infidèle. Il s'est mis à sortir beaucoup de son côté, et j'ai vu très très souvent pleurer maman.

YAP: Est-ce qu'elle vous a jamais expliqué pourquoi?

HdeB: Maman serrait les dents. Vous savez qu'il y avait un secret de famille que j'ai seulement appris après la mort de ma mère. Nous savions que mon grand-père avait fait faillite, mais ce que nous ne savions pas c'est qu'il avait fait de la prison. Maman ne nous l'avait jamais dit, jamais, jamais, jamais. C'est par une vieille amie de maman à qui j'ai rendu visite après sa mort que je l'ai appris. J'étais allée lui porter un souvenir de maman et elle m'a raconté que mon grand-père avait fait de la prison. "Et votre pauvre grand-mère!" Ma grand-mère était pourtant un peu fière. Et j'imagine l'effort pour elle. D'abord elle adorait son mari. Dans ma famille, je crois que les femmes sont beaucoup plus épouses que mères. Ma grand-mère a été une mère assez froide mais une épouse très dévouée à son mari. Maman a été une très bonne épouse, très dévouée. Elle adorait papa, mais papa ne l'a pas rendue heureuse. Et avec nous elle a souvent été très maladroite. Et Simone et moi, d'ailleurs, n'avons pas eu envie d'avoir des enfants.

YAP: A cause des malheurs de votre grand-mère et de votre mère?

HdeB: Peut-être. Un jour quand j'avais déjà cinquante ans, j'ai demandé à ma mère: "Maman, écoute, qu'est-ce que c'est que ce secret de famille?" Elle m'a dit: "C'est que ta grand-mère avait mis son argenterie au mont de piété." Elle ne m'a jamais dit: "Ton grand-père a fait de la prison." Elle en a terriblement souffert.

YAP: Surtout de la faillite de son père?

HdeB: Justement son amie me disait aussi: "Je suis sûre que votre père l'a rendue très malheureuse." Mais elle ne me l'a jamais dit, elle ne se plaignait jamais. Elle est devenue cependant très dure parce que ça lui faisait mal et quelquefois alors ça sortait même sur nous. Elle était injuste avec nous, elle était amère, colérique sans raison. C'est une femme qui souffrait. Elle faisait semblant de ne pas souffrir de la pauvreté. Alors, par exemple, il y avait trois classes dans le chemin de fer, et nous voyagions en troisième classe. Ça nous humiliait beaucoup, mais on ne le disait pas. On disait, "Oh, au fond, j'aime bien voyager en troisième classe." Enfin, je crois qu'il vaut mieux, si on souffre d'une chose, de dire "Vraiment j'en souffre." C'est plus sain. C'est assez malsain de se cacher la vérité. Je me rends compte qu'elle avait été malheureuse. Les enfants ne se rendent pas compte. Je me suis dit: "Elle pleure pourquoi? Pourquoi est-ce qu'elle pleure tellement?"

YAP: Elle n'a jamais essayé de vous expliquer les causes de son malheur?

HdeB: Ah, non, et on ne demande pas ça à sa mère. Et puis papa était très égoïste. Un jour papa a dit à maman: "Françoise, au cirque il y a un fakir. Pour ton anniversaire je t'emmènerai voir le fakir." Alors maman a dit: "Oh, écoute, le fakir, ça ne m'amuse pas. Je déteste les fakirs. Je n'ai pas du tout envie d'y aller." Alors le jour de son anniversaire, il a dit: "J'ai pris quatre places pour le cirque pour aller voir le fakir." Il a toujours été comme ça. Il était très très égoïste.

YAP: Ça a dû rendre la vie très difficile pour votre mère.

HdeB: Bien sûr, maman a souffert beaucoup plus parce qu'elle avait un mari très infidèle. Je sais qu'une fois—oh, j'avais déjà dix-huit ans—il est rentré à huit heures du matin. Maman était à la messe, elle était partie en pleurant à la petite messe, et papa m'a dit: "Oh, tu sais, Hélène, j'ai joué au bridge . . ." et j'ai dit: "Ecoute, papa, si ça t'amuse tu raconteras ça à maman, mais pas à moi."

YAP: Est-ce que votre mère a accepté sans contester tout ce qu'il disait?

HdeB: Même maman ne l'aurait pas cru cette fois-là. Papa avait dix ans de plus que maman. Il avait bien vécu, avec de jolies maîtresses. Il avait décidé de se marier et il avait été chercher en province une jeune fille belle, riche, et vertueuse. Maman était belle et vertueuse, mais elle n'était plus riche. Elle avait une dot mais elle n'a jamais été payée. Et je sais que ça l'a toujours remuée. Et notre bonne qui aimait beaucoup papa me disait: "Ah, votre papa il est bien. Il n'a jamais reproché à votre maman que sa dot n'ait pas été payée." Bien sûr, on ne doit pas reprocher à sa femme de ne pas apporter d'argent. Il aurait été ignoble de le lui reprocher.

YAP: Mais c'était la tradition, n'est-ce pas?

HdeB: Oui. Il a été floué parce qu'il avait épousé une jeune fille riche et puis cette jeune fille finalement n'était plus riche. Mais c'est ça, c'était la France bourgeoise. Enfin, vous avez lu Balzac . . . Du reste, toute mon enfance, vous savez, je n'avais pas envie de me marier, et je me suis dit: "J'ai le droit de travailler parce que je n'aurai pas de dot, et une fille sans dot ne se marie pas." Mes parents avaient des amis, en Limousin, une dame qu'on allait voir tous les ans. Nous jouions au tennis avec ses fils, qui étaient du reste de beaux garçons, mais que nous n'aurions jamais eu envie d'épouser. Et tous les ans avec tact la dame disait à maman: "Vous savez, mes fils n'épouseront jamais une jeune fille qui n'aurait pas au moins cent mille francs de dot." A l'époque, cent mille francs c'était quelque chose. Cette femme lui disait en effet: "Vos filles ne sont pas pour nos fils." Alors, maman me disait ça mais ça ne me faisait aucune importance. Je n'avais pas du tout envie de les épouser.

YAP: La société a vraiment changé depuis.

HdeB: Oui, quoique . . . je vous ai dit que j'ai eu une interview pour *Marie-Claire* dernièrement avec une femme de trente-cinq ans. Je lui disais que notre mère lisait nos lettres quand nous avions dix-huit et seize ans, ou dix-sept et dix-neuf ans. Elle m'a dit: "Ma mère aussi lisait nos lettres, quand j'avais quinze ans . . . je suis sûre qu'il y a encore des femmes qui lisent les lettres de leurs filles." Et non seulement ça mais maman jetait celles qui ne lui plaisaient pas.

YAP: Alors, pendant votre adolescence vous avez commencé à vous révolter un peu contre la tradition de la famille. Et qu'est-ce que vous avez fait?

HdeB: Eh bien, notre premier acte d'indépendance, c'était d'aller nous promener dans les rues pendant que nos parents étaient sortis. Ils allaient beaucoup dîner en ville. Quand ils étaient invités à dîner, on savait qu'ils ne rentreraient pas avant minuit. Alors, oh, peut-être de neuf heures à onze heures, nous allions nous promener dans les rues bien sages, mais ça marchait, c'était une aventure, de se promener seules le soir. Jamais on ne nous aurait permis de sortir seules le soir.

YAP: Il fallait toujours avoir vos parents avec vous?

HdeB: Ah oui, le soir. Dans la journée tout de même nous allions encore toutes seules, mais le soir on ne sortait pas seules. Aussi une fois nous avons même été jusqu'à aller prendre un café crème à la Rotonde. Ça c'était la grande révolte contre famille et patrie.

YAP: Vous aviez apparemment besoin d'échapper un peu à l'influence de vos parents pendant votre adolescence.

HdeB: Maman a été très maladroite avec moi. On a tout fait, on n'y est pas arrivé heureusement, on a tout fait pour me faire détester Simone. Puisque on me la donnait en exemple, et puis, tout ce que faisait Simone était bien. Moi, j'étais la petite qui n'était pas tellement bien acceptée, vous comprenez. Ils voulaient un fils. Et c'est pour ça que quand les femmes enceintes que je rencontre disent: "Oh, je veux un fils," je leur dis: "Ecoutez, il ne faut pas miser sur un fils ou une fille, il faut accepter l'enfant que vous aurez, parce que c'est affreux de ne pas être accepté. Il ne faut pas comprendre que j'étais une enfant martyre. Maman était très affectueuse avec moi, mais elle me faisait sentir que enfin je n'étais pas grand-chose. Elle cherchait tout de même à m'humilier.

YAP: De quelle façon vous humiliait-elle?

HdeB: Il y a une histoire que je raconte toujours, parce qu'elle m'a beaucoup marquée. Un jour où maman parlait à la famille des succès de Simone, elle disait: "Vous savez, Simone a encore été première." Et j'ai dit: " Moi aussi, maman, j'ai été première." "Oh, pour toi c'est plus facile." Ce n'était pas plus facile. J'avais deux ans et demi de moins, j'étais deux classes en dessous, ce n'était pas plus facile.

YAP: Et Simone a compris cela.

HdeB: J'ai toujours dit que si Simone n'avait pas été aussi gentille et aussi intelligente, elle aurait pu me briser. Vraiment j'aurais pu tomber dans la mélancolie. C'est très mauvais pour un enfant d'être écrasé. Mais Simone m'a valorisée. Et je l'admirais plus que j'admirais mes parents. Et comme je l'admirais plus que personne, du moment qu'elle m'estimait, du moment que j'avais l'estime de Simone, c'est que j'étais estimable. C'était très important. Et vous savez, si je n'avais pas eu assez de confiance en moi, je n'aurais jamais pu faire de peinture, parce que pour créer il faut une grande confiance en soi. Or cette confiance en moi, on a tout fait pour la détruire. Mais alors Simone, elle me l'a donnée. Peut-être que c'est ce que je lui dois le plus.

YAP: Elle a dit dans son autobiographie que pendant votre adolescence vous étiez plus belle qu'elle.

HdeB: C'est-à-dire que je n'ai pas eu d'âge ingrat. Elle a eu un âge ingrat très dur. Je crois qu'elle avait eu une petite vie très heureuse, et puis elle a eu les difficultés de quatorze ans. Il y avait quelque chose qui n'allait plus dans ses rapports avec nos parents, dans ses rapports aussi avec

Dieu, parce qu'elle commençait à se demander si Dieu existait. Vous savez, on se pose des questions quand on a une mère très catholique et un père incroyant. Une mère qui dit: "Oh, la Sainte Vierge a encore fait un miracle à Lourdes" et un père qui lui dit: "Mais si la Sainte Vierge est capable de faire des miracles pourquoi est-ce qu'elle ne ferait pas repousser une jambe?" Et ma mère disait que c'était puisque ça c'est trop facile à croire. A cause de tout ça, on se pose des questions. A quatorze ans, Simone était très très brillante élève, mais dans sa vie privée elle avait certainement des problèmes. Ça n'allait plus du tout. Elle avait été une très jolie petite fille, et puis elle est devenue une très jolie jeune fille, mais il y a eu un an entre quatorze et quinze ans où vraiment moi j'ai été plus jolie. Je n'ai pas eu d'âge ingrat.

YAP: Est-ce que vous avez bien connu la mère de Zaza pendant votre adolescence?

HdeB: Oh, bien sûr. Mme Lacoin, c'était un personnage.

YAP: Et comment était-elle?

HdeB: Une assez belle femme. Je ne me la rappelle qu'avec un chapeau. Je suis sûre que chez elle elle ne portait pas de chapeau. Elle sortait des cours un chapeau sur la tête, un grand chapeau. Elle était très gentille. Elle était beaucoup plus adroite que maman. Simone me disait: "Mais les petits Lacoin, vraiment ils font tout ce qu'ils veulent." Un jour d'audition Zaza allait jouer un morceau de piano qu'elle avait beaucoup de mal à faire et sa mère jurait: "Tu n'y arriveras pas, tu n'arriveras pas." Elle l'a réussi et elle s'est retournée et a tiré sa langue à sa mère. Pour Simone et moi, c'était impensable que nous fassions ça. Tirer la langue à votre mère, c'était . . . Alors Zaza a scandalisé les demoiselles du Cours Désir mais sa mère a ri. Sa mère était très coulante pour les enfants. Mais, mais, justement, après, quand ils avaient dix-huit ans, alors à ce moment-là . . . Zaza adorait sa mère. Comme elle avait été très gentille, l'air très gentille, très coulante, très affectueuse, on ne peut pas se révolter contre une mère pareille. Tandis que maman, qui était très maladroite, qui nous heurtait, qui était quelquefois très brutale, on se révolte en ce moment-là.

YAP: Et on a besoin de pouvoir se révolter.

HdeB: C'est beaucoup plus sain. La révolte c'est sans doute très pénible pour les parents, mais je crois que c'est très sain. Zaza ne s'est pas révoltée et elle en est morte. Simone en a raconté l'histoire que vous connaissez bien. Madame Lacoin était une belle femme du Midi, très affable, mais en même temps elle était très mondaine. Elle pensait qu'aller au bal c'était un devoir autant que d'aller à la messe. Un devoir social. Zaza ne s'est jamais révoltée. Parce que, justement, on ne se révoltait pas contre Mme Lacoin.

YAP: Faisiez-vous un grand effort pour faire plaisir à votre mère?

HdeB: Généralement, mais pas toujours. Simone avait une amie que j'aimais beaucoup. Et comme elle se mariait, elle nous a invitées. Alors j'ai dit oui, ça me ferait plaisir d'y aller. Je ne sais pas pourquoi, mais maman m'a dit: "Non, tu n'as pas besoin d'y aller, tu n'iras pas à ce mariage." "Pourquoi?" "Tu n'iras pas, tu n'iras pas, tu n'iras pas." J'ai dit: "Si, j'irai," puis j'y ai été. Alors elle a été très peinée, très coléreuse. Mais maman était comme ça, quand elle se mettait une chose dans la tête. Alors elle a été chez Mme Lacoin, et puis Mme Lacoin m'a convoquée et m'a dit: "Je sais bien que ta mère n'a pas toujours été une très bonne éducatrice mais quand même vous lui devez du respect," etc.

YAP: Mme Lacoin pensait donc qu'il fallait toujours obéir à sa mère.

HdeB: Quand j'étais petite, bien sûr, je lui ai obéi, mais là, je n'ai pas obéi. J'y ai été. C'est pour ça qu'elle a été parler à Mme Lacoin. Ah, non, j'ai commencé à désobéir. Parce que je trouvais que c'était idiot. Et Simone aussi, Simone aussi. Maman commençait à trouver que Simone avait une mauvaise influence sur moi. Elle voulait m'empêcher de voir Simone. Comment est-ce qu'on peut empêcher deux soeurs qui vivent ensemble de se voir?

YAP: On aurait pensé qu'elle préférerait que vous soyez ensemble.

HdeB: Non, parce qu'elle se rendait compte que Simone avait perdu la foi. Elle espérait encore faire de moi une jeune fille bien sage. Elle avait compris que Simone ne serait plus jamais une jeune fille bien sage.

YAP: Elle était jalouse aussi peut-être.

HdeB: Elle était jalouse aussi peut-être. Je me rappelle une fois, j'avais écrit à Simone, en cachet de maman, puisque Simone était justement chez Zaza dans les Landes, et puis j'ai dû aller mettre la lettre à la poste. Et elle m'a surprise. Moi, j'avais dix-sept ans déjà. Elle a ouvert la lettre et elle l'a lue. J'ai été folle de rage. Et puis je lui en ai tellement voulu. C'était très maladroit. Maman a été très maladroite. Et en même temps, ah, elle était tellement sans méchanceté, la pauvre, mais . . .

YAP: Elle faisait de son mieux mais elle ne savait pas comment . . .

HdeB: Ah, vous savez, elle s'était trop préparée à ce rôle de mère de famille. Elle avait suivi des conférences, et puis, comme je vous ai dit, les rapports entre mère et filles étaient tellement faussement montés. On disait par exemple: "Une jeune fille n'a pas de meilleure amie que sa mère. Une jeune fille doit tout dire à sa mère." Or, je ne crois qu'aucune jeune fille ne dit tout à sa mère. Est-ce que vous avez toujours tout dit à votre mère?

YAP: Mais non. Quand j'étais très petite, peut-être, mais après ça . . .

HdeB: Je suis sûre que même si on n'a pas fait des choses extraordinaires, on n'a pas envie de tout dire. Et maman ne nous permettait pas d'avoir une vie personnelle. C'est pour ça que nous nous étions révoltées. Quand j'étais petite, au Cours Désir, les mamans avaient le droit d'assister aux cours. Jusqu'à l'âge de dix ans. Et maman ne manquait pas un de mes cours. Avec son ouvrage, elle faisait des grandes tapisseries au petit point, des recouverts de fauteuils, des tapisseries au petit point . . .

YAP: Tous les jours?

HdeB: Enfin, nous avions des cours deux fois par semaine. Deux fois par semaine elle était là, derrière la table. Et alors si je disais une bêtise—bon, ça arrive quand on est enfant de dire une bêtise—la bêtise était repartie, toute la famille savait que j'avais dit une bêtise. Enfin, il y a une histoire que je trouve très très caractéristique des faux rapports qu'on nous montrait entre mère et fille. Nous étions de petites catholiques. Et avant la première communion, tous les ans il y avait la retraite. On passait trois ou quatre jours, toute la journée, au Cours Désir, mais sans aller en classe. On allait à la chapelle du Cours Désir. On écoutait l'aumônier, qui nous faisait de grands sermons, et c'était une journée assez sage, très très paisible. Et puis nous devions écrire nos pensées les plus secrètes sur un carnet. Mais maman lisait mon carnet. Et puis quelquefois elle se moquait un peu de moi. C'est maladroit, parce que nous n'avions pas le droit d'avoir une vie personnelle. Et les enfants ont besoin d'une vie personnelle. C'est pour ça que quand je vois aujourd'hui des parents qui veulent faire un ami de leurs enfants et qui veulent les accompagner en classe, je crois que c'est triste.

YAP: Les enfants ont besoin de se séparer de leurs parents.

HdeB: Nous avons eu encore une grande marge de liberté parce que maman faisait des visites toute la journée, beaucoup de visites, et Simone et moi nous nous dévouions à nos jeux. C'était très secret, et si une grande personne entrait comme nous jouions, on cessait immédiatement de jouer.

YAP: Une vie personnelle enfin.

HdeB: Mais on l'a volée, cette vie personnelle. Et ça ne lui plaisait pas encore. Quand maman nous entendait, elle essayait d'écouter. Et je vais vous raconter une histoire. Je crois que ça va vous amuser. Il s'agit justement de la retraite. La veille de la première communion, l'aumônier a dit—maman était là, naturellement elle était toujours là, dans la tribune, elle écoutait tout—"Mes enfants, ce soir, vous devriez vous asseoir sur les genoux de votre chère maman, vous lui direz 'Maman, je vous demande pardon de tout le mal que j'ai pu vous faire.'" Et je me suis dit: "Maman attend que je fasse ça." Et j'ai senti toute petite que c'était en effet de la comédie. Et je ne l'ai pas fait. Elle m'a dit: "Ah, tu n'es pas venue te réfugier auprès de moi." Et je n'ai pas expliqué pourquoi mais elle a dû comprendre. J'en ai senti vraiment la comédie, l'hypocrisie, la sottise enfin. Bon, nos vrais rapports c'était quelquefois des scènes. Quelquefois maman pleurait, elle pleurait facilement parce qu'elle était malheureuse. Elle pleurait, et puis je l'embrassais et on s'était réconciliées.

YAP: Il y avait beaucoup d'affection quand même.

HdeB: Dans la famille il y avait beaucoup d'affection, beaucoup de cris, beaucoup de colères. Nous étions tous les quatre forts. Papa était très violent. Et en effet maman était violente aussi. Et je pense que Simone et moi nous avions chacune notre violence. Moi j'étais la moins violente. Mais enfin, quand même, nous tous entrions en colère. Nous étions capables d'entrer en colère.

YAP: Il est quelquefois très nécessaire de pouvoir exprimer sa colère.

HdeB: Oui. Mais c'était une famille agitée, ce n'était pas une famille paisible. Pas du tout, pas du tout. Et plus nous grandissions, moins c'était paisible. Alors Simone me défendait toujours. Elle était toujours de mon côté. Elle a su m'aider plus que moi je n'ai pu l'aider, parce que tout de même elle était plus grande que moi.

YAP: Et le rôle de la religion? Vous avez été élevée comme une bonne petite catholique.

HdeB: J'ai été très pieuse. J'y ai cru, tout en me disant: "Oh, mon Dieu, que la vie serait belle si Dieu n'existait pas." Je crois que si je n'avais pas été croyante, ma révolte aurait été beaucoup plus directe. J'ai été vraiment très croyante.

YAP: Jusqu'à quel âge? Est-ce que vous avez jamais parlé avec votre mère de votre changement d'attitude?

HdeB: J'ai dû le cacher, parce que je savais qu'avec Simone, quand elle en avait parlé, elle avait eu un grand chagrin. Alors le dimanche matin, tous les dimanches matins, je faisais semblant d'aller à la messe, et j'allais au Musée du Louvre. Je connaissais—maintenant il a beaucoup changé—je connaissais le Musée du Louvre vraiment comme ma poche. Je connaissais la moindre petite salle.

YAP: C'était peut-être le commencement de votre inspiration artistique.

HdeB: J'ai beaucoup vu de peintures, bonnes et mauvaises.

YAP: Et vous l'avez toujours caché à votre mère?

HdeB: Ah oui. Et même je lui ai toujours caché que Lionel et moi ne nous sommes mariés que civilement. Je lui ai toujours fait croire que nous étions mariés religieusement. Et comme je me suis mariée au Portugal pendant la guerre, c'était facile à lui faire croire. Alors elle m'a dit mais comment, parce que normalement il faut un certificat de baptême. Et je lui ai dit: "Mais écoutez, c'était la guerre." J'ai été baptisée en Limousin, parce que ma marraine, c'était ma tante Hélène, la soeur de papa qui habitait à La Grillère. "Mais écoutez, au Portugal je ne pouvais pas quand même demander mon certificat de baptême." C'est ce que j'ai dit à maman. "Et puis Lionel est protestant, oui, mais on s'est mariés à la sacristie. Puisque c'était la guerre . . ." Parce que vous savez, vous devez le savoir parce que votre famille a été catholique, c'est pire de se marier civilement que de vivre ensemble. Maman n'était pas très très sûre que j'étais croyante.

YAP: Elle ne posait pas de questions, elle préférait ne pas savoir.

HdeB: Je crois qu'elle préférait ne pas me poser de questions personnelles. Elle a dit à une de mes cousines: "Oh, pas la peine d'aller au ciel si je n'y retrouve pas tous les miens." Elle se demandait tout de même si papa, Simone et moi nous allions au ciel. Et ça lui faisait de la peine.

YAP: Ça a dû être bien difficile pour elle. Il y a toute cette histoire de la raison pour laquelle Mme Lacoin ne voulait pas que Zaza épouse Merleau-Ponty, et c'était parce que lui était un enfant illégitime, n'est-ce pas? Mais Simone ne le savait pas.

HdeB: Ah, non. Ce qu'elle a dit dans ses mémoires, c'est tout ce qu'elle savait, elle a vraiment dit tout ce qu'elle savait. Mais du reste c'est une telle horreur d'aller dire à Maurice Merleau-Ponty, qui n'en savait rien: "Vous n'êtes pas le fils de votre père. Vous êtes un enfant illégitime. Vous et votre soeur vous êtes des enfants illégitimes." Et alors c'est pour ça que Merleau-Ponty, pensant qu'il n'était pas assez bien pour Zaza, s'est un peu retiré.

YAP: La famille de Zaza était une famille bien pensante.

HdeB: Oh là là. Oh là là. Justement, ils étaient tous tellement d'accord que Zaza ne pouvait pas s'échapper. Tandis que moi, dans ma famille, toutes les femmes allaient à la messe, aucun homme n'y allait. Le dimanche matin, tous les hommes, mon grand-père, mes oncles, papa, restaient au lit et les femmes allaient à la messe. Alors, on pensait quand même que la religion, c'est bon pour les femmes et les enfants. Et puis on disait que les hommes, c'était la partie tout de même la plus intelligente et la plus extraordinaire de la famille. Alors pourquoi est-ce qu'ils ne croient pas en Dieu, quand même? On se pose la question. Parce que vraiment c'est pour les femmes et les enfants.

YAP: Et les membres de la famille comme la cousine Jeanne par exemple . . .

HdeB: Oh, mais son père n'allait pas à la messe. C'était le frère de papa. Il n'allait pas à la messe non plus. Sa mère était aussi comme maman, une jeune fille provinciale. Elle était de Périgueux, maman était de Verdun. Nous allions à la messe tous les dimanches et il n'y avait guère que des femmes et des enfants. Très peu d'hommes pratiquaient, et on se moquait d'eux. Les autres se moquaient un petit peu d'eux. Mon père se moquait d'eux. Nous avions un ou deux hommes pratiquants dans la famille, et ça me faisait de la peine parce que la famille les rejetait. Aucun homme ne pratiquait.

YAP: Est-ce que vous avez considéré votre mère comme modèle à un certain moment de votre vie?

HdeB: Oh non, jamais. Jamais, non. Non, parce que je ne l'ai jamais sentie vraiment heureuse. D'abord parce qu'il y a eu la guerre, et après ça parce que papa l'a rendue malheureuse. Non, très petite, jusqu'à cinq ans, . . . il n'y avait pas de problème. Mais je ne crois pas qu'un enfant de cinq ans se dise: "Ma mère est un modèle." Elle est unique, alors tout est bien, les parents sont parfaits, tout est parfait. Et puis le jour où nous avons commencé à nous poser des questions, nous nous sommes rendu compte que maman n'était pas heureuse. Au fond, j'ai toujours été une révoltée. Je crois que je suis devenue vraiment féministe sans le savoir très jeune. Parce que j'étais assez révoltée par la vie des femmes. J'ai un souvenir, par exemple. Maman était rentrée d'un goûter de dames et elle me disait: "Oh, Madame une Telle"—cette dame avait perdu un fils à la guerre—"dit: 'J'ai eu vingt ans de bonheur parfait.'"

Peut-être pour se consoler de la mort de son fils. Et je me suis dit: "Mais ce bonheur-là, moi je n'en veux pas." Je me suis vraiment révoltée même contre le bonheur de ces dames: "Moi, je veux une autre vie." Je ne sais pas pourquoi, mais je sais que j'ai commencé très très très très jeune. J'ai refusé, cela commençait par le refus de la vie des femmes qui m'entouraient. Je ne savais pas absolument ce que je voulais, mais c'est déjà quelque chose.

YAP: Est-ce vrai, ce que Simone a dit dans *Une Mort très douce,* que votre mère se sentait plus à l'aise avec vous qu'avec Simone?

HdeB: Oui. Simone l'intimidait. Moi je ne l'intimidais pas.

YAP: Et pourquoi? Qu'est-ce qui a fait la différence? Simone était plus osée dans ce qu'elle lui disait?

HdeB: Simone faisait attention mais elle ne trouvait pas de point de contact avec maman. Moi j'en trouvais. J'entrais plus facilement dans des petites conversations, plus féminines si vous voulez. Je lui parlais de ses amies, de ses petites histoires. Elle sentait que ça n'intéressait pas Simone. Elle avait un petit peu peur de la supériorité intellectuelle de Simone. Elle avait peur que Simone ne la juge pas bien. Je ne sais pas, moi, j'étais plus ... elle me sentait plus proche, mais Simone lui faisait un petit peu peur.

YAP: Le portrait de votre mère que Simone a présenté dans ses oeuvres, est-ce que vous croyez que c'est un portrait assez vrai?

HdeB: Oh oui, très vrai. Mais je trouve qu'il y a des jugements un peu durs. Justement quelquefois elle est un peu dure dans ses mémoires, parce qu'elle a des rancunes de petite fille qu'on n'efface pas, des rongeurs, blessures qui ne s'arrangent pas. Elle a raconté certains épisodes qui l'ont blessée dans son enfance. Mais je trouve que dans *Une Mort très douce* elle a vraiment compris maman, ce qu'était la vie de maman ... les souffrances de maman, la tristesse, pourquoi maman était cette jeune femme ... Vous savez, on se révolte contre la dureté d'une mère. Mais quand on comprend que cette dureté vient d'un malheur profond, alors on comprend. Elle était neurasthénique, et c'est vrai, ce n'est pas gai pour les enfants d'être élevés par une mère neurasthénique, mais elle avait des raisons d'être neurasthénique. Elle était très malheureuse et elle avait l'air de penser que si elle disait qu'elle était très malheureuse, ça veut dire: "Georges, tu me rends trop malheureuse." Jamais, jamais, jamais. Elle disait: "Je suis heureuse, je suis très heureuse en ménage." Son intime amie, celle qui m'a raconté beaucoup de choses, m'a dit:

"Mais vous savez, jamais, jamais elle n'a avoué qu'elle était malheureuse." Je savais qu'elle était malheureuse.

YAP: Ça l'aurait aidée de l'avouer.

HdeB: Ça l'aurait aidée de le lui avouer, à cette amie. C'était une femme gentille qui l'aimait beaucoup et qu'elle aimait beaucoup. Mais elle ne se confiait pas.

YAP: C'était sans doute à cause de son tempérament. Et ça ne faisait pas partie de son éducation non plus.

HdeB: Ça ne faisait pas partie de son éducation, bien sûr. C'était l'époque. Et puis elle admettait que sa mère n'avait jamais eu de rapports très intimes avec elle. Sa mère avait toujours été assez froide.

YAP: Mais elle, elle n'a jamais été vraiment froide avec vous et avec Simone?

HdeB: Non, non, pas froide. Maman nous embrassait beaucoup, elle aimait beaucoup nous embrasser. Toute la famille est affectueuse. Moi, c'est pour ça que je me plais tellement en Italie. On s'embrassait beaucoup. Je crois qu'en Amérique on s'embrasse très peu en famille, n'est-ce pas?

YAP: Ça dépend. Dans les familles d'une tradition européenne, et surtout méditerranéenne, on s'embrasse tout le temps. Les hommes mêmes. Et ça semble peut-être un peu étrange pour les autres Américains d'héritage plutôt anglo-saxon.

HdeB: Une fois, j'ai vu un petit garçon qui partait pour l'école. Sa mère allait l'embrasser et il a dit: "Non, on n'embrasse pas les garçons." C'est important quand même qu'en Europe un enfant n'a pas peur de laisser sa mère l'embrasser.

YAP: Est-ce que vous avez jamais considéré la possibilité d'avoir des enfants vous-même?

HdeB: Non. J'ai une amie qui fait une enquête pour le journal *Autrement* sur la question de la maternité, et elle est venue m'interviewer justement sur mon non-désir d'enfant. Alors la directrice, enfin la rédactrice-en-chef, lui a dit de me poser la question: "Est-ce que la création remplace les enfants?" Je lui ai dit que c'est une question idiote. Je n'ai pas remplacé un désir d'enfant parce que je n'ai jamais eu un désir d'enfant et je ne crois pas avoir été stérile. Je n'ai aucune raison de penser que j'ai été stérile. Mais simplement je n'ai pas voulu d'enfant parce que j'avais une telle ambition de peintre que je savais que ç'aurait été très très difficile de faire mon métier avec des enfants, même un enfant. Un enfant, ça vous absorbe. On n'a pas le droit de sacrifier l'enfant. Un mari on peut le sacrifier dans certaines occasions. Bon, s'il est malade, on s'occupe de lui, mais enfin dans l'ensemble, un adulte, il a sa vie. Mais un enfant, il vit par vous. Je n'ai pas voulu courir ce risque.

YAP: C'est une question de temps.

HdeB: En partie. Beaucoup de peintres, surtout d'artistes comme moi, ont besoin de temps. J'ai toujours eu besoin de beaucoup de temps. J'ai toujours travaillé comme si je devais vivre cent ans. Je ne sais pas si je vivrai cent ans. Je ne suis pas jeune, mais j'aurai eu le temps de beaucoup travailler.

YAP: Que pensez-vous de la façon contemporaine d'élever les enfants?

HdeB: Je crois que dans mon village on les élève très mal. Je connais des jeunes couples qui élèvent très bien leurs enfants, il y a encore des gens qui les élèvent bien. Mais j'ai l'impression que justement les gens qui élèvent bien leurs enfants, ils ont compris qu'un enfant n'est pas un copain. On disait: "Que les enfants fassent tout ce qu'ils veuillent." J'ai eu une amie, il y a vraiment longtemps, qui disait: "Il ne faut pas que je donne des complexes à mon fils." Et j'ai connu une famille, une famille assez aisée, très bonne bourgeoisie. Ils ont eu quatre fils. Et ils ont eu pour principe qu'il ne faut jamais contrarier un enfant. Même si l'enfant se promène au bord d'un précipice, il ne faut rien dire, il faut que les enfants fassent ce qu'ils veulent. Le résultat, c'est quatre enfants qui n'avaient vraiment eu pas de problèmes, qui étaient choisis, qui avaient des parents qui les aimaient, qui avaient tout pour être heureux, et tous les quatre se sont drogués. Un a commencé à quatorze ans, il y en a un qui s'en est sorti, et l'aîné est à vingt-cinq ans complètement gâteux. Alors ce n'est pas une réclame pour une éducation très permissive.

YAP: Très differente de votre éducation à vous.

HdeB: Ah oui. Je ne crois pas non plus qu'il faut battre les enfants, mais je pense qu'il faut un peu d'autorité. Maman nous traitait souvent sévèrement, mais ça c'est une chose que je n'aurais jamais reproché à ma mère. On nous donnait un certain sens de la discipline, et ça m'a aidée toute ma vie. Si on fait une chose très librement, comme je fais la peinture, si on n'est pas discipliné, alors on n'arrive à rien. Ecoutez, quelquefois les gens me disent: "Mais vous travaillez quand vous êtes inspirée?" Et je dis: "Je travaille quand c'est l'heure de travailler."

YAP: Votre soeur avait elle aussi ce besoin de travailler.

HdeB: Je pense que ce n'est pas mal. Et je pense que mes parents ont dû me donner aussi cette discipline. Alors, maintenant dans mon village, les enfants, les parents vraiment démissionnent, mais je pense que les paysans sont toujours en retard sur la bourgeoisie. Cette démission de la bourgeoisie, c'est maintenant qu'elle vient dans mon village. Résultat: les enfants sont très mal élevés, des petits vandales. J'en sais quelque chose parce qu'on m'a cassé beaucoup de choses chez moi. Et ces enfants ne sont pas plus heureux.

YAP: Quels sont les conseils que vous donneriez à une femme de vingt ans en ce qui concerne le mariage, la maternité, la vie en général?

HdeB: C'est difficile de donner des conseils. Je lui dirais surtout de faire ce qu'elle a envie de faire. Je suis sûre que le seul conseil qu'on peut donner aux jeunes, c'est de faire ce qu'ils ont envie de faire profondément. Pas faire ce que la femme croit bon, parce qu'elle a entendu d'ailleurs que c'était bien, ou parce qu'elle pense que les gens trouveront que c'est bien. Il faut faire exactement ce qu'on a profondément envie de faire. Je crois que c'est ça le seul conseil que je puisse jamais donner aux jeunes.

Notes

Author's note: All translations in the text from the original French are my own.

Introduction

1. Margaret Sanger, *Motherhood in Bondage* (London: Brentano's Ltd., 1928).

2. Philip Wylie, *Generation of Vipers*. (New York: Farrar and Rinehart, 1942).

3. Hans Sebald, *Momism: The Silent Disease of America* (Chicago: Nelson Hall, 1976).

4. Betty Friedan, *The Feminine Mystique* (New York: W. W. Norton & Company, 1963).

5. Betty Friedan, *The Second Stage* (New York, Summit Books, 1981), p. 258.

6. Shirley L. Radl, *Mother's Day Is Over* (New York: Charterhouse l, 1973).

7. Jessie Bernard, *The Future of Motherhood* (New York: The Dial Press, 1974).

8. Adrienne Rich, *Of Woman Born* (New York: W. W. Norton & Company, 1976).

9. Albert Memmi, *Dominated Man* (Boston: Beacon, 1968), pp. 150–51, as quoted in Rich, ibid., p. 251.

10. Dorothy Dinnerstein, *The Mermaid and the Minotaur, Sexual Arrangements and Human Malaise* (New York: Harper & Row, 1976).

11. Nancy Friday, *My Mother/My Self, The Daughter's Search for Identity* (New York: Dell Publishing Company, 1977), p. 19.

12. Albert Camus, *The Stranger* (New York: Vintage Books, Random House, 1946).

13. Nancy Chodorow, *The Reproduction of Mothering* (Berkeley: University of California Press, 1978).

14. Kim Chernin, *In My Mother's House* (New Haven and New York: Ticknor and Fields, 1983).

15. Christina Crawford, *Mommie Dearest* (New York: Berkley Publishing Corporation, 1981).

16. Kim Chernin, *The Hungry Self* (New York: Times Books, Random House, 1985).

17. Carole Klein, *Mothers and Sons* (Boston: Houghton Mifflin Company, 1984).

18. Mercedes Lynch Maloney and Anne Maloney, *The Hand That Rocks the Cradle* (Englewood Cliffs, New Jersey: Prentice Hall, 1985).

19. Julie Kettle Gundlac, *My Mother before Me* (Secaucus, New Jersey: Lyle Stewart, 1986).

20. Beppie Harrison, *The Shock of Motherhood* (New York: Scribners, 1986).

21. Phyllis Chesler, *Mothers on Trial* (New York: McGraw-Hill, 1986).

22. Sue Miller, *The Good Mother* (New York: Harper & Row, 1986).

23. Danièle, "Un Accouchement, un avortement," *Les Temps Modernes*, no. 333/334 (April/May 1974), p. 1831: "Un avortement n'est pas, on ne me le fera pas croire, une péripétie médicale comme l'arrachage d'une dent."

24. *Les Temps Modernes*, no. 333–334 (April-May 1974), p. 2028: "Tout seul on n'est rien."

25. Françoise Collin, "Féminitude et féminisme," *Cahiers du GRIF*, no. 1 (November 1973), pp. 5–22.

26. Françoise Collin, "Les Enfants de tous," *Cahiers du GRIF*, no. 9/10 (December 1975), p. 4: "Mariées ou non, nous sommes toutes . . . d'une certaine manière des 'mères célibataires.'"

27. Françoise Collin, "Humour en amour," *Cahiers du GRIF*, no. 17/18 (September 1977), p. 5: "La maternité semble, en bonheur ou en malheur, paralysante."

28. Françoise d'Eaubonne, "La Mère indifférente," *Cahiers du GRIF*, no. 17/18 (September 1977), p. 28: "de se prolonger et de léguer le meilleur de lui à un être jeune qu'il aide à devenir adulte, qu'il veut rendre quelqu'un d'utile et d'heureux."

29. Julia Kristeva, Interview, *Cahiers du GRIF*, no. 32 (Winter 1982) p. 8: "Dans toute relation passionnelle on retrouve l'ombre de la mère."

30. Yvonne Knibiehler and Catherine Fouquet, *L'Histoire des mères, du Moyen Age à nos jours* (Paris: Editions Montalba, 1980).

31. Ibid., p. 168: "Toute femme est une école . . . et c'est d'elle que les générations reçoivent vraiment leur croyance."

32. Elisabeth Badinter, *L'Amour en plus* (Paris: Flammarion, 1980).

33. Ibid., p. 470: "Apparemment, l'amour maternel n'est plus l'apanage des femmes."

34. Luce Irigaray, *Et l'une ne bouge pas sans l'autre* (Paris: Les Editions de Minuit, 1979), p. 7: "Avec ton lait, ma mère, j'ai bu la glace. Et me voilà maintenant avec ce gel à l'intérieur."

35. Luce Irigaray, *Le Corps-à-corps avec la mère* (Ottawa: Les Editions de la Pleine Lune, 1981), p. 21: "telle la mère vers laquelle on ne devrait pas se retourner."

36. Ibid., p. 23: "La blessure imparable, et irréparable, est celle de la coupure du cordon."

37. Ibid., p. 86: "Donc une mère, c'est quoi? Quelqu'une qui fait des gestes commandés, stéréotypés, qui n'a pas de langage personnel et qui n'a pas d'identité."

38. Christine Collange, *Moi, ta mère* (Paris: Fayard, 1985), p. 42.

39. Ibid., p. 161: "femmes héroïques, femmes pélicanes qui sacrifiaient leur destinée personnelle pour remplir leur mission maternelle."

40. Ibid., p. 172: "Plus j'y réfléchis, moins je suis convaincue qu'il soit absolument indispensable que mes enfants me 'tuent' pour devenir adultes."

41. Anne-Marie de Vilaine, Laurence Gavarini, Michèle Le Coadic, "Avant-Propos," *Maternité en mouvement,* a collective work (Grenoble: Presses Universitaires de Grenoble, 1986), p. 12: "d'une part, analyser notre rapport ambivalent et complexe à notre mère, à la Mère, au maternel, d'autre part, combler le vide théorique du mouvement des femmes en France concernant la maternité."

42. Jacqueline Feldman, "Au risque de les perdre . . . ," *Maternité en mouvement,* p. 32: "Féminisme, la liberté d'être; maternité, l'attachement à des êtres; féminisme, la révolte contre la société; maternité, tout le poids de la responsabilité sociale."

43. Elisabeth Badinter, "La Solution: une mutation des pères . . . ," *Maternité en mouvement,* p. 37: "effaçant de bonne grâce la femme qui demeure sous la mère."

44. Michèle Le Coadic, "Pour une convivialité conflictuelle," *Maternité en mouvement,* p. 52: "un risque de mort appelé sacrifice de soi."

45. Françoise Gavarini, "L'Institution des rôles et la négation de l'amour," *Maternité en mouvement,* p. 55: "faisant de nos rapports une préparation à ses désirs. Tu as été pleinement mère, et totalement absente. Femme, où es-tu? Je ne t'ai jamais rencontrée."

46. Ibid., p. 56: "Maternité, je te hais. . . . Tu as transformé ma puissance créatrice en procréation, . . . ces vies sorties de ma vie et de ma rencontre avec un Autre, en objets familiaux."

47. Anne-Marie de Vilaine, "Mère/fille/mère: j'aurais aimé nous inventer une autre histoire . . . ," *Maternité en mouvement,* p. 58: "Comment peut-on revendiquer la sororité entre femmes et refuser toute solidarité avec la mère? Qu'est-ce qui fait qu'une femme n'a plus le droit à notre écoute, notre sympathie, notre compréhension parce qu'elle est notre mère?"

48. Annie Leclerc, "Enfantement et création," *Maternité en mouvement,* p. 129: "Quand l'enfant devient le plus haut degré d'expression possible de la mère, sa réalisation ultime, quelle perte de soi pour la mère, quelle chaîne pour l'enfant!"

49. Françoise Hurstel, "Sans regret," Interview with Hélène de Beauvoir, *Autrement,* no. 90 (May 1987), p. 104: "Ils l'ont étouffée tout simplement. Et c'est la folie et la mort qui ont été sa seule issue."

50. Corinne Alexandre Garner, "Fils de . . . ," *Autrement,* no. 90, p. 37: "Si, adulte, il sait qu'elle ne peut physiquement le suivre partout, il découvre qu'elle est encore partout, toujours, non pas avec lui, mais en lui."

51. Jean-Marc Terrasse, "Et demain . . . ," Interview with Elisabeth Badinter, *Autrement,* no. 90, p. 49: "Un vampire, il est chronophage, il vous vole votre temps."

52. Jean-Marc Terrasse, "Règlement de contes," *Autrement,* no. 90, p. 111: "La mère tente de tuer la fille devenue femme mais c'est la fille qui tuera la femme dans la mère en devenant femme à son tour. Sa féminité exclut et annihile celle de la mère."

53. Jean-Jacques Rousseau, *Les Confessions,* as quoted in *Autrement,* no. 90, p. 219: "Je coûtai la vie à ma mère, et ma naissance fut le premier de mes malheurs."

Chapter 1

1. Simone de Beauvoir, *Quand prime le spirituel* (Paris: Gallimard, 1979), p. vii: "J'avais mis beaucoup de moi-même dans cet ouvrage. J'étais en révolte contre le spiritualisme qui m'avait longtemps opprimée et je voulais exprimer ce dégoût à travers l'histoire de jeunes femmes que je connaissais et qui en avaient été les victimes plus ou moins consentantes."

2. Ibid., p. 144: "Je sais ce que c'est qu'un homme; ils parlent d'idéal mais ils sont pleins d'ignobles désirs."

3. Ibid., p. 139: "Crois bien que si je n'avais pensé qu'à mon plaisir, tu ne serais pas de ce monde."

4. Ibid., p. 137: "Ils ont l'air de me tenir pour responsable . . . moi aussi j'ai envie d'être débarrassée d'elle . . . je vais la secouer un peu. Tes devoirs d'Etat à présent sont ceux d'une épouse et d'une mère, c'est immoral ce refus de remplir ta mission de femme . . . un pauvre parasite, un déchet, comme la cousine Marie, voilà ce qu'elle va devenir, ça fait beau dans une famille; Jésus a maudit le figuier stérile, je saurai l'obliger à accepter son rôle social, à remplir la destinée que Vous lui avez assignée; toutes ses amies sont mariées."

5. Ibid., p. 135: "Elle est comme j'étais à son âge, trop sensible; c'est à moi d'être forte pour elle."

6. Ibid., p. 146: "J'ai été comme toi; mais on apprend à ne pas s'écouter."

7. Ibid., p. 145: "C'était atroce de torturer cette enfant, mais il fallait penser à son salut, non à son bonheur."

8. Ibid., p. 160: "Depuis trois ans je n'ai pas cessé de lutter; pour chacun des livres que j'ai lus, chaque sortie, chaque pensée, j'ai lutté. Je m'étais juré de ne jamais causer à maman aucune peine et je n'ai pas cessé de la tourmenter. Quand je lui cédais, je me sentais méprisable; quand je résistais, je me haïssais. . . . Je n'en peux plus, Chantal."

9. Ibid., p. 175: "J'étais si heureuse quand j'étais petite. . . . Il faudra que je vous dise un jour, Pascal, ce que maman a su faire de notre enfance."

10. Ibid., p. 134: "Jamais je n'aurais dû lui permettre de continuer ses études, ça a été ma première faute, on devient compliqué et orgueilleux. Je hais ces intellectuels . . . . Je ne laisserai pas les premiers venus compromettre son salut. La marier au plus vite."

11. Ibid., p. 138: "Jadis, c'était d'elle seule que dépendaient les joies et les peines de son enfant."

12. Ibid., p. 188: "Anne, ma petite sainte, . . . prie pour moi, pauvre pécheresse. Aide-moi à accepter sans murmure d'avoir été l'instrument de ta souffrance, de ton salut."

13. Ibid., p. 7: "Mme Drouffe avait pour Marcelle une dévotion passionnée, mais elle n'était ni très intelligente, ni très cultivée; Marcelle l'adorait, naturellement, cependant elle se sentait très seule auprès de sa mère: souvent elle ne pouvait pas s'empêcher de lui répondre avec dureté."

14. Ibid., p. 204: "J'étais dans la vie comme une visiteuse qui n'ose toucher à rien; maman

et Marcelle . . . avaient ainsi des airs de parents pauvres: seul Denis paraissait chez lui et c'était à lui qu'il fallait s'adresser pour obtenir la clef qui ouvre toutes les portes."

15. Ibid., p. 248: "Le monde brillait comme un sou neuf; je ne savais pas encore ce que je voulais en faire mais tout était possible puisque au centre des choses, à cette place que Denis avait laissée vide, voici que je me trouvais moi-même."

16. Ibid., p. 13: "Ces êtres d'exception, c'étaient aussi des hommes, de grands enfants maladroits comme sont tous les hommes. Elle eût aimé mettre de l'ordre dans leurs chambres, vérifier le noeud de leur cravate et recoudre leurs boutons comme elle faisait pour Pascal. Son admiration pour eux se nuança d'une affection maternelle."

17. Ibid., p. 36: "bouleversée de voir cet enfant sur qui elle veillait maternellement pendant le jour se métamorphoser en un jeune mâle impérieux."

18. Ibid., p. 62: "Quel idéal de vie libre, intelligente et heureuse elle devait représenter pour ces enfants!"

19. Ibid., p. 70: "un univers infiniment riche et pourtant accessible."

20. Ibid., p. 83: "tous deux éclatant de jeunesse, tous deux purs et beaux."

21. Ibid., p. 84: "Sur un invisible autel se célèbrent les mystères de la jeunesse et de l'amour et j'incline mon front avec ferveur."

22. Ibid., p. 85: "Si quelque fée bienveillante ne se penchait sur la jeunesse et sur l'amour, ces fleurs fragiles seraient vite brisées par les mains grossières des hommes. J'aime que grâce à moi, un peu plus de beauté, un peu plus de bonheur aient embaumé un instant le monde."

23. Ibid., p. 100: "Ils auraient pu me compromettre. . . . Toute cette boue!"

24. Ibid.: "Les voilà entièrement reprises par leurs familles. . . . Un moment elle médita tristement sur l'ingratitude de l'enfance."

25. Ibid., p. 101: "A l'aurore de ces jeunes vies se dresserait pour jamais sa fine silhouette, . . . une silhouette un peu énigmatique, un peu paradoxale dont l'apparition dans un vieux lycée de province avait été un tel éblouissement."

26. Ibid., p. 91: "une grosse bosse au milieu du ventre."

27. Ibid., p. 93: "une mystérieuse pourriture . . . en train de s'épanouir."

28. Ibid., p. 102: "Elle ferait des tricots, le soir elle écouterait la T.S.F., elle essaierait d'aimer son enfant, pour se consoler. Andrée la verrait deux fois par an peut-être, et bientôt elles n'auraient plus rien à se dire."

29. Ibid., p. 91: "Porter toute l'année la même robe, déjeuner au lycée pour six francs, ne jamais voyager, ne jamais sortir, cela permettait d'être épousée un jour par un petit fonctionnaire désireux d'améliorer son train de vie."

30. Ibid., p. 103: "Un jour, malgré tout, je finirai bien par ne plus être jeune."

31. Ibid., p. 120: "Je trouve horrible qu'on puisse en être réduit à se servir de sa tête comme d'un gagne-pain. Tout mon avenir, le pain que je mangerai: mon charbon, mes souliers, c'est de mon cerveau que je dois tout attendre. Un cerveau, c'est fragile, c'est si fragile."

32. Ibid., p. 121: "Etre assise dans une chambre tiède et caresser sans mots cette tête d'archange qu'il poserait enfin sur ses genoux; pas de baisers."

33. Ibid., p. 127: "Elle n'a pas envie que sa fille soit comme nous; on la comprend."

34. Mary Evans, *Simone de Beauvoir, A Feminist Mandarin* (London and New York: Tavistock, 1985).

35. Judith Okely, *Simone de Beauvoir* (New York: Virago/Pantheon, 1986), p. 23.

36. Terry Keefe, *Simone de Beauvoir* (London: Harrap, 1983), p. 144.

Chapter 2

1. Appendix A.

2. Simone de Beauvoir, *L'Invitée* (Paris: Gallimard, 1943), p. 142: "Quand Françoise se retrouvait dans cet appartement, il lui semblait que toutes ces années ne l'avaient menée nulle part; le temps s'étalait autour d'elle en une mare stagnante et douceâtre. Vivre c'était vieillir."

3. Claude Francis and Fernande Gontier, *Les Ecrits de Simone de Beauvoir* (Paris: Gallimard, 1979).

4. *L'Invitée*, p. 386: "Avec étonnement, elle contempla un instant cette rue affairée, lucide, où toutes choses avaient un air raisonnable. Et puis elle se retourna vers la chambre engluée d'angoisse où les pensées obsédantes poursuivaient leur ronde sans trêve."

5. Ibid., p. 9: "Elle ne regrettait pas que Pierre ne fût pas auprès d'elle, il y avait des joies qu'elle ne pouvait pas connaître en sa présence: toutes les joies de la solitude; elles les avait perdues depuis huit ans, et parfois elle en éprouvait comme un remords . . . c'était étrange de redevenir quelqu'un, tout juste une femme."

6. Ronald Hayman, *Sartre, A Life* (New York: Simon and Schuster, 1987).

7. *L'Invitée*, p. 15: "roses comme ceux d'un enfant ensommeillé."

8. Ibid., p. 49: "C'était indéniable, elle avait des sentiments maternels pour Gerbert; maternels, avec une discrète nuance incestueuse."

9. Claude Francis and Fernande Gontier, *Simone de Beauvoir* (Paris: Librairie Académique Perrin, 1985).

10. *L'Invitée*, p. 20: "Xavière lui appartenait; rien ne donnait jamais à Françoise des joies si fortes que cette espèce de possession. . . . Les gestes de Xavière, sa figure, sa vie même avaient besoin de Françoise pour exister."

11. Ibid., p. 311: "Xavière était rivée à elle . . . tout ce qui arrivait à Xavière lui arrivait à travers Françoise, et fût-ce en dépit d'elle-même, Xavière lui appartenait."

12. Ibid., p. 286: "absolument ligotée."

13. Ibid., p. 264: "Elle comprenait enfin quel miracle avait fait irruption dans sa vie . . . mille merveilles allaient naître par la grâce de ce jeune ange exigeant."

14. Ibid., p. 191: "Cette petite sorcière . . . Elle regarde les choses avec ses yeux tout

neufs; et voilà que les choses se mettent à exister pour nous, juste comme elle les voit. . . . Grâce à elle, c'est une vraie nuit de Noël que nous vivons cette année."

15. Ibid., p. 37: "C'était scandaleux: elle avait tellement l'impression de dominer Xavière, de la posséder jusque dans son passé et dans les détours encore imprévus de son avenir! et cependant il y avait cette volonté butée contre laquelle sa propre volonté se brisait."

16. Ibid., p. 42: "C'était Françoise désormais qui l'emporterait à travers la vie. 'Je la rendrai heureuse,' décida-t-elle avec conviction."

17. Ibid., p. 118: "Avec Xavière les choses s'alourdissaient tout de suite: on avait l'impression de marcher dans la vie avec des kilos de terre glaise sous les semelles."

18. Ibid., p. 212: "C'était terrible tout ce temps qu'elle dévorait. On n'avait plus jamais de loisir, ni de solitude, ni même simplement de repos: on arrivait à un état de tension inhumaine."

19. Ibid., p. 364: "Elle fuirait jusqu'au bout du monde pour échapper à ses tentacules avides qui voulaient la dévorer toute vive."

20. Ibid., p. 42: "Leurs doigts restaient emmêlés . . . fondante, abandonnée, [Xavière] lui était tout entière livrée."

21. Ibid., p. 76: "Elle revit un autre visage, enfantin, désarmé qui s'appuyait sur son épaule, par un petit matin gris; elle n'avait pas su le retenir, il s'était effacé, il était perdu peut-être à jamais."

22. Ibid., p. 22: "Je ne me souviens que de vous . . . comme vous étiez belle!"

23. Ibid., p. 351: "une union totale qui confondrait leurs joies, leurs inquiétudes, leurs tourments."

24. Ibid., p. 306: "Elle sentait contre sa poitrine les beaux seins tièdes de Xavière, elle respirait son haleine charmante; était-ce du désir? Mais, que désirait-elle? Ses lèvres contre ses lèvres? Ce corps abandonné entre ses bras? Elle ne pouvait rien imaginer, ce n'était qu'un besoin confus de garder tourné vers elle à jamais ce visage d'amoureuse et de pouvoir dire passionnément: elle est à moi."

25. Ibid., p. 309: "Xavière lui reprochait-elle son effacement discret? Avait-elle souhaité que Françoise lui fît violence et s'imposât à son amour?"

26. Ibid., p. 46: "une petite fille aimante et désarmée dont on aurait voulu couvrir de baisers les joues nacrées."

27. Ibid., p. 78: "Il y a quelque chose d'enfantin en elle qui m'écoeure un peu, elle sent encore le lait."

28. Ibid., p. 166: "Elle choisit le moins rouge des sandwiches; il avait un goût étrange, mais ce n'était pas si mauvais."

29. Ibid., p. 167: "Ces traits charmants composaient une honnête figure d'enfant et non un masque inquiétant de magicienne."

30. Ibid., p. 285: "Ses regards transfiguraient les moindres objets."

31. Ibid.: "enchantement joyeux."

32. Ibid., p. 396: "Ça vous est si difficile de vivre. . . . Laissez-moi vous aider."

33. Jean-Paul Sartre, *Les Mains sales* (Paris: Gallimard, 1948), p. 215: "Tu es un môme qui a de la peine à passer à l'âge d'homme mais tu feras un homme très acceptable si quelqu'un te facilite le passage. . . . Je te garderai près de moi et je t'aiderai."

34. *L'Invitée,* p. 67: "une femme en face d'un homme."

35. Ibid., p. 228: "Cette austère petite vertu, ça semblait sacrilège de la penser comme une femme avec des désirs de femme."

36. Ibid., p. 259: "Cette perle noire, cet ange austère, avec ses mains caressantes d'homme Pierre en ferait une femme pâmée. Elle le regarda avec une espèce d'horreur."

37. Ibid., p. 179: "Jamais elle ne serait une femme qui possède l'exacte maîtrise de son corps. . . . C'était cela que ça signifiait trente ans: une femme faite"

38. Ibid., p. 66: "Comment peut-on accepter de vivre par programme, avec des emplois du temps et des devoirs à faire comme en pension!"

39. Ibid., p. 68: "C'est encore une de vos belles inventions, les concerts! Qu'on puisse avoir envie de musique à heure fixe! Mais c'est extravagant."

40. Ibid., p. 213: "A quoi ça servait-il? Elle ne réussissait qu'à leur empoisonner leurs joies, et à se rendre odieuse à ses propres yeux."

41. Ibid., p. 135: "Vous êtes sans tache. Ça m'éblouit tellement, je ne peux plus croire que vous existiez pour de vrai."

42. Ibid., p. 396: "[Elle] se mit à l'embrasser avec une dévotion exaltée; c'étaient là des baisers sacrés qui purifiaient Xavière de toutes les souillures et qui lui rendaient le respect d'elle-même. Sous ces lèvres douces, Françoise se sentait si noble, si éthérée, si divine, que son coeur se souleva; elle souhaitait une amitié humaine, et non ce culte fanatique et impérieux dont il lui fallait être l'idole docile."

43. Ibid., p. 163: "à la fois comme une idole et comme un paillasson."

44. Ibid., p. 139: "Elle a beau t'aimer de tout son coeur, pour sa petite âme possessive, tu es quand même le plus grand obstacle entre elle et moi."

45. Ibid., p. 168: "A côté de Xavière, elle se sentait si sèche."

46. Ibid., p. 340: "Ce n'était pas seulement un sanctuaire où Xavière célébrait son propre culte; c'était une serre chaude où s'épanouissait une végétation luxuriante et vénéneuse, c'était un cachot d'hallucinée dont l'atmosphère moite collait au corps."

47. Ibid., p. 357: "Sous le vain prétexte de se garder pure, elle avait fait le vide en elle."

48. Ibid., p. 419: "Jamais Françoise n'arriverait à lui faire comprendre qu'elle ne lui demandait pas de déployer pour elle la grâce de son corps, ni les séductions de son esprit, mais seulement de la laisser participer à sa vie."

49. Ibid., p. 20: "annexé à sa vie cette petite existence triste."

50. Ibid., p. 126: "une vivante catastrophe qui envahissait sournoisement sa vie."

51. Ibid., p. 131: "une intrusion étrangère."

52. Ibid., p. 46: "une petite fille aimante et désarmée."

53. Ibid., p. 186: "un petit morceau du monde tiède et désarmé."

54. Ibid., p. 76: "enfantin, désarmé."

55. Ibid., p. 130: "naïveté désarmante."

56. Ibid., p. 179: "Aucun héroïsme, aucune absurdité n'y pourraient rien changer."

57. Jean-Paul Sartre, *Lettres au Castor et à quelques autres* (Paris: Gallimard, 1983).

58. *L'Invitée*, p. 297: "Elle n'avait aucune prise sur cette petite âme butée ni même sur le beau corps de chair qui la défendait; un corps tiède et souple, accessible à des mains d'homme mais qui se dressait devant Françoise comme une armure rigide."

59. Ibid., p. 360: "traversée d'une envie farouche de battre Xavière, de la fouler aux pieds."

60. Ibid., p. 397: "Dans un élan de rage impuissante, Françoise souhaita de serrer dans ses mains cette petite tête dure jusqu'à la faire éclater."

61. Ibid.: "cette douloureuse présence étrangère qui sans cesse lui barrait la route."

62. Ibid., p. 442: "Ce n'était pas seulement sa présence, c'était son existence même que Xavière aurait voulu effacer."

63. Ibid., p. 494: "N'y avait-il aucun moyen d'anéantir cet orgueil insolent?"

64. Ibid., p. 496: "Xavière elle-même proclamerait sa défaite; il n'y avait pas de victoire possible sans son aveu."

65. Ibid., p. 374: "Xavière ne se renonçait jamais; si haut qu'elle vous situât, même lorsqu'elle vous chérissait, on restait un objet pour elle.... Elle sourit. Il faudrait tuer Xavière."

66. Hazel Barnes, *The Literature of Possibility* (Lincoln: University of Nebraska Press, 1959), p. 124.

67. Maurice Merleau-Ponty, *Sens et non-sens* (Paris: Les Editions Nagel, 1966).

68. Annie-Claire Jaccard, *Simone de Beauvoir* (Zurich: Juris, 1968), p. 98: "D'une part, il traite l'autre en objet annexable et d'autre part il aimerait que celui-ci soit une source créatrice pour le couple."

69. Jean-Raymond Audet, *Simone de Beauvoir face à la mort* (Lausanne: L'Age d'Homme, 1979), p. 15: "Immédiatement se noue entre les deux une espèce de relation mère-fille (assez louche d'ailleurs)."

70. Ibid., p. 41: "une sorte d'infanticide philosophique cruel et inutile."

71. Carol Ascher, *Simone de Beauvoir: A Life of Freedom.* (Boston: Beacon Press, 1981).

72. Ibid., p. 56.

73. Martha Noel Evans, *Masks of Tradition.* (Ithaca: Cornell University Press, 1987), p. 93.

74. Ibid., p. 100.

75. Ibid.

76. Simone de Beauvoir, *La Force de l'âge* (Paris: Gallimard, 1960), p. 350: "ce vertige que j'avais connu à côté de Zaza."

77. Ibid., p. 615: "Si j'avais choisi d'en faire une meurtrière, c'est que je préférais n'importe quoi à la soumission."

78. Ibid., pp. 348–49: "Ce dénouement ... a eu pour moi une valeur cathartique. D'abord, en tuant Olga sur le papier, je liquidai les irritations, les rancunes que j'avais pu éprouver à son égard; je purifiai notre amitié de tous les mauvais souvenirs qui se mélangeaient aux bons. Surtout, en déliant Françoise, par un crime, de la dépendance où la tenait son amour pour Pierre, je retrouvai ma propre autonomie."

Chapter 3

1. Simone de Beauvoir, *Le Sang des autres* (Paris: Gallimard, 1945), p. 15: "Du matin au soir, elle courait de droite et de gauche, dans une fuite sans fin, poussant pendant des heures le fauteuil roulant de la vieille gouvernante paralysée, causant des doigts et des lèvres avec sa cousine sourde. Elle n'aimait pas la vieille gouvernante, ni la cousine. Ce n'était pas pour elles qu'elle se dépensait. C'était à cause de cette odeur sans joie qui s'infiltrait dans la maison."

2. Ibid., p. 19: "Elle s'est arrêtée, et pour contenir la poussée stupide elle a étendu ses petits bras; j'étais convaincu que si papa ne l'avait pas empoignée, s'il avait étendu lui aussi ses grands bras d'homme, la foule subjuguée aurait repris son pas tranquille. Mais mon père ne songeait pas à arrêter la marche aveugle du monde."

3. Ibid., pp. 21–22: "C'était insensé de vouloir changer quelque chose au monde, à la vie; les choses étaient déjà assez déplorables si l'on se gardait d'y toucher. Tout ce que condamnait son coeur et sa raison, elle s'acharnait à le défendre: mon père, le mariage, le capitalisme. . . . Il fallait se tapir dans un coin, se faire le plus petit possible et plutôt que tenter un effort perverti d'avance, tout accepter."

4. Ibid., p. 34: "Avec quel emportement de justice hargneuse elle prenait parti pour cet homme qu'elle n'aimait pas!"

5. Ibid.: "une autre voix au-dedans d'elle qui suppliait: qu'il ne parle pas, pas encore; qu'on me le laisse encore un peu de temps."

6. Ibid., p. 32: "Nous étions libres, libres de salir nos âmes, de gâcher nos vies; elle ne prenait que la liberté d'en souffrir."

7. Ibid., pp. 35–36: "Elle n'avait que moi. . . . Mais comment la défendre contre elle-même?"

8. Ibid., p. 170: "'Ah! je ne peux pas te donner de conseils.' . . . Quand nous étions petits, elle nous avait appris farouchement à ne pas mentir; mais elle non plus, elle n'était plus sûre de rien: ni de la prudence, ni de la charité, ni de la vérité."

9. Ibid., p. 170: "On a beau faire; on est toujours responsable."

10. Ibid., p. 154: "Je me sentais pareil à ma mère, rasant les murs, fuyant les regards qui m'eussent renvoyé ma véridique image."

11. Ibid., p. 234: "Avec tant de joie il avait ... fait raser les cheveux trop riches, trop serrés qu'il tenait de sa mère!"

12. Ibid., p. 293: "Je n'ai pas faim, mais il faut que je mange. Ma mère ne mange pas: elle me regarde. Il ne faut pas qu'elle sache. *Elle sait. Je sais qu'elle sait. Elle ne me pardonnera jamais.*"

13. Ibid., p. 294: "Soudain j'ai cinq ans, j'ai peur et j'ai froid, je voudrais que ma mère me borde dans mon lit, qu'elle m'embrasse longtemps; je voudrais rester ici: je me coucherais dans ma vieille chambre, blotti dans mon passé, et peut-être je dormirais: 'Il faut que je parte.'"

14. Ibid.: "Elle mourra sans m'avoir pardonné."

15. Ibid., p. 272: "Ils étaient alléchés par l'éclat de la situation qui s'offrait à leur fille, mais ils la blâmaient de se compromettre avec l'envahisseur."

16. Ibid., p. 298: "Elle me tuera! . . . Ah! je m'en vais. Donnez-moi ma potion, vite. . . . Dites-lui de revenir vite. Ils me tueront!"

17. Ibid., pp. 108–9: "Ce mariage . . . ça faisait partie des mythes; on en parlait avec sérieux, mais personne n'y croyait pour de bon."

18. Ibid., p. 94: "Elle me harcelait de questions: on aurait dit qu'elle me prenait pour Dieu le Père."

19. Ibid., p. 124: "Il n'est pas question qu'Hélène garde cet enfant, comprenez-vous?"

20. Ibid., p. 127: "Sous sa peau enfantine, il y avait cette chose qu'elle nourrissait de son sang."

21. Ibid., p. 129: "Je refusais d'agir sur son destin et j'avais disposé d'elle aussi brutalement que par un viol."

22. Ibid., p. 131: "Sa jeunesse et sa gaieté s'écoulaient de son ventre avec un gargouillement obscène."

23. Ibid., p. 109: "Tu ne comptes pas rester vierge toute ta vie?"

24. Ibid.: "Tu crois qu'il n'y a que toi au monde avec qui je puisse coucher?"

25. Ibid., p. 202: "Tu trouverais absurde qu'on ait des enfants, n'est-ce pas?"

26. Ibid., p. 202: "Faire naître un enfant, l'empêcher de naître . . . c'est aussi absurde. C'est indifférent."

27. Ibid., pp. 205–6: "Autrefois, tu expliquais qu'il suffirait de vous croiser les bras; on ne pourrait rien faire sans vous."

28. Ibid., p. 264: "Il lui sembla soudain qu'elle sentait le poids de l'enfant sur ses genoux, et l'appel de ces yeux pleins de reproche."

29. Ibid., p. 300: "Si on courait tous ensemble sur l'agent? Si on lui arrachait l'enfant? Mais personne ne bougeait."

30. Ibid., p. 295: "Deux huîtres dans une coquille."

31. Ibid., p. 307: "La coquille s'était brisée: elle existait pour quelque chose, pour quelqu'un."

32. Ibid., pp. 43–44: "Elle comptait marcher près de lui sans obstacle vers la gloire et le bonheur."

33. Ibid., p. 161: "cette bergerie fraternelle où Denise prétendait vivre, un paradis humain bien ratissé, où coulaient les vertus abondantes, où le mérite, la vérité, la beauté pendaient aux arbres comme des fruits dorés."

34. Ibid., p. 104: "Yvonne ne faisait rien d'autre que coudre, éplucher des pommes de terre, et soigner une malade imaginaire; et cependant sa vie ne semblait pas absurde; c'était même satisfaisant de penser qu'Yvonne existait, juste comme elle était, penchée sur son ouvrage dans sa chambre solitaire."

35. Ibid., p. 22: "cette prudence insensée."

36. Ibid., p. 128: "C'était une si petite fille. Et déjà son corps connaissait cette souffrance aiguë de femme."

37. Ibid., p. 307: "La terre entière était une présence fraternelle."

38. Beauvoir, *La Force de l'âge*, p. 377: "Je pensai: 'Cela vaut la peine d'écrire si on peut créer la fraternité avec des mots.'"

39. Hélène Nahas, *La Femme dans la littérature existentielle* (Paris: Presses Universitaires de France, 1957), p. 103: "comme un gros chat sensuel et somnolent, qui a renoncé à toute activité créatrice. Elle a produit un enfant et l'a vu s'éloigner d'elle."

40. Georges Hourdin, *Simone de Beauvoir et la liberté* (Paris: Les Editions du Cerf, 1962).

41. Elaine Marks, *Simone de Beauvoir: Encounters with Death* (New Brunswick, New Jersey: Rutgers University Press, 1973), p. 38.

42. Robert D. Cottrell, *Simone de Beauvoir* (New York: Frederick Ungar, 1975), p. 53.

43. Ascher, *Simone de Beauvoir*.

Chapter 4

1. Simone de Beauvoir, *Les Bouches inutiles* (Paris: Gallimard, 1945), p. 107: "Maître d'Avesnes a toujours écouté votre voix. Suppliez-le. Persuadez-le. Il est bon, il est juste. Il cédera à vos prières."

2. Ibid., pp. 55–56: "Me la donner? Pensez-vous que je consentirais à l'enfermer dans ma maison et à lui dire: voilà que je suis toute ta part sur terre? Je n'ai pas l'âme d'un geôlier."

3. Ibid., p. 65: "Crois-tu que je ne t'ai pas entendu gémir toutes ces nuits? Il est parti: tu pleures. Il revient: tu pleures. Est-ce ma fille, cette chair à souffrance?"

4. Ibid., p. lll: "Ce sera ton enfant, Clarice; ton avenir, ton bonheur."

5. Ibid.: "Sois heureuse et ma vie n'aura pas été tout à fait vaine."

6. Ibid., p. 55: "C'est une enfant. Elle connaîtra plus tard que j'ai agi pour son bien."

7. Ibid., p. 54: "J'admire que vous osiez tailler, rogner, construire dans des matériaux de chair vive."

8. Ibid., p. 119: "L'amour et la joie dont je l'ai frustrée, qui les lui rendra? Ah! criminelle! Je pensais: plus tard, elle sera heureuse. Mais sa vie s'est arrêtée ici, dans la souffrance et la haine; elle est morte avec ce poids écrasant sur son coeur: le poids de ma volonté stupide."

9. Ibid.: "Comment ai-je osé croire que le monde était une pâte docile qu'il m'appartenait de façonner à mon gré?"

10. Ibid., p. 54: "Ne connaîtras-tu jamais cette joie? Jeter les yeux autour de toi et penser: ceci est mon oeuvre."

11. Ibid., p. 53: "Je sais tout ce que je vous dois. Vous avez été pour ma soeur et pour moi plus qu'une mère. Mais permettez qu'à présent je dirige ma vie sans secours."

12. Ibid., p. 56: "Si un homme et une femme se sont jetés d'un même élan vers un même avenir, dans l'oeuvre qu'ils ont construite ensemble, dans les enfants qu'ils ont engendrés, dans ce monde tout entier qu'a modelé leur volonté commune, ils se retrouvent confondus d'une manière indissoluble."

13. Ibid., p. 34: "Je ne suis pas la femme qui convient à un échevin. Je ne ressemble pas à ma mère."

14. Ibid., p. 56: "Clarice n'est pas de votre espèce."

15. Ibid., p. 98: "Rien n'est à moi, sauf cette petite vie qui bouge dans mon ventre et qui demain s'arrachera de moi."

16. Ibid., p. lll: "Mon enfant naîtra. Ne voudrez-vous pas lui sourire?"

17. Ibid., p. 59: "Il est jeune encore. Il changera, tu le changeras."

18. Ibid., p. 112: "Mensonge ce jour où j'ai mis Clarice au monde."

19. Ibid., p. 48: "Un an! Mon heure sera passée! Vaucelles sera perdue ou sauvée; c'est aujourd'hui, dans la famine, dans la peur, qu'elle est à prendre. Ah! sentir toute cette force en moi et n'en rien faire."

20. Ibid., p. 105: "Vaucelles est à prendre. Il faut la prendre."

21. Ibid., p. 130: "C'était pour le bien de Vaucelles. Jamais vos faibles coeurs ne seront capables de lui donner le destin que je rêvais pour elle. Entre mes mains, elle fût devenue la reine des Flandres et du monde."

22. Nahas, *La Femme.*

23. Cottrell, *Simone de Beauvoir,* p. 66.

24. Marie-Claire Pasquier, unpublished talk on "Simone de Beauvoir as playwright: *Les Bouches inutiles,*" Simone de Beauvoir Colloquium, Columbia University, April 4–6, 1985.

25. Virginia Fichera, "Simone de Beauvoir and 'The Woman Question': *Les Bouches inutiles,*" *Yale French Studies,* "Simone de Beauvoir: Witness to a Century," no. 72 (1986), p. 59.

Chapter 5

1. Simone de Beauvoir, *Tous les hommes sont mortels* (Paris: Gallimard, 1946), p. 40: "Vous m'avez harcelé pour que je me remette à vivre. Eh bien, maintenant, il faut me rendre la vie supportable."

2. Ibid., p. 123: "sourire à ses petits-enfants."

3. Ibid., p. 124: "me donna un fils que nous appelâmes Tancrède."

4. Ibid., p. 363: "En haut de la montagne, il y avait une femme qui me faisait signe: Catherine; elle m'attendait. Dès que j'aurais touché sa main je serais sauvé. Mais le

sol s'enfonçait sous mes pas . . . j'eus à peine le temps de lever la main en criant: Catherine! et je fus englouti dans une boue brûlante."

5. Ibid., p. 149: "Nous vieillirons sans avoir eu de jeunesse. . . . Qui nous rendra les années que vous nous volez?"

6. Ibid., p. 161: "Tant que ma mère était vivante, j'ai patienté. Mais c'est assez. . . . Vous avez régné votre temps. Maintenant c'est mon tour."

7. Mark, 10:15

8. *Tous les hommes sont mortels*, p. 189: "J'entendais ne partager mon fils avec personne."

9. Ibid., p. 192: "Il me doit la vie, il me doit le monde."

10. Ibid., p. 193: "Je sentais la chaleur de mes mains qui pénétrait sa chair, je sentais sous ma paume ses jeunes muscles, sa peau tendre, ses os fragiles, et il me semblait lui façonner un corps tout neuf. Je pensai avec passion: je serai toujours là pour te sauver de tous les maux. Tendrement j'emportai dans mes bras mon fils auquel j'avais donné deux fois la vie."

11. Simone de Beauvoir, *Pyrrhus et Cinéas* (Paris: Librairie Gallimard, 1944).

12. *Tous les hommes sont mortels*, p. 197: "Tout mon amour ne lui servait à rien. . . . Voilà qu'il voulait tenir sa vie entre ses propres mains, ses mains neuves et maladroites; mais pouvait-on enfermer cette vie dans une serre pour la cultiver sans danger? Etouffée, ligotée, elle perdrait son éclat et son parfum."

13. Ibid., p. 202.

14. Ibid., p. 204: "Je n'avais pas le droit de l'empêcher d'accomplir son destin d'homme, ce destin sur lequel je ne pouvais rien."

15. Ibid., p. 207: "Juste un trou dans le ventre; et vingt ans de soins, vingt ans d'espoir et d'amour étaient anéantis. . . . Il mourait glorieux, comblé; comme si sa victoire eût été une vraie victoire . . . il mourait, ayant fait ce qu'il voulait faire, il était à jamais un héros triomphant."

16. Ibid., p. 212: "J'ai laissé Antoine maître de sa vie, et il l'a perdue; il est mort pour rien. Je ne recommencerai pas une pareille faute."

17. Ibid., p. 210: "C'est peut-être pour cela qu'Antoine a choisi de mourir: vous ne lui aviez pas laissé d'autre manière de vivre."

18. Ibid., p. 226: "Si je n'avais pas voulu si impérieusement son bonheur, elle eût aimé, souffert, vécu. Je l'avais perdue plus sûrement que je n'avais perdu Antoine."

19. Ibid., p. 232: "Il s'agit de ma lignée."

20. Ibid., 237: "Rien ne sera livré aux caprices des hommes ni aux hasards du sort. Ce sera la raison qui gouvernera la terre: ma raison."

21. Ibid., p. 277: "Sa puissance est mon oeuvre, son bonheur est mon oeuvre. Je construis un monde et j'ai donné à cet homme sa vie."

22. Ibid., p. 285: "Comment avais-je un jour osé me dire: 'J'ai donné à cet homme la vie et le bonheur'? Il fallait donc dire aujourd'hui: 'C'est moi qui lui ai donné ces yeux éteints, cette bouche douloureuse et ce coeur frissonnant; son malheur est mon oeuvre."

23. Ibid., p. 399: "J'avais besoin d'elle pour vivre."

24. Ibid., p. 415: "Pourquoi lui avais-je cédé? Elle avait voulu un enfant, et voilà que s'accomplissaient dans son ventre d'étranges et dangereuses alchimies."

25. Ibid., pp. 418–19: "J'avais de l'amitié pour ces enfants parce que Marianne les avait portés dans son ventre; mais ce n'étaient pas mes enfants; une fois j'avais eu un fils, un fils à moi: il était mort à vingt ans."

26. Ibid., p. 439: "Ne pourrais-je pas la faire vivre à travers moi?"

27. Ibid., p. 454: "J'avais envie de parler d'elle; depuis longtemps elle est morte; mais pour Armand c'est aujourd'hui qu'elle commençait à exister; elle pouvait ressusciter dans son coeur belle, jeune, ardente. —Elle avait foi dans la science. Elle croyait comme vous au progrès, à la raison, à la liberté. Elle était passionnément dévouée au bonheur de l'humanité. . . . Elle était si vivante; tout ce qu'elle touchait vivait: les fleurs, les idées."

28. Ibid., p. 485: "C'est notre enfant."

29. Ibid., p. 520: "Demain il faudra lutter encore. Mais aujourd'hui nous sommes vainqueurs."

30. Ibid., p. 497: "Je me soucie de tout et de tous. C'est comme ça que je suis faite."

31. Ibid., p. 511: "De toutes les femmes que j'ai connues, c'est la plus généreuse et la plus passionnée, c'est la plus noble, la plus pure."

32. Simone de Beauvoir, *La Force des choses*, vol. 1 (Paris: Gallimard, 1963), p. 96: "Sa défection ne refuse pas à l'Histoire son sens: elle indique seulement que la rupture des générations est nécessaire pour aller de l'avant."

33. Barnes, *The Literature of Possibility*.

34. Cottrell, *Simone de Beauvoir*, p. 72.

35. Keefe, *Simone de Beauvoir*, p. 178.

Chapter 6

1. Simone de Beauvoir, *Le Deuxième Sexe*, vol. 1 (Paris: Gallimard, 1949), p. 43: "L'espèce réaffirme ses droits."

2. Ibid., vol. 1, p. 308: "c'est beau comme un tour de prestidigitation. La mère apparaît douée de la puissance mirifique des fées."

3. Ibid., vol. 2, p. 497: "Il y a deux cas où l'adolescente a peine à échapper à son emprise: si elle a été ardemment couvée par une mère anxieuse; ou si elle a été maltraitée par une 'mauvaise mère' qui lui a insufflé un profond sentiment de culpabilité; au premier cas leurs rapports souvent frisaient l'homosexualité . . . la jeune fille cherchera dans des bras nouveaux ce même bonheur. Dans le second cas, elle éprouvera un besoin ardent d'une 'bonne mère' qui la protège contre la première, qui écarte la malédiction qu'elle a sur sa tête."

4. Ibid., vol. 2, p. 380: "La femme ne souhaite pas réincarner un individu en un autre mais ressusciter une situation: celle qu'elle a connue petite fille, à l'abri des adultes; elle a été profondément intégrée au foyer familial, elle y a goûté la paix d'une

quasi-passivité; l'amour lui rendra sa mère aussi bien que son père, il lui rendra son enfance."

5. Ibid., vol. 1, p. 322.

6. Ibid., vol. 1, p. 329: "Souvent il ne lui semble plus merveilleux mais horrible qu'un corps parasite doive proliférer à l'intérieur de son corps; l'idée de cette monstrueuse enflure l'épouvante. . . . Les images d'enflure, de déchirure, d'hémorragie vont la hanter."

7. Ibid., vol. 2, p. 15: "vouée au maintien de l'espèce et à l'entretien du foyer."

8. Ibid., vol. 2, p. 126: "Les vingt premières années de la vie féminine sont d'une extraordinaire richesse; la femme . . . découvre le monde et son destin. A vingt ans, maîtresse d'un foyer, liée à jamais à un homme, un enfant dans les bras, voilà sa vie finie pour toujours. Les vraies actions, le vrai travail sont l'apanage de l'homme."

9. Ibid., vol. 2, pp. 132–133: "Le plus souvent, la naissance d'un enfant les oblige à se cantonner dans leur rôle de matrone; il est actuellement fort difficile de concilier travail et maternité."

10. Ibid., vol. 1, p. 76: "On ne saurait obliger directement la femme à enfanter: tout ce qu'on peut faire c'est l'enfermer dans des situations où la maternité est pour elle la seule issue; la loi ou les moeurs lui imposent le mariage, on interdit les mesures anticonceptionnelles et l'avortement, on défend le divorce."

11. Ibid., vol. 1, p. 84: "Ce n'est pas en donnant la vie, c'est en risquant sa vie que l'homme s'élève au-dessus de l'animal; c'est pourquoi dans l'humanité la supériorité est accordée non au sexe qui engendre mais à celui qui tue."

12. Ibid., vol. 1, p. 152: "Toute femme qui fait en sorte qu'elle ne puisse engendrer autant d'enfants qu'elle pourrait se rend coupable d'autant d'homicides."

13. Ibid., vol. 1, p. 47: "la révolte de l'organisme contre l'espèce qui prend possession de lui."

14. Ibid., vol. 1, p. 206: "L'homme répugne à retrouver dans la femme qu'il possède l'essence redoutée de la mère."

15. Ibid., vol. 1, p. 198: "A travers tout le respect dont l'entoure la société, la fonction de gestation inspire une répulsion spontanée."

16. Ibid., vol. 1, p. 103: "Ce n'est pas la mère qui engendre ce qu'on appelle son enfant: elle n'est que la nourrice du germe versé dans son sein; celui qui engendre, c'est le père. La femme comme un dépositaire étranger reçoit le germe et s'il plaît aux dieux elle le conserve."

17. Ibid., vol. 1, p. 238:: "la suprême victoire masculine . . . la réhabilitation de la femme par l'achèvement de sa défaite."

18. Ibid., vol. 1, p. 305: "La fille est pour la mère à la fois son double et une autre, à la fois la mère la chérit impérieusement et elle lui est hostile."

19. Ibid., vol. 1, p. 428: "Plus la jeune fille mûrit, plus l'autorité maternelle lui pèse."

20. Ibid., vol. 2, p. 180: "presque les mots de l'amant."

21. Ibid., vol. 2, p. 185: "La *mater dolorosa* fait de ses souffrances une arme dont elle use sadiquement."

22. Ibid., vol. 2, p. 192: "Mère passionnée ou mère hostile, l'indépendance de l'enfant ruine ses espoirs."

23. Ibid., vol. 2, p. 54: "L'idéal du bonheur s'est toujours matérialisé dans la maison, chaumière ou château; elle incarne la permanence et la séparation. C'est entre ses murs que la famille se constitue en une cellule isolée et qu'elle affirme son identité par-delà le passage des générations; le passé mis en conserve sous forme de meubles et de portraits d'ancêtres préfigure un avenir sans risque . . . "

24. Ibid., vol. 2, p. 169: "La mère souhaite à la fois garder dans son ventre le trésor de chair qui est un précieux morceau de son moi et se débarrasser d'un gêneur."

25. Ibid., vol. 2, p. 194: "accepter sa défaite."

26. Ibid., vol. 2, pp. 296–97: "rare mélange de générosité et de détachement pour trouver dans la vie de ses enfants un enrichissement sans se faire leur tyran ni les changer en bourreaux."

27. Nancy Friday, *My Mother/My Self.*

28. *Le Deuxième Sexe*, vol. 2, p. 294: "La vie va se poursuivre sans elle; elle n'est plus *la* Mère: seulement un chaînon . . . elle n'est plus qu'un individu fini, périmé."

29. Ibid., vol. 2, p. 299: "bien rare que la femme trouve dans sa postérité—naturelle ou élue—une justification de sa vie déclinante. . . . Elle se sait inutile."

30. Ibid., vol. 2, p. 146: "On répète à la femme depuis son enfance qu'elle est faite pour engendrer et on lui chante la splendeur de la maternité. Tout est justifié par ce merveilleux privilège qu'elle détient de mettre des enfants au monde. Et voilà que l'homme, pour garder sa liberté, . . . demande à la femme de renoncer à son triomphe de femelle."

31. Jean-Paul Sartre, *L'Age de raison* (Paris: Gallimard, 1945).

32. *Le Deuxième Sexe*, vol. 2, p. 148: "La seule chose sûre, c'est ce ventre fourragé et saignant, ces lambeaux de vie rouge, cette absence de l'enfant."

33. Ibid., vol. 2, p. 198: "l'entreprise la plus délicate, la plus grave aussi qui soit: la formation d'un être humain."

34. Ibid., vol. 2, p. 291: "Rien de plus rare que celle qui respecte authentiquement en son enfant la personne humaine, qui reconnaît sa liberté jusque dans ses échecs, qui assume avec lui les risques impliqués par tout engagement."

35. Ibid., vol. 2, p. 196: "la femme capable de vouloir avec désintéressement le bonheur d'un autre."

36. Ibid., vol. 2, p. 455: "Faute de crèches, de jardins d'enfants convenablement organisés, il suffit d'un enfant pour paralyser entièrement l'activité de la femme."

37. Ibid., vol. 2, p. 496: "sentirait autour d'elle un monde androgyne et non un monde masculin."

38. Nahas, *La Femme*, p. 4.

39. Geneviève Gennari, *Simone de Beauvoir* (Paris: Editions Universitaires, 1959), p. 90.

40. Ibid., p. 97: "reste étrangère à l'histoire d'amour très simple et très profonde qui se joue entre la mère et l'enfant."

41. Hourdin, *Simone de Beauvoir*, p. 125: "Que nous le voulions ou non, la femme jusqu'à plus ample découverte est faite en partie pour stabiliser et civiliser l'homme, pour porter, mettre au monde, allaiter et élever des enfants."

42. Ibid., p. 126: "la seule voie de salut."

43. Ibid.: "qui ont accompli leur destin et trouvé leur libre accomplissement dans les tâches de la famille et de la maternité, qu'il est ridicule de ramener à la pure animalité."

44. Serge Julienne-Caffié, *Simone de Beauvoir* (Paris: Gallimard, 1966).

45. Suzanne Lilar, *Le Malentendu du "Deuxième Sexe"* (Paris: Presses Universitaires de France, 1970), p. 151: "Beauvoir n'est pas moins féroce à l'égard de la maternité que du mariage."

46. Ibid.: "Il n'est rien de viril qui ne puisse se retrouver chez la femme, rien de féminin—jusqu'à la vocation maternelle—qui ne puisse se retrouver chez l'homme."

47. Jean Leighton, *Simone de Beauvoir on Women* (Cranbury, New Jersey: Associated University Presses, 1975), p. 8.

48. Ibid., p.29.

49. Ibid., p. 35.

50. Ibid., p. 43.

51. Cottrell, *Simone de Beauvoir*, p. 104.

52. Ibid., p. 105.

53. Konrad Bieber, *Simone de Beauvoir* (Boston: G. K. Hall, 1979), p. 127.

54. "Six Experts Discuss *The Second Sex*," *Saturday Review,* February 21, 1953.

55. Ascher, *Simone de Beauvoir*, p. 126.

56. Ibid., p. 127.

57. Ibid., p. 134.

58. Ibid., p. 141.

59. Anne Whitmarsh, *Simone de Beauvoir and the Limits of Commitment* (Cambridge: Cambridge University Press, 1981), p. 147.

60. Jacques J. Zéphir, *Le Néo-féminisme de Simone de Beauvoir* (Paris: Denoël/Gonthier, 1982).

61. Simone de Beauvoir, "Réponse à quelques femmes et à un homme," *Le Nouvel Observateur*, no. 382 (March 6–12, 1972), p. 40, as quoted in Zéphir, *Le Néo-féminisme*, p. 79: "Ce n'est pas moi qui veux imposer ma manière de vivre à toutes les femmes, puisque au contraire je milite pour leur liberté: liberté de la maternité, de la contraception, de l'avortement; les fanatiques, ce sont certaines mères de famille qui n'admettent pas qu'on suive un autre chemin que le leur."

62. Keefe, *Simone de Beauvoir*, p. 106.

63. Donald L. Hatcher, *Understanding "The Second Sex"* (New York: Peter Lang, 1984), p. 117.

64. Ibid., p. 120.

65. Ibid., p. 266.

66. Mary Evans, *Simone de Beauvoir*, p. 57.

67. Ibid., p. 59.

68. Ibid., p. 67.

69. Judith Okely, *Simone de Beauvoir*, p. 7.

70. Ibid., p. 8.

71. Ibid., p. 60.

72. Ibid., p. 66.

73. Ibid., p. 76.

74. Ibid., p. 77.

75. Ibid., pp. 93–94.

76. Ibid., p. 97.

77. Ibid., p. 98.

78. Ibid., p. 116.

Chapter 7

1. Simone de Beauvoir, *Les Mandarins* (Paris: Gallimard, 1954), p. 31: "une nette agressivité par rapport à ma mère. . . . L'ambivalence des sentiments que je porte à ma fille provient de mon inimitié à l'égard de ma mère, de mon indifférence envers moi-même."

2. Ibid., p. 48: "S'il a voulu si vite un enfant, c'est sans doute parce que je ne suffisais pas à justifier son existence; peut-être aussi cherchait-il une revanche contre cet avenir sur lequel il n'avait plus de prise."

3. Ibid., p. 3: "Je ne l'ai pas désirée; c'est Robert qui a souhaité tout de suite un enfant. J'en ai voulu à Nadine de déranger notre tête-à-tête."

4. Ibid., pp. 61–62: "Jamais elle ne s'est résignée à appartenir à la même espèce que moi; quand je lui expliquai qu'elle allait bientôt être réglée et ce que ça signifiait, elle m'a écoutée avec une attention hagarde et puis elle a fracassé contre le sol son vase préféré. Avec la première souillure, sa colère a été si puissante qu'elle est restée dix-huit mois sans saigner."

5. Ibid., p. 346: "La motocyclette demeurait à ses yeux le symbole de tous les plaisirs virils dont elle n'était pas la source et qu'elle ne pouvait pas non plus partager."

6. Ibid., p. 171: "Les femmes, ça végète toujours. . . . Regarde-toi par exemple: tu t'en tires, soit, tu as des clients; mais enfin, tu ne seras jamais Freud."

7. Ibid., p. 201: "Je suppose qu'au fond, je suis faite pour avoir un mari et des enfants comme toutes les femmes. Je récurerai mes casseroles et je pondrai un chiard tous les ans."

8. Ibid., p. 59: "Peut-être l'aurais-je soulagée si je l'avais prise dans mes bras en lui disant: 'Ma pauvre petite fille, pardonne-moi de ne pas t'aimer davantage.'"

9. Ibid., p. 28: "Cette année-là, nous avons été des amies, ma fille et moi."

10. Ibid., p. 61: "Si je l'avais aimée davantage, nos rapports auraient été différents: peut-être aurais-je su l'empêcher de mener une vie que je blâme."

11. Ibid.: "Tu appelles ça vivre! Franchement, ma pauvre maman, tu crois que tu as vécu? Causer avec papa la moitié de la journée et soigner des cinglés pendant l'autre moitié, tu parles d'une existence! ... J'aimerais mieux finir dans un bordel que de me promener dans la vie avec des gants de chevreau glacé: jamais tu ne les enlèves, tes gants."

12. Ibid., p. 72: "Qu'arriverait-il si j'ôtais mes gants? Si je ne les ôtais pas ce soir, les enlèverais-je jamais?"

13. Ibid., p. 78: "Plus jamais je n'essaierais d'arracher mes gants de chevreau glacé: c'est trop tard.... Maintenant mes gants sont greffés à ma peau, pour les ôter il faudrait m'écorcher."

14. Beauvoir, *La Force de l'âge*, p. 490: "Elle continuait ... à me reprocher de lui mesurer avarement mon temps. 'Vous êtes une horloge dans un frigidaire!' gémissait-elle."

15. Beauvoir, *La Force des choses*, vol. 1, p. 316: " Elle m'en voulait encore de l'avoir sacrifiée à mon travail, et cette rancune se retournait contre ce que j'écrivais; elle me répétait, de manière indirecte mais transparente: 'C'est tellement triste d'être un écrivain de second ordre.'"

16. *Les Mandarins*, p. 200: "J'aurais beau rester auprès d'elle, Je ne réussirais pas à la protéger.... Je ne pouvais lui donner ni l'amour ni le bonheur. Que je lui étais inutile! ... je lis sans effort en elle, et je ne sais rien faire pour elle."

17. Ibid., p. 503: "J'espère que je vais vite me découvrir une vocation de grand-mère."

18. Ibid., p. 576: "Un jour, elle aura mon âge et je ne serai plus là. Elle est la réalité de l'avenir et de l'oubli."

19. Ibid., p. 578: "J'ai imaginé la voix de Nadine, énorme et indigne: 'Tu n'aurais pas dû! tu n'avais pas le droit!' ... Je ne peux pas leur infliger mon cadavre et tout ce qui s'en suivra dans leurs coeurs à eux: Robert penché sur ce lit, Lewis dans la maison de Parker avec des mots qui dansent devant ses yeux, les sanglots furieux de Nadine."

20. Ibid.: "Elle serait entrée, elle m'aurait vue sur le lit, le corps convulsé: quelle horreur!"

21. *La Force des choses*, vol. 1, p. 376: "Anne n'a pas l'étoffe d'une suicidée; mais son retour au consentement quotidien ressemble plutôt à une défaite qu'à un triomphe."

22. *Les Mandarins*, p. 550: "Ces deux femmes se seraient fait tuer l'une pour l'autre et pourtant il y avait entre elles quelque chose qui ne collait pas. Nadine devenait beaucoup plus agressive et beaucoup plus butée quand sa mère était là."

23. Ibid.: "Je l'aime bien, mais souvent elle m'agace; je suppose que c'est pareil pour elle. Ça n'a rien de rare, c'est comme ça les rapports de famille."

24. Ibid., p. 502: "Allons, donne-moi un conseil; je vois bien que tu en meurs d'envie."

25. Ibid.: "Bien sûr, si tu demandes à un homme s'il veut un enfant, il prend peur; mais quand l'enfant est là, il est enchanté."

26. Ibid., p. 543: "Elle se résignait mal à n'être plus qu'une mère de famille . . . elle donnait [au bébé] son biberon avec autorité, avec patience, elle mettait son point d'honneur à être une mère compétente, elle avait acquis de solides principes de puériculture et un tas d'objets hygiéniques; mais jamais Henri n'avait surpris de vraie tendresse dans ses yeux quand elle s'occupait de Maria. Même avec ce bébé elle gardait ses distances, elle restait toujours murée en elle-même."

27. Ibid., p. 557: "Ah! vous avez bonne mine quand vous êtes là tous les trois à me regarder avec des airs de juge! . . . Vous êtes de grandes personnes et je ne suis qu'une enfant. Ce qui m'amuse ne vous amuse pas, c'est normal."

28. Ibid., p. 281: "n'avoir plus besoin de maman et être sûre de ne jamais redevenir pauvre."

29. Ibid., p. 471: "Josette ne m'a jamais servi à rien. Elle s'est compromise d'une manière parfaitement inutile."

30. Ibid., p. 476: "Quelles armes lui avait-on données? quels principes? quels espoirs? Il y avait eu les gifles de sa mère, la muflerie des mâles, l'humiliante beauté."

31. Ibid., p. 177: "Henri . . . c'est moi qui l'ai fait; je l'ai créé comme il crée les personnages de ses livres."

32. *La Force des choses*, vol. l, p. 367: "Le pivot de sa vie, c'est la vie des autres: son mari, sa fille; cette dépendance, qui l'apparente à la majorité des femmes, m'intéressait."

33. Barnes, *The Literature of Possibility*, p. 231.

34. Julienne-Caffié, *Simone de Beauvoir*, p. 72.

35. Hourdin, *Simone de Beauvoir*, p. 142.

36. Leighton, *Simone de Beauvoir on Women*, p. 84.

37. Ibid., p. 96.

38. Ibid., p. 108.

39. Ibid., p. 123.

40. Ibid., p. 172.

41. Ibid.

42. Keefe, *Simone de Beauvoir*, p. 193.

43. Leighton, *Simone de Beauvoir on Women*, p. 180.

44. *La Force des choses*, vol. l, p. 369: "Au départ, je comptais me venger sur Nadine de certains traits qui m'avaient heurtée chez Lise et chez plusieurs de mes cadettes, entre autres, une brutalité sexuelle qui révélait déplaisamment leur frigidité, une agres-

sivité qui compensait mal leur sentiment d'infériorité. . . . Peu à peu, . . . je me mis à voir des excuses; Nadine me parut plutôt victime que blâmable."

Chapter 8

1. Appendix B.

2. Simone de Beauvoir, *Mémoires d'une jeune fille rangée* (Paris: Gallimard, 1958), p. 25: "Un neuf nous eût toutes deux déshonorées."

3. Ibid., p. 43: "Ainsi vivions-nous, elle et moi, dans une sorte de symbiose, et sans m'appliquer à l'imiter, je fus modelée par elle. Elle m'inculqua le sens du devoir, ainsi que des consignes d'oubli de soi et d'austérité. . . . J'appris de maman à m'effacer, à contrôler mon langage, à censurer mes désirs, à dire et à faire exactement ce qui devait être dit et fait. Je ne revendiquais rien et j'osais peu de chose."

4. Ibid., p. 17: "Quand on touche à Simone, elle devient violette."

5. Ibid., p. 41: "La chaleur de son affection rachetait ses sautes d'humeur. Plus impeccable et plus lointaine, elle n'eût pas si profondément agi sur moi."

6. Appendix B., pp. 361, 377.

7. *Mémoires d'une jeune fille rangée*, p. 191: "Simone aimerait mieux se mettre toute nue que de dire ce qu'elle a dans la tête."

8. Ibid., p. 225: "Naturellement, à ta mère tu ne veux rien dire."

9. Christiane Rochefort, *Les Petits Enfants du siècle* (Paris: Editions Bernard Grasset, 1961).

10. Appendix A, pp. 328, 342.

11. *Mémoires d'une jeune fille rangée*, pp. 107–8: "Si elle m'avait souvent contrariée, je crois qu'elle m'eût précipitée dans la révolte. Mais dans les choses importantes—mes études, le choix de mes amies—elle intervenait peu; elle respectait mon travail et même mes loisirs, ne me demandant que de menus services: moudre le café, descendre la caisse à ordures. J'avais l'habitude de la docilité, et je croyais que, en gros, Dieu l'exigeait de moi; le conflit qui m'opposait à ma mère n'éclata pas."

12. Ibid., p. 172: "Elle me demanda avec un peu d'embarras 'où j'en étais du point de vue religieux'. Mon coeur se mit à battre: 'Eh bien, dis-je, voilà quelque temps que je ne crois plus'. Son visage se décomposa: 'Ma pauvre petite!' dit-elle. Elle ferma la porte, pour que ma soeur n'entendît pas la suite de notre entretien; d'une voix implorante, elle ébaucha une démonstration de l'existence de Dieu, puis elle eut un geste d'impuissance, et s'arrêta, les larmes aux yeux. Je regrettai de lui avoir fait de la peine, mais je me sentais bien soulagée: enfin j'allais pouvoir vivre à visage découvert."

13. Ibid., p. 175: "Les yeux au ciel, ma mère priait pour mon âme; ici-bas, elle gémissait sur mes égarements: toute communication était coupée entre nous."

14. Ibid., p. 191: "Ma mère m'avait dit souvent qu'elle avait souffert de la froideur de bonne-maman, et qu'elle souhaitait être pour ses filles une amie; mais comment aurait-elle pu causer avec moi de personne à personne? J'étais à ses yeux une âme

en péril, une âme à sauver: un objet. La solidité de ses convictions lui interdisait la moindre concession."

15. Hélène de Beauvoir, *Souvenirs*, comp. Marcelle Routier (Garamont: Librairie Séguier, 1987).

16. *Mémoires d'une jeune fille rangée*, p. 87: "Ma mère nous laissa entendre que les nouveau-nés sortaient par l'anus, et sans douleur. Elle parlait d'un ton détaché; mais cette conversation n'eut pas de suite: plus jamais je n'abordai avec elle ces problèmes et elle n'en souffla plus mot."

17. Ibid., p. 104: "On l'enveloppa de bandages si bien que j'eus tout le jour l'impression de cacher dans mon corsage une encombrante infirmité."

18. Ibid., p. 12: "J'émergeais saine et sauve de l'aventure qui m'avait tour à tour réduite en foetus et changée en matrone."

19. Chernin, *The Hungry Self.*

20. *Mémoires d'une jeune fille rangée*, p. 58: "Dans la vie, je le savais, il en va tout autrement: une mère de famille est toujours flanquée d'un époux; mille tâches fastidieuses l'accablent. Quand j'évoquai mon avenir, ces servitudes me parurent si pesantes que je renonçai à avoir des enfants à moi; ce qui m'importait, c'était de former des esprits et des âmes: je me ferai professeur, décidais-je."

21. Ibid., p. 87: "Je ne me souviens pas d'avoir ruminé les phénomènes de la grossesse et de l'accouchement, ni de les avoir intégrés à mon avenir; j'étais réfractaire au mariage et à la maternité, et je ne me sentis sans doute pas concernée."

22. Ibid., p. 103: "J'avais imaginé que la confrérie féminine dissimulait soigneusement aux hommes sa tare secrète."

23. Ibid., p. 108: "Son éducation, son milieu l'avaient convaincue que pour une femme la maternité est le plus beau des rôles: elle ne pouvait le jouer que si je tenais le mien, mais je refusais aussi farouchement qu'à cinq ans d'entrer dans les comédies des adultes."

24. Ibid., p. 112: "Car alors elle saurait que je savais: je ne pouvais pas supporter cette idée. Je ne redoutais pas une réprimande. J'étais irréprochable. Mais j'avais une peur panique de ce qui se passerait dans sa tête. Peut-être se croirait-elle obligée d'avoir une conversation avec moi: cette perspective m'épouvantait parce que, au silence qu'elle avait toujours gardé sur ces problèmes, je mesurais sa répugnance à les abor-der. . . . La connaissance que j'en avais deviendrait, à travers la conscience de ma mère, un scandale qui nous souillerait toutes deux."

25. Ibid., p. 142: "Mettre neuf enfants au monde comme l'a fait maman, ça vaut bien autant que d'écrire des livres."

26. Ibid., p. 141: "rabâcher à l'infini la même ennuyeuse ritournelle."

27. Ibid., p. 144: "Je songeai sans répugnance au mariage. L'idée de maternité me restait étrangère, je m'étonnais que Zaza s'extasiât devant des nouveau-nés fripés."

28. Ibid., p. 212: "Je n'y voyais plus mon salut mais ma perte."

29. Ibid., p. 221: "Mademoiselle Lambert ne 'vivait' pas. Elle faisait des cours et travaillait à une thèse: je trouvais cette existence bien aride."

30. Ibid., pp. 226–27: "Le mariage, pour quoi faire? Elever des enfants ou corriger des devoirs, c'était la même inutile ritournelle. . . . Mademoiselle Lambert comme ma mère égrenaient des journées mortes, elles se contentaient de s'occuper. En vérité, le mal dont je souffrais, c'était d'avoir été chassée du paradis de l'enfance et de n'avoir pas retrouvé une place parmi les hommes."

31. Ibid., p. 238: "J'ai trop vécu les yeux tournés vers le passé et sans pouvoir m'arracher à l'émerveillement de mes souvenirs d'enfance."

32. Ibid., p. 241: "Quand je sortais avec mes parents ou avec les Mabille, une infranchissable pellicule s'interposait entre le monde et moi."

33. Ibid., pp. 270–71: "Jamais ma mère n'aurait accepté d'y mettre les pieds. . . . J'éprouvais une grande satisfaction à me savoir radicalement hors la loi."

34. Ibid., p. 319: "Je souhaitais seulement l'amour, écrire de bons livres, avoir quelques enfants, 'avec des amis à qui dédier mes livres et qui apprendront la pensée et la poésie à mes enfants'. J'accordais au mari une part bien minime."

35. Ibid., p. 325: "Je souhaitai vivement que cette image ne figurât pas dans mon avenir."

36. Ibid., p. 92: "une belle quadragénaire, brune, aux yeux de feu, au sourire appuyé. Elle tempérait par une soigneuse amabilité son aisance de souveraine."

37. Ibid., p. 116: "Moi, si j'avais commis une incongruité, ma mère l'eût ressentie dans la honte: mon conformisme traduisait sa timidité."

38. Ibid., p. 117: "Zaza me confia aussi que Madame Mabille—à qui elle attribuait des trésors de charme, de sensibilité, de fantaisie—avait souffert de l'incompréhension d'un mari ennuyeux comme un livre d'algèbre. Je me rends compte aujourd'hui qu'elle éprouvait pour son père une répulsion physique. Sa mère l'avertit très tôt, et avec une crudité méchante, des réalités sexuelles: Zaza comprit précocement que Madame Mabille avait haï dès la première nuit et à jamais les étreintes conjugales."

39. Ibid., p. 118: "Sa patience, ses sourires, recouvraient, je crois, une grande froideur."

40. Ibid., p. 121: "Elle essayait de faire entrer mon acte dans le circuit des politesses adultes. Je m'aperçus à cet instant que je ne l'aimais plus du tout."

41. Ibid., pp. 277–78: "Madame Mabille suivait avec ses enfants une habile politique; tout petits, elles les traitait avec une indulgence enjouée; plus tard, elle restait libérale dans les petites choses; quand il s'agissait d'affaires sérieuses, son crédit était intact."

42. Ibid., p. 278: "celle-ci s'était prise à ses sourires: l'amour autant que le respect paralysait ses révoltes."

43. Ibid., p. 253: "Se nourrir devenait une entreprise de longue haleine, et harassante."

44. Ibid., p. 332: "Ma petite, la femme n'aime pas; c'est l'homme qui aime."

45. Ibid., p. 278: "cette mère et toute cette famille entre nous."

46. Ibid., p. 178: "Mes amies, et Zaza elle-même, jouaient avec aisance leur rôle mondain; elles paraissaient au 'jour' de leur mère, servaient le thé, souriaient, disaient aimablement des riens; moi je souriais mal, je ne savais pas faire du charme, de l'esprit ni même des concessions!"

47. Ibid., p. 248: "Je l'aime tellement, voyez-vous, que cela m'est plus dur que tout de lui causer toute cette peine que je lui cause et d'aller contre sa volonté."

48. Ibid., pp. 276–77: "Je me demandais si à la longue Zaza ne se laisserait pas convaincre que son devoir de chrétienne était de fonder un foyer."

49. Ibid., p. 303: "Je vous avoue que je suis effrayée de reprendre mon existence d'il y a trois mois. Le très respectable formalisme dont vivent la plupart des gens de 'notre milieu' m'est devenu insupportable."

50. Ibid., p. 304: "Heureusement, Zaza m'aime beaucoup."

51. Ibid., p. 358: "N'ayez pas de chagrin, maman chérie, dit-elle. Dans toutes les familles il y a du déchet: c'est moi le déchet."

52. Ibid., p. 208: "Sa mère, sa soeur m'entoureraient de leur tendresse, mes parents se radouciraient: je redeviendrais celle que tout le monde aimait, je reprendrais ma place dans cette société hors de laquelle je n'envisageais que l'exil."

53. Ibid., p. 297: "[Il] n'espérait guère pouvoir aimer une femme d'amour; il était trop exclusivement attaché à sa mère."

54. Hourdin, *Simone de Beauvoir*, p. 46: "aussi solide . . . que son mari était léger."

55. Ibid., p. 46: "faussement puritaine."

56. Ibid., p. 53: "milieu . . . spirituellement médiocre."

57. Ibid., p. 187–88: "Nous désirons rejoindre le plan de Dieu en participant à son acte de création, en donnant naissance, à partir de deux libertés réunies, à des libertés nouvelles. . . . Jean-Paul Sartre et Simone de Beauvoir sont orphelins de Dieu. C'est peut-être parce qu'ils se refusent au simple amour créateur des hommes. Ayant rejeté leur passé familial, n'ayant aucun visage d'enfant à leurs côtés, n'ayant pas d'avenir autre que dans leurs livres, ils sont véritablement seuls."

58. Francis Jeanson, *Simone de Beauvoir ou l'entreprise de vivre* (Paris: Editions du Seuil, 1966), p. 140: "Sans doute cela n'est-il point sans rapport avec la remarquable sensibilité au charme féminin dont la quasi-totalité de cette oeuvre m'apparaît imprégnée."

59. Ibid., p. 142: "engluée dans sa condition féminine, physiquement irresponsable (sa vitalité incontrôlée, ses humeurs) et moralement mystifiée (par une triple soumission, à Dieu, à son mari, aux conventions de leur milieu social)."

60. Annemarie Lasocki, *Simone de Beauvoir ou l'entreprise d'écrire* (La Haye: Martinus Nijhoff, 1971).

61. Marks, *Simone de Beauvoir*, p. 51.

62. Cottrell, *Simone de Beauvoir*, p. 9.

63. Ibid., p. 13.

64. Leighton, *Simone de Beauvoir on Women*, p. 194.

65. Ibid.

66. Ibid., p. 197.

67. Ibid., p. 198.

68. Ibid., p. 202.

69. Ibid., p. 203.

70. Ibid., p. 205.

71. Ascher, *Simone de Beauvoir*, p. 13.

72. Ibid., p. 21.

73. Whitmarsh, *Simone de Beauvoir*, p. 7.

74. Ibid., pp. 10–11.

75. Keefe, *Simone de Beauvoir*, p. 9.

76. Ibid., p. 12.

77. Ibid., p. 32.

78. Mary Evans, *Simone de Beauvoir*, p. 3.

79. Ibid., p. 8.

80. Ibid., p. 5.

81. Ibid., p. 12.

82. Okely, *Simone de Beauvoir*, p. 30.

83. Ibid., p. 38.

84. Ibid., pp. 42–43.

85. Catherine Portuges, "Attachment and Separation in *The Memoirs of a Dutiful Daughter*," *Yale French Studies*, no. 72 (New Haven: Yale University Press, 1986), p. 114.

86. Renée Winegarten, *Simone de Beauvoir*. (Oxford: Berg Publishers Limited, 1988), p. 12.

87. Appendix A, pp. 329, 343.

88. Appendix B, pp. 363, 379.

Chapter 9

1. Simone de Beauvoir, *La Force de l'âge* (Paris: Librairie Gallimard, 1960), p. 18: "J'avais liquidé mon passé; je m'engageai sans réserve dans notre histoire."

2. Ibid., p. 20: "Je conservais de bonnes relations avec mes parents, mais ils avaient perdu sur moi toute emprise."

3. Ibid., p. 58: "J'avais laissé tomber presque toutes les obligations qui m'ennuyaient: tantes, cousins, amies d'enfance. Je déjeunais assez souvent chez mes parents: comme nous évitions les querelles, nous avions peu de sujets de conversation; ils ignoraient à peu près tout de ma vie."

4. Ibid., p. 474: "Grâce à cette équivoque, je ne me trouvai pas en conflit avec mes parents."

5. Ibid., p. 82: "Je me sentais si peu d'affinités avec mes parents que d'avance les fils, les filles que je pourrais avoir m'apparaissaient comme des étrangers; j'escomptais de

leur part ou de l'indifférence, ou de l'hostilité tant j'avais eu d'aversion pour la vie de famille."

6. Ibid., p. 87: "Ma mère s'emportait contre les employés de la gare, mon père insultait les voyageurs qui partageaient notre compartiment, et tous deux se querellaient. . . . Ah! je m'étais bien promis que ma vie serait différente!"

7. Ibid., p. 139: "A la sortie du lycée mon coeur se serrait quand je pensais qu'elles allaient rentrer dans un intérieur aussi fermé, aussi morne que celui où j'avais étouffé à leur âge."

8. Ibid., p. 479: "Je reconnaissais cette chaude bêtise qui avait obscurci mon enfance: elle accablait officiellement le pays tout entier."

9. Ibid., p. 566: "Je ne retrouvai pas grand-chose du passé."

10. Ibid., p. 82: "Il se suffisait, il me suffisait. Et je me suffisais."

11. Ibid.: "Pour risquer de les compromettre, il aurait fallu qu'un enfant représentât à mes yeux un accomplissement aussi essentiel qu'une oeuvre: ce n'était pas le cas."

12. Ibid., p. 83: "Enfanter, c'est accroître vainement le nombre des êtres qui sont sur terre, sans justification."

13. Ibid.: "Je n'ai pas eu l'impression de refuser la maternité; elle n'était pas mon lot; en demeurant sans enfant, j'accomplissais ma condition naturelle."

14. Ibid., p. 20: "En un sens nous étions tous deux sans famille."

15. Ibid., pp. 376–77: "On dira sans doute que Sartre fut pour moi un substitut du père, et Olga le succédané d'un enfant: aux yeux de ces doctrinaires, il n'existe jamais de relations adultes; ils ignorent la dialectique qui de l'enfance à la maturité . . . transforme les relations affectives."

16. Ibid., p. 99: "J'avais tout à leur apprendre: cette idée me piquait. . . . Je me réjouissais presque autant de leurs progrès que si j'en avais fait moi-même."

17. Ibid., p. 164: "Mais qu'étions-nous? Pas de mari, d'enfant, de foyer, aucune surface sociale, et vingt-six ans: à cet âge, on a envie de peser sur terre."

18. Ibid., p. 169: "commission départementale de la natalité et de la protection de l'enfance."

19. Ibid., p. 237: "Le conflit qui oppose classiquement l'adolescent à ses parents prit chez elle une forme particulièrement pénible parce que soudain ils incarnaient ce que, plus ou moins consciemment, ils lui avaient eux-mêmes appris à mépriser: le bon ordre, la sagesse des nations, les coutumes établies et tout le sérieux de cet âge adulte qu'elle voyait approcher avec horreur. Elle s'en voulait de les avoir déçus, car elle avait toujours tenu passionnément à leur estime; mais leur revirement, leur défection l'emplissaient de rancune."

20. Ibid., p. 262: "Ensemble, nous haïssions les foules dominicales, les dames et les messieurs comme il faut, la province, les familles, les enfants et tous les humanismes."

21. André Gide, *Les Nourritures terrestres.* (Paris: Editions Gallimard, 1917), p. 69: "Familles, je vous hais!"

22. *La Force de l'âge*, p. 265: "Son rôle était tout de même celui d'une enfant, aux prises avec un couple d'adultes qu'unissait une complicité sans faille. . . . Nous n'avions pas établi avec elle de véritables relations d'égalité, mais plutôt nous l'avions annexée."

23. Ibid., p. 250: "Par son impétuosité, par son extrémisme, Olga l'incarnait avec éclat."

24. Ibid., p. 348: "En tuant Olga sur le papier, je liquidai les irritations, les rancunes que j'avais pu éprouver à son égard: je purifiai notre amitié de tous les mauvais souvenirs qui se mélangeaient aux bons."

25. Ibid., p. 491: "A mes yeux, sa vitalité, ses dons l'emportaient de loin sur ses disgrâces."

26. Ibid., p. 39: "Madame Lemaire se consacrait à [son mari], à ses enfants, à de vieilles parentes, à diverses épaves, elle avait renoncé à vivre pour son compte."

27. Ibid., p. 374: "Si elle a quelque chose dans le ventre, qu'elle le sorte!"

28. Ibid., p. 109: "Une mère chérie et révérée depuis le berceau peut conserver un terrible ascendant, même si on déplore l'étroitesse de ses idées et ses abus d'autorité; jugé, blâmé, un mari cesse d'inspirer du respect."

29. Ibid., p. 376: "La malédiction qui pèse sur la plupart des femmes, la dépendance, me fut épargnée. Gagner sa vie, en soi ce n'est pas un but; mais par là seulement on atteint une solide autonomie intérieure."

30. Ibid., p. 371: "Non seulement nous étions, comme tous les bourgeois, protégés du besoin, et, comme tous les fonctionnaires, de l'insécurité, mais nous n'avions pas d'enfants, pas de famille, pas de responsabilités: des elfes."

31. Ibid., p. 170: "de soutenir les doctrines hitlériennes en exigeant que la femme fût reléguée au foyer."

32. Ibid., p. 138: "La procréation en particulier ne devait pas être subie, mais lucidement consentie."

33. Jaccard, *Simone de Beauvoir*, p. 88: "Grâce au trio, l'être pense approcher le monde extérieur et entrer en contact avec lui tout en restant à l'intérieur de sa coquille protectrice."

34. Lasocki, *Simone de Beauvoir*, p. 183: "l'esclavage politique ou familial dans les rapports sociaux."

35. Keefe, *Simone de Beauvoir*, pp. 34–35.

Chapter 10

1. Simone de Beauvoir, *La Force des choses*, vol. 1 (Paris: Editions Gallimard, 1963), pp. 494–95: "Je retrouve, à cinquante ans de distance, la vieille idée de mon père: 'La femme est ce que son mari la fait.' Il se trompait bien; il n'a pas entamé d'un cheveu la jeune dévote façonnée par le couvent des Oiseaux."

2. Simone de Beauvoir, *Une Mort très douce* (Paris: Gallimard, 1964), p. 147: "Elle jouait souvent le rôle essentiel: elle se confondait avec Sartre, et nous étions heureuses ensemble. Et puis le rêve tournait au cauchemar: pourquoi habitais-je de nouveau avec elle? Comment étais-je retombée sous sa coupe? Notre relation ancienne survivait donc en moi sous sa double figure: une dépendance chérie et détestée."

3.   Hélène de Beauvoir, *Souvenirs*, p. 234.

4.   Appendix B, pp. 360, 377.

5.   Appendix A, pp. 328, 342–43.

6.   *La Force des choses*, vol. 1, p. 316: "Elle m'en voulait encore de l'avoir sacrifiée à mon travail et cette rancune se retournait contre ce que j'écrivais."

7.   Ibid., vol. 1, p. 317: "Elle avait espéré compenser par la maternité les tristesses de son premier âge, mais ces tristesses l'avaient mal préparée à choyer une petite fille avec qui elle s'identifiait trop et trop peu."

8.   Ibid., vol. 2, p. 508: "Vous me rappelez ma mère."

9.   Ibid., vol. 1, p. 266: "J'aurais refusé toute valeur au sentiment maternel et à l'amour: non. J'ai demandé que la femme les vécût en vérité et librement, alors que souvent ils lui servent d'alibi."

10.   Ibid., vol. 2, p. 304: "maternité heureuse."

11.   Ibid., vol. 1, p. 19: "Avoir vingt ou vingt-cinq ans en septembre 44, cela paraissait une énorme chance: tous les chemins s'ouvraient.... Leur gaieté fortifiait la mienne. Auprès d'eux, j'avais leur âge."

12.   Ibid., vol. 2, p. 273: "d'apprendre ce que pensent les jeunes, ce qu'ils savent, ce qu'ils veulent, comment ils vivent."

13.   Ibid., vol. 2, p. 507: "L'avenir est dans leurs mains et si dans leurs projets je reconnais les miens, il me semble que ma vie se prolonge par-delà de ma tombe. Je me plais en leur compagnie; cependant le réconfort qu'ils m'apportent est douteux: perpétuant ce monde, ils me le volent.... Quelle supériorité d'être vivant!"

14.   Ibid., vol. 2, p. 169: "J'ai eu une envie aiguë d'être jeune."

15.   Ibid., vol. 1, p. 92: "Nos pieuses enfances bourgeoises créaient un lien entre nous; mais nous y réagissions de manières différentes. Il gardait la nostalgie des paradis perdus: pas moi. Il se plaisait avec les gens âgés, il se défiait des jeunes que je préférais de loin aux vieux."

16.   Ibid., vol. 1, p. 145: "encore plus étouffante que la mienne."

17.   Ibid., vol. 2, p. 495: "Ça pèse, ça résiste, une jeunesse."

18.   Ibid., vol. 1, p. 328: "une formidable Déesse-Mère."

19.   Ibid., vol. 2, p. 232: "Elle a des enfants et un métier qui doit éprouver les nerfs et les coeurs: encore une de ces jeunes femmes superactives à qui je tire mon chapeau."

20.   Ibid., vol. 2, p. 511: "Au mieux, si on me lit, le lecteur pensera: elle en avait vu des choses!"

21.   Ibid.: "Si du moins elle avait enrichi la terre; si elle avait engendré ... quoi? une colline? une fusée? Mais non. Rien n'aura eu lieu."

22.   Ibid.: "cette mine d'or à mes pieds, toute une vie à vivre."

23.   Ibid.: "Tournant un regard incrédule vers cette crédule adolescente, je mesure avec stupeur à quel point j'ai été flouée."

24. Jeanson, *Simone de Beauvoir*, p. 200: "le dépassement décisif d'une attitude adolescente (et assez typiquement petite-bourgeoise), caractérisée par une extrême réserve à l'égard de ses plus proches amis et par l'absolu secret dont elle entourait alors son propre dialogue avec elle-même."

25. Ibid., p. 200: "Cette femme . . . a choisi de se mettre à nu sous nos yeux, bien plus qu'aucune 'strip-teaseuse' ne le fera jamais."

26. Madeleine Descubes, *Connaître Simone de Beauvoir* (Paris: Editions Resma, 1974), p. 62.

27. Lasocki, *Simone de Beauvoir*, p. 124: "Elle profitait de sa 'jeunesse retrouvée.'"

Chapter 11

1. Simone de Beauvoir, *Une Mort très douce* (Paris: Editions Gallimard, 1964), p. 27: "Pour moi, ma mère avait toujours existé et je n'avais jamais sérieusement pensé que je la verrais disparaître un jour, bientôt. Sa fin se situait, comme sa naissance, dans un temps mythique."

2. Ibid., p. 16: "Elle avait l'âge de mourir."

3. Ibid., p. 28: "Je me rendis compte que l'accident de ma mère me frappait beaucoup plus que je ne l'avais prévu. Je ne savais pas trop pourquoi. Il l'avait arrachée à son cadre, à son rôle, aux images figées dans lesquelles je l'emprisonnais."

4. Ibid., p. 97: "Les parents ne comprennent pas leurs enfants, mais c'est réciproque."

5. Ibid., pp. 45–46: "Plus d'une fois elle s'est plainte à moi de la sécheresse de sa mère. Bonne-maman, à cinquante ans, était une femme distante et même hautaine, qui riait peu, cancanait beaucoup, et ne témoignait à maman qu'une affection très convention-nelle; fanatiquement dévouée à son mari, ses enfants n'avaient tenu dans sa vie qu'une place secondaire."

6. Appendix B, pp. 351, 367.

7. *Une Mort très douce*, p. 46: "Jusqu'aux approches de mon adolescence, maman m'a attribué les plus hautes qualités intellectuelles et morales: elle s'identifiait à moi; elle humiliait et ravalait ma soeur: c'était la cadette, rose et blonde, et sans s'en rendre compte maman prenait sur elle sa revanche."

8. Ibid., p. 45: "Elle se remémorait tout un passé d'amertume."

9. Ibid., pp. 147–48: "La tristesse de notre échec, dont je croyais avoir pris mon parti, m'est revenue au coeur. . . . Il n'était pas en mon pouvoir d'effacer les malheurs d'enfance qui condamnaient maman à me rendre malheureuse et à en souffrir en retour."

10. Ibid., p. 95: "Notre brève explication sur mon incroyance nous a réclamé à toutes deux un considérable effort. J'ai eu de la peine en voyant ses larmes. Mais j'ai vite réalisé qu'elle pleurait sur son échec sans se soucier de ce qui se passait en moi."

11. Ibid.: "Une entente serait restée possible si, au lieu de demander à tout le monde des prières pour mon âme, elle m'avait donné un peu de confiance et de sympathie. Je sais maintenant ce qui l'en empêchait: elle avait trop de revanches à prendre, de blessures à panser pour se mettre à la place d'autrui."

12. Ibid., pp. 130–31: "La religion était le pivot et la substance de sa vie .... Son abstention me convainc ... que prier était pour elle un exercice qui exigeait de l'attention, de la réflexion, un certain état d'âme. Elle savait ce qu'elle aurait dû dire à Dieu: 'Guérissez-moi. Mais que votre volonté soit faite: j'accepte de mourir.' Elle n'acceptait pas. En ce moment de vérité, elle ne voulait pas prononcer des mots insincères. Elle ne s'accordait pas cependant le droit de se rebeller. Elle se taisait."

13. Hélène de Beauvoir, *Souvenirs*, p. 243: "Papa, Simone et moi, nous avions à ses yeux mené des vies pas bien du tout. Elle refusait d'y penser, de penser à la mort, à l'autre monde, parce que, mon dieu! retrouverait-elle papa, qui était loin d'être un saint? La rejoindrions-nous, nous qui étions loin d'être des saintes? Nous qui fûmes toute sa vie."

14. *Une Mort très douce*, p. 51: "On sait assez que chez l'homme l'habitude tue le désir. Maman avait perdu sa première fraîcheur et lui sa fougue. Pour la réveiller, il recourait aux professionnelles."

15. Ibid., p. 51: "Que le mariage bourgeois soit une institution contre nature, son cas suffirait à m'en convaincre. L'alliance passée à son doigt l'avait autorisée à connaître le plaisir; ses sens étaient devenus exigeants; à trente-cinq ans, dans la force de l'âge, il ne lui était plus permis de les assouvir."

16. Ibid., pp. 53–54: "Elle s'est précipitée dans la seule issue qui s'offrît à elle: se nourrir des jeunes vies dont elle avait la charge. 'Moi du moins, je n'ai jamais été égoïste, j'ai vécu pour les autres', m'a-t-elle dit plus tard. Oui; mais aussi par eux. Possessive, dominatrice, elle aurait voulu nous tenir tout entières dans le creux de sa main. Mais c'est au moment où cette compensation lui est devenue nécessaire que nous avons commencé à souhaiter de la liberté, de la solitude."

17. Ibid., p. 43: "Quand mon père est mort, je n'ai pas versé un pleur. J'avais dit à ma soeur: 'Pour maman, ça sera pareil.'"

18. Ibid., pp. 46–47: "corsetée des principes les plus rigides: bienséances provinciales et morale de couvent."

19. Hélène de Beauvoir, *Souvenirs*, p. 29: "Rien n'avait préparé ma mère à élever à Paris deux petites filles qui ne pourraient mener la même existence qu'elle. Maman avait une conception totalement tyrannique de la maternité: les filles devaient être étroitement, inconditionnellement liées à leur mère. Son axiome favori, qu'elle avait puisé dans un livre de Marcel Prévost, était: 'Une jeune fille a deux amies, sa mère et son aiguille.' C'était le genre de principe qu'elle nous inculquait."

20. *Une Mort très douce*, pp. 60–61: "Ma mère ... a vécu contre elle-même. Riche d'appétits, elle a employé toute son énergie à les refouler et elle a subi ce reniement dans la colère. Dans son enfance, on a comprimé son corps, son coeur, son esprit, sous un harnachement de principes et d'interdits. On lui a appris à serrer elle-même étroitement ses sangles. En elle subsistait une femme de sang et de feu: mais contrefaite, mutilée et étrangère à soi."

21. Ibid., p. 21: "que mon père vieillissant, devenu hypocondriaque, remplissait des éclats de sa mauvaise humeur."

22. Ibid., p. 109: "Je m'étais attachée à cette moribonde. Tandis que nous parlions dans la pénombre, j'apaisais un vieux regret: je reprenais le dialogue brisé pendant mon adolescence et que nos divergences et notre ressemblance ne nous avaient jamais

permis de renouer. Et l'ancienne tendresse que j'avais crue tout à fait éteinte ressuscitait, depuis qu'il lui était possible de se glisser dans des mots et des gestes simples."

23. Ibid., p. 26: "C'étaient des phrases routinières, mécaniques comme la respiration, mais tout de même animées par sa conscience: impossible de les entendre sans gêne. Je m'attristais du contraste entre la vérité de son corps souffrant et les billevesées dont sa tête était farcie."

24. Ibid., pp. 97–98: "Je frappais. J'entendais un petit gémissement, le frottement de ses pantoufles sur le plancher, encore un soupir, et je me promettais que cette fois je trouverais des sujets de conversation, un terrain d'entente. Au bout de cinq minutes la partie était perdue: nous avions si peu d'intérêts communs! Je feuilletais ses livres: nous ne lisions pas les mêmes. Je la faisais parler, je l'écoutais, je commentais. Mais, parce qu'elle était ma mère, ses phrases déplaisantes me déplaisaient plus que si elles étaient sorties d'une autre bouche."

25. Ibid., p. 98: "Je sais que tu ne me trouves pas intelligente."

26. Ibid., p. 60: "Elle redoutait de 'passer pour une idiote' à nos yeux. Elle continua donc d'entretenir des brumes dans sa tête et de dire oui à tout sans s'étonner de rien."

27. Hélène de Beauvoir, *Souvenirs*, pp. 69–70: "Si elles font des études, elles seront plus intelligentes que moi. Simone est déjà plus intelligente, je ne veux pas avoir deux filles plus intelligentes, donc Hélène ne passera pas son baccalauréat."

28. *Une Mort très douce*, p. 94: "Toi, tu me fais peur."

29. Ibid., p. 59: "On ne l'avait habituée ni à voir clair en elle, ni à user de son propre jugement. Il lui fallait s'abriter derrière des autorités."

30. Ibid., p. 96: "J'étais le soutien de la famille, en quelque sorte son fils. D'autre part j'étais un écrivain connu. . . . Souvent choquée par le contenu de mes livres, elle était flattée par leur succès. Mais par l'autorité qu'il me conférait à ses yeux, il aggravait son malaise."

31. Ibid., p. 15: "Elle avait l'air si confuse de déranger, si éperdument reconnaissante de ce qu'on faisait pour elle: elle fendait le coeur."

32. Ibid., p. 27: "Aucun corps n'existait moins pour moi—n'existait davantage. Enfant, je l'avais chéri; adolescente, il m'avait inspiré une répulsion inquiète; c'est classique; et je trouvai normal qu'il eût conservé ce double caractère répugnant et sacré: un tabou. Tout de même, je m'étonnai de la violence de mon déplaisir. Le consentement insouciant de ma mère l'aggravait."

33. Ibid., p. 146: "oubliant mon dégoût pour ce lit nuptial où j'étais née, où mon père était mort."

34. Ibid., p. 75: "Sa nudité ne me gênait plus: ce n'était plus ma mère, mais un pauvre corps supplicié."

35. Ibid., p. 103: "Le monde s'était réduit aux dimensions de sa chambre. . . . Ma vraie vie se déroulait auprès d'elle et n'avait qu'un but: la protéger."

36. Ibid., pp. 43–44: "Je parlai à Sartre de la bouche de ma mère, telle que je l'avais vue le matin et de tout ce que j'y déchiffrais: une gloutonnerie refusée, une humilité presque servile, de l'espoir, de la détresse, une solitude—celle de sa mort, celle de sa vie—qui ne voulait pas s'avouer. Et ma propre bouche, m'a-t-il dit, ne m'obéissait

plus: j'avais posé celle de maman sur mon visage et j'en imitais malgré moi les mimiques. Toute sa personne, toute son existence s'y matérialisaient et la compassion me déchirait."

37. Ibid., p. 19: "J'imaginais sa détresse. Elle croyait au ciel; mais malgré son âge, ses infirmités, ses malaises, elle était farouchement accrochée à la terre et elle avait de la mort une horreur animale."

38. Ibid., p. 39: "J'étais fascinée par ce mouvement de succion, à la fois avide et retenu, par cette lèvre ombragée d'un léger duvet, qui se gonflait comme elle se gonflait dans mon enfance quand maman était mécontente ou gênée."

39. Ibid., p. 48: "Le visage de maman, avec ce léger duvet qui ombrageait sa lèvre supérieure, trahissait une chaude sensualité.... J'ai été saisie par le rayonnement de son sourire, lié pour moi d'une manière mystérieuse à cette chambre dont elle sortait; je reconnaissais à peine dans cette fraîche apparition la grande personne respectable qui était ma mère."

40. Ibid., p. 71: "Nous retrouvions le sourire qui avait ébloui notre petite enfance, un radieux sourire de jeune femme. Entre-temps, où s'était-il perdu?"

41. Ibid., p. 132: "Maman aimait la vie comme je l'aime et elle éprouvait devant la mort la même révolte que moi."

42. Ibid., p. 85: "Sa maladie avait fracassé la carapace de ses préjugés et de ses prétentions."

43. Ibid.: "Sa beauté, son sourire ressuscités exprimaient un paisible accord avec elle-même et, sur ce lit d'agonie, une espèce de bonheur."

44. Ibid., p. 37: "Plus intime avec elle que moi, elle lui était aussi plus attachée."

45. Ibid., p. 97: "Elle pensait que je la jugeais. Poupette, 'la petite,' moins respectée que moi—et qui, ayant été moins marquée par maman, n'avait pas hérité de sa raideur—avait avec elle des rapports plus libres."

46. Ibid., pp. 65–66: "Tu as vu mourir papa et bonne-maman; moi, j'étais loin . . . maman, c'est moi qui la prends en charge. Et puis, j'ai envie de rester avec elle."

47. Ibid., pp. 134–35: "Quand quelqu'un de cher disparaît, nous payons de mille regrets poignants la faute de survivre. Sa mort nous découvre sa singularité unique . . . il nous semble qu'il aurait dû tenir plus de place dans notre vie: à la limite toute la place. Nous nous arrachons à ce vertige: il n'était qu'un individu parmi d'autres. Mais comme on ne fait jamais tout son possible, pour personne—même dans les limites, contestables, qu'on s'est fixées—il nous reste encore bien des reproches à nous adresser."

48. Ibid., p. 135: "A l'égard de maman nous étions surtout coupables, ces dernières années, de négligences, d'omissions, d'abstentions. Il nous a semblé les avoir rachetées par ces journées que nous lui avons consacrées, par la paix que lui donnait notre présence, par les victoires remportées contre la peur et la douleur. Sans notre vigilance têtue, elle aurait souffert bien davantage."

49. Ibid., p. 103: "C'est bête! pour une fois que je vous ai toutes les deux à ma disposition, je suis malade!"

50. Ibid., p. 147: "D'ordinaire je pensais à elle avec indifférence. Pourtant, dans mon sommeil . . . elle jouait souvent le rôle essentiel: elle se confondait avec Sartre, et nous étions heureuses ensemble. Et puis le rêve tournait au cauchemar: pourquoi habitais-je de nouveau avec elle? Comment étais-je retombée sous sa coupe? Notre relation ancienne survivait donc en moi sous sa double figure: une dépendance chérie et détestée. Elle a ressuscité dans toute sa force quand l'accident de maman, sa maladie, sa fin eurent cassé la routine qui réglait à présent nos rapports. . . . La 'petite maman chérie' de mes dix ans ne se distingue plus de la femme hostile qui opprima mon adolescence; je les ai pleurées toutes les deux en pleurant ma vieille mère."

51. Hélène de Beauvoir, *Souvenirs*, p. 243: "Tout se passa comme si, aux approches de la mort, se révélait à nous la jeune femme qu'elle aurait pu être. Elle recommanda à nos petites cousines: 'Profitez de la vie, mes petites.' Elle usa même d'une expression très 1900: 'Levez la jambe tant que vous le pouvez. Moi je ne l'ai pas assez levée!' . . . Elle nous stupéfia, nous qui pensions connaître notre mère."

52. *Une Mort très douce*, p. 78: "'Je dis toujours à mes petites-nièces: mes petites, profitez de la vie. —Je comprends pourquoi elles t'aiment tant. Mais tu n'aurais pas dit ça à tes filles?' Alors maman, soudain sévère: 'A mes filles? Ah! non!'"

53. Ibid., p. 48: "Rien, jamais, n'abolit notre enfance."

54. Marks, *Simone de Beauvoir*, p. 101.

55. Ibid., p. 104.

56. Ibid., pp. 101–2.

57. Ibid., p. 104.

58. Ibid., p. 110.

59. Ibid.

60. Cottrell, *Simone de Beauvoir*, p. 134.

61. Ibid., p. 135.

62. Ibid., p. 136.

63. Ibid., p. 137.

64. Bieber, *Simone de Beauvoir*, p. 92.

65. Ibid., p. 93.

66. Keefe, *Simone de Beauvoir*, p. 60.

67. Ibid., p. 61.

68. *Une Mort très douce*, p. 144: "Elle devenait un personnage, cette femme effacée, si rarement nommée."

69. Appendix B, pp. 361, 377.

Chapter 12

1. Simone de Beauvoir, *Tout compte fait* (Paris: Gallimard, 1972), p. 169: "Ce livre avait

encore un caractère autobiographique. Quand je l'eus achevé, je me suis promis de ne plus parler de moi d'ici longtemps."

2. Simone de Beauvoir, *Les Belles Images* (Paris: Gallimard, 1966), p. 9: "Elle est entrée à la radio par la petite porte, en 45, et elle est arrivée à la force des poignets, en travaillant comme un cheval, en piétinant ceux qui la gênaient."

3. Ibid., p. 17: "'C'est sa mère, elle a de l'affection pour elle. Mais c'est aussi une étrangère. Derrière les images qui virevoltent dans les miroirs, qui se cache? Peut-être personne du tout."

4. Ibid.: "Dominique pose des questions, par principe, mais elle trouverait indiscret que Laurence lui donne des réponses inquiétantes, ou simplement détaillées."

5. Ibid., pp. 21–22: "Tu ne sais pas ce que c'est que d'avoir des souliers déchirés et de sentir à travers sa chaussette qu'on a marché sur un crachat. Tu ne sais pas ce que c'est d'être toisée par des copines aux cheveux bien lavés et qui se poussent du coude. Non, tu ne sortiras pas avec cette tache sur ta jupe, va te changer."

6. Ibid., p. 21: "une magnifique poupée de métal."

7. Ibid., p. 46: "Non, crie Laurence, sans voix. Maman! ma pauvre maman!"

8. Ibid., p. 51: "Elle dit des mots cueillis jadis sur les lèvres de sa mère; dignité, sérénité, courage, respect de soi, faire bonne figure, se conduire avec classe, avoir le beau rôle. Dominique ne répond rien."

9. Ibid., p. 52: "Et Dominique, a-t-elle jamais aimé? peut-elle aimer? . . . Sa souffrance même ne l'humanise pas. C'est comme d'entendre grincer une langouste, un bruit inarticulé, n'évoquant rien, sinon la douleur toute nue. Bien plus intolérable que si on pouvait la partager."

10. Ibid., p. 71: "qui s'est taillé son chemin dans la vie à coups de hache, écrasant, écartant tout ce qui la gênait et soudain impuissante et se débattant avec rage."

11. Ibid., pp. 95–96: "Le seul remède, ce serait de le tuer: Dominique souffrirait beaucoup moins."

12. Ibid., p. 117: " Il fait si noir dans ce coeur, des serpents s'y tordent."

13. Ibid., pp. 124–25: "Que ce serait facile si Laurence pouvait la prendre dans ses bras, lui caresser les cheveux, comme avec Catherine. Ce qui la déchire, c'est cette répulsion qui se mêle à sa pitié: comme elle aurait pitié d'un crapaud blessé, sans se décider à le toucher. Elle a horreur de Gilbert, mais aussi de sa mère."

14. Ibid., p. 176: "Il se rendait compte qu'il l'avait mal jugée, que sa mondanité, son ambition, c'était une forme de vitalité. Et justement, il avait besoin de quelqu'un de vivant à ses côtés."

15. Chernin, *The Hungry Self.*

16. *Les Belles Images,* p. 25: "Laurence . . . avait essayé de croire en Dieu, en une autre vie où tout était compensé. Dominique avait été parfaite: elle lui avait permis de parler avec un prêtre, elle l'avait même choisi intelligent."

17. Ibid., p. 55: "J'aurais aimé m'asseoir dans le noir avec une petite fille de mon âge, et rire et chuchoter. Mais Dominique disait toujours: 'Elle est sûrement très sympa-

thique, ta camarade, mais, ma pauvre petite, elle est tellement ordinaire.' Marthe a eu une amie, la fille d'un ami de papa, bouchée et sotte. Moi non. Jamais."

18. Ibid., p. 172: "C'est précieux, une amitié. Si j'avais une amie, je lui parlerais au lieu de rester prostrée."

19. Ibid., p. 43: " Il me semblait n'avoir plus d'avenir: Jean-Charles, les petites en avaient un; moi pas; alors à quoi bon me cultiver? Cercle vicieux: je me négligeais, je m'ennuyais et je me sentais de plus en plus dépossédée de moi."

20. Ibid., p. 44:: "Pourquoi existe-t-on? Ce n'est pas mon problème. On existe. Il s'agit de ne pas s'en apercevoir, de prendre son élan, de filer d'un trait jusqu'à la mort."

21. Ibid., p. 67: "Elle a l'impression que les gens lui sont juxtaposés, ils n'habitent pas en elle; sauf ses filles, mais ça doit être organique."

22. Ibid., p. 122: "Faudra-t-il qu'elle devienne une femme comme moi, avec des pierres dans la poitrine et des fumées de soufre dans la tête?"

23. Ibid., pp. 135–36: "C'est effrayant de penser qu'on marque ses enfants rien que par ce qu'on est.... Les humeurs quotidiennes, les hasards d'un mot, d'un silence, toutes ces contingences qui devraient s'effacer derrière moi, ça s'inscrit dans cette enfant qui rumine et qui se souviendra, comme je me souviens des inflexions de voix de Dominique. Ça semble injuste. On ne peut pas prendre la responsabilité de tout ce qu'on fait–ne fait pas."

24. Ibid., p. 158: "Placide et grasse, sa mère bavardait avec une autre grosse femme, tout en faisant aller et venir une voiture d'enfant avec un bébé dedans; insensible à la musique, à la nuit, elle jetait parfois un regard bovin sur la petite inspirée.... Une charmante fillette qui deviendrait cette matrone."

25. Ibid.: "Non. Je ne voulais pas.... Je refusais qu'un jour elle ressemblât à sa mère, ne se rappelant même pas avoir été cette adorable ménade. Petite condamnée à mort, affreuse mort sans cadavre. La vie allait l'assassiner. Je pensai à Catherine qu'on était en train d'assassiner."

26. Ibid., p. 175: "Et de nouveau fond sur elle l'image qu'elle refoule avec le plus de violence, qui surgit dès que sa vigilance se relâche: Jean-Charles, papa, Dominique, souriant comme sur une affiche américaine vantant une marque de oat-meal. Réconciliés, s'abandonnant ensemble aux gaietés de la vie de famille."

27. Ibid., p. 180: "Ils la forceront à manger, ils lui feront tout avaler ... tout ce qu'elle vomit, sa vie, celle des autres avec leurs fausses amours, leurs histoires d'argent, leurs mensonges. Ils la guériront de ses refus, de son désespoir. Non."

28. Ibid., p. 133: "Si sûr de son bon droit; furieux si nous dérangeons l'image qu'il se fait de nous, petite fille, jeune femme exemplaires, se foutant de ce que nous sommes pour de bon."

29. Ibid., pp. 180–81: "Et Catherine? lui clouer les paupières? Non! ... Je ne permettrai pas qu'on lui fasse ce qu'on m'a fait.... Cette femme qui n'aime personne, insensible aux beautés du monde, incapable même de pleurer, cette femme que je vomis."

30. Ibid., p. 183: "Pour moi les jeux sont faits.... Mais les enfants auront leur chance. Quelle chance? elle ne le sait même pas."

31. Ibid., p. 57: "Précieux instants à jamais perdus. Pour elles aussi, un jour, ils seront perdus à jamais. Quel dommage! Les empêcher de grandir. Ou alors . . . quoi?"

32. Simone de Beauvoir, *Tout compte fait* (Paris: Gallimard, 1972), p. 172.

33. Cottrell, *Simone de Beauvoir*, p. 138.

34. Ibid., p. 139.

35. Bieber, *Simone de Beauvoir*, p. 172.

36. Ibid.

37. Ibid.

38. Ibid., p. 173.

39. Ascher, *Simone de Beauvoir*, p. 177.

40. Keefe, *Simone de Beauvoir*, p. 205.

41. Ibid., p. 209.

42. Ibid., p. 212.

Chapter 13

1. Simone de Beauvoir, "L'Age de discrétion," in *La Femme rompue* (Paris: Gallimard, 1967), p. ll: "où traînent encore des livres, des papiers, un vieux pull-over gris, un pyjama violet, cette chambre que je ne me décide pas à transformer parce que je n'ai pas le temps, pas l'argent, parce que je ne veux pas croire que Philippe ait cessé de m'appartenir."

2. Ibid., p. 20: "Pourquoi me suis-je acharnée à faire de Philippe un intellectuel alors qu'André l'aurait laissé s'engager dans d'autres chemins? Enfant, adolescente, les livres m'ont sauvée du désespoir; cela m'a persuadée que la culture est la plus haute des valeurs."

3. Ibid., p. 22: "Soudain il est apparu. . . . Il m'a serrée très fort en disant des mots joyeux et je me suis abandonnée à la tendresse du veston de flanelle contre ma joue."

4. Ibid.: "Toujours je l'oublie; toujours elle est là. . . . Je l'ai vite effacée. J'étais seule avec Philippe comme au temps où je le réveillais chaque matin d'une caresse sur le front."

5. Ibid., p. 33: "Je les connais ces jeunes femmes 'dans le vent'. On a un vague métier, on prétend se cultiver, faire du sport, bien s'habiller, tenir impeccablement son intérieur, élever parfaitement ses enfants, mener une vie mondaine, bref réussir sur tous les plans. Et on ne tient vraiment à rien. Elles me glacent le sang."

6. Ibid., p. 25: "En petites phrases mesurées, elle a laissé entendre ce qu'elle pensait de nous. . . . Nous vivons, coupés du monde, dans des laboratoires et des bibliothèques. . . . Elle n'est pas stupide à ce point-là, Irène. Elle existe, elle compte, elle a annulé la victoire que j'ai remportée avec Philippe, contre lui, pour lui."

7. Ibid., p. 27: "C'est moi qui ai façonné sa vie. Maintenant j'y assiste du dehors, en témoin distant. C'est le sort commun à toutes les mères: mais qui s'est jamais consolé en se disant que son sort est le sort commun?"

8. Ibid., p. 31: "Qu'est-ce que j'ai imaginé? Parce qu'il était exigeant je me suis crue indispensable. Parce qu'il se laisse facilement influencer j'ai cru l'avoir créé à mon image.... Sa vérité, c'est moi qui la détenais. Et il choisit de s'éloigner de moi, de briser nos complicités, de refuser la vie qu'au prix de tant d'efforts je lui avais bâtie. Il deviendra un étranger."

9. Ibid., p. 35: "On n'est pas un salaud parce qu'on refuse de partager vos entêtements séniles."

10. Ibid., p. 36: "Tout est fini entre Philippe et moi."

11. Ibid., p. 37: "Devant les planches nues, des larmes me sont montées aux yeux. Tant de souvenirs émouvants, bouleversants, délicieux se levaient en moi. Je leur tordrais le cou. Il m'avait quittée, trahie, bafouée, insultée. Jamais je ne le lui pardonnerais."

12. Ibid., p. 41: "Marié, passé de l'autre côté."

13. Ibid., p. 45: "Moins capricieux, moins nonchalant, il aurait eu moins besoin de moi. Il n'aurait pas été si délicieusement tendre s'il n'avait rien eu à se faire pardonner."

14. Ibid., p. 54: "Ma petite, ma chérie, je t'en prie, ne me déteste pas. Je ne peux pas vivre brouillé avec toi. Je t'en prie. Je t'aime tant."

15. Ibid., p. 55: "Je n'en dors plus. Mais je ne veux pas te perdre, aie pitié de moi, tu me rends si malheureux!"

16. Ibid., p. 56: "Pour toi l'amour, il faut que ça se mérite.... Je me suis donné assez de mal pour ne pas démériter. Tous mes désirs—être aviateur, ou coureur automobile, ou reporter, l'action, l'aventure—tu les tenais pour des caprices; je les ai sacrifiés, pour te faire plaisir. La première fois que je ne te cède pas, tu te brouilles avec moi.... Je n'allais tout de même pas t'obéir toute ma vie. Tu es trop tyrannique. Au fond tu n'as pas de coeur, seulement de la volonté de puissance.... Eh bien! adieu, méprise-moi tout ton soûl, je me passerai de toi."

17. Ibid., p. 19: "Elles m'entraînent dans leur avenir, par-delà ma tombe."

18. "Monologue," p. 93: "Piquer une crise de nerfs devant le petit m'ouvrir les veines sur leur paillasson. Toutes ces pouffiasses elles ont un homme pour les protéger des gosses pour les servir et moi zéro; ça ne peut pas durer."

19. Ibid., pp. 117–18: "Et si je me tuais devant lui crois-tu que ça lui ferait un beau souvenir? ... je me descendrai dans son salon je m'ouvrirai les veines quand ils se ramèneront il y aura du sang partout et je serai morte."

20. Ibid., p. 97: "Je la tenais oui j'étais ferme mais j'étais tendre toujours prête à bavarder avec elle je voulais être son amie ... Mais quel caractère ingrat! Elle est morte et alors? Les morts ne sont pas des saints. Elle ne coopérait pas elle ne me confiait rien."

21. Ibid., p. 98: "J'avais beaucoup à donner à Sylvie j'en aurais fait une fille bien; et moi je n'exigeais rien d'elle. J'étais tout dévouement. Cette ingratitude!"

22. Ibid., p. 102: "Sylvie la petite ingrate je voulais qu'elle ait un vrai foyer et une mère irréprochable une femme mariée la femme d'un banquier."

23. Ibid., p. 104: "Tant d'efforts de luttes de drames de sacrifices: en vain. L'oeuvre de ma vie volatilisée. Je ne laissais rien au hasard; et le plus cruel des hasards s'est mis au travers de ma route."

24. Ibid., p. 112: "Oui, si j'étais de ces mères qui se lèvent à sept heures du matin on l'aurait sauvée moi je vis sur un autre rythme ce n'est pas criminel comment aurais-je deviné? J'étais toujours là quand elle revenait du lycée beaucoup de mères ne peuvent pas en dire autant prête à bavarder avec elle à l'interroger c'est elle qui s'enfermait dans sa chambre sous prétexte de travailler. Jamais je ne lui ai manqué."

25. Ibid.:"Tu l'as tuée!"

26. Ibid., pp. 88–89: "Nanard était le roi. Elle le prenait dans son lit le matin je les entendais se chatouiller ... elle se baladait à travers son bordel de chambre à moitié à poil dans son peignoir de soie blanche taché et troué de brûlures de cigarettes il se collait à ses cuisses ça lève le coeur les mères avec leurs petits mâles."

27. Ibid., p. 95: "Je ne voulais pas que ma fille devienne une putain comme ma mère. A soixante-dix ans des jupes au genou de la peinture sur toute la figure!"

28. Ibid., pp. 104–5: "Ma mère; une mère c'est tout de même une mère je ne lui ai rien fait c'est elle qui m'a bousillé mon enfance elle m'a insultée elle a osé me dire ... Je veux qu'elle retire ce qu'elle m'a dit je ne continuerai pas à vivre avec ce cri dans mes oreilles une fille ne supporte pas d'être maudite pas sa mère même si c'est la dernière des putes."

29. Ibid., p. 97: "J'aurais baisé les mains de ma mère si elle s'était conduite comme ça avec moi."

30. Ibid., p. 103: "mal habillée négligée talochée rabrouée par sa concierge de mère toujours au bord des larmes."

31. Ibid., p. 97: "Je le gâterai ça leur fera rentrer dans la gorge leurs calomnies et leurs mensonges."

32. Ibid., p. 118: "Mon Dieu! Faites que vous existiez! Faites qu'il y ait un ciel et un enfer où je me promènerai dans les allées du paradis avec mon petit garçon et ma fille chérie et eux tous ils se tordront dans les flammes de l'envie je les regarderai rôtir et gémir je rirai je rirai et les enfants riront avec moi. Vous me devez cette revanche mon Dieu. J'exige que vous me la donniez."

33. "La Femme rompue," p. 125: "Voilà une des raisons—la principale—pour lesquelles je n'ai aucune envie de m'astreindre à un métier; je supporterais mal de n'être pas totalement à la disposition des gens qui ont besoin de moi. Je passe presque toutes mes journées au chevet de Colette. Sa fièvre ne tombe pas. . . . Des idées terrifiantes me traversent la tête."

34. Ibid., p. 139: "Elle n'est pas moins intelligente que sa soeur; la chimie l'intéressait, ses études marchaient bien, c'est dommage qu'elle les ait arrêtées. Que va-t-elle faire de ses journées? Je devrais l'approuver; elle a choisi la même voie que moi: mais j'avais Maurice."

35. Ibid., p. 195: "La médecine, telle que papa l'exerçait dans son Cabinet de Bagnolet, je pensais qu'il n' y avait pas de plus beau métier. Mais pendant ma première année, j'ai été boulversée, écoeurée, débordée par l'horreur quotidienne. J'ai flanché plusieurs fois."

36. Ibid., p. 186: "C'était moi l'égoïste, moi qui n'avais pas hésité à lui faire lâcher l'internat, qui aurais voulu le maintenir toute sa vie dans la médiocrité pour le garder à la

maison, qui suis jalouse de son travail: une castratrice . . . il ne souhaitait pas se marier tout de suite, je le savais, et pour l'enfant on aurait pu se débrouiller."

37. Ibid.: "possessive, impérieuse, envahissante avec mes filles comme avec lui."

38. Ibid.: "Tu as poussé Colette à faire un mariage idiot; et c'est pour t'échapper que Lucienne est partie."

39. Ibid., p. 213: "Son sentimentalisme, son besoin de sécurité, sa timidité, sa passivité, il m'en rendait responsable."

40. Ibid., p. 216: "Elle a ri: si je suis bête, elle veut bien l'être aussi. Elle m'aime tendrement, ça au moins on ne me l'ôtera pas. Mais l'ai-je écrasée? . . . S'est-elle étiolée à vivre dans mon ombre?"

41. Ibid., p. 219: "La pauvre, elle s'était donné beaucoup de mal et rien n'était réussi. Je la regardais avec les yeux de Maurice. Son appartement manque de charme, c'est certain. . . . Ils ne sortent pas, ils ont peu d'amis. . . . De nouveau je me suis demandé avec terreur: est-ce ma faute si la brillante lycéenne de quinze ans est devenue cette jeune femme éteinte?"

42. Ibid., p. 162: "Les pères n'ont jamais exactement les filles qu'ils souhaitent parce qu'ils se font d'elles une certaine idée à laquelle elles devraient se plier. Les mères les acceptent telles qu'elles sont. Colette avait besoin avant tout de sécurité et Lucienne de liberté; je les comprends toutes les deux. Chacune à sa manière, Colette si sensible, si humaine, Lucienne si énergique, si brillante, je les trouve tout à fait réussies."

43. *Mémoires d'une jeune fille rangée*, p. 42: "Mon père me traitait comme une personne achevée; ma mère prenait soin de l'enfant que j'étais."

44. "La Femme rompue," p. 213: "Est-ce qu'avec une mère différente—moins anxieuse, moins présente—Lucienne aurait supporté la vie de famille?"

45. Ibid., p. 236: "Elle ne m'aime pas; elle me le dira."

46. Ibid.: "Alors j'effacerais tout ce qui est mal, tout ce qui me nuit, je remettrais les choses en place entre Maurice et moi."

47. Ibid., p. 246: "Quand tu mises sur l'amour conjugal, tu prends une chance d'être plaquée à quarante ans, les mains vides."

48. Ibid.: "Non, bien sûr. Tu vois où ça mène."

49. Ibid., p. 250: "Tu as toujours eu un sens très exagéré de tes responsabilités."

50. Ibid.: "Selon elle, ce qui compte dans une enfance, c'est la situation psychanalytique, telle qu'elle existe à l'insu des parents, presque malgré eux. L'éducation, dans ce qu'elle a de conscient, de délibéré, ça serait très secondaire. Mes responsabilités seraient nulles."

51. Ibid., pp. 249–50: "Je trouve cette existence aride. . . . Ça aussi, c'est sûrement de ma faute, ce refus de l'amour: mon sentimentalisme l'a écoeurée, elle s'est travaillée pour ne pas me ressembler. . . . Elle n'est pas la fille forte, rayonnante, équilibrée que j'imaginais de Paris."

52. Ibid., p. 134: "J'ai eu du mal à admettre que tous les enfants mentent à leur mère. Pas à moi! Je ne suis pas une mère à qui on ment; pas une femme à qui on ment. Orgueil imbécile."

53. Ibid., p. 177: "ne néglige pas du tout sa fille. Elle lui apprend à se débrouiller seule, à vivre par elle-même, et elle a bien raison."

54. Ibid., p. 155: "Les femmes qui ne font rien ne peuvent pas blairer celles qui travaillent."

55. Ibid., p. 237: "Est-ce que je sais qui je suis? Peut-être une espèce de sangsue qui se nourrit de la vie des autres: celle de Maurice, de nos filles, de tous ces pauvres 'chiens mouillés' à qui je prétendais venir en aide. Une égoïste qui refuse de lâcher prise."

56. Ibid., p. 251: "L'ambition? Je n'en avais pas d'autre que de créer du bonheur autour de moi. Je n'ai pas rendu Maurice heureux. Et mes filles ne le sont pas non plus. Alors? Je ne sais plus rien. Non seulement pas qui je suis mais comment il faudrait être. . . . Comment vivre sans croire à rien ni à moi-même?"

57. Beauvoir, *Tout compte fait*, p. 176.

58. Ibid., p. 180.

59. Cottrell, *Simone de Beauvoir*, p. 143.

60. Annie Ophir, *Regards féminins* (Paris: Denoël/Gontier, 1976), p. 19.

61. Ibid., p. 22: "Ironie du sort ou mise en garde contre les mères intellectuelles?"

62. Ibid., p. 28: "Il a transgressé toutes les limites, il a rompu les conventions sociales qui permettaient de maintenir aux yeux de tous l'idée de la dignité humaine."

63. Ibid., pp. 47–48: "La mère . . . est la Voleuse par excellence. Elle a monopolisé, donc volé à Murielle, le Père et le Frère."

64. Ibid., p. 48: "Mais le pire de tout: la mère a volé à Murielle la belle image qu'elle avait d'elle-même en tant que mère. . . . La mère-momie est un vampire qui se nourrit de la vie des Autres et surtout de celle de sa fille Murielle."

65. Yolanda Astarita Patterson, "Entretien avec Simone de Beauvoir (20 juin 1978)," *The French Review* 52, no. 5 (April 1979).

66. Ophir, *Regards féminins*, p. 64: "son double rôle d'Épouse chérie et de Mère indispensable. "

67. Ibid., p. 65: "Admettre que son mari et ses filles ont évolué signifie se mettre en question en tant qu'Epouse et Mère, constater qu'en dehors de ces rôles, il n'y a plus PERSONNE."

68. Ibid., p. 86: "son terne double."

69. Bieber, *Simone de Beauvoir*, p. 174.

70. Ibid., p. 176.

71. Ibid., p. 179.

72. Carolyn A. Durham, "Patterns of Influence: Simone de Beauvoir and Marie Cardinal," *The French Review* 60, no. 3 (February 1987), p. 345.

73. Ibid., p. 346.

Chapter 14

1. Simone de Beauvoir, *La Vieillesse* (Paris: Gallimard, 1970), p. 34: "La fonction reproductrice est brutalement interrompue à un âge relativement jeune."

2. Ibid., p. 47: "Toute sociète . . . exalte la vigueur, la fécondité, liées à la jeunesse; elle redoute l'usure et la stérilité de la vieillesse."

3. Ibid., p. 399: "Du jour . . . où il se trouve astreint à reproduire sa vie, l'individu, enfermé dans un métier, voit son univers se rétrécir, ses projets se raréfier."

4. Ibid., p. 89: "Une protection plus efficace, c'est celle qu'assure aux vieux parents l'amour de leurs enfants."

5. Ibid., p. 283: "Ceux-ci ne s'occupent pas d'eux, ils ont sacrifié en vain leurs habitudes."

6. Ibid., p. 143: "Aussitôt sortis des jupes de leurs mères, les enfants sont tout de suite traités en petits adultes."

7. Ibid., p. 279: "et son rôle de grand-mère lui apporte de nouvelles possibilités."

8. Ibid., p. 389: "perdre une certaine image d'eux-mêmes que détenait le défunt; avec celui-ci s'engloutit une enfance, une adolescence dont il était seul à garder un certain souvenir."

9. Ibid., p. 393: "Toute sa vie ma mère a été marquée par son enfance, mais à la fin elle évoquait plus souvent encore avec rancune la préférence que son père avait manifestée à sa soeur cadette."

10. Ibid., p. 398: "Si les souvenirs affectifs qui réveillent l'enfance sont si précieux, c'est parce que, pendant un bref instant, ils nous remettent en possession d'un avenir sans limites."

11. Ibid., p. 402: "Presque partout la cellule familiale a éclaté."

12. Ibid., p. 460: "'Il dit n'avoir aucun sentiment pour ses arrière-petits-enfants qui de leur côté l'ignorent.'"

13. Ibid., p. 459: "A partir de là, on est menacé par la solitude et ses tristesses."

14. Ibid., p. 497: "L'équilibre affectif des gens âgés dépend surtout de leurs rapports avec leurs enfants."

15. Ibid., p. 498: "Avec sa fille, la mère cherche une identification. Mais la fille n'a pas toujours surmonté la classique hostilité de l'adolescence; elle maintient sa volonté de s'affranchir de sa mère en la tenant à distance; la vieille femme en souffre et lui en veut. De son côté, elle a traversé une phase de 'sentiment oedipien inversé' quand sa fille, devenue adulte, a menacé sa propre jeunesse: leurs rapports ultérieurs dépendent beaucoup de la manière dont cette crise a été liquidée."

16. Ibid.: "Les sentiments les plus chaleureux et les plus heureux des personnes âgées sont ceux qu'elles nourrissent pour leurs petits-enfants."

17. Ibid., p. 499: "Du fait que la femme se valorise ordinairement en tant que mère la rivalité avec la fille ou avec la bru peut sur ce terrain être très aiguë."

18. Ibid., p. 500: "Elle ressuscite leur propre jeunesse, elle les emporte dans l'infini de l'avenir; c'est la meilleure défense contre la morosité qui menace le grand âge."

19. Ibid., p. 513: "Toute leur vie soumises à leur mari, dévouées à leurs enfants, elles peuvent enfin se soucier d'elles-mêmes."

20. Ibid., p. 567: "La vie garde un prix tant qu'on en accorde à celle des autres, à travers l'amour, l'amitié, l'indignation, la compassion. Alors demeurent des raisons d'agir ou de parler."

21. Lasocki, *Simone de Beauvoir*, p. 149: "Nous avions vu que les rapports entre parents et enfants avaient plutôt été balayés de l'oeuvre beauvoirienne, l'auteur ayant pensé avoir réglé les siens propres avec ses parents."

22. *La Vieillesse*, p. 469, as quoted in Marks, *Simone de Beauvoir*, p. 125: "De même que les parents, les époux anxieux ne sont pas ceux qui aiment le plus, mais ceux qui éprouvent un manque au coeur de leurs sentiments."

23. Kathleen Woodward, "Simone de Beauvoir: Aging and Its Discontents" (unpublished manuscript dated January 1985), p. 17.

24. Ibid., p. 24.

25. Ibid., p. 20.

26. Simone de Beauvoir, *Tout compte fait,* pp. 14–15: "Jeune, gaie et fière d'avoir réussi un premier enfant, elle a eu avec moi des rapports tendres et chaleureux."

27. Ibid., p. 47: "Mon exemple montre d'une manière frappante combien un individu est tributaire de son enfance. La mienne m'a permis de prendre un bon départ."

28. Ibid., p. 29: "Si ma mère avait été moins indiscrète et moins tyrannique, les limites de son intelligence m'auraient moins gênée: la rancune n'aurait pas oblitéré l'affection que je lui portais."

29. Ibid.: "Si tous deux s'étaient montrés amicaux, j'aurais tout de même été en opposition avec leur manière de vivre et de penser; j'aurais plus ou moins étouffé à la maison et je me serais sentie seule: mais non pas rejetée, exilée, trahie. . . . C'est la seule période de ma vie qui m'ait laissé des regrets. . . . De dix-sept à vingt ans, l'attitude de mes parents m'a profondément peinée."

30. Ibid.: "Ma mère était si timorée et si despotique qu'elle n'aurait pas su nous inventer des plaisirs et qu'elle aurait répugné à nous laisser nous divertir sans elle."

31. Ibid., p. 28: "Aurais-je à mener un jour l'existence grise et plate de ma mère?"

32. Appendix B, pp. 351, 367.

33. *Tout compte fait*, p. 31: "J'aurais connu les déchirements qui sont ceux de tant de jeunes femmes, ligotées par l'amour et la maternité sans avoir oublié leurs anciens rêves."

34. Ibid., pp. 145–46: "J'ai aperçu ma mère—une jeune et belle silhouette sans visage— qui se tenait au bord d'une étendue d'eau lumineuse qu'il me fallait traverser pour la rejoindre . . . mais il n'y avait pas de barque pour le franchir. . . . On était obligé de s'aventurer dans l'eau où on risquait de se noyer. Cependant, je devais avertir ma mère qu'un grand danger la menaçait."

35. Ibid., p. 157: "Ma mère vient de se tuer."

36. Ibid., p. 169: "gravées en moi à jamais."

37. Ibid., p. 22: "Pourquoi a-t-elle échoué dans la mort alors qu'elle aurait souhaité vivre, aimer, écrire peut-être? Quelles ont été ses malchances? Avant tout, je pense, celle de sa petite enfance: moins appréciée par son père que sa soeur aînée, passionnément attachée à une mère affectueuse mais peu disponible, sous son apparente désinvolture elle était très vulnérable et manquait de confiance en soi: c'est ce que confirment les derniers mots qu'elle a prononcés: 'Je suis un déchet'."

38. Ibid., pp. 629–30: "Zaza avait l'esprit critique et bien des aspects de sa religion l'ont laissée perplexe; si elle n'y a pas renoncé, c'est à cause de l'amour inconditionné et douloureux qu'elle avait voué à sa mère: elle ne voulait pas intérieurement s'éloigner d'elle."

39. Ibid., p. 131: "Comme beaucoup de femmes 'relatives' elle vivait dans le souci."

40. Jean-Paul Sartre, *Les Mots* (Paris: Gallimard, 1964), p. 18: "Pauvre Anne-Marie: passive, on l'eût accusée d'être une charge; active, on la soupçonnait de vouloir régenter la maison. . . . Il ne fallut pas longtemps pour que la jeune veuve redevînt mineure: une vierge avec tache."

41. *Tout compte fait*, p. 132: "Il n'a rien compris à son enfance."

42. Ibid., p. 128: "J'ai été deux fois mariée et mère, et je suis toujours vierge."

43. Ibid., p. 131: "En s'insurgeant contre les préjugés qui avaient brimé sa jeunesse et contre les idées que son mari lui avait imposées, elle se vengeait de tous ceux qui l'avaient tyrannisée. Vers 62, elle se sentait tout à fait libérée: 'C'est seulement maintenant, à quatre-vingt-quatre ans, que je me suis vraiment affranchie de ma mère', nous dit-elle."

44. Ibid., p. 132: "Je nous revois le soir, rassemblés sous la lampe, mes parents, mes frères et moi. Mais je me rends compte qu'en fait, on ne se parlait pas. Chacun était tout seul."

45. Ibid., p. 136: "frappé par la farouche dureté de son visage. Il a eu l'impression que la vie avait écrasé et affadi, sans cependant la briser, une femme que sa constitution disposait à la passion, à la ténacité et même à la violence."

46. Ibid., p. 86: "Sa mère, qui dans sa jeunesse avait nourri des ambitions qu'elle n'avait pas pu satisfaire, avait voulu prendre sa revanche à travers sa fille. Toute petite, elle lui fit donner des leçons de piano, de chant et de danse."

47. Ibid., p. 91: "En public, ses parents étaient fiers d'elle; à la maison, son attitude rétive les exaspérait; ils prétendaient s'ingérer dans sa vie et elle ne le supportait pas. Ils voulaient la 'mater', elle était indomptable. . . . Cette histoire éveillait des échos en moi. Mais j'étais plus âgée, je dépendais moins de mes parents quand j'avais souffert de leur malveillance et elle ne s'était pas manifestée avec autant de brutalité."

48. Ibid., p. 118: "Lire! qu'est-ce que vous pensez! Je ne lis même pas un journal! Vous ne savez pas comme c'est absorbant de dresser un enfant!"

49. Ibid., p. 35: "La seule nouveauté pour eux c'est celle qu'apportent la naissance et le développement de leurs enfants: elle se perd au jour le jour dans la monotonie quotidienne."

50. Ibid., p. 56: "Quand on a été mal aimé dans son enfance et qu'on a adopté le point de vue de ses parents, on a constitué de soi une image dont on ne se débarrasse jamais."

51. Ibid., p. 620: "Mécontente de son sort, elle ne veut pas que celui de ses filles soit plus clément et elle réclame d'autant plus âprement le maintien de son status qu'elle en souffre davantage."

52. Ibid., pp. 625–26: "Je déplore l'esclavage imposé à la femme à travers les enfants et les abus d'autorité auxquels ceux-ci sont exposés. Les parents font entrer leurs enfants dans leurs jeux sado-masochistes, projetant sur eux leurs fantasmes, leurs obsessions, leurs névroses. C'est une situation éminemment malsaine. . . . Comme beaucoup de féministes, je désire l'abolition de la famille, mais sans trop savoir par quoi la remplacer."

53. Bieber, *Simone de Beauvoir*, p. 101.

54. Ibid., p. 105.

55. Ascher, *Simone de Beauvoir*, p. 47.

56. Zéphir, *Le Néo-féminisme*, p. 80: "On voit bien le sérieux d'une telle position et à quel point il est stupide et malhonnête de prétendre que son opposition à la famille et au mariage proviendrait de ce qu'elle en est elle-même privée et qu'elle n'aimerait pas voir les autres femmes y trouver le bonheur."

57. Keefe, *Simone de Beauvoir*, p. 40.

58. Ibid., p. 41.

Chapter 15

1. Simone de Beauvoir, *La Cérémonie des adieux* (Paris: Gallimard, 1981), p. 139: "Si la vieillesse est, comme certains le disent, la perte de la curiosité, alors il n'était pas du tout vieux."

2. Ibid., p. 28: "une équipée assez sotte."

3. Jean-Paul Sartre, *Lettres au Castor*.

4. *La Cérémonie des adieux*, p. 138: "Trop de jeunes personnes! 'Mais ça m'est utile.' . . . Et je pense qu'en effet c'est beaucoup à elles qu'il devait le goût de vivre. Il m'a déclaré avec une complaisance naïve: 'Je n'ai jamais plu davantage aux femmes.'"

5. Ibid., p. 49.

6. Ibid., p. 84: "En sortant, Sartre me déclara qu'il continuerait à fumer."

7. Ibid., p. 283: "Je me suis fait une culture musicale qui n'était pas différente de celle de ma mère."

8. Ibid., p. 539: "Il me semble que la plus grande chance était sans conteste de naître dans une famille universitaire, c'est-à-dire dans une famille d'intellectuels d'un certain genre."

9. Ibid., p. 425: "L'argent que nous donnait mon grand-père, l'argent avec lequel il nous faisait vivre ma mère et moi; ma mère m'expliquait que ce n'était pas le mien."

Ensuite elle s'est remariée, et l'argent de mon beau-père était encore moins le mien que celui de mon grand-père."

10. Ibid., p. 546: "Et ça ne vous gênait pas de vous trouver en opposition sur un point si important avec votre famille, que vous respectiez, que vous aimiez bien? — Ma foi, non."

11. Ibid., p. 415: "Est-ce que vous avez été trop chouchouté, cajolé, embrassé, par la mère, par le grand-père, et vous êtes-vous raidi contre ça? — C'est possible."

12. Ibid., p. 401: "L'abandon de ma mère m'était très désagréable. Bien qu'il fût assez rare chez elle, la pauvre!"

13. Ibid., p. 444: "J'avais eu un rôle privilégié dans la vie de ma mère les années précédentes et il m'était ôté puisqu'il y avait cet homme qui vivait avec elle et qui avait le rôle principal. Avant, j'étais un prince par rapport à ma mère, maintenant je n'étais qu'un prince de second ordre."

14. Ibid., p. 38: "Il ne voulait surtout pas se retrouver au Père-Lachaise entre sa mère et son beau-père."

15. Ibid., p. 373: "J'avais certainement un sentiment assez sexuel pour ma mère."

16. Ibid., p. 382: "La domination venait de l'enfance. Mon grand-père dominait ma grand-mère. Mon beau-père dominait ma mère."

17. Ibid., p. 246: "Ma mère lisait peu, mais enfin, de temps en temps, elle lisait un livre, un de ceux qu'on lisait à l'époque."

18. Ibid., p. 327: "J'ai eu une enfance dans laquelle on a beaucoup parlé et abusivement de mon intelligence . . . j'ai été amené à me penser comme un petit prince."

19. Ibid., p. 486: "Je venais d'un milieu bourgeois qui . . . n'avait même pas entendu parler de la lutte des classes. Ma mère, et même mon grand-père, ne savaient pas ce que c'était."

20. Ibid., pp. 249–50: "Mes parents vivaient cinquante ans en arrière en ce qui concerne la culture et la vie."

21. Ibid., p. 320: "La pauvre femme ne connaissait rien à tout ça, elle avait eu un père qui avait eu la légion d'honneur, et un mari qui avait la légion d'honneur. Il lui paraissait que son fils devait l'avoir."

22. Ibid., p. 186: "Moi je savais que mon beau-père ne s'en souciait pas. De sorte que ça a été, constamment, le type contre lequel j'écrivais. Toute ma vie; et le fait d'écrire, c'était contre lui."

23. Ibid., p. 251: "Un auteur comme Stendhal, je l'ai lu avec les gens de mon âge et contre ceux qui étaient plus âgés, même les professeurs."

24. Ibid., p. 259: "A partir du moment où je me suis installé chez ma mère, j'ai consenti à posséder certaines choses, comme par exemple une bibliothèque."

25. Ibid.: "Ma mère, après la mort de mon beau-père, voulait que j'habite chez elle. —Oui, je sais. Bon, alors, pour en revenir à la lecture."

26. Ibid., p. 357: "J'aime toujours mieux les jeunes que les vieux . . . quand je parle avec le chef mao qui n'a pas trente ans, je suis plus à l'aise qu'avec un type de c inquante

ou soixante ans. . . . La plupart des maos n'ont pas d'amitié pour moi, ni moi pour eux, on fait le travail ensemble . . . il y en a un pour qui j'ai une amitié réelle, c'est Victor."

27. Ibid., p. 359: "Moi, j'ai le sentiment de mon âge, et ça me rajeunit de parler avec de jeunes femmes."

28. Ibid., p. 529: "J'aime bien voir Victor, mais au bout d'un moment nous avons une conversation de personne à personne; ce n'est pas un jeune homme qui vient voir un vieillard."

29. Ibid., p. 46: "Je n'ai jamais souhaité avoir un fils, jamais, et je ne recherche pas dans mes rapports avec des hommes plus jeunes que moi un substitut du rapport paternel."

30. Ibid., p. 55: "D'un air joyeux, il nous a dit un soir, à Bost et à moi, que son amitié avec eux le rajeunissait. Il regrettait seulement d'être un peu trop âgé pour qu'elle fût tout à fait fructueuse."

31. Ibid., pp. 55–56: "Je suis content de vos rapports avec moi. Il va de soi que je n'existe pour vous qu'autant que je vous suis utile. Cela je l'approuve pleinement. Mais quand il s'agit de faire de l'action en commun, il y a de l'amitié, c'est-à-dire un rapport qui dépasse l'action entreprise, un rapport de réciprocité. Voilà le sens profond de mon rapport avec vous. . . . Si vous me remettez en question et que je me conteste pour être avec vous, j'aide dans la mesure de mes moyens à créer une société où il y aura encore des philosophes, des hommes d'un type nouveau, manuels-intellectuels, mais qui se poseront la question: Qu'est-ce que l'homme?"

32. Ibid., p. 141: "Je regrettais qu'une partie de la vie de Sartre me fût désormais fermée."

33. Ibid., p. 150: "Victor, au lieu de l'aider à enrichir sa propre pensée, faisait pression sur lui pour qu'il la reniât."

34. Ibid.: "Je n'ai pas caché à Sartre l'étendue de ma déception. Il en a été surpris. Mais il n'en a mis que plus d'entêtement à faire paraître immédiatement l'entretien."

35. Ibid., p. 151: "Militant et philosophe, Victor réaliserait le 'nouvel intellectuel' dont Sartre rêvait et qu'il aurait contribué à faire exister. Douter de Victor, c'était renoncer à cette vivante prolongation de lui-même, plus importante pour lui que les suffrages de la postérité. Donc il avait choisi, malgré toutes ses résistances, de croire en lui."

36. Ibid., p. 553: "L'oeuvre qu'on fait, à la fois si elle doit réussir dépasse le public présent, vivant, existant, et s'adresse aussi bien à un public futur."

37. Ibid., p. 86: "Vous êtes une bonne *épouse* ."

38. Ibid., p. 155: "Il m'a tendu la bouche. J'ai embrassé sa bouche, sa joue."

39. Jean Clémentin, "Un homme qui a fait ce qu'il avait à faire," *Le Canard enchaîné*, December 2, 1981, p. 2: "Faute de pouvoir être quelqu'un par lui-même, il ambitionne de se faire l'héritier spirituel, le légataire intellectuel de J.-P. Sartre."

40. Keefe, *Simone de Beauvoir*, p. 65.

41. Okely, *Simone de Beauvoir*, p. 142.

42. Richard Sennett, "Trials of Mutual Freedom," *The Atlantic*, May 1984, p. 116.

43. Ibid., p. 117.

44. Ibid., p. 118.

45. Ibid., p. 119.

46. Ruth Rosen, "Living as If Life Really Matters," *San Francisco Chronicle Review Section,* July 8, 1984, p. 3.

47. Anatole Broyard, "Books of The Times," *The New York Times,* April 19, 1984, p. 21.

48. Douglas Johnson, *The New York Times Book Review,* April 1984, p. 11.

49. Hazel E. Barnes, "Beauvoir and Sartre: The Forms of Farewell," *Philosophy and Literature* 9, no. 1 (April 1985), p. 32.

50. Ibid., p. 39.

51. Ibid., p. 36.

Chapter 16

1. Francis Jeanson, Interviews of November 9 and 10, 1965, in *Simone de Beauvoir,* pp. 250–98.

2. John Gerassi, "Simone de Beauvoir: *The Second Sex* 25 Years Later," *Society* 13, no. 2 (February 1976), pp. 79–85.

3. Josée Dayan and Malka Ribowska, *Simone de Beauvoir,* text of a film shot in April 1978 (Paris: Gallimard, 1979).

4. Cathy Bernheim and Antoine Spire, "Simone de Beauvoir: le désaveu," *Le Matin,* December 5, 1985, p. 26: "Je suis née dans le bonheur total. Je suis née dans la sérénité, moi."

5. Jeanson, *Simone de Beauvoir* pp. 254–56: "Ni rapport proprement moral, ni rapport charnel, ni rapport . . . humain, presque! Ça se passait entièrement du côté de ma mère. . . . C'est elle qui a compté d'abord; et quand il s'est mis à compter à son tour, elle comptait tout de même encore pour moi, mais, évidemment, mon attitude à son égard s'est faite plus hostile."

6. Ibid., p. 257: "Oui, en effet, je m'autorisais de mon père pour être intelligente et de ma mère pour rester une enfant."

7. Catherine David, "Beauvoir elle-même," *Le Nouvel Observateur,* January 22, 1979, pp. 82–90.

8. Appendix A, pp. 330, 344.

9. Madeleine Chapsal, *Les Ecrivains en personne* (Paris: Julliard, 1960), pp. 17–37, as quoted in Francis et Gontier, *Les Ecrits de Simone de Beauvoir,* p. 383.

10. Jeanson, *Simone de Beauvoir,* p. 276: "Je n'ai pas eu d'enfants, mais je n'en avais jamais vraiment souhaité, et je ne regrette aucunement de ne pas en avoir."

11. Beauvoir, "Réponse à quelques femmes et à un homme," as quoted in Zéphir, *Le Néo-féminisme,* p. 79: "Pour moi qui n'en souhaitais pas, et qui voulais avant tout accomplir une oeuvre, ç'a été une chance de n'en pas avoir. Ce n'est pas moi qui veux imposer ma manière de vivre à toutes les femmes, puisque au contraire je milite pour

leur liberté: liberté de la maternité, de la contraception, de l'avortement; les fanatiques, ce sont certaines mères de famille qui n'admettent pas qu'on suive un autre
chemin que le leur."

12. Alice Schwarzer, *Simone de Beauvoir aujourd'hui. Six entretiens* (Paris: Mercure de
France, 1984), p. 56: "Ma relation avec Sartre était telle . . . que je n'ai jamais éprouvé
le désir d'avoir un enfant. Je n'avais pas tellement envie d'avoir une reproduction de
Sartre—il me suffisait—ni de moi-même: je me suffisais."

13. Ibid., p. 57: "Absolument pas! Je n'ai jamais regretté de ne pas avoir d'enfant."

14. Dayan and Ribowska, *Simone de Beauvoir*, film text, p. 73: "Je n'ai jamais regretté de
ne pas avoir d'enfants. J'aime beaucoup mieux les amitiés, j'aime beaucoup mieux
des relations, oui, que j'ai choisies, que celles qui m'auraient été imposés par la
maternité."

15. Jeanson, *Simone de Beauvoir*, p. 275: "Mon image d'avant, une certaine image de
jeunesse qu'on prolonge toujours plus ou moins, s'était cassée, et je ne parvenais pas
à me reconnaître dans cette femme qui pouvait en effet être mère, presque grand-
mère."

16. Simone de Beauvoir, preface to *Avortement: Une Loi en procès. L'affaire de Bobigny*
(Paris: Gallimard, 1973), as quoted in Francis and Gontier, *Les Ecrits de Simone de
Beauvoir*, p. 513.

17. Michèle Souvenot, "Les Aveux de Simone de Beauvoir," *Le Journal du dimanche*, April
22, 1984, p. 7: "J'ai rajouté mon nom à celui des autres, sans hésitation. Et pourtant,
c'était un mensonge. Cet acte, l'avortement, je ne l'ai jamais accompli."

18. Dayan and Ribowska, *Simone de Beauvoir*, film text, p. 34: "C'est toi qui me valorisais."

19. Patterson, "Entretien avec Simone de Beauvoir (20 juin 1978)," p. 750: "C'était une
espèce d'oppression que le savoir, en un sens je les opprimais de mon savoir."

20. Schwarzer, *Six entretiens*, p. 97: "Absolument pas! . . . Les rapports mère-fille sont
généralement catastrophiques."

21. Dayan and Ribowska, *Simone de Beauvoir*, film text, pp. 72–73: "Il s'agit de relations
bien meilleures que celles qui existent généralement entre mères et filles."

22. Curtis Cate, "Europe's First Feminist Has Changed the Second Sex," *The New York
Times Magazine*, July ll, 1971, p. 39: "If this suggestively incestuous relationship (which
a liaison between an older woman and a much younger man always is) did not fulfill
a latent maternal instinct she had long since stifled, it did at least give Beauvoir a
sense of springtime rebirth."

23. Schwarzer, *Six entretiens*, p. 23: "Elle n'a pas d'enfant—et pourtant une grande partie
de la nouvelle génération voit en elle un modèle."

24. Dayan and Ribowska, *Simone de Beauvoir*, film text, p. 75: "Je n'ai pas à donner des
solutions à des gens et les gens n'ont pas à attendre des solutions de moi."

25. *Simone de Beauvoir Society Newsletter* (Menlo Park, California: Simone de Beauvoir
Society, June 1985), p. 4. For further information about the Simone de Beauvoir
Society and its publications, please contact Yolanda Astarita Patterson, 440 La Mesa
Drive, Menlo Park, California 94025.

26.   Appendix A, pp. 331, 345.

27.   Josyane Savigneau, "Une mère symbolique," *Le Monde,* April 16, 1986, p. 19: "Dans sa vie privée comme dans son combat public, Simone de Beauvoir, notre 'mère symbolique', a forcé le temps. Partout, elle était là. Qu'elles ignorent ou non Simone de Beauvoir, les femmes qui, aujourd'hui, ont pris place parmi les 'créateurs' et les 'décideurs', celles avec qui il faut désormais compter, lui doivent quelque chose. . . . Ces femmes-là sont la descendance de cette femme sans enfant, de cette vieille dame au turban suranné, au regard tendu, qui, obstinément, pendant plus de soixante ans, en dépit des calomnies, des insultes, puis, pis, de la dérision, a affirmé qu'être née femme n'est pas une faute."

28.   Appendix A, pp. 331, 345.

29.   Jeanson, *Simone de Beauvoir,* p. 264: "Ce serait une erreur de penser que, pour être féministe, il faut ne pas avoir d'enfants: loin de là!"

30.   Ibid., pp. 282–83: "La maternité peut *toujours* avoir une valeur positive, quand ce ne serait que de renseigner les femmes sur elles-mêmes . . . si l'on n'est pas expressément requis par d'autres choses, cela doit être assez passionnant, la découverte de ce qu'est un enfant."

31.   Betty Friedan, *It Changed My Life: Writings on the Women's Movement* (New York: Random House, 1976), p. 313.

32.   Ibid., p. 314.

33.   Ibid.

34.   Schwarzer, *Six entretiens,* p. 80: "Ah non! Je ne la refuse pas! Je pense seulement qu'aujourd'hui c'est un drôle de piège pour une femme. C'est pourquoi je con-seillerais à une femme de ne pas devenir mère. Mais je n'en fais pas un jugement de valeur. Ce qui est à condamner, ce ne sont pas les mères, mais l'idéologie qui incite toutes les femmes à devenir mères, et les conditions dans lesquelles elles doivent l'être."

35.   Dayan and Ribowska, *Simone de Beauvoir,* film text, p. 72: "Si on enlevait à la femme la mauvaise conscience qui lui vient d'une manière atavique à travers sa propre mère, sa propre grand-mère, bon, après ça, la maternité, pourquoi pas? C'est une chose assez belle, en effet, que de voir naître, grandir, se développer un être humain. Mais étant donné la situation actuelle, c'est pour la femme un piège dans lequel elle ne peut que laisser sa liberté et son bonheur."

36.   Margaret A. Simons and Jessica Benjamin, "Simone de Beauvoir: An Interview," *Feminist Studies* 5, no. 2 (Summer 1979), p. 341.

37.   Simone de Beauvoir, with Maria Craipeau, "Aujourd'hui Julien Sorel serait une femme," (*France Observateur,* no. 514, March 1960), as quoted in Francis and Gontier, *Les Ecrits de Simone de Beauvoir,* p. 378.

38.   Patterson, "Entretien avec Simone de Beauvoir (20 juin 1978)," p. 746: "Si elle a des enfants, c'est la fin de sa carrière, en général ça s'arrête. Il y a une grosse distance entre tout ce que peut espérer une adolescente qui aime des choses, qui aime lire, qui aime étudier, etc., et puis quand elle se trouve à faire le ménage, avec les enfants, etc., il y a beaucoup de choses qui meurent en elle."

39. Preface to *Avortement: Une Loi en procès,* as quoted in Francis and Gontier, *Les Ecrits de Simone de Beauvoir,* p. 511: "Au lieu de dire à la petite fille, quand elle a deux, trois ou quatre ans: 'Tu seras vouée à laver la vaisselle', on lui dit: 'Tu seras vouée à être maman', on lui donne des poupées, on exalte la maternité de façon que, quand elle devient une jeune fille, elle ne pense qu'à une chose, c'est se marier et avoir des enfants. On l'a convaincue qu'elle ne serait pas une femme complète si elle n'a pas d'enfant."

40. Schwarzer, 1982 interview, *Six entretiens,* p. 120: "Aussi longtemps que l'on considère que la tâche principale de la femme est de faire des enfants, elle ne s'occupera pas de politique, de technologie—et elle ne disputera pas aux hommes leur suprématie."

41. Beauvoir, September 1966 lecture in Japan, as quoted in Francis and Gontier, *Les Ecrits de Simone de Beauvoir,* p. 459: "Elle appartient à son mari, à ses enfants. A n'importe quel moment, le mari ou les enfants peuvent venir lui demander une explication, une aide, un service et elle est obligée de les satisfaire. Elle appartient à la famille, au groupe, elle ne s'appartient pas à elle-même."

42. Simone de Beauvoir, "La Condition féminine," *La Nef,* no. 5, January-March 1961, pp. 121–27, as quoted in Francis et Gontier, *Les Ecrits de Simone de Beauvoir,* p. 402.

43. Simone de Beauvoir, preface to *La Grand'Peur d'aimer* by Dr. Lagroua Weill-Hallé (Ed. Julliard-Sequana, 1960; Ed. Gonthier, Paris, 1961), as quoted in Francis and Gontier, pp. 397–400.

44. Ibid., p. 398: "L'homme peut s'évader de l'enfer domestique alors qu'elle s'y consume."

45. Preface to *Avortement: Une Loi en procès,* as quoted in Francis and Gontier, *Les Ecrits de Simone de Beauvoir,* p. 505: "Un avortement correctement exécuté est une opération aussi bénigne que l'extraction d'une dent: moins dangereuse qu'un accouchement."

46. Hélène Pedneault and Marie Sabourin, "Simone de Beauvoir féministe," interview *La Vie en rose,* March 1984, p. 29: "Nous avons maintenant la gratuité de l'avortement, une conquête énorme, et la contraception est tout à fait répandue. Et il y a vraiment des lois qui insistent beaucoup sur l'égalité des droits, des salaires, de l'embauche, et sur l'antisexisme à l'école. Et ça, ça me semble très important."

47. September 1966 lecture in Japan, as quoted in Francis and Gontier, *Les Ecrits de Simone de Beauvoir,* p. 424: "Du point de vue de ce que j'appellerai sa dignité personnelle, du point de vue de son bonheur, de son équilibre, la femme ne peut pas s'accomplir si elle se borne à être épouse et mère."

48. Friedan, *It Changed My Life,* p. 311.

49. Patterson, "Entretien avec Simone de Beauvoir (20 juin 1978)," p. 748: "Si elles travaillent dehors, elles sont moins sur le dos des enfants, et puis elles ont un horizon un peu plus ouvert quand même. Mais celles qui sont complètement au foyer n'ont que ça, alors elles exercent un pouvoir sur leur enfant."

50. Ibid.: "Pour moi, je trouve que la famille n'existe pas."

51. Beauvoir, "Réponse à quelques femmes et à un homme," as quoted in Francis and Gontier, *Les Ecrits de Simone de Beauvoir*, p. 499: "Les parents font entrer les enfants dans leurs jeux sado-masochistes, projetant sur eux leurs fantasmes, leurs obsessions, leurs névroses. . . . Sans parler des enfants martyrs, le monde des enfants névrosés que produit notre société est impressionnant."

52. Pedneault and Sabourin, "Simone de Beauvoir féministe," p. 30: "Ce n'est surtout pas au nom de la maternité que les femmes doivent être pacifistes. On essaie trop souvent de les enfermer dans une espèce de ghetto en disant: 'C'est parce que vous êtes des mères'. Alors là, je ne suis pas d'accord. C'est parce qu'elles sont des êtres humains qu'elles doivent se battre pour le pacifisme."

53. Simons and Benjamin, "Simone de Beauvoir," p. 340.

54. Gerassi, "Simone de Beauvoir," p. 81.

55. Simons and Benjamin, "Simone de Beauvoir," p. 341.

56. Schwarzer, 1976 interview, *Six entretiens*, p. 77: "Je crois qu'il ne faut pas qu'une femme se laisse prendre au piège des enfants et du mariage. Même si une femme a envie d'avoir des enfants, elle doit bien réfléchir aux conditions dans lesquelles elle devra les élever, parce que la maternité, actuellement, est un véritable esclavage. Les pères et la société laissent aux femmes, et à elles seules, la responsabilité des enfants. Ce sont les femmes qui restent à la maison quand les enfants sont malades. Ce sont elles les responsables quand l'enfant échoue. Et si une femme veut quand même un enfant, il vaudrait mieux qu'elle l'ait sans se marier, parce que le mariage, c'est le plus grand piège."

57. Liliane Lazar, "Conversation avec Simone de Beauvoir, février 1983," *Simone de Beauvoir Studies* 2 (Fall 1984), p. 9: "Je pense qu'il ne faut plus de mariage. . . . L'engagement de deux êtres qui ont devant eux soixante ans de vie chacun, puisque maintenant on vit très longtemps, est quelque chose d'absurde. . . ."

58. Appendix A, pp. 331–32, 346.

59. Ibid., pp. 332, 346.

60. Preface to *Avortement: Une Loi en procès*, as quoted in Francis and Gontier, *Les Ecrits de Simone de Beauvoir* pp. 508–9. "Celle qui se rebelle contre la maternité forcée est sur le chemin d'une rébellion plus générale."

Chapter 17

1. Jules Renard, *Poil de carotte* (Paris: Gallimard, 1957).

2. Hervé Bazin, *Vipère au poing* (Paris: Bernard Grasset, 1948).

3. Marie Cardinal, *Les Mots pour le dire* (Paris: Bernard Grasset, 1975).

4. Marguerite Duras, *Un Barrage contre le Pacifique* (Paris: Gallimard, 1950).

5. Paule Marshall, *Brown Girl, Brownstones* (New York: The Feminist Press, 1981, original copyright 1959).

6. Colette, *Sido* (Paris: Librairie Hachette, 1901).

7. Sylvia Plath, *Letters Home* (New York: Bantam, 1975).

8. Yasushi Inoue, *Chronicle of My Mother,* trans. Jean Oda Moy (Tokyo, New York, and San Francisco: Kodansha International, 1982).

9. Annie Ernaux, *Une Femme* (Paris: Gallimard, 1987).

10. Deirdre Bair, "Reflections on Life: 'Working' with Simone de Beauvoir," *Simone de Beauvoir Studies* 3 (1985–86), p. 34.

11. Carolyn Grassi, "Thinking of Simone de Beauvoir," *Simone de Beauvoir Studies* 3 (1985–86), p. 54.

12. Hazel Barnes, "Simone de Beauvoir and Later Feminism," *Simone de Beauvoir Studies* 4 (1987), p. 8.

Bibliography

Ascher, Carol. *Simone de Beauvoir: A Life of Freedom*. Boston: Beacon Press, 1981.

Astruc, Alexandre, and Michel Contat. *Sartre*. Full text from a film shot in February-March 1972. Paris: Gallimard, 1977.

Audet, Jean-Raymond. *Simone de Beauvoir face à la mort*. Lausanne: L'Age d'Homme, 1979.

Autrement, no. 90, "La Mère" (May 1987).

Badinter, Elisabeth. *L'Amour en plus*. Paris: Flammarion, 1980.

―――. "La Solution: une mutation des pères." In *Maternité en mouvement*, pp. 37–38. Grenoble: Presses Universitaires de Grenoble, 1986.

Bair, Deirdre. "Reflections on Life: *Working* with Simone de Beauvoir," *Simone de Beauvoir Studies* 3 (1985–86), pp. 29–36.

Barnes, Hazel. "Beauvoir and Sartre: The Forms of Farewell." *Philosophy and Literature* 9, no. 1 (April 1985), pp. 21–40.

―――. *The Literature of Possibility*. Lincoln: University of Nebraska Press, 1959.

―――. "Simone de Beauvoir and Later Feminism." *Simone de Beauvoir Studies*, 4 (1987), pp. 5–34.

Bazin, Hervé. *Vipère au poing*. Paris: Bernard Grasset, 1948.

Beauvoir, Hélène de. *Souvenirs*. Compiled by Marcelle Routier. Garamont: Librairie Séguier, 1987.

Beauvoir, Simone de. *Les Belles Images*. Collection Folio, no. 243. Paris: Gallimard, 1966.

―――. *Les Bouches inutiles*. Paris: Gallimard, 1945.

―――. *La Cérémonie des adieux*. Followed by interviews with Jean-Paul Sartre, August–September 1974. Paris: Gallimard, 1981.

―――. "La Condition féminine," *La Nef*, no. 5 (January–March 1961), pp. 121–27.

―――. *Le Deuxième Sexe*. 2 vols. Collection Idées, nos. 152–53. Paris: Gallimard, 1949.

―――. *La Femme rompue*. Collection Folio, no. 76. Paris: Gallimard, 1967.

―――. *La Force de l'âge*. Paris: Gallimard, 1960.

―――. *La Force des choses*. 2 vols. Livre de poche, nos. 2539–40. Paris: Gallimard, 1963.

―――. *L'Invitée*. Livre de poche, nos. 793–94. Paris: Gallimard, 1943.

―――. *Les Mandarins*. Paris: Gallimard, 1954.

―――. *Mémoires d'une jeune fille rangée*. Paris: Gallimard, 1958.

―――. *Une Mort très douce*. Collection Folio, no. 137. Paris: Gallimard, 1964.

―――. Preface to *Avortement: Une Loi en procès. L'affaire de Bobigny*. Ed. Association "Choisir." Paris: Gallimard, 1973.

―――. Preface to *La Grand'Peur d'aimer* by Dr. Lagroua Weill-Hallé. Ed. Julliard-Sequana, 1960. Paris: Gonthier, 1961.

_____ . "Présentation," "Les Femmes s'entêtent." *Les Temps Modernes,* nos. 333–34 (April–May 1974), pp. 1719–20.

_____ . *Pyrrhus et Cinéas.* Paris: Gallimard, 1944.

_____ . *Quand prime le spirituel.* Paris: Gallimard, 1979.

_____ . "Réponse à quelques femmes et à un homme." *Le Nouvel Observateur,* no. 382 (March 6–12, 1972), pp. 40–42.

_____ . *Le Sang des autres.* Collection Folio no. 363. Paris: Gallimard, 1945.

_____ . *Tout compte fait.* Collection Folio, no. 1022. Paris: Gallimard, 1972.

_____ . *Tous les hommes sont mortels.* Collection Folio, no. 533. Paris: Gallimard, 1946.

_____ . *La Vieillesse.* Paris: Gallimard, 1970.

Bernard, Jessie. *The Future of Motherhood.* New York: The Dial Press, 1974.

Bernheim, Cathy, and Antoine Spire. "Simone de Beauvoir: le désaveu." *Le Matin,* December 5, 1985, pp. 26–27.

Bieber, Konrad. *Simone de Beauvoir.* Boston: G. K. Hall, 1979.

Brée, Germaine. *Women Writers in France: Variations on a Theme.* New Brunswick, New Jersey: Rutgers University Press, 1973.

Broyard, Anatole. "Books of The Times." *The New York Times,* April 19, 1984, p. 21.

Camus, Albert. *The Stranger.* New York: Vintage Books, Random House, 1946.

Cardinal, Marie. *Les Mots pour le dire.* Paris: Bernard Grasset, 1975.

Cate, Curtis. "Europe's First Feminist Has Changed the Second Sex." *The New York Times Magazine,* July 11, 1971, pp. 32–44.

Chapsal, Madeleine. In *Les Ecrivains en personne,* pp. 17–37. Paris: Julliard, 1960.

Chernin, Kim. *In My Mother's House.* New Haven and New York: Ticknor & Fields, 1983.

_____ . *The Hungry Self.* New York: Times Books, Random House, 1985.

Chesler, Phyllis. *Mothers on Trial.* New York: McGraw-Hill, 1986.

Chodorow, Nancy. *The Reproduction of Mothering.* Berkeley: University of California Press, 1978.

Clémentin, Jean. "Un homme qui a fait ce qu'il avait à faire." *Le Canard enchaîné,* December 2, 1981, p. 2.

Cohen-Solal, Annie. *Sartre.* Paris: Gallimard; New York: Pantheon, 1985.

Collange, Christine. *Moi, ta mère.* Paris: Fayard, 1985.

Colette. *Sido.* Paris: Librairie Hachette, 1901.

Collin, Françoise. "Les enfants de tous." *Cahiers du GRIF,* no. 9/10 (December 1975), pp. 3–9.

_____ . "Féminitude et féminisme." *Cahiers du GRIF,* no. 1 (November 1973), pp. 5–22.

_____ . "Humour en amour." *Cahiers du GRIF,* no. 17/18, "Mères femmes" (September 1977), pp. 3–6.

Cottrell, Robert D. *Simone de Beauvoir.* New York: Frederick Ungar, 1975.

Craipeau, Maria, and Simone de Beauvoir. "Aujourd'hui Julien Sorel serait une femme." *France Observateur,* no. 514 (March 1960).

Crawford, Christina. *Mommie Dearest.* New York: Berkley Publishing Corporation, 1981.

Danièle. "Un Accouchement, un avortement." *Les Temps Modernes,* nos. 333–34 (April–May 1974), pp. 1831–44.

David, Catherine. "Beauvoir elle-même." *Le Nouvel Observateur,* January 22, 1979, pp. 82–90.

Dayan, Josée and Malka Ribowska. *Simone de Beauvoir.* Text of a film shot in April 1978. Paris: Gallimard, 1979.

Descubes, Madeleine. *Connaître Simone de Beauvoir.* Paris: Editions Resma, 1974.

Dinnerstein, Dorothy. *The Mermaid and the Minotaur, Sexual Arrangements and Human Malaise.* New York: Harper & Row, 1976.

Duras, Marguerite. *Un Barrage contre le Pacifique*. Paris: Gallimard, 1950.

Durham, Carolyn A. "Patterns of Influence: Simone de Beauvoir and Marie Cardinal." *The French Review* 60, no. 3 (February 1987), pp. 341–48.

d'Eaubonne, Françoise. *Une Femme nommée Castor. Mon amie Simone de Beauvoir*. Sofinem/Encre, 1986.

———. "La Mère indifférente." *Cahiers du GRIF*, nos. 17/18, "Mères femmes," (September 1977) pp. 25–28.

Ernaux, Annie. *Une Femme*. Paris: Gallimard, 1987.

Evans, Martha Noel. *Masks of Tradition*. Ithaca: Cornell University Press, 1987.

Evans, Mary. *Simone de Beauvoir, A Feminist Mandarin*. London and New York: Tavistock, 1985.

Feldman, Jacqueline. "Au risque de les perdre . . . ." In *Maternité en mouvement*, pp. 32–36. Grenoble: Presses Universitaires de Grenoble, 1986.

Fichera, Virginia. "Simone de Beauvoir and 'The Woman Question': *Les Bouches inutiles*." *Yale French Studies*, no. 72 (1986), pp. 50–64.

Francis, Claude and Fernande Gontier. *Les Ecrits de Simone de Beauvoir*. Paris: Gallimard, 1979.

———. *Simone de Beauvoir*. Paris: Librairie Académique Perrin, 1985.

Friday, Nancy. *My Mother / My Self, The Daughter's Search for Identity*. New York: Dell, 1977.

Friedan, Betty. *The Feminine Mystique*. New York: W. W. Norton, 1963.

———. *It Changed My Life: Writings on the Women's Movement*. New York: Random House, 1976.

———. *The Second Stage*. New York, Summit, 1981.

Gagnebin, Laurent. *Simone de Beauvoir ou le refus de l'indifférence*. Paris: Editions Fischbacher, 1968.

Garner, Corinne Alexandre. "Fils de . . . ." *Autrement*, no. 90 (May 1987), pp. 34–38.

Gavarini, Françoise. "L'Institution des rôles et la négation de l'amour." In *Maternité en mouvement*, pp. 55–56. Grenoble: Presses Universitaires de Grenoble, 1986.

Gennari, Geneviève. *Simone de Beauvoir*. Paris: Editions Universitaires, 1959.

Gerassi, John. "Simone de Beauvoir: *The Second Sex* 25 Years Later." *Society* 13, no. 2 (February 1976), pp. 79–85.

Gide, André. *Les Nourritures terrestres*. Paris: Gallimard, 1917.

———. *L'Immoraliste*. Paris: Mercure de France, 1902.

Grassi, Carolyn. "Thinking of Simone de Beauvoir." *Simone de Beauvoir Studies* 3, (1985–86), p. 54.

Gundlac, Julie Kettle. *My Mother before Me*. Secaucus, New Jersey: Lyle Stewart, 1986.

Harrison, Beppie. *The Shock of Motherhood*. New York: Scribners, 1986.

Hatcher, Donald L. *Understanding "The Second Sex."* New York: Peter Lang, 1984.

Hayman, Ronald. *Sartre, A Life*. New York: Simon & Schuster, 1987.

Henry, A. M. *Simone de Beauvoir ou l'échec d'une chrétienté*. Paris: Arthème Fayard, 1961.

Hourdin, Georges. *Simone de Beauvoir et la liberté*. Paris: Les Editions du Cerf, 1962.

Hurstel, Françoise. "Sans regret." Interview with Hélène de Beauvoir. *Autrement*, no. 90, "La Mère" (May 1987), pp. 100–105.

Ibsen, Henrik. *A Doll's House*. In *Four Great Plays by Henrik Ibsen*. Translated by R. Farquharson Sharp. New York: Bantam, 1959.

Inoue, Yasushi. *Chronicle of My Mother*. Translated by Jean Oda Moy. Tokyo, New York, and San Francisco: Kodansha International, 1982.

Irigaray, Luce. *Et l'une ne bouge pas sans l'autre*. Paris: Les Editions de Minuit, 1979.

———. *Le Corps-à-corps avec la mère*. Ottawa: Les Editions de la Pleine Lune, 1981.

Jaccard, Annie-Claire. *Simone de Beauvoir*. Zurich: Juris, 1968.

Jeanson, Francis. *Simone de Beauvoir ou l'entreprise de vivre*. Paris: Editions du Seuil, 1966.

Johnson, Douglas. *The New York Times Book Review,* April 1984, p. 11.

Julienne-Caffié, Serge. *Simone de Beauvoir*. Paris: Gallimard, 1966.

Keefe, Terry. *Simone de Beauvoir*. London: Harrap, 1983.

Klein, Carole. *Mothers and Sons*. Boston: Houghton Mifflin, 1984.

Knibiehler, Yvonne, and Catherine Fouquet. *L'Histoire des mères, du Moyen Age à nos jours*. Paris: Editions Montalba, 1980.

Kristeva, Julia. Interview, *Cahiers du GRIF,* no. 32 (Winter 1982), pp. 7–23.

Lasocki, Annemarie. *Simone de Beauvoir ou l'entreprise d'écrire*. La Haye: Martinus Nijhoff, 1971.

Lazar, Liliane. "Conversation avec Simone de Beauvoir, février 1983." *Simone de Beauvoir Studies* 2 (Fall 1984), pp. 5–ll.

Leclerc, Annie. "Enfantement et création." In *Maternité en mouvement,* pp. 128–29. Grenoble: Presses Universitaires de Grenoble, 1986.

Le Coadic, Michèle. "Pour une convivialité conflictuelle." In *Maternité en mouvement,* pp. 52–54. Grenoble: Presses Universitaires de Grenoble, 1986.

Leighton, Jean. *Simone de Beauvoir on Woman*. Foreword by Henri Peyre. Cranbury, New Jersey: Associated University Presses, 1975.

Lilar, Suzanne. *Le Malentendu du "Deuxième Sexe"*. Paris: Presses Universitaires de France, 1970.

Madsen, Alex. *Hearts and Minds. The Common Journey of Simone de Beauvoir and Jean-Paul Sartre*. New York: Morrow Quill Paperbacks, 1977.

Maloney, Mercedes Lynch, and Anne Maloney. *The Hand That Rocks the Cradle*. Englewood Cliffs, New Jersey: Prentice Hall, 1985.

Marks, Elaine. *Simone de Beauvoir: Encounters with Death*. New Brunswick, New Jersey: Rutgers University Press, 1973.

Marshall, Paule. *Brown Girl, Brownstones*. New York: The Feminist Press, 1981. Original copyright 1959.

Mauriac, François. *Le Noeud de vipères*. Paris: Bernard Grasset, 1933.

Merleau-Ponty, Maurice. *Sens et non-sens*. Paris: Les Editions Nagel, 1966.

Miller, Sue. *The Good Mother*. New York: Harper & Row, 1986.

Moubachir, Chantal. *Simone de Beauvoir ou le souci de différence*. Paris: Seghers, 1972.

Musset, Alfred de. "La Nuit de mai." In Ramon Guthrie and George E. Diller, *French Literature and Thought since the Revolution*. New York: Harcourt Brace, 1942, pp. 116–21.

Nahas, Hélène. *La Femme dans la littérature existentielle*. Paris: Presses Universitaires de France, 1957.

Okely, Judith. *Simone de Beauvoir*. New York: Virago/Pantheon, 1986.

Ophir, Annie. *Regards féminins*. Preface by Simone de Beauvoir. Paris: Denoël/Gontier, 1976.

Pasquier, Marie-Claire. "Simone de Beauvoir as playwright: *Les Bouches inutiles*." Paper read at the Simone de Beauvoir Colloquium, Columbia University, April 4–6, 1985.

Patterson, Yolanda Astarita. "Entretien avec Simone de Beauvoir (20 juin 1978)." *The French Review* 52, no. 5 (April 1979), pp. 745–54 .

———— . "Interview with Hélène de Beauvoir, Trebiano," June 22, 1986. Appendix B.

———— . "Interview with Simone de Beauvoir, rue Schoelcher, September 14, 1985. Appendix A.

Pedneault, Hélène, and Marie Sabourin. "Simone de Beauvoir féministe." Interview. *La Vie en rose* (March 1984), pp. 25–36.

Plath, Sylvia. *Letters Home*. New York: Bantam, 1975.

Portuges, Catherine. "Attachment and Separation in *The Memoirs of a Dutiful Daughter.*" *Yale French Studies*, no. 72, pp. 107-18. New Haven: Yale University Press, 1986.

Radl, Shirley L. *Mother's Day Is Over.* New York: Charterhouse l, 1973.

Renard, Jules. *Poil de carotte.* Paris: Gallimard, 1957.

Rich, Adrienne. *Of Woman Born.* New York: W. W. Norton, 1976.

Rochefort, Christiane. *Les Petits Enfants du siècle.* Paris: Editions Bernard Grasset, 1961.

Rosen, Ruth. "Living as if Life Really Matters." *San Francisco Chronicle*, review section, July 8, 1984, p. 3.

Roth, Philip. *Portnoy's Complaint.* New York: Random House, 1969.

Sanger, Margaret. *Motherhood in Bondage.* London: Brentano's, 1928.

Sartre, Jean-Paul. *L'Age de raison.* Paris: Gallimard, 1945.

————. *Le Diable et le bon Dieu.* Paris: Gallimard, 1951.

————. *Huis Clos, suivi de Les Mouches.* Paris: Gallimard, 1947.

————. *Lettres au Castor et à quelques autres.* Edited by Simone de Beauvoir. Paris: Gallimard, 1983.

————. *Les Mains sales.* Paris: Gallimard, 1948.

————. *La Mort dans l'âme.* Paris: Gallimard, 1949.

————. *Les Mots.* Collection Folio, no. 24. Paris: Gallimard, 1964.

————. *La Nausée.* Paris: Gallimard, 1938.

Saturday Review. 'Six Experts Talk about *The Second Sex.*" February 21, 1953.

Savigneau, Josyane. "Une mère symbolique." *Le Monde,* April 16, 1986, p. 19.

Schwarzer, Alice. *Simone de Beauvoir aujourd'hui. Six entretiens.* Paris: Mercure de France, 1984.

Sebald, Hans. *Momism: The Silent Disease of America.* Chicago: Nelson Hall, 1976.

Sennett, Richard. "Trials of Mutual Freedom." *The Atlantic,* May 1984, pp. 116–19.

Simone de Beauvoir Society Newsletter. Edited by Yolanda Astarita Patterson. Menlo Park, California: Simone de Beauvoir Society, June 1985.

Simone de Beauvoir Studies. Vols. l–5. Menlo Park, California: Simone de Beauvoir Society, 1983–88.

Simons, Margaret A., and Jessica Benjamin. "Simone de Beauvoir: An Interview." *Feminist Studies* 5, no. 2 (Summer 1979), pp. 330–45.

"Six Experts Discuss *The Second Sex.*" *Saturday Review,* February 21, 1953.

Souvenot, Michèle. "Les Aveux de Simone de Beauvoir." *Le Journal du dimanche,* April 22, 1984, p. 7.

Les Temps Modernes, nos. 333–34 (April–May 1974).

Terrasse, Jean-Marc. "Et demain. . . ." Interview with Elisabeth Badinter. *Autrement,* no. 90 (May 1987), pp. 48–53.

————. "Règlement de contes." *Autrement,* no. 90 (May 1987), pp. 110–11.

Van der Berghe, Christian Louis. *Dictionnaire des idées: Simone de Beauvoir.* The Hague: Mouton, 1967.

Vilaine, Anne-Marie de. "Mère/fille/mère: j'aurais aimé nous inventer une autre histoire. . . ." In *Maternité en mouvement,* pp. 58–61. Grenoble: Presses Universitaires de Grenoble, 1986.

Vilaine, Anne-Marie de, Laurence Gavarini, and Michèle Le Coadic. *Maternité en mouvement.* Grenoble: Presses Universitaires de Grenoble, 1986.

Whitmarsh, Anne. *Simone de Beauvoir and the Limits of Commitment.* Cambridge: Cambridge University Press, 1981.

Winegarten, Renée. *Simone de Beauvoir.* Oxford: Berg, 1988.

Woodward, Kathleen. "Simone de Beauvoir: Aging and Its Discontents." Unpublished manuscript dated January 1985.

Woolf, Virginia. *A Room of One's Own*. New York: Harcourt Brace, 1929.

Wylie, Philip. *Generation of Vipers*. New York: Farrar & Rinehart, 1942.

Yale French Studies. no. 72, "Simone de Beauvoir: Witness to a Century." New Haven: Yale University Press, 1986.

Yalom, Marilyn. *Maternity, Mortality, and the Literature of Madness*. University Park and London: The Pennsylvania State University Press, 1985.

Zéphir, Jacques J. *Le Néo-féminisme de Simone de Beauvoir*. Paris: Denoël/Gonthier, 1982.

Index